1 KINGS

VOLUME 10

THE ANCHOR BIBLE is a fresh approach to the world's greatest classic. Its object is to make the Bible accessible to the modern reader; its method is to arrive at the meaning of biblical literature through exact translation and extended exposition, and to reconstruct the ancient setting of the biblical story, as well as the circumstances of its transcription and the characteristics of its transcribers.

THE ANCHOR BIBLE is a project of international and interfaith scope: Protestant, Catholic, and Jewish scholars from many countries contribute individual volumes. The project is not sponsored by any ecclesiastical organization and is not intended to reflect any particular theological doctrine. Prepared under our joint supervision, THE ANCHOR BIBLE is an effort to make available all the significant historical and linguistic knowledge which bears on the interpretation of the biblical record.

THE ANCHOR BIBLE is aimed at the general reader with no special formal training in biblical studies; yet it is written with the most exacting standards of scholarship, reflecting the highest technical accomplishment.

This project marks the beginning of a new era of cooperation among scholars in biblical research, thus forming a common body of knowledge to be shared by all.

William Foxwell Albright
David Noel Freedman
GENERAL EDITORS

THE ANCHOR BIBLE

1 KINGS

♦

A New Translation
with Introduction and Commentary

MORDECHAI COGAN

THE ANCHOR BIBLE
Doubleday
New York   London   Toronto   Sydney   Auckland

THE ANCHOR BIBLE
PUBLISHED BY DOUBLEDAY
a division of Random House, Inc.
1540 Broadway, New York, New York 10036

THE ANCHOR BIBLE DOUBLEDAY, and the portrayal of an
anchor with the letters A and B are trademarks of
Doubleday, a division of Random House, Inc.

Library of Congress Cataloging-in-Publication Data

Bible. O.T. Kings, 1st. English. Cogan. 2000.
   1 Kings: a new translation with introduction and commentary /
     Mordechai Cogan.— 1st ed.
     p. cm. — (The Anchor Bible ; v. 10)
   Includes bibliographical references and indexes.
   ISBN 0-385-02992-6 (alk. paper)
    1. Bible. O.T. Kings, 1st—Commentaries.   I. Title: First Kings
   II.Cogan, Mordechai.   III. Title.   III. Bible. English.
   Anchor Bible. 1964; v. 10.

BS192.2.A1 1964 .G3 vol. 10
[BS1333]
220.7'7 s—dc21
[222'.53077]   00–043177
                              CIP

First Edition

10 9 8 7 6 5 4 3 2 1

PREFACE

♦

The Anchor Bible commentary on the book of Kings began as the project of Prof. Hayim Tadmor, who in 1980 invited me to collaborate with him, and in 1988, we completed the first volume, *2 Kings*. Academic and public responsibilities caused many delays in the continuance of this joint work, and in 1996, I assumed the task of writing the commentary on *1 Kings* and the Introduction to both volumes. I wish to express my appreciation to Prof. Tadmor for many years of stimulating research together and to thank him for commenting on the final draft of the manuscript of the present volume.

The editor of the Anchor Bible series, Prof. David Noel Freedman, has been a constant source of support and informed counsel. His critical and challenging comments, in a correspondence that has continued faithfully over several years, have made this work a better book, for which I am most grateful. A number of his interpretations, where they differ from my own, are presented in his name (with the initials DNF).

During the academic year 1999–1998, the composition of the book of Kings was the topic of a graduate seminar at The Hebrew University; the student presentations clarified a number of important issues treated in the Introduction.

I owe special thanks to Judah Troen, a student at the Institute of Jewish Studies at The Hebrew University and a very dear personal friend, who prepared the bibliography; in addition, he was a ready and wise interlocutor, with whom a considerable number of thorny issues concerning Kings were threshed out. *Těšu'ôt ḥēn ḥēn lěkā.*

A grant from the Research Committee of the Faculty of Humanities of The Hebrew University of Jerusalem helped in preparing the final manuscript. Vogel Alter and Patrice Kaminski were responsible for the illustrational reproductions.

The production of this book was carried through under the watchful and considerate eye of Andrew R. Corbin, Editor at the Doubleday Religious Publishing Division. The painstaking copy editing of Beverly Fields saved me many an embarrassment, for which I am most grateful.

Finally, a personal reflection: Writing a commentary on a book of the Bible is a humbling experience, for no sooner does one delve into the task than he is confronted with the prodigious literary production that the millennium-old commentary genre has generated. These works introduce the reader to the issues that engaged earlier generations and, if attentive, he or she may observe the individual behind the commentary, for a commentary is, by its very nature, an individual reading of the text at hand, as it reflects both the interests and the training of its writer. From my first days at the University of Pennsylvania close to four decades ago, I found myself challenged by the proposition enunciated by E. A. Speiser that the Bible can only be understood through the prism of the languages and culture of ancient Mesopotamia. Much of my academic career has been devoted to probing Speiser's assertion, with the period of the Israelite monarchy serving as its prime testing ground. Indeed, the texts and archaeology of the ancient Near East have made it possible for our generation, more than previous ones, to unravel the secrets of the sacred text. The historical-philological examination has been extended beyond all imaginable limits through an ongoing intercourse with the world of Israel's neighbors. Another lesson from my school days, acquired at the feet of my esteemed mentor, Moshe Greenberg, taught me the great value of consulting traditional Jewish biblical exegesis. So, as a son of Israel and resident of the State of Israel, I culled untold insights from this rich trove; from it and from the research published in Modern Hebrew, I gained both knowledge and understanding. In the commentary that follows, I share my personal engagement with Kings in the hope that it will contribute to the contemporary discourse and perhaps even find its place in the continuum of the exegetical tradition.

May He who "gives strength to the weary, fresh vigor to the spent" (Isa 40:29) grant me wisdom and good health to continue "to magnify His Teaching and to glorify it" (42:21).

Jerusalem and Beer-sheba
Adar Sheni 5760
March 2000

CONTENTS

◆

ABBREVIATIONS

◆

PRINCIPAL ABBREVIATIONS

AASF   Annales Academiae Scientiarum Fennicae
AASOR   Annual of the American Schools of Oriental Research
AB   Anchor Bible
ABD   *Anchor Bible Dictionary*. Edited by D. N. Freedman. 6 vols. New York: Doubleday, 1992
ABL   *Assyrian and Babylonian Letters Belonging to the Kouyunjik Collections of the British Museum*. Edited by R. F. Harper. 14 vols. Chicago: University of Chicago Press, 1892–1914
ADD   *Assyrian Deeds and Documents*. C. H. W. Johns. 4 vols. Cambridge: Deighton-Bell, 1898–1923
AfO   *Archiv für Orientforschung*
AHw   *Akkadisches Handwörterbuch*. W. von Soden. 3 vols. Wiesbaden: Harrassowitz, 1965–1981
AJBA   *Australian Journal of Biblical Archaeology*
AJSL   *American Journal of Semitic Languages and Literatures*
ANEP   *The Ancient Near East in Pictures Relating to the Old Testament*. Edited by J. B. Pritchard. 2d ed. Princeton: Princeton University Press, 1969
ANET   *Ancient Near Eastern Texts Relating to the Old Testament*. Edited by J. B. Pritchard. 3d ed. Princeton: Princeton University Press, 1969
AnOr   Analecta Orientalia
AOAT   Alter Orient und Altes Testament
AOS   American Oriental Series
ARI   *Assyrian Royal Inscriptions*. A. K. Grayson. 2 vols. RANE. Wiesbaden: Harrassowitz, 1972–1976
ArOr   *Archiv Orientální*
AS   Assyriological Studies
ASORDS   American Schools of Oriental Research Dissertation Series
ASTI   *Annual of the Swedish Theological Institute*
ATD   Das Alte Testament Deutsch
BA   *Biblical Archaeologist*
BAR   *Biblical Archaeology Review*
BARead   *Biblical Archaeologist Reader*. Vols. 2–3. Garden City: Doubleday, 1964–1970
BASOR   *Bulletin of the American Schools of Oriental Research*
BDB   Brown, F., S. R. Driver, and C. A. Briggs. *A Hebrew and English Lexicon of the Old Testament*. Oxford: Clarendon, 1907
BH^3 *Biblia Hebraica*. Edited by R. Kittel. 3d ed. Stuttgart, 1937
BHS   *Biblia Hebraica Stuttgartensia*. Stuttgart: Deutsche Bibelstiftung, 1983
Bib   *Biblica*
BibOr   Biblica et Orientalia

BIES   *Bulletin of the Israel Exploration Society (= Yediot)*
BiOr   *Bibliotheca Orientalis*
BIOSCS   *Bulletin of the International Organization for Septuagint and Cognate Studies*
BJRL   *Bulletin of the John Rylands University Library of Manchester*
BJPES   *Bulletin of the Jewish Palestine Exploration Society (= Yediot, later BIES)*
BKAT   Biblischer Kommentar, Altes Testament. Edited by M. Noth and H. W. Wolff
B-L   Bauer, H., and P. Leander. *Historische Grammatik der hebräischen Sprache.* Halle: Niemeyer, 1918–1922
BWANT   Beiträge zur Wissenschaft vom Alten und Neuen Testament
BZAW   Beihefte zur Zeitschrift für die alttestamentliche Wissenschaft
CAD   *The Assyrian Dictionary of the Oriental Institute of the University of Chicago.* Edited by I. J. Gelb et al. Chicago: Oriental Institute, 1956–
CAH   Cambridge Ancient History
CahRB   Cahiers de la Revue biblique
CBC   Cambridge Bible Commentary on the New English Bible
CBQ   *Catholic Biblical Quarterly*
CBQMS   Catholic Biblical Quarterly Monograph Series
CBSC   Cambridge Bible for Schools and Colleges
ConBOT   Coniectanea Biblica: Old Testament
DDD   *Dictionary of Deities and Demons in the Bible.* Edited by K. van der Toorn, B. Becking, and P. W. van der Horst. Leiden: Brill, 1995
DJD   Discoveries in the Judaean Desert
EA   El-Amarna Tablets. According to the edition of J. A. Knudtzon. *Die el-Amarna-Tafeln.* VAB 2. Leipzig: Hinrichs, 1908–1915. Reprint, Aalen, 1964. Continued in A. F. Rainey, *El-Amarna Tablets 359–379.* 2d revised ed. Kevelaer: Butzon & Bercker, 1978
EHAT   Exegetisches Handbuch zum Alten Testament
ErIsr   *Eretz-Israel*
EncJud   *Encyclopaedia Judaica.* 16 vols. Jerusalem: Keter, 1972
EncMiqr   *Encyclopedia Miqra'it* (Encyclopaedia Biblica). 8 vols. Jerusalem, 1950–1982
FOTL   The Forms of the Old Testament Literature
FRLANT   Forschungen zur Religion und Literatur des Alten und Neuen Testaments
GKC   *Gesenius' Hebrew Grammar.* Edited by E. Kautzch. Translated by A. E. Cowley. 2d ed. Oxford: Clarendon, 1910. Cited by section.
HAR   *Hebrew Annual Review*
HAT   Handbuch zum Alten Testament
HCOT   Historical Commentary on the Old Testament
Hen   *Henoch*
HSAT   *Die Heilige Schrift des Alten Testament.* Edited by E. Kautzsch and A. Bertholet. 4th ed. Tübingen: Mohr (Siebeck), 1922–1923
HSM   Harvard Semitic Monographs
HSS   Harvard Semitic Studies
HUCA   *Hebrew Union College Annual*
IB   *Interpreter's Bible.* Edited by G. A. Buttrick et al. 12 vols. New York: Abingdon, 1951–1957
ICC   International Critical Commentary

IDB	*Interpreter's Dictionary of the Bible*. Edited by G.A. Buttrick. 4 vols. Nashville: Abingdon, 1962
IEJ	*Israel Exploration Journal*
Int	*Interpretation*
JANES	*Journal of the Ancient Near Eastern Society of Columbia University*
JAOS	*Journal of the American Oriental Society*
JB	Jerusalem Bible
JBL	*Journal of Biblical Literature*
JBLMS	Journal of Biblical Literature Monograph Series
JCS	*Journal of Cuneiform Studies*
JNES	*Journal of Near Eastern Studies*
JPOS	*Journal of the Palestine Oriental Society*
JQR	*Jewish Quarterly Review*
JSOT	*Journal for the Study of the Old Testament*
JSOTSup	Journal for the Study of the Old Testament Supplement Series
JSS	*Journal of Semitic Studies*
JTS	*Journal of Theological Studies*
JWH	*Journal of World History*
KAI	*Kanaanäische und aramäische Inschriften*. H. Donner and W. Röllig. 3 vols. Wiesbaden: Harrossowitz,1962
KB	L. Koehler and W. Baumgartner. *Hebräisches und aramäisches Lexikon zum Alten Testament*. 3d ed. Leiden: Brill, 1967
KEHAT	Kurzgefasstes exegetisches Handbuch zum Alten Testament
KHC	Kurzer Hand-Commentar zum Alten Testament
KJV	King James Version
LÄ	*Lexikon der Ägyptologie*. Edited by W. Helck, E. Otto, and W. Westendorf. Wiesbaden: Harassowitz, 1972
Leš	*Lešonénu*
Luc.	Lucianic recensions of LXX
LXX	Septuagint, according to *Septuaginta*. Edited by A. Rahlfs
MT	Masoretic Text
MUSJ	*Mélanges de l'Université Saint-Joseph*
NAB	New American Bible
NCB	New Century Bible
NEAEHL	*New Encyclopedia of Archaeological Excavations in the Holy Land*. Edited by E. Stern. 4 vols. Jerusalem: Israel Exploration Society, 1993
NEB	New English Bible
NIBC	New International Bible Commentary
NJB	New Jerusalem Bible
NJPSV	New Jewish Publication Society of America Version
NRSV	New Revised Standard Version
OBO	Orbis biblicus et orientalis
OG	Old Greek
OIP	Oriental Institute Publications
OL	Old Latin
OLP	Orientalia lovaniensia periodica
Or	*Orientalia*
OTL	Old Testament Library
OtSt	*Oudtestamentische Studiën*

PEQ	*Palestine Exploration Quarterly*
PJ	*Palästina-Jahrbuch*
RANE	Records of the Ancient Near East
RB	*Revue biblique*
RHJE	*Revue de l'histoire juive en Égypte*
RHPR	*Revue d'histoire et de philosophie religieuses*
RIMA	The Royal Inscriptions of Mesopotamia, Assyrian Periods
RlA	*Reallexikon der Assyriologie.* Edited by E. Ebeling et al. Berlin: de Gruyter, 1928–
RSO	*Rivista degli studi orientali*
RSV	Revised Standard Version
SAA	State Archives of Assyria
SAAS	State Archives of Assyria Studies
SBLDS	Society of Biblical Literature Dissertation Series
SBLMS	Society of Biblical Literature Monograph Series
SBT	Studies in Biblical Theology
ScrHier	Scripta Hierosolymitana
Sem	*Semitica*
SHCANE	Studies in the History and Culture of the Ancient Near East
SOTSMS	Society for Old Testament Studies Monograph Series
ST	*Studia Theologica*
Syr.	Syriac, according to *The Old Testament in Syriac according to the Peshitta Version.* Edited by H. Gottlieb and E. Hammershaimb
TAPS	Transactions of the American Philosophical Society
Tg.	Targum, according to *The Bible in Aramaic.* Edited by A. Sperber
TDOT	*Theological Dictionary of the Old Testament.* Edited by G. J. Botterweck et al. Grand Rapids: Eerdmans, 1974–
TLZ	*Theologische Literaturzeitung*
TWAT	*Theologisches Wörterbuch zum Alten Testament.* Edited by G. J. Botterweck and H. Ringgren. Stuttgart: Kohlhammer, 1970–
TynBul	*Tyndale Bulletin*
TZ	*Theologische Zeitschrift*
UF	*Ugarit-Forschungen*
VAB	Vorderasiatische Bibliothek
VT	*Vetus Testamentum*
VTSup	Vetus Testamentum Supplements
WBC	Word Bible Commentary
WHJP	*World History of the Jewish People*
WO	*Die Welt des Orients*
WSS	Avigad, N. *Corpus of West Semitic Stamp Seals.* Jerusalem: Israel Academy of Sciences and Humanities, 1997
ZA	*Zeitschrift für Assyriologie*
ZAW	*Zeitschrift für die alttestamentliche Wissenschaft*
ZDMG	*Zeitschrift der deutschen morgenländischen Gesellschaft*
ZDPV	*Zeitschrift des deutschen Palästina-Vereins*

OTHER ABBREVIATIONS AND SIGNS

ad, ad loc.	at, at the place
Akk	Akkadian
ANE	Ancient Near East(ern)
Ar	Arabic
Aram	Aramaic
BCE	Before the Common Era (= BC)
BH	Biblical Hebrew
ca.	circa, approximately
cf.	"compare with" or "see"
col., cols.	column, columns
D	the Deuteronomic source
Dtr	Deuteronom(ist)ic History
E	the Elohistic source
e.g.	for example
Eg	Egyptian
esp.	especially
E.T.	English Translation
et al.	and others
fem.	feminine
Fs.	Festschrift (honorary volume)
Gk	Greek
Heb	Hebrew
ibid.	in the same place
idem	the same, previously mentioned
i.e.	that is
J	the Yahwist source
Kh.	Khirbet
LBH, LH	Late Biblical Hebrew
lit.	literally
loc. cit.	in the place cited
masc.	masculine
MH	Mishnaic Hebrew
MS, MSS	manuscript, manuscripts
NA	Neo-Assyrian
NB	Neo-Babylonian
n., nn.	note, notes
n.b.	note well
no.	number
opp.	opposite
OT	Old Testament
P	the Priestly source
part.	participle
pass.	passive
Phoen	Phoenician
pl.	plural
sg.	singular

Sum	Sumerian
s.v.	under the word
Ug	Ugaritic
v., vv.	verse, verses
viz.	namely
Vulg.	Vulgate (Latin version of the Bible)
WSem	West Semitic
(words)	words added for purposes of translation
⟨words⟩	words added to MT
« »	words omitted from MT
16*, 24* [etc.]	asterisks denote page numbers of English-language part of Hebrew collections
*špṭ [etc.]	asterisks on Hebrew words denote the consonants of verbal roots

LIST OF MAPS AND ILLUSTRATIONS

◆

MAPS

ILLUSTRATIONS

1 AND 2 KINGS
A TRANSLATION

◆

THE REIGN OF SOLOMON

The Accession of Solomon

1 ¹Now King David was old, advanced in years; they would cover him with clothes, but he could not get warm. ²His servants said to him: "Let them search for a young virgin for my lord the king, and she will attend the king and be his housekeeper; she will lie in your bosom and my lord the king will be warm." ³So they searched for a beautiful girl throughout all the territory of Israel. They found Abishag the Shunammite and brought her to the king. ⁴Now the girl was very beautiful indeed, and she became housekeeper to the king and she served him; yet the king did not have relations with her.

⁵Now Adonijah son of Haggith went about boasting: "*I* will be king." He acquired a chariot and horsemen and fifty outrunners. ⁶Yet his father never once caused him displeasure by saying: "Why have you done this?" He was, moreover, very handsome, and he was the one born after Absalom. ⁷He conspired with Joab son of Zeruiah and with Abiathar the priest, and they supported Adonijah; ⁸but Zadok the priest and Benaiah son of Jehoiada and Nathan the prophet and Shimei and Rei and David's warriors were not with Adonijah.

⁹Then Adonijah slaughtered sheep, oxen, and fatlings by the stone Zoheleth near En-rogel, and he invited all his brothers, the king's sons, and all the men of Judah, the king's servants; ¹⁰but he did not invite Nathan the prophet and Benaiah and the warriors and Solomon his brother. ¹¹Then Nathan said to Bathsheba, Solomon's mother: "Have you not heard that Adonijah son of Haggith has become king and our lord David did not know? ¹²Now let me give you advice, so that you may save your life and the life of your son Solomon. ¹³Go and come to the King David and say to him: 'Did not *you* my lord the king swear to your handmaid: "Solomon your son shall be king after me and he shall sit upon my throne"? Then why has Adonijah become king?' ¹⁴While you are still talking there with the king, *I* will come in after you and confirm your words."

¹⁵So Bathsheba came to the king in his chamber. — Now the king was very old and Abishag the Shunammite was attending the king. — ¹⁶Bathsheba bowed and prostrated herself before the king. The king said: "What is the matter?" ¹⁷She said to him: "My lord, *you* swore by YHWH your God to your handmaid: 'Solomon your son shall rule after me and *he* shall sit upon my throne.' ¹⁸And now Adonijah has become king and you, my lord the king, did not know. ¹⁹He slaughtered oxen and fatlings and sheep in great quantity and he invited all the king's sons and Abiathar the priest and Joab, commander of the army, but Solomon your servant he did not invite. ²⁰And you, my lord the king, the eyes of all Israel are upon you, to tell them who will sit upon the throne of my lord

---

* The translation is based on the Hebrew text established in the commentary and not the Masoretic Text.

the king after him. ²¹(Otherwise,) when my lord the king sleeps with his ancestors, I and my son Solomon will be considered wrongdoers."

²²Now she was still talking with the king when Nathan the prophet came in. ²³They told the king: "Nathan the prophet is here"; and he came before the king and prostrated himself before the king with his face to the ground. ²⁴Nathan said: "My lord the king, did *you* say: 'Adonijah shall reign after me and *he* shall sit on my throne'? ²⁵For he has gone down today and has slaughtered oxen, fatlings, and sheep in great quantity. He invited all the king's sons and the officers of the army and Abiathar the priest, and they are now eating and drinking in his presence and saying: 'May King Adonijah live!' ²⁶But *me*, your servant, and Zadok the priest and Benaiah son of Jehoiada and Solomon your servant he did not invite. ²⁷Has this matter come about by order of my lord the king, and you have not informed your servant who shall sit on the throne of my lord the king after him?"

²⁸King David answered and said: "Call Bathsheba to me." She came before the king and stood before the king. ²⁹The king swore, saying: "By the life of YHWH who rescued me from every adversity: ³⁰As I swore to you by YHWH, God of Israel: 'Solomon your son shall reign after me and *he* shall sit on my throne in my stead,' so I will do this very day." ³¹Bathsheba bowed facing the ground and she prostrated herself to the king, and she said: "May my lord, King David, live forever!"

³²Then King David said: "Call Zadok the priest and Nathan the prophet and Benaiah son of Jehoiada to me." They came before the king. ³³The king said to them: "Take your lord's servants with you, and have Solomon my son ride my own mule and bring him down to Gihon. ³⁴There Zadok the priest and Nathan the prophet shall anoint him as king over Israel; then you shall blow the horn and say: 'May King Solomon live!' ³⁵Go up after him, and he will come in and sit on my throne and *he* shall reign in my stead; for it is he that I have appointed to become ruler of Israel and Judah." ³⁶Benaiah son of Jehoiada answered the king and said: "Amen. May YHWH the God of my lord the king so order. ³⁷As YHWH has been with my lord the king, so may he be with Solomon, and may he make his throne greater than the throne of my lord, King David."

³⁸So Zadok the priest and Nathan the prophet and Benaiah son of Jehoiada and the Cherethites and the Pelethites went down; they had Solomon ride on King David's mule, and they led him to Gihon. ³⁹Zadok the priest took the horn of oil from the Tent and anointed Solomon. They blew the horn and all the people said: "May King Solomon live!" ⁴⁰Then all the people went up after him; the people were playing pipes and rejoicing with great joy, so that the earth was split by their sound.

⁴¹Now Adonijah and all the invited who were with him heard (it) just as they finished eating. When Joab heard the sound of the horn, he said: "Why the sound of the city in uproar?" ⁴²He was still speaking when Jonathan son of Abiathar the priest came. Adonijah said: "Come, for you are a worthy man and you bring good news." ⁴³Jonathan answered and said to Adonijah: "On the contrary. Our lord, King David, has made Solomon king. ⁴⁴The king sent with him

Zadok the priest and Nathan the prophet and Benaiah son of Jehoiada and the Cheretheites and the Pelethites. They had him ride on the king's mule, ⁴⁵and Zadok the priest and Nathan the prophet anointed him king at Gihon. They went up from there rejoicing, and the city was in an uproar. That is the sound you heard. ⁴⁶Furthermore, Solomon sat on the royal throne. ⁴⁷And furthermore, the king's servants came to bless our lord King David: 'May God make the name of Solomon better than your name, and may he make his throne greater than your throne.' Then the king bowed low on the bed. ⁴⁸And furthermore, thus said the king: 'Blessed be YHWH, God of Israel, who has given this day someone to sit on my throne and my eyes behold it.' ⁴⁹Thereupon, all the invitees of Adonijah trembled, and so they left; each went his own way.

⁵⁰Adonijah, fearing Solomon, immediately went and took hold of the horns of the altar. ⁵¹They told Solomon: "Adonijah is in fear of King Solomon, and here he has taken hold of the horns of the altar, and said: 'Let King Solomon swear to me today that he will not kill his servant with the sword.'" ⁵²Solomon said: "If he will be a worthy man, a hair of his will not fall to the ground, but if he is caught in a wrongdoing, he shall die." ⁵³King Solomon sent and they took him down from the altar; he came and prostrated himself to King Solomon, and Solomon said to him: "Go home."

Solomon Takes Charge

2 ¹Now the time of David's death drew near, so he charged Solomon his son: ²"I am going the way of all the earth; be strong and be a man! ³Keep the mandate of YHWH your God, following his ways, keeping his statutes, his commands, and his laws and his warnings, as written in the Teaching of Moses, in order that you may be successful in all that you do and wherever you turn; ⁴so that YHWH will fulfill his promise that he made concerning me: 'If your offspring watch their way to walk before me faithfully, with all their heart and all their soul, then no one of your line shall be cut off from the throne of Israel.'

⁵Furthermore, *you* know what Joab son of Zeruiah did to me, what he did to two officers of the army of Israel, Abner son of Ner and Amasa son of Jether. He killed them, and so brought about the blood of war in peacetime and put the blood of war on the girdle that is on his loins and the sandals that are on his feet. ⁶Act in accordance with your wisdom so that his white head does not go down in peace to Sheol. ⁷But with the sons of Barzillai the Gileadite be loyal, and let them be among those that eat at your table, for they took me in when I fled from Absalom your brother. ⁸Now you have with you Shimei son of Gera, a Benjaminite from Bahurim; *he* cursed me with a grievous curse on the day I was going to Mahanaim. But *he* came down to the Jordan to meet me and I swore by YHWH: 'I will not kill you by the sword.' ⁹However now, you should not clear him, for you are a wise man and you will know what to do to him, so as to bring down his white head in blood to Sheol."

¹⁰So David slept with his ancestors, and he was buried in the City of David. ¹¹The years that David reigned over Israel were forty years; in Hebron he

reigned seven years, and in Jerusalem he reigned thirty-three years. [12]And Solomon sat on the throne of David his father, and his kingdom was firmly established.

[13]Then Adonijah son of Haggith came to Bathsheba mother of Solomon. She said: "Do you come in peace?" He said: "In peace." [14]He said: "I have something to say to you." She said: "Speak." [15]He said: "*You* know that to me the kingship belonged and that to me all Israel looked to rule, but the kingship turned away and became my brother's, for it was from YHWH that it became his. [16]And now, I have one request to ask of you. Do not refuse me." She said to him: "Speak." [17]He said: "Please talk to King Solomon—for he will not refuse you—to give me Abishag the Shunammite as wife." [18]Bathsheba said: "Very well. *I* will speak to the king on your behalf."

[19]So Bathsheba came to King Solomon to speak to him about Adonijah. The king rose to greet her, and he bowed down to her. He sat on his throne, and he had a throne set for the king's mother, and she sat on his right. [20]Then she said: "I have one small request to ask of you. Do not refuse me." The king said to her: "Ask, my mother, for I will not refuse you." [21]She said: "Let Abishag the Shunammite be given to Adonijah your brother as wife." [22]King Solomon answered and said to his mother: "And why do you ask for Abishag the Shunammite for Adonijah? Ask the kingship for him! For he is my older brother! For him, for Abiathar the priest, and for Joab son of Zeruiah!" [23]Then King Solomon swore by YHWH: "So may God do to me and even more, for Adonijah spoke this way at the cost of his life. [24]Now, by the life of YHWH, who has established me and seated me on the throne of David my father and who has made a house for me as he promised, this day Adonijah shall be put to death!" [25]King Solomon instructed Benaiah son of Jehoiada; he struck him down, and he died.

[26]To Abiathar the priest, the king said: "Go to Anathoth, to your fields; for though you are a man marked to die, I will not put you to death at this time, for you carried the Ark of the Lord YHWH before David my father and because you bore all the hardships that my father bore." [27]So Solomon ousted Abiathar from being priest of YHWH, in fulfillment of the word of YHWH that he had spoken concerning the house of Eli at Shiloh.

[28]When the news reached Joab—Joab had sided with Adonijah but had not sided with Absalom—Joab fled to the Tent of YHWH and took hold of the horns of the altar. [29]Solomon was told that Joab had fled to the Tent of YHWH and that he was by the altar; so Solomon sent Benaiah son of Jehoiada (with orders): "Go, strike him down!" [30]Benaiah came to the Tent of YHWH and he said to him: "Thus said the king: 'Come out!'" He said: "No, for here I will die!" Benaiah brought back word to the king: "This is how Joab spoke and how he answered me." [31]The king said to him: "Do as he spoke, and strike him down and bury him; so you will remove from me and my father's house (the guilt of) the innocent blood that Joab shed. [32]And YHWH will bring back his blood on his own head, for he fell upon two men more righteous and better than he, and he killed them with the sword—and my father did not know—Abner son of

Ner, commander of the army of Israel, and Amasa son of Jether, commander of the army of Judah. ³³(The guilt of) their blood will come back on the head of Joab and the heads of his offspring forever, but upon David and his offspring and his house and his throne there will peace forever from YHWH." ³⁴So Benaiah son of Jehoiada went up and struck him down and killed him; he was buried at his home in the steppe. ³⁵The king appointed Benaiah son of Jehoiada over the army in his place; the king appointed Zadok the priest in place of Abiathar.

³⁶Then the king sent and called for Shimei; he said to him: "Build yourself a house in Jerusalem and stay there, and do not go out from there anywhere else. ³⁷For on the day that you go out and cross Wadi Kidron, know full well that you shall surely die. Your blood will be on your own head." ³⁸Shimei said to the king: "The matter is fine. As my lord the king has spoken, so shall your servant do." And so Shimei stayed in Jerusalem for a number of years. ³⁹Now three years later, two servants of Shimei ran away to Achish son of Maacah, king of Gath; Shimei was told: "Your servants are in Gath." ⁴⁰So Shimei immediately saddled his ass and went to Gath, to Achish, in search of his servants. Shimei went and brought his servants from Gath. ⁴¹Solomon was told that Shimei had gone from Jerusalem to Gath and had returned. ⁴²The king sent and called for Shimei, and he said to him: "Did I not have you swear by YHWH and warned you: 'On the day that you leave and go anywhere, you know full well that you shall surely die.' And you said to me: 'The matter is fine. I accept.' ⁴³So why did you not keep the oath of YHWH and the order that I gave you?" ⁴⁴The king said to him: "*You* know all the wrong that you harbored in your heart, which you did to David my father; so YHWH has brought down your wrongdoing on your own head. ⁴⁵King Solomon is blessed, and the throne of David shall be established before YHWH forever." ⁴⁶Then the king ordered Benaiah son of Jehoiada; he went out and struck him down, and he died. Thus, the kingdom was firmly in Solomon's hand.

The King's Visit to Gibeon and the Grant of Wisdom

3 ¹Solomon became the son-in-law of Pharaoh king of Egypt; he married Pharaoh's daughter and brought her to the City of David until he completed building his house and the House of YHWH and the wall of Jerusalem round about. ²Only the people were sacrificing at the high places, because a house for the name of YHWH had not been built up to those days. ³Now Solomon loved YHWH, following the statutes of David his father; only he was sacrificing and making offerings at the high places.

⁴The king went to Gibeon to sacrifice there, for that was the great high place. Solomon used to sacrifice a thousand burnt offerings on that altar. ⁵At Gibeon, YHWH appeared to Solomon in a dream by night. God said: "Ask, what shall I give you?" ⁶Solomon said: "*You* have acted with great loyalty toward your servant David my father, as he walked before you in truth and in righteousness and integrity with you. You have kept this great loyalty toward him and given

him a son sitting on his throne as it is today. [7]Now then, YHWH, my God, *you* have made your servant king in place of David my father, yet I am a little child. I have no experience to lead. [8]And your servant is among your people that you have chosen, a great people, so numerous they cannot be numbered and cannot be counted. [9]So, give your servant an understanding heart to judge your people, to distinguish between good and bad; for who can judge this vast people of yours?" [10]The Lord was pleased that Solomon had asked this thing. [11]God said to him: "Because you asked for this and did not ask for long life for yourself, and you did not ask for riches for yourself and did not ask for the life of your enemies, but you asked for yourself understanding in hearing justice, [12]now I do as you have spoken. I give you a heart of wisdom and understanding; there was no one like you before you, and there will not be anyone like you after you. [13]And even though you did not ask, I give you both riches and honor, that there will not be any king like you during your lifetime. [14]And if you follow my ways, keeping my statutes and commands as your father David did, I will give you long life." [15]Solomon awoke and, indeed, it was a dream. When he came to Jerusalem, he stood before the Ark of the covenant of YHWH; he sacrificed burnt offerings and presented offerings of well-being and made a banquet for all his servants.

The Judgment of a Wise King

3   [16]Then two prostitutes came to the king and stood before him. [17]One woman said: "If it please my lord, I and this woman live in the same house; and I gave birth while she was in the house. [18]On the third day after my delivery, this woman also gave birth; we were alone, no outsider was with us in the house, just the two of us in the house. [19]Now the son of this woman died during the night because she lay on him. [20]She got up in the middle of the night and took my son from beside me while your maidservant was sleeping, and she laid him in her bosom, and she laid her dead son in my bosom. [21]When I got up in the morning to nurse my son, here he is, dead! But I looked carefully at him in the morning, and here he was not my son whom I had borne." [22]The other woman said: "No! For my son is the live one; your son is the dead one!" And this one was saying: "No! Your son is the dead one; my son is the live one!" Thus they argued before the king. [23]The king said: "This one says: 'This is my son, the live one; your son is the dead one.' And the other says: 'No! Your son is the dead one and my son the live one!'" [24]The king said: "Bring me a sword." They brought a sword before the king. [25]The king said: "Cut the live son in two! And give half to one and half to the other." [26]But the woman whose son was the live one said to the king, for she was overcome with compassion for her son: "Please, my lord, give her the live child, but by no means, don't kill him. And the other one was saying: "Neither I nor you shall have him! Cut him!" [27]The king replied: "Give her the live infant and by no means, don't kill him. She is his mother." [28]When all Israel heard of the judgment rendered by the king, they were in awe of the king, for they saw that God's wisdom was in him to do justice.

The Administration of Solomon's Kingdom

4 ¹King Solomon was king over all Israel.

²These were his officers:

Azariah son of Zadok, the priest;

³Elihoreph and Ahijah sons of Shisha, scribes;

Jehoshaphat son of Ahilud, the recorder;

⁴and Benaiah son of Jehoiada, over the army;

and Zadok and Abiathar, priests;

⁵and Azariah son of Nathan, over the prefects;

and Zabud son of Nathan, priest (and) friend of the king;

⁶and Ahishar, over the household;

and Adoniram son of Abda, over the levy.

⁷Solomon had twelve prefects for all Israel, and they provided for the king and his household; each had to provide for one month a year. ⁸These were their names:

Son of Hur in Mount Ephraim;

⁹Son of Deker in Makaz and in Shaalbim and Beth-shemesh and Elon-beth-hanan;

¹⁰Son of Hesed in Aruboth—in his charge were Socoh and all the land of Hepher;

¹¹Son of Abinadab—all the district of Dor. Taphath the daughter of Solomon was his wife;

¹²Baana son of Ahilud—Taanach and Megiddo and all of Beth-shean, near Zarethan, south of Jezreel, from Beth-shean to Abel-meholah up to the other side of Jokmeam;

¹³Son of Geber in Ramoth-gilead—in his charge were the villages of Jair son of Manasseh in the Gilead; in his charge was the region of Argob in the Bashan, sixty large cities with walls and bronze bars;

¹⁴Ahinadab son of Iddo—Mahanaim;

¹⁵Ahimaaz in Naphtali; he, too, married a daughter of Solomon, Basemath;

¹⁶Baana son of Hushai in Asher and Bealoth;

¹⁷Jehoshaphat son of Paruah in Issachar;

¹⁸Shimei son of Ela in Benjamin;

¹⁹Geber son of Uri in the land of Gilead, the land of Sihon king of the Amorites and Og king of Bashan;

and one prefect in the land ⟨of Judah⟩.

²⁰Judah and Israel were as many as the sand by the sea; eating, drinking, and making merry. 5 ¹Now Solomon ruled over all the kingdoms from the River, (through) the land of the Philistines to the border of Egypt; they brought tribute and served Solomon all his lifetime.

²Solomon's board for one day was thirty *kors* of fine flour, and sixty *kors* of flour, ³ten fat oxen, and twenty pasture-fed oxen, and one hundred sheep, besides deer and gazelles, roebucks and fattened fowl.

⁴Indeed, he held sway over all "Beyond-the-River," from Tiphsah to Gaza, over all the kings of "Beyond-the-River." He enjoyed peace on all sides round

about. ⁵Judah and Israel dwelled securely, each person at the foot of his vine and at the foot of his fig tree, from Dan to Beer-sheba, all the days of Solomon.

⁶Solomon had forty thousand stalls for the horses of his chariot force and twelve thousand horsemen. ⁷These prefects provided for King Solomon and all those who came to King Solomon's table, each one in his month; they let nothing be lacking. ⁸They (also) brought the barley and straw for the horses and steeds to the appointed place, each according to his charge.

Solomon's Wisdom

5   ⁹God granted Solomon wisdom and exceedingly much understanding, and breadth of heart, as the sand on the seashore. ¹⁰Solomon's wisdom was greater than the wisdom of all the Kedemites and all the wisdom of Egypt. ¹¹He was wiser than all men, than Ethan the Ezrahite, and Heman and Chalkol and Darda, the sons of Mahol; and his fame was in all the nations round about. ¹²He uttered three thousand proverbs, and his songs were a thousand and five. ¹³He spoke of trees, from the cedar that is in Lebanon to the hyssop that grows out of the wall; he spoke of beasts and of birds and of creeping things and of fish. ¹⁴They came from all peoples to hear Solomon's wisdom, (sent) by all the kings of the earth who had heard of his wisdom.

Negotiations with Hiram

5   ¹⁵Hiram king of Tyre sent his servants to Solomon when he heard that he had been anointed king in place of his father, for Hiram had always loved David. ¹⁶Solomon sent (in reply) to Hiram: ¹⁷"You knew that my father David could not build a house for the name of YHWH his God because of the wars that surrounded him, until YHWH made them subject to him. ¹⁸Now YHWH my God has given me rest all around; there is no adversary and no misfortune. ¹⁹And so I intend to build a house for the name of YHWH my God, as YHWH promised David my father: 'Your son, whom I shall set upon your throne in your place, *he* will build the house for my name.' ²⁰Now, then, give orders to cut cedars in the Lebanon for me; my servants will be beside your servants, and I will pay you for your servants whatever you say. *You* know that we have no one who knows how to cut trees like the Sidonians."

²¹When Hiram heard Solomon's words, he was greatly pleased; he said: "Blessed be YHWH today, who has given David a wise son over this great people." ²²Hiram sent (in reply) to Solomon: "I have heard what you sent to me. *I* will do all that you wish in the matter of the cedar trees and juniper trees. ²³My servants will bring (the trees) down from the Lebanon to the sea and *I* will make them into rafts in the sea (and deliver them) to the place you shall send to me; there I will have them broken up and *you* can transport them. You, for your part, will fulfill my wish by providing food for my household." ²⁴So it was (that) Hiram would provide Solomon with all the cedar and juniper trees he

wished, [25]and Solomon provided Hiram with twenty thousand *kors* of wheat as food for his household and twenty *kors* of beaten oil. These Solomon provided Hiram yearly. [26]YHWH granted Solomon wisdom, as he had promised him; and there was peace between Hiram and Solomon, and the two of them concluded a treaty.

[27]King Solomon raised a levy from all Israel, and the levy was thirty thousand men.

[28]He sent them to the Lebanon, ten thousand a month in rotation; one month they would be in the Lebanon and two months at home. Adoniram was Over-the-levy.

[29]Solomon had seventy thousand basket carriers and eighty thousand quarriers in the mountains, [30]excluding the officers of Solomon's prefects who were in charge of the work, three thousand three hundred, who oversaw the people doing the work. [31]The king gave orders to quarry large stones, quality stone, in order to lay the foundation of the house with hewn stone. [32]Solomon's builders and Hiram's builders and the Gebalites fashioned (them); thus they prepared the timber and the stone to build the house.

The Construction of the Temple

6 [1]It was in the four hundred and eightieth year after the departure of the Israelites from the land of Egypt, in the fourth year of the reign of Solomon over Israel, in the month of Ziv, that is the second month, he built the House for YHWH.

[2]The House that King Solomon built for YHWH was sixty cubits long, twenty ⟨cubits⟩ wide, and thirty cubits high. [3]The porch in front of the main hall was twenty cubits long along the width of the House, ten cubits deep in front of the House. [4]He made windows for the House, splayed and latticed. [5]He built an extension on the walls of the House, that is, the walls of the House around the main hall and the shrine; he made side-chambers all around. [6]The lowest side-chamber was five cubits wide, the middle one was six cubits wide, the third one, seven cubits wide; for he made recesses in the House on the outside all around, so as not to fasten onto the walls of the House. [7]Concerning the building of the House, it was built of undressed stone from the quarry; no hammers or ax or any iron tool was heard in the House during its building. [8]The opening of the lowest (side-chamber) was on the right side of the House; spiral stairs went up to the middle (side-chamber) and from the middle to the third. [9]So he built the House and completed it; he roofed the House with coffers in rows of cedar wood. [10]He built the extension along the entire House, (each story) five cubits in height; he paneled the House with cedar wood.

[11]The word of YHWH came to Solomon: [12]"As to this House that you are building, if you will follow my statutes and obey my rules and keep my commands, following them, then I will fulfill my promise to you that I made to David your father. [13]I will dwell among the Israelites and I will not forsake my people Israel."

[14]Solomon built the House and he completed it. [15]He built the walls of the House on the inside with cedar planks from the floor of the House up to the beams of the roof; he overlaid (them) with wood on the inside. He overlaid the floor of the House with juniper planks. [16]He built twenty cubits in the rear of the House with cedar planks from the floor up to the beams; he built it on the inside as a shrine, the Holy of Holies. [17]The House was forty cubits (long), that is, the main hall in front of it. [18]The cedar for the House on the inside was carved with gourds and open flowers; everything was of cedar; no stone was seen.

[19]He prepared a shrine in the House in the innermost part to place there the Ark of YHWH's covenant. [20]The interior of the shrine was twenty cubits long and twenty cubits wide and twenty cubits high; he overlaid it with refined gold; he (also) overlaid the cedar altar. [21]Solomon overlaid the House on the inside with refined gold; he drew chains in front of the shrine, and he overlaid it with gold. [22]He overlaid the entire House with gold, until completing the entire House; and the entire altar belonging to the shrine he overlaid with gold. [23]In the shrine, he made two cherubs of pinewood; it was ten cubits high. [24]One wing of the cherub was five cubits, and the other wing of the cherub was five cubits; it was ten cubits from wing tip to wing tip. [25]The other cherub was ten cubits; the two cherubs had the same size and the same shape. [26]The height of one cherub was ten cubits, and so was that of the other cherub. [27]He placed the cherubs in the inner House; and the wings of the cherubs were spread out so that the wing of one touched the wall, and the wing of the second cherub touched the second wall, and their wings that were toward the inside touched each other. [28]He overlaid the cherubs with gold.

[29]He carved round all the walls of the House carved figures of cherubs, palmettes, and open flowers, (both) on the inside and out; [30]and he overlaid the floor of the House with gold, (both) inside and out. [31]As for the entrance to the shrine, he made doors of pinewood; the jamb (and) the doorposts were a fifth (of the wall). [32]As for the two doors of pinewood, he carved on them carved figures of cherubs, palmettes, and open flowers, and he overlaid (them) with gold and hammered out the gold on the cherubs and the palmettes. [33]Similarly, for the entrance to the main hall, he made doorposts of pinewood, a fourth (of the wall), [34]and two doors of juniper wood, with two folding leaves for one door and two folding leaves for the other door. [35]He carved cherubs, palmettes, and open flowers (on them) and overlaid (them) with gold, applied evenly on the engravings.

[36]He built the inner court with three courses of hewn stone and a course of cedar beams.

[37]In the fourth year, in the month of Ziv, the House of YHWH was founded; [38]and in the eleventh year, in the month of Bul, that is the eighth month, the House was completed according to all its details and all its specifications. It took seven years to build it.

The Palace Complex

7 ¹And it took Solomon thirteen years to build his house. Thus he completed his entire house.

²He built the House of the Forest of Lebanon, one hundred cubits long and fifty cubits wide and thirty cubits high, with four rows of cedar columns, and cedar beams on the columns; ³and it was roofed with cedar from above, over the planks that were on the columns, forty-five (in number), fifteen to a row; ⁴and splayed (windows), (in) three rows, facing each other, three times; ⁵and all the entrances and doorposts had squared frames, and opposite, facing each other, three times.

⁶He made the porch of columns, fifty cubits long and thirty cubits wide, and a porch was in front of them, and columns with a canopy was in front of them.

⁷He made the porch of the throne where he was to give judgment—the porch of judgment, and it was roofed with cedar from floor to beams.

⁸And his house in which he was to reside, the other court within the porch, was of like construction; and he made a house like this porch for Pharaoh's daughter, whom Solomon had married.

⁹All these buildings were of quality stone, hewn to measure, smoothed with a smoothing tool, inside and out, from the foundation to the coping, from outside to the great court; ¹⁰and it was founded (upon) quality stone, large stones, stones of ten cubits and stones of eight cubits, ¹¹and above were quality stones, hewn to measure, and cedar wood. ¹²And the great court, round about, three rows of hewn stone and a row of cedar beams; and (likewise) the inner court of the House of YHWH and the porch of the house.

The Furnishings of the Temple

7 ¹³King Solomon sent to bring Hiram from Tyre; ¹⁴he was the son of a widow of the tribe of Naphtali, and his father was a Tyrian, a coppersmith. He was endowed with wisdom, understanding, and knowledge to perform all work in bronze. He came to King Solomon and did all his work.

¹⁵He fashioned the two columns of bronze; eighteen cubits, the height of one column; a cord of twelve cubits could encompass the one column ⟨and its thickness was four fingers, (it was) hollow; and so was⟩ the second column. ¹⁶He made two capitals to put on top of the columns, cast in bronze; five cubits, the height of one capital; five cubits, the height of the second capital; ¹⁷lattices, latticework, festoons, chainwork for the capitals on top of the columns—seven for the one capital and seven for the second capital. ¹⁸He made the pomegranates, two rows around the one lattice to cover the capitals that were on top of the columns; and so he made for the second capital. ¹⁹And (the) capitals that were on top of the columns, lilywork, in the main hall, four cubits, ²⁰and (the) capitals on the two columns, even above, close by the belly that was opposite the lattice and the pomegranates, two hundred in rows around the second capital. ²¹He set up the columns for the porch of the main hall. He set up the

right-hand column and named it Jachin, and he set up the left-hand column and named it Boaz; [22]and on top of the columns, lilywork. The work of the columns was finished.

[23]He made the Sea, cast (of metal), ten cubits from rim to rim, circular, five cubits high and thirty cubits its line all around; [24]and gourds under its rim encircling it all around for ten cubits, encompassing the Sea round about, two rows of gourds, cast during its casting; [25]standing on twelve oxen, three facing north and three facing west and three facing south and three facing east, with the Sea on them from above and their hind quarters (turned) inward; [26]its thickness (was) a hand's breadth, and its rim was like the rim of a cup, (like) a lily flower; it could hold two thousand *baths*.

[27]He (Hiram) made the stands, ten (of) bronze; the length of one stand four cubits, its width four cubits, and its height three cubits. [28]This was the construction of the stand(s). They had frames and frames between the crosspieces; [29]and on the frames between the crosspieces, lions, oxen, and cherubs, and so on the frames. Above and below the lions and the oxen, spirals of hammered work. [30]Each stand had four bronze wheels and bronze axles, and its four legs had shoulder pieces under the laver; the shoulder pieces were cast with spirals at each end. [31]Its mouth within the crown and above (it) for one cubit; its mouth was round like the construction of a pedestal, one and one-half cubits, and there were carvings even on its mouth. Now their frames were square, not round. [32]There were four wheels under the frames, and the axletrees of the wheels were in the stand; the height of each wheel was one and one-half cubits. [33]The construction of the wheels was like the construction of a chariot wheel: their axletrees and their rims and their spokes and their hubs were all cast. [34]There were four shoulder pieces at the four corners of each stand; its shoulder pieces were part of the stand. [35]At the top of the stand, a half-cubit high, (the mouth) was circular; at the top of the stand, its supports and its frames were part of it. [36]He engraved on the panels 《   》 cherubs, lions, and palms, with spirals at each end round about. [37]In this manner, he made the ten stands, a single casting, one measure and one form for all of them.

[38]He made ten bronze lavers; each laver contained forty *baths*, each laver being four cubits; there was one laver on each stand for the ten stands. [39]He placed five stands on the right side of the House and five on the left side of the House, and he placed the Sea at the right side of the House toward the southeast.

[40]Hiram made the pots and the shovels and the sprinkling bowls. Thus, Hiram brought to a close all the work that he did for King Solomon (on) the House of YHWH:

[41]Columns—two;

the bowls of the capitals that were on top of the columns—two;

the latticework—two—to cover the two bowls of the capital that were on top of the columns;

[42]the pomegranates—four hundred—for the two latticeworks, two rows of pomegranates for each latticework to cover the two bowls that were over the columns;

⁴³the stands—ten;
  the lavers—ten—(those) on the stands;
⁴⁴the Sea—one;
  the cattle—twelve—beneath the Sea;
⁴⁵the pots, the shovels, and the sprinkling bowls—
all these vessels that Hiram made for King Solomon for the House of YHWH
were of burnished bronze. ⁴⁶In the plain of the Jordan, the king cast them in the
thick earth, between Succoth and Zarethan. ⁴⁷Solomon left all the vessels out
of account because of their very great number; the weight of the bronze was
not ascertained.
  ⁴⁸Solomon made all the vessels of the House of YHWH:
  the altar, of gold;
  the table upon which was the showbread, of gold;
⁴⁹the lampstands, five on the right and five on the left, in front of the shrine,
    of refined gold;
  the flowers, the lamps, and the tongs, of gold;
⁵⁰the basins, the snuffers, the bowls, the ladles, and the firepans, of refined gold;
  and the hinges of the doors to the inner house, the Holy of Holies, (and) the
  doors of the house, of the main hall, of gold.
⁵¹Thus, all the work that King Solomon did for the House of YHWH was finished. Solomon brought the votive objects of his father, David, the silver, the
gold, and the vessels (and) deposited (them) in the treasury of the House of
YHWH.

The Inauguration of the Temple

8   ¹Then Solomon assembled the elders of Israel—all the heads of the tribes,
the ancestral chieftains of the Israelites to King Solomon—in Jerusalem, to
bring up the Ark of YHWH's covenant from the City of David, that is, Zion.
²All the men of Israel assembled before King Solomon in the month of
Ethanim—at the Festival—that is, the seventh month. ³When all the elders of
Israel had come, the priests carried the Ark, ⁴and they brought up the Ark of
YHWH and the Tent of Meeting and all the holy vessels that were in the Tent;
the priests and the Levites brought them up. ⁵(All the while) King Solomon
and the whole assembly of Israel who were present with him before the Ark
were sacrificing sheep and oxen, so numerous that they could not be numbered or be counted. ⁶The priests brought the Ark of YHWH's covenant to its
place, to the shrine of the House, to the Holy of Holies, beneath the wings of
the cherubs; ⁷for the cherubs spread wings over the place of the Ark; and the
cherubs formed a canopy over the Ark and its poles from above. ⁸The poles
were so long that the ends of the poles could be seen from the sanctuary in
front of the shrine; but they could not be seen outside. They are there until this
day. ⁹There is nothing in the Ark save the two tablets of stone that Moses placed
there at Horeb, when YHWH made a covenant with the Israelites when they
left the land of Egypt.

¹⁰As the priests left the sanctuary, the cloud filled the House of YHWH; ¹¹the priests could not stand in attendance because of the cloud, for the presence of YHWH had filled the House of YHWH. ¹²Then Solomon said:

> YHWH intended to dwell in thick cloud.
> ¹³I have indeed built a princely House for you,
>   a place for your dwelling forever.

¹⁴Then the king turned around and blessed all the congregation of Israel; all the congregation of Israel was standing. ¹⁵He said: "Blessed be YHWH, God of Israel, who with his own mouth promised David my father and with his own hand fulfilled (his promise): ¹⁶'From the day I brought my people Israel out from Egypt, I have not chosen a city out of all the tribes of Israel to build a house for my name to be there; but I chose David to be over my people Israel.' ¹⁷Now my father David had in mind to build a house for the name of YHWH, God of Israel. ¹⁸But YHWH said to David my father: 'Whereas you had in mind to build a house for my name, you have done well by these thoughts. ¹⁹However, *you* shall not build the house, but your son who shall issue from your loins, *he* shall build the house for my name.' ²⁰YHWH has fulfilled the promise he made, and I have succeeded my father David and sat on the throne of Israel as YHWH promised; and I have built the House for the name of YHWH, God of Israel. ²¹I have set a place there for the Ark in which is YHWH's covenant that he made with our ancestors when he brought them out from the land of Egypt."

²²Solomon stood before the altar of YHWH opposite all the congregation of Israel; he spread his palms heavenward ²³and said: "YHWH, God of Israel, there is no god like you, in heaven above or on earth below, keeping with loyalty the covenant with your servants who serve you wholeheartedly, ²⁴who kept your promise to your servant David my father; with your own mouth you promised and with your own hands you fulfilled, as it is today. ²⁵So, now, YHWH, God of Israel, keep your promise to your servant, David my father: 'No one of your line sitting on the throne of Israel shall be cut off at my instance, if your sons watch their way to serve me as you served me.' ²⁶Now, then, ⟨YHWH,⟩ God of Israel, may the promise that you made to David my father be confirmed.

²⁷But, indeed, can God dwell on earth? Here the heavens and the highest heavens cannot contain you; how much less this House that I have built? ²⁸Yet, turn to the prayer and the supplication of your servant, O YHWH, my God, to listen to the praise and the prayer that your servant offers before you this day, ²⁹that your eyes may be open toward this House night and day, to the place of which you said: 'My name shall be there'; that you might listen to the prayer that your servant offers toward this place. ³⁰Listen to the supplication of your servant and your people Israel, which they will pray toward this place. *You* shall listen in your dwelling in heaven, listen and forgive.

³¹If a man wrongs his neighbor, and the latter utters an imprecation against him to curse him, and the curse is taken before your altar in this House; ³²then *you* shall listen in heaven and act; judge your servants, condemning the wicked

by bringing his way on his head and acquitting the righteous by rewarding him according to his innocence.

³³When your people Israel are defeated by an enemy because they have sinned against you and then return to you and praise your name and pray and make supplication to you in this House, ³⁴then *you* shall listen in heaven; forgive the sin of your people Israel and restore them to the land you gave to their ancestors.

³⁵When the heavens are shut up and there is no rain, because they have sinned against you, and they pray to this place and praise your name, turning from their sin so that you answer them; ³⁶then *you* shall listen in heaven; forgive the sin of your servants, your people Israel, so that you teach them the good way that they should follow. Grant rain to your land that you gave to your people as an inheritance.

³⁷If there is famine in the land; if there be pestilence; if there be blight, mildew, locusts, hoppers; if their enemy presses upon them in one of their cities — whatever the plague or the sickness (may be) — ³⁸every prayer (and) every supplication that any one of your people Israel shall have, each of whom knows his own affliction, when he spreads his palms to this house, ³⁹then *you* shall listen in heaven, your dwelling place, and forgive and act. Render to each man according to his ways as you will know his heart, for you alone know the hearts of all men, ⁴⁰so that they may fear you all the days that they live on the land that you gave to our ancestors.

⁴¹Moreover, to the foreigner, who is not of your people Israel, who shall come from a distant land because of your name — ⁴²for they shall hear of your great name and your strong hand and your outstretched arm — who shall come and pray toward this House, ⁴³*you* shall listen in heaven, your dwelling place, and act in accord with all that the foreigner asks of you, so that the peoples of the earth may know your name, to fear you as do your people Israel and know that your name is proclaimed over this House that I have built.

⁴⁴When your people go out to war against their enemy, wherever you shall send them, and they pray to YHWH in the direction of the city that you have chosen and the House that I have built for your name, ⁴⁵listen in heaven to their prayer and their supplication and act justly toward them.

⁴⁶When they sin against you — for there is no person who does not sin — and you are angry at them and deliver them to an enemy who carries them off as captives to his country, far or near, ⁴⁷and then they take it to heart in the land of their captivity, they repent, and make supplication to you in the land of their captors: 'We have sinned and we have acted perversely ⟨and⟩ we have acted wickedly.' ⁴⁸If they return to you with all their heart and with all their soul in the land of their enemies who captured them, and if they pray to you in the direction of their land that you gave their ancestors, the city that you chose and the House that I have built for your name, ⁴⁹listen in heaven, your dwelling place, to their prayer and their supplication and act justly toward them, ⁵⁰forgive your people who have sinned against you, for all their transgressions by which they transgressed against you, and cause their captors to have mercy upon

them so that they will show them mercy. [51]For they are your people and your inheritance, whom you brought out from Egypt, from the midst of the iron furnace, [52]so may your eyes be open to the supplication of your servant and the supplication of your people Israel, to listen to them whenever they call out to you. [53]For *you* have set them apart for yourself as an inheritance out of all the peoples of the earth, as you promised through Moses your servant when you brought our ancestors out from Egypt, O Lord YHWH."

[54]When Solomon finished offering all this prayer and supplication to YHWH, he rose from before the altar of YHWH, from kneeling with his palms spread heavenward; [55]he stood and blessed all the congregation of Israel in a loud voice: [56]"Blessed be YHWH who has given rest to his people Israel according to all he promised. Not one word of all the good things that he promised through his servant Moses has gone unfulfilled. [57]May YHWH our God be with us as he was with our ancestors. May he not abandon us and not forsake us. [58]May he turn our hearts toward him, to follow all his ways and keep his commands and his statutes and his laws that he commanded our ancestors. [59]And may these my words that I have made in supplication before YHWH be close to YHWH our God day and night, that he do justice with his servant and with his people Israel, as each day requires; [60]that all the peoples of the earth shall know that YHWH, he is God; there is no other. [61]May your heart be fully with YHWH our God, following his statutes, and keeping his commands, as on this day."

[62]Now the king and all Israel with him offered sacrifice before YHWH. [63]Solomon offered the sacrifice of well-being, in which he offered to YHWH twenty-two thousand oxen and one hundred twenty thousand sheep. Thus, the king and all the Israelites inaugurated the House of YHWH. [64]On that day, the king consecrated the center of the court that was in front of the House of YHWH; for it was there that he made the burnt offerings and the meal offerings and the fat of the offerings of well-being—the bronze altar that was before YHWH was too small to hold (all) the burnt offerings and the meal offerings and the fat of the offerings of well-being.

[65]At that time, Solomon celebrated the Festival; all Israel was with him, a great assembly from Lebo-hamath to the Wadi of Egypt, before YHWH our God for seven days and seven days, fourteen days. [66]On the eighth day, he dismissed the people and they blessed the king. They went home happy and glad at heart for all the good that YHWH had done for David his servant and Israel his people.

YHWH's Second Appearance to Solomon

9 [1]Now when Solomon had completed building the House of YHWH and the king's house and everything that Solomon's desire wished to do, [2]YHWH appeared to Solomon a second time, as he had appeared to him in Gibeon. [3]YHWH said to him: "I have heard your prayer and your supplication that you have made before me. I have consecrated this House that you have built to place my name there forever, and my eyes and my heart shall be there for all

time. ⁴As for you, if you will walk before me as David your father walked with integrity and with uprightness, doing all that I commanded you, keep my statutes and my rules, ⁵then I will establish your royal throne over Israel forever, as I promised concerning David your father: 'No one of your line shall be cut off from the throne of Israel.' ⁶But if you turn from me, you and your children, and do not keep my commands (and) my statutes that I have given you, and you go and worship other gods and bow down to them, ⁷then I will cut Israel off the land that I have given them, and I will dismiss this House that I have consecrated for my name. Israel shall become a proverb and a byword among all the peoples. ⁸And this House will be a ruin; everyone who passes by will be appalled and whistle. And when they say: 'Why did YHWH do this to this land and to this House?' ⁹they will be told: 'Because they forsook YHWH their God, who brought their fathers out of the land of Egypt, and embraced other gods and bowed to them and worshiped them. Therefore YHWH brought all this evil upon them.'"

The Further Works of Solomon

9   ¹⁰Now at the end of the twenty years it had taken Solomon to build the two houses, the House of YHWH and the king's house—¹¹Hiram king of Tyre had supplied Solomon with cedar and juniper trees and gold, as much as he wished—then King Solomon gave Hiram twenty cities in the land of the Galilee. ¹²But when Hiram went from Tyre to see the cities that Solomon had given him, they did not please him. ¹³He said: "What are these cities that you have given me, my brother?" He named them The Land of Cabul, (their name) until this day. ¹⁴Hiram sent the king one hundred and twenty talents of gold.

¹⁵This is the matter of the levy that King Solomon raised to build the House of YHWH, his house, the Millo, the wall of Jerusalem, Hazor, Megiddo, and Gezer.—¹⁶Pharaoh king of Egypt had come up and captured Gezer; he burned it down and killed the Canaanites who lived in the city. Then he gave it as a marriage gift to his daughter, Solomon's wife.—¹⁷Solomon built Gezer, Lower Beth-horon, ¹⁸Baalath, Tamar in the Steppe, in the land, ¹⁹and all the store-cities that belonged to Solomon and the chariot cities and the cavalry cities—all Solomon's desire that he had for building in Jerusalem and in Lebanon and in all the territory of his rule. ²⁰All the people who remained from the Amorites, the Hittites, the Perizzites, the Hivites, the Jebusites, who were not Israelite,—²¹their children who remained in the land after them, whom the Israelites could not doom to destruction—Solomon imposed corvée upon them until this day. ²²But Solomon did not enslave the Israelites, for they were the armed force, his servants, his officers, his adjutants, his chariot officers, and his horsemen.

²³These were the officers of prefects who were in charge of Solomon's work, five hundred and fifty who oversaw the people doing the work.

²⁴But the daughter of Pharaoh went up from the City of David to her house, which he built for her. Then he built the Millo.

[25]Solomon used to sacrifice burnt offerings and offerings of well-being three times a year on the altar that he built for YHWH, and used to offer incense with it that was before YHWH. Thus he set up the House (of YHWH).

[26]King Solomon built a fleet at Ezion-geber, which is near Eloth on the shore of the Red Sea, in the land of Edom. [27]Hiram sent his servants in the fleet, shipmen who were experienced on the sea, with Solomon's servants. [28]They came to Ophir; there they acquired gold: four hundred and twenty talents that they delivered to King Solomon.

The Visit of the Queen of Sheba

10   [1]Now the queen of Sheba had been hearing of Solomon's fame for the sake of the name of YHWH, so she came to test him with hard questions. [2]She came to Jerusalem with a very large force, camels bearing spices, a very great amount of gold, and precious stones. When she came to Solomon, she told him everything she had in her mind, [3]and Solomon replied to all her questions; there was nothing hidden from the king that he could not tell her. [4]When the queen of Sheba saw all of Solomon's wisdom, the house that he built, [5]the food of his table, the seating of his servants, the post of his attendants and their dress, his cupbearers, and the burnt offerings that he brought to the House of YHWH, she was left breathless. [6]She said to the king: "It was true what I heard in my country about your affairs and your wisdom. [7]But I did not believe the things until I came and my own eyes saw; indeed, they did not tell me half of it. You have more wisdom and wealth than the report I heard. [8]Happy are your people. Happy are these your servants, who wait upon you continuously, who can hear your wisdom. [9]Blessed be YHWH your God who has delighted in you, setting you on the throne of Israel; because of YHWH's love of Israel forever, he made you king to do justice and righteousness." [10]Then she gave the king one hundred twenty talents of gold and a very large quantity of spices and precious stones. There was never again such a large quantity of spices as that which the queen of Sheba gave King Solomon.— [11]Moreover, Hiram's fleet, which carried gold from Ophir, brought from Ophir a very large amount of *almug* wood and precious stones. [12]The king made supports from the *almug* wood for the House of YHWH and the king's house, and harps and lyres for the singers. Such *almug* wood has not come or been seen to this day.— [13]King Solomon gave the queen of Sheba all she desired, whatever she asked, besides what he gave her as befitted King Solomon. Then she and her servants left and returned to her country.

Concluding Notes on Solomon's Wealth and Trade

10   [14]Now the weight of the gold that was received by Solomon in a single year was six hundred sixty-six gold talents, [15]besides (what came) from traders and the business of merchants, and all the Arab kings, and the governors of the land.

¹⁶King Solomon made two hundred large shields of beaten gold; six hundred (shekels) of gold went into one large shield; ¹⁷three hundred bucklers of beaten gold, three minas of gold went into one buckler. The king put them in the House of the Forest of Lebanon.

¹⁸The king made a great ivory throne and overlaid it with pure gold. ¹⁹The throne had six steps; the back of the throne had a rounded top. There were arms on each side of the seat, with two lions standing beside the arms. ²⁰And twelve lions were standing there on the six steps on each side. There was nothing like it ever made in any kingdom.

²¹All King Solomon's drinking vessels were of gold; all the vessels in the House of the Forest of Lebanon were of refined gold; there were none of silver, (for) it was considered of no value in Solomon's days. ²²For the king had a Tarshish fleet on the sea with Hiram's fleet. Once every three years, the Tarshish fleet would arrive carrying gold and silver, ivories, apes, and peacocks.

²³Thus, King Solomon exceeded all the kings of the earth in wealth and wisdom. ²⁴All the world sought an audience with Solomon in order to hear his wisdom which God had put in his heart. ²⁵And each one brought his tribute: silver vessels, gold vessels, garments, arms, spices, horses, and mules, according to the yearly due.

²⁶Solomon assembled chariots and horsemen; he had one thousand four hundred chariots and twelve thousand horsemen. He stationed them in the chariot cities and with the king in Jerusalem. ²⁷Solomon made silver (as plentiful) in Jerusalem as stones, and he made the cedars as plentiful as the sycamores in the Shephelah. ²⁸The source of Solomon's horses was Egypt and Cilicia; the king's merchants purchased them in Cilicia. ²⁹A chariot exported from Egypt cost six hundred shekels of silver and a horse one hundred fifty; and similarly, they exported (them) to all the kings of the Hittites and the kings of Aram.

Solomon's Apostasy

11 ¹Now King Solomon loved many foreign women; besides Pharaoh's daughter, (there were) women from the Moabites, Ammonites, Edomites, Sidonians, Hittites, ²from the nations of which YHWH said to the Israelites: "You should not join with them and *they* should not join with you, for they surely will entice you after their gods." To such (women) Solomon held fast out of love. ³He had seven hundred wives of royal rank and three hundred concubines; and his wives enticed him. ⁴In Solomon's old age, his wives enticed him after other gods, and his heart was not fully with YHWH his God as was the heart of David his father. ⁵Solomon followed Ashtoreth, god of the Sidonians, and Milcom, the abomination of the Ammonites. ⁶Solomon did what was displeasing to YHWH and was not loyal to YHWH as David his father. ⁷Then Solomon built a high place for Chemosh, the abomination of Moab on the mountain east of Jerusalem, and for Molech, the abomination of the Ammonites. ⁸Thus he did for all of his foreign wives, who sacrificed and offered to their gods.

⁹YHWH was incensed at Solomon, for he had turned away from YHWH God of Israel, who had appeared to him twice ¹⁰and had commanded him about this matter of not following other gods; but he did not keep what YHWH commanded. ¹¹YHWH said to Solomon: "Because this was your will, and you did not keep my covenant and my statutes which I commanded you, I most certainly will tear the kingdom away from you and give it to your servant. ¹²But I will not do it during your days, for the sake of David your father, but I will tear it away from your son. ¹³Still, I will not tear away the whole kingdom; I will give your son one tribe for the sake of David my servant and for the sake of Jerusalem, which I have chosen."

The Rebellions of Hadad and Rezon

11   ¹⁴So YHWH raised up an adversary for Solomon, Hadad the Edomite; he was of the royal line in Edom. ¹⁵Now, when David was fighting Edom—at the time that Joab the army commander went to bury the slain, having killed every male in Edom, ¹⁶for Joab and all Israel stayed there for six months until they wiped out all males in Edom—¹⁷Hadad together with some Edomite men, his father's servants, fled in the direction of Egypt. Hadad was still a young lad. ¹⁸They set out from Midian and came to Paran; they took some men with them from Paran and they came to Egypt, to Pharaoh, king of Egypt, who gave him a house, arranged for his maintenance, and gave him land. ¹⁹Hadad found very much favor with Pharaoh, and so he gave him in marriage his wife's sister, the sister of the *Tahpenes*, (that is) the queen mother. ²⁰The sister of the *Tahpenes* bore him a son, Genubath; the *Tahpenes* weaned him in Pharaoh's house, and Genubath remained in Pharaoh's house with Pharaoh's children. ²¹When Hadad heard in Egypt that David slept with his ancestors and that Joab the army commander was dead, Hadad said to Pharaoh: "Permit me to leave, so that I can go to my own country." ²²Pharaoh said to him: "But what are you lacking with me that you want to go to your own country?" He said: "Nothing, but do let me leave."

²³God raised up an adversary for him, Rezon son of Eliada, who had fled from Hadadezer, king of Zobah, his lord. ²⁴He gathered men about him and became a leader of a band, when David slew them. They went to Damascus and lived there, and he became king in Damascus. ²⁵He was an adversary of Israel all the days of Solomon, together with the harm that Hadad (caused); he was hostile toward Israel and became king over Aram.

Jeroboam—Intimations of Kingship; Solomon's Death

11   ²⁶Now Jeroboam son of Nebat, an Ephraimite from Zeredah—the name of his widowed mother was Zeruah—was a servant of Solomon; he raised his hand against the king. ²⁷This is the account of his raising his hand against the king. Solomon built the Millo (and) closed the breach in the City of David, his

father. ²⁸Now the man Jeroboam was a capable man. Solomon took note of how the young man performed his task, and so he put him in charge of all the corvée of the House of Joseph.

²⁹At that time, Jeroboam had left Jerusalem, and the prophet Ahijah the Shilonite met him on the road; he was wearing a new robe. When the two of them were alone in the open country, ³⁰Ahijah took hold of the new robe he had on and tore it into twelve pieces. ³¹He said to Jeroboam: "Take ten pieces for yourself, for thus says YHWH, God of Israel: 'I am about to tear the kingdom out of Solomon's hands, and I will give you ten tribes. ³²But one tribe shall be his for the sake of David, my servant, and for the sake of Jerusalem, the city I have chosen out of all the tribes of Israel. ³³For he has forsaken me and bowed down to Ashtoreth the goddess of the Sidonians, Chemosh, the god of Moab, and Milcom, the god of the Ammonites, and has not followed my ways to do what was pleasing to me and (keep) my statutes and rules, as David his father. ³⁴But I will not take all the kingdom away from him, for I will keep him a ruler as long as he lives, for the sake of David, my servant, whom I chose and who kept my commandments and my statutes. ³⁵But I will take the kingdom away from his son and give it to you—the ten tribes. ³⁶To his son will I give one tribe, so that there be a lamp for David my servant forever before me in Jerusalem, the city that I have chosen for myself to establish my name there. ³⁷But it is you that I will take, and you shall reign over all you desire, and you shall be king over Israel. ³⁸If you obey all that I command you and follow my ways and do what is pleasing to me, keeping my statutes and commandments as David my servant did, then I will be with you and I will build a lasting dynasty for you as I did for David. I will give Israel to you ³⁹and, in view of this, I will humble David's descendants, but not forever.'"

⁴⁰Solomon sought to kill Jeroboam, but Jeroboam promptly fled to Egypt to Shishak, king of Egypt; he stayed in Egypt until Solomon's death.

⁴¹The rest of the history of Solomon and all that he did and his wisdom are indeed recorded in the Book of the Deeds of Solomon. ⁴²The length of Solomon's reign in Jerusalem over all Israel was forty years. ⁴³So Solomon slept with his ancestors and was buried in the City of David, his father. Rehoboam his son succeeded him.

HISTORY OF THE DIVIDED KINGDOM

Rehoboam's Aborted Coronation

12 ¹Rehoboam went to Shechem, for all Israel had come to Shechem to make him king. ²When Jeroboam son of Nebat learned of this—he was still in Egypt where he had fled from King Solomon—Jeroboam returned from Egypt. ³They sent for him, and Jeroboam and the whole assembly of Israel came and spoke to Rehoboam: ⁴"Your father made our yoke heavy. You, then, lighten the hard labor of your father and the heavy yoke which he imposed upon us and

we shall serve you." [5]He said to them: "Go away for three days and then come back to me." So the people went away.

[6]King Rehoboam then took counsel with the elders who had served Solomon his father during his lifetime: "How do you advise answering this people?" [7]They spoke to him: "If you become a servant of this people today and serve them and answer them by speaking kind words, then they will be your servants forever." [8]But he rejected the advice that the elders gave him and took counsel with the youngsters who had grown up with him, those who were serving him. [9]He said to them: "What do you advise that we answer this people who spoke to me: 'Lighten the yoke that your father imposed upon us'"? [10]Then the youngsters who had grown up with him said: "Thus you should say to this people who spoke to you: 'Your father made our yoke heavy; and you, lighten it for us!' Thus you should speak to them: 'My little thing is thicker than my father's loins. [11]Now my father burdened you with a heavy yoke, and I will add to your yoke; my father disciplined you with whips, and I will discipline you with scourges.'"

[12]Jeroboam and all the people came to Rehoboam on the third day, as the king had said: "Come back to me on the third day." [13]The king answered the people harshly and he rejected the advice that the elders had given him. [14]He spoke with them in accordance with the youngsters' advice: "My father made your yoke heavy, and I will add to your yoke. My father disciplined you with whips, and I will discipline you with scourges." [15]The king did not listen to the people, for YHWH had brought this about in order to fulfill the promise that YHWH had spoken through Ahijah the Shilonite to Jeroboam son of Nebat. [16]When all Israel saw that the king had not listened to them, the people answered the king:

> What share have we in David?
> No lot in the son of Jesse!
> To your tents, O Israel,
> Now look to your own house, O David!

So the Israelites went to their homes. [17]But as for the Israelites who lived in the towns of Judah, Rehoboam ruled over them.

[18]King Rehoboam dispatched Adoram, who was in charge of the corvée, but all Israel stoned him to death. With effort, King Rehoboam had mounted his chariot to flee to Jerusalem. [19]Thus Israel has been in rebellion against the House of David until this day.

An Independent Israel

12   [20]All Israel heard that Jeroboam had returned; they summoned him to the assembly and made him king over all Israel. Only the tribe of Judah followed the House of David.

[21]Rehoboam came to Jerusalem and assembled all the House of Judah and the tribe of Benjamin—one hundred eighty thousand select soldiers—to fight

against the House of Israel in order to restore the kingship to Rehoboam son of Solomon. [22]But the word of God came to Shemaiah, the man of God: [23]"Say to Rehoboam son of Solomon, king of Judah, and to all the House of Judah, and Benjamin and the rest of the people: [24]Thus said YHWH: 'You shall not set out to make war against your kinsmen, the Israelites. Let each man return home, for this matter has been brought about by Me.'" They heeded the word of YHWH and turned back in accordance with the word of YHWH.

The Reign of Jeroboam (Israel)

12 [25]Jeroboam built Shechem in the hill country of Ephraim and dwelled there. Then he went out from there and built Penuel. [26]Jeroboam said to himself: "Now the kingdom will revert to the House of David. [27]If this people (continues) to go up to offer sacrifice in the House of YHWH in Jerusalem, the heart of this people will turn back to their lord, to Rehoboam, king of Judah; they will kill me and return to Rehoboam, king of Judah." [28]So the king took counsel. He made two golden calves, and he said to them: "Enough going up to Jerusalem! Here are your gods, O Israel, who brought you up from the land of Egypt." [29]He set up one in Bethel, and the other he assigned to Dan. — [30]This matter was indeed sinful. — The people went ahead of that one as far as Dan. [31]He made a shrine of the high place and he appointed some of the people priests who were not Levites. [32]Jeroboam established a festival in the eighth month on the fifteenth day of the month, like the Festival in Judah, and he ascended the altar. This he did in Bethel, sacrificing to the calves that he made; and he stationed in Bethel the priests of the high places that he had appointed.

The Man of God from Judah

12 [33]So he ascended the altar that he made in Bethel on the fifteenth day of the eighth month, the month in which he invented on his own to establish a festival for the Israelites. As he ascended the altar to offer sacrifice, 13 [1]there came a man of God from Judah to Bethel by YHWH's word. Just as Jeroboam was standing on the altar to offer sacrifice, [2]he called out against the altar by YHWH's word: "O altar, altar! Thus said YHWH: 'A son shall be born to the House of David, Josiah by name, and he shall slaughter upon you the priests of the high places who offer sacrifices upon you, and human bones shall be burned upon you.'" [3]On that day, he gave a portent: "This is the portent that YHWH has foretold: 'The altar shall break apart, and the ashes upon it shall be spilled.'" [4]When the king heard the word of the man of God that he called out against the altar in Bethel, Jeroboam stretched out his hand from the top of the altar and said: "Seize him!" But the hand that he stretched out against him withered and he could not draw it back to himself. [5]The altar broke apart, and the ashes were spilled from the altar, in accordance with the portent the man of God had given by YHWH's word. [6]Then the king addressed the man of God:

"Please entreat YHWH your God and pray on my behalf that my hand may be restored to me." The man of God entreated YHWH, and the hand of the king was restored to him and became as at first. [7]Then the king spoke to the man of God: "Come home with me and take some food, and I shall give you a gift." [8]But the man of God said to the king: "If you were to give me half your house, I would not come with you, nor will I eat bread, nor will I drink water in this place, [9]for thus he has ordered me by the word of YHWH: 'You shall not eat bread or drink water, nor shall you return by the road you came.'" [10]So he left by a different road and did not return by the road he had come to Bethel.

[11]There was a certain old prophet living in Bethel. His son came and told him all the things that the man of God had performed that day in Bethel; (and) the words that he had spoken to the king, they told them to their father. [12]Their father said to them: "Which road did he take?" His sons had seen the road that the man of God who came from Judah had taken. [13]He said to his sons: "Saddle an ass for me!" They saddled an ass for him and he mounted it [14]and set out after the man of God. He found him sitting under a terebinth and said to him: "Are you the man of God who came from Judah?" He said: "I am." [15]He said to him: "Come home with me and eat some bread." [16]He said: "I cannot go back with you or enter your home; I cannot eat bread or drink water with you in this place. [17]For the order I have by YHWH's word is: 'You shall not eat bread or drink water there; nor shall you return by the road you came.'" [18]He said to him: "I, too, am a prophet like you, and an angel spoke to me by YHWH's word: 'Bring him back with you to your house; let him eat bread and drink water.'" He was lying to him. [19]So he went back with him, and he ate bread and drank water in his house.

[20]While they were sitting at the table, the word of YHWH came to the prophet who had brought him back. [21]He announced to the man of God who had come from Judah: "Thus said YHWH: 'Because you rebelled against the order of YHWH and have not obeyed the command that YHWH your God gave you [22]but have gone back and eaten bread and drunk water in the place of which He spoke: "Do not eat bread and do not drink water," your corpse shall not come to the grave of your ancestors.'" [23]After he had eaten bread and had drunk, he saddled the ass for him—belonging to the prophet who had brought him back—[24]and he set out. On the way, a lion came upon him and killed him. His corpse was left lying on the road, with the ass standing by it and the lion standing by the corpse. [25]Now some people were passing by, and they saw the corpse lying on the road and the lion standing by the corpse; they came and told it in the town where the old prophet lived. [26]When the prophet who had brought him back from the road heard it, he said: "It is the man of God who rebelled against the order of YHWH! YHWH handed him over to the lion who mauled him to death, in accordance with the word of YHWH that he foretold to him." [27]Then he spoke to his sons: "Saddle the ass for me!" and they saddled (it). [28]He set out and found his corpse lying on the road; the ass and the lion were standing by the corpse; the lion had not eaten the corpse, nor had it mauled the ass. [29]The prophet lifted the corpse of the man of God, laid it on the ass,

and brought it back; the old prophet came back to the town to mourn over him and to bury him. [30]He laid the corpse in his own grave, and they mourned over him: "Alas, my brother!" [31]After he had buried him, he said to his sons: "When I die, bury me in the grave where the man of God is buried; lay my bones next to his bones, [32]for the word that he announced by YHWH's word against the altar in Bethel and against all the shrines of the high places in the towns of Samaria shall surely come about."

[33]After this incident, Jeroboam did not turn back from his evil way. He kept on appointing some of the people as priests of the high places; anyone who so desired, he would install as priest at the high places. [34]By this matter it became a sin for the House of Jeroboam to its utter destruction from the face of the earth.

A Prophetic Oracle of Doom against Jeroboam

14 [1]At that time, Abijah son of Jeroboam fell ill. [2]Jeroboam said to his wife: "Come now, disguise yourself so that no one will recognize that you are the wife of Jeroboam and go to Shiloh. Ahijah the prophet is there, the one who foretold that I would be king over this people. [3]Take with you ten (loaves of) bread, some wafers, and a flask of honey and go to him. He will tell you what will happen to the lad." [4]The wife of Jeroboam did so. She set out to go to Shiloh, and she came to the house of Ahijah. Now Ahijah could not see, for his eyes had grown dim with old age.

[5]YHWH had said to Ahijah: "The wife of Jeroboam is coming to inquire (of YHWH) through you about her son who is ill. Thus and thus you shall speak to her. And when she comes, she will be hiding her identity." [6]When Ahijah heard the sound of her footsteps as she came in the doorway, he said: "Come in, wife of Jeroboam. Why is it that you are hiding your identity? I have been sent with a harsh message for you. [7]Go, say to Jeroboam: 'Thus said YHWH, the god of Israel: "Because I elevated you from among the people and made you ruler over my people Israel, [8]and I tore the kingdom from the House of David and gave it you, yet you have not been like my servant David, who kept my commandments and who followed me with all his heart, doing only what pleased me; [9]you have acted worse than all who preceded you. You have gone and made for yourself other gods, molten images to anger me, and me you cast off behind your back. [10]Therefore, I will bring disaster upon the House of Jeroboam, and I will cut off every male belonging to Jeroboam, even the restricted and the abandoned in Israel. I will stamp out the House of Jeroboam as one burns dung completely. [11]Those of Jeroboam('s kin) who die in the city, the dogs will eat; those who die in the field, the birds of heaven will eat."' For YHWH has spoken. [12]As for you, hurry back to your home; as soon as you set foot in the town, the child will die. [13]And all Israel will lament him and bury him, for he alone of (the House of) Jeroboam shall be brought to burial, for in him alone of all the House of Jeroboam has some good been found by YHWH, the god of Israel. [14]Then YHWH will raise up for himself a king over Israel who will

destroy the House of Jeroboam this very day, even right now! [15]YHWH will strike Israel like a reed that sways in water and will uproot Israel from this good land that he gave to their ancestors; he will scatter them beyond the River (Euphrates), because they made their poles of Asherah, angering YHWH; [16]and he will hand Israel over because of the sins of Jeroboam which he committed and because he caused Israel to sin."

[17]The wife of Jeroboam set out immediately and came to Tirzah. As soon as she set foot on the threshold of her house, the lad died. [18]They buried him, and all Israel mourned over him, in accord with the word of YHWH, which he had spoken through his servant, Ahijah the prophet.

[19]The rest of the history of Jeroboam, how he fought and how he reigned, are indeed recorded in the History of the Kings of Israel. [20]Jeroboam had reigned twenty-two years, and he slept with his ancestors. Nadab his son succeeded him.

The Reign of Rehoboam (Judah)

14 [21]Now Rehoboam son of Solomon became king in Judah. Rehoboam was forty-one years old when he became king, and he reigned seventeen years in Jerusalem, the city that YHWH chose to place his name there out of all of the tribes of Israel. His mother's name was Naamah, the Ammonitess. [22]Judah did what was displeasing to YHWH; they incensed him more than their ancestors had done by their sins that they committed. [23]They, too, built for themselves high places and pillars and poles of Asherah on every lofty hill and under every fresh tree. [24]There were even male prostitutes in the land; they practiced all of the abominations of the nations whom YHWH dispossessed before the Israelites.

[25]In the fifth year of King Rehoboam, Shishak king of Egypt marched against Jerusalem. [26]He carried off the treasures of the House of YHWH and the treasures of the royal palace; he carried off everything. He (even) took the golden bucklers that Solomon had made. [27]King Rehoboam had bronze bucklers made to replace them, and he would entrust them to the officers of the outrunners who guard the entrance to the royal palace. [28]Whenever the king went to the House of YHWH, the outrunners would carry them and then return them to the guardroom of the outrunners.

[29]The rest of the history of Rehoboam and all that he did are indeed recorded in the History of the Kings of Judah. [30]There was war between Rehoboam and Jeroboam all the years. [31]Rehoboam slept with his ancestors, and he was buried with his ancestors in the City of David, and the name of his mother was Naamah the Ammonitess. Abijam his son succeeded him.

The Reign of Abijam (Judah)

15 [1]In the eighteenth year of King Jeroboam son of Nebat, Abijam became king over Judah. [2]He reigned three years in Jerusalem; his mother's name was Maacah, daughter of Abishalom. [3]He followed all the sinful ways of his father

that he practiced before him, and his heart was not fully with YHWH his God as was the heart of David his ancestor. [4]For the sake of David, YHWH his God gave him a lamp in Jerusalem by establishing his son after him and by maintaining Jerusalem.

[5]For David had done what was pleasing to YHWH and did not stray from all that he commanded him all the days of his life, except in the matter of Uriah the Hittite. [6]Now there was war between Rehoboam and Jeroboam all his days. [7]The rest of the history of Abijam and all that he did are indeed recorded in the History of the Kings of Judah. There was war between Abijam and Jeroboam. [8]Abijam slept with his ancestors, and they buried him in the City of David. Asa his son succeeded him.

The Reign of Asa (Judah)

15   [9]In the twentieth year of Jeroboam, Asa became king over Judah. [10]And he reigned forty-one years in Jerusalem, and his mother's name was Maacah, daughter of Abishalom. [11]Asa did what was pleasing to YHWH like David his ancestor. [12]He expelled the male prostitutes from the land and removed all the idols that his ancestors had made. [13]He even deposed his mother, Maacah, from (serving as) queen mother, because she had made a horrid object for Asherah. Asa cut down her horrid object and burned (it) in Wadi Kidron. [14]But the high places were not removed; yet Asa was loyal to YHWH throughout his life. [15]He brought his father's sacred objects and his own sacred objects into the House of YHWH—silver, gold, and vessels.

[16]There was war between Asa and Baasha king of Israel all their days. [17]Baasha king of Israel marched against Judah, and he built Ramah so as to prevent anyone from going out and coming in to Asa king of Judah. [18]So Asa took all the remaining silver and gold in the treasuries of the House of YHWH and the treasuries of the royal palace, and he handed them over to his servants. King Asa sent them to Ben-hadad son of Tabrimmon son of Hezion, king of Aram, who reigned in Damascus (with this message): [19]"There is a treaty between me and you (as there was) between my father and your father. Now I am sending you a bribe of silver and gold. Go, break your treaty with Baasha king of Israel so that he may withdraw from me." [20]Ben-hadad acceded to King Asa and sent his army officers against the towns of Israel; he attacked Ijon, Dan, Abel-beth-maacah, and all Chinneroth—all the land of Naphtali. [21]When Baasha heard (about this), he stopped building Ramah and stayed in Tirzah. [22]Then King Asa mustered all Judah, with no exemptions; they carried away the stones and the timber of Ramah, which Baasha had built, and King Asa built Geba of Benjamin and Mizpah with them.

[23]The rest of ≪   ≫ the history of Asa and all his exploits and all that he did and the cities that he built are indeed recorded in the History of the Kings of Judah. But in his old age, he became ill with a foot ailment. [24]Asa slept with his ancestors, and he was buried with his ancestors in the City of David, his ancestor. Jehoshaphat his son succeeded him.

The Reign of Nadab (Israel)

15   ²⁵Nadab son of Jeroboam became king over Israel in the second year of Asa king of Judah, and he reigned over Israel for two years. ²⁶He did what was displeasing to YHWH and followed the way of his father and the sin that he caused Israel to commit. ²⁷Baasha son of Ahijah of the House of Issachar conspired against him. Baasha struck him down at Gibbethon of the Philistines, while Nadab and all Israel were besieging Gibbethon. ²⁸Baasha killed him in the third year of Asa king of Judah, and he succeeded him. ²⁹As soon as he became king, he struck down all the House of Jeroboam; he did not leave a soul belonging to Jeroboam until he destroyed it, just as YHWH had promised through his servant Ahijah the Shilonite, ³⁰because of the sins that Jeroboam committed and by which he caused Israel to sin, thereby angering YHWH, God of Israel. ³¹The rest of the history of Nadab and all that he did are indeed recorded in the History of the Kings of Israel. ³²There was war between Asa and Baasha king of Israel all their days.

The Reign of Baasha (Israel)

15   ³³In the third year of Asa king of Judah, Baasha son of Ahijah became king over all Israel in Tirzah for twenty-four years. ³⁴He did what was displeasing to YHWH; he followed the way of Jeroboam and the sin that he caused Israel to commit. 16 ¹The word of YHWH came to Jehu son of Hanani concerning Baasha: ²"Since I have elevated you from the dust and have made you ruler over my people Israel, but you followed the way of Jeroboam and caused my people Israel to sin, angering me with their sins, ³I am going to stamp out Baasha and his House. I will make your House like the House of Jeroboam son of Nebat. ⁴Those of Baasha('s kin) who die in the city the dogs will eat; those of his (kin) who die in the field the birds of heaven will eat. ⁵The rest of the history of Baasha and what he did and his exploits are indeed recorded in the History of the Kings of Israel. ⁶Baasha slept with his ancestors and was buried in Tirzah. Elah his son succeeded him. ⁷Moreover, there was the word of YHWH concerning Baasha and his House through Jehu son of Hanani the prophet, because of all the evil that he did in displeasing YHWH, angering him by his actions and becoming like the House of Jeroboam, and because he struck it down.

The Reign of Elah (Israel)

16   ⁸In the twenty-sixth year of Asa king of Judah, Elah son of Baasha became king over Israel in Tirzah for two years. ⁹His servant Zimri, commander of half the chariotry, conspired against him. While he was in Tirzah, drinking himself drunk in the house of Arza, "Over the Household" at Tirzah, ¹⁰Zimri came, attacked him, and killed him in the twenty-seventh year of Asa king of Judah. He succeeded him as king. ¹¹At his accession, as soon as he took the throne, he

struck down all the House of Baasha, not leaving a single male, neither kins-men nor friends. [12]Zimri destroyed all the House of Baasha in accordance with the word of YHWH, which he spoke against Baasha through Jehu the prophet, [13]because of all the sins of Baasha and the sins of Elah his son that they com-mitted and caused Israel to commit, angering YHWH the God of Israel with their emptiness. [14]The rest of the history of Elah and all that he did are indeed recorded in the History of the Kings of Israel.

The Reign of Zimri (Israel)

16   [15]In the twenty-seventh year of Asa king of Judah, Zimri became king in Tirzah for seven days; it was while the army was encamped against Gibbethon of the Philistines. [16]When the encamped army heard that Zimri had conspired and had even killed the king, all Israel made Omri, the commander of the army, king over Israel that very day in the camp. [17]Then Omri together with all Israel withdrew from Gibbethon and laid siege to Tirzah. [18]When Zimri saw that the city had been captured, he went into the citadel of the palace and burned down the palace over him, and he died; [19]because of the sins that he committed, by doing what was displeasing to YHWH, by following the way of Jeroboam, and the sin that he committed by causing Israel to sin. [20]The rest of the history of Zimri and the conspiracy that he formed are indeed recorded in the History of the Kings of Israel.

The Reign of Omri (Israel)

16   [21]Then the people Israel were divided into two; half of the people followed Tibni son of Ginath to make him king; the (other) half followed Omri. [22]The people who followed Omri prevailed over the people who followed Tibni son of Ginath. Tibni died, and Omri became king.

[23]In the thirty-first year of Asa king of Judah, Omri became king over Israel for twelve years; in Tirzah he was king for six years. [24]He bought the hill of Samaria from Shemer for two talents of silver. He built (on) the hill and named the city that he built Samaria, after Shemer, the owner of the hill. [25]Omri did what was displeasing to YHWH; he was worse than all who preceded him. [26]He followed all the way of Jeroboam son of Nebat and his sin that he caused Israel to commit, angering YHWH the God of Israel with their emptiness. [27]The rest of the history of Omri, what he did and the exploits he undertook, are indeed recorded in the History of the Kings of Israel. [28]Omri slept with his ancestors and was buried in Samaria. Ahab his son succeeded him.

The Reign of Ahab (Israel): Introduction

16   [29]Ahab son of Omri became king over Israel in the thirty-eighth year of Asa king of Judah. Ahab son of Omri reigned over Israel in Samaria for twenty-two years. [30]Ahab son of Omri did what was displeasing to YHWH, more than

all who preceded him. [31]Now, as if it had been a slight thing to follow the sins of Jeroboam, he took as wife Jezebel, daughter of Ethbaal, king of the Sidonians, and he went and served Baal and bowed down to him. [32]He erected an altar for Baal (in the) House of Baal that he built in Samaria. [33]Ahab (also) made the pole of Asherah. Ahab did more to anger YHWH God of Israel than all the kings of Israel who preceded him.

[34]In his days, Hiel of Bethel built Jericho. At the cost of Abiram his eldest son, he laid its foundation, and with Segub his youngest son he set its doors, in accordance with the word of YHWH, which he spoke through Joshua son of Nun.

Elijah and the Great Drought

17   [1]Elijah the Tishbite, one of the residents of Gilead, said to Ahab: "By the life of YHWH, God of Israel, whom I serve, there will be no dew or rain these years, except by my word."

[2]The word of YHWH came to him: [3]"Go away from here; turn eastwards and hide in Wadi Cherith, east of the Jordan. [4]You will drink from the wadi, and I have ordered the ravens to feed you there." [5]So he proceeded to do according to the word of YHWH. He went and stayed in Wadi Cherith, east of the Jordan. [6]The ravens would bring him bread and meat in the morning and bread and meat in the evening, and he would drink from the wadi. [7]After some time, the wadi dried up because there was no rain in the land.

[8]Then the word of YHWH came to him: [9]"Up, go to Zarephath of Sidon and stay there. Now I have ordered a certain widow there to feed you." [10]So he set right out for Zarephath. When he came to the entrance of the town, there was a widow gathering wood. He called to her: "Please bring me a little water in a vessel so I can drink." [11]As she went to bring (it), he called to her: "Please bring me a bit of bread in your hand." [12]She said: "By the life of YHWH, your God, I have nothing baked, only a handful of flour in the jug and a little oil in the flask. Here I am gathering a few sticks, so that I can go in and prepare it for myself and my son. We shall it eat and then we shall die." [13]Elijah said to her: "Have no fear. Come, do as you have said. But first make me a small cake from it and bring it out to me, and afterwards make (something) for yourself and your son. [14]For thus said YHWH, the God of Israel: 'The jug of flour shall not give out and the flask of oil shall not fail, until the day that YHWH gives rain on the face of the earth.'" [15]She went and did according to Elijah's word. She ate, she and he and her household for some time. [16]For the jug of flour did not give out and the flask of oil did not fail, according to the word of YHWH which he spoke through Elijah.

[17]Sometime afterward, the son of the woman, the mistress of the house, fell ill; his illness became so severe that he had no breath left in him. [18]She said to Elijah: "What have I to do with you, man of God? Did you come to me to call attention to my sin and kill my son?" [19]He said to her: "Give me your son!" He took him from her bosom and brought him up to the roof chamber where he was staying and laid him on his bed. [20]He called to YHWH: "YHWH, my God,

will you bring harm even to the widow with whom I lodge by killing her son?" [21]He stretched out on the child three times; he called to YHWH: "YHWH my God. Let the child's life return to his body." [22]YHWH heard Elijah's call; the child's life returned to his body and he revived. [23]Then Elijah took the child and brought him down from the roof chamber into the house and gave him to his mother. Elijah said: "See, your son is alive." [24]The woman said to Elijah: "Now indeed I know that you are a man of God and that the word of YHWH in your mouth is true."

The Contest on Mount Carmel

18 [1]A long time passed, and in the third year, the word of YHWH came to Elijah: "Go, present yourself to Ahab so that I may give rain on the face of the earth." [2]So Elijah went to present himself to Ahab.

Now the famine was severe in Samaria. [3]Ahab called Obadiah, "Over the Household."—Obadiah greatly feared YHWH. [4]When Jezebel slaughtered the prophets of YHWH, Obadiah had taken a hundred prophets and hidden them fifty in a cave and continually provided them with bread and water.—[5]Ahab said to Obadiah: "Come, let us go through the land to all the springs of water and to all of the wadis. Perhaps we shall find some grass to keep the horses and mules alive and not have to destroy any of the beasts." [6]They divided the land between them to go through it; Ahab went one way by himself and Obadiah went another way by himself.

[7]Now as Obadiah was on the way, he was suddenly met by Elijah. He recognized him and fell on his face and said: "Is it you, my lord, Elijah?" [8]He said to him: "It is I. Go, say to your lord: 'Elijah is here!'" [9]He said: "What is my sin that you hand your servant over to Ahab to have me killed? [10]By the life of YHWH your God, there is no nation or kingdom to which my lord has not sent to search for you. And when they said: 'He is not (here),' he had that kingdom or nation swear that they could not find you. [11]And now you say: 'Go, say to your lord: "Elijah is here!"' [12]And it will happen, I leave you and the spirit of YHWH will carry you to somewhere I do not know; and when I come to tell Ahab and he does not find you, he will kill me, though your servant has feared YHWH from my youth. [13]Has my lord not been told what I did when Jezebel was killing the prophets of YHWH, how I hid a hundred of the prophets of YHWH by fifties in a cave and provided them with bread and water? [14]And now you say: 'Go, say to your lord: "Elijah is here!"' He will kill me!" [15]Elijah said: "By the life of YHWH of hosts whom I serve, today I will present myself to him."

[16]So Obadiah went to meet Ahab, and he told him; and Ahab went to meet Elijah. [17]When Ahab saw Elijah, Ahab said to him: "Is that you, troubler of Israel?" [18]He said: "I have not troubled Israel, but you have and your father's house, by your abandoning YHWH's commands; you followed the Baals! [19]Now then, send, gather all Israel to me at Mount Carmel, as well as the four hundred and fifty prophets of Baal and the four hundred prophets of Asherah who eat at Jezebel's table."

²⁰Ahab sent to all the Israelites and gathered the prophets at Mount Carmel. ²¹Elijah approached all the people and said: "How long will you keep hopping between the two boughs? If YHWH is God, follow him, and if Baal, follow him." But the people did not answer him a word. ²²Then Elijah said to the people: "I alone have remained as a prophet of YHWH, and the prophets of Baal are four hundred and fifty. ²³Let two bulls be given to us; let them choose one bull for themselves, cut it up, and place it on the wood but not set fire (to it). And I will prepare the other bull and place it on the wood but not set fire (to it). ²⁴Then you will call on the name of your god, and I will call on the name of YHWH, and the god who answers by fire, he is God." All the people answered: "The matter is good!"

²⁵Elijah said to prophets of Baal: "Choose one bull for yourselves and prepare (it) first, for you are many; call on the name of your god, but do not put fire (to it)." ²⁶So they took the bull that was given to them, and they prepared (it), and they called on the name of Baal from morning until noon: "O Baal. Answer us!" But there was no sound and no one answering. They hopped about the altar they had made. ²⁷At noon, Elijah mocked them; he said: "Call loudly. For he is a god. Maybe he is in conversation, or he is occupied, or may be on the way, or perhaps he is asleep and will wake up." ²⁸So they called loudly and they gashed themselves, as was their custom, with swords and spears until blood spilled over them. ²⁹When the noon passed, they raved until the hour of the meal offering. But there was no sound and no one answering and no response.

³⁰Then Elijah said to all the people: "Come up to me." All the people came up to him. Then he proceeded to repair the destroyed altar of YHWH. ³¹Elijah took twelve stones according to the number of the tribes of the sons of Jacob— to whom the word of YHWH came: "Israel shall be your name"—³²and with the stones, he built an altar in the name of YHWH. He made a trough around the altar with a capacity of about two *seahs* of seed. ³³He arranged the wood, cut up the bull, and placed it on the wood. ³⁴He said: "Fill four jars with water and pour (it) on the offering and on the wood." He said: "Do it a second time," and they did it a second time. He said: "Do it a third time," and they did it a third time. ³⁵The water ran around the altar and he also filled the trough with water. ³⁶At the time of the meal offering, Elijah the prophet came forward and said: "YHWH, God of Abraham, Isaac, and Israel! Let it be known today that you are God in Israel and that I am your servant, and by your command I have done all these things. ³⁷Answer me, YHWH, answer me, so that this people will know that you, YHWH, are God, and it is *you* who have turned their hearts backward." ³⁸Then YHWH's fire descended and consumed the offering, the wood, the stones, and the dust, and licked up the water that was in the trough. ³⁹When the people saw this, they fell on their faces and said: "YHWH, He is God. YHWH, He is God." ⁴⁰Then Elijah said to them: "Seize the prophets of Baal. Let no one of them escape." They seized them, and Elijah took them down to Wadi Kishon and slaughtered them there.

⁴¹Elijah said to Ahab: "Go up, eat and drink, for there is the sound of roaring rain." ⁴²So Ahab went up to eat and drink, while Elijah went up to the top of

Carmel. He crouched on the ground and put his face between his knees. [43]He said to his attendant: "Go up. Look toward the sea." He went up and looked, and he said: "There is nothing." Seven times he said: "Go back." [44]On the seventh time, he said: "There is a cloud as small as a man's hand rising from the sea." He said: "Go. Say to Ahab: 'Hitch up (your chariot) and go down, so that the rain will not stop you.'" [45]By that time, the skies grew dark with clouds and wind; then there was a heavy rain. Ahab mounted up and went to Jezreel; [46]and, as the hand of YHWH had come upon Elijah, he bound up his loins and ran in front of Ahab all the way to Jezreel.

Elijah's Journey to Horeb

19 [1]Ahab told Jezebel all that Elijah had done and how he killed all the prophets by the sword. [2]Whereupon, Jezebel sent a messenger to Elijah: "May the gods do thus (to me) and even more if by this time tomorrow I have not made your life like the life of one of them." [3]He was afraid, and so he set out to save his life.

He came to Beer-sheba, which is in Judah, and he left his attendant there, [4]while he himself went a day's journey into the steppe. He came and sat down under a broom tree; he prayed that he might die and said: "Enough! Now, O YHWH, take my life, for I am no better than my ancestors." [5]Then he lay down and fell asleep under a broom tree. Suddenly, an angel was touching him and said to him: "Get up! Eat!" [6]He looked and there, at his head, was a cake (baked on a hot) stone and a flask of water. He ate and drank and then lay down again. [7]The angel of YHWH came back a second time; he touched him and said: "Get up! Eat, for the road is too much for you." [8]So he got up and ate and drank. Then he walked by the strength of that food forty days and forty nights to the mountain of God, Horeb.

[9]There he went into a cave, and there he spent the night. Suddenly, the word of YHWH came to him. He said to him: "What are you doing here, Elijah?" [10]He said: "I have been most zealous for YHWH, the God of hosts, for the Israelites have abandoned your covenant, your altars they have destroyed, and your prophets they have killed by the sword. And I, I alone am left, and they have sought my life to take it." [11]He said: "Go out and stand on the mountain before YHWH. Lo, YHWH is passing by, and a great and mighty wind, rending mountains and shattering rocks is before YHWH. But YHWH is not in the wind. And after the wind, an earthquake. But YHWH is not in the earthquake. [12]And after the earthquake, fire. But YHWH is not in the fire. And after the fire, the sound of sheer silence." [13]When Elijah heard (this), he covered his face with his cloak; he went out and stood at the entrance of the cave. Then a voice came to him and said: "What are you doing here, Elijah?" [14]He said: "I have been most zealous for YHWH, the God of hosts, for the Israelites have abandoned your covenant, your altars they have destroyed, and your prophets they have killed by the sword. And I, I alone am left, and they sought to take my life."

¹⁵Then YHWH said to him: "Go, be on your way, toward the wilderness of Damascus. You are to go and anoint Hazael as king over Aram, ¹⁶and Jehu son of Nimshi you will anoint as king over Israel, and Elisha son of Shaphat of Abel-meholah you will anoint as prophet in your place. ¹⁷Whoever escapes the sword of Hazael, Jehu shall kill, and whoever escapes the sword of Jehu, Elisha shall kill. ¹⁸I will leave seven thousand in Israel, every knee that has not bent to Baal and every mouth that has not kissed him."

¹⁹So he went from there, and he found Elisha son of Shaphat; he was plowing. There were twelve teams ahead of him, and he was with the twelfth. Elijah went over to him and threw his cloak over him. ²⁰He left the oxen and ran after Elijah and said: "Let me kiss my father and my mother, and then I will follow you." He said to him: "Go. Go back. For what have I done to you?" ²¹He turned from him; and he took a yoke of oxen and slaughtered them, and with the ox-gear he boiled their meat; then he gave to the people and they ate. Then he rose and followed Elijah and became his attendant.

Ahab and Ben-hadad: The Early Wars

20 ¹Now Ben-hadad king of Aram gathered all his forces, with him thirty-two kings and horses and chariots. He advanced and laid siege to Samaria and attacked it. ²He sent messengers to Ahab king of Israel within the city. ³He said to him: "Thus says Ben-hadad: 'Your silver and your gold are mine. And your wives and your finest children are mine.'" ⁴The king of Israel replied and said: "As your word, my lord, the king. I and all I have are yours." ⁵The messengers returned and said: "Thus says Ben-hadad: 'I sent to you saying: "Your silver and your gold, your wives and your sons you will give me." ⁶Indeed, this time tomorrow I will send my servants to you, and they will search through your house and the houses of your servants, and all your eyes' delight that they put their hands on they will take away.'" ⁷Then the king of Israel summoned all of the elders of the land and said: "Know now and take note that this fellow is looking for trouble. When he sent to me for my wives and for my sons, for my silver and for my gold, I did not hold back (anything) from him." ⁸All the elders and all the people said to him: "Do not obey and do not consent!" ⁹So he said to Ben-hadad's messengers: "Say: 'To my lord, the king: (According to) all that you sent to your servant the first time I shall do; but this thing I cannot do.'" The messengers went and brought him back this word. ¹⁰Then Ben-hadad sent to him and said: "May the gods do thus to me and even more if the dust of Samaria will be sufficient for handfuls for all the army that is in my train." ¹¹The king of Israel replied and said: "Speak: 'The one who girds up should not boast as the one who unbuckles.'" ¹²Now when (Ben-hadad) heard this word—he was drinking, he and the kings at Succoth—he said to his servants: "Set (the attack)!" And they set upon the city.

¹³Now a certain prophet approached Ahab king of Israel and said: "Thus said YHWH: 'Have you seen this great multitude? I am going to give it into your hands today, and you will know that I am YHWH.'" ¹⁴Ahab said: "Through

whom?" He said: "Thus says YHWH: 'Through the attendants of the district officers.'" He said: "Who will prepare the battle?" He said: "You." [15]So he mustered the attendants of the district officers, and there were two hundred thirty-two and, after them, he mustered all the army, all the Israelites, seven thousand. [16]They set out at noon, while Ben-hadad was drinking himself drunk at Succoth, he and the kings, the thirty-two kings who were aiding him. [17]The attendants of the district officers went out first. Ben-hadad sent, and they told him: "Some men have come out from Samaria." [18]He said: "If they have come out for peace, take them alive; if they have come out for war, take them alive."

[19]When these went out from the city—the attendants of the district officers and the troops that were behind them—[20]each struck down his man. So Aram fled, and Israel pursued them. Ben-hadad king of Aram fled on horse with (some of) the horsemen. [21]The king of Israel set out and attacked the horses and chariots and inflicted a great blow upon Aram.

[22]Then the prophet approached the king of Israel and said to him: "Go, be resolute, and take careful note of what you should do; for at the turn of the year, the king of Aram will march against you." [23]Now the servants of the king of Aram said to him: "Their gods are mountain gods; therefore, they have overpowered us. But if we fight them in the plain, we will surely overpower them. [24]This is the thing you should do: remove the kings, each from his position, and appoint governors in their place. [25]Then you should tally for yourself a force like the force that deserted you, horse for horse, chariot for chariot; and let us fight them in the plain. We will surely overpower them." He listened to them, and he did so.

[26]At the turn of the year, Ben-hadad mustered the Arameans, and he advanced to Aphek to do battle with Israel. [27]Meanwhile the Israelites were mustered and provisioned, and set out to meet them. The Israelites encamped opposite them like two exposed (flocks of) goats, while the Arameans filled the land. [28]Then the man of God approached and said to the king of Israel: "Thus said YHWH: 'Because the Arameans have said: "YHWH is God of the mountains and not God of the valleys," I am going to give all of this great multitude over to you, and you shall know that I am YHWH.'"

[29]They encamped opposite each other for seven days. On the seventh day, the battle was joined and the Israelites struck down one hundred thousand Aramean foot soldiers in one day. [30]The remaining ones fled to Aphek into the city; and the wall fell upon the twenty-seven thousand men remaining. Ben-hadad (also) fled and came into the city, into an inner room. [31]His servants said to him: "Now we have heard that the kings of the House of Israel are kings of loyalty. Let us put sackcloth on our loins and ropes on our heads and go out to the king of Israel. Perhaps he will spare your life." [32]So they girded sackcloth on their loins and ropes on their heads and came to the king of Israel. They said: "Your servant Ben-hadad says: 'Please let me live!'" He said: "Is he still alive? He is my brother." [33]The men were looking for an omen and they quickly seized upon it, and they said: "Ben-hadad is indeed your brother." He said: "Go, bring him." Ben-hadad came out to him, and he took him up into his chariot.

³⁴(Ben-hadad) said to him: "I shall return the cities that my father took from your father, and you may set up bazaars in Damascus as my father set up in Samaria." (Ahab said:) "And I, for my part, shall free you under this treaty." He made a treaty with him and freed him.

³⁵Now one of the Sons of the Prophets said to his fellow, by the word of YHWH: "Do strike me!" But the man refused to strike him. ³⁶He said to him: "Because you did not obey YHWH, as soon as you leave me, a lion will attack you." He left him, and a lion came upon him and attacked him. ³⁷Then he met another man and he said: "Do strike me!" The man struck hard and wounded him. ³⁸The prophet went and waited for the king on the road, and he disguised himself with a wrapping over his eyes. ³⁹Now, as the king was passing by, he appealed to the king and said: "Your servant went out into the thick of battle. Suddenly a man came over and brought a man to me and said: 'Guard this man. If he is missing, it will be your life for his life, or you will weigh out a talent of silver.' ⁴⁰Your servant was busy here and there, and he got away." The king of Israel said: "That is your sentence. You yourself have determined (it)." ⁴¹He quickly removed the wrapping from his eyes, and then the king of Israel recognized him as one of the prophets. ⁴²He said to him: "Thus said YHWH: 'Because you have freed the man I have doomed, your life shall be for his life and your people for his people.'" ⁴³So the king of Israel went home, irritated and angry; and he came to Samaria.

Naboth's Vineyard

21 ¹Sometime afterward. Naboth the Jezreelite had a vineyard in Jezreel next to the palace of Ahab, king of Samaria. ²Ahab spoke to Naboth: "Sell me your vineyard that I may have it as a vegetable garden, for it is next to my house, and I will give you in its place a vineyard better than it. (Or) if you like, I will pay you its price in silver." ³Naboth said to Ahab: "Far be it from me by YHWH that I should sell my ancestral inheritance to you."

⁴Ahab came home irritated and angry because of the matter that Naboth the Jezreelite had told him: "I will not sell you my ancestral inheritance." He lay down on his bed, turned his face away, and would not eat. ⁵His wife Jezebel came to him, and she spoke to him: "Why is your spirit irritated and you do not eat?" ⁶He told her: "I spoke to Naboth the Jezreelite, and I said to him: 'Sell me your vineyard, or if you wish, I will give you a vineyard in its place.' But he said: 'I will not sell you my vineyard.'" ⁷Then Jezebel his wife said to him: "Now *you* will exercise kingship over Israel! Get up, eat, and cheer up! *I* will give you the vineyard of Naboth the Jezreelite!"

⁸So she wrote letters in Ahab's name and sealed (them) with his seal; she sent the letters to the elders and the nobles of his town, who lived with Naboth. ⁹(Thus) she wrote in the letters: "Proclaim a fast and seat Naboth at the head of the people, ¹⁰and seat two worthless men opposite him. Have them testify against him: 'You have cursed God and king.' Then take him out and stone him to death."

¹¹The men of his town, the elders and the nobles who lived in his town, did as Jezebel had sent them, just as she had written in the letters she sent them. ¹²They proclaimed a fast and seated Naboth at the head of the people. ¹³Two worthless men came and sat opposite him and testified against him, the worthless men against Naboth in front of the people: "Naboth has cursed God and king." They took him outside the town and stoned him to death. ¹⁴Then they sent to Jezebel: "Naboth has been stoned to death."

¹⁵When Jezebel heard that Naboth had been stoned to death, Jezebel said to Ahab: "Up, take possession of the vineyard of Naboth the Jezreelite that he refused to sell to you for silver, for Naboth is not alive; he is dead." ¹⁶When Ahab heard that Naboth was dead, Ahab set out to go down to the vineyard of Naboth the Jezreelite to take possession of it.

¹⁷Then the word of YHWH came to Elijah the Tishbite: ¹⁸"Up, go down to meet Ahab, king of Israel, who (resides) in Samaria. He is now in Naboth's vineyard; he went down there to take possession of it. ¹⁹Tell him: 'Thus said YHWH: "Have you murdered and also taken possession?" Thus said YHWH: "In the place where the dogs licked the blood of Naboth, the dogs shall lick your blood, even yours!" ' "

²⁰Ahab said to Elijah: "Have you found me, my enemy?" He said: "I have found (you). Because you have given yourself over to doing what displeases YHWH, ²¹I will bring disaster upon you, and I will stamp you out. I will cut off (every) male belonging to Ahab, even the restricted and the abandoned in Israel. ²²I will make your house like the House of Jeroboam son of Nebat and the House of Baasha son of Ahijah, because of the provocation with which you provoked (me, i.e., YHWH), causing Israel to sin. — ²³Even against Jezebel YHWH spoke: 'The dogs shall devour Jezebel in the plot of Jezreel.' — ²⁴Those of Ahab('s kin) who die in the city, the dogs will eat; those who die in the field, the birds of heaven will eat." — ²⁵Indeed, there was no one like Ahab who had given himself over to doing what displeased YHWH, whom Jezebel his wife instigated. ²⁶He acted abominably by following the idols, just as the Amorites had done, whom YHWH had dispossessed before the Israelites. —

²⁷When Ahab heard these words, he rent his garments and put sackcloth on his body. He fasted and lay in sackcloth and went about subdued. ²⁸Then the word of YHWH came to Elijah the Tishbite: ²⁹"Have you seen how Ahab has humbled himself before me? Because he humbled himself before me, I shall not bring the disaster in his days; in the days of his son, I shall bring the disaster upon his house."

Ahab at Ramoth-gilead

22 ¹They stayed at home for three years, (as) there was no war between Aram and Israel. ²But in the third year, Jehoshaphat king of Judah went down to the king of Israel. ³The king of Israel said to his servants: "Do you know that Ramoth-gilead belongs to us? But we keep silent about taking it from the king

of Aram." ⁴He said to Jehoshaphat: "Will you go with me to battle at Ramoth-gilead?" Jehoshaphat said to the king of Israel: "I am (ready) as you are; my forces are as your forces; my horses are as your horses." ⁵Then Jehoshaphat said to the king of Israel: "Inquire of YHWH today." ⁶So the king of Israel assembled the prophets, about four hundred persons, and he said to them: "Shall I go to battle against Ramoth-gilead or shall I refrain?" They said: "Advance! The Lord will give (it) into the hand of the king." ⁷But Jehoshaphat said: "Is there not another prophet of YHWH here that we may inquire through him?" ⁸The king of Israel said to Jehoshaphat: "There is another person to inquire of YHWH through him, but I hate him, for he does not prophesy good about me but only evil—(this) Micaiah son of Imlah!" Jehoshaphat said: "The king should not say such a thing!" ⁹So the king of Israel called one of his eunuchs and said: "Quickly bring Micaiah son of Imlah."

¹⁰Now the king of Israel and Jehoshaphat king of Judah were sitting on their thrones, dressed in robes at the threshing floor at the entrance of the gate of Samaria, and all the prophets were prophesying before them. ¹¹Zedekiah son of Chenaanah made himself horns of iron, and he said: "Thus says YHWH: With these you shall gore Aram until their end." ¹²And all the prophets prophesied the same: "Advance to Ramoth-gilead and be successful, for YHWH will give (it) into the hand of the king." ¹³The messenger who had gone to call Micaiah told him: "Look here! The words of the prophets are unanimous in being good for the king. Let your word be like the word of one of them, and speak good." ¹⁴Micaiah said: "By the life of YHWH, only what YHWH says to me will I speak."

¹⁵When he came to the king, the king said to him: "Micaiah, shall we go to battle against Ramoth-gilead, or shall we refrain?" He said to him: "Advance and be successful, for YHWH will give (it) into the hand of the king." ¹⁶The king said to him: "How many times have I put you under oath that you should speak to me only the truth in the name of YHWH." ¹⁷He said: "I saw all Israel scattered on the mountains, like sheep without a shepherd. YHWH said: 'These have no masters. Let each one return to his home in peace.'" ¹⁸The king of Israel said to Jehoshaphat: "Did I not tell you (that) he would not prophesy good about me but only evil?" ¹⁹He said: "Therefore, hear the word of YHWH. I saw YHWH sitting on his throne and all the host of heaven in attendance to his right and to his left. ²⁰YHWH said: 'Who will entice Ahab so that he will advance and fall at Ramoth-gilead?' One said thus and one said thus. ²¹Then a spirit came forward and stood before YHWH and said: 'I will entice him.' YHWH said to him: 'How?' ²²He said: 'I will go out and be a lying spirit in the mouth of all his prophets.' He said; 'You will entice, and indeed you will succeed. Go out and do so!' ²³Here, then, YHWH has put a lying spirit in the mouth of these prophets of yours, for YHWH has spoken evil against you." ²⁴Then Zedekiah son of Chenaanah stepped up and struck Micaiah on the cheek and said: "Which (way) did the spirit of YHWH pass from me to speak to you?" ²⁵Micaiah said: "You will see on that day when you go into the innermost room to hide." ²⁶Then the king of Israel said: "Take Micaiah and turn him over to Amon, governor of the city and Joash, the king's son, ²⁷and say: 'Thus says

the king: "Put this fellow in prison, and feed him scant bread and scant water until I return safely." '" ²⁸Micaiah said: "If you do return safely, YHWH has not spoken through me."《 》

²⁹So the king of Israel and Jehoshaphat king of Judah advanced to Ramoth-gilead. ³⁰The king of Israel said to Jehoshaphat: "I will disguise myself and go into battle, but you, wear your robes." Then the king of Israel disguised himself and went into battle. ³¹Now the king of Aram had ordered his chariot officers— (there were) thirty-two: "Do not battle with the small or the great, but only with the king of Israel." ³²When the chariot officers saw Jehoshaphat, they said: "He is surely the king of Israel." They turned toward him for battle; then Jehoshaphat cried out. ³³When the chariot officers saw that he was not the king of Israel, they turned back from him. ³⁴But one man drew his bow innocently, and he hit the king of Israel between the joints of the armor. He said to his driver: "Turn your hand and get me out of the camp, for I am wounded." ³⁵The battle raged that day, and the king was propped up in the chariot facing Aram. He died that evening, and the blood from his wound spilled out into the hollow of the chariot. ³⁶A cry went through the camp at sundown: "Every man to his city! Every man to his land!" ³⁷So the king died and was brought to Samaria. They buried the king in Samaria. ³⁸They washed off the chariot at the pool of Samaria, and the dogs licked his blood, and the whores bathed, in accordance with YHWH's word that he had spoken.

³⁹The rest of the history of Ahab and all that he did and the house of ivory that he built and all the cities that he built are indeed recorded in the History of the Kings of Israel. ⁴⁰So Ahab slept with his ancestors. Ahaziah his son succeeded him.

The Reign of Jehoshaphat (Judah)

22   ⁴¹Jehoshaphat son of Asa became king over Judah in the fourth year of Ahab king of Israel. ⁴²Jehoshaphat was thirty-five years old when he became king, and he reigned twenty-five years in Jerusalem. His mother's name was Azubah daughter of Shilhi. ⁴³He followed all the way of his father Asa; he did not stray from it, doing what was pleasing to YHWH. ⁴⁴But the high places were not removed; the people continued to sacrifice and make offerings at the high places. ⁴⁵Jehoshaphat made peace with the king of Israel. ⁴⁶The rest of the history of Jehoshaphat and the exploits he undertook and how he fought, are indeed recorded in the History of the Kings of Judah.

⁴⁷He stamped out from the land the rest of the male prostitutes who remained from the days of his father Asa. ⁴⁸There was no king in Edom; a prefect was king. ⁴⁹Jehoshaphat built Tarshish ships to go to Ophir for gold; but he did not go, for the ships were wrecked at Ezion-geber. ⁵⁰Then Ahaziah son of Ahab said to Jehoshaphat: "Let my servants go with your servants in the ships." But Jehoshaphat did not consent.

⁵¹So Jehoshaphat slept with his ancestors, and he was buried with his ancestors in the City of David his ancestor. Jehoram, his son, succeeded him.

The Reign of Ahaziah (Israel)

⁵²Ahaziah son of Ahab became king over Israel in Samaria in the seventeenth year of Jehoshaphat king of Judah; he reigned two years over Israel. ⁵³He did what was displeasing to YHWH. He followed the way of his father and the way of his mother and the way of Jeroboam son of Nebat, who caused Israel to sin. ⁵⁴He worshipped Baal and bowed down to him, so that he angered YHWH, God of Israel, just as his father had done.   **2 Kings 1** ¹Moab rebelled against Israel after the death of Ahab.

Elijah and Ahaziah

1   ²Now Ahaziah fell through the lattice in his upper chamber at Samaria and was injured. So he sent messengers, instructing them, "Go, inquire of Baal-zebub, god of Ekron, whether I shall recover from this injury." ³The angel of YHWH then spoke to Elijah the Tishbite, "Up, go meet the messengers of the king of Samaria and speak to them, 'Is it for lack of a god in Israel that you are going to inquire of Baal-zebub, god of Ekron? ⁴Therefore, thus says YHWH, "You shall not leave the bed you are upon, for you shall certainly die!"'" And so Elijah set out.

⁵When the messengers returned to him (Ahaziah), he said to them, "Why have you returned?" ⁶They said to him, "A man came to meet us and said to us, 'Go, return to the king who sent you and speak to him, "Thus says YHWH: Is it for lack of a god in Israel that you send to inquire of Baal-zebub, god of Ekron? Therefore, you shall not leave the bed you are upon, for you shall certainly die!"'" ⁷He said to them, "What was the appearance of the man who came to meet you and who spoke these things to you?" ⁸They said to him, "A hairy man, girt with a leather belt around his waist." And he said, "It is Elijah the Tishbite."

⁹Then he sent an officer of fifty and his company of fifty to him. He climbed up to where he was, for he was sitting on a hilltop, and spoke to him, "O Man of God, the king orders, 'Come down!'" ¹⁰But Elijah replied and spoke to the officer of fifty, "And if I am a man of God, let fire descend from heaven and consume you and your company of fifty." Whereupon fire descended from heaven and consumed him and his company of fifty. ¹¹So again he sent another officer of fifty and his company of fifty. He climbed up and spoke to him, "Man of God, thus says the king, 'Come down quickly!'" ¹²But Elijah replied and spoke to him, "If I am a man of God, let fire descend from heaven and consume you and your company of fifty." Whereupon an awesome fire descended from heaven and consumed him and his fifty men. ¹³So again he sent a third officer of fifty and his company of fifty. When the third officer of fifty climbed up and drew near, he fell on his knees in front of Elijah, and pleaded with him and said, "O man of God, do value my life and the lives of these fifty men, your servants. ¹⁴Indeed, fire descended from heaven and consumed the first two officers of fifty and their companies of fifty, so now value my life." ¹⁵Then the

angel of YHWH spoke to Elijah, "Go down with him. Do not be afraid of him." So he left and went down with him to the king. [16]He spoke to him, "Thus says YHWH, 'Since you sent messengers to inquire of Baal-zebub, the god of Ekron, as if there were no god in Israel to consult his word, therefore, you shall not leave the bed you are upon, for you shall certainly die.'" [17]And so he died in accordance with YHWH's word, which Elijah had pronounced.

Jehoram, ⟨his brother,⟩ succeeded him, in the second year of Jehoram, son of Jehoshaphat king of Judah, because he did not have a son. [18]The rest of the history of Ahaziah (and) what he did are indeed recorded in the annals of the kings of Israel.

Elijah's Ascent to Heaven; Succession of Elisha

2 [1]Now when YHWH was about to take Elijah up to heaven in a storm, Elijah and Elisha were going from Gilgal. [2]Elijah said to Elisha, "Stay here, please, for YHWH has sent me to Beth-el." But Elisha said, "By the life of YHWH and by your life, I will not leave you." So they went down to Beth-el. [3]The Sons of the Prophets who were at Beth-el came out to Elisha and said to him, "Do you know that YHWH will take your master from you today?" He said, "I know it, too. Keep silent!"

[4]Then Elijah said to him, "Elisha, stay here, please, for YHWH has sent me to Jericho." But he said, "By the life of YHWH and by your life, I will not leave you." So they came to Jericho. [5]The Sons of the Prophets, who were at Jericho came up to Elisha and said to him, "Do you know that YHWH will take your master from you today?" He said, "I know it, too. Keep silent!"

[6]Then Elijah said to him, "Stay here, please, for YHWH has sent me to the Jordan." But he said, "By the life of YHWH and by your life, I will not leave you." So the two of them went on. [7]Fifty men of the Sons of the Prophets went and stood opposite at a distance, while the two of them stood by the Jordan. [8]Elijah took his mantle, rolled it up, and struck the waters; it parted in two. Then they both crossed over on dry land. [9]As they were crossing, Elijah said to Elisha, "Ask what I may do for you before I am taken from you." Elisha said, "If only a double share of your spirit would belong to me." [10]He replied, "You have asked a difficult thing. But if you see me being taken from you, you will have it; and if not, it will not be." [11]Now as they went on, walking and talking, fiery chariots with fiery horses appeared and separated them one from the other, and Elijah went up to heaven in the storm. [12]All the while, Elisha looked on and kept shouting, "My father, my father! The chariots of Israel and its horsemen!" And he saw him no more. Then he took hold of his garments and rent them in two.

[13]He picked up Elijah's mantle, which had fallen from him, and went back and stood by the bank of the Jordan. [14]He took Elijah's mantle, which had fallen from him, and as he struck the waters, and he said, "Where, indeed, is YHWH, God of Elijah?" When he struck the waters, they parted in two, and Elisha crossed over. [15]The Sons of the Prophets, who were at Jericho, saw him from

the other side, and they said, "Elijah's spirit has come to rest upon Elisha." So they went to meet him and bowed down to the ground before him.

[16]They said to him, "There are fifty able-bodied men among us, your servants. Let them go and search for your master. Maybe YHWH's wind has carried him and thrown him against one of the mountains or into one of the ravines." But he said, "Don't send (them)!" [17]They pressed him until he was embarrassed, so that he said, "Send!" They sent fifty men who searched for three days, but they did not find him. [18]When they came back to him—he was staying in Jericho—he said to them, "Didn't I tell you, 'Do not go'?"

THE ELISHA CYCLE

Sweetening the Waters

2   [19]The men of the city said to Elisha, "The city's location is a good one, as my lord can see, but the water is bad and the land miscarries." [20]He said, "Bring me a new flask, and put salt in it"; and they brought (it) to him. [21]Then he went out to the water source and threw the salt into it, and said, "Thus says YHWH, 'I have healed these waters. Death and miscarriage shall issue from there no longer.'" [22]So the water has remained healed until this day, in accordance with Elisha's word which he spoke.

Youngsters at Beth-el Punished

2   [23]He went from there up to Beth-el. As he was on the way, some young boys came out of the city and mocked him. They said, "Be off, baldy! Be off, baldy!" [24]He turned around and, looking at them, he cursed them by the name of YHWH. Whereupon two she-bears came out of the forest and mauled forty-two of the youngsters. [25]From there, he went to Mount Carmel and from there he returned to Samaria.

Jehoram's Campaign against Mesha of Moab

3   [1]Jehoram son of Ahab became king over Israel in Samaria in the eighteenth year of Jehoshaphat king of Judah; he reigned twelve years. [2]He did what was displeasing to YHWH, yet not like his father and his mother; he removed the pillar of Baal which his father had made. [3]Yet he held fast to the sinful way of Jeroboam son of Nebat who caused Israel to sin; he did not stray from it.

[4]Now Mesha king of Moab was a sheep-breeder and he used to pay tribute to the king of Israel: one hundred thousand lambs and the wool of one hundred thousand rams. [5]But when Ahab died, the king of Moab rebelled against the king of Israel. [6]One day, King Jehoram left Samaria and enlisted all the Israelites.

⁷He went and sent a message to Jehoshaphat king of Judah: "The king of Moab has rebelled against me. Will you join me in battle against Moab?" He said, "I will go! I am (ready) as you are; my forces are as your forces; my horses as your horses." ⁸He said, "Which road shall we take?" and he said, "The Desert of Edom Road."

⁹So the king of Israel, the king of Judah, and the king of Edom set out, and they circled about for seven days. There was no water for the camp or for the animals in their train, ¹⁰when the king of Israel said, "Alas! YHWH must have summoned these three kings in order to hand them over to the Moabites." ¹¹Jehoshaphat said, "Isn't there a prophet of YHWH here through whom we may inquire of YHWH?" One of the servants of the king of Israel replied, "Elisha son of Shaphat is here, who poured water on the hands of Elijah." ¹²Jehoshaphat said, "He certainly has YHWH's word!" And so the king of Israel, Jehoshaphat, and the king of Edom went down to him. ¹³Elisha said to the king of Israel, "What have I to do with you? Go to your father's prophets and your mother's prophets!" The king of Israel said, "No! For YHWH must have summoned these three kings in order to hand them over to the Moabites." ¹⁴And Elisha said, "By the life of YHWH of hosts whom I serve, were it not for Jehoshaphat king of Judah whom I hold in respect, I would not look at you or even take note of you. ¹⁵Now, then, bring me a musician!"—for when a musician played, the hand of YHWH used to come upon him. ¹⁶He said, "Thus says YHWH, 'This wadi shall produce pools upon pools.' ¹⁷For thus says YHWH, 'You shall not see wind and you shall not see rain, yet that wadi shall fill up with water and you, your flocks, and your herds shall drink. ¹⁸But this is a trifle for YHWH, so he will deliver Moab over to you. ¹⁹You shall destroy every fortified city, ≪ ≫ cut down every good tree, stop up every spring, and ruin every fertile plot with stones.'" ²⁰So it happened in the morning, at the hour of the meal offering, that water came in from the direction of Edom and the land was filled with water.

²¹Meanwhile, all Moab had heard that the kings had marched to make war on them, and so every one who could bear arms was called up, and they were stationed at the border. ²²When they rose that morning, and the sun was shining on the water, the Moabites saw the water in front of them red as blood. ²³They said, "It is blood! The kings are utterly destroyed; they have killed one another. Now, then, to the spoil, Moab!" ²⁴But when they came to the Israelite camp, the Israelites sprang up and attacked the Moabites, who fled before them. They moved against Moab on the attack, ²⁵destroying the cities, throwing stones into every fertile plot, filling it up, stopping up every spring, and cutting down every good tree, leaving only the stones of Kir-haresheth (intact), which the slingers surrounded and attacked.

²⁶When the king of Moab saw that the war was too much for him, he took seven hundred swordsmen with him to break through to the king of Edom; but they failed. ²⁷Then he took his eldest son who was to succeed him and offered him as a sacrifice on the (city) wall. There was great wrath against the Israelites and so they broke camp and returned to (their own) land.

A Helper in Times of Distress

4   ¹A certain woman, the wife of one of the Sons of the Prophets, cried out to Elisha, "Your servant, my husband, has died. You know that your servant feared YHWH; but a creditor has come to take away my two children as his slaves." ²Elisha said to her, "What can I do for you? Tell me, what do you have in the house?" She said, "Your maidservant has nothing at all in the house, except for a container of oil." ³He said, "Go out and borrow vessels from all your neighbors, empty vessels. Do not skimp! ⁴When you come back, close the door behind you and your sons, and pour (oil) into all these vessels and set aside the full ones." ⁵And so she left him. When she closed the door behind her and her sons, they kept bringing (vessels) to her and she kept pouring. ⁶When the vessels were full, she said to her son, "Bring me another vessel." He said to her, "There is not another vessel." Then the oil stopped. ⁷She came and told the man of God, and he said, "Go, sell the oil and pay off your debt, and you and your sons can live on the remainder."

⁸One day, Elisha was passing through Shunem, where there was a wealthy woman who insisted that he take some food. And whenever he passed through, he would stop there for some food. ⁹She said to her husband, "Now I know for sure that the man of God who always passes by our place is holy. ¹⁰Let us make a small roof chamber by the wall, and put a bed, a table, a chair, and a lamp for him there; and whenever he visits us, he can stay there." ¹¹One day, he visited there; he stopped by the roof chamber and rested there. ¹²He said to Gehazi, his attendant, "Call the Shunammite woman!" He called her and she presented herself. ¹³He said to him, "Please say to her, 'You have shown all this concern for us. What can we do for you? Can I speak on your behalf to the king or to the commander-in-chief?'" But she said, "I dwell among my kinsfolk." ¹⁴He said, "Then what can we do for her?" Gehazi said, "Still, she has no child and her husband is old." ¹⁵He said, "Call her." He called her and she stood in the doorway. ¹⁶He said, "At this season, next year, you shall embrace a son." She said, "Do not, my lord, man of God, do not deceive your maidservant." ¹⁷The woman did conceive, and she bore a child at the season next year of which Elisha had spoken to her.

¹⁸The child grew up. One day, he went out to his father among the reapers. ¹⁹He said to his father, "My head, my head!" He said to his servant, "Carry him to his mother." ²⁰He carried him and brought him to his mother. He sat on her knees until midday and then he died. ²¹She went up and laid him on the bed of the man of God, then closed (the door) on him and went out. ²²She called her husband and said, "Send me one of the servants and one of the she-asses so that I can hurry to the man of God and return." ²³He said, "Why are you going to him today? It is not the new moon or the Sabbath." She said, "All is well!"

²⁴She saddled the she-ass and then said to her servant, "Lead on and proceed! Do not slow the riding for me, unless I tell you." ²⁵So she went and came to the man of God on Mount Carmel. The man of God saw her from a distance; he said to Gehazi his attendant, "Here is that Shunammite woman. ²⁶Now, run

to greet her and say to her, 'Is all well with you? Is your husband well? Is your child well?'" She answered, "All is well." [27]When she came to the man of God on the mountain, she grabbed hold of his feet. Gehazi stepped forward to push her away; but the man of God said, "Let her alone, for she is embittered, yet YHWH had hidden it from me and not told me." [28]She said, "Did I ask for a son of my lord? Did I not say, 'Do not deceive me'?" [29]Then he said to Gehazi, "Get yourself ready and take my staff with you and go! If you meet anyone, do not greet him, and if anyone greets you, do not answer him. Place my staff on the face of the lad." [30]The mother of the lad said, "By the life of YHWH and by your life, I will not leave you!" He got up and followed her.

[31]Gehazi went on ahead of them, and he placed the staff on the lad's face, but there was no sound and no response. So he went back to meet him and told him, "The lad did not wake up." [32]Elisha entered the house and there was the lad dead, laid out on his bed. [33]He went in and closed the door on both of them and then prayed to YHWH. [34]He got up (on the bed) and lay down on top of the boy; he put his mouth to his mouth, his eyes to his eyes, his palms on his palms, and crouched upon him. And the child's body became warm. [35]Then he walked up and down about the house, and got up (on the bed), and crouched upon him. The lad sneezed seven times and the lad opened his eyes. [36]He called Gehazi and said, "Call this Shunammite woman." He called her and she came to him; he said, "Pick up your son!" [37]She came in and fell at his feet, prostrating herself on the ground. Then she picked up her son and went out.

[38]Elisha came again to Gilgal, at the time of famine in the land. As the Sons of the Prophets sat in front of him, he said to his attendant, "Set the big pot (on the fire) and cook some porridge for the Sons of the Prophets." [39]One (of them) went out into the field to gather herbs and found a wild vine; he collected a skirt-full of bitter apples from it. When he returned, he sliced them into the porridge pot, for he did not know (what they were). [40]They poured it for the men to eat, and as they were eating the porridge, they shouted, "There's death in the pot, man of God!" They couldn't eat (it). [41]He said, "Then bring some flour." He threw (it) into the pot and said, "Pour out for the men and let them eat." And now there was nothing harmful in the pot.

[42]A man came from Baal-shalisha and brought the man of God some bread of the first fruits, twenty barley loaves, and some fresh ears of grain. He said, "Give it to the people that they may eat." [43]But his attendant said, "How can I set this before a hundred people?" He said, "Give it to the people that they may eat, for thus says YHWH, 'They will eat and leave some over.'" [44]So he set it before them, and they ate and had some left over, in accordance with YHWH's word.

The Conversion of Naaman

5   [1]Now Naaman, commander of the army of the king of Aram, was greatly esteemed by his master and held in favor, for through him YHWH had given victory to Aram. But this valorous man was a leper. [2]Once, when the Aramaeans

were raiding, they took captive a young girl from the land of Israel, and she served Naaman's wife. ³She said to her mistress, "If only my master would present himself before the prophet who is in Samaria, he would cure him of his leprosy." ⁴[Naaman] came and told his master word for word what the girl from the land of Israel had said, ⁵The king of Aram said, "Come, then, let me send a letter to the king of Israel."

He set out and took with him ten talents of silver, six thousand (shekels of) gold and ten changes of clothing. ⁶He brought the letter to the king of Israel, (which read) thus: "Now when this letter reaches you, know that I am sending Naaman my servant to you, that you may cure him of his leprosy." ⁷When the king of Israel read the letter, he rent his clothes and said, "Am I God, to take life or to give life, that this fellow sends to me to cure a man of leprosy. Surely you must see that he is picking a quarrel with me." ⁸When Elisha, the man of God, heard that the king of Israel had rent his clothes, he sent (a message) to the king: "Why have you rent your clothes? Let him come to me and he will learn that there is a prophet in Israel."

⁹So Naaman came with his horses and chariots and waited at the entrance of the house for Elisha. ¹⁰Elisha sent a messenger to say to him, "Go and bathe seven times in the Jordan so that your flesh may be restored and so that you may be clean." ¹¹Naaman was angered and left; he said, "Here I thought that he would surely come out and stand and invoke YHWH his God by name, and wave his hand over the spot and cure the leper. ¹²Are not the Abana and the Pharpar, the rivers of Damascus, better than all the waters of Israel? Can I not bathe in them and be cleansed!?" He turned and left in a rage. ¹³But his servants went up to him and spoke to him; they said, "Sir, if the prophet had told you (to do) a difficult thing, would you not do it? How much more when he said to you, 'Bathe and be clean.'" ¹⁴So he went down and dipped himself in the Jordan seven times in accordance with the word of the man of God, and his flesh was restored as the flesh of a little child and he was clean.

¹⁵He returned to the man of God, he and his entire company, and came and stood before him and said, "Now I know that there is no God in all the world except in Israel. So please accept a gift from your servant." ¹⁶He said, "As YHWH lives, whom I serve, I will not accept anything." He pressed him to accept, but he refused. ¹⁷Then Naaman said, "If not, then let your servant be given two mules' load of earth; for your servant will no longer offer burnt offering or sacrifice to other gods except to YHWH. ¹⁸But may YHWH forgive your servant for this one thing: when my master enters the House of Rimmon to bow down there, and he leans on my arm, and I bow down in the house of Rimmon—when I bow down in the House of Rimmon, may YHWH forgive me for this thing." ¹⁹He said to him, "Go in peace."

He had gone a short distance ²⁰when Gehazi the attendant of Elisha, the man of God thought, "Here my master has spared this Aramaean Naaman by not receiving from him what he brought. As YHWH lives, I will run after him and get something from him." ²¹So Gehazi hurried after Naaman. When Naaman saw someone running after him, he climbed down from his chariot to meet him and said, "Is everything well?" ²²He said, "It is well. My master sent me to say, 'Just now two young men of the Sons of the Prophets from the hill country of Ephraim have come to me. Please give them a talent of silver and two changes of clothes.'" ²³Naaman said, "Kindly take two talents," and he pressed him. Then he tied up two talents of silver in two bags, in addition to two changes of clothing and he gave (them) to two of his servants, and they carried (them) ahead of him. ²⁴When he reached the citadel, he took (them) from them and deposited (them) in his house. He dismissed the men and they left.

²⁵As for him, he went in and stood before his master; Elisha said to him, "Where from, Gehazi?" He said, "Your servant has not gone anywhere." ²⁶He said to him, "Was I not there in spirit when the man got down from his chariot to meet you? Is this a time to accept silver and to accept clothes and olive groves and vineyards and sheep and cattle and male and female slaves? ²⁷Naaman's leprosy will now cling to you and to your descendants forever." He left his presence, as leprous as snow.

The Floating Axhead

6   ¹The sons of the Prophets said to Elisha, "See now, the place where we meet with you is too cramped for us. ²Let us go to the Jordan, and each person will take a beam from there and we will build ourselves a place to meet in." He said, "Go!" ³Then one of them said, "Will you please come with your servants?" He said, "I will come"; ⁴and so he went with them. When they came to the Jordan, they cut down trees. ⁵As one of them was felling a beam, the ax head fell into the water. He cried out, "Alas, my master, it was borrowed!" ⁶The man of God said, "Where did it fall?" He showed him the place. Then he cut off a stick and threw it in there, and he made the ax head float. ⁷He said, "Pick it up!" So he reached out and took it.

Elisha at Dothan: The Seeing and the Blind

6   ⁸Now the king of Aram was at war with Israel. Once he took counsel with his servants, "Attack at such and such a place." ⁹But the man of God sent to the king of Israel, "Be careful not to pass by that place, for the Aramaeans attack there." ¹⁰So the king of Israel sent to the place of which the man of God had told him; he would warn it and would be on guard there, more than once or twice. ¹¹This matter infuriated the king of Aram, so he called his servants and said to them, "Won't you tell me who among us is supporting the king of Israel?" ¹²One of his servants said, "No, my lord king, it is Elisha, the prophet in Israel who tells the king of Israel the words you speak in your bedroom." ¹³He said, "Go and find out where he is and I will send to seize him." It was reported to him, "He is in Dothan." ¹⁴So he sent there horses and chariots, a strong force; they came at night and surrounded the city.

¹⁵The servant of the man of God went out early and lo, a force with horses and chariots was all around the city. His attendant said to him, "Alas, master,

what shall we do?" [16]He said, "Fear not! There are more on our side than with them." [17]Then Elisha prayed and said, "YHWH, open his eyes and let him see." YHWH opened the eyes of the attendant, and he saw the hill filled with fiery horses and chariots all around Elisha.

[18]When (the Aramaeans) came against him, Elisha prayed to YHWH and said, "Please strike this people with a blinding light"; and he struck them with a blinding light in accordance with the word of Elisha. [19]Then Elisha said to them, "This is not the road and this is not the city. Follow me and I will lead you to the man you are looking for." He led them to Samaria. [20]When they entered Samaria, Elisha said, "YHWH, open the eyes of these men and let them see." YHWH opened their eyes, and they saw that they were inside Samaria. [21]The king of Israel said to Elisha when he saw them, "Shall I strike (them) down, father?" [22]He said, "Do not strike! Are these ones whom you have captured with your sword and bow, that you would strike (them) down? Set food and water before them, and let them eat and drink and then go back to their master." [23]So he set a lavish feast for them; and they ate and drank. Then he sent them off and they went back to their master. And the Aramaean bands no longer raided the land of Israel.

A Famine in Samaria

6   [24]Some time later, Ben-hadad king of Aram gathered all his troops and marched and laid siege to Samaria. [25]There was a great famine in Samaria, for they were besieging it until a donkey's head was (sold) for eighty (shekels) of silver and a quarter of a *qab* of "dove's dung" was five (shekels) of silver.

[26]Once when the king of Israel was walking on the city wall, a woman appealed to him, "Help, my lord king!" [27]He said, "No! Let YHWH help you! From where can I get help for you, from the threshing floor or from the winepress?" [28]Then the king said to her, "What is the matter?" She said, "This woman said to me, 'Give up your son so that we may eat him today; and tomorrow we will eat my son.' [29]So we cooked my son and we ate him. But when I said to her the next day, 'Give up your son so that we may eat him,' she had hidden her son." [30]When the king heard the words of the woman, he rent his clothes; and as he walked along the wall, the people could see that he was wearing sackcloth underneath. [31]He said, "Thus and more may God do to me, if the head of Elisha son of Shaphat remains on his shoulders this day."

[32]Now Elisha was sitting in his house and the elders were sitting with him, when (the king) sent ahead a man. But before the messenger came, he said to the elders, "Do you see, this son of a murderer has sent to cut off my head. Look, when the messenger comes, close the door and press him against the door. No doubt the sound of his master's feet follows him." [33]While he was still talking with them, the king came down to him and said, "Indeed this evil is from YHWH. Why should I still have hope in YHWH?"

7   [1]Then Elisha said, "Hear the word of YHWH, thus said YHWH, 'This time tomorrow, a *seah* of choice flour shall be (sold) for a shekel, and two *seahs* of

barley for a shekel at the market price of Samaria.'" [2]The adjutant, upon whom the king leans, answered the man of God, "Even if YHWH were to make floodgates in the sky, could this come to pass?" He said, "You shall see it with your own eyes, but you shall not eat of it."

[3]There were four men, lepers, at the entrance to the gate. They said to one another, "Why are we sitting here until we die? [4]If we say we will go into the city, there is famine in the city and we shall die there. And if we sit here, we shall die. Come, let us desert to the Aramaean camp. If they let us live, we shall live; if they put us to death, we shall die." [5]They set out at dusk to go to the Aramaean camp; but when they came to the edge of the Aramaean camp, there was not a person there. [6]For YHWH had caused the Aramaean army to hear the sound of chariots (and) the sound of horses, the sound of a great force, so that they said to one another, "The king of Israel has hired the kings of the Hittites and the kings of Egypt against us to attack us." [7]They started to flee at dusk; they abandoned their tents, their horses, and their asses, the camp as it was, and they fled for their lives.

[8]When those lepers came to the edge of the camp, they went into one tent, and they ate and drank and then carried off silver and gold and clothing from it, and went and hid them. They came back and went into another tent; they carried off (things) from it and went and hid them. [9]Then they said to one another, "We are not doing right. This day is a day of good tidings and we are keeping silent. If we wait until morning light, punishment will overtake us. Come, let us go and inform the palace." [10]They went and called to the gatekeepers and informed them, "We came to the Aramaean camp, and there was not a person there nor the sound of anyone, just the horses tied up, and the asses tied up, and the tents as they were."

[11]The gatekeepers called out and it was reported inside the palace. [12]The king got up in the night and said to his servants, "I will tell you what the Aramaeans have done to us. They know that we are starving, so they left their camp to hide in the field, thinking, 'When they come out of the city, we will take them alive and then enter the city.'" [13]One of his servants answered and said, "Let a few of the remaining horses that are still here be taken; (in any case) they are like the many Israelites ≪ ≫ who have already perished, and let us send and find out."

[14]They took two chariot teams, and the king sent them after the Aramaean army, with orders: "Go and find out." [15]They followed them as far as the Jordan; and the entire way was filled with clothing and equipment which the Aramaeans had thrown off in their haste. The messengers returned and told the king. [16]Then the people went out and plundered the Aramaean camp. Thus a *seah* of choice flour was (sold) for a shekel and two *seah*s of barley for a shekel, in accordance with the word of YHWH.

[17]Now the king had appointed his adjutant, upon whom he leans, in charge of the gate. The people trampled him to death in the gate, just as the man of God had spoken when the king came down to him. [18]For when the man of God spoke to the king, "Two *seah*s of barley shall be (sold) for a shekel and a *seah* of

choice flour for a shekel this time tomorrow at the market price of Samaria," [19]the adjutant answered the man of God and said, "Even if YHWH were to make flood gates in the sky, could this come to pass?" He said, "You shall see it with your own eyes, but you shall not eat of it." [20]This is exactly what happened to him. The people trampled him to death in the gate.

The Shunammite's Land Claim

8   [1]Once Elisha spoke to the woman whose son he had revived, "Up, go, you and your household, and live wherever you will, for YHWH has decreed a seven-year famine, and it has already come upon the land." [2]The woman proceeded to act in accordance with the word of the man of God; she and her household went and lived in the land of the Philistines for seven years. [3]At the end of the seven years, the woman returned from the land of the Philistines and she went to appeal to the king concerning her house and her field. [4]Now the king was talking to Gehazi, the attendant of the man of God: "Tell me all of the great deeds that Elisha has performed." [5]And as he was telling the king how (Elisha) had revived the dead, the woman whose son he had revived was appealing to the king concerning her house and her field. Gehazi said, "My lord king, this is the woman and this is her son whom Elisha revived." [6]The king questioned the woman and she told him. Then the king assigned a eunuch to her, with orders: "Restore everything that belongs to her and all the income from her field, from the day she left the country until now."

Elisha and the Kings of Damascus

8   [7]Elisha came to Damascus at a time when Ben-hadad the king of Aram was ill. It was reported to him: "The man of God has arrived here." [8]The king said to Hazael, "Take a gift with you and go meet the man of God; inquire of YHWH through him, 'Will I recover from the illness?'" [9]Hazael went to meet him and took with him a gift of all the best of Damascus, forty camel loads! He came and stood before him and said, "Your son Ben-hadad, king of Aram, has sent me to you to ask, 'Will I recover from this illness?'" [10]Elisha said to him, "Go, tell him, 'You will surely recover.' But YHWH has shown me that he will surely die." [11]He kept his face motionless for a long while; then the man of God wept. [12]Hazael said, "Why does my lord weep?" He said, "Because I know the harm that you will bring upon the Israelites: you will set their fortresses on fire; you will put their young men to the sword; you will dash their little ones in pieces and rip open their pregnant women." [13]Hazael said, "Who is your servant, (but) a dog, that he should do such a great thing?" Elisha said, "YHWH has shown me you as king of Aram." [14]He left Elisha and returned to his lord, who said to him, "What did Elisha say to you?" He said, "He said to me, 'You will surely recover.'" [15]The next day, he took a cloth and dipped it in water; he spread it over his face and he died. So Hazael succeeded him.

HISTORY OF THE DIVIDED MONARCHY RESUMED

The Reign of Jehoram (Israel)

8   [16]In the fifth year of Joram son of Ahab, king of Israel, « » Jehoram son of Jehoshaphat, king of Judah, became king. [17]He was thirty-two years old when he became king, and he reigned eight years in Jerusalem. [18]He followed the ways of the kings of Israel, just as the house of Ahab had done, for Ahab's daughter was his wife; he did what was displeasing to YHWH. [19]But YHWH was unwilling to destroy Judah for the sake of David his servant, for he had promised to give him and his offspring a lamp for all time. [20]In his days, Edom rebelled against the authority of Judah and set up its own king. [21]Joram crossed over to Zair with all his chariots. He set out by night and attacked the Edomites, who had surrounded him and his chariot officers. But the army fled back to their homes. [22]So Edom has rebelled against the authority of Judah, until this day. Then Libnah rebelled at that time. [23]The rest of the history of Joram and all that he did are indeed recorded in the annals of the kings of Judah. [24]So Joram slept with his ancestors and he was buried with his ancestors in the City of David. Ahaziah his son succeeded him.

The Reign of Ahaziah (Israel)

8   [25]In the twelfth year of Joram son of Ahab, king of Israel, Ahaziah son of Jehoram, king of Judah, became king. [26]He was twenty-two years old when he became king and he reigned one year in Jerusalem; his mother's name was Athaliah daughter of Omri, king of Israel. [27]He followed the ways of the House of Ahab and did what was displeasing to YHWH just like the House of Ahab, for he was a son-in-law of the house of Ahab. [28]He joined Joram son of Ahab in battle against Hazael king of Aram at Ramoth-Gilead; but the Aramaeans defeated Joram.

[29]But King Joram had gone back to Jezreel to recover from the wounds which the Aramaeans had inflicted on him at Ramah in his battle with Hazael king of Aram; and Ahaziah son of Jehoram king of Judah had come down to see Joram son of Ahab in Jezreel for he was ill.

Revolt in Israel: Jehu's Accession

9   [1]Now Elisha the prophet summoned one of the Sons of the Prophets and said to him, "Get yourself ready, and take this flask of oil with you, and go to Ramoth-Gilead. [2]When you arrive, look for Jehu son of Jehoshaphat son of Nimshi; go and have him get up from the rest of his companions and take him into an inner room. [3]Then take the flask of oil and pour (some) on his head and

say, 'Thus said YHWH, "I anoint you king over Israel."' Then open the door and flee. Do not delay." ⁴So the attendant, the prophet's attendant, went to Ramoth-Gilead.

⁵When he arrived, there were the army officers sitting (together). He said, "Commander, I have a message for you!" Jehu said, "For which one of us?" He said, "For you, commander." ⁶He got up and went inside. (The lad) poured the oil on his head and said to him, "Thus said YHWH, the God of Israel, 'I anoint you king over the people of YHWH, over Israel. ⁷You shall strike down the house of Ahab your master; thus will I avenge on Jezebel the blood of my servants, the prophets, the blood of all the servants of YHWH. ⁸All the House of Ahab shall perish and I will cut off every male belonging to Ahab, even the restricted and the abandoned in Israel. ⁹I shall make the House of Ahab like the House of Jeroboam son of Nebat and the House of Baasha son of Ahijah. ¹⁰And as for Jezebel, the dogs shall devour (her) in a plot at Jezreel, with no one to bury (her).'" Then he opened the door and fled.

¹¹Jehu went outside to the servants of his master. They said to him, "Is all well? Why did this madman come to you?" He said to them, "You know this man and the way he talks." ¹²They said, "A lie! Do tell us!" He said, "Thus and thus he said, 'Thus said YHWH, "I anoint you king over Israel."'" ¹³Quickly, each one took his garment and put it under him on the bare steps; they blew the horn and said, "Jehu is king!" ¹⁴Thus Jehu son of Jehoshaphat son of Nimshi formed a conspiracy against Joram.

Joram had been on guard at Ramoth-Gilead, he and all Israel, against Hazael king of Aram. ¹⁵But King Joram had gone back to Jezreel to recover from the wounds which the Aramaeans had inflicted on him in his battle with Hazael king of Aram.

Jehu said, "If this is your wish, let no one leave the town to go and report in Jezreel." ¹⁶Then Jehu mounted up and went to Jezreel—that was where Joram was laid up, and Ahaziah king of Judah had come down to see Joram. ¹⁷The lookout standing on the tower in Jezreel saw Jehu's troop as it was coming; he said, "I see a troop!" Joram said, "Take a rider and send out to meet them and have him ask, 'Is all well?'" ¹⁸The horseman went to meet him and said, "Thus said the king, 'Is all well?'" Jehu said, "What concern is it of yours whether all is well? Fall in behind me!" The lookout reported, "The messenger reached them, but is not coming back." ¹⁹Then he sent a second horseman; when he reached them, he said, "Thus said the king, 'Is all well?'" Jehu said, "What concern is it of yours whether all is well? Fall in behind me!" ²⁰The lookout reported, "He reached them, but is not coming back. And the driving is like the driving of Jehu son of Nimshi, for he drives like a madman." ²¹Joram said, "Hitch up!" They hitched up his chariot, and Joram king of Israel and Ahaziah king of Judah went out, each in his own chariot; they went out to meet Jehu. They met him by the plot of Naboth the Jezreelite. ²²When Joram saw Jehu, he said, "Is all well, Jehu?" He said, "What is this 'Is all well?' while the harlotries of your mother Jezebel and her many sorceries (continue)?" ²³Joram turned his hands and fled, and he said to Ahaziah, "Treason, Ahaziah!" ²⁴But Jehu drew his bow and hit Joram between the shoulders—the arrow went through his heart—and he collapsed in his chariot. ²⁵Then (Jehu) said to Bidkar his adjutant, "Take and throw him in the plot of land belonging to Naboth the Jezreelite. Remember how you and I were riding side by side behind Ahab, when YHWH made this pronouncement about him, ²⁶'I swear, as surely as I saw the blood of Naboth and the blood of his sons last night, by YHWH's word, I will requite you in this very plot, by YHWH's word.' So now, take and throw him in the plot in accordance with the word of YHWH."

²⁷When Ahaziah king of Judah saw (this), he fled by the road to Beth-haggan. Jehu pursued him and said, "Him, too! Shoot him!" ⟨They shot him⟩ in his chariot at the ascent of Gur near Ibleam. He fled to Megiddo and died there. ²⁸His servants drove him to Jerusalem, and they buried him in his own tomb with his ancestors in the City of David.

²⁹In the eleventh year of Joram son of Ahab, Ahaziah became king of Judah.

³⁰Jehu came to Jezreel. When Jezebel heard (of this), she painted her eyes with kohl and dressed her hair and she looked out of the window. ³¹Jehu was coming through the gate. She said, "Is all well, Zimri, his master's killer?" ³²He looked up toward the window and said, "Who is on my side? Who?" Two or three eunuchs looked out toward him. ³³He said, "Throw her down!" They threw her down, and some of her blood spattered on the wall and on the horses; he trampled her. ³⁴He went in and ate and drank, and said, "Look after this cursed one; bury her. After all, she is a princess." ³⁵They went to bury her, but they found nothing of her save the skull, the feet, and the palms of the hands. ³⁶They returned and reported to him. He said, "It is the word of YHWH which he spoke through his servant Elijah the Tishbite, 'Dogs shall devour the flesh of Jezebel in the plot of Jezreel, ³⁷and the carcass of Jezebel shall be like dung on the field in the plot of Jezreel, so that no one will be able to say "This is Jezebel."'"

10 ¹Ahab had seventy sons in Samaria. Jehu wrote letters and sent (them) to Samaria, to the officials of the city and to the elders and to the guardians (of the sons) of Ahab, thus, ²"Now, when this letter reaches you, since your master's sons are with you and you have chariots and horses, a fortified city and weapons, ³choose the best and most suitable of your master's sons and place him on his father's throne, and fight for your master's house." ⁴But they were very much frightened and said, "Here two kings could not stand up to him, how can we stand?" ⁵The royal steward and the governor of the city and the elders and the guardians sent to Jehu, "We are your servants, so whatever you tell us, we will do. We will not make anyone king. Do whatever pleases you." ⁶He wrote them a letter a second time: "If you are on my side and will obey me, then take the heads of the men, your master's sons, and come to me at this time tomorrow to Jezreel." Now the princes, seventy men, were with the nobles of the city who were rearing them. ⁷When the letter reached them, they took the princes and slaughtered (all) seventy men; they put their heads in baskets and sent them to him in Jezreel. ⁸A messenger came and reported to him, "They have brought the heads of the princes." He said, "Put them in two heaps at the entrance of the gate until morning." ⁹In the morning, he went out and stood

(there); he said to all the people, "You are innocent! Here I conspired against my master and killed him, but who has struck down all of these? ¹⁰Take note, then, that nothing of YHWH's word which YHWH spoke against the House of Ahab shall go unfulfilled; for YHWH has done what he promised through his servant Elijah." ¹¹Then Jehu struck down all who were left of the House of Ahab in Jezreel, all his nobles, his intimates, his priests, until he had left no survivor.

¹²He then set out to go to Samaria. On the way, when he was at Beth-eked of the shepherds, ¹³he met the kinsmen of Ahaziah king of Judah. He said, "Who are you?" They said, "We are the kinsmen of Ahaziah. We have come down (to inquire) after the welfare of the princes and the sons of the queen-mother." ¹⁴He said, "Take them alive!" They took them alive and slaughtered them at the pit in Beth-eked, forty-two men, and did not leave a single one of them.

¹⁵He went on from there and he met Jehonadab son of Rechab (coming) to meet him. He greeted him and said to him, "Is your heart true (to mine), as my heart is to your heart?" Jehonadab said, "It is indeed." (Jehu said,) "Give (me) your hand." He gave him his hand and (Jehu) lifted him up into the chariot. ¹⁶He said, "Come with me and see my zeal for YHWH." So he took him along in his chariot. ¹⁷When he came to Samaria, he struck down all who were left of (the House of) Ahab in Samaria until he had destroyed it, in accordance with the word of YHWH, which he spoke to Elijah.

¹⁸Then Jehu assembled all the people and said to them, "Ahab served Baal a little; Jehu will serve him much! ¹⁹Invite all the prophets of Baal, all his ministrants, and all his priests to me; let no one be missing, for I am having a great sacrifice for Baal. Whoever is missing shall not live!" Jehu was acting craftily in order to destroy the ministrants of Baal. ²⁰Jehu said, "Convoke a solemn assembly for Baal," and so it was proclaimed. ²¹Jehu sent (word) throughout all Israel and all the ministrants of Baal came; there was no one who did not come. They came into the House of Baal, and the House of Baal was filled from end to end. ²²He said to the man in charge of the wardrobe, "Issue garments to all the ministrants of Baal." He issued the garments to them. ²³Then Jehu and Jehonadab son of Rechab came to the House of Baal; he said to the ministrants of Baal, "Check carefully that there are no servants of YHWH here among you, but only ministrants of Baal alone." ²⁴Then they went into offer sacrifices and burnt offerings. Now Jehu had assigned eighty men outside and had said, "For any one of the men that I hand over to you who escapes, it shall be a life for a life." ²⁵When he finished presenting the burnt offering, Jehu said to the outrunners and the adjutants, "Come in and strike them down! Let no one get away!" The outrunners and the adjutants struck them down with the sword; they left (them) lying (there). Then they went into the interior of the House of Baal. ²⁶They brought out the sacred pillar of the House of Baal and burned it. ²⁷They tore down the sacred pillar of Baal and then tore down the House of Baal, turning it into a latrine until today. ²⁸Thus Jehu rooted out Baal from Israel.

²⁹Yet Jehu did not abandon the sins of Jeroboam son of Nebat, who caused Israel to sin (with regard to) the golden calves at Bethel and at Dan. ³⁰YHWH said

to Jehu, "Since you have done well by pleasing me, carrying out all that I had in mind against the House of Ahab, four generations of your descendants shall sit on the throne of Israel." [31]But Jehu did not follow carefully the teaching of YHWH, the God of Israel, with all his heart; he did not stray from the sinful way of Jeroboam, who caused Israel to sin.

[32]In those days, YHWH began to reduce Israel. Hazael struck at them on all the borders of Israel: [33]from the Jordan on the east, all the land of the Gilead—the Gadites, the Reubenites, the Manassites—from Aroer by wadi Arnon, including the Gilead and the Bashan.

[34]The rest of the history of Jehu and all that he did and all his exploits are indeed recorded in the annals of the kings of Israel. [35]So Jehu slept with his ancestors and was buried in Samaria. Jehoahaz his son succeeded him. [36]Jehu had reigned over Israel for twenty-eight years in Samaria.

Revolt in Judah: Athaliah Dethroned

11 [1]When Athaliah mother of Ahaziah saw that her son was dead, she set out to destroy all the royal line. [2]But Jehosheba daughter of king Joram, sister of Ahaziah took Joash son of Ahaziah and stole him away from where the princes were being killed in the bed chamber, him and his nurse. He was hidden from Athaliah and so was not killed. [3]He was in hiding with her in the House of YHWH for six years, while Athaliah ruled the country.

[4]Now in the seventh year, Jehoiada sent for the captains of the hundreds of the Carites and the outrunners and had them come to him in the House of YHWH. He made an alliance with them and had them take an oath in the House of YHWH. Then he showed them the king's son. [5]He ordered them, "This is what you must do: a third of you who come on duty on the sabbath will keep guard over the palace, [6]a third at the Sur Gate, and a third at the gate behind the outrunners will guard the House ≪   ≫. [7]Two units of yours, everyone who goes off duty on the sabbath, shall guard the House of YHWH for the king. [8]You shall surround the king all about, every man with his weapons in hand, and whoever comes to the ranks shall be killed. Be with the king in his comings and his goings."

[9]The captains of the hundreds did just as Jehoiada the priest ordered; each took his men—those who came on duty on the sabbath and those who go off duty on the sabbath—and they came to Jehoiada the priest. [10]The priest gave the captains of the hundreds King David's spears and quivers that were in the House of YHWH. [11]The outrunners, each with his weapons in hand, stood from the south end of the House to the north end of the House, at the altar and the House, all about the king. [12]Then (Jehoiada) brought out the king's son and placed the diadem and the jewels upon him. They made him king and they anointed him; they clapped their hands and shouted, "Long live the king!"

[13]When Athaliah heard the sound of the outrunners (and) the People, she came to the People in the House of YHWH. [14]She saw the king standing by the pillar, as was the custom, the officers with the trumpets beside the king, and all

the People of the Land rejoicing and blowing trumpets. Athaliah rent her garments and shouted, "Treason, treason!" [15]Jehoiada the priest ordered the captains of the hundreds in charge of the troops and said to them, "Take her out through the ranks and anyone who follows her, put to the sword"; for the priest thought, "She should not be put to death in the House of YHWH." [16]They took her away by force, and she entered the palace through the Horses Entrance; there she was put to death.

[17]Then Jehoiada made a covenant between YHWH and the king and the People that they should be a people belonging to YHWH, and between the king and the people. [18]Then all the People of the Land came to the House of Baal; they tore it down, and its altars and images they smashed to bits. They killed Mattan, the priest of Baal in front of the altars. (Jehoiada) the priest set guards over the House of YHWH, [19]and he took the captains of the hundreds, the Carites and the outrunners and all the People of the Land, and they led the king down from the House of YHWH. They entered the palace through the Gate of the Outrunners. And he sat upon the royal throne. [20]All the People of the Land rejoiced and the city was quiet, whereas Athaliah they put to death by the sword in the palace.

The Reign of Jehoash (Judah)

12 [1]Jehoash was seven years old when he became king. [2]In the seventh year of Jehu, Jehoash became king, and he reigned forty years in Jerusalem; his mother's name was Zibiah from Beer-sheba. [3]Jehoash did what was pleasing to YHWH all his days, just as Jehoiada the priest had instructed him. [4]Yet the high places were not removed; the people continued to sacrifice and make offerings at the high places.

[5]Jehoash said to the priests, "All the silver brought as sacred donations to the House of YHWH—silver of the census tax, silver from the valuation of persons, or any silver that a man may voluntarily bring to the House of YHWH—[6]let the priests take for themselves, each from his acquaintance, and they shall repair the House wherever damage may be found."

[7]But in the twenty-third year of Jehoash, the priests had not (yet) made repairs on the House. [8]So King Jehoash summoned Jehoiada the priest and the (other) priests and said to them, "Why are you not repairing the House? Now, do not keep silver from your acquaintances, but donate it for the repair of the House." [9]The priests agreed not to take silver from the people, nor to make repairs on the Temple.

[10]Then Jehoiada the priest took a chest and bored a hole in its side, and he set it near the altar, on the right as one enters the House of YHWH; and the priests, keepers of the threshold, would put there all the silver brought to the House of YHWH. [11]Whenever they saw that there was much silver in the chest, the king's scribe and the high priest would come and tie (it) up and count the silver found in the House of YHWH. [12]They would give the silver that was

weighed over to the workmen in charge of the House of YHWH; they used it to pay the carpenters and builders working in the House of YHWH, [13]and the masons and stone cutters, to buy timber and quarry stone to repair the House of YHWH, and for all other expenditures needed to repair the House. [14]However, no silver basins, snuffers, sprinkling bowls, or trumpets — vessels of gold and silver of any kind — were made for the House of YHWH from the silver brought into the House of YHWH. [15]But they paid it to the workmen who repaired the House of YHWH. [16]Furthermore no accounting was made with the men to whom the silver was given to pay the workmen, for they dealt honestly. [17]Silver from guilt offerings and from sin offerings was not given over to the House of YHWH; it belonged to the priests.

[18]Then Hazael king of Aram marched and fought against Gath and captured it; he set out to attack Jerusalem. [19]So Jehoash king of Judah took all the sacred objects dedicated by Jehoshaphat, Jehoram, and Ahaziah, his ancestors, the kings of Judah, and his sacred objects, and all the gold found in the treasuries of the House of YHWH and the palace and he sent (them) to Hazael king of Aram, who then withdrew from Jerusalem.

[20]The rest of the history of Joash and all that he did are indeed recorded in the annals of the kings of Judah. [21]His servants rose up and formed a conspiracy; they killed Joash at Beth-millo, which leads down to Silla. [22]The servants who killed him were Jozabad son of Shimeath and Jehozabad son of Shomer. He died and was buried with his ancestors in the City of David. Amaziah his son succeeded him.

The Reign of Jehoahaz (Israel)

13 [1]In the twenty-third year of Joash son of Ahaziah king of Judah, Jehoahaz son of Jehu became king over Israel in Samaria for seventeen years. [2]He did what was displeasing to YHWH. He followed the sinful way of Jeroboam son of Nebat, who caused Israel to sin; he did not stray from it. [3]YHWH was incensed at Israel, and so he handed them over to Hazael king of Aram and Ben-hadad son of Hazael for many years. [4]But Jehoahaz implored YHWH and YHWH heard him, for he saw the oppression of Israel, how the king of Aram had oppressed them. [5]So YHWH gave Israel a deliverer and they were freed from the authority of Aram. The Israelites lived peacefully as in former times. [6]But they did not stray from the sinful way of the House of Jeroboam who had caused Israel to sin; they followed it. There was even a pole of Asherah in Samaria. [7]Jehoahaz was left with no force, except fifty horsemen, ten chariots, and ten thousand foot soldiers; for the king of Aram had destroyed them and crushed them like dust. [8]The rest of the history of Jehoahaz and all that he did and his exploits are indeed recorded in the annals of the kings of Israel. [9]So Jehoahaz slept with his ancestors and was buried in Samaria. Joash his son succeeded him.

The Reign of Joash (Israel)

13   ¹⁰In the thirty-seventh year of Joash king of Judah, Jehoash son of Jehoahaz became king over Israel in Samaria for sixteen years. ¹¹He did what was displeasing to YHWH. He did not stray from all the sinful way of Jeroboam son of Nebat who caused Israel to sin; he followed it. ¹²The rest of the history of Joash and all that he did and his exploits, that he fought with Amaziah king of Judah, are indeed recorded in the annals of the kings of Israel. ¹³So Joash slept with his ancestors—Jeroboam took the throne—and Joash was buried in Samaria with the kings of Israel.

A Prophecy of Victory; The Death of Elisha

13   ¹⁴Now Elisha fell ill with a sickness of which he was to die. Joash king of Israel went down to him; he wept over him and said: "My father, my father. The chariots of Israel and its horsemen!" ¹⁵Elisha said to him, "Take a bow and arrows," and he took a bow and arrows. ¹⁶Then he said to the king of Israel, "Put your hand to the bow." He put his hand (to the bow), and Elisha placed his hands on the king's hands ¹⁷and said, "Open the window facing east." He opened (it). Elisha said, "Shoot" and he shot. He said, "An arrow of victory for YHWH. An arrow of victory over Aram. You will defeat Aram at Aphek completely." ¹⁸Then he said, "Take the arrows," and he took (them). He said to the king of Israel, "Strike the ground!" He struck three times and stopped. ¹⁹But the man of God was angry at him and said, "Had you struck five or six times, then you would have defeated Aram completely. Now you will defeat Aram (only) three times." ²⁰Then Elisha died and was buried.

Moabite bands used to raid the land with the start of the year. ²¹Once, they were burying a man and they spotted such a band. They threw the body into the grave of Elisha and left. When the body touched the bones of Elisha, it came alive and stood on its feet.

²²Hazael king of Aram oppressed Israel all the days of Jehoahaz. ²³But YHWH was gracious and had mercy upon them. He showed regard for them because of his covenant with Abraham, Isaac, and Jacob. He would not destroy them, and so has not rid himself of them until now. ²⁴When Hazael king of Aram died, Ben-hadad his son succeeded him. ²⁵Jehoash son of Jehoahaz recaptured the cities from Ben-hadad son of Hazael, which had been taken in war from Jehoahaz his father. Joash defeated him three times and thus recovered the cities of Israel.

The Reign of Amaziah (Judah)

14   ¹In the second year of Joash son of Joahaz king of Israel, Amaziah son of Joash king of Judah became king. ²He was twenty-five years old when he became king, and he reigned twenty-nine years in Jerusalem. His mother's name was Jehoaddan from Jerusalem. ³He did what was pleasing to YHWH,

yet not like David his ancestor; he did just as Joash his father had done. [4]Yet the high places were not removed; the people continued to sacrifice and to make offerings at the high places. [5]When the kingdom was firmly in his hand, he put to death those of his servants who had attacked the king his father. [6]But he did not put to death the sons of the attackers, in accordance with what is written in the book of the Teaching of Moses which YHWH commanded: Fathers shall not be put to death for their children; children shall not be put to death for their fathers. Each shall be put to death only for his own sin.

[7]He defeated ten thousand Edomites in the Valley of Salt, and he captured Sela in battle and named it Joktheel, (as it is called) until this day.

[8]Then Amaziah sent messengers to Jehoash son of Jehoahaz son of Jehu king of Israel: "Come, let us meet face to face!" [9]Jehoash king of Israel responded to Amaziah king of Judah, "The thistle in Lebanon sent a message to the cedar in Lebanon, 'Give your daughter in marriage to my son.' But a wild animal in Lebanon passed by and trampled the thistle. [10]You certainly did defeat Edom, but then it has carried you away. Enjoy your honor, and do stay at home! Now why provoke trouble in which you and Judah will fall?" [11]But Amaziah did not take heed. So Jehoash king of Israel set out and they met face to face, he and Amaziah king of Judah, at Beth-shemesh in Judah. [12]Judah was routed by Israel, and they all fled to their homes. [13]Jehoash king of Israel captured Amaziah king of Judah son of Jehoash son of Ahaziah at Beth-shemesh. Then he marched to Jerusalem, and breached the walls of Jerusalem from the Ephraim Gate to the Corner Gate, a distance of four hundred cubits. [14]He carried off all the gold and the silver and all the vessels which were found in the House of YHWH and in the royal treasuries and hostages, and then returned to Samaria.

[15]The rest of the history of Jehoash (and) what he did and his exploits, and how he fought with Amaziah king of Judah are indeed recorded in the annals of the kings of Israel. [16]So Jehoash slept with his ancestors and he was buried in Samaria with the kings of Israel. Jeroboam his son succeeded him.

[17]Amaziah son of Joash king of Judah lived fifteen years after the death of Jehoash son of Jehoahaz king of Israel. [18]The rest of the history of Amaziah is indeed recorded in the annals of the kings of Judah. [19]A conspiracy was formed against him in Jerusalem, and so he fled to Lachish. But they sent after him to Lachish and killed him there. [20]They brought him (back) on horses, and he was buried in Jerusalem with his ancestors in the City of David. [21]Then all the People of Judah took Azariah—he was then sixteen years old—and they made him king to succeed his father Amaziah. [22]It was he who rebuilt Elath and restored it to Judah, after the king slept with his ancestors.

The Reign of Jeroboam II (Israel)

14   [23]In the fifteenth year of Amaziah son of Joash king of Judah, Jeroboam son of Joash became king over Israel in Samaria for forty-one years. [24]He did what was displeasing to YHWH. He did not stray from all the sinful ways of Jeroboam son of Nebat who caused Israel to sin. [25]It was he who restored the boundaries

of Israel from Lebo-hamath to the Sea of the Arabah, in accordance with the word of YHWH the God of Israel, which he spoke through his servant Jonah son of Amittai, the prophet from Gath-hahepher. [26]For YHWH saw Israel's affliction was very bitter indeed; there was no one but the restricted and the abandoned, and no one to help Israel. [27]YHWH did not speak of blotting out Israel's name from under the heavens, and so he rescued them through Jeroboam son of Joash. [28]The rest of the history of Jeroboam and all that he did, and his exploits, how he fought and restored Damascus and Hamath for Israel, are indeed recorded in the annals of the kings of Israel. [29]So Jeroboam slept with his ancestors ⟨and was buried in Samaria⟩ with the kings of Israel. Zechariah his son succeeded him.

The Reign of Azariah (Judah)

15 [1]In the twenty-seventh year of Jeroboam, king of Israel, Azariah son of Amaziah king of Judah became king. [2]He was sixteen years old when he became king and he reigned fifty-two years in Jerusalem. His mother's name was Jecoliah, from Jerusalem. [3]He did what was pleasing to YHWH, just as Amaziah his father had done. [4]Yet the high places were not removed; the people continued to sacrifice and make offerings at the high places. [5]YHWH struck the king so that he was a leper until the day of his death. He resided in *Beth ha-ḥophshith*, while Jotham, the king's son, was royal steward and judged the People of the Land. [6]The rest of the history of Azariah and all that he did are indeed recorded in the annals of the kings of Judah. [7]So Azariah slept with his ancestors and they buried him with his ancestors in the City of David. Jotham, his son, succeeded him.

From Zechariah to Pekah: The Decline of Israel

15 [8]In the thirty-eighth year of Azariah king of Judah, Zechariah son of Jeroboam became king over Israel in Samaria for six months. [9]He did what was displeasing to YHWH, just as his ancestors had done. He did not stray from the sinful ways of Jeroboam son of Nebat, who caused Israel to sin. [10]Shallum son of Jabesh conspired against him. He attacked him at Ibleam and killed him; and he succeeded him as king. [11]The rest of the history of Zechariah is recorded in the annals of the kings of Israel. [12]This was in accord with the word of YHWH which promised Jehu, "Four generations of your descendants shall sit on the throne of Israel." And so it was.

[13]Shallum son of Jabesh became king in the thirty-ninth year of Uzziah king of Judah, and he reigned one month in Samaria. [14]Menahem son of Gadi set out from Tirzah and came to Samaria. He attacked Shallum son of Jabesh in Samaria and killed him; and he succeeded him as king. [15]The rest of the history of Shallum and the conspiracy which he formed are recorded in the annals of the kings of Israel.

[16]Then Menahem attacked Tappuah and all who were in it and its border areas from Tirzah, because it would not open (its gates). He defeated it, and even ripped open all its pregnant women.

[17]In the thirty-ninth year of Azariah king of Judah, Menahem son of Gadi became king over Israel for ten years in Samaria. [18]He did what was displeasing to YHWH; he did not stray from the sinful ways of Jeroboam son of Nebat, who caused Israel to sin. [19]In his days, Pul king of Assyria marched against the country. Menahem paid Pul a thousand talents of silver so that he would support him in holding on to the kingdom. [20]Menahem levied the silver from Israel: every man of means had to pay the king of Assyria fifty shekels of silver per person. Then the king of Assyria withdrew and did not remain there in the country. [21]The rest of the history of Menahem and all that he did are indeed recorded in the annals of the kings of Israel. [22]So Menahem slept with his ancestors and Pekahiah his son succeeded him.

[23]In the fiftieth year of Azariah king of Judah, Pekahiah son of Menahem became king over Israel in Samaria for two years. [24]He did what was displeasing to YHWH; he did not stray from the sinful ways of Jeroboam son of Nebat, who caused Israel to sin. [25]Pekah son of Remaliah, his adjutant, conspired against him. He attacked him in Samaria in the citadel of the palace ≪ ≫ with the help of fifty Gileadites, and killed him; and he succeeded him as king. [26]The rest of the history of Pekahiah and all that he did are recorded in the annals of the kings of Israel.

[27]In the fifty-second year of Azariah king of Judah, Pekah son of Remaliah became king over Israel in Samaria for twenty years. [28]He did what was displeasing to YHWH; he did not stray from the sinful ways of Jeroboam son of Nebat, who caused Israel to sin. [29]In the days of Pekah king of Israel, Tiglath-pileser king of Assyria came and took Ijon, Abel-beth-maachah, Janoah, Kedesh, Hazor— the Gilead and the Galilee—all the land of Naphtali. He exiled their population to Assyria. [30]Hoshea son of Elah conspired against Pekah son of Remaliah. He attacked and killed him; and he succeeded him as king, in the twentieth year of Jotham son of Uzziah. [31]The rest of the history of Pekah and all that he did are recorded in the annals of the kings of Israel.

The Reign of Jotham (Judah)

15   [32]In the second year of Pekah son of Remaliah king of Israel, Jotham son of Uzziah king of Judah became king. [33]He was twenty-five years old when he became king, and he reigned sixteen years in Jerusalem. His mother's name was Jerusha daughter of Zadok. [34]He did what was pleasing to YHWH; he did just as Uzziah his father had done. [35]Yet the high places were not removed; the people continued to sacrifice and to make offerings at the high places. He built the Upper Gate of the House of YHWH. [36]The rest of the history of Jotham and all that he did are indeed recorded in the annals of the kings of Judah. [37]In those days, YHWH first loosed Rezin king of Aram and Pekah son of Remaliah

against Judah. ³⁸So Jotham slept with his ancestors, and he was buried with his ancestors in the City of David his ancestor. Ahaz his son succeeded him.

The Reign of Ahaz (Judah)

16 ¹In the seventeenth year of Pekah son of Remaliah, Ahaz son of Jotham king of Judah became king. ²Ahaz was twenty years old when he became king, and he reigned sixteen years in Jerusalem. He did not do what was pleasing to YHWH, his God, like David, his ancestor, ³but he followed the ways of the kings of Israel; he even passed his son through fire, imitating the abominations of the nations whom YHWH dispossessed before the Israelites. ⁴He sacrificed and made offerings at the high places, on the hills, and under every leafy tree.

⁵Then Rezin king of Aram and Pekah son of Remaliah king of Israel came to do battle against Jerusalem. They besieged Ahaz, but they were not able to attack.

⁶At that time, the king of Edom restored Elath to Edom, he drove out the Judahites from Elath. Edomites came to Elath and settled there until this day.

⁷Ahaz sent messengers to Tiglath-pileser king of Assyria: "I am your servant and your son. Come, rescue me from the hand of the king of Aram and from the hand of the king of Israel who are attacking me." ⁸Ahaz took the silver and the gold stored in the House of YHWH and in the palace treasury, and sent a bribe to the king of Assyria. ⁹The king of Assyria responded to his plea; the king of Assyria proceeded against Damascus. He captured it and exiled its population to Kir, and put Rezin to death.

¹⁰Now when King Ahaz went to Damascus to greet Tiglath-pileser, king of Assyria, he saw the altar in Damascus; whereupon King Ahaz sent a model of the altar and a plan with all details for its construction to Uriah the priest. ¹¹Uriah the priest built the altar, according to all that King Ahaz had sent him from Damascus; Uriah the priest completed it by the time King Ahaz returned from Damascus. ¹²When the king returned from Damascus and inspected the altar, he approached the altar and ascended it; ¹³he offered his burnt offering and his meal offering; he poured out his libation, and he dashed the blood of his offering of well-being against the altar. ¹⁴As for the bronze altar which (had stood) before YHWH, he moved (it) from the front of the House, from between the altar and House of YHWH, and placed it on the north side of the (new) altar. ¹⁵King Ahaz then ordered Uriah the priest: "On the great altar, offer the morning burnt offering and the evening meal offering and the king's burnt offering and his meal offering and the burnt offering of all the People of the Land, and their meal offerings and their libations. All the blood of the burnt offerings and all the blood of the sacrifices you shall dash against it. The bronze altar will be for me to frequent." ¹⁶Uriah the priest did just as King Ahaz ordered.

¹⁷King Ahaz stripped off the frames of the wheeled stands and removed the basin from them; he took down the (bronze) Sea from the bronze oxen that supported it and placed it on the stone pavement. ¹⁸He also removed from the House of YHWH the sabbath covering built in the House and the king's outer entrance, (all) on account of the king of Assyria.

¹⁹The rest of the history of Ahaz and what he did are indeed recorded in the annals of the kings of Judah. ²⁰So Ahaz slept with his ancestors and he was buried with his ancestors in the city of David. Hezekiah, his son, succeeded him.

The Reign of Hoshea (Israel): The Fall of Samaria

17 ¹In the twelfth year of Ahaz, king of Judah, Hoshea son of Elah became king over Israel in Samaria for nine years. ²He did what was displeasing to YHWH, yet not as the kings of Israel who had preceded him. ³Shalmaneser king of Assyria marched against him, and Hoshea became his vassal and rendered him tribute. ⁴But when the king of Assyria discovered that Hoshea was part of a conspiracy, for he had sent envoys to Sais ⟨to⟩ the king of Egypt and withheld the yearly tribute to the king of Assyria, the king of Assyria arrested him and put him in prison. ⁵The king of Assyria invaded the whole country; he marched against Samaria and laid siege to it for three years. ⁶In the ninth year of Hoshea, the king of Assyria captured Samaria. He exiled Israel to Assyria and resettled them in Halah and on the Habor, the river of Gozan, and in the cities of Media.

A Homily on the Fall of the Northern Kingdom

17 ⁷Now, because the Israelites sinned against YHWH, their God, who brought them up from the land of Egypt, from under the control of Pharaoh, king of Egypt, by revering other gods; ⁸and followed the statutes of the nations, whom YHWH dispossessed before the Israelites, and of the kings of Israel which they practiced, ⁹the Israelites ascribed untruths to YHWH, their God; and built themselves high places in all their cities, from watchtower to fortified city; ¹⁰and set up pillars and sacred poles for themselves on every lofty hill and under every leafy tree; ¹¹and made offerings there, at all the high places, as the nations whom YHWH exiled before them; and did evil things, angering YHWH; ¹²and worshipped idols, about which YHWH had said to them, "Do not do this thing!" ¹³YHWH even warned Israel and Judah by every prophet and every seer, "Turn back from your evil ways and keep my commands and my statutes, in accord with all the Law which I commanded your ancestors, and which I sent to you through my servants, the prophets."

¹⁴But they did not listen. They were as stiff-necked as their ancestors had been, who did not trust YHWH, their God. ¹⁵Moreover they spurned his statutes, and his covenant which he made with their ancestors, and the warnings which he had given to them; and they went after emptiness and became empty themselves, and after the fashion of the neighboring nations which YHWH commanded them not to imitate. ¹⁶They abandoned all the commands of YHWH, their God; they made themselves molten images — two calves; they made a pole of Asherah; they bowed down to all the heavenly host; they worshipped Baal; ¹⁷they passed their sons and their daughters through fire; they practiced divination and sorcery; they gave themselves up to doing what was displeasing to

YHWH, making him angry. [18](Because of all this,) YHWH was very angry with Israel, and he removed them from his sight; only the tribe of Judah was left.

[19]But even Judah did not keep the commands of YHWH, their God; they followed the statutes practiced by the Israelites. [20]Thus YHWH spurned all the seed of Israel; he afflicted them by handing them over to plunderers, until he rid himself of them.

[21]When he tore Israel away from the House of David, they made Jeroboam son of Nebat king; Jeroboam led Israel away from following YHWH and caused them to sin greatly. [22]The Israelites follows all the sinful ways practiced by Jeroboam; they did not stray from it; [23]until YHWH removed Israel from his sight, as he had foretold through all his servants, the prophets. So Israel was exiled from its land to Assyria, until this day.

Samaria Resettled

17   [24]The king of Assyria then brought (people) from Babylon, Cutha, Avva, Hamath, Sepharvaim, and settled them in the cities of Samaria in place of the Israelites. They took possession of Samaria and settled in its cities. [25]Now at the beginning of their settlement there, they did not revere YHWH, so YHWH let lions loose against them, and they were killing some of them. [26]It was reported to the king of Assyria, "The nations whom you exiled and settled in the cities of Samaria did not know the rites of the god of the land, and so he let lions loose against them. They are preying upon them, because they do not know the rites of the local god!" [27]The king of Assyria ordered, "Have one of the priests whom I exiled from there sent back there. Let him go and settle there and teach them the rites of the god of the land." [28]Thus one of the priests exiled from Samaria came and settled in Bethel; he taught them how to revere YHWH. [29]But each nation made its own gods and set (them) up in the shrines of the high places which the Samarians had made, each nation in the city in which it was living. [30]The people of Babylon made Succoth-benoth; the people of Cutha made Nergal; the people of Hamath made Ashima; [31]the Avvites made Nibhaz and Tartak; and the Sepharvites were burning their sons in fire to Adrammelech and Anammelech, gods of Sepharvaim. [32]And they revered YHWH; they appointed some of their own number priests at the high places and they officiated for them at the shrines of the high places. [33]They revered YHWH and (at the same time) they served their own gods, after the rites of the nations from among whom they had been exiled.

[34]Until this day, they follow the(ir) earlier practices: they do not revere YHWH, and they do not do as required by their statutes and their practice—the Teaching and the command which YHWH commanded the sons of Jacob, whose name he changed to Israel. [35]YHWH had made a covenant with them, and he commanded them, "Do not revere other gods. Do not bow down to them; do not serve them; do not sacrifice to them. [36]For it is only YHWH, who brought you up from the land of Egypt, with great power and outstretched arm whom you shall revere; to him you shall bow down; to him you shall sacrifice.

[37]Carefully observe the statutes and the rules—the Teaching and the command which he wrote down for you—forever. Do not revere other gods. [38]Do not forget the covenant which he made with you; do not revere other gods. [39]For it is only YHWH your God that you shall revere, and he shall deliver you from all your enemies." [40]But they did not listen; rather they follow their earlier practices.

[41]Now these nations revered YHWH and they served their idols (at the same time); even their sons and grandsons behave as did their ancestors, until this day.

THE KINGDOM OF JUDAH UNTIL THE EXILE

The Reign of Hezekiah: Reform and Rebellion

18 [1]It was in the third year of Hoshea son of Elah, king of Israel, that Hezekiah son of Ahaz, king of Judah, became king. [2]He was twenty-five years old when he became king, and he reigned twenty-nine years in Jerusalem. His mother's name was Abi, daughter of Zechariah. [3]He did what was pleasing to YHWH, just as David, his ancestor, had done. [4]It was he who abolished the high places, and broke the sacred pillars, and cut down the pole of Asherah and smashed the bronze serpent that Moses had made; for until those very days the Israelites were offering sacrifices to it. It was called Nehushtan. [5]In YHWH God of Israel he put his trust; there was no one like him among all the kings of Judah following him, or among those before him. [6]He was loyal to YHWH; he did not turn away from him, but kept the commands which YHWH had given to Moses. [7]And so YHWH was with him; in all that he undertook, he was successful. He rebelled against the king of Assyria and was his vassal no longer. [8]He defeated the Philistines as far as Gaza and its border areas, from watchtower to fortified city.

[9]It was in the fourth year of King Hezekiah—that is, the seventh year of Hoshea, son of Elah, king of Israel—that Shalmaneser, king of Assyria, marched against Samaria and laid siege to it; [10]he captured it at the end of three years. In the sixth year of Hezekiah, that is the ninth year of Hoshea, king of Israel, Samaria was captured. [11]The king of Assyria exiled Israel to Assyria and he settled them in Halah and on the Habor, the river of Gozan, and in the cities of Media; [12]for they had not obeyed YHWH, their God; they violated his covenant—all that Moses, YHWH's servant, commanded. They would not obey and would not behave.

Sennacherib's Campaign to Judah

18 [13]In the fourteenth year of King Hezekiah, Sennacherib, king of Assyria, attacked all of Judah's fortified cities and seized them. [14]Whereupon Hezekiah, king of Judah, sent a message to the king of Assyria at Lachish: "I admit my guilt. Withdraw from me and whatever you will impose upon me, I shall bear." The king of Assyria then imposed (a payment of) three hundred talents of silver and

thirty talents of gold upon Hezekiah, king of Judah. [15]And so Hezekiah turned over all the silver stored in the House of YHWH and in the palace treasury. [16]At that time Hezekiah stripped the doors of the Temple Hall and the posts which he himself had plated and delivered them to the king of Assyria.

[17]The king of Assyria dispatched the Tartan, the Rab-saris, and the Rab-shakeh from Lachish to King Hezekiah in Jerusalem, together with a large force. They marched up to Jerusalem and took up positions by the conduit of the Upper Pool on the Fuller's Field Road; [18]and they called for the king. Eliakim son of Hilkiah, the royal steward Shebna the scribe, and Joah son of Asaph the recorder came out to them.

[19]The Rab-shakeh spoke to them, "Tell Hezekiah, thus said the Great King, the king of Assyria, 'What is this confidence of yours? [20]Do you think that plans and arming for war can emerge from empty talk? Now, in whom have you put your trust that you rebelled against me? [21]Here now, you put your trust in this splintered reed staff, in Egypt; that if someone leans upon it, it pierces his palm and punctures it. That's Pharaoh, king of Egypt, to all who put their trust in him! [22]And if you tell me, It is in YHWH our God that we put our trust! Is he not the one whose high places and altars Hezekiah removed, and then ordered throughout Judah and Jerusalem, You must worship before this altar in Jerusalem? [23]Now, come make a wager with my master, the king of Assyria: I will give you two thousand horses, if you will be able to supply riders for them. [24]And so, how could you turn down ≪   ≫ one of my master's minor servants and trust in Egypt for chariots and horsemen? [25]Now was it without YHWH that I marched against this place to destroy it? YHWH said to me, 'Attack this country and destroy it!'"

[26]Eliakim son of Hilkiah, Shebna, and Joah then said to the Rab-shakeh, "Please speak Aramaic with your servants; we understand it. Do not speak Judean with us within earshot of the people on the wall." [27]But the Rab-shakeh answered them, "Was it to your master and to you that my master has sent me to speak these words? Was it not rather to the men sitting on the wall, who, together with you, will have to eat their own excrement and drink their own urine?" [28]Then the Rab-shakeh stepped forward and called out loudly in Judean, ≪   ≫ "Hear the message of the Great King, the king of Assyria. [29]Thus said the king, 'Do not let Hezekiah deceive you, for he cannot save you from me.' [30]And do not let Hezekiah have you put your trust in YHWH, by saying, 'YHWH will surely save us; and this city will not be handed over to the king of Assyria.' [31]Do not listen to Hezekiah; for thus said the king of Assyria, 'Send me a gift and surrender to me! Then each one of you will eat of his own vine and of his own fig tree and will drink the water of his own cistern; [32]until I come to transfer you to a land like your own land, a land of grain and new wine, a land of bread and vineyards, a land of olive oil and honey. Stay alive and don't die.' Do not listen to Hezekiah, when he incites you by saying, 'YHWH will save us!' [33]Did any of the gods of the(se) nations ever save his land from the king of Assyria? [34]Where are the gods of Hamath and Arpad? Where

are the gods of Sepharvaim? ≪   ≫ ⟨Where are the gods of Samaria?⟩ Did they save Samaria from me? [35]Who of all the gods of the countries was able to save his land from me, that YHWH should be able to save Jerusalem from me?" [36]They remained silent ≪   ≫ and did not answer a word, for it was the king's order, "Do not answer him!"

[37]Thereupon Eliakim son of Hilkiah, the royal steward, Shebna the scribe, Joah son of Asaph the recorder came to Hezekiah, with their garments rent, and reported the Rab-shakeh's message to him.

19   [1]When King Hezekiah heard this, he rent his garments and put on sackcloth and entered the House of YHWH. [2]He sent Eliakim, the royal steward, Shebna the scribe and the elder priests, dressed in sackcloth, to Isaiah son of Amoz, the prophet. [3]They told him, "Thus said Hezekiah, 'This day is a day of distress, of rebuke, and of contempt. Children have come to the breach, but there is no strength for the birth. [4]Perhaps YHWH your God will listen to all the words of the Rab-shakeh, whom his master the king of Assyria sent to taunt the living God and will punish him for the words which YHWH your God has heard. So do offer a prayer for this last remnant!'"

[5]Now when the servants of King Hezekiah came to Isaiah, [6]Isaiah said to them, "Speak thus to your master: Thus said YHWH, 'Do not be frightened by the words you have heard by which these attendants of the king of Assyria reviled me. [7]Behold, I will put a spirit in him, so that he will hear a report and return to his own country, and I will strike him down by the sword and his own country.'"

[8]Now the Rab-shakeh withdrew, and since he heard that the camp had moved from Lachish, he found the king of Assyria engaged in battle at Libnah. [9]He (the king of Assyria) received a report about Tirhakah, king of Ethiopia: He has set out to do battle with you. So again he sent messengers to Hezekiah: [10]"Speak thus to Hezekiah, king of Judah, 'Do not let your God deceive, the one in whom you put your trust, by thinking that Jerusalem will not be given over to the king of Assyria. [11]Now surely you have heard what the kings of Assyria did to all the lands—destroying them! And you—will you be saved? [12]Did the gods of the nations save them whom my ancestors destroyed, Gozan and Haran and Reseph and the Edenites of Telassar? [13]Where is the king of Hamath and the king of Arpad and the king of Lair, Sepharvaim, Hena, and Iwwah?'"

[14]Hezekiah received the letter from the messengers and read it. He then went up to the House of YHWH; Hezekiah spread it out before YHWH, [15]and Hezekiah prayed before YHWH, "O YHWH, God of Israel, enthroned upon the cherubim, You, alone, are God of all the kingdoms of the earth. It was You who made heaven and earth. [16]Turn your ear, O YHWH, and listen; open your eyes, O YHWH, and look. Listen to the message that Sennacherib has sent to taunt the living God. [17]It is true, O YHWH, that the kings of Assyria have laid waste the nations and their lands, [18]and put their gods to fire—for they are not gods, but only man's handicraft, mere wood and stone; thus they were able to

destroy them. ¹⁹But now, O YHWH, our God, save us from his hand, so that all the kingdoms of the earth may know that You, YHWH, alone, are God."

²⁰Then Isaiah son of Amoz sent a message to Hezekiah: "Thus said YHWH, God of Israel, 'I have heard your prayer to me concerning Sennacherib, king of Assyria. This is what YHWH has spoken concerning him:

²¹ "Maiden Daughter Zion
despises you, scorns you.
Daughter Jerusalem
shakes her head after you.
²² Whom have you taunted and reviled?
Against whom have you raised your voice?
And raised your eyes heavenward?
Against the Holy One of Israel!
²³ Through your messengers you taunted YHWH, by saying,
With my many chariots, it was I.......
I ascended mountain peaks, the far reaches of the Lebanon.
I felled its tallest cedars, its choicest firs.
I entered its remotest lodge, its rich woodlands.
²⁴ It was I who dug and drank strange waters,
And with the soles of my feet I dried up the Niles of Egypt.
²⁵ Have you not heard? From of old, I did it.
In ancient days, I fashioned it. Now I have brought it about—
and it is: Fortified cities crashing into ruined heaps,
²⁶ Their inhabitants powerless, dismayed, and confounded.
They were like grass in the field, and fresh pasture;
Like straw on rooftops, blasted by the east wind.
²⁷ ⟨Your every action⟩ and your every pursuit, I know. ≪   ≫
²⁸ Because you have raged against me, and your uproar rings in my ears,
I will put my hook in your nose and my bridle through your lips,
and turn you back on the very road by which you came.
²⁹ This shall be the sign for you:
This year you shall eat from the aftergrowth,
next year from the self-sown;
but in the third year, sow and reap,
plant vineyards and enjoy their fruit.
³⁰ The remaining survivors of the house of Judah shall add on
roots below and produce fruit above.
³¹ For a remnant shall emerge out of Jerusalem,
And a survivor from Mount Zion. The zeal of YHWH shall effect this.
³² Therefore, thus said YHWH concerning the king of Assyria:
He shall not enter this city, nor shall he shoot an arrow there.
He shall not move up defenses before it,
nor throw up a siege mound against it.
³³ He shall go back by the same road he came; but into this city,

he shall not enter. The word of YHWH.

³⁴ For I will defend this city and save it, for my own sake
   and for the sake of David, my servant."'"

³⁵That night, YHWH's angel went out and struck the Assyrian camp—
185,000 men! At daybreak there were dead bodies all about.

³⁶So Sennacherib, king of Assyria, broke camp and left. He returned to Nin-
eveh, where he resided. ³⁷Once, as he was worshipping in the House of Nisroch,
his god, Adrammelech and Sharezer, ⟨his sons⟩, struck him down with the
sword and then fled to the land of Ararat. Esarhaddon, his son, became king.

Hezekiah's Illness and Recovery

20 ¹In those days, Hezekiah became mortally ill. The prophet Isaiah son of
Amoz came to him and said to him, "Thus said YHWH, 'Prepare your testament, for you are about to die; you shall not recover.'" ²Whereupon he turned
toward the wall and prayed to YHWH, ³"Please, O YHWH, remember how I
served you faithfully and loyally, and did what was pleasing to you." And Hezekiah wept bitterly. ⁴Isaiah had not left the middle courtyard, when the word of
YHWH came to him: ⁵"Return and say to Hezekiah, ruler of my people, 'Thus
said YHWH, God of David your ancestor: I have heard your prayer; I have seen
your tears. Now, then, I will heal you. Within three days you shall go up to the
House of YHWH. ⁶I will add fifteen years to your life. I will save you and this
city from the hand of the king of Assyria, and I will protect this city, for my own
sake and for the sake of David my servant.'" ⁷Then Isaiah said, "Fetch a fig cake."
They brought one and placed it upon the boil and he recovered. ⁸Hezekiah
said to Isaiah, "What is the sign that YHWH will heal me and that within three
days I shall go up to the House of YHWH?" ⁹Isaiah replied, "This will be the
sign for you from YHWH, that YHWH will perform what he promised: The
shadow has moved ahead ten steps; can it return ten steps?" ¹⁰Hezekiah said, "It
is easy for the shadow to lengthen ten steps; not so for it to go back ten steps."
¹¹So the prophet Isaiah called to YHWH, and He moved the shadow back
the ten steps which ⟨the sun⟩ had gone down on the Ahaz dial.

The Embassy of Merodach-baladan

20 ¹²At that time, Merodach-baladan son of Baladan, king of Babylon, sent
letters and a gift to Hezekiah, for he had heard that Hezekiah had taken ill.
¹³Hezekiah was pleased with them and he showed the envoys his entire store-
house—the silver, the gold, the spices and the fine oil, his armory, and everything in his treasuries. There was not a thing in his residence or in his realm
that Hezekiah did not show them.

¹⁴Then Isaiah the prophet came to King Hezekiah and asked him, "What did
these men say? And from where did they come to you?" Hezekiah replied,

"They came from a distant land, from Babylon." [15]And he said, "What did they see in your residence?" Hezekiah said, "They saw everything in my residence. There was not a thing in my treasures that I did not show them." [16]Thereupon Isaiah said to Hezekiah, "Hear the word of YHWH, [17]'Now, in days to come, everything in your residence and that which your ancestors have amassed up until today shall be carried off to Babylon. Nothing shall be left behind,' said YHWH. [18]And some of your very own offspring, whom you will have fathered, will be taken captive to serve as eunuchs in the palace of the king of Babylon." [19]Hezekiah said to Isaiah, "The word of YHWH which you announced is just." For he thought: At least there will be peace and security in my lifetime.

[20]The rest of the history of Hezekiah and all his exploits, and how he constructed the pool and the conduit to bring water into the city, are indeed recorded in the annals of the kings of Judah. [21]So Hezekiah slept with his ancestors and Manasseh his son succeeded him.

The Reign of Manasseh

21 [1]Manasseh was twelve years old when he became king and he reigned fifty-five years in Jerusalem. His mother's name was Hephzibah. [2]He did what was displeasing to YHWH, imitating the abominations of the nations whom YHWH dispossessed before the Israelites. [3]He rebuilt the high places which Hezekiah his father had destroyed; he erected altars to Baal; he made a pole of Asherah, just as Ahab king of Israel had done; he bowed down to all the heavenly host and worshipped them. [4]He built altars in the House of YHWH, of which YHWH had said, "In Jerusalem, I will establish My name." [5]He built altars to all the heavenly host in the two courtyards of the House of YHWH. [6]He passed his son through fire; he practiced soothsaying and sorcery, and dealt with persons who consult ghosts and spirits, greatly displeasing YHWH to his anger. [7]He set the idol of Asherah, which he made, in the House, of which YHWH had said to David and to Solomon his son, "In this House and in Jerusalem which I have chosen out of all the tribes of Israel, I will establish My name forever. [8]And I will not cause Israel to wander again from the land which I gave to their ancestors, provided that they will carefully observe all that I commanded them—all the Teaching which my servant Moses commanded them." [9]But they did not listen, and Manasseh misled them to do evil, more than the nations whom YHWH destroyed before the Israelites.

[10]Then YHWH spoke through his servants, the prophets, [11]"Since Manasseh, king of Judah has done these abominable things, worse than anything the Amorites before him did, and has caused Judah to sin with his idols; [12]therefore, thus said YHWH, God of Israel, 'I am about to bring disaster on Jerusalem and Judah, so that it will resound in both ears of all who hear it. [13]I will stretch the measuring line of Samaria and the plummet of the House of Ahab over Jerusalem; and I will wipe out Jerusalem, as a plate is wiped clean and turned over on its face. [14]I will abandon the remnant of My inheritance and hand them over to their enemies, so that they become spoil and plunder for all their ene-

mies, [15]because they did what was displeasing to Me. They have been angering me ever since the day that their ancestors left Egypt, until this day!'"

[16]And what is more, Manasseh shed innocent blood, so much so that he filled Jerusalem from end to end, apart from causing Judah to sin by displeasing YHWH.

[17]The rest of the history of Manasseh and all that he did and his sinful acts are indeed recorded in the annals of the kings of Judah. [18]So Manasseh slept with his ancestors and he was buried in the garden of his residence, in the garden of Uzza; and Amon his son succeeded him.

The Reign of Amon

21   [19]Amon was twenty-two years old when he became king, and he reigned two years in Jerusalem. His mother's name was Meshullemeth, daughter of Haruz, from Jotbah. [20]He did what was displeasing to YHWH, just as Manasseh his father had done. [21]He followed all his father's ways; he worshipped the idols which is father worshipped and he bowed down to them. [22]He abandoned YHWH, the God of his fathers, and did not follow YHWH's way.

[23]Amon's courtiers plotted against him, and they killed the king in his residence. [24]But the People of the Land killed all those who had plotted against King Amon, and the People of the Land set Josiah, his son, on the throne as his successor. [25]The rest of the history of Amon (and) what he did are indeed recorded in the annals of the kings of Judah. [26]They buried him in his own tomb in the garden of Uzza, and Josiah his son succeeded him.

The Reign of Josiah: The Great Reform

22   [1]Josiah was eight years old when he became king, and he reigned thirty-one years in Jerusalem. His mother's name was Jedidah, daughter of Adaiah from Bozkath. [2]He did what was pleasing to YHWH; he followed all the ways of David, his ancestor, straying neither to the right nor to the left.

[3]In the eighteenth year of King Josiah, the king sent Shaphan, the scribe, son of Azaliah, son of Meshullam, to the House of YHWH: [4]"Go to Hilkiah the high priest and have him sum up the silver that has been brought to the House of YHWH, which the keepers of the threshold have collected from the people. [5]Let them deliver it to the workmen in charge of the House of YHWH, and they will pay it to the workmen of the House of YHWH, who are to repair the House, [6]to the carpenters, builders, masons, and to buy timber and quarry stone for repairing the House. [7]Note that the silver delivered to them is not to be audited, for they deal honestly."

[8]Hilkiah the high priest said to Shaphan the scribe, "I have found the book of the Teaching in the House of YHWH." Hilkiah gave the book to Shaphan and he read it. [9]Shaphan the scribe came to the king and reported back to the king, "Your servants have melted down the silver found in the House, and they

delivered it to the workmen in charge of the House of YHWH." [10]Then Shaphan the scribe told the king, "Hilkiah the priest gave me a book," and Shaphan read it before the king. [11]When the king heard the words of the book of the Teaching, he rent his garments. [12]The king then ordered Hilkiah the priest, Ahikam son of Shaphan, Achbor son of Micaiah, Shaphan the scribe, and Asaiah the king's servant, [13]"Go, inquire of YHWH on my behalf, on behalf of the people, and on behalf of all Judah concerning the words of this book that has been found. For great indeed is YHWH's wrath that has been kindled against us, because our ancestors did not obey the words of this book, to do all that is prescribed for us."

[14]So Hilkiah the priest, Ahikam, Achbor, Shaphan, and Asaiah went to Huldah the prophetess, wife of Shallum, son of Tikvah, son of Harhas, the keeper of the wardrobe—she lived in Jerusalem in the Mishneh quarter—and they spoke with her. [15]She said to them, "Thus said YHWH, God of Israel, 'Say to the man that sent you to me, [16]"Thus said YHWH: I am about to bring disaster on this place and on its inhabitants, all the words in the book which the king of Judah has read. [17]Because they have abandoned Me and they made offerings to other gods, so as to anger Me by all their practices, My wrath is burning against this place and it will not be extinguished." [18]But as for the king of Judah, who sent you to inquire of YHWH, thus you shall say to him, "Thus said YHWH, God of Israel: As for the things which you heard, [19]since you took fright and you humbled yourself before Me, when you heard that I promised to turn this place and its inhabitants into a horror and a curse, and you rent your garments and wept before Me, I, too, have heard—the word of YHWH." [20]Therefore I will gather you to your ancestors, and you will be gathered to your grave in peace. You will not behold all the disasters which I am bringing on this place.'" So they reported back to the king.

23 [1]Then the king sent for all the elders of Judah and Jerusalem to assemble before him. [2]The king went up to the House of YHWH, and with him all the men of Judah, all the residents of Jerusalem, the priests, and the prophets, all the people, young and old. He read out to them all the words of the book of the covenant which was found in the House of YHWH. [3]The king stood by the pillar and he concluded the covenant before YHWH, to follow YHWH, to keep his commandments, his injunctions, and his laws with all their heart and soul, to uphold the terms of this covenant written in this book. And all the people committed themselves to the covenant.

[4]The king then ordered Hilkiah the high priest, the deputy priests, and the keepers of the threshold to remove from the Hall of YHWH all the objects made for Baal, Asherah, and all the heavenly host. He burned them outside of Jerusalem on the terraces of the Kidron and had their ashes carried to Bethel. [5]He put an end to the idolatrous priests who had been installed by the kings of Judah to offer sacrifices at the high places in the cities of Judah and the environs of Jerusalem—those who sacrificed to Baal, to the sun and moon and planets, all the heavenly host. [6]He removed the (idol of) Asherah from the House of YHWH to the Kidron Valley outside Jerusalem; he burnt it in the

Kidron Valley and beat it to dust, and then scattered the dust over the common burial ground. [7]He tore down the houses of the sacred males within the House of YHWH, where women weave coverings for Asherah.

[8]He brought in all the priests from the cities of Judah, and defiled the high places where the priests had offered sacrifices, from Geba to Beer-Sheba. And he tore down the high places of the gates, by the entrance of the gate of Joshua, governor of the city, on a person's left at the city gate. [9]But the priests of the high places did not ascent the altar of YHWH in Jerusalem, though they ate unleavened bread together with their fellow (priests). [10]He defiled the Topheth in the Ben-hinnom Valley, so that no one could pass his son or daughter through fire to Molech. [11]He did away with the horses which the kings of Judah had dedicated to the sun, at the entrance to the House of YHWH, near the chamber of Nathan-melech, the officer of the precincts; and he burnt the chariots of the sun. [12]The king tore down the altars on the roof of the upper chamber of Ahaz that the kings of Judah had made, and the altars that Manasseh had made in the two courtyards of the House of YHWH. He hastily removed them from there, and he threw their rubble into the Kidron Valley. [13]The king defiled the high places east of Jerusalem, south of the Mount of the Destroyer, which Solomon king of Israel had built for Ashtoreth, the detestation of Sidon, for Chemosh, the detestation of Moab, and for Milcom, the abomination of the Ammonites. [14]He broke the sacred pillars; he cut down the sacred poles, and filled their places with human bones.

[15]Moreover the altar in Bethel, the high place which Jeroboam, son of Nebat, had made, causing Israel to sin, even that altar and the high place, he tore down. He burned the high place, making dust of it, and burned the pole of Asherah. [16]When Josiah looked about and saw the graves which were there on the mountainside, he sent and took the bones out of the graves. He burned (them) on the altar, and thus defiled it, in accordance with the word of YHWH foretold by the man of God, who had foretold these things. [17]He asked, "What is this marker I see?" The men of the city replied, "The grave of the man of God who came from Judah. He foretold all these things which you did to the altar at Bethel." [18]He then ordered, "Leave it alone! Let no one disturb his bones." So they spared his bones and the bones of the prophet, who came from Samaria. [19]Josiah also removed the shrines of the high places in the cities of Samaria which the kings of Israel had made to provoke ⟨YHWH's anger⟩. He did to them just as he had done in Bethel. [20]He slaughtered all the priests of the high places who were there on the altars, and burned human bones on them. Then he returned to Jerusalem.

[21]The king issued an order to all his people: "Celebrate the Passover of YHWH your God, as prescribed in this Book of the Covenant." [22]Indeed, a Passover such as this had not been celebrated since the days of the Judges who judged Israel and all the days of the kings of Israel and the kings of Judah; [23]only in the eighteenth year of King Josiah was such a Passover of YHWH celebrated in Jerusalem. [24]Moreover, Josiah stamped out those who consult ghosts and spirits, the household images and the idols, all the detestations which had

appeared in the land of Judah and in Jerusalem, in order to fulfill the words of the Teaching written in the book which Hilkiah the priest found in the House of YHWH. [25]There was no king like him before, who turned back to YHWH with all his heart, with all his soul, and with all his might, in accord with the entire Teaching of Moses; and after him, no one arose like him.

[26]Yet YHWH did not turn away from his great wrath which had flamed up against Judah, for all the things by which Manasseh angered him. [27]YHWH said, "I will also remove Judah from my sight as I removed Israel; for I will spurn this city which I have chosen, Jerusalem, and this House of which I said, 'My name shall be there.'"

[28]The rest of the history of Josiah and all that he did are indeed recorded in the annals of the kings of Judah. [29]In his days, Pharaoh Necho, king of Egypt, set out for the river Euphrates to the king of Assyria. When King Josiah confronted him, (Necho) put him to death at Megiddo as soon as he had seen him. [30]His attendants drove his body from Megiddo and brought him to Jerusalem; and they buried him in his own tomb. Then the People of the Land took Jehoahaz son of Josiah and anointed him; they made him king to succeed his father.

The Reign of Jehoahaz

23   [31]Jehoahaz was twenty-three years old when he became king, and he reigned three months in Jerusalem. His mother's name was Hamutal, daughter of Jeremiah of Libnah. [32]He did what was displeasing to YHWH, just as his ancestors had done. [33]Pharaoh Necho imprisoned him at Riblah in the land of Hamath, ending his reign in Jerusalem, and he imposed an indemnity on the land of one hundred talents of silver and a talent of gold. [34]Then Pharaoh Necho made Eliakim son of Josiah king to succeed Josiah his father, changing his name to Jehoiakim. He took Jehoahaz and brought him to Egypt, where he died. [35]Jehoiakim paid Pharaoh the silver and the gold, but assessed the land so as to pay the amount set by Pharaoh. He exacted the silver and the gold from the People of the Land, each according to his assessment, so as to pay Pharaoh Necho.

The Reign of Jehoiakim

23   [36]Jehoiakim was twenty-five years old when he became king, and he reigned eleven years in Jerusalem. His mother's name was Zebidah daughter of Pedaiah of Rumah. He did what was displeasing to YHWH, just as his ancestors had done.

24   [1]In his days, Nebuchadnezzar, king of Babylon marched forth; and Jehoiakim became his vassal for three years. Then he turned and rebelled against him. [2]YHWH let loose bands of Chaldeans, Aramaeans, Moabites, and Ammonites against him. He let them loose against Judah to destroy it, in accordance with the word of YHWH spoken through his servants to the prophets. [3]This was entirely YHWH's intent, directed against Judah, to remove them from his sight,

because of all the sins that Manasseh committed; ⁴and also because of the innocent blood which he shed. He filled Jerusalem with innocent blood so that YHWH would not forgive. ⁵The rest of the history of Jehoiakim and all that he did are indeed recorded in the annals of the kings of Judah. ⁶So Jehoiakim slept with his ancestors and Jehoiachin his son succeeded him. ⁷The king of Egypt did not leave his country any more, for the king of Babylon seized all that had belonged to the king of Egypt, from the Wadi of Egypt to the River Euphrates.

The Exile of Jehoiachin

24 ⁸Jehoiachin was eighteen years old when he became king and he reigned three months in Jerusalem. His mother's name was Nehushta, daughter of Elnathan from Jerusalem. ⁹He did what was displeasing to YHWH, just as his father had done.

¹⁰At that time, the troops of Nebuchadnezzar, king of Babylon, marched against Jerusalem, and the city came under siege. ¹¹When Nebuchadnezzar, king of Babylon, arrived at the city—his troops were (still) besieging it— ¹²Jehoiachin, king of Judah, surrendered to the king of Babylon: he, his mother, his courtiers, his officers, and his officials. The king of Babylon, in the eighth year of his reign, took him prisoner. ¹³He carried off from there all the treasures of the House of YHWH and of the palace, and he broke up all the gold objects in the Hall of YHWH which Solomon, king of Israel, had made, as YHWH had foretold. ¹⁴He exiled all of Jerusalem—all the officers and all the warriors, ten thousand exiles, and all the craftsmen and the smiths. Only the poorest of the land were left behind. ¹⁵He exiled Jehoiachin to Babylonia; and he took into exile from Jerusalem to Babylonia the king's mother, the king's wives, his officials, and the notables of the land, ¹⁶and all the warriors, seven thousand, and the craftsmen and the smiths, one thousand—all brave men, trained soldiers. The king of Babylon brought them as exiles to Babylon. ¹⁷The king of Babylon set Mattaniah, Jehoiachin's uncle, on the throne as his successor and changed his name to Zedekiah.

The Reign of Zedekiah: The Fall of Jerusalem

24 ¹⁸Zedekiah was twenty-one years old when he became king, and he reigned eleven years in Jerusalem. His mother's name was Hamutal, daughter of Jeremiah from Libnah. ¹⁹He did what was displeasing to YHWH, just as Jehoiakim had done. ²⁰Because of YHWH's wrath did these things happen to Jerusalem and Judah, until he rid himself of them. Thus Zedekiah rebelled against the king of Babylon.

25 ¹In the ninth year of Zedekiah's reign, in the tenth month, on the tenth day of the month, Nebuchadnezzar king of Babylon marched against Jerusalem, he and all his forces, and he encamped against it. They built a siege wall all about, ²so that the city was under siege until the eleventh year of King Zedekiah.

³⟨In the fourth month,⟩ on the ninth day of the month, the hunger became severe in the city; even the People of the Land had no bread. ⁴Thus the city was breached. ⟨Zedekiah⟩ and all the soldiers ⟨fled⟩ by night, leaving through the gate between the two walls which was near the king's garden; and though the Chaldeans were all around the city, he made off by the Arabah road. ⁵But the Chaldean forces pursued the king and overtook him in the steppes of Jericho, as all his troops dispersed.

⁶They captured the king and brought him to the king of Babylon at Riblah. He passed sentence upon him. ⁷They slaughtered Zedekiah's sons before his own eyes and (then) blinded Zedekiah. He put him in fetters and had him brought to Babylon.

⁸In the fifth month, on the seventh day of the month—it was the nineteenth year of King Nebuchadnezzar, king of Babylon—Nebuzaradan the chief cook, an officer of the king of Babylon, came to Jerusalem. ⁹He burned the House of YHWH and the Palace and all the houses of Jerusalem—every large house he burned down. ¹⁰All the Chaldean forces that were with the chief cook tore down the walls of Jerusalem all about. ¹¹Then Nebuzaradan the chief cook exiled the rest of the people left in the city and those who had deserted to the king of Babylon—the rest of the masses. ¹²But from the poor of the land, the chief cook left some to be vine dressers and field workers.

¹³The Chaldeans broke up the bronze columns in the House of YHWH, and the stands and the bronze Sea in the House of YHWH; and they carried the bronze away to Babylon. ¹⁴They took the pots, the shovels, the snuffers, the spoons, all the bronze vessels used in the service. ¹⁵The chief cook took the fire pans and the sprinkling bowls, those of gold and of silver. ¹⁶The weight of all these vessels was incalculable: two columns, one Sea, and the stands, which Solomon had made for the Temple. ¹⁷The height of one column was eighteen cubits and its capital was bronze. The height of the capital was five cubits, and on the capital all around was a meshwork with pomegranates, all of bronze. The other column was exactly like it, with its meshwork.

¹⁸The chief cook took Seraiah the high priest, Zephanaiah the deputy priest, and three keepers of the threshold. ¹⁹And from the city, he took an official who was in charge of the fighting men and five of the king's personal attendants who were found in the city, and the scribe of the army commander who mustered the People of the Land, as well as sixty of the People of the Land who were in the city. ²⁰Nebuzaradan the chief cook took them and brought them to the king of Babylon at Riblah. ²¹The king of Babylon had them struck down and put to death in Riblah in the land of Hamath. Thus Judah was exiled from its land.

Gedaliah, a Babylonian Governor in Judah

25 ²²Now as for the people left in the land of Judah, those whom Nebuchadnezzar king of Babylon left behind, he appointed Gedaliah son of Ahikam son of Shaphan over them. ²³When all the officers of the army, they and their men,

heard that the king of Babylon had appointed Gedaliah, they came to Gedaliah at Mizpah: Ishmael son of Nethaniah, Johanan son of Kareah, Seraiah son of Tanhumeth the Netophathite and Jaazaniah son of the Maacathite, they and their men. ²⁴Gedaliah gave his oath to them and their men: "Do not be afraid to serve the Chaldeans. Stay in the land; serve the king of Babylon and it will go well with you." ²⁵But in the seventh month, Ishmael son of Methaniah son of Elishama, one of the royal line, came with ten men and they struck down Gedaliah and he died, as well as the Judaeans and the Chaldeans who were at Mizpah with him. ²⁶Then all the people, young and old and the army officers set out and went to Egypt, for they were afraid of the Chaldeans.

Epilogue: Release of Jehoiachin

25   ²⁷In the thirty-seventh year of the exile of Jehoiachin king of Judah, in the twelfth month, on the twenty-seventh day of the month, Evil-merodach, king of Babylon, in his accession year, pardoned Jehoiachin king of Judah ⟨and released him⟩ from prison. ²⁸He spoke kindly to him and set his throne above those of the kings who were with him in Babylon. ²⁹He changed his prison garb and he received permanent provisions by his favor for life. ³⁰His allowance was a permanent allowance from the king, daily for life.

INTRODUCTION

◆

INTRODUCTION TO THE
BOOK OF KINGS

◆

1. FOREWORD

The Introduction to Kings that follows reviews and reworks the introductory remarks presented in *2 Kings*, in which the focus was primarily on the biblical book of 2 Kings (Cogan and Tadmor 1988, 1–11; also Cogan 1990); this new discussion surveys both books and represents the views of the present author alone.

The commentary presents the reader with a literary division of Kings that in many instances abandons the familiar chapter divisions (on which, see below, Section 2). In a number of cases, this division follows the reigns of each king of Judah and Israel as marked off by the author of Kings; but in other cases, the extensive blocks of material inserted into these reigns (e.g., the block between 1 Kgs 16:29–33 and 22:39–40) require a separation into constituent literary units in order to achieve effective exegesis (see the remarks of Talshir 1996). The order of presentation in each unit follows a standard model: Translation–Notes–Comment. The Translation is a new rendition of the Masoretic Text (MT). The detailed Notes that follow clarify textual and linguistic matters, in a sense, justifying the translation. In addition, persons and places are identified, and attention is called to the world of the ancient Near East, the background for much of what is related in Kings. The third subdivision, the Comment, contains a discussion of the structure of the individual units and their themes, paying specific attention to literary and form-critical issues. In addition, inasmuch as Kings is a book of "history," an evaluation of the unit as a source for historical reconstruction is offered. These historical remarks are at best *Vorarbeiten* (preliminaries) to a consecutive History of Israel yet to be written, since other perspectives—in addition to a perspective of the author–historian of Kings—have to be studied before such a history can properly be written (see further below, Section 8). (The division of the Comment into several sections is noted by headings in *1 Kings*, a practice not followed in *2 Kings*, though the same points are treated in both books.)

The bibliography of close to a thousand books and articles includes only the works cited in the commentary; it in no way aims to be comprehensive but reflects the commentator's selection of the discussions that have contributed to his understanding of Kings.

2. NAME OF THE BOOK AND ITS PLACE IN THE CANON

The book of Kings is the fourth book in the "First (or Early) Prophets," the first section of the second major division of the Bible (*Tôrâ, Nĕbî'îm, Kĕtûbîm,* from which the currently popular acronym *Tanak* is derived). Kings is referred to as a single book—*sēper mĕlākîm*—in the Talmud (*b. B. Bat.* 14b–15a), where its composition is credited to the prophet Jeremiah. Not until the printing of the *Bomberg Rabbinic Bible* (Venice, 1517) was the division into two books introduced into Jewish tradition (see Note on 2 Kgs 1:1). Within Greek tradition, Samuel and Kings were considered a continuous work, and they were divided into the four books of "Kingdoms" (or "Reigns," Thackeray's term); this practice was followed by the Vulgate and the translations based upon it; thus, First and Second Kings became Third and Fourth Kingdoms.[1] The verse division is a part of the Masoretic tradition, which counted 1534 verses in Kings. The chapter division (as well as verse numbering) is of early medieval Christian origin and is noted in a Hebrew manuscript as early as ca. 1330; it was introduced into the *Bomberg Bible* alongside the Masoretic versification (Ginsburg 1966, 25–26).

---

[1] See Note at 1 Kgs 2:12 for the Lucianic notation on this division. The oft-repeated suggestion that the division into the two books of Kings (as well as Samuel) was a scribal convenience, halving the material at an appropriate spot in order to fit the text onto two scrolls, might have to be shelved, inasmuch as the practice at Qumran was to prepare long scrolls in order to accommodate books with as many as 66 chapters, such as Isaiah. Nor is the "present partition [of Samuel and Kings] arbitrary, the History of Succession being interrupted" (Bentzen 1961, 2:96); Kings begins where it should, with the accession of Solomon (see full discussion in Comment on 1 Kgs 1). [DNF: "But Isaiah has 17,000 words while Kings is over 25,000 words. Is it coincidence that only the three longest books of the Hebrew Bible are divided: Kings 25,000+, Samuel 24,000+, Chronicles 24,000+? The next longest is Jeremiah with about 22,000—not divided. . . . The division may well have originated with the LXX because the number of words in a translated book may be 50% more than in Hebrew."]

3. TEXT AND VERSIONS

The goal of the present commentary is to elucidate the Hebrew text of Kings as set by the Masoretic tradition and preserved in the two oldest manuscripts, the Aleppo Codex (ca. 915; published in *Miqra'ot Gedolot 'Haketer'*) and the Leningrad Codex (dated 1009; published in BHS). The fragments of scrolls of the book of Kings from the Dead Sea caves, some thousand years older, reflect texts quite similar to MT.[2] The Greek traditions, on the other hand, especially the Lucianic recension,[3] present a widely different text at several junctures. The divergencies include alternate positioning of whole sections of the text (e.g., MT 1 Kgs 22:41–51 appears in LXX after 16:28 and again in 1 Kgs 22); chronological reckonings for the reigns of Omri down through Jehu that vary greatly from MT; repetition of individual verses joined together in creative blocks (e.g., 1 Kgs 2:35[a–o] and 2:46[a–l])—all of this is in addition to the scattered words and phrases that suggest that the translations were based on *Vorlagen* other than MT.

One of the most significant results of the study of the biblical texts from the Dead Sea has been the recovery of the state of text-stabilization during the final centuries of the Second Temple. The evidence shows that, though the biblical books were considered canonical, the text of these books was still in flux, and because they had not reached verbal, let alone letter stabilization, they circulated in multiple recensions (see Greenberg 1956; 1978, 141–44). This state of affairs certainly prevailed centuries earlier, at the time of the first Greek translation. Given this picture of textual fluidity, it seems presumptuous to think that one can recover the "original" book of Kings by applying time-honored text-critical procedures—that is, comparing MT and the ancient translations (retroverted into Hebrew) and adopting the "best" reading (for a recent defense of this approach, see Trebolle Barrera 1982). Most text critics now admit to the subjectivity of this enterprise (see Tov 1992, 410). Furthermore, some of the ancient translations may be witnesses to the growth and development of the biblical books within learned circles and various communities (see, e.g., the Note on the Miscellanies in the LXX at 1 Kgs 2:46 [below, pp. 171–72]), and so they should be studied as part of the history of the interpretation of the Bible. In the present commentary on Kings, therefore, reference to non-Masoretic readings has been kept to a minimum; the readings that are most often cited by commentators in order to "correct" MT are cited in the Notes to the Translation.

---

[2] The Kings texts from Qumran include: 4QKgs (4Q54), the upper part of two columns on seven fragments, 1 Kgs 7:20–21; 25–27; 29–42; 50 (or 51?); 51–8:9; 16–18, published by Trebolle Barrera 1995; 5QKgs (5Q2), three fragments of the first column of 1 Kgs 1:16–37, published by Milik 1962; 6QKgs (6Q4), a rare example of a biblical scroll copied on papyrus, eighteen or so identifiable fragments and dozens of pieces with single words and/or letters, 1 Kgs 3:12–14; 12:28–31; 22:28–31; 2 Kgs 5:26; 6:32; 7:8–10; 7:20–8:5; 9:1–2; 10:19–21, published by Baillet 1962.

[3] A convenient statement on the characteristics of this recension can be found in Shenkel 1968, 5–21; Fernandez Marcos 1984.

Only when MT is incontrovertibly faulty is a suggestion proffered to emend the text, with due use being made of the versional evidence.

4. ON THE TRANSLATION

The flush of translations of the Bible into contemporary English that have appeared during the last quarter of the twentieth century may seem to the reader to have made the production of yet another translation here a superfluous task. After all, most of the "Bible-sounding" relics from Elizabethan days that were found in pre–World War II renditions have made way for their equivalents in modern idiom. In addition, many of the newer translations are based on the advances in our understanding of Biblical Hebrew, greatly aided by comparative Semitic philology. A key aspect of the new approach to translating "Biblical Hebrew into English" is the recognition that "a Hebrew term may have several nuances, depending on the context, and it is incorrect, if not misleading, to reproduce that term by a single English term throughout" (Orlinsky 1969, 25). Thus, in the drive to free the ancient text from perceived "mechanical translations," the modern versions have chosen clarity over consistency, doing away with the ambiguous turn of phrase.

The translation offered in the present work has on the whole taken another tack. Motivated by the example of Buber and Rosenzweig in their epochal rendering of the Bible into German,[4] I have attempted to reflect the built-in echoes of the original Hebrew by maintaining consistency in English renditions. Thus, for example, ḥesed is "loyalty" in all of its occurrences (see Note on 1 Kgs 3:6); contrast the variety offered in NAB: ḥesed is "constant friendship" (1 Kgs 2:7); "constant love" (3:6); and "to be trusted" (20:31); NJPSV offers "deal graciously" (2:7); "kindness" (3:6); "magnanimous" (20:31). At the same time, the careful reader will note inconsistencies in application of this guideline (and admittedly so) because care was taken not to forfeit the clarity and understandability of the vernacular, even in the simplest cases. The Hebrew noun ʿēṣ is "tree, wood, timber, lumber," and consequently, "trees" are cut in 1 Kgs 5:20, but "wood" is used in making doors for the Temple in 6:31–34. Verbs are the most notorious parts of speech to translate, so that here, too, there are some cases of multiple renderings. Hebrew *yādōʿa, "to know" is rendered "have relations with" rather than "know" in 1 Kgs 1:4, because in that sense, our English dictionaries indicate that "know" is archaic; but a few verses later, it remains "know" (1:18). The

---

[4] "Absolute word choice is aimed at grasping the meaning of the individual word, at liberating its original concreteness from the encrustation of ordinary abstraction. Relative word choice is aimed at preserving the biblically intended relation between two or more words related by their roots, or sometimes merely by their sounds . . . alliteration and assonance, and to a still greater degree repetitions of words, phrases, and sentences cannot be understood in aesthetic terms alone; rather such patterns belong for the most part to the matter and character of the biblical message itself, and rendering them rightly is one of the central tasks of the translation" (Buber and Rosenzweig 1994, 81–82).

reader or speaker of Hebrew hears *yāda‘* twice and knows just how far the old king had declined; the reader of this commentary will find an appropriate note, calling attention to this repetition, which would otherwise go unnoticed in reading the translation alone.

It may be argued that this approach leads to literalness and to wooden translations. Yet this is exactly what a proper rendition calls for: literalness that maintains ambiguity; in this way, the text is left open to the reader. Thus, for example, Heb *qoṭen* in 1 Kgs 12:10 is "little thing"; the translations that commit to "little finger"—and they are the majority—curtail one of the joys of reading the Bible, that of being an active participant in the interpretive process.[5]

Finally, note should be taken of the italicized pronouns in my translation of 1 Kings, found mostly in direct speech. This translational practice seeks to represent the presence of an independent personal pronoun together with a finite verb. Since the verb form in Hebrew already indicates person, an added pronoun, far from being otiose, is understood to express emphasis, and in oral presentation would bear tonal stress.[6]

5. LANGUAGE AND PHILOLOGY

Even a cursory reading of the Notes to the rendering of the Hebrew text of Kings into English reveals the heavy reliance of the Commentary upon the evidence of cognate Semitic languages in elucidating many words and phrases.[7] In this use, the lead has been taken from the early Hebrew grammarians, who understood the inherent value of this method. Rabbi Jonah Ibn-Janah remarked in the introduction to his grammatical treatise *Sēper Hā-riqmâ*:

> I also found that the Rabbis, of blessed memory, who are a model in all matters, in explaining a strange word in our language cite evidence from a similar one in other languages . . . (*b. Šabb.* 63a–b; *b. Yebam.* 94b; *b. Šabb.* 31b; *b. Roš Haš.* 26a) from Greek, Persian, Arabic, African and other languages. And having seen their practice, we shall not refrain from citing evidence, where there is no evidence from the Hebrew, from what we have found similar and appropriate in Arabic; for after Aramaic, it is more like our language than any other one. (Ibn-Janah 1964, 17–18)

The modern rediscovery of forgotten Semitic languages and the advancement in their linguistic analysis that has marked the close of the twentieth century have

---

[5] For an enlightening discussion of the goals and method of the translators of the Authorized Version (KJV), who sought "transparency which makes it possible for the reader to see the original clearly," see Hammond 1987.

[6] For an essay to identify the various psychological factors concerning this use of the pronoun, see Muraoka 1985, 47–59.

[7] See the earlier discussion with reference to 2 Kings in Cogan and Tadmor 1988, 7–8; also Cogan 1990, 22–24.

placed the comparative method on a firm footing. Moreover, as has become abundantly clear, the political and commercial integration of the kingdoms of Israel and Judah into the Syro-Mesopotamian sphere was a fact of life throughout the age of the monarchies. The historical circumstances were such that the speakers of Biblical Hebrew found themselves exposed to the languages of both allies and conquerors, leading ultimately to the development of mutilingualism. Thus, the prime referents for the current study have been the Assyrian and Babylonian dialects of Akkadian as well as Aramaic.

Lexical clarifications abound. For example, the timber brought from the forests of Lebanon for the construction of the Temple included *běrôš* (cf. 1 Kgs 5:22), now identifiable as "juniper" (Akk *burāšu*); on the other hand, the imported *'almūggîm* in 1 Kgs 10:11, traditionally "coral," turns out to be the wood of the *elammakku* tree, known to have been favored by kings and craftsmen, though its name remains unspecifiable. Moving from the inanimate to the human world, the titles of the personages at foreign courts can be fixed for the first time from contemporary documents: Tahpenes is not a personal name but the Egyptian term for a "wife of the king" (1 Kgs 11:19), and Nebuzaradan, the official charged with overseeing Jerusalem's destruction (cf. 2 Kgs 25:8), is known to have borne the honorific "the chief cook" (*rab ṭabbāḥîm*). Beyond individual lexemes, many Hebrew idioms have been recovered through comparison with their semantic equivalents in Akkadian. Thus, Ahab's question prior to his engagement with Ben-hadad employs the unique turn of phrase *ye'sōr hammilḥāmâ*, literally, "tie/bind the battle" (1 Kgs 20:14), that means "prepare the battle array," as does Akk *tāḥaza kaṣāru*. By similar analogy, the nuance of Heb **yšb* as "stay at home, do nothing" (1 Kgs 22:1) is suggested. In the gate of Samaria, the fixed "market price" (Heb *ša'ar*) was likely posted, just as it was in the city gates of many Mesopotamian cities (cf. 2 Kgs 7:1).

One can easily imagine the place of honor that these languages would have enjoyed had the documentary treasures of the ancient Near East been available to the early masters a millennium ago.

6. COMPOSITION OF THE BOOK OF KINGS

A half-millennium ago, Isaac Abarbanel (1437–1508) reflected on the composition of Kings, most likely drawing upon his experience at the court of King Alfonso V of Portugal.

> There is no doubt that it was the custom in Israel, as it is today among the nations, to record in a book all matters concerning monarchs and their deeds, and these books are called *dibrê hayyāmîm*, as the events and their outcomes were written for each king. Among these stories and tales were (both) essential as well as superfluous items, for the purpose of the story was solely the recording of all the deeds of the kings, day by day. There were also items written on demand, as it is the manner of scribes, who as spokesmen, may

praise or denigrate in excessive manner in line with their loves and hates. Now when the Holy One commanded the prophet (Jeremiah) to commit to writing the matters of the kings, the purpose of the telling was not like the matter of *dibrê hayyāmîm*. It was only to report the development of the generations and the chain of kings one after another, and to make known their righteousness or wickedness and the reward that they would receive from the Lord for their deeds or the punishment . . . [so the prophet] omitted many items which were in the books *dibrê hayyāmîm*, such as the tales and deeds of kings and their bravery, and city building. Inasmuch as he regularly refers to the book *dibrê hayyāmîm*, it was not appropriate or necessary [for these items to be included] in this book [= the book of Kings]. (from Abarbanel's Second Introduction to Kings)

This premodern description of the composition of Kings may lack critical terminology, but in its overall conception it resembles the stance of many current commentators: the author of the book of Kings refers to a number of sources that he apparently used in working up his profiles of the kings of Israel and Judah. There were others, unnamed but clearly present, that have been identified by modern criticism using textual analysis, that entered his treatise on the fate of the monarchy. A clarification of the nature of these sources follows.

SOURCES

The sources designated within Kings are: (a) *The History of the Kings of Israel* and *The History of the Kings of Judah*; (b) *The Book of the Deeds of Solomon*; undesignated sources; (c) Prophetic tales and narratives; and (d) Temple records.

a. *The History of the Kings of Israel and The History of the Kings of Judah*

The author of Kings put his readers on notice that there was much more to be known about the achievements of the monarchy than he had included in his own composition and that it was available in the two books—*spr dbry hymym* of Israel and *spr dbry hymym* of Judah—translated in 1 Kings as "History" ("Annals" in 2 Kings).[8] All notices to these books are in the closing regnal formulas. Reference to the *History of the Kings of Israel* is made 17 times, for all but two of Israel's monarchs (Joram and Hoshea). In addition, the phrase "(all) that he did" appears 13 times (1 Kgs 15:31; 16:5, 14, 27; 22:39; 2 Kgs 1:18; 10:34; 13:8, 12 [= 14:15]; 14:28; 15:21, 26, 31); "(all) his heroic deeds" appears 6 times (1 Kgs 16:5, 27; 2 Kgs 10:34; 13:8, 12 [= 14:15 "how he fought with Amaziah king of Judah"]; 14:28); "the conspiracy that he formed" appears twice (1 Kgs 16:20;

---

[8] The suggestion (Mowinckel 1963, 17–18) that the two titles are two parts of a single book, written in Judah, where an interest in the important events in Israel was expressed, has not won many adherents.

2 Kgs 15:15); "that he fought" twice (1 Kgs 14:19; 2 Kgs 14:28); "the house of ivory that he built and all the cities that he built" once (1 Kgs 22:39); and "how he fought and restored Damascus and Hamath for Israel" once (2 Kgs 14:28).

Reference to the *History of the Kings of Judah* is made 15 times, for all but five of Judah's monarchs (Ahaziah, Athaliah, Jehoahaz, Jehoiachin, Zedekiah): the phrase "(all) that he did" appears 12 times (1 Kgs 14:29; 15:7, 23; 2 Kgs 8:23; 12:20; 15:6, 36; 16:19; 21:17, 25; 23:28; 24:5); "(all) his heroic deeds" 3 times (1 Kgs 15:23; 22:46; 2 Kgs 20:20); "the cities that he built" once (1 Kgs 15:23); "the pool which he made . . ." once (2 Kgs 20:20); and "the sin that he sinned" once (2 Kgs 21:17).

Comparison of the items noted for each book indicates that there was no substantial difference between the Histories of the two kingdoms; both contained records of royal undertakings in war and public works, of conspiracies against the crown, and of cultic misdeeds. From the parsimonious style of many of the references—most contain just three words!—one cannot determine how detailed the reports on individual reigns were—that is, whether they were just summaries or fuller accounts. If the entries were chronologically organized, which seems likely, then the author of Kings may have found in them a handy source for the basic facts that served him in constructing his pragmatic framework: the name of a king, date of accession, age at accession, and length of reign. (This does not obviate the availability to the author of separate King Lists; rather it suggests another avenue of chronological information.)

Using the categories the author of Kings himself established, one may suggest that when referring to the following incidents, he found them recorded in the Histories (they all appear outside the closing regnal formulas): royal undertakings in war (including attacks by foreign rulers)—1 Kgs 14:25–26, 30; 15:16–21; 2 Kgs 10:32–33; 12:18–19; 13:5, 7, 22, 24–25; 14:7, 25; 16:5, 7–9; 17:3–6; 18:13–16; 23:29–30; public works—1 Kgs 16:24, 34; 22:49; 2 Kgs 14:22; conspiracies against the crown—2 Kgs 14:19–20; 15:10, 14, 16, 25, 30. To these can be added: royal illnesses—1 Kgs 15:23; 2 Kgs 15:5; foreign relations—1 Kgs 16:31; 22:48; 2 Kgs 1:1; 8:20–22; 15:19–20, 29; 16:6; 23:33–35; 24:1–2; and, if we broaden the category of "cultic misdeeds" (said of Manasseh) to include all royal attention to cultic matters—1 Kgs 15:13–14; 2 Kgs 18:4.

The referral notices to the Histories bear a certain similarity to the bibliographical footnotes one often finds in modern works: "For further reading, see. . . ." This similarity, however, is only surface deep, and account should be taken of the author's intended audience. If Kings was written for the population at large, it is not likely that the author was inviting them to visit the palace or Temple library/archives. Such repositories would not have been open to the public. Moreover, the vast majority of the populace was unschooled in letters, and reading material as such was very limited.[9] So, if written for a general audi-

---

[9] The statement "that there were readers and writers in ancient Israel, and that they were by no means rare" (Lemaire 1992, 1005, quoting A. R. Millard), is a bit overdrawn. The idea that the alphabet, rather than a syllabary, made for a generally literate population does not sufficiently consider the

ence, Kings would most likely have been read aloud at public gatherings; and by noting that there was much more to tell about a particular monarch in the History than he had related, the author lent credibility to his own work; that is, the listener was asked to believe that he was acquainted with this composition and might have made selective use of it.[10]

On the other hand, if the author of Kings was writing for the scribes and literati (among whom he may have been counted), in this case as well it does not seem that he was recommending research in the archives; some of his scribal readers may have been the very ones whose job it was to record the daily operation of the kingdom and to prepare royal inscriptions. For this audience, too, the referral notice contained a suggestion of authenticity, which they could readily check if a question arose.

What emerges, then, is that *spr(y) dbry hymym* were compositions that surveyed and summarized the monarchic period in both kingdoms. They were commonly known and were held to be authoritative, since they were likely based on firsthand source material: records of wars, tribute payments, royal projects, and so forth.[11] It is hard to say what their original purpose was. Were they compiled for private use at the behest of the king? Or did the initiative stem from scribal circles, which might suggest that they be seen as an "intellectual" exercise? If so, perhaps they were never meant to be part of a public discourse. Whatever the case, we are indeed fortunate that the author of Kings made use of *The History of the Kings of Israel* and *The History of the Kings of Judah*,[12] for his references are the closest we are likely to get to the archives and libraries of ancient Israel.[13]

b. *The Book of the Deeds of Solomon*

The Book of the Deeds of Solomon (*spr dbry šlmh*) is the third work referred to by the author, in which one could read about "all that he [= Solomon] did and

---

social and economic factors that prevented the spread of reading at large. See the stimulating remarks of Warner 1980; see also Haran 1988, and Whitt 1995, 2395–96.

[10] This is not an endorsement of the view set forth by Garbini (1981), who compared the referrals in Kings to the larger number of these notices in Chronicles, which he takes, for both books, to be literary inventions of their respective authors. For Chronicles, see the summary discussion in Japhet 1993, 19–23; also Schniedewind 1997, 215.

[11] Thus, the somewhat whimsical picture drawn by Van Seters (1983, 301) of the author of Kings traveling around the country reading and copying cuneiform (!) inscriptions so as to tell the story of the Assyrian conquest of Samaria and their battles in Judah can be set aside. We are thus also spared having to credit him with a knowledge of hieroglyphs and/or demotic (cf. 1 Kgs 14:25–26; 2 Kgs 23:34–35)! Nor need we wonder what stelae were left standing undamaged after the withdrawal of the conqueror so that our author could peruse them.

[12] The use of the English word "history" follows the definition of "history" in the *Oxford English Dictionary*: "a relation of incidents (in later use, only those confessedly true)."

[13] I am aware that I have transferred the task of surveying and collecting the bits and the pieces of monarchic history from the author of Kings to the authors of the Histories, inasmuch as the Kings author was not an antiquarian, as his own remarks indicate. The Histories, on the other hand, might have been drawn up over generations, successively growing with time.

his wisdom" (1 Kgs 11:41). The extended treatment of Solomon's reign (1 Kgs 3–11) is characterized by its emphasis on the king's wisdom and wealth (3:5–14; 5:9–14; 10:14–25) and includes a variety of administrative documents (1 Kgs 4:2–6, 7–19), inventories (e.g., 7:41–45), and reports (11:14–25), stories (3:16–27), a snippet of a poem (8:12–13), and even a late legend (10:1–13). These features, unexampled in other parts of Kings, suggest that the author excerpted from *The Book of the Deeds of Solomon*, whose provenance may have been some of the wise men at the court of Jerusalem (see further in Comment on 1 Kgs 11). These savants projected the image of their king as "wiser than all men" (5:11), a portrayal that was continually polished down to the reign of Hezekiah, under whose direction Solomonic lore was copied and collected (cf. Prov 25:1).[14]

c. *Prophetic Tales and Narratives*

A considerable block of material, undesignated as such, treats the lives and works of a host of prophets and men of God, mostly from the kingdom of Israel. The prophets include: from *Israel*—Ahijah the Shilonite (1 Kgs 11:29–38; 14:1–18); Jehu son of Hanani (1 Kgs 16:1–4, 7); Elijah (1 Kgs 17–19; 21; 2 Kgs 1:1–2:18); Elisha (2 Kgs 2:19–25; 3:3–9:13; 13:14–21); Micaiah son of Imlah (1 Kgs 22:2–38); Jonah son of Amittai (2 Kgs 14:25); and unnamed men of God (1 Kgs 13:1–32; 20:13–14, 22, 28, 35–43). From *Judah*—Isaiah (2 Kgs 19–20); Huldah (2 Kgs 22:13–20); and unnamed prophets (2 Kgs 21:10–15).

The cycle of stories concerning Elijah and Elisha dominates the history of Israel. These two prophetic leaders were revered in the circles of "the sons of the prophets," where they were remembered for their wondrous acts. Concerning Elisha, tales circulated about how he sweetened the bitter waters at Jericho (2 Kgs 2:19–21), increased a needy widow's oil supply (4:1–7), improved and extended the food for his hungry followers (4:38–41; 42–44), recovered an ax lost in the water (6:1–7), and quickened the dead (4:8–37). The prophet's blessing was considered to have healing powers (cf. 5:3, 11), but his curse brought death (2:23–24). His repute reached the court in Samaria (8:4–6) and beyond to Damascus (5:1–4), where, as legend had it, the prophet once visited (8:7). This man of God is depicted as involved in political affairs, supporting the rebellions of Jehu (9:1–13) and Hazael (8:7–15); he intervened directly in the wars with Aram–Damascus (6:8–23) and foretold of victory (13:14–19). The stories as they now appear are the products of long development. Many have retained their short anecdotal form, and they bear the markings of oral transmission.[15]

---

[14] Na'aman has suggested that the "Deeds of Solomon" "was apparently a school text written in the 'high school' of Jerusalem and used for educational and tutorial purposes (1997b, 77).

[15] A remarkable feature of these legends is the preservation of morphological and lexical items that suggest a Northern dialect of Hebrew, especially in quoted speech. This was first pointed out by Burney 1903, 208–9; and recently reviewed and refined by Sivan and Schniedewind 1997; see, too, Notes on 2 Kgs 4:28; 6:4; and Comment on 2 Kgs 4.

Others appear as expanded tales that include much local color and often close with a moral lesson; growth of this kind may have taken place in the preliterary stage. Chronological and historical questions are of no importance because the tales are associatively linked and, in this received form, they were inserted into Kings. (Rofé [1988a] has presented a useful classification of this material in which he traces the *legenda* as they evolved from wonder tale to parable.)

Of a different quality are the Elijah traditions. Though they likely had their origin in the same circles as the traditions concerning Elisha, the individual stories about Elijah now operate as scenes in an integrated narrative whose overriding theme is the struggle against Baal worship in Israel. In the present text, Elijah confronts the royal sponsors of the foreign cult by predicting an extended drought; then appear vignettes of the prophet's miraculous sustenance by the ravens (1 Kgs 17:2–7) and by the woman from Zarephath (17:8–16). The tale of his resuscitation of the woman's son (17:17–24) is nonessential to the plot; it recalls a similar good act by Elisha, a recollection that exemplifies the nature of these prophetic tales—they wander freely between master and disciple.[16] The religious conflict comes to a head in the contest on Mount Carmel, where YHWH bests Baal; Israel is won back to its God, and the drought is ended (18:20–46). The additional tale of YHWH's revelation to Elijah on Horeb (1 Kgs 19:1–18) now reads as a postscript, as if the victory over Baal was somehow incomplete; the prophet was to appoint new leadership because the final battle would be engaged in the next generation. With regard to the Horeb episode, note should be taken of the legendary motifs that the Elijah tale shares with those associated with the archetypical prophet Moses (see details in Comment to 1 Kgs 19:1–21). Assuming the primacy of the Mosaic traditions, the assimilation of such motifs into the Elijah cycle indicates the respect and reverence in which Elijah was held in the circles that transmitted the stories of his life's work.

Another discrete set of prophetic announcements concerning the fate of the kings of Israel is identifiable. It reflects prophetic involvement in the selection of monarchs during the recurring instability of the Northern Kingdom. The reports of these prophecies are highly stylized and include: (1) the prediction of the rise to the throne of a new king (1 Kgs 11:29–30 [announced by Ahijah]), followed sometime later by (2) prophetic criticism and the prediction of the downfall of a designated king, employing well-known curse formulas (14:7–11, 14 [against Jeroboam]; 16:1–4, 7 [against Baasha]; 21:21–24; 2 Kgs 9:7–10 [against Ahab]). Even the favored House of Jehu, the longest to rule in Samaria, anointed by Elisha's attendant (2 Kgs 9:1–6), was not immune to this sort of censure (cf. 2 Kgs 10:29–30). The thrust of this prophetic critique is the disloyalty of the kings to YHWH—specifically, their holding fast to the idolatries of Jeroboam son of Nebat.

---

[16] The present configuration of the story and its moral stance cannot be taken to mean that the Elijah tale is secondary, borrowed from a similar one in the Elisha tradition; it simply is witness to a more-developed stage of recital, not to origins. [DNF: "Similarly, stories wander between father and son (Abraham and Isaac both are involved in 'wife–sister' episodes)."]

In contrast to this varied repertoire of prophetic lore from Israel, reports of prophets in Judah are few: only two are known, Isaiah and Huldah, and both are associated with reform-minded kings—Hezekiah and Josiah. Hezekiah sought Isaiah's intercession with YHWH at the time of the Assyrian threat to Jerusalem (2 Kgs 19:1–7; cf. 20–34) and consulted the prophet during his illness (20:1–11). Josiah inquired of YHWH through Huldah concerning the "words of this book that has been found" (2 Kgs 22:12–20). Both prophets offered encouragement to these faithful scions of the House of David in their hours of stress: Isaiah promised victory over Sennacherib; Huldah spoke of personal well-being for Josiah.

d. *Temple Records*

Another source for the author of Kings that sometimes has been suggested (especially in the early critical commentaries) is Temple records. This is based on the abundant references to the Solomonic Temple, its construction and dedication (1 Kgs 6–8), the frequent use of Temple funds to pay off foreign invaders (e.g., 1 Kgs 14:25; 15:18; see below), and the detailed descriptions of innovations (2 Kgs 16:10–16) and renovations of the building (e.g., 2 Kgs 12:5–17; 22:3–9). Yet the centrality of the Temple within the ideological-historiographical structure of the book of Kings does not necessarily require that the source of the Temple-related reports be that institution. This is not to disallow that record-keeping of income and outlay, dedications as well as pillage, was part of the standard operating procedure in the Jerusalem Temple, as it was in cult establishments throughout the ancient world. One should not, however, overlook the fact that the kings of the Davidic dynasty saw themselves as more than patrons of the Temple; thus, they appear directly responsible for its upkeep, even to the point of censuring the priests and instructing them on allocation of incomes (2 Kgs 12:5–17), and they, not the priesthood, are the ones who sponsored cultic reform in Judah (e.g., 1 Kgs 15:12–13 [Asa]; 2 Kgs 18:4 [Hezekiah]; 21:3–7 [Manasseh]; 23:4–14 [Josiah]). Not even in the architectural plans of the Temple building laid out in 1 Kgs 6 is there anything particularly "priestly." All of these chapters in the history of the Temple may well be of monarchic inception, of various dates that are not always attainable (see Montgomery and Gehman, 37–38).[17]

At the same time, the relatively large number of reported cases of forced withdrawals from the Temple treasury—either taken to ward off a threat to Jerusalem (cf. 1 Kgs 14:25–26 [Shishak]; 15:16–21 [Baasha]; 2 Kgs 12:18–19 [Hazael]; 16:5,

---

[17] In two reports, that of the Temple repair undertaken by Joash (2 Kgs 12:5–17) and that of the altar reform of Ahaz (16:10–16), a number of technical terms does suggest an affinity to the Priestly writings of the Pentateuch. But in both instances, the presence of the high priest alongside the king, who is the prime mover, can explain this echo of sacral terminology; see comments, ad loc., and discussion in Paran 1989, 309–30, 358.

7–9 [Pekah and Rezin]; 18:13–16 [Hezekiah]) or taken as booty (cf. 2 Kgs 14:14 [Jehoash]; 24:13 and 25:13–17 [Nebuchadnezzar])—suggests that the data might derive from Temple records; the case of Shishak's raid, with its singular example of a year-date (1 Kgs 14:25), points to a putative Temple chronicle of sorts. The present statements, formulated uniformly in a "threat-payment-rescue" pattern, which include references to the royal treasury as well as to the Temple (he took "the treasures of the House of YHWH and the treasures of the royal palace"), might well be the workup of the author of Kings. Note should also be taken of the inventories of cultic equipment (1 Kgs 7:41–45, 48–50; 2 Kgs 25:13–17), which also may have been derived from Temple records.

The discrimination of the various sources that have been brought together in the composition of Kings calls for a remark on ancient stylistics and editorial procedure. The book's author does not seem to have made any effort at erasing the telltale signs of the individual sources; each was left to speak out in its own distinctive idiom and particular statement—hence its visibility. This procedure has led to some unevenness in the narrative, occasionally to the point of blatant contradiction, observable especially within the large block of prophetic material in 1 Kgs 17–2 Kgs 9. Thus, for example, Elijah's foretold punishment of Ahab—that his blood would be licked by dogs in the very spot in Jezreel where Naboth was executed, bringing his dynasty to an end (1 Kgs 21:19–22)—is twice confounded: Ahab died in battle and his body was returned to Samaria for burial (22:37–38), and it wasn't until a decade later that the last of the Omride kings was eliminated (cf. 2 Kgs 9:24–26). Tension is also observable between the individual sources and the editorial framework. For instance, the claim that peace and security were Solomon's lot during his entire reign (cf. 1 Kgs 5:1, 5) does not stand up when considered alongside the accounts of the uprisings against Solomon in Edom and Damascus that took place soon after the death of David (cf. 11:14–25; see especially v. 25). Similarly, the view of the Temple as YHWH's chosen dwelling (8:12–13) is not supported by the statement that YHWH does not reside within the Temple, not even in the heavens or in the highest heavens (v. 27). There are even cases in which the author of Kings seems to have unwittingly introduced inconsistencies by employing hyperbole and generalizing statements (e.g., 1 Kgs 14:9; 2 Kgs 17:23; 25:21–22; on this matter, see Cogan, forthcoming c). To suggest that these inelegancies and others are the result of secondary, postauthorial additions of extraneous material into an originally unified book of Kings sidesteps the issue by positing the existence of late annotators who were insensitive to the disruptions that their additions caused. The approach adopted in this commentary assumes that the textual tensions are likely the signs of a literary canon that out of respect for tradition sought to preserve its very variety, while at the same time holding converse with it (see the remarks on "composite artistry" by Alter 1981, 132–33; also Na'aman 1997, 169).

AUTHORSHIP

The identification of the sources and their utilization in the composition of Kings lead directly to the question of the book's author. This nameless personage has been dubbed the Deuteronomist or Deuteronomistic Historian (hereafter Dtr), owing to the telltale signs that indicate his adoption of Deuteronomic thought and its application in conceptualizing the history of Israel. Among the key Deuteronomic tenets addressed in Kings are the call for steadfast loyalty to YHWH by observing the Teaching of Moses, and the centralization of the cult at the chosen place. Thus, in the pragmatic framework created by Dtr, which ties the entire work together, the following particulars are recorded for each monarch: name, age at accession (for the kings of Judah), length of reign, mother's name (for the kings of Judah), evaluation, reference to source, death and burial, name of successor. The judgment formulations, "doing what was pleasing to YHWH" and "doing what was displeasing to YHWH," find their explication in the standard set by David in his exemplary behavior: he "walked with integrity and with uprightness, doing all that I commanded . . . keeping my statutes and my rules" (1 Kgs 9:4). Many of Judah's kings were judged to have been loyal to YHWH, but only two were unreservedly acclaimed—Hezekiah and Josiah; both undertook cultic reforms that closed down local shrines (i.e., "the high places"), thereby centralizing all worship at the single sanctuary in Jerusalem in accord with Deuteronomic law (cf. Deut 12). The renewal of the covenant between the people of Judah and their God as overseen by Josiah (2 Kgs 23:1–3, 25) is the highlight of monarchic activity and of the book of Kings. Contrariwise, Israel's kings were judged whether or not they "followed the ways of Jeroboam son of Nebat, who sinned and caused Israel to sin," Jeroboam having led Israel away from the lawful cult of YHWH in Jerusalem to worship the golden calves he set up at the shrines in Dan and Bethel. (For a convenient list of the Deuteronomistic phraseology that accompanies the evaluations in Kings, see S. R. Driver 1913, 200–203; and extensively, Weinfeld 1972, 320–59.)

The seminal thesis of Martin Noth (1981 [1957]), in which he posited a comprehensive Deuteronomistic History (the books of Joshua through Kings), has dominated all recent discussion concerning the composition of Kings. Noth posited a single Deuteronomistic author, who, writing in the mid–sixth century BCE, produced a unified work that depicted Israel's "ever-intensifying decline" (Noth 1981, 79), due to its neglect of the way of YHWH. The book of Kings treated the crucial and final stage in this epic that set out Israel's history from the occupation of Canaan to its Exile from the Promised Land.[18] In the law of the king in Deut 17:13–20, dynastic longevity is conditioned on the monarch's faithfulness to the Teaching of Moses; in Kings, monarchic behavior becomes

---

[18] The premonarchic and Davidic chapters of this history need not detain us, since they are discussed in detail by Boling and Wright 1982, 41–72 (Joshua); Boling 1975, 29–38 (Judges); and McCarter 1980, 18–30 (1 Samuel); 1984, 4–19 (2 Samuel).

determinative for the fate of all Israel. The Deuteronomist developed his survey using traditional materials culled from a number of sources; these were occasionally glossed in order to accommodate them within the overall scheme of history. At key transition periods, Dtr inserted speeches (1 Kgs 2:2–4; 8:14–61), divine addresses (e.g., 1 Kgs 9:2–9; 2 Kgs 21:10–15), or third-person summaries (e.g., 2 Kgs 17:7–23) in which the authorial viewpoint finds expression: YHWH's forbearance notwithstanding, the judgment to send Israel into exile was a just and deserved punishment for a sinning nation.

Noth's proposal that a single author was responsible for Kings has prompted much debate, the result being a somewhat daunting proliferation of refinements and reconfigurations of the original thesis. (The main discussions are conveniently surveyed by Provan 1988, 1–31; McKenzie 1991, 1–19; 1992; and Knoppers 1993, 16–54.) Especially disturbing to the unified view of authorship are the terminological variations in the Dtr framework; in addition, an unevenness of viewpoint can be detected in a number of authorial passages (see the works of Bin-Nun 1968; H. Weippert 1972; Halpern and Vanderhooft 1991).[19]

In the present commentary, a modified version of the view associated with Frank Moore Cross and his students has been adopted, namely, that Kings developed in two stages: the first major edition appeared during the reign of Josiah and was redacted and extended in a second edition during the Exile (Cross 1973; see R. D. Nelson 1981; Friedman 1981). The two pervasive themes of Kings, the sins of Jeroboam and the promise to David of an eternal dynasty, find their culmination in the actions of Josiah. The sundering of the monarchy because of Solomon's apostasy left a "lamp for David" in Jerusalem (1 Kgs 11:36) that awaited the birth of a distant offspring—Josiah is specifically named in 13:2—who would purge Judah and Israel of its idolatries and reunite the kingdom under a renewed covenant with YHWH (2 Kgs 23). "The historian [= Dtr₁] has combined his motifs of the old covenant forms of the league and of the north, with those taken from the royal theology of the Davidids to create a complex and eloquent program" in support of the Josianic reform, during which time he wrote (Cross 1973, 285). This hopeful outlook needed to be revised after the fall of Jerusalem and the end of the monarchy. A second, exilic Deuteronomist (= Dtr₂) introduced the idea of conditionality to the Davidic promise (cf., e.g.,1 Kgs 2:4; 8:25; 9:6) and thus explained Judah's fate as inevitable, given Manasseh's grave sin (2 Kgs 21:10–15; cf. the reworked passage, 22:16–20).

The substrata of Cross's Dtr₁ can be further delineated. In this first edition of Kings, prominence is given to the history of the kingdom of Israel in which

---

[19] The inclination expressed by Long (1984, 21), "that 1 and 2 Kings, and the Dtr history, were composed by one person and remain essentially a unified work," is based on "what we know of ancient modes of composition and with the literary facts of the Bible." But until there are ample studies of contemporary ancient Near Eastern works similar to Kings, their composition as well as their stylistics, such pleading might best be held in abeyance. Van Seters's survey of "Mesopotamian Historiography" is a competent point of departure (1983, 55–99) that needs to be augmented by additional original investigations.

Dtr$_1$ appears to have made maximum use of available Northern traditions (cf., e.g., 2 Kgs 14:8–13, for an Israelite report that depicts a Davidic king in an uncomplimentary fashion, while the framework judges him favorably). The wholesale incorporation of Israelite prophetic materials, while accommodable within the Deuteronomistic outlook, goes beyond what is necessary for a historical survey and creates an imbalance, considering the fact that similar prophetic traditions from Judah are absent. Moreover, the lengthy Dtr peroration on YHWH's rejection of Israel because of its apostate ways (2 Kgs 17:7–23) makes it hard to understand how a Deuteronomist could author verses that attest to YHWH's favor toward a number of Israel's kings. For example, "Jehoahaz implored YHWH and YHWH heard him, for he saw the oppression of Israel . . . so YHWH gave Israel a deliverer" (2 Kgs 13:4–5); "But YHWH was gracious and had mercy upon them. He showed regard for them because of his covenant with Abraham, Isaac, and Jacob. He would not destroy them, and so has not rid himself of them until now" (13:23); "It was he [= Jeroboam II] who restored the boundaries of Israel . . . in accordance with the word of YHWH the God of Israel, which he spoke through his servant Jonah son of Amittai, the prophet from Gath-hahepher . . . YHWH did not speak of blotting out Israel's name from under the heavens, and so he rescued them through Jeroboam son of Joash" (14:25–27). Such indications, taken together with the special group of prophecies concerning Israel's early dynasties (see above), suggest that Dtr$_1$ made use of a Northern prophetic composition that surveyed Israel's checkered history and called for repentance and a return to YHWH. This Israelite work likely included a critique of the calves of Jeroboam, since such criticism was first raised in the North by the prophet Hosea (10:5–8;13:2). A pre-Dtr composition of this sort could have reached Judah after 720 BCE with the refugees who fled Assyrian-occupied Israel where, a century later, the composition was to serve as the inspiration for the Deuteronomistic view of the monarchy (for somewhat differing perspectives and evaluations of northern "prophetic historiography," see McKenzie 1985; and Rofé 1988a, 75–105; 1991, in which the scope and shape of an "Ephraimite history" are delineated).

An additional word is in order concerning Dtr$_1$'s interest in the prophetic traditions, because his interest goes well beyond particular events in which prophets participated. For the author, folktale and legend, historical short story, and doom prophecy are all on the same footing; all are joined into a single whole by the rubric "in accordance with the word of YHWH, which (the prophet) spoke."[20] This conforms with the Deuteronomic test of true prophecy: "If the prophet speaks in the name of YHWH and the word does not come true, that word was not spoken by YHWH" (Deut 18:22). Thus, Dtr regularly noted fulfillment of the word of YHWH (cf. 1 Kgs 2:27; 12:15; 13:26; 14:18; 15:29; 16:12; 17:16; 22:38; 2 Kgs 2:22; 4:44; 7:16–18; 14:25; 23:15–17; 24:13). Even promises

---

[20] The fundamental study of this aspect of Deuteronomic and Deuteronomistic historiography is by von Rad 1966b; and earlier, 1953, 74–91.

from earlier parts of the Deuteronomistic history, such as the promise of the prophet Nathan to David concerning the future dynasty, are recalled on their accomplishment (1 Kgs 8:20; see also 2:27). A number of prophecies appear to have been adjusted to fit circumstances as they later developed (see, e.g., 1 Kgs 21:28–29); and the naming of Josiah and the acts of revenge he would perform against the altar in Bethel in 1 Kgs 13:2 has all the marks of an *ex eventum* prophecy inserted to create the desired balance. The prophecy concerning the future pillage of Jerusalem and the exile of Judah's princes, ascribed to Isaiah (2 Kgs 20:16–18), is similarly a fiction, having its denouement in 2 Kgs 24:11–13. On the other hand, Huldah's promise to Josiah that he would die in peace (2 Kgs 22:20), when in fact he was put to death (23:29), is the only prophecy in Kings that goes unfulfilled, a sure sign of its authenticity.[21]

Conspicuous by their absence from this mosaic of prophetic activity are the literary prophets whose words and deeds are preserved in the Latter Prophets. True, Isaiah son of Amoz is central to the drama during the Assyrian siege of Jerusalem (2 Kgs 19), and there is a passing reference to Jonah son of Amittai (14:25). But it is the otherwise unheard-of Huldah to whom Josiah turns (22:14) and not Jeremiah. Also absent from Kings is any reference to the predominant theme of literary prophecy: social justice and its decisive role in determining Israel's fate. On this issue, Deuteronomic thought took an independent stand and, in line with other Pentateuchal sources, held that steadfast loyalty to YHWH, Israel's one and only God, was the measure for length of days in the Promised Land. For this reason the nationalistic prophecies of Jonah son of Amittai and those of Isaiah that backed the Davidic king and promised the rescue of Jerusalem could be assimilated within Kings. In sum, the prophets in Kings function as spokesmen of YHWH, calling lawbreakers to order, and as witnesses to impending punishment. Note, for instance, the characterization in the homily on Israel's fall: "YHWH even warned Israel and Judah by every prophet and every seer, 'Turn back from your evil ways and keep my commands and my statues, in accord with all the Law which I commanded your ancestors, and which I sent to you through my servants, the prophets'" (2 Kgs 17:13).

Turning to Dtr₂ and his additions to the first edition of Kings, chronologically these cover the last quarter-century of the Judean monarchy, from the death of Josiah to the murder of Gedaliah (2 Kgs 23:26–25:26). *The History of the Kings of Judah* is not quoted after 24:5 (the reign of Jehoiakim), which suggests

---

[21] Often Dtr can be seen to have preserved conflicting viewpoints, presenting them in what might be perceived as inharmonious juxtaposition. Thus, for example, the ancient poem associated with the dedication of the Temple in 1 Kgs 8:12–13 declares the House of YHWH to be the deity's earthly residence, a view that is immediately corrected by expressions of Deuteronomic theology whereby the Temple is spoken of as the home of YHWH's name (vv. 16, 19, 20), for indeed even "the heavens and the highest heavens cannot contain you" (v. 27). In similar fashion, Ahab's death at Ramoth-gilead reported in the prophetic tale (1 Kgs 22:35) stands alongside an earlier framework note that the king died a natural death (v. 40; see Note, ad loc.); similarly, the promise of Josiah's peaceful demise (2 Kgs 22:20) is contradicted by his violent end at Megiddo (23:29). Such "discrepancies" are signs of ancient compositional technique that did not favor editing out other views.

that Dtr$_2$ likely described events that he personally witnessed. The evaluations of the last kings of Judah in the framework passages are colorless and are essentially a copy of the previous judgments, "He did what was displeasing to YHWH just as his ancestors/father/Jehoiakim had done," because Manasseh had been branded the arch-sinner, whose behavior had determined Jerusalem's downfall (cf. 24:3). Further explanations were unnecessary, and a homily like the one over the fall of Samaria (17:7–23) was not composed. The end of the book of Kings does not hold out any message of hope, such as can be found in other (later?) Deuteronomistic writings (cf. Deut 4:4–29; 30:1–10), and one might even suggest that the dispiritedness of Dtr$_2$ reflects the view of someone who wrote close to the time of the conquest and exile.[22] Perhaps he was no other than Dtr$_1$, who had seen the high hopes of a revitalized Judah under Josiah shattered, and so he reedited his earlier work, giving it its present pessimistic tone (on the late postscript in 25:27–30, see Comment ad loc.).[23]

7. CHRONOLOGY

The chronological presentation in the book of Kings is the most systematic of any in the Bible.[24] The framework passages give the following data for each of the kings of Judah and Israel: the length of his reign and a synchronic note concerning the regnal year of his royal contemporary in the neighboring kingdom; in addition, for the kings of Judah, his age at accession and his mother's name are recorded. The alternating presentation of monarchs in the two kingdoms follows a set pattern: the reign of a king in one kingdom (A) is set out and if, during this term, his counterpart in the neighboring kingdom (B) dies and is replaced, then upon the death of king (A), the presentation shifts to kingdom (B); the kings of kingdom (B) are presented until there is a death in kingdom (A), whereupon a shift back to kingdom (A) takes place.

It cannot be determined whether the Deuteronomistic author of Kings had access to original chronological data or whether such data was already incorporated into *The History of the Kings of Judah* and *The History of the Kings of Israel*, the composite works that he refers to at the close of his presentation of each reign (see Lewy 1927, 7; Begrich 1929, 173–74). It stands to reason that these "Histories" were arranged chronologically, but just how comprehensive they were and what their relation to archival data was cannot be said (on this issue, see above in Section 6). The lengths of the reigns ultimately derive from

---

[22] He may have been one of the (many?) Judeans who did not go into exile but gathered around Gedaliah at Mizpah; see Noth (1981, 142) for a similar suggestion concerning his single Dtr, who as one who had "stayed in the land" would not relate to any express expectation for the future.

[23] Other Dtr$_2$ passages identified in Kings include: 1 Kgs 2:4; 8:25; 9:4–9; 2 Kgs 17:7–18, 20:17–19; 21:10–15; 22:16–20 (~ 20aα); 23:25b–25:26.

[24] The following is based, in part, on the article "Chronology" (Cogan 1992), in which a brief survey of the history of research can be found.

the king lists of each kingdom, and the synchronisms might have been available in a document that arranged the names of the rulers of the two kingdoms and their reigns synchronically (as exemplified in the Synchronistic Chronicle from Assyria; see ANET, 272–73). If the author was responsible for the synchronisms, then it must be assumed that material from the kingdom of Israel reached Jerusalem soon after the fall of Samaria in 722 BCE in order for it to have been available to him at the time of the first edition of Kings during the reign of Josiah. Obtaining data from Judahite sources would have been no problem. In explanations of the chronological scheme of Kings, it is assumed that an attempt was made to integrate the inherent differences between the sources, which caused some contradictions. But since the Deuteronomist had no firsthand knowledge of the chronology of the Northern Kingdom, reconciliation of conflicting data could not always be achieved—for example, the synchronization of the reigns of Jotham and Ahaz, kings of Judah (2 Kgs 15:32 and 16:1), with the bloated figure of a 20-year reign for Pekah of Israel (2 Kgs 15:27). Whatever the case, the synchronisms may be emblematic of the ideal single monarchy under the House of David.

Absolute chronology is achieved through the correlation of biblical dates with extrabiblical ones that are fixed astronomically. In this regard, the Assyrian Eponym lists and Eponym Chronicle (Akk *līmu*, "eponym," a high official after whom the year was named; see RlA 2.412–56; Millard 1994b) are vital; king lists and chronicles also provide important data (RlA 6.86–135). For example, a general notation such as "In the days of Pekah king of Israel, Tiglath-pileser king of Assyria came . . ." (2 Kgs 15:29) can be fixed by reference to the notation in the Eponym Chronicle that the Assyrian king campaigned in Philistia in 734 and besieged Damascus for two years, 733–732 (see Note on 2 Kgs 15:29). The Babylonian Chronicle, in addition to providing a year-by-year précis of the reign of Nebuchadnezzar, also records the date of Jerusalem's surrender, which is only vaguely referred to in 2 Kgs 24:11–12 (see Note, ad loc.). Egyptians materials are less helpful in these matters because there are serious questions at critical junctures due to gaps in the documentation (see Note on Shishak's campaign at 1 Kgs 14:25).

Several terms dominate the discussion of the chronology of the monarchies:

a. *Regnal Year.* The official "royal year" was reckoned from the start of the New Year. According to the Mishnah (*m. Roš Haš.* 1:1), "the New Year for kings and pilgrimage festivals" was counted from the month of Nisan (March–April), as was the practice in Mesopotamia; but this statement may reflect postbiblical practice. Scholars are divided on whether the regnal year ran from Nisan to Nisan, or Tishri to Tishri, or whether different calendars were in force in Judah and Israel, with shifts made at certain junctures. Though the evidence is inconclusive, it appears that a Nisan calendar was in use in Judah, while in Israel, a Tishri calendar was used. The half-year difference between the two kingdoms can be seen in the notice of the 6-month reign of Zechariah of Israel (2 Kgs 15:8), which is synchronized with the 38th year of Azariah of Judah, while the 1-month reign of Azariah's successor, Shallum, is in the 39th year of Azariah

(2 Kgs 15:13). In Judah, the regnal year had passed, while in Israel, the regnal year had not yet ended; if it had, Zechariah would have been credited with 2 years (by nonaccession reckoning; see below).

b. *Accession Year.*   The "accession year" is the period from the king's taking the throne until the start of the New Year (Heb *šěnat molkô*; cf. 2 Kgs 25:27; Akk *rēš šarrūti*; see Note, ad loc.).

c. *Accession Year (or Postdating) System.*   This system counts the years of a king's reign only from the first full regnal year after the accession year. Assyrian and Babylonian chronologies employ the postdating system throughout.

d. *Nonaccession Year (or Antedating) System.*   This system does not recognize an accession year but counts the first year of a king's reign from his actual taking of the throne; thus, in the antedating system, the last year of the deceased king and the first one of his successor, which are the same year, are both counted. Antedating was employed in Egypt for most of its history. In Judah and Israel, the chronological data can, for the most part, be understood on the assumption that the nonaccession system in counting regnal years was in use. However, toward the middle or end of the 7th century, under the strong assimilatory pressures of the Mesopotamian empires, Judah seems to have adopted the accession year system.

e. *Co-regency.*   This term refers to the designation of a royal heir during the lifetime of the reigning monarch. Evidence for co-regency is available from Egypt. In neither Israel or Judah does it seem to have been the regular practice; generally, unusual historical circumstances led to the appointment of a co-regent in order to insure the continuity of the ruling family on the throne. The number of cases of co-regency explicitly recorded in Kings is not great; sometimes the synchronisms lead one to suspect a period of co-regency—an overlap in the total regnal years of both kings (e.g., 2 Kgs 14:21 and 15:5).

There is no textual support for the claim sometimes made (see Wellhausen 1875, 621; Koch 1978; Hughes 1990, 36–41) that the chronology of the monarchy was compromised in order to fit it into a second 480-year period, which followed the first 480 years (from the Exodus until the construction of Temple was begun; cf. 1 Kgs 6:1; and Note, ad loc.). This second period is conjectured to have included 430 years for the Davidic monarchy, plus a 50-year Exile. But nowhere does Dtr or any other ancient writer calculate these numbers, arrived at after much manipulation.

The chronology of the monarchy presented in this commentary has been calculated following these principles. The dates assigned to each monarch (see appropriate Notes) and tabulated in Appendix 2 have been worked out earlier (Cogan 1992, 1007–10). Other studies, utilizing many of the above principles, arrive at different results (see, among others, Albright 1945; Jepsen 1964; Tadmor 1970; Thiele 1983).

A major divergence from the chronology of the Divided Monarchy as presented by MT appears in Lucianic manuscripts of the LXX, especially for the period from Omri to Jehu (after which it follows MT; LXX[B] agrees with Luc. up until 1 Kgs 22). According to MT synchronisms, Omri's 12-year reign includes

4 years during which he contended with Tibni over the throne of Israel (cf. 1 Kgs 16:15, 23). An alternate construing of the text preserved in the Old Greek translation gives Omri all 12 years as sole ruler (16:23), and it not only reworks all of the succeeding synchronisms with the kings of Judah, but it also reorders the sequence of presentation of their reigns—for example, 1 Kgs 22:41–51 appears as 1 Kgs 16:28a–h (in which Jehoshaphat comes to the throne in the 11th year of Omri). It also identifies the king of Judah in 2 Kgs 3 as Ahaziah (as opposed to MT's Jehoshaphat). Shenkel argued that the Old Greek chronology is original and that MT is a secondary development adjusted to accommodate the prophetic narratives concerning Elijah and Elisha (Shenkel 1968; cf. Miller 1967, 281–84). But as Gooding has pointed out (1970), a number of the calculations (e.g., in LXX^B Zimri is assigned 7 years), the omitted synchronisms, and the repositioned textual units do not recommend themselves as original. This divergent system may represent the earliest preserved attempt at resolving imagined difficulties in the MT chronology (see also Thiele 1983, 88–94).

Finally, unlike modern histories that favor strict chronologies, Kings exhibits sequential departures that may seem somewhat jarring. For example, after the complete defeat of the Assyrian army and the retreat of Sennacherib reported in 2 Kgs 19:35–36, unexpected reference is made to the Assyrian threat to Jerusalem, still in the future (cf. 20:6). This break with expected chronological sequence was caused by the precedence given by Dtr to the story of the city's salvation, putting off the chronologically earlier story of Hezekiah's illness until 2 Kgs 20. In like manner, the revolts against Solomon that broke out early in his reign were gathered together under the rubric "YHWH raised up an adversary for Solomon" and inserted into Solomon's old age (cf. 1 Kgs 11:14–25), set there as evidence that his apostasy did not go unpunished. Chronological considerations are forfeited for the didactic lesson.[25]

8. HISTORY: BIBLICAL TEXT, ARCHAEOLOGY, AND EXTRABIBLICAL DOCUMENTATION

Every reader of Kings confronts the view of the Deuteronomistic author(s) that YHWH, God of Israel, was active in history. "It is a course of events shaped by the word of Yahweh, continually intervening to direct and to deliver, and steadily pressing these events towards their fulfillment in history" (von Rad 1966b, 221). Therefore, it is only natural that a commentary on Kings devote effort to elucidating the nature of the reported historical traditions. This exercise seeks to separate the actual from the legendary, the real from the ideal. Judgments concerning the historicity of events as divergent as a battlefield victory and a conversation in the king's private chamber are of potential interest to the reader whose sole concern is with literary matters, as well as to one devoted

---

[25] Similar chronological manipulations are exhibited in Chronicles (on which see Cogan 1985).

to the moral and religious teachings of the book. But for the historian, they are more than a heuristic exercise; they are vital, for only with a clear literary analysis of the text in hand can one proceed with the reconstruction of the history of ancient Israel.

In this reconstruction, the literary analysis and evaluation of the biblical reports are commonly juxtaposed with the evidence from archaeology and extrabiblical documentation. Archaeology, by its very nature, uncovers the physical setting against which the events were played out but often not described by the ancient writer; perhaps he assumed that his audience needed no introduction to the surroundings with which it was familiar. Thus, for example, the four-room house typical of many Israelite sites in the Iron Age (see A. Mazar 1990, 485–89) helps the modern reader imagine the "small roof chamber" in which Elisha stayed whenever he visited Shunem (cf. 2 Kgs 4:10). Actual horned altars of various sizes and construction enliven the actions of Adonijah and Joab (cf. 1 Kgs 1:50; 2:28). The decommissioning of one such altar, graphically revealed at Tel Beer-sheba in the secondary, profane use made of its stones, may be evidence for cultic reform similar to the reforms accredited to Hezekiah and Josiah (cf. Note on 2 Kgs 23:8). The Temple of Solomon and its furnishings described in unusual detail in 1 Kgs 6 and 7:13–51 would remain an obscure blueprint were it not for the archaeological unearthing of comparable temples and shrines, mostly from Syro-Phoenician sites (see Notes and Comments, ad loc.). The other great project of Solomon, the fortification of his kingdom, can now be evaluated in light of the walls and gates at many major sites; these monumental structures were surely constructed at great expense of means and manpower (cf. 1 Kgs 9:15–23; 11:27–28). But it is this last item that illustrates the evidential limits of the archaeological record. The gateways excavated at Hazor, Megiddo, and Gezer share a common plan, but their dating is disputed (see A. Mazar 1990, 384–87), with some archaeologists firmly convinced that they are of Solomonic provenance in accord with 1 Kgs 9:15 (see, e.g., Dever 1997, 232–42), while others argue for construction a century later, in the days of Ahab (e.g., Finklestein 1990). Throughout the Notes in the Commentary, the reader will find reference to the pertinent archaeological discussions, and a sampling of the prominent finds is illustrated.

The other witnesses to the monarchic period that require a hearing in the historical evaluation of the biblical record come from extrabiblical documentation. Precious little has been recovered from the land of Israel, whether in Hebrew or in any other ancient language. Besides the six-line Siloam Inscription, only a few fragments of stone monuments have reached us. The recent discovery at Tel Dan of three pieces of the Aramaic stela of Hazael (see Appendix 1, no. 3), the first for a ruler of Aram–Damascus, increased by almost one hundred percent the written evidence of this sort. This dearth, however, is made up for by the many hundreds of ostraca and engraved seals that shed invaluable light on mundane matters but are of little use in dealing with the larger political scene, which is the focus of much of Kings. Thus, for example, the blessings of "YHWH of Samaria and his Asherah" from an inscription discovered at Kuntillet ʿAjrud may point to the popular veneration of this Canaanite goddess (see Note on 2 Kgs 21:7). In the rare instances where coordinating extrabiblical reports are available—for example, the raid of Shishak (cf. 1 Kgs 14:25), the campaigns of Tiglath-pileser III (2 Kgs 15:29), Sennacherib (2 Kgs 18:13–19:36), Nebuchadnezzar (2 Kgs 24)—it is well to remember that Israel's neighbors recorded military encounters, tax and tribute payments, conquests and the exile of populations. That is to say, they recorded only events of immediate self-interest to the victors.[26] The internal history of the kingdoms of Israel and Judah went unnoted and must, in the end, be recovered from an analysis of the book of Kings.

The extrabiblical documents have been translated anew and are presented in Appendix I in the present volume and in 2 *Kings*, Appendix 1.

---

[26] See the remarks on the discovery and early use of the Mesopotamian documentation in the mid–nineteenth century in Cogan and Tadmor 1988, 4–5.

9. OUTLINE OF HISTORICAL EVENTS

TABLE 1: SYNCHRONOUS OUTLINE OF HISTORICAL EVENTS IN 1 KINGS

DATE	UNITED KINGDOM OF ISRAEL AND JUDAH	
970		
	SOLOMON, SON OF DAVID (968–928)	
	Revolts in Edom and Damascus	11:14–25
	Construction of Temple and palace complex	5:14–7:51
960	Dedication of Temple	8:1–66
950		
	Cession of Cabul territory to Tyre	9:10–13
940		
930		

DATE	KINGDOM OF ISRAEL	KINGDOM OF JUDAH	
	JEROBOAM, SON OF NEBAT (928–907)	REHOBOAM, SON OF SOLOMON (928–911)	
	Independent kingdom in Northern Israel 12:20	Shishak's raid	14:25–26
920			
910		ABIJAH, SON OF REHOBOAM (911–908)	

TABLE 1, *cont.*

KINGDOM OF ISRAEL		KINGDOM OF JUDAH	
		ASA, SON OF ABIJAH (908–867)	
NADAB, SON OF JEROBOAM (907–906)			
Assassinated by Baasha	15:27–28		
BAASHA, SON OF AHIJAH (906–883)			
900 Blockade of Judah	15:17		
Aramean invasion of Galilee	15:20	Renewed treaty with Damascus	15:18–19
890			
		Cultic reforms	15:11–13
ELAH, SON OF BAASHA (883–882)			
Assassinated by Zimri	16:9–10		
ZIMRI (882)			
Commits suicide after 7 days			
TIBNI, SON OF GINATH (882–878)/			
OMRI (882–871)			
4–year civil war in Israel	16:21–22		
880 Omri gains ascendancy	16:23		
Samaria becomes Israel's capital	16:24		
AHAB, SON OF OMRI (873–852)			
870		JEHOSHAPHAT, SON OF ASA (870–846)	
Construction at Samaria	22:39		
860 First engagements with			
Damascus	20:1–34		
853 Participation in coalition against			
Assyria at Qarqar			
Further battles with Aram–		Alliance with Israel against	
Damascus		Damascus	
King dies in battle	22:1–38		
850			

BIBLIOGRAPHY

◆

BIBLIOGRAPHY

1. COMMENTARIES ON 1 KINGS

Abarbanel, Don Isaac
1957   *Pērûš ʿal nĕbîʾîm rišônîm*. Jerusalem: Torah ve Daʿat.
Barnes, W. E.
1908   *The Two Books of Kings*. CBSC. Cambridge: Cambridge University Press.
Benzinger, I.
1899   *Die Bücher der Könige*. KHC. Freiburg: Mohr.
Burney, C. F.
1903   *Notes on the Hebrew Text of the Book of Kings*. Oxford. [Reprinted, New York: Ktav, 1970]
DeVries, S. J.
1985   *1 Kings*. WBC. Waco, Tex.: Word.
Ehrlich, A. B.
1900   *Mikrâ ki-Pheschutô*, vol. 2. Berlin: Poppelauer.
1914   *Randglossen zur Hebräischen Bibel*, vol. 7. Leipzig: Hinrichs.
Eissfeldt, O.
1922   *Könige*. Volume 1 of *HSAT*. 4th ed. Tübingen: Mohr.
Gersonides (acronym of Levi ben Gershon)
1995   Commentary in *Mikraʾot Gedolot 'Haketer.'*
Graetz, H.
1894   *Emendationes in Plerosque Sacrae Scripturae Veretis Testamenti Libros*. Breslau: Schleische Buchdrukerei.
Gray, J.
1979   *I and II Kings*. OTL. 3d ed. Philadelphia: Westminster.
Grotius, H.
1660   *In Critici sacri*. Edited by J. Pearson. Annotatores ad Libros Historicus 2. London.
Haupt, P. (*See* Stade and Schwally)
Honor, L. L.
1955   *Book of Kings 1: A Commentary*. New York: Union of American Hebrew Congregations.
Jones, G. H.
1984   *I and 2 Kings*. 2 vols. NCB. Grand Rapids, Mich.: Eerdmans.
Joüon, P.
1912   Notes de critique textuelle. *MUSJ* 5:473–85.

Author's note: All refererences to commentaries cite the author's name, or name and page numbers (without a date). Dates are used in the documentation style for other references to the bibliography).

Kittel, R.
1900   *Die Bücher der Könige*. HAT. Göttingen: Vandenhoeck & Ruprecht.

Klostermann, A.
1887   *Die Bücher Samuels und der Könige*. Kurzgefasste Kommentare. Edited by
          H. L. Strack and O. Zöckler. Nördlingen: Beck.

Landersdorfer, S.
1927   *Die Bücher der Könige*. Bonn: Hanstein.

Long, B. O.
1984   *1 Kings*. FOTL 9. Grand Rapids, Mich.: Eerdmans.

Malbim (acronym of Meir Loeb ben Jehiel Michael)
1957   *Sefer Mikra'e Kodesh on Prophets and Writings*, vol. 3. Jerusalem: Pardes.

Mikra'ot Gedolot 'Haketer': Kings I and II
1995   M. Cohen, editor. Ramat-Gan: Bar Ilan University Press.

Moffatt, J.
n.d.   *The Old Testament: A New Translation*. London: Hodder and Stoughton.

Montgomery, J. A., and H. S. Gehman
1951   *The Book of Kings*. ICC. Edinburgh: T. & T. Clark.

Mulder, M.
1998   *1 Kings 1–11*. Volume 1 of *I Kings*. HCOT. Leuven: Peeters.

Nelson, R. D.
1987   *First and Second Kings*. Interpretation. Atlanta: John Knox.

Noth, M.
1968   *Könige I*. BKAT. Neukirchen-Vluyn: Neukirchener Verlag.

Perles, F.
1922   *Annalekten zur Textkritik des Alten Testament*. Leipzig: Engel.

Provan, I. W.
1995   *1 and 2 Kings*. NIBC. Peabody, Mass.: Hendrickson.

Qara, R. Joseph
1995   Commentary in *Mikra'ot Gedolot 'Haketer.'*

Qimḥi, David
1995   Commentary in *Mikra'ot Gedolot 'Haketer.'*

Rashi (acronym of Rabbi Solomon ben Isaac)
1995   Commentary in *Mikra'ot Gedolot 'Haketer.'*

Rehm, M.
1979   *Das erste Buch der Könige*. Wurzburg: Echter.

Robinson, J.
1972   *The First Book of Kings*. CBC. Cambridge: Cambridge University Press.

Šanda, A.
1912   *Die Bücher der Könige*. EHAT. Münster: Aschendorffsche.

Skinner, J.
1893   *I and II Kings*. Century Bible. Edinburgh: T. C. & E. C. Jack, n.d. [ca. 1893]

Snaith, N. H.
1954   *The First and Second Books of Kings*. Pages 3–338 in vol. 3 of *IB*. New York:
          Abingdon.

Stade, B., and F. Schwally, with notes by P. Haupt
   1904   *The Books of Kings.* The Sacred Books of the Old Testament. Leipzig: Hinrichs.

Thenius, O.
   1873   *Die Bücher der Könige.* 2d ed. KEHAT. Leipzig: Hirzel.

Walsh, J. T.
   1996   *1 Kings.* Berit Olam. Collegeville, Minn.: Liturgical Press.

Wiseman, D. J.
   1993   *1 and 2 Kings.* Tyndale Old Testament Commentaries. Leicester: Inter-Varsity Press.

Würthwein, E.
   1977   *Das Erste Buch der Könige, Kapitel 1–16.* ATD. Göttingen: Vandenhoeck & Ruprecht.
   1984   *Die Bücher der Könige: 1. Kön. 17–2. Kön. 25.* ATD. Göttingen: Vandenhoeck & Ruprecht.

2. BOOKS AND ARTICLES

Aberbach, M., and L. Smolar
   1967   Aaron, Jeroboam and the Golden Calves. *JBL* 86:129–40.

Abramski, S.
   1978   The Resurrection of the Kingdom of Damascus and Its Historiographic Record. Pages 17–43 in *Studies in Bible and the Ancient Near East Presented to S. E. Loewenstamm.* Edited by Y. Avishur and Y. Blau. Jerusalem: Rubinstein. [Hebrew]

Abu Assaf, A.
   1990   *Der Tempel von ʿAin Dara.* Mainz: Von Zabern.

Ackerman, S.
   1992   *Under Every Green Tree: Popular Religion in Sixth-Century Judah.* HSS 46. Atlanta: Scholars Press.
   1993   The Queen Mother and the Cult in Ancient Israel. *JBL* 112:385–401.

Aharoni, Y.
   1959   The Province-List of Judah. *VT* 9:225–46.
   1963   Tamar and the Roads to Elath. *IEJ* 13:30–42.
   1965   The Carmel as the Israel–Tyre Border. Pages 56–62 in *Western Galilee and the Coast of Galilee.* Jerusalem: Israel Exploration Society. [Hebrew]
   1970   Mount Carmel as Border. Pages 1–7 in *Archäologie und Altes Testament: Fs. K. Galling.* Edited by A. Kutschke and E. Kutsch. Tübingen: Mohr (Siebeck).
   1976   The Solomonic Districts. *Tel Aviv* 3:5–15.
   1979   *The Land of the Bible: A Historical Geography.* Rev. ed. Philadelphia: Westminster.
   1982   *The Archaeology of the Land of Israel.* Philadelphia: Westminster.

Aḥituv, S.
   1984   *Canaanite Toponyms in Ancient Egyptian Documents.* Jerusalem: Magnes.

Ahlström, G. W.

1963   *Aspects of Syncretism in Israelite Religion.* Lund: Gleerup.

1982   *Royal Administration and National Religion in Ancient Palestine.* SHCANE 1. Leiden: Brill.

1985   The Cultroom at ʿEn Gev. *Tel Aviv* 12:93–95.

1993a   *The History of Ancient Palestine from the Palaeolithic Period to Alexander's Conquest.* JSOTSup 146. Sheffield: Sheffield Academic Press.

1993b   Pharaoh Shoshenq's Campaign in Palestine. Pages 1–17 in *History and Traditions of Early Israel: Studies Nielsen.* Edited by A. Lemaire and B. Otzen. VTSup 50. Leiden: Brill.

Albenda, P.

1986   *The Palace of Sargon, King of Assyria.* Paris: Éditions Recherche sur les Civilisations.

Albright, W. F.

1925   The Administrative Divisions of Israel and Judah. *JPOS* 5:17–54.

1933   Archaeological and Topographical Explorations in Palestine and Syria. *BASOR* 49:23–31.

1936   Zabul Yam and Thapit Nahar in the Combat between Baal and the Sea. *JPOS* 16:17–20.

1942a   Two Cressets from Marissa and the Pillars of Jakhin and Boaz. *BASOR* 85:18–27.

1942b   A Votive Stele Erected by Ben-Hadad I of Damascus to the God Melqart. *BASOR* 87:23–29.

1945   The Chronology of the Divided Monarchy of Israel. *BASOR* 100:16–22.

1950   The Judicial Reform of Jehoshaphat. Pages 61–82 in *A. Marx Jubilee Volume.* New York: Jewish Theological Seminary.

1955   New Light on Early Recensions of the Hebrew Bible. *BASOR* 140:27–33.

1969a   *Yahweh and the Gods of Canaan.* Garden City, N.Y.: Doubleday.

1969b   *Archaeology and the Religion of Israel.* 5th ed. Garden City, N.Y.: Doubleday.

1975   Syria, the Philistines and Phoenicia. Pages 507–36 in *The Middle East and the Aegean Region c. 1380–1000 B.C.* Volume 2/2 of *CAH.* Cambridge: Cambridge University Press.

Alfrink, B.

1943   L'expression *skb ʿm ʾbwtyw. OtSt* 2:106–18.

Alt, A.

1913   Israels Gaue unter Salomo. Pages 1–19 in *Alttestamentliche Studien Rudolf Kittel zum 60. Geburtstag dargebracht.* BZAW 13. Leipzig: Hinrichs. [= Alt 1953, 76–89]

1935   Das Gottesurteil auf dem Karmel. Pages 1–18 in *Festschrift Georg Beer zum 70. Geburtstage.* Stuttgart: Kohlhammer. [= Alt 1953, 135–49]

1937   Galiläische Probleme. *PJ* 33:52–88. [= Alt 1953, 363–74]

1950   Menschen ohne Namen. *ArOr* 18:9–24. [= Alt 1959, 198–213]

1951a   Die Weisheit Salomons. *TLZ* 36:139–44. [= Alt 1953, 90–99. E.T.: Solomonic Wisdom. Pages 102–12 in *Studies in Ancient Israelite Wisdom.* Edited by J. L. Crenshaw. New York: Ktav, 1976]

1951b   Das Königtum in den Reichen Israel und Juda. *VT* 1:2–22. [= Alt 1953, 116–34. E.T.: Alt 1966, 241–59]

1953   *Kleine Schriften zur Geschichte des Volkes Israel,* vol. 2. Munich: Beck.

1954   Der Stadtstaat Samaria. *Berichte und die Verhandlungen der Sächsischen Akademie der Wissenschaften zur Leipzig. Phil.-hist. Klasse.* 101/5. [= Alt 1959, 258–302]

1959   *Kleine Schriften zur Geschichte des Volkes Israel,* vol. 3. Munich: Beck.

1966   *Essays on Old Testament History and Religion.* Oxford: Blackwell.

Alter, R.
1981   *The Art of Biblical Narrative.* New York: Basic.

Anbar, M.
1988   La "Reprise." *VT* 38:391–98.

Andersen, F. I.
1966   The Socio-juridical Background of the Naboth-Incident. *JBL* 85:46–57.

Andreasen, N. A.
1983   The Role of the Queen Mother in Israelite Society. *CBQ* 45:179–94.

Ap-Thomas, D. R.
1956   Notes on Some Terms Relating to Prayer. *VT* 6:225–41.
1983   All the King's Horses? A Study of the Term פרש (I Kings 5.6 [EVV., 4.26] etc.). Pages 135–51 in *Proclamation and Presence: Old Testament Essays in Honour of G. H. Davies.* Corrected ed. Edited by J. I. Durham and J. R. Porter. Macon, Ga.: Mercer University Press.

Arav, R., and M. Bernett
2000   The *bit ḫilāni* at Bethsaida: Its Place in Aramaean/Neo-Hittite and Israelite Palace Architecture in the Iron Age II. *IEJ* 50:47–81.

Artzi, P.
1954   Sablum = *sbl. BIES* 18:66–70.

Ash, P. S.
1995   Solomon's? District? List. *JSOT* 67:67–86.
1998   Jeroboam I and the Deuteronomistic Historian's Ideology of the Founder. *CBQ* 60:16–24.

Avigad, N.
1953   The Epitaph of a Royal Steward from Siloam. *IEJ* 3:137–52.
1964   The Seal of Jezebel. *IEJ* 14:174–76.
1979   A Group of Hebrew Seals from the Hecht Collection. Pages 119–26 in *Festschrift R. Hecht.* Jerusalem: Koren.
1980   The Chief of the Corvée. *IEJ* 30:170–73.
1986   *Hebrew Bullae from the Time of Jeremiah: Remnants of a Burnt Archive.* Jerusalem: Israel Exploration Society.
1989   The Inscribed Pomegranate from the "House of the Lord." *Israel Museum Journal* 8:7–16.
1997   *Corpus of West Semitic Stamp Seals.* Jerusalem: Israel Academy of Sciences and Humanities, Israel Exploration Society, Institute of Archaeology.

Avishur, Y., and M. Heltzer
1997   *Studies on the Royal Administration in Ancient Israel in the Light of Epigraphic Sources.* Jerusalem: Akademon. [Hebrew]

Avi-Yonah, M.
1952   Mount Carmel and the God of Baalbek. *IEJ* 2:118–24.
1954   בחורים. Page 46 in vol. 2 of *EncMiqr.*

Bagnani, G.
    1954   The Molten Sea of Solomon's Temple. Pages 114–17 in *The Seed of Wisdom: Essays in Honour of T. J. Meek*. Edited by W. S. McCullough. Toronto: University of Toronto Press.

Baillet, M.
    1962   Grotte 6. Pages 107–12 in *Les "petites grottes" de Qumran*. Edited by M. Baillet, J. T. Milik, and R. de Vaux. DJD 3. Oxford: Clarendon.

Ball, E.
    1977   A Note on I KINGS xxii.28. *JTS* 28:90–94.

Barkai, G.
    1989   The Priestly Benediction on Silver from Keteph Hinnom in Jerusalem. *Cathedra* 52:37–76.
    1997   The Megerah and the Tephahot. *Shnaton* 11:32–45.

Barnett, R. D.
    1956   Phoenicia and the Ivory Trade. *Archaeology* 9:87–97.
    1973   Monkey Business. *JANES* 5:1–5.
    1977   *Illustrations of Old Testament History*. 2d ed. London: British Museum.
    1982   *Ancient Ivories in the Middle East*. Qedem 14. Jerusalem: Israel Exploration Society.

Barnett, R. D., and M. Falkner
    1962   *The Sculptures of Tiglath-pileser III (745–727 B.C.)*. London: British Museum.

Barrick, W. B.
    1992   High Place. Pages 195–200 in vol. 3 of *ABD*.
    1996   On the Meaning of בית-ה/במות and בתי-במות and the Composition of the Kings History. *JBL* 115:621–41.

Barthélemy, D.
    1982   *Critique textuelle de l'ancien testament*. OBO 50/1. Göttingen: Vandenhoeck & Ruprecht.

Bartlett, J. R.
    1976   An Adversary against Solomon: Hadad the Edomite. *ZAW* 88:205–26.
    1989   *Edom and the Edomites*. JSOTSup 77. Sheffield: JSOT Press.

Becking, Bob
    1992   *The Fall of Samaria: An Historical and Archaeological Study*. SHCANE 2. Leiden: Brill.

Begrich J.
    1929   *Die Chronologie der Könige von Israel und Juda und die Quellen des Rahmen der Königbücher*. Tübingen: Mohr.
    1933   Jesaja 14,28–32: Ein Beitrag zur Chronologie der israelitisch-judäischen Königzeit. *ZDMG* 86:66–79.
    1940–41   Sofer und mazkir: Ein Beitrag zur inneren Geschichte des davidisch-salomonischen Grossreiches und das Königreiches Juda. *ZAW* 58:1–29.

Ben-Barak, Z.
    1985   The Case of Naboth in the Light of Documents from Mesopotamia: A New Perspective. Pages 15–20 in *Division A: The Period of the Bible* of *Proceedings of the Ninth World Congress of Jewish Studies*. Jerusalem: World Union of Jewish Studies. [Hebrew]

1991   The Status and Right of the *Gebira*. *JBL* 110:23–34.

Ben-Dov, M.
1976   *Nph*: A Geographical Term of Possible "Sea-People" Origin. *Tel Aviv* 3:70–73.

Ben-Tor, A., and D. Ben-Ami
1998   Hazor and the Archaeology of the Tenth Century B.C.E. *IEJ* 48:1–37.

Bentzen, A
1961   *Introduction to the Old Testament*. 2 vols. Copenhagen: Gad.

Ben-Zvi, E.
1991   The Account of the Reign of Manasseh in II Reg 21, 1–18 and the Redactional History of the Book of Kings. *ZAW* 103:355–74.
1993   Prophets and Prophecy in the Compositional and Redactional Notes in I–II Kings. *ZAW* 105:331–51.

Berlin, A.
1983   *Poetics and Interpretation of Biblical Narrative*. Sheffield: Almond.

Beuken, W. A. M.
1989   No Wise King without a Wise Woman (I Kings iii 16–28). *OtSt* 25:1–10.

Binger, T.
1997   *Asherah: Goddesses in Ugarit, Israel and the Old Testament*. JSOTSup 232. Sheffield: Sheffield Academic Press.

Bin-Nun, S. R.
1968   Formulas from Royal Records of Israel and of Judah. *VT* 18:14–32.
1975   *The Tawananna in the Hititte Empire*. Heidelberg: Carl Winter.

Biram, A.
1953   *Mas ʿobed. Tarbiz* 23:137–42.

Biran, A.
1985   On the Identification of Anathoth. *ErIsr* 18 (Avigad Volume): 209–14.
1994   *Biblical Dan*. Jerusalem: Israel Exploration Society–Hebrew Union College–Jewish Institute of Religion.

Biran, A., and J. Naveh
1995   The Tel Dan Inscription: A New Fragment. *IEJ* 45:1–18.

Bird, P. A.
1997   The End of the Male Cult Prostitute: A Literary-Historical and Sociological Analysis of Hebrew *qadeš-qedešim*. Pages 37–80 in *Congress Volume: Cambridge, 1995*. VTSup 66. Leiden: Brill.

Blenkinsopp, J.
1972   *Gibeon and Israel*. Cambridge: Cambridge University Press.
1974   Did Saul Make Gibeon His Capital? *VT* 24:1–7.

Bloch-Smith, E.
1994   "Who Is the King of Glory?" Solomon's Temple and Its Symbolism. Pages 18–31 in *Scripture and Other Artifacts: Essays on the Bible and Archaeology in Honor of Philip J. King*. Edited by M. D. Coogan, J. C. Exum, L. E. Stager. Louisville: Westminster and John Knox.

Boer, P. A. H. de
1955   "Vive le roi!" *VT* 5:225–31.

Boling, R. G.
1975   *Judges*. AB 6A. Garden City, N.Y.: Doubleday.

Boling, R. G., and G. E. Wright
1982   *Joshua*. AB 6. Garden City, N.Y.: Doubleday.

Bordreuil, P.
1975   Inscriptions sigillaires ouest-sémitiques, II: Un cachet hebreu récemment
            acquis par le Cabinet des médailles de la Bibliothèque Nationale. *Syria*
            52:107–18.

Born, A. von den
1965   Zum Tempelweihespruch (1 Kgs 8:12f). *OtSt* 14:235–44.

Brauner, R. A.
1974   "To Grasp the Hem," and 1 Samuel 15:27. *JANES* 6:35–38.

Brekelmans, C. H. W.
1982   Solomon at Gibeon. Pages 53–59 in *Von Kanaan bis Kerala: Fs. J. P. M.
            van der Ploeg*. AOAT 211. Neukirchen-Vluyn: Neukirchener Verlag.

Brettler, M.
1991   The Structure of 1 Kings 1–11. *JSOT* 49:87–97.

Brichto, H. C.
1963   *The Problem of "Curse" in the Hebrew Bible*. JBLMS 13. Philadelphia:
            Society of Biblical Literature and Exegesis.

Bright, J.
1981   *A History of Israel*. 3d ed. Philadelphia: Westminster.

Brin, G.
1966   On the Title *bn hmlk*. *Leš* 31:5–20.

Brinkman, J. A.
1968   *A Political History of Post-Kassite Babylonia, 1158–722 B.C.* AnOr 43.
            Rome: Pontifical Biblical Institute.

Buber, M.
1960   *The Prophetic Faith*. New York: Harper & Row.
1994   On Word Choice in Translating the Bible: *In Memorium* Franz Rosen-
            zwieg. Pages 73–89 in *Scripture and Translation*, by Buber and Rosenzweig.
            Bloomington: Indiana University Press.

Buber, M., and F. Rosenzweig
1994   *Scripture and Translation*. Bloomington: Indiana University Press.

Busink, T. A.
1970   *Der Tempel Salomos*. Volume 1 of *Der Tempel von Jerusalem von Salomo
            bis Herodes*. Leiden: Brill.

Campbell, A. F.
1986   *Of Prophets and Kings: A Late Ninth-Century Document (1 Samuel 1–
            2 Kings 10)*. CBQMS 17. Washington, D.C.: Catholic Biblical Association.

Canciani, F., and G. Pettinato
1965   Salomos Thron: Philologische und archäologische Erwägungen. *ZDPV*
            81:88–108.

Caquot, A.
1961   Ahiya de Silo et Jéroboam 1ᵉʳ. *Sem* 11:18–19.

Carr, D. M.
1991   *From D to Q: A Study of Early Jewish Interpretations of Solomon's Dream at Gibeon*. SBLMS 44. Atlanta, Ga.: Scholars Press.

Carroll, R. P.
1969   The Elijah-Elisha Sagas: Some Remarks on Prophetic Succession in Ancient Israel. *VT* 19:400–415.

Casson, L.
1971   *Ships and Seamanship in the Ancient World*. Princeton: Princeton University Press.

Cassuto, U.
1975   *Bible and Ancient Oriental Texts*. Volume 2 of *Biblical and Oriental Studies*. Jerusalem: Magnes.

Childs, B. S.
1980   On Reading the Elijah Narratives. *Int* 34:128–37.

Clements, R. C.
1988   Solomon and the Origins of Wisdom in Israel. Pages 23–35 in *Perspectives on the Hebrew Bible: Essays in Honor of Walter J. Harrelson*. Edited by J. Crenshaw. Macon, Ga.: Mercer University Press.

Cody, A.
1965   Le titre égyptien et le nom propre du scribe de David. *RB* 72:381–93.

Cogan, M.
1985   The Chronicler's Use of Chronology as Illuminated by Neo-Assyrian Royal Inscriptions. Pages 197–209 in *Empirical Models for Biblical Criticism*. Edited by J. Tigay. Philadelphia: University of Pennsylvania Press.
1986   "The City That I Chose": The Deuteronomistic View of Jerusalem. *Tarbiz* 55:301–9.
1990   Through the Commentator's Looking Glass. Pages 21–27 in *Division A: The Bible and Its World* of *Proceedings of the Tenth World Congress of Jewish Studies*. Jerusalem: World Union of Jewish Studies.
1992   Chronology. Pages 1002–11 in vol. 1 of *ABD*.
1994   *Joel: Introduction and Commentary*. Mikra Leyisraʾel. Tel-Aviv and Jerusalem: Am Oved and Magnes. [Hebrew]
Forthcoming a   Locating *māt Ḫatti* in Neo-Assyrian Inscriptions. *Beer-sheva* 15.
Forthcoming b   "For in Him Alone of All the House of Jeroboam Has Some Good Been Found by YHWH, God of Israel" (1 Kings 14:13): On the Odyssey of Interpretations. *Fs. Aḥituv*.
Forthcoming c   A Slip of the Pen? On Josiah's Actions in Samaria (2 Kings 23:15–20). *Fs. Weinfeld*. Edited by C. Cohen, S. Paul, and A. Hurvitz. Winona Lake, Ind.: Eisenbrauns.

Cogan, M., and H. Tadmor
1988   *II Kings: A New Translation with Introduction and Commentary*. AB 11. New York: Doubleday.

Cohen, H. R.
1978   *Biblical Hapax Legomena in the Light of Akkadian and Ugaritic*. SBLDS 37. Missoula, Mont.: Scholars Press.

Cohen, M., editor
  1995   *Mikra'ot Gedolot 'Haketer': Kings I and II*. Ramat-Gan: Bar Ilan University Press.

Cohen, M. A.
  1965   The Role of the Shilonite Priesthood in the United Monarchy of Ancient Israel. *HUCA* 36:59–98.
  1975   In All Fairness to Ahab: A Socio-Political Consideration of the Ahab-Elijah Controversy. *ErIsr* 12 (Glueck Volume): 87*–94*.

Cohn, R. L.
  1982   The Literary Logic of 1 Kings 17–19. *JBL* 101:333–50.
  1985   Literary Technique in the Jeroboam Narrative. *ZAW* 97:23–35.

Coote, R. B.
  1981   Yahweh Recalls Eljiah. Pages 115–20 in *Traditions in Transformation: Turning Points in Biblical Faith* (F. M. Cross Fs.). Edited by B. Halpern and J. D. Levenson. Winona Lake, Ind.: Eisenbrauns.

Cowley, A. E.
  1923   *Aramaic Papyri of the Fifth Century* B.C. Oxford: Oxford University Press.

Cross, F. M.
  1973   The Themes of the Book of Kings and the Structure of the Deuteronomistic History. Pages 274–89 in *Canaanite Myth and Hebrew Epic*. Cambridge: Harvard University Press.
  1998   *From Epic to Canon: History and Literature in Ancient Israel*. Baltimore: Johns Hopkins University Press.
  1999   King Hezekiah's Seal Bears Phoenician Imagery. *BAR* 22:42–45.

Cross, F. M., and D. N. Freedman
  1952   *Early Hebrew Orthography: A Study of the Epigraphic Evidence*. AOS 36. New Haven, Conn.: American Oriental Society.
  1955   The Song of Miriam. *JNES* 14:237–50.

Crowfoot, J. W., and G. M. Crowfoot
  1938   *Early Ivories from Samaria*. London: Palestine Exploration Fund.

Dalley, S., and J. N. Postgate
  1984   *The Tablets from Fort Shalmaneser*. London: British School of Archaeology in Iraq.

Danelius, E.
  1967–68 The Sins of Jeroboam Ben-Nabat. *JQR* 58:95–114, 204–23.

Davey, C. J.
  1980   Temples of the Levant and the Buildings of Solomon. *TynBul* 31:107–46.

Davies, G. E.
  1979   *The Way of the Wilderness*. SOTSMS 5. Cambridge: Cambridge University Press.
  1989   "*Urwot*" in 1 Kings 5:6 (EVV 4:26) and the Assyrian Horse Lists. *JSS* 34:25–38.

Day, J.
  1992   Asherah. Pages 483–87 in vol. 1 of *ABD*.
  1995   Foreign Semitic Influence on the Wisdom of Israel and Its Appropriation in the Book of Proverbs. Pages 55–70 in *Wisdom in Ancient Israel. Essays in Honour of J. A. Emerton*. Edited by J. Day, R. P. Gordon, and H. G. M. Williamson. Cambridge: Cambridge University Press.

Dearman, J. A., and J. M. Miller
1983 The Melqart Stele and the Ben Hadads of Damascus: Two Studies. *PEQ* 115:95–101.

Debus, J.
1967 *Die Sünde Jeroboams*. FRLANT 93. Göttingen: Vandenhoeck and Ruprecht.

Deller, K.
1984 Assyrisch um/nzarḫu und Hebräisch ʿäzraḥ. ZA 74:235–39.

Demsky, A.
1973 Geba, Gibeah, and Gibeon: An Historico-Geographic Riddle. *BASOR* 212:26–31.

De Ordorico, M.
1995 *The Use of Numbers and Quantifications in the Assyrian Royal Inscriptions*. SAAS 3. Helsinki: Neo-Assyrian Text Corpus Project.

Deurloo, K. A.
1989 The King's Wisdom in Judgement: Narration as Example (I Kings iii). *OtSt* 25:11–21.

Deutsch, R.
1997 *Messages from the Past*. Tel Aviv: Archaeological Center Publications.

Dever, W. G.
1971 Further Excavations at Gezer, 1967–1971. *BA* 34:94–132.
1982 Monumental Architecture in Ancient Israel in the Period of the United Monarchy. Pages 269–306 in *Studies in the Period of David and Solomon and Other Essays*. Edited by T. Ishida. Winona Lake, Ind.: Eisenbrauns.
1997 Archaeology and the "Age of Solomon": A Case-Study in Archaeology and Historiography. Pages 217–52 in *The Age of Solomon: Scholarship at the Turn of the Millennium*. Edited by L. K. Hardy. Leiden: Brill.

Dever, W. G., et al.
1970 *Gezer 1*. Jerusalem: Hebrew Union College.

DeVries, S. J.
1978 *Prophet against Prophet*. Grand Rapids, Mich.: Eerdmans.
1979 A Reply to G. Gerleman on *malkê ḥesed* in 1 Kings xx 31. *VT* 29:359–62.

Donner, H.
1959 Amt und Herkunft des Amtes des Königinmutter im Alten Testament. Pages 105–46 in *J. Friedrich Festschrift zum 65. Geburtstag*. Heidelberg: Carl Winter.
1977 The Separate States of Israel and Judah. Pages 381–434 in *Israelite and Judaean History*. Edited by J. H. Hayes and J. M. Miller. London: SCM.

Dothan, T.
1992 Bronze Wheels from Tel Miqne-Ekron. *ErIsr* 23 (Biran Volume): 148–54.

Dougherty, R. P.
1925 Cuneiform Parallels to Solomon's Provisioning System. Pages 23–65 in AASOR 5. New Haven: Yale University Press.

Drinkard, J. F.
1979 ʿAl Pene as "East of." *JBL* 98:285–86.

Driver, G. R.
1937 Linguistic and Textual Problems: Isaiah i–xxxix. *JTS* 38:36–50.

1955   Birds in the Old Testament. *PEQ* 87:5–20, 129–40.
1957   *Aramaic Documents of the Fifth Century* B.C. Oxford: Clarendon.
1960   Abbreviations in the Masoretic Text. *Textus* 1:112–31.
1966   Forgotten Hebrew Idioms. *ZAW* 78:1–7.

Driver, S. R.
1892   *Hebrew Tenses*. Oxford: Clarendon.
1913   *An Introduction to the Literature of the Old Testament*. 9th ed. Edinburgh:
          T. & T. Clark.

Edelman, D. V.
1995   Solomon's Adversaries Hadad, Rezon and Jeroboam: A Trio of "Bad Guy"
          Characters Illustrating the Theology of Immediate Retribution. Pages 166–
          91 in *The Pitcher is Broken: Memorial Essays for G. W. Ahlström*. Edited by
          S. W. Holloway and L. K. Handy. JSOTSup 190. Sheffield: Sheffield Aca-
          demic Press.

Eissfeldt, O.
1940–41   Lade und Stierbild. *ZAW* 58:190–215.
1965   *The Old Testament: An Introduction*. New York: Harper & Row.
1967   "Bist Du Elia, so bin Ich Isebel" (I Kön. xix 2). Pages 65–70 in *Hebräische
          Wortforschung (Fs. W. Baumgarten)*. VTSup 16. Leiden: Brill.

Elat, M.
1977   *Economic Relations in the Lands of the Bible c.1000–539* B.C. Jerusalem:
          Mosad Bialik and Israel Exploration Society. [Hebrew]
1982   Tarshish and the Problem of Phoenician Colonisation in the Western
          Mediterranean. *OLP* 13:55–61.

Elgavish, D.
1998   *The Diplomatic Service in the Bible and the Ancient Near East*. Jerusalem:
          Magnes. [Hebrew]

Eph'al, I.
1982   *The Ancient Arabs*. Jerusalem: Magnes.
1991   "The Samarian(s)" in the Assyrian Sources. Pages 36–45 in *Ah Assyria . . . :
          Studies in Assyrian History and Ancient Near Eastern Historiography Pre-
          sented to Hayim Tadmor*. Edited by M. Cogan and I. Eph'al. ScrHier 33.
          Jerusalem: Magnes.
1994   "You Are Defecting to the Chaldeans" (Jer. 37:13). *ErIsr* 24 (Malamat Vol-
          ume): 18–22.
Forthcoming On the Common Literary Expressions of the Ancient Semites. *Fs.
          M. Weinfeld*. Edited by C. Cohen, S. Paul, and A. Hurvitz. Winona Lake,
          Ind.: Eisenbrauns.

Evans, C. D.
1983   Naram-Sin and Jeroboam: The Archetypal *Unheilsherrscher* in Mesopota-
          mian and Biblical Historiography. Pages 97–125 in *Scripture in Context II:
          More Essays on the Comparative Method*. Edited by W. W. Hallo, J. C.
          Moyer, and L. G. Perdue. Winona Lake, Ind.: Eisenbrauns.

Evans, D. G.
1966   Rehoboam's Advisers at Shechem and Political Institutions in Israel and
          Sumer. *JNES* 25:273–79.

Ewald, H.
1870 *Ausführliches Lehrbuch der Hebräischen Sprache des Alten Bundes.* 8th ed. Leipzig: Hahn.

Eynikel, E.
1996 *The Reform of King Josiah and the Composition of the Deuteronomistic History. OtSt* 33.

Fales, F. M., and J. N. Postgate
1992 *Imperial Administrative Records, Part I: Palace and Temple Administration.* SAA 7. Helsinki: Helsinki University Press.

Federn, W.
1960 Dahamunzu (KBo V 6 iii 8). *JCS* 14:33.

Feldman, L. H.
1995 Josephus' Portrait of Solomon. *HUCA* 66:103–67.

Feliks, Y.
1957 *Plant World of the Bible.* Ramat-Gan: Masada. [Hebrew]
1981 *Nature and Man in the Bible.* London: Soncino.

Fensham, F. C.
1969 The Treaty between the Israelites and Tyrians. Pages 71–87 in *Congress Volume: Rome, 1968.* VTSup 17. Leiden: Brill.
1980 A Few Observations on the Polarisation between Yahweh and Baal in I Kings 17–19. *ZAW* 92:227–36.

Fenton (Yinon), P. B.
1994 The Head between the Knees. *Da'at* 32–33:19–29. [Hebrew] [French Translation: *Revue d'histoire et de philosophie religieuses* 72/4 (1992): 413–26]

Fernandez Marcos, N.
1984 The Lucianic Text in the Book of Kingdoms: From Lagarde to the Text Pluralism. Pages 161–74 in *De Septuaginta: Studies in Honour of John William Wevers.* Edited by A. Pietersma and C. Cox. Mississauga, Ont.: Benben.

Finkelstein, I.
1990 On Archaeological Methods and Historical Considerations: Iron Age II Gezer and Samaria. *BASOR* 277/278:109–30.

Finkelstein, J. J.
1973 The Goring Ox. *Temple Law Quarterly* 46:169–290.

Fishbane, M.
1985 *Biblical Interpretation in Ancient Israel.* Oxford: Clarendon.

Fitzmyer, J. A.
1970 *Luke 1–9.* AB 28. New York: Doubleday.

Flanagan, J. W.
1972 Court History or Succession Document? A Study of 2 Samuel 9–20 and 1 Kings 1–2. *JBL* 91:172–81.

Fleming, D. E.
1999 If El Is a Bull, Who Is a Calf?: Reflections on Religion in Second-Millennium Syria–Palestine. *ErIsr* 26 (Cross Volume): 23*–27*.

Fokkelman, J. P.
1981   *Narrative Art and Poetry in the Books of Samuel*, vol. 1. Assen: Van Gorcum.

Forshey, H. O.
1992   Court Narrative (2 Samuel 9–1 Kings 2). Pages 1172–79 in vol. 1 of *ABD*.

Forti, T.
1996   Animal Images in the Didactic Rhetoric of the Book of Proverbs. *Bib* 77:48–63.

Fox, M. J.
1986   Egyptian Onomastica and Biblical Wisdom. *VT* 36:302–10.

Fox, N.
1996   Royal Officials and Court Families: A New Look at the ילדים (*yĕlādîm*) in 1 Kings 12. *BA* 59:225–32.

Freedman, D. N.
1993   Kingly Chronologies: Then and Later. *ErIsr* 24 (Malamat Volume): 41*–65*.

Freedman, D. N., and M. O'Connor
1983   "כרוב *kerub*." Pages 322–34 in vol. 4 of *TWAT*.

Friedman, R. E.
1981   From Egypt to Egypt: Dtr^1 and Dtr^2. Pages 167–92 in *Traditions in Transformation: Turning Points in Biblical Faith* (F. M. Cross Fs.). Edited by B. Halpern and J. D. Levenson. Winona Lake, Ind.: Eisenbrauns.
1987   *Who Wrote the Bible?* New York: Harper & Row.

Frisch, A.
1991a   Structure and Its Significance: The Narrative of Solomon's Reign (1 Kings 1–12.24). *JSOT* 51:3–14.
1991b   The Narrative of Solomon's Reign: A Rejoinder. *JSOT* 51:22–24.

Fritz, V.
1987   Temple Architecture: What Can Archaeology Tell Us about Solomon's Temple? *BAR* 13:38–49.
1992   Die Kapitelle der Saulen des Salomonischen Tempels. *ErIsr* 23 (Biran Volume): 36*–42*.
1996   Monarchy and Re-urbanization: A New Look at Solomon's Kingdom. Pages 187–95 in *The Origins of the Ancient Israelite States*. Edited by V. Fritz and P. R. Davies. JSOTSup 228. Sheffield: Sheffield Academic Press.

Frymer-Kensky, T.
1992   *In the Wake of the Goddess*. New York: Free Press.

Gal, Z.
1985   Cabul, Jiphtah-El and the Boundary between Asher and Zebulun in Light of Archaeological Evidence. *ZDPV* 101:114–27.

Galling, K.
1937   *Biblisches Reallexikon*. Tübingen: Mohr.
1955   Beitrag. Pages 219–41 in *Ezechiel*. Edited by G. Fohrer. Tübingen: Mohr.

Garber, P.L.
1951   Reconstructing Solomon's Temple. *BA* 14:2–24.

Garbini, G.
1981   Le fonti citate nel "Libro dei Re." *Hen* 3:26–46.

Garfinkel, S.
1987   Of Thistles and Thorns: A New Approach to Ezekiel II 6. *VT* 37:426–37.
Ginsberg, H. L.
1967   The Omrid-Davidid Alliance and Its Consequences. Pages 91–93 in *Papers*. Volume 1 of *Proceedings of the Fourth World Congress of Jewish Studies*. Jerusalem: World Union of Jewish Studies.
Ginsburg, C. D.
1966   *Introduction to the Massoretico-Critical Edition of the Hebrew Bible*. New York: Ktav. [Reprint of 1897 ed.]
Ginzberg, L.
1928   *The Legends of the Jews*. 6 vols. Philadelphia: Jewish Publication Society.
Gitin, S., T. Dothan, and J. Naveh
1997   A Royal Dedicatory Inscription from Ekron. *IEJ* 47:1–16.
Glatt, D. A.
1993   *Chronological Displacement in Biblical and Related Literatures*. SBLDS 139. Atlanta: Scholars Press.
Glueck, N.
1965   Ezion-geber. *BA* 28:7–87.
1967   *Ḥesed in the Bible*. Cincinnati: Hebrew Union College Press.
Goldwasser, J.
1949   Siamun's Campaign in Palestine. *BJPES* 14:82–84.
Good, R. M.
1979   The Israelite Royal Steward in the Light of Ugaritic ʿl bt. *RB* 86:580–82.
Goodfriend, E. A.
1992   Prostitution. Pages 505–10 in vol. 5 of *ABD*.
Gooding, D.W.
1965a   Pedantic Timetabling in the 3rd Book of Reigns. *VT* 15:153–66.
1965b   The Septuagint's Version of Solomon's Misconduct. *VT* 15:325–35.
1967a   Temple Specifications: A Dispute in Logical Arrangement between the MT and the LXX. *VT* 17:143–72.
1967b   The Septuagint's Rival Versions of Jeroboam's Rise to Power. *VT* 17:173–89.
1968   The Shimei Duplicate and Its Satellite Miscellanies in 3 Reigns ii. *JSS* 13:76–92.
1969a   Problems of Text and Midrash in the Third Book of Reigns. *Textus* 7:1–29.
1969b   Text Sequence and Translation-Revision in 3 Reigns IX,10–X,13. *VT* 19:448–63.
1970   Review of Shenkel 1968. *JTS* 21:118–31.
1976   *Relics of Ancient Exegesis: A Study of the Miscellanies in 3 Reigns 2*. SOTSMS 4. Cambridge: Cambridge University Press.
Gordon, R. P.
1995   A House Divided: Wisdom in the Old Testament Narrative Traditions. Pages 94–105 in *Wisdom in Ancient Israel. Essays in Honour of J. A. Emerton*. Edited by J. Day, R. P. Gordon, and H. G. M. Williamson. Cambridge: Cambridge University Press.
Görg, M.
1974   Die Gattung des sogennanten Tempelweihspruch (1 Kgs 8:12f). *UF* 6:55–63.

Grayson, A. K.
  1976   Studies in Neo-Assyrian History: The Ninth Century B.C. *BiOr* 33:134–45.
  1996   *Assyrian Rulers of the Early First Millenium BC II (858–745 BC)*. RIMA 3. Toronto: University of Toronto Press.
Grdseloff, B.
  1947   Édóm, d'après les sources égyptiennes. *RHJE* 1:69–100.
Green, A. R.
  1978   Solomon and Siamun: A Synchronism between Dynastic Israel and the Twenty-First Dynasty of Egypt. *JBL* 97:353–67.
  1979   Israelite Influence at Shishak's Court. *BASOR* 233:59–62.
  1983   David's Relations with Hiram: Biblical and Josephan Evidence for Tyrian Chronology. Pages 373–97 in *The Word of the Lord Shall Go Forth: Essays in Honor of David Noel Freedman in Celebration of His Sixtieth Birthday*. Edited by C. L. Meyers and M. O'Connor. Philadelphia: American Schools of Oriental Research / Winona Lake, Ind.: Eisenbrauns.
Greenberg, M.
  1956   The Stabilization of the Text of the Hebrew Bible. *JAOS* 76:157–67. [= Greenberg 1995, 191–208]
  1957   The Hebrew Oath Particle ḤAY/ḤĒ. *JBL* 76:34–39.
  1978   The Use of the Ancient Versions for Interpreting the Hebrew Text. Pages 131–48 in *Congress Volume: Göttingen, 1977*. VTSup 29. Leiden: Brill. [= Greenberg 1995, 209–25]
  1981   You Turned Their Hearts Backward (1 Kgs 18:37). Pages 52–66 in *Studies in Aggadah, Targum and Jewish Liturgy in Memory of Joseph Heinemann*. Edited by E. Fleisher and J. J. Petuchowski. Jerusalem: Magnes and Hebrew Union College. [Hebrew]
  1983a   *Biblical Prose Prayer*. Berkeley: University of California Press.
  1983b   *Ezekiel 1–20*. AB 22. Garden City, N.Y.: Doubleday.
  1994   Hittite Royal Prayers and Biblical Petitionary Psalms. Pages 15–27 in *Neue Wege der Psalmenforschung*. Edited by K. Seybold and E. Zenger. Freiburg: Herder.
  1995   *Studies in the Bible and Jewish Thought*. Philadelphia: Jewish Publication Society.
  1997   *Ezekiel 21–37*. AB 22A. Garden City, N.Y.: Doubleday.
Greenfield, J. C.
  1962   Cherethites and Pelethites. Page 557 in vol. 1 of *IDB*.
  1967   Ugaritic Lexicographical Notes. *JCS* 21:89–93.
  1977   *Našû-nadānu* and Its Congeners. Pages 87–91 in *Essays on the Ancient Near East: Studies in Memory of Jacob Joel Finkelstein*. Edited by M. de Jong Ellis. Memoirs of the Connecticut Academy of Arts and Sciences 19. Hamden, Conn.: Archon.
Greenfield, J. C., and M. Mayerhoffer
  1967   The ʾAlgummim/ʾAlmuggim Problem Reexamined. Pages 83–89 in *Hebräische Wortforschung (Fs. W. Baumgarten)*. VTSup 16. Leiden: Brill.
Gressmann, H.
  1907   Das Salomonische Urteil. *Deutsche Rundschau* 130:212–38.
Gruber, M. I.
  1980   *Aspects of Nonverbal Communication in the Ancient Near East*. Studia Pohl: Dissertationes 12. 2 vols. Rome: Pontifical Biblical Institute.

1983   The *qādēš* in the Book of Kings and Other Sources. *Tarbiz* 52:167–76.
1987   Hebrew *daʻăbôn nepeš* 'Dryness of Throat': From Symptom to Literary
            Convention. *VT* 37:365–69.

Gunkel, H.
1906   *Elias, Jahve und Baal.* Tübingen: Mohr.

Gunn, D. M.
1978   *The Story of King David.* JSOTSup 6. Sheffield: JSOT Press.

Gutmann, J., editor
1976   *The Temple of Solomon: Archaeological Fact and Medieval Tradition in
            Christian, Islamic and Jewish Art.* AAR and SBL, Religion and the Arts 3.
            Missoula, Mont.: Scholars Press.

Haak, R. D.
1983   The "Shoulder" of the Temple. *VT* 33:271–78.

Hallo, W. W.
1988   The Nabonassar Era and Other Epochs in Mesopotamian Chronology and
            Chronography. Pages 175–90 in *A Scientific Humanist: Studies in Memory
            of Abraham Sachs.* Edited by E. Leichty, M. de J. Ellis, and P. Gerardi.
            Occasional Publications of the Samuel Noah Kramer Fund 9. Philadel-
            phia: University Museum.

Halpern, B.
1974   Sectionalism and the Schism. *JBL* 93:519–32.

Halpern, B., and D. S. Vanderhooft
1991   The Editions of Kings in the 7th–6th Centuries B.C.E. *HUCA* 62:179–244.

Hammond, G.
1987   English Translations of the Bible. Pages 647–66 in *The Literary Guide to
            the Bible.* Edited by R. Alter and F. Kermode. Cambridge: Harvard Univer-
            sity Press.

Haran, M.
1959   The Ark and the Cherubim: Their Symbolic Significance in Biblical
            Ritual. *IEJ* 9:30–38, 89–94.
1978   *Temples and Temple-Service in Ancient Israel.* Oxford: Oxford University
            Press. [Reprinted, Winona Lake, Ind.: Eisenbrauns, 1985]
1984   *Ezekiel.* Volume 12 of *Encyclopaedia Olam Ha-Tanakh.* Ramat Gan: Revi-
            vim. [Hebrew]
1988   On the Diffusion of Literacy and Schools in Ancient Israel. Pages 81–95
            in *Congress Volume: Jerusalem, 1986.* VTSup 40. Leiden: Brill.
1999   The Books of the Chronicles "of the Kings of Judah" and "of the Kings of
            Israel": What Sort of Books Were They? *VT* 49:156–64.

Hareuveni, E.
1929   Studies in the Names of the Plants of the Land of Israel. *Leš* 2:176–83.

Harris, R.
1990   Images of Women in the Gilgamesh Epic. Pages 219–30 in *Lingering over
            Words: Fs. Moran.* Edited by T. Abusch, J. Huehnergard, and P. Steinkeller.
            HSS 37. Atlanta, Ga.: Scholars Press.

Harris, Z. S.
1936   *A Grammar of the Phoenician Language.* AOS 8. New Haven, Conn.: Amer-
            ican Oriental Society.

Hauptmann, A., et al.
  1992   Early Copper Produced at Feinan, Wadi Arabah, Jordan: The Composition
            of the Ores and Copper. *Archaeomaterials* 6:1–33.
Hayes, J. H., and J. M. Miller, editors
  1977   *Israelite and Judaean History*. London: SCM.
Heaton, E. W.
  1974   *Solomon's New Men: The Emergence of Ancient Israel as a National State*.
            London: Thames & Hudson.
Held, M.
  1965   Studies in Comparative Semitic Lexicography. Pages 395–406 in *Studies
            in Honor of Benno Landsberger on His Seventy-Fifth Birthday*. AS 16. Chi-
            cago: University of Chicago Press.
  1968   The Root *zbl/sbl* in Akkadian, Ugaritic and Biblical Hebrew. *JAOS* 88:90–96.
  1985   Marginal Notes to the Biblical Lexicon. Pages 93–103 in *Biblical and
            Related Studies Presented to Samuel Iwry*. Edited by A. Kort and S. Mor-
            schauser. Winona Lake, Ind.: Eisenbrauns.
Heltzer, M.
  1987   The Neo-Assyrian *šakintu* and the Biblical *sokenet* (I Reg. 1,4). Pages 87–90
            in *La femme dans le proche-orient antique*. Paris: Éditions recherche sur
            les civilisations.
Hentschel, G.
  1977   *Die Elijah-Erzahlungen*. Leipzig: St. Benno.
Herrmann, S.
  1953–54   Die Königsnovelle in Ägypten und Israel: Ein Beitrag zur Gattungs-
            geschichte in den Geschichtsbüchern des Alten Testaments. *Wissen-
            schaftliche Zeitschrift der Karl Marx Universität, Leipzig* 3:33–44. [E.T.:
            The Royal Novella in Egypt and Israel: A Contribution to the History of
            Genre in the Historical Books of the Old Testament. Pages 493–515 in
            *Reconsidering Israel and Judah: Recent Studies on the Deuteronomistic
            History*. Sources for Biblical and Theological Study 8. Winona Lake, Ind.:
            Eisenbrauns, 2000]
  1964   Operationen Pharao Schoschenks I. im östlichen Ephraim. *ZDPV*
            80:55–79.
Hess, R. S.
  1996   A Typology of West Semitic Place Name Lists with Special Reference to
            Joshua 13–21. *BA* 59:160–70.
  1997   The Form and Structure of the Solomonic District List in 1 KINGS 4:7–19.
            Pages 279–92 in *Crossing Borders and Linking Horizons: Studies in Honor
            of Michael C. Astour on His Eightieth Birthday*. Edited by G. D. Young,
            M. W. Chavalas, and R. E. Averbeck. Bethesda, Md.: CDL.
Hillers, D. R.
  1964   *Treaty-Curses and the Old Testament Prophets*. Rome: Pontifical Biblical
            Institute.
Hoenig, S. B.
  1979   Tarshish. *JQR* 69:181–82.
Hoftijzer, J.
  1989   Philological Notes on I Kings xi 14. *OtSt* 25:29–37.

Holder, J.
1988   The Presuppositions, Accusations, and Threats of 1 Kings 14:1–18. *JBL* 107:27–38.

Honeyman, A. M.
1944   Some Developments of the Semitic Root *'by. JAOS* 64:81–82.

Horowitz, W.
1998   *Mesopotamian Cosmic Geography.* Mesopotamian Civilizations 8. Winona Lake, Ind.: Eisenbrauns.

Hrouda, B.
1972–75   "Ḫilāni, bīt." Pages 406–9 in vol. 4 of *RlA*.

Hughes, G. R., editor
1954   *Reliefs and Inscriptions at Karnak III: The Bubastite Portal.* Chicago: University of Chicago Press.

Hughes, J.
1990   *Secrets of the Times: Myth and History in Biblical Chronology.* JSOTSup 66. Sheffield: Sheffield Academic Press.

Hulse, E. V.
1971   Joshua's Curse and the Abandonment of Ancient Jericho: Schistosomiasis as a Possible Medical Explanation. *Medical History* 15:376–86.

Hurowitz, V. A.
1992   *I Have Built You an Exalted House: Temple Building in the Bible in Light of Mesopotamian and Northwest Semitic Writings.* JSOTSup 115. Sheffield: Sheffield Academic Press.
1994   Inside Solomon's Temple. *Bible Review* 10:24–37, 50.
1995a   Solomon's Golden Vessels (I Kings 7:48–50) and the Cult of the First Temple. Pages 151–64 in *Pomegranates and Golden Bells: Studies in Biblical, Jewish, and Near Eastern Ritual, Law, and Literature in Honor of Jacob Milgrom.* Edited by D. P. Wright, D. N. Freedman, and A. Hurvitz. Winona Lake, Ind.: Eisenbrauns.
1995b   The Form and the Fate of the Tabernacle: Reflections on a Recent Proposal. *JQR* 86:127–51.
1998   Ascending the Mountain of the Lord: A Glimpse into the Solomonic Temple. Pages 215–23 in *Capital Cities: Urban Planning and Spiritual Dimensions. Proceedings of the Symposium Held on May 27–29, 1996, Jerusalem, Israel—Bible Lands Museum Jerusalem.* Edited by Joan Goodnick Westenholz. Publications no. 2. Jerusalem: Bible Lands Museum.

Hurvitz, A.
1970   Linguistic Observations on the Biblical Usage of the Priestly Term עדה. *Tarbiz* 40:261–67.
1982   *A Linguistic Study of the Relationship between the Priestly Source and the Book of Ezekiel.* CahRB 20. Paris: Gabalda.

Ibn-Janah, J.
1896   *Sepher Haschoraschim: Wurzelwörterbuch der hebräischen Sprache von Abulwalîd Merwân Ibn Gnâh, aus dem Arabischen in's Hebräische übersetzt von Jehuda Ibn Tibbon.* Edited by W. Bacher. Berlin: Itzkowski.
1964   *Sēper Hā-riqmâ.* Edited by M. Wilensky. Jerusalem: Academy of the Hebrew Language.

Ikeda, Y.
1982   Solomon's Trade In Horses and Chariots in Its International Setting. Pages
            215–38 in *Studies in the Period of David and Solomon and Other Essays.*
            Edited by T. Ishida. Winona Lake, Ind.: Eisenbrauns.
1991   King Solomon and His Red Sea Trade. Pages 113–32 in *Near Eastern
            Studies: Dedicated to H.I.H. Prince Takahito Mikasa on the Occasion of His
            Seventy-Fifth Birthday.* Edited by M. Mori, H. Ogawa, and M. Yoshikawa.
            Wiesbaden: Harrassowitz.

Ishida, T.
1977   *The Royal Dynasties in Ancient Israel.* BZAW 142. Berlin: de Gruyter.
1982   Solomon's Succession to the Throne of David: A Political Analysis. Pages
            175–87 in *Studies in the Period of David and Solomon and Other Essays.*
            Edited by T. Ishida. Winona Lake, Ind.: Eisenbrauns. [Revised version,
            Ishida 1999, 102–36]
1985   "Solomon Who Is Greater Than David": Solomon's Succession in 1 Kings
            I–II in the Light of the Inscription of Kilamua, King of YUɔDY-Samɔal.
            Pages 145–53 in *Congress Volume: Salamanca, 1983.* Edited by J. A. Emer-
            ton. VTSup 36. Leiden: Brill. [Revised version, Ishida 1999, 166–74]
1987   Adonijah the Son of Haggith and His Supporters: An Inquiry into Prob-
            lems about History and Historiography. Pages 165–87 in *The Future of
            Biblical Studies: The Hebrew Scriptures.* Edited by R. E. Friedman and
            H. G. M. Williamson. Atlanta, Ga.: Scholars Press. [Revised version, Ishida
            1999, 102–36]
1991   The Succession Narrative and Esarhaddon's Apology: A Comparison.
            Pages 166–73 in *Ah Assyria . . . : Studies in Assyrian History and Ancient
            near Eastern Historiography Presented to Hayim Tadmor.* Edited by
            M. Cogan and I. Ephʿal. ScrHier 33. Jerusalem: Magnes. [Revised version,
            Ishida 1999, 175–85]
1993   The Story of Abner's Murder: A Problem Posed by the Solomonic Apolo-
            gist. *ErIsr* 24 (Malamat Volume): 109*–13*. [Revised version, Ishida 1999,
            158–65]
1999   *History and Historical Writing in Ancient Israel: Studies in Biblical Histo-
            riography.* SHCANE 16. Leiden: Brill.

Japhet, S.
1993   *I and II Chronicles.* OTL. Philadelphia: Fortress.

Jepsen, A.
1956   *Die Quellen des Königsbuches.* 2d ed. Halle [Salle]: Max Niemeyer.
1964   Zur Chronologie der Könige von Israel und Juda. Pages 4–48 in *Unter-
            suchungen zur israelitisch-jüdischen Chronologie.* BZAW 88. Berlin: de
            Gruyter.
1971   Gottesmann und Prophet. Pages 171–82 in *Probleme biblischer Theologie.*
            Munich.

Joüon, P.
1923   *Grammaire de l'hébreu biblique.* Rome: Pontifical Biblical Institute.

Kalimi, I.
1990   The Land of Moriah, Mount Moriah, and the Site of Solomon's Temple
            in Biblical Historiography. *Harvard Theological Review* 83:345–62.
1995   The Contribution of the Literary Study of Chronicles to the Solution of
            Its Textual Problems. *Biblical Interpretation* 3:190–212.

Kallai, Z.
1960   *The Northern Boundaries of Judah*. Jerusalem: Magnes. [Hebrew]
1986   *Historical Geography of the Bible*. Jerusalem: Magnes / Leiden: Brill.
1987   Studies concerning Solomon's Districts. Pages 196–209 in *Studies in Bible in Memory of U. Cassuto*. Jerusalem: Magnes. [Hebrew]

Kapelrud, A. S.
1963   Temple Building, a Task for Gods and Kings. *Or* 32:56–62.

Katzenstein, H. J.
1960   The Royal Steward (*Asher ʿal ha-Bayith*). *IEJ* 10:149–54.
1997   *The History of Tyre*. 2d ed. Beer-sheva: Ben-Gurion University of the Negev.

Kaufmann, Y.
1957   The Stories concerning David and Solomon. *Molad* 15:97–102. [Hebrew] [= Kaufmann 1966, 169–79]
1960   *The Religion of Israel*. Chicago: University of Chicago Press.
1964   The Opening Stories concerning Solomon's Reign. Pages 87–93 in *Sefer M. H. Segal*. Jerusalem: Israel Bible Society. [Hebrew] [= Kaufmann 1966, 197–204]
1966   *From the Furnace of the Biblical Creation: Collected Essays*. Tel-Aviv: Dvir. [Hebrew]

Kenik, H. A.
1983   *Design for Kingship: The Deuteronomistic Narrative Technique in 1 Kings 3:4–15*. SBLDS 69. Chico, Calif.: Scholars Press.

Kenyon, K.
1971   *Royal Cities of the Old Testament*. New York: Shocken.

Keys, G.
1996   *The Wages of Sin: The Reappraisal of the "Succession Narrative."* JSOTSup 221. Sheffield: Sheffield Academic Press.

Kitchen, K. A.
1965   *Theological Students' Fellowship Bulletin*, no. 41:17.
1971   Punt and How to Get There. *Or* 40:184–207.
1973   *The Third Intermediate Period in Egypt (1100–650 BC)*. Warminster: Aris & Phillips.
1989   Two Notes on the Subsidiary Rooms of Solomon's Temple. *ErIsr* 20 (Yadin Volume): 107*–12*.

Klein, J.
1979   The Reading and Pronunciation of the Sumerian Word for 'Monkey'. *JCS* 31:149–60.

Knauf, E. A.
1997   Le Roi est mort, vive le Roi!: A Biblical Argument for the Historicity of Solomon. Pages 81–95 in *The Age of Solomon: Scholarship at the Turn of the Millennium*. Edited by L. W. Handy. SHCANE 11. Leiden: Brill.

Knoppers, G. N.
1993   *Two Nations under God: The Deuteronomistic History of Solomon and the Dual Monarchies*, vol. 1. HSM 52. Atlanta: Scholars Press.
1994   *Two Nations under God: The Deuteronomistic History of Solomon and the Dual Monarchies*, vol. 2. HSM 53. Atlanta: Scholars Press.

1995   Prayer and Propoganada: Solomon's Dedication of the Temple and the
          Deuteronomist's Program. *CBQ* 57:229–54.

Koch, K.
1978   Die mysteriosen Zahlen der judäischen Könige und die apokalyptischen
          Jahrwochen. *VT* 28:433–41.

Kochavi, M.
1989   The Identification of Zeredah, Home of Jeroboam Son of Nebat, King of
          Israel. *ErIsr* 20 (Yadin Volume): 198–201. [Hebrew]
1996   The Land of Geshur: History of a Region in the Biblical Period. *ErIsr* 25
          (Aviram Volume): 184–201. [Hebrew]
1998   The Ancient Road from the Bashan to the Mediterranean. Pages 25–47 in
          *From the Ancient Sites of Israel: Essays on Archaeology, History and The-
          ology in Memory of Aapeli Saarisalo (1896–1986)*. Edited by T. Eskola and
          E. Junkkaala. Helsinki: Theological Institute of Finland.

Koehler, L.
1937   Hebräische Vokabeln. *ZAW* 55:161–74.

Kogut, S.
1986   On the Meaning and Syntactical Status of *hnh* in Biblical Hebrew. Pages
          133–54 in *Studies in Bible*. Edited by S. Japhet. ScrHier 31. Jerusalem:
          Magnes.

Koopmans, W. T.
1991   The Testament of David in 1 Kings II 1–10. *VT* 41:429–49.

Kwasman, T.
1988   *Neo-Assyrian Legal Documents in the Koujunjik Collection of the British
          Museum*. Studia Pohl: Series Maior 14. Rome: Pontifical Biblical Institute.

Labuschagne, C. J.
1974   The *našû-nadānu* Formula and Its Biblical Equivalent. Pages 176–80 in
          *Travels in the World of the Old Testament: Studies Presented to Prof. M. A.
          Beek at the Occasion of His Sixty-Fifth Birthday*. Edited by H. van Voss,
          P. H. J. Houwink Ten Cate, and N. A. van Uchelen. Assen: Van Gorcum.

Lambert, W. G.
1960   *Babylonian Wisdom Literature*. Oxford: Clarendon. [Reprinted, Winona
          Lake, Ind.: Eisenbrauns, 1996]
1972–75   Himmel. Pages 411–12 in vol. 4 of *RlA*.

Lamon, R. S., and G. M. Shipton
1939   *Megiddo I*. Chicago: University of Chicago Press.

Lance, H. D.
1967   Gezer in the Land and in History. *BA* 30:34–47.
1976   Solomon, Siamun, and the Double Ax. Pages 209–23 in *Magnalia Dei:
          The Mighty Acts of God—Essays on the Bible and Archaeology in Memory
          of G. Ernest Wright*. Edited by F. M. Cross, W. E. Lemke, P. D. Miller.
          Garden City, N.Y.: Doubleday.

Landsberger, B.
1964   Einige unerkannt gebliebene oder verkannte Nomina des Akkadischen.
          WO 3:48–79.
1967   Akkadisch-hebräische Wortgleichungen. Pages 176–204 *Hebräische Wort-
          forschung (Fs. W. Baumgarten)*. VTSup 16. Leiden: Brill.

Langlamet, F.
1976   Pour ou contre Salomon?: La redaction prosalomienne de I Rois I–II. *RB* 83:321–79, 481–529.

Lasine, S.
1989   The Riddle of Solomon's Judgment and the Riddle of Human Nature in The Hebrew Bible. *JSOT* 45:61–86.

Lassner, J.
1993   *Demonizing the Queen of Sheba.* Chicago: University of Chicago Press.

Leibowitz, E., and G. Leibowitz
1989–90 Solomon's Judgment. *Beth Mikra* 35:242–44.

Lemaire, A.
1988   Hadad l'Édomite ou Hadad l'Araméen? *Biblische Notizen* 43:14–18.
1991   Hazel de Damas, roi d'Aram. Pages 91–108 in *Marchands, diplomates et empereurs: Études sur la civilisation mesopotamiene offertes à Paul Garelli.* Edited by D. Charpin and F. Joannes. Paris: Éditions Recherche sur les Civilisations.
1992   Writing and Writing Materials. Pages 999–1008 in vol. 6 of *ABD.*
1995   Wisdom in Solomonic Historiography. Pages 106–18 in *Wisdom in Ancient Israel: Essays in Honour of J. A. Emerton.* Edited by J. Day, R. P. Gordon, and H. G. M. Williamson. Cambridge: Cambridge University Press.
2000   Tarshish-Tarsisi: Problème de topographie historique biblique et assyrienne. Pages 44–62 in *Studies in Historical and Geography and Biblical Historiography Presented to Zecharia Kallai.* VTSup 81. Leiden: Brill.

Lemke, W. E.
1976   The Way of Obedience: I Kings 13 and the Structure of the Deuteronomistic History. Pages 301–26 in *Magnalia Dei: The Mighty Acts of God—Essays on the Bible and Archaeology in Memory of G. Ernest Wright.* Edited by F. M. Cross, W. E. Lemke, P. D. Miller. Garden City, N.Y.: Doubleday.

Levenson, J. D.
1981   From Temple to Synagogue: 1 Kings 8. Pages 143–66 in *Traditions in Transformation: Turning Points in Biblical Faith.* Edited by B. Halpern and J. D. Levenson. Winona Lake, Ind.: Eisenbrauns.

Lewis, D. M.
1987   The King's Dinner (Polyaenus IV 3,32). Pages 79–87 in *Achaemenid History II: The Greek Sources.* Edited by H. Sarcisi-Weerdenburg and A. Kuhrt. Leiden: Nederlands Institut voor het Nabije Oosten.

Lewis, T. J.
1992a   Belial. Pages 654–56 in vol. 1 of *ABD.*
1992b   Dead, Abode of the. Pages 100–105 in vol. 2 of *ABD.*

Lewy, J.
1927   *Die Chronologie der Könige von Israel und Juda.* Giessen: Alfred Töpelmann.

Licht, J.
1978   *Storytelling in the Bible.* Jerusalem: Magnes.

Lie, A. G.
1929   *The Inscriptions of Sargon II, King of Assyria.* Paris: Geuthner.

Lieberman, S.
1950   *Hellenism in Jewish Palestine*. New York: Jewish Theological Seminary.
Limor, O.
1988   The Grave of David on Mt. Zion: The Sources of the Tradition. Pages 11–
        23 in *Jews, Samaritans and Christians in Byzantine Palestine*. Edited by
        D. Jacobi and Y. Tsafrir. Jerusalem: Ben-Zvi Institute. [Hebrew]
Lingen, A. van der
1992   Bw'-yṣ' ("To Go Out and To Come In") as a Military Term. *VT* 42:59–66.
Lipiński, E.
1969   Le Ben-hadad II de la Bible et l'histoire. Pages 157–73 in *The Ancient
        Near East as Related to the Bible and the Holy Land*. . . . Volume 1 of *Pro-
        ceedings of the Fifth World Congress of Jewish Studies*. Jerusalem: World
        Union of Jewish Studies.
1974   Le recit de 1 rois xii 1–19 à la lumière de l'ancien usage de l'Hébreu et de
        nouveaux textes de Mari. *VT* 24 :430–37.

Liver, J.
1953   The Chronology of Tyre at the Beginning of the First Millennium B.C.
        IEJ 3:113–20.
1967   The Book of the Acts of Solomon. *Bib* 48:75–101.
1968a   נגיד. Pages 753–55 in vol. 5 of *EncMiqr*.
1968b   נשיא. Pages 981–82 in vol. 5 of *EncMiqr*.
1971   עלי, בני עלי. Pages 231–33 in vol. 6 of *EncMiqr*.
1979   קהל. Pages 66–70 in vol. 7 of *EncMiqr*.
Liverani, M.
1990   *Prestige and Interest: International Relations in the Near East ca. 1600–
        1100 B.C.* Padua: Sargon srl.
Loewenstamm, S. E.
1956   Notes on the Alalakh Tablets. *IEJ* 6:217–25.
1962   מידה כנגד מידה. Pages 845–49 in vol. 4 of *EncMiqr*.
1969   The Lord is My Strength and My Glory. *VT* 19:464–70.
1986   נחלת ה׳. Pages 155–92 in *Studies in Bible*. Edited by S. Japhet. ScrHier 31.
        Jerusalem: Magnes
Long, B. O.
1983   The Form and Significance of 1 Kings 22:1–38. Pages 193–208 in vol. 3 of
        Isac Leo Seeligmann Volume. Edited by A. Rofé and Y. Zakovitch. Jerusa-
        lem: Rubinstein.
Loretz, O.
1974   Der Torso eines kanaanäisch-israelitischen Tempelweihespruches in 1 Kön
        8:12–13. *UF* 6:478–80.
Luckenbill, D. D.
1924   *The Annals of Sennacherib*. OIP 2. Chicago: University of Chicago Press.
Mach, R., and J. H. Marks
1960   The Head upon the Knees: A Note to I Kings 18:42. Pages 68–73 in *The
        World of Islam: Studies in Honour of Phillip K. Hitti*. Edited by J. Kritzeck
        and R. B. Winder. London: Macmillan.
Malamat, A.
1958   The Kingdom of David and Solomon in Its Contact with Egypt and Aram
        Naharaim. *BA* 21:96–102. [= *BARead* 2:89–98]

1963a   Aspects of the Foreign Policy of David and Solomon. *JNES* 22:1–17.
1963b   Kingship and Council in Israel and Sumer: A Parallel. *JNES* 22:247–53.
1965a   Origins of Statecraft in the Israelite Monarchy. *BA* 28:34–65. [= *BARead* 3:163–98]
1965b   Campaigns to the Mediterranean by Iahdunlin and Other Early Mesopotamian Rulers. Pages 365–73 in *Studies in Honor of Benno Landsberger on His Seventy-Fifth Birthday*. AS 16. Chicago: University of Chicago Press.
1973   The Aramaeans. Pages 134–55 in *Peoples of Old Testament Times*. Edited by D. J. Wiseman. Oxford: Oxford University Press.
1982   A Political Look at the Kingdom of David and Solomon and its Relations with Egypt. Pages 189–204 in *Studies in the Period of David and Solomon and Other Essays*. Edited by T. Ishida. Winona Lake, Ind.: Eisenbrauns.
1999   Naamah, the Ammonite Princess, King Solomon's Wife. *RB* 106:35–40.

Mallul, M.
1986   "Sissiktu" and "sikku": Their Meaning and Function. *BiOr* 43:20–36.

Manor, D. W.
1992   Timnaʿ (Place). Pages 553–56 in vol. 6 of *ABD*.

Mare, W. H.
1992   Serpent's Stone. Pages 116–17 in vol. 5 of *ABD*.

Martin, W. J.
1969   "Dischronologized" Narrative in the Old Testament. Pages 179–86 in *Congress Volume: Rome, 1968*. VTSup 17. Leiden: Brill.

Mazar, A.
1982   The "Bull Site": An Iron Age I Open Cult Site. *BASOR* 247:27–42.
1990   *Archaeology of the Land of the Bible, 10,000–586 B.C.E.* New York: Doubleday.

Mazar, B.
1944   Givath Elohim. *BJPES* 8:35–37. [= B. Mazar 1975, 80–83]
1946–47 King David's Scribe and the Officialdom of the United Monarchy of Israel. *BJPES* 13:105–14. [Hebrew] [E.T.: B. Mazar 1986, 126–38]
1950   The Excavations at Tell Qasîle. *IEJ* 1:194–218.
1957   Pharaoh Shishak's Campaign to the Land of Israel. Pages 57–76 in *Volume du Congress: Strasbourg, 1956*. VTSup 4. Leiden: Brill. [= B. Mazar 1986, 139–50]
1960a   The Cities of the Territory of Dan. *IEJ* 10:65–77.
1960b   The Cities of the Priests and the Levites. Pages 193–205 in *Congress Volume: Oxford, 1959*. VTSup 7. Leiden: Brill.
1962   The Aramean Empire and Its Relations with Israel. *BA* 25:97–120. [= *BARead* 2:127–51. Revised version, B. Mazar 1986, 151–72]
1964   The Military Elite of King David. Pages 248–67 in *ʿOz le-David*. Jerusalem: Israel Bible Society. [Hebrew] [= B. Mazar 1986, 83–103. Shortened English version: *VT* 13 (1963): 310–20]
1975a   *Cities and Districts in Eretz Israel*. Jerusalem: Mosad Bialik and Israel Exploration Society. [Hebrew]
1975b   *The Mountain of the Lord*. Garden City, N.Y.: Doubleday.
1986   *The Early Biblical Period: Historical Essays*. Jerusalem: Israel Exploration Society.
1989   The House of Omri. *ErIsr* 20 (Yadin Volume): 215–19. [Hebrew]

Mazar, E., and B. Mazar
　1989　　*Excavations in the South of the Temple Mount: The Ophel of Biblical Jeru-salem.* Qedem 29. Jerusalem: Israel Exploration Society.

Mazor, L.
　1988　　The Origin and Evolution of the Curse upon the Rebuilder of Jericho: A Contribution of Textual Criticism to Biblical Historiography. *Textus* 14:1–26.

McCarter, P. K.
　1980　　*I Samuel.* AB 8. Garden City, N.Y.: Doubleday.
　1984　　*II Samuel.* AB 9. Garden City, N.Y.: Doubleday.

McKane, W.
　1986　　*Jeremiah I–XXV.* ICC. Edinburgh: T. & T. Clark.

McKenzie, S. L.
　1985　　The Prophetic History and the Redaction of Kings. *HAR* 10:203–20.
　1991　　*The Trouble with Kings: The Composition of the Book of Kings in the Deuteronomistic History.* VTSup 42. Leiden: Brill.
　1992　　Deuteronomistic History. Pages 160–68 in vol. 2 of *ABD*.

Mendels, D.
　1987　　Hellenistic Writers of the Second Century B.C. on the Hiram-Solomon Relationship. *Studia Phoenicia* 5:429–41.

Mendelsohn, I.
　1962a　　On Corvée Labor in Ancient Canaan and Israel. *BASOR* 167:31–35.
　1962b　　Slavery in the OT. Pages 383–91 in vol. 4 of *IDB*.

Meshel, Z.
　1975　　On the Problem of Tell el-Halifa, Eilat and Ezion Geber. *ErIsr* 12 (Glueck Volume): 49–56. [Hebrew]

Mettinger, T. N. D.
　1971　　*Solomonic State Officials.* ConBOT 5. Lund: Gleerup.
　1995　　Cherubim. Pages 362–67 in *DDD*.

Meyers, C. L.
　1976　　*The Tabernacle Menorah.* ASORDS 2. Missoula, Mont.: Scholars Press.
　1983　　Jachin and Boaz in Religious and Political Perspective. *CBQ* 45:167–78.
　1992a　　Lampstand. Pages 141–43 in vol. 4 of *ABD*.
　1992b　　Temple, Jerusalem. Pages 350–68 in vol. 6 of *ABD*.

Milgrom, J.
　1970　　*Studies in Levitical Terminology, I.* Berkeley: University of California Press.
　1978　　Priestly Terminology and the Political and Social Structure of Pre-monarchic Israel. *JQR* 69:65–81.
　1990　　*Numbers.* The JPS Torah Commentary. Philadelphia: Jewish Publication Society.
　1991　　*Leviticus 1–16.* AB 3. New York: Doubleday.

Milik, J. T.
　1962　　Textes de la grotte 5Q. Pages 171–72 in *Les "petites grottes" de Qumrân.* Edited by M. Baillet, J. T. Milik, and R. de Vaux. DJD 3. Oxford: Clarendon.

Millard, A. R.
　1989a　　The Doorways of Solomon's Temple. *ErIsr* 20 (Yadin Volume): 135*–39*.

1989b   Does the Bible Exaggerate King's Solomon's Golden Wealth? *BAR* 15:20–34.

1991   Large Numbers in Assyrian Royal Inscriptions. Pages 213–22 in *Ah Assyria . . . : Studies in Assyrian History and Ancient Near Eastern Historiography Presented to Hayim Tadmor*. Edited by M. Cogan and I. Eph'al. ScrHier 33. Jerusalem: Magnes.

1994a   Story, History, and Theology. Pages 37–64 in *Faith, Tradition, and History: Old Testament Historiography in Its Near Eastern Context*. Edited by A. R. Millard, J. K. Hoffmeier, and D. W. Baker. Winona Lake, Ind.: Eisenbrauns.

1994b   *The Eponyms of the Assyrian Empire, 910–612 BC*. SAAS 2. Helsinki: Neo-Assyrian Text Corpus Project.

1994c   King Solomon's Shields. Pages 286–95 in *Scripture and Other Artifacts: Essays on the Bible and Archaeology in Honor of Philip J. King*. Edited by M. D. Coogan, J. C. Exum, and L. E. Stager. Louisville: Westminster and John Knox.

1997   King Solomon in His Ancient Context. Pages 30–53 *in The Age of Solomon: Scholarship at the Turn of the Millennium*. Edited by L. W. Handy. SHCANE 11. Leiden: Brill.

Millard, A. R., and P. Bordreuil
1982   A Statue from Syria with Assyrian and Aramaic Inscriptions. *BA* 45:135–41.

Miller, J. M.
1966   The Elisha Cycle and the Accounts of the Omride Wars. *JBL* 85:441–55.
1967   Another Look at the Chronology of the Early Divided Monarchy. *JBL* 86:276–88.
1968   "So Tibni Died" (1 Kings xvi.22). *VT* 18:392–94.
1969   The Rest of the Acts of Jehoahaz (I KINGS 20–22 1–38). *ZAW* 80:337–42.

Miller, J. M., and J. H. Hayes
1986   *A History of Ancient Israel and Judah*. Philadelphia: Westminster.

Milson, D.
1986   The Design of the Royal Gates at Megiddo, Hazor and Gezer. *ZDPV* 102:87–92.

Monson, J. H.
1996   Solomon's Temple and the Temple at 'Ain Dara. *Qadmoniot* 29:33–38. [Hebrew]

Montgomery, J. A.
1930   The Year-Eponymate in the Hebrew Monarchy. *JBL* 49:311–19.
1932   The Supplement at the End of 3 Kingdoms 2 (I Reg. 2). *ZAW* 50:124–29.

Moore, G. F.
1895   *Judges*. ICC. Edinburgh: T. & T. Clark.

Morag, S.
1983   The Yemenite Tradition of the Bible: The Transition Period. Pages 137–49 in *Estudios Masoréticos (V Congreso de la IOMS)*. Madrid: Textos y Estudios "Cardinal Cisneros."

Moran, W. L.
1963   The Ancient Near Eastern Background of the Love of God in Deuteronomy. *CBQ* 25:77–87.

Motzki, H.
1975   Ein Beitrag zum Problem des Stierkultes in der Religionsgeschichte Israels. *VT* 25:470–85.

Mowinckel, S.
1934   "The Spirit" and the "Word" in the Pre-exilic Reforming Prophets. *JBL* 53:199–227.
1962   Drive and/or Ride in O.T. *VT* 12:278–99.
1963   Israelite Historiography. *ASTI* 2:4–26.

Muhly, J. D.
1973   *Copper and Tin*. Pages 155–535 in Transactions of the Connecticut Academy of Arts and Sciences 43. Hamden, Conn.: Archon.

Muilenburg, J.
1961   The Linguistic and Rhetorical Usages of the Particle כי in the Old Testament. *HUCA* 32:135–60.

Mulder, M. J.
1972   Versuch zur Deutung von *sokenet* in 1. Kön I 2, 4. *VT* 22:43–54.
1989   Solomon's Temple and YHWH's Exclusivity. *OtSt* 25:49–62.

Mullen, E. T.
1992   Divine Assembly. Pages 214–17 in vol. 2 of *ABD*.

Munn-Rankin, J. M.
1956   Diplomacy in Western Asia in the Early Second Millennium B.C. *Iraq* 18:68–110.

Muraoka, T.
1985   *Emphatic Words and Structures in Biblical Hebrew*. Jerusalem: Magnes / Leiden: Brill.

Na'aman, N.
1986   *Borders and Districts in Biblical Historiography*. Jerusalem: Simor.
1992   Israel, Edom and Egypt in the 10th Century B.C.E. *Tel Aviv* 19:71–93.
1997a   Prophetic Stories as Sources for the Histories of Jehoshaphat and the Omrides. *Bib* 78:153–73.
1997b   Sources and Composition in the History of Solomon. Pages 57–80 in *The Age of Solomon: Scholarship at the Turn of the Millennium*. Edited by L. W. Handy. SHCANE 11. Leiden: Brill.
1998   Shishak's Campaign to Palestine as Reflected by the Epigraphic, Biblical and Archaeological Evidence. *Zion* 63:247–76.

Napier, B. D.
1959   The Omrides of Jezreel. *VT* 9:366–78.

Naveh, J.
1990   Nameless People. *IEJ* 40:108–23.

Nelson, H. N.
1944   The Significance of the Temple in the Ancient Near East: The Egyptian Temple. *BA* 7:44–53. [= *BARead* 1:147–57]

Nelson, R. D.
1981   *The Double Redaction of the Deuteronomistic History*. JSOTSup 18. Sheffield: Sheffield Academic Press.
1991   The Role of the Priesthood in the Deuteronomistic History. Pages 132–47 in *Congress Volume: Leuven, 1989*. Edited by J. A. Emerton. VTSup 43. Leiden: Brill.

Neufield, E.
1978   Apiculture in Ancient Palestine (Early and Middle Iron Age) within the Framework of the Ancient Near East. *UF* 10:219–47.

Norin, S.
1988   The Age of the Siloam Inscription and Hezekiah's Tunnel. *VT* 48:37–48.

North, R.
1967   Ophir/Parvaim and Petra/Jotheel. Pages 197–202 in *Papers*. Volume 1 of *Proceedings of the Fourth World Congress of Jewish Studies*. Jerusalem: World Union of Jewish Studies.

Noth, M.
1928   *Die Israelitischen Personennamen im Rahmen der Gemeinsemitischen Namengebung*. BWANT 3/10. Stuttgart: Kohlhammer.
1938   Die Wege der Pharaonenheere in Palästina und Syrien, IV: Schoschenkliste. *ZDPV* 61:277–304.
1960   *The History of Israel*. Rev. ed. New York: Harper.
1981   *The Deuteronomistic History*. JSOTSup 15. Sheffield: JSOT Press.

Obbink, H. T.
1929   Jahwebilder. *ZAW* 47:264–74.

O'Brien, Mark A.
1989   *The Deuteronomistic History Hypothesis: A Reassessment*. OBO 92. Freiburg: Universitäts Verlag / Göttingen: Vandenhoeck & Ruprecht.

Olmstead, A. T.
1913   Source Study and the Biblical Text. *AJSL* 30:1–35.
1915   The Oldest Book of Kings. *AJSL* 31:169–214.

Olyan, S. M.
1982   Zadok's Origins and the Tribal Politics of David. *JBL* 101:177–93.

Oppenheim, A. L.
1941   Idiomatic Akkadian. *JAOS* 61:251–71.
1944   The Significance of the Temple in the Ancient Near East: The Mesopotamian Temple. *BA* 7:54–63. [= *BARead* 1:158–68]
1954–56   Sumerian: inim.gar; Akk: *egirru* = Greek: *kledon*. *AfO* 17:49–55.
1956   *The Interpretation of Dreams in the Ancient Near East*. TAPS 46/3. Philadelphia: American Philosophical Society.

Orlinsky, H. M.
1940   On the Commonly Proposed *LEK W[E]NA'ABOR* of I Kings 18 5. *JBL* 59:515–17.
1969   *Notes on the New Translation of the Torah*. Philadelphia: Jewish Publication Society.

Orni, E., and E. Efrat
1980   *Geography of Israel*. 4th ed. Jerusalem: Israel Universities Press.

Ottosson, M.
1969   *Gilead: Tradition and History*. ConBOT 3. Lund: Gleerup.

Ouellette, J.
1969   Le vestibule du Temple de Salomon: Était-il un Bīt Ḫilani? *RB* 76:365–78.
1972   The *Yaṣia'* and the *Ṣ[e]la'ot*: Two Mysterious Structures in Solomon's Temple. *JNES* 31:187–91.

1976   The Basic Structure of Solomon's Temple and Archaeological Research. Pages 1–20 in *The Temple of Solomon: Archaeological Fact and Medieval Tradition in Christian, Islamic and Jewish Art*. Edited by J. Gutmann. AAR and SBL, Religion and the Arts 3. Missoula, Mont.: Scholars Press.

Paran, M.
1989   *Forms of the Priestly Style in the Pentateuch*. Jerusalem: Magnes. [Hebrew]

Parker, K. I.
1988   Repetition as a Structuring Device in 1 Kings 1–11. *JSOT* 42:19–27.

Parpola, S.
1970   *Neo-Assyrian Toponyms*. Kevelaer: Butzon & Bercker / Neukirchen-Vluyn: Neukirchener Verlag.
1983   *Letters from Assyrian Scholars to the Kings Esarhaddon and Assurbanipal*. AOAT 5/2. Neukirchen-Vluyn: Neukirchener Verlag.

Patai, R.
1939   The "Control of Rain" in Ancient Palestine. *HUCA* 14:251–86.

Patrich, J.
1986   The *Messibah* of the Temple according to the Tractate *Middot*. *IEJ* 36:215–33.

Paul, S.
1991   *Amos*. Hermeneia. Minneapolis: Fortress.

Pintore, F.
1970   I dodici intendenti di Salomone. *RSO* 45:177–207.

Pitard, W. T.
1987   *Ancient Damascus: A Historical Study of the Syrian City-State from Earliest Times until Its Fall to the Assyrians in 732 B.C.E.* Winona Lake, Ind.: Eisenbrauns.

Plein, I.
1966   Erwägungen zur Überlieferung von I Reg 11:26–14:20. *ZAW* 78:8–24.

Pope, M. H.
1962   Oaths. Pages 575–77 in vol. 3 of *IDB*.
1977   *Song of Songs*. AB 7C. Garden City, N.Y.: Doubleday.

Porten, B.
1967   The Structure and Theme of the Solomon Narrative (I Kings 3–11). *HUCA* 38:93–128.

Porter, J.
1981   *Bny hnby'ym*. *JTS* 32:423–29.

Postgate, J. N.
1969   *Neo-Assyrian Royal Grants and Decrees*. Studia Pohl: Series Maior 1. Rome: Pontifical Biblical Institute.
1974   *Taxation and Conscription in the Assyrian Empire*. Studia Pohl: Series Maior 3. Rome: Pontifical Biblical Institute.

Powell, M. A.
1992   Weights and Measurements. Pages 897–908 in vol. 6 of *ABD*.

Pratico, G. D.
1986   A Re-appraisal of the Site Archaeologist Nelson Glueck Identified as King Solomon's Red Sea Port. *BAR* 12:24–35.

Pritchard, J. B.
1974   *Solomon and Sheba*. London: Phaidon.
1978   *Recovering Sarepta, a Phoenician City*. Princeton: Princeton University Press.

Provan, I. W.
1988   *Hezekiah and the Book of Kings*. BZAW 172. Berlin: de Gruyter.

Qimron, E.
1974   *Lwl* and *blwl*. *Leš* 38:225–27.

Raban, A.
1998   Near Eastern Harbors: Thirteenth–Seventh Centuries BCE. Pages 428–38 in *Mediterranean Peoples in Transition*. Edited by S. Gitin, A. Mazar, and E. Stern. Jerusalem: Israel Exploration Society.

Rabin, C
1982a   שׁוֹר. Page 387 in vol. 8 of *EncMiqr*.
1982b   תוכיים. Pages 464–65 in vol. 8 of *EncMiqr*.

Rabinowitz, I.
1984   ʾAZ Followed by Imperfect Verb-Form in Preterite Contexts: A Redactional Device in Biblical Hebrew. *VT* 34:53–62.

Rad, G. von
1953   *Studies in Deuteronomy*. SBT 9. London: SCM.
1962   *Old Testament Theology*, vol. 1. New York: Harper & Row.
1965   *Old Testament Theology*, vol. 2. New York: Harper & Row.
1966a   The Beginnings of Historical Writing in Ancient Israel. Pages 166–204 in *The Problem of the Hexateuch and Other Essays*. New York: McGraw-Hill.
1966b   The Deuteronomic Theology of History in *I* and *II Kings*. Pages 205–21 in *The Problem of the Hexateuch and Other Essays*. New York: McGraw-Hill.

Rainey, A. F.
1962   Administration in Ugarit and the Samaria Ostraca. *IEJ* 12:62–63.
1969   The Satrapy "Beyond the River." *AJBA* 1:51–78.
1970   Compulsory Labor Gangs in Ancient Israel. *IEJ* 20:191–202.
1971   שׁישׁק. Pages 655–56 in vol. 6 of *EncMiqr*.
1975a   Notes on Some Proto-Sinaitic Inscriptions. *IEJ* 25:106–16.
1975b   Institutions: Family, Civil and Military. Pages 69–107 in *Ras Shamra Parallels*, vol. 2. Edited by L. R. Fisher. AnOr 50. Rome: Pontifical Biblical Institute.
1987–89   Tell Gerisa and the Territory of the Tribe of Dan. Pages 59–72 in *Israel: People and Land*, 5–6. Tel-Aviv: Land of Israel Museum. [Hebrew]

Redford, D. B.
1972   Studies in Relations between Palestine and Egypt during the First Millennium B.C. Pages 141–56 in *Studies in the Ancient Palestinian World*. Edited by J. W. Wevers and D. B. Redford. Toronto: University of Toronto Press.
1973   Studies in Relations between Palestine and Egypt during the First Millennium B.C., II: The Twenty-Second Dynasty. *JAOS* 93:3–17.
1992   *Egypt, Canaan, and Israel in Ancient Times*. Princeton: Princeton University Press.

Reider, J.
1952–53   Contributions to the Scriptural Text. *HUCA* 24:85–106.

Reif, S.
1972   Dedicated to *hnk*. *VT* 22:495–501.

Reis, P. T.
1994   Vindicating God: Another Look at 1 Kings XIII. *VT* 44:376–86.

Revell, E. J.
1993   Language and Interpretation in 1 Kings 20. Pages 103–13 in *The Frank Talmage Memorial Volume 1*. Edited by B. Walfish. Haifa: Haifa University Press.

Reviv, H.
1989a   Jeroboam's Rule over His Kingdom. *Shnaton* 10:169–78.
1989b   *The Elders in Ancient Israel*. Jerusalem: Magnes.
1993   *The Society in the Kingdoms of Israel and Judah*. Jerusalem: Mosad Bialik. [Hebrew]

Roberts, J. J. M.
1970   A New Parallel to I Kings 18:28–29. *JBL* 89:76–77.

Robinson, H. P.
1991   Elijah at Horeb, 1 Kings 19:1–18: A Coherent Narrative? *RB* 98:513–36.

Roesel, H. N.
1984   Zu den "Gauen" Salomons. *ZDPV* 100:84–90.

Rofé, A.
1988a   *The Prophetical Stories*. Jerusalem: Magnes.
1988b   The Vineyard of Naboth: The Origin and Message of the Story. *VT* 38:89–104.
1991   Ephraimite versus Deuteronomistic History. Pages 221–35 in *Storia e tradizioni di Israele: Scritti in onore di J. Alberto Soggin*. Edited by D. Garrone and F. Israel. Brescia: Paideia.

Rogerson, J., and P. Davies
1996   Was the Siloam Tunnel Built by Hezekiah? *BA* 59:138–49.

Röllig, W.
1980–83   "*Laba'um*." Page 410 in vol. 6 of *RlA*.

Rosenberg, R.
1982   The Concept of Biblical "Belial." Pages 35–40 in *Division A: The Period of the Bible* of *Proceedings of the Eighth World Congress of Jewish Studies*. Jerusalem: World Union of Jewish Studies.

Rost, L.
1926   *Die Überlieferung von der Thronfolge Davids*. BWANT 3/6. Stuttgart: Kohlhammer. [E.T.: *The Succession to the Throne of David*. Sheffield: Almond, 1982]

Roth, W.
1982   The Story of the Prophet Micaiah (1 Kings 22) in Historical-Critical Interpretation,1876–1976. Pages 105–37 in *The Biblical Mosaic*. Edited by R. M. Polzin and E. Rothman. Philadelphia: Fortress / Chico, Calif.: Scholars Press.

Rothenberg, B.
1962   Tell el-Kheleifeh: Ezion-geber—Eilath. *PEQ* 94:44–56.
1970   An Archeological Survey of South Sinai: First Season, 1967/68—Preliminary Report. *PEQ* 102:4–29.

Rupprecht, K.
1977   *Der Tempel von Jerusalem.* BZAW 144. Berlin: de Gruyter.
Safran, J.
1985   Ahuzath and the Pact of Beer-Sheba. *Beer-sheva* 2:121–30. [Hebrew]
Saggs, H. W. F.
1955   The Nimrud Letters, 1952: Part II. *Iraq* 17:126–54.
Savran, G.
1987   1 and 2 Kings. Pages 146–64 in *The Literary Guide to the Bible.* Edited by
        R. Alter and F. Kermode. Cambridge: Harvard University Press.
Schiffman, L. H.
1999   The House of the Laver in the Temple Scroll. *ErIsr* 26 (Cross Volume):
        169*–75*.
Schley, D. G.
1987   I Kings 10:26–29: A Reconsideration. *JBL* 106:595–601.
Schneidewind, W. M.
1997   *The Word of God in Transition: From Prophet to Exegete in the Second
        Temple Period.* JSOTSup 197. Sheffield: Sheffield Academic Press.
Schoors, A.
1981   The Particle *ki. OtSt* 2 (*Remembering All the Way . . .*): 240–76.
Schulman, A. R.
1979a   Diplomatic Marriage in the Egyptian New Kingdom. *JNES* 38:177–93.
1979b   Königstochter. Pages 659–61 in vol. 3/21 of *LÄ*.
Scott, R. B. Y.
1939   The Pillars Jachin and Boaz. *JBL* 58:143–49.
1955   Solomon and the Beginnings of Wisdom in Israel. Pages 262–79 in *Wis-
        dom in Israel and in the Ancient Near East.* Edited by M. Noth and
        D. Winton Thomas. VTSup 3. Leiden: Brill.
1965   *Proverbs, Ecclesiastes.* AB 18. Garden City, N.Y.: Doubleday.
1970   Weights and Measurements of the Bible. Pages 345–58 in *BARead*, vol. 3.
Seebass, H.
1967   Zur Königserhebung Jeroboams I. *VT* 17:325–33.
1968   Die Verwerfung Jeroboams I. und Salomons durch die Prophetie des
        Ahia von Silo. WO 4:162–82.
1976   Zur Teilung der Herrschaft Salomons nach I Reg 11:29–39. *ZAW* 88:363–76.
Seeligmann, I. L.
1954   Problems of Prophecy in Israel. *ErIsr* 3 (Cassuto Volume): 125–32. [= Seelig-
        mann 1992, 171–88]
1963   Menschliches Heldentum und Göttliche Hilfe: Die doppelte Kausalität
        im alttestamentlichen Geschichtsdenken. *TZ* 19:385–411. [= Seeligmann
        1992, 62–81]
1971   From Historical Reality to Historiosophic Viewpoint in the Bible. *Peraqim*
        2:273–313. [= Seeligmann 1992, 102–40]
1978   Die Auffassung von der Prophetie in der Deuteronomistischen und
        Chronistischen Geschichtsschreibung (mit ein Exkurs über das Buch
        Jeremia). Pages 254–84 in *Congress Volume: Göttingen, 1977.* VTSup 29.
        Leiden: Brill. [= Seeligmann 1992, 205–28]
1992   *Studies in Biblical Literature.* Jerusalem: Magnes. [Hebrew]

Seger, J. D.
    1992   Gath. Pages 908–9 in vol. 2 of *ABD*.

Selms, A. van
    1957   The Origin of the Title "The King's Friend." *JNES* 16:118–23.

Shenkel, J. D.
    1968   *Chronology and Recensional Development in the Greek Text of Kings.*
                HSM 1. Cambridge: Harvard University Press.

Shiloh, Y.
    1971   Review of: M. L. Buhl and S. Holm-Nielsen, *Shiloh: The Danish Exca-*
                vations at Tull Sailun, Palestine, in 1926, 1929, 1932 and 1963 — The Pre-
                Hellenistic Remains. IEJ 21:67–69.
    1977   The Proto-Aeolic Capital: The Israelite "Timorah" (Palmette) Capital.
                PEQ 109:39–52.
    1984   *Excavations at the City of David, I: 1978–1982.* Qedem 19. Jerusalem:
                Israel Exploration Society.

Shupak, N.
    1985   Some Idioms Connected with the Concept of "Heart" in Egypt and the
                Bible. Pages 202–12 in *Pharaonic Egypt.* Edited by S. Israelit-Groll. Jeru-
                salem: Magnes.

Silberman, L. H.
    1974   The Queen of Sheba in Judaic Tradition. Pages 65–84 in *Solomon and*
                Sheba. Edited by J. B. Pritchard. London: Phaidon.

Simon, U.
    1976   1 Kings 13: A Prophetic Sign-Denial and Persistence. *HUCA* 47:81–117.
    1997   Elijah's Battle against Baal Worship: The Role of the Prophet in Return-
                ing the People to Its God. Pages 189–278 in *Reading Prophetic Narratives.*
                Jerusalem: Bialik. [Hebrew]

Simpson, W. K.
    1973   *The Literature of Ancient Egypt.* New Haven: Yale University Press.

Sivan, D., and W. Schniedewind
    1993   Letting Your "Yes" Be "No" in Ancient Israel: A Study of the Asservative *lʾ*
                and *hlʾ. JSS* 38:209–26.
    1997   The Elijah-Elisha Narratives: A Test Case for the Northern Dialect of
                Hebrew. *JQR* 87:303–37.

Smith, S.
    1953   On the Meaning of *Goren. PEQ* 85:42–45.

Smith, W. R.
    1956   *The Religion of the Semites.* New York: Meridian. [Reprint of 1894 ed.]

Soden, W. von
    1950   Akkadisch *taʾu* und Hebräisch *taʾ* als Raumbezeichnungen. *WO* 1:356–61.

Soggin, J. A.
    1975   Tibni, King of Israel in the First Half of the 9th Century BC. Pages 50–55
                in *Old Testament and Oriental Studies.* BibOr 29. Rome: Pontifical Bibli-
                cal Institute.
    1977   The Davidic-Solomonic Kingdom. Pages 332–80 in *Israelite and Judaean*
                History. Edited by J. H. Hayes and J. M. Miller. London: SCM.

1982 Compulsory Labor under David and Solomon. Pages 259–67 in *Studies in the Period of David and Solomon and Other Essays*. Edited by T. Ishida. Winona Lake, Ind.: Eisenbrauns.

Spanier, K.
1994 The Queen Mother in the Judaean Royal Court. Pages 75–88 in *Division A: The Bible and Its World* of *Proceedings of the Eleventh World Congress of Jewish Studies*. Jerusalem: World Union of Jewish Studies.

Speiser, E. A.
1950 On Some Articles of Armor and Their Names. *JAOS* 70:47–49.
1952 The "Elative" in West-Semitic and Akkadian. *JCS* 6:81–92. [= Speiser 1967, 465–93]
1958 The *muškênum*. *Or* 27:19–28. [= Speiser 1967, 332–43]
1960 "People" and "Nation" of Israel. *JBL* 79:157–63. [= Speiser 1967, 160–70]
1961 The Verb SHR in Genesis and Early Hebrew Movements. *BASOR* 164:23–28. [= Speiser 1967, 97–105]
1963 Background and Function of the Biblical *Nasiʾ*. *CBQ* 25:111–17. [= Speiser 1967, 113–22]
1964 *Genesis*. AB 1. Garden City, N.Y.: Doubleday.
1965 *Pālil* and Cogeners: A Sampling of Apotropaic Symbols. Pages 389–94 in *Studies in Honor of Benno Landsberger on his Seventy-Fifth Birthday*. AS 16. Chicago: University of Chicago Press.
1967 *Oriental and Biblical Studies: Collected Writings of E. A. Speiser*. Edited by J. J. Finklestein and M. Greenberg. Philadelphia: University of Pennsylvania Press.

Stager, L. E.
1988 Shemer's Estate. *BASOR* 277:93–107.

Stamm, J. J.
1967 Hebräische Frauennamen. Pages 301–39 in *Hebräische Wortforschung (Fs. W. Baumgarten)*. VTSup 16. Leiden: Brill.
1971 Zwei alttestamentliche Königsnamen. Pages 443–52 in *Near Eastern Studies in Honor of William Foxwell Albright*. Edited by H. Goedicke. Baltimore: Johns Hopkins Press.

Stein, D.
1993 The Queen of Sheba versus Solomon: Riddles and Commentary in Midrash Mishle I. *Jewish Folklore* 15:7–35.

Steiner, R. C.
1989 New Light on the Biblical Millo from Hatran Inscriptions. *BASOR* 276:15–24.

Stern, E.
1994 *Dor: Ruler of the Seas*. Jerusalem: Israel Exploration Society.

Stinespring, W. F.
1962 Temple, Jerusalem. Pages 534–60 in vol. 4 of *IDB*.

Stol, M.
1993 Biblical Idiom in Akkadian. Pages 246–49 in *The Tablet and the Scroll: Near Eastern Studies in Honor of William W. Hallo*. Edited by M. E. Cohen, D. C. Snell, and D. B. Weisberg. Bethesda, Md.: CDL.

Strange, J.
1966   The Inheritance of Dan. *ST* 20:120–39.

Streck, M.
1916   *Assurbanipal und die letzten assyrischen Könige bis zum Untergange Nineveh's.* VAB 7. Leipzig: Hinrichs.

Sutcliffe, E. F.
1958   Simultaneity in Hebrew: A Note on 1 Kings i.41. *JSS* 3:80–81.

Sweeny, M. A.
1995   The Critique of Solomon in the Josianic Edition of the Deuteronomic History. *JBL* 114:607–22.

Tadmor, H.
1958   The Campaigns of Sargon II of Assur: A Chronological-Historical Study. *JCS* 12:22–40.
1961   Que and Muṣri. *IEJ* 11:143–50.
1968   "The People" and the Kingship in Ancient Israel: The Role of Political Institutions in the Biblical Period. *JWH* 11:46–68.
1970   The Chronology of the First Temple Period. *WHJP* 4/1:44–60.
1982   Traditional Institutions and the Monarchy: Social and Political Tensions in the Time of David and Solomon. Pages 239–57 in *Studies in the Period of David and Solomon and Other Essays.* Edited by T. Ishida. Winona Lake, Ind.: Eisenbrauns.

Tadmor, H., and M. Cogan
1979   Ahaz and Tiglath-Pileser in the Book of Kings: Historiographic Considerations. *Bib* 60:491–508.

Talmon, S.
1958   Divergences in Calendar-Reckoning in Ephraim and Judah. *VT* 8:48–74. [Reprinted, pp. 113–39 in *King, Cult and Calendar in Ancient Israel: Collected Studies.* Jerusalem: Magnes, 1986]
1978   The Presentation of Synchroneity and Simultaneity in Biblical Narrative. Pages 9–26 in *Studies in Hebrew Narrative Art throughout the Ages.* Edited by J. Heinemann and S. Werses. ScrHier 27. Jerusalem: Magnes. [Reprinted, pp. 112–33 in *Literary Studies in the Hebrew Bible: Form and Content.* Jerusalem: Magnes / Leiden: Brill, 1993]

Talmon, S., and W. W. Fields
1989   The Collocation *mštyn bqyr wᶜṣwr wᶜzwb* and Its Meanings. *ZAW* 101:85–112.

Talshir, Z.
1981–82   The Detailing Formula "*wzh (h)dbr. . . .*" *Tarbiz* 51:23–35.
1989   *The Duplicate Story of the Divison of the Kingdom (LXX 3 Kingdoms xii 24a–z).* Jerusalem: Simor. [Hebrew]
1990   The Image of the Edition of the Book of Kings as Reflected in the Septuagint. *Tarbiz* 59:249–302.
1996a   The Contribution of Diverging Traditions Preserved in the Septuagint to Literary Criticism of the Bible. Pages 21–40 in *VIII Congress of the IOSCS: Paris, 1992.* Society of Biblical Literature Septuagint and Cognate Studies 41. Atlanta: Scholars Press.

1996b   Towards the Structure of the Book of Kings: Formulaic Synchronism and Story Synchronism (1 Kings 12–2 Kings 17). Pages 73*–88* in *Texts, Temples, and Traditions: A Tribute to Menahem Haran*. Edited by M. V. Fox, V. A. Hurowitz, et al. Winona Lake, Ind.: Eisenbrauns. [Hebrew]

Talstra, Eep
1987   *Solomon's Prayer: Synchrony and Diachrony in the Composition of 1 Kings 8, 14–61*. Kampen: Kok Pharos.

Tcherikover, V.
1959   *Hellenistic Civilization and the Jews*. Philadelphia: Jewish Publication Society.

Thiel, W.
1991   Deuteronomistische Redaktionsarbeit in den Elia-Erzählungen. Pages 148–71 in *Congress Volume: Leuven, 1989*. Edited by J. A. Emerton. VTSup 43. Leiden: Brill.

Thiele, E. R.
1983   *The Mysterious Numbers of the Hebrew Kings*. Grand Rapids, Mich.: Zondervan.

Thomson, H. C.
1960   A Row of Cedar Beams. *PEQ* 92:57–63.

Tigay, J. H.
1996   *Deuteronomy*. The JPS Torah Commentary. Philadelphia: Jewish Publication Society.

Timm, Stephan
1982   *Die Dynastie Omri*. FRLANT 124. Göttingen: Vandenhoeck & Ruprecht.

Toorn, K. van der
1992a   Prison. Pages 468–69 in vol. 5 of *ABD*.
1992b   Prostitution (Cultic). Pages 510–13 in vol. 5 of *ABD*.

Tov, E.
1984   The LXX Additions (Miscellanies) in 1 Kings 2 (3 Reigns 2). *Textus* 11:89–113.
1992   Textual Criticism (OT). Pages 393–412 in vol. 6 of *ABD*.

Trebolle Barrera, J.
1982   Redaction, Recension, and Midrash in the Books of Kings. *BIOSCS* 15:12–35.
1995   4QKgs. Pages 171–83 in *Qumran Cave 4:IX: Deuteronomy, Joshua, Judges, Kings*. Edited by E. Ulrich, F. M. Cross, et al. DJD 14. Oxford: Clarendon.

Tsafrir, Y.
1975   The Levitic City of Beth-Shemesh in Judah or in Naphtali. *ErIsr* 12 (Glueck Volume): 44–45.

Tvedtnes, J. A.
1982   Egyptian Etymologies for Biblical Cultic Paraphernalia. Pages 215–21 in *Egyptological Studies*. Edited by S. Israelit-Groll. ScrHier 28. Jerusalem: Magnes.

Tzori, N.
1967   Abel-Meholah. *BIES* 31:132–35.

Ullendorff, E.
1963   The Queen of Sheba. *BJRL* 45:486–504.
1974   The Queen of Sheba in Ethiopian Tradition. Pages 104–14 in *Solomon and Sheba*. Edited by J. B. Pritchard. London: Phaidon.

Ulrich, E., and F. M. Cross, et al.
1995   *Qumran Cave 4:IX: Deuteronomy, Joshua, Judges, Kings*. DJD 14. Oxford: Clarendon.

Ussishkin, D.
1966a   Building IV in Hamath and the Temples of Solomon and Tell Tayanat. *IEJ* 16:104–10.
1966b   King Solomon's Palace and Building 1723 in Megiddo. *IEJ* 16:174–86.
1970   The Necropolis from the Time of the Kingdom of Judah at Silwan, Jerusalem. *BA* 33:34–46.
1973   King Solomon's Palaces. *BA* 36:78–105.
1980   Was the "Solomonic" Gate at Megiddo built by King Solomon? *BASOR* 239:1–18.
1993   *The Village of Silwan*. Jerusalem: Israel Exploration Society and Yad Izhak Ben-Zvi.
1994   Gate 1567 at Megiddo and the Seal of Shema, Servant of Jeroboam. Pages 410–28 in *Scripture and Other Artifacts: Essays on the Bible and Archaeology in Honor of Phillip J. King*. Edited by M. D. Coogan, J. C. Exum, and L. E. Stager. Louisville: Westminster and John Knox.
1997   Jezreel, Samaria and Megiddo: Royal Cities of Omri and Ahab. Pages 351–64 in *Congress Volume: Cambridge, 1995*. Edited by J. A. Emerton. VTSup 66. Leiden: Brill.

Van Beek, G. W.
1960   Frankincense and Myrrh. *BA* 23:69–95. [= *BARead* 2:99–126]
1974   The Land of Sheba. Pages 40–63 in *Solomon and Sheba*. Edited by J. B. Pritchard. London: Phaidon.

Van Seters, J.
1983   *In Search of History*. New Haven and London: Yale University Press.
1997   Solomon's Temple: Fact and Ideology in Biblical and Near Eastern Historiography. *CBQ* 59:45–57.

Van Winkle, D. W.
1989   1 Kings XIII: True and False Prophecy. *VT* 39:31–43.

Vanoni, G.
1984   *Literarkritik und Grammatik: Untersuchung der Widerholungen und Spannungen in 1 Kön. 11.12*. Münchener Universität Schriften: Arbeiten Text und Sprache Altes Testament 21. St. Ottilien: EOS.

Vaughan, P. H.
1974   *The Meaning of "Bama" in the Old Testament*. SOTSMS 3. Cambridge: Cambridge University Press.

Vaux, R. de
1939   Titres et fonctionnaires égyptiens a la cour de David et de Salomon. *RB* 48:394–405.
1961   *Ancient Israel*. New York: McGraw-Hill.
1971a   The Religious Schism of Jeroboam I. Pages 97–110 in *The Bible and the Ancient Near East*. New York: Doubleday.

1971b   The Prophets of Baal on Mount Carmel. Pages 238–51 in *The Bible and the Ancient Near East*. New York: Doubleday.

Veijlo, T.
1975   *Die ewige Dynastie*. AASF B 193. Helsinki: Suomalainen Tiedeakatemia.

Vincent, L.-H.
1956   *Jerusalem de l'Ancien Testament*. Paris: Gabalda.

Walsh, J. T.
1995   The Characterization of Solomon in First Kings 1–5. *CBQ* 57:471–93.

Waltke, B. K., and M. O'Connor
1990   *An Introduction to Biblical Hebrew Syntax*. Winona Lake, Ind.: Eisenbrauns.

Warner, S.
1980   The Alphabet: An Innovation and Its Diffusion. *VT* 30:81–90.

Watson, P. F.
1974   The Queen of Sheba in Christian Tradition. Pages 115–45 in *Solomon and Sheba*. Edited by J. B. Pritchard. London: Phaidon.

Watt, W. M.
1974   The Queen of Sheba in Islamic Tadition. Pages 85–103 in *Solomon and Sheba*. Edited by J. B. Pritchard. London: Phaidon.

Weinfeld, M.
1972   *Deuteronomy and the Deuteronomic School*. Oxford: Clarendon. [Reprinted, Winona Lake, Ind.: Eisenbrauns, 1992]
1982   The Counsel of the "Elders" to Rehoboam and Its Implications. *Maarav* 3:27–53.
1991   *Deuteronomy 1–11*. AB 5. New York: Doubleday.

Weippert, H.
1972   Die "deuteronomistischen" Beurteilungen der Könige von Israel und Juda und das Problem der Redaktion der Königsbücher. *Bib* 53:301–39.
1983   Die Ätiologie des Nordreiches und seines Königshauses (1 Reg 11 29–40). *ZAW* 95:344–75.
1988   Ahab el campeador?: Redaktionsgeschichtliche Untersuchungen zu 1 Kön 22. *Bib* 69:457–79.
1992   Die Kesselwagen Salomos. *ZDPV* 108:8–41.

Weippert, H., and M. Weippert
1989   Zwei Frauen vor dem Königsgericht: Einzelfragen der Erzählung von "Salomoschen Urteil." Pages 133–60 in *Door het oog van de profeten: Exegetische studies aangeboden aan prof. dr. C. van Leeuwen*. Edited by B. E. J. H. Becking, et al. Utrechtse Theologische Reeks 8. Utrecht.

Weippert, M.
1961   Gott und Stier. *ZDPV* 77:93–117.
1980–83   Libanon. Pages 641–50 in vol. 6 of *RlA*.

Weisman, Z.
1996   *Political Satire in the Bible*. Jerusalem: Mosad Bialik. [Hebrew]

Weiss, M.
1984   *The Bible from Within*. Jerusalem: Magnes.
1987   The Story on the Beginnings of Job. Pages 335–90 in *Scriptures in Their Own Light: Collected Essays*. Jerusalem: Magnes. [Hebrew]

Weiss, R.
1968   Textual Notes. *Textus* 6:127–31.

Wellhausen, J.
1875   Die Zeitrechnung des Buches der Könige seit der Theilung des Reiches. *Jahrbücher für deutsche Theologie* 29:607–40.
1899   *Die Composition des Hexateuchs.* 4th ed. Berlin: Reimer. [Reprinted, Berlin: de Gruyter, 1963]

Wevers, J. W.
1950   Exegetical Principles Underlying the Septuagint Text of 1 Kings ii 12–xxi 43. *OtSt* 8:300–322.

White, M. C.
1997   *The Elijah Legends and Jehu's Coup.* Brown Judaic Studies 311. Atlanta, Ga.: Scholars Press.

Whitt, W. D.
1995   The Story of the Semitic Alphabet. Pages 2379–97 in *Civilizations of the Ancient Near East.* Edited by J. Sasson. New York: Scribner's.

Whybray, R. N.
1968   *The Succession Narrative: A Study of II Sam. 9–20; I Kings 1 and 2.* SBT 2/9. Naperville, Ill.: Allenson.

Wightman, G. J.
1990   The Myth of Solomon. *BASOR* 277/278:5–23.

Williamson, H. G. M.
1982   *1 and 2 Chronicles.* NCB. Grand Rapids, Mich.: Eerdmans.
1991   Jezreel in the Biblical Texts. *Tel Aviv* 18:72–92.

Wiseman, D. J.
1953   *The Alalakh Tablets.* London: British Institute of Archaeology at Ankara.

Wolde, E. van
1995   Who Guides Whom?: Embeddedness and Perspective in Biblical Hebrew and in 1 Kings 3:16–28. *JBL* 114:623–45.

Woude, A. S. van der
1989   Zur Geschichte der Grenze zwischen Juda und Israel. *OtSt* 25:38–47.

Wright, G. E.
1967   The Provinces of Solomon (1 Kings 4:7–19). *ErIsr* 8 (Sukenik Volume): 58*–68*.

Würthwein, E.
1973   Die Erzählung von Gottesmann aus Juda in Bethel: Zur Komposition von 1 Kön 13. Pages 181–89 in *Wort und Geschichte: Elliger Festschrift.* Edited by H. Gese and H. Ruger. Neukirchen-Vluyn: Neukirchener Verlag.
1983   Elijah at Horeb: Reflections on I Kings 19.9–18. Pages 152–66 in *Proclamation and Presence: Old Testament Essays in Honour of G. H. Davies.* Corrected ed. Edited by J. I. Durham and J. R. Porter. Macon, Ga.: Mercer University Press.

Wyatt, N.
1995   Asherah. Columns 183–95 in *DDD.*

Wylie, C. C.
1949   On King Solomon's Molten Sea. *BA* 12:86–90.

Yadin, Y.
1955 Some Aspects of the Strategy of Ahab and David (I Kings 20; II Samuel 11). *Bib* 36:332–51.
1958 Solomon's City Wall and Gate at Gezer. *IEJ* 8:80–86.
1963 *The Art of Warfare in Biblical Lands.* New York: McGraw-Hill.
1972 *Hazor.* The Schweich Lectures, 1970. The British Academy. Oxford: Oxford University Press.

Yaron, R.
1958 A Ramissid Parallel to 1 K ii 33, 44–45. *VT* 8:432–33.

Yeivin, S.
1942–44 Abijam, Asa, and Maacah, Daughter of Abishalom. *BJPES* 10:116–19.
1959 Jachin and Boaz. *PEQ* 91:6–22.
1959–60 Did the Kingdoms of Israel Have a Maritime Policy? *JQR* 50:193–228.
1960 The Date of the Seal "Belonging to Shema (the) Servant (of) Jeroboam." *JNES* 19:205–12.
1968 מקדש שלמה. Pages 328–46 in vol. 5 of *EncMiqr.*
1979a The Divided Kingdom. Pages 126–79, 330–40 in vol. 4/1 of *WHJP.*
1979b Administration. Pages 147–71 in vol. 5 of *WHJP.*

Younger, K. L.
1990 *Ancient Conquest Accounts.* JSOTSup 98. Sheffield: Sheffield Academic Press.

Zakovitch, Y.
1979 The Purpose of Narrations in Scripture concerning Purchase of Possessions. *Beth Mikra* 76:17–21.
1981–82 A Still, Small Voice. *Tarbiz* 51:329–46.
1984 The Tale of Naboth's Vineyard (1 Kings 21). Pages 379–405 in M. Weiss, *The Bible from Within.* Jerusalem: Magnes.
1991 *"And You Shall Tell Your Son . . .": The Concept of the Exodus in the Bible.* Jerusalem: Magnes.

Zalevsky, S.
1973 The Revelation of God to Solomon in Gibeon. *Tarbiz* 42:214–58.

Zertal, A.
1992 Arubboth. Pages 465–67 in vol. 1 of *ABD.*

Zohary, M.
1982 *Plants of the Bible.* Cambridge: Cambridge University Press.

Zori, N.
1966 Abel-Meholah. *BIES* 31:132–35.

Zwickel, W.
1999 *Der Salomonische Tempel.* Mainz: von Zabern.

TRANSLATION, NOTES, AND COMMENTS

◆

THE REIGN OF SOLOMON

◆

I. THE ACCESSION OF SOLOMON

(1:1–53)

1 ¹Now King David was old, advanced in years; they would cover him with clothes, but he could not get warm. ²His servants said to him: "Let them search for a young virgin for my lord the king, and she will attend the king and be his housekeeper; she will lie in your bosom and my lord the king will be warm." ³So they searched for a beautiful girl throughout all the territory of Israel. They found Abishag the Shunammite and brought her to the king. ⁴Now the girl was very beautiful indeed, and she became housekeeper to the king and she served him; yet the king did not have relations with her.

⁵Now Adonijah son of Haggith went about boasting: "I will be king." He acquired a chariot and horsemen and fifty outrunners. ⁶Yet his father never once caused him displeasure by saying: "Why have you done this?" He was, moreover, very handsome, and he was the one born after Absalom. ⁷He conspired with Joab son of Zeruiah and with Abiathar the priest, and they supported Adonijah; ⁸but Zadok the priest and Benaiah son of Jehoiada and Nathan the prophet and Shimei and Rei and David's warriors were not with Adonijah.

⁹Then Adonijah slaughtered sheep, oxen, and fatlings by the stone Zoheleth near En-rogel, and he invited all his brothers, the king's sons, and all the men of Judah, the king's servants; ¹⁰but he did not invite Nathan the prophet and Benaiah and the warriors and Solomon his brother. ¹¹Then Nathan said to Bathsheba, Solomon's mother: "Have you not heard that Adonijah son of Haggith has become king and our lord David did not know? ¹²Now let me give you advice, so that you may save your life and the life of your son Solomon. ¹³Go and come to the King David and say to him: 'Did not *you* my lord the king swear to your handmaid: "Solomon your son shall be king after me and he shall sit upon my throne"? Then why has Adonijah become king?' ¹⁴While[a] you are still talking there with the king, *I* will come in after you and confirm your words."

¹⁵So Bathsheba came to the king in his chamber.—Now the king was very old and Abishag the Shunammite was attending the king.—¹⁶Bathsheba bowed and prostrated herself before the king. The king said: "What is the matter?" ¹⁷She said to him: "My lord, *you* swore by YHWH your God to your handmaid: 'Solomon your son shall rule after me and *he* shall sit upon my throne.' ¹⁸And

---

[a] Many MSS and versions read *whnh* for MT *hnh*, v. 22; *waw* lost through haplography.

now Adonijah has become king and you,[b] my lord the king, did not know. [19]He slaughtered oxen and fatlings and sheep in great quantity and he invited all the king's sons and Abiathar the priest and Joab, commander of the army, but Solomon your servant he did not invite. [20]And you,[c] my lord the king, the eyes of all Israel are upon you, to tell them who will sit upon the throne of my lord the king after him. [21](Otherwise,) when my lord the king sleeps with his ancestors, I and my son Solomon will be considered wrongdoers."

[22]Now she was still talking with the king when Nathan the prophet came in. [23]They told the king: "Nathan the prophet is here"; and he came before the king and prostrated himself before the king with his face to the ground. [24]Nathan said: "My lord the king, did *you* say: 'Adonijah shall reign after me and *he* shall sit on my throne'? [25]For he has gone down today and has slaughtered oxen, fatlings, and sheep in great quantity. He invited all the king's sons and the officers of the army[d] and Abiathar the priest, and they are now eating and drinking in his presence and saying: 'May King Adonijah live!' [26]But *me*, your servant, and Zadok the priest and Benaiah son of Jehoiada and Solomon your servant he did not invite. [27]Has this matter come about by order of my lord the king, and you have not informed your servant[e] who shall sit on the throne of my lord the king after him?"

[28]King David answered and said: "Call Bathsheba to me." She came before the king and stood before the king. [29]The king swore, saying: "By the life of YHWH who rescued me[f] from every adversity: [30]As I swore to you by YHWH, God of Israel: 'Solomon your son shall reign after me and *he* shall sit on my throne in my stead,' so I will do this very day." [31]Bathsheba bowed facing the ground[g] and she prostrated herself to the king, and she said: "May my lord, King David, live forever!"

[32]Then King David said: "Call Zadok the priest and Nathan the prophet and Benaiah son of Jehoiada to me." They came before the king. [33]The king said to them: "Take your lord's servants with you, and have Solomon my son ride my own mule and bring him down to Gihon. [34]There Zadok the priest and Nathan the prophet shall anoint him as king over Israel; then you shall blow the horn and say: 'May King Solomon live!' [35]Go up after him, and he will come in and sit on my throne and he shall reign in my stead; for it is he that I have appointed to become ruler of Israel and Judah." [36]Benaiah son of Jehoiada answered the king and said: "Amen. May YHWH the God of my lord the king so order. [37]As YHWH has been with my lord the king, so may he be[h] with Solo-

---

[b] Read *'th* with many MSS and Luc., LXX, Vulg., Syr., Tg. (some MSS), for MT: *'th*, "now"; cf. Minhat Shay.

[c] Many MSS and LXX and Syr. read *'th*, "now."

[d] Lucianic recension reads: "Joab commander of the army"; see Josephus, *Ant.* 7.352; other versions follow MT; see note.

[e] Read with qere *'bdk* for ketib *'bdyk* ("your servants").

[f] Lit., "rescued my life."

[g] MT: *'rṣ*; sebirin and several MSS: *'rṣh*, cf. vv. 23, 52.

[h] Read with ketib (as jussive) *yhy*; qere *yhyh* (also 5QKgs).

mon, and may he make his throne greater than the throne of my lord, King David."

³⁸So Zadok the priest and Nathan the prophet and Benaiah son of Jehoiada and the Cherethites and the Pelethites went down; they had Solomon ride on King David's mule, and they led him to Gihon. ³⁹Zadok the priest took the horn of oil from the Tent and anointed Solomon. They blew the horn and all the people said: "May King Solomon live!" ⁴⁰Then all the people went up after him; the people were playing pipes and rejoicing with great joy, so that the earth was split by their sound.

⁴¹Now Adonijah and all the invited who were with him heard (it) just as they finished eating. When Joab heard the sound of the horn, he said: "Why the sound of the city in uproar?" ⁴²He was still speaking when Jonathan son of Abiathar the priest came. Adonijah said: "Come, for you are a worthy man and you bring good news." ⁴³Jonathan answered and said to Adonijah: "On the contrary. Our lord, King David, has made Solomon king. ⁴⁴The king sent with him Zadok the priest and Nathan the prophet and Benaiah son of Jehoiada and the Cheretheites and the Pelethites. They had him ride on the king's mule, ⁴⁵and Zadok the priest and Nathan the prophet anointed him king at Gihon. They went up from there rejoicing, and the city was in an uproar. That is the sound you heard. ⁴⁶Furthermore, Solomon sat on the royal throne. ⁴⁷And furthermore, the king's servants came to bless our lord King David: 'May God^i make the name of Solomon better than your name, and may he make his throne greater than your throne.' Then the king bowed low on the bed. ⁴⁸And furthermore, thus said the king: 'Blessed be YHWH, God of Israel, who has given this day someone to sit on my throne and my eyes behold it.'" ⁴⁹Thereupon, all the invitees of Adonijah trembled, and so they left; each went his own way.

⁵⁰Adonijah, fearing Solomon, immediately went and took hold of the horns of the altar. ⁵¹They told Solomon: "Adonijah is in fear of King Solomon, and here he has taken hold of the horns of the altar, and said: 'Let King Solomon swear to me today that he will not kill his servant with the sword.'" ⁵²Solomon said: "If he will be a worthy man, a hair of his will not fall to the ground, but if he is caught in a wrongdoing,^j he shall die." ⁵³King Solomon sent and they took him down from the altar; he came and prostrated himself to King Solomon, and Solomon said to him: "Go home."

---

^i Read with many MSS, qere, LXX, and Vulg. *'lhym* for ketib *'lhyk*; Lucianic recension and Tg.: *yhwh*; see Note.

^j Lit., "if a wrong be found in him."

NOTES

1 1. *advanced in years.* The idiom *b' bymym* appears again in Gen 18:11; 24:1; Josh 13:1; 23:1, 2. According to the chronological data given in 2 Sam 5:4 and 1 Kgs 2:11, David would have been close to seventy years old at this time.

but he could not get warm. The verb in the imperfect indicates repeated attempts that failed. The vocalization in BHS, Aleppo Codex, and the overwhelming majority of MSS is *yiḥam*; a minority have the lengthened form *yēḥam*, on which see GKC, 67g, p. Modern speculation diagnoses the king's infirmity as "advanced arteriosclerosis" (DeVries).

2. *His servants said to him*. The quoted remark is the suggestion of one of the servants, as seen by the singular "my lord the king."

she will attend the king. That is, "she will serve him." The idiom *ʿmd lpny*, "to stand before," suggests being at someone's beck and call—e.g., courtiers (1 Kgs 10:8); a prophet serving YHWH (1 Kgs 17:1; 18:15; 2 Kgs 3:14; 5:16). For the equivalent Akk idiom *ina pān uzzuzzu*, see Oppenheim 1941, 258.

his housekeeper. Hebrew *sōkenet* in fem. appears only here, the masc. *sōkēn* in Isa 22:15 with reference to Shebna (cf. 2 Kgs 18:18). The suggested derivation from Akk *šaknu*, "governor, commander" (CAD Š/1, 180–92; see, e.g., Noth) is uncalled-for, given the evidence from mid-second-millennium Alalakh, Ugarit, and Amarna of **skn*, "to care for," in WSem and Canaanite; note the forms *sākinu* (CAD S, 76) and *sūkinu* (CAD S, 354). In *Hiphil*, **skn* conveys "to be familiar with, close to"; cf. Num 22:30; Ps 139:3; Job 22:21. There is not the slightest hint that she was the king's concubine, not even in 1 Kgs 2:22 (see Note there) or that the maid was meant to obtain "a high position at court," replacing the old queen (so Mulder). Even less likely is that she was destined to run the royal harem (as proposed by Heltzer 1987 on the basis of the Neo-Assyrian title *šakintu*, for which see CAD Š/1, 165–66). Her duties were confined to nursing the failing king; cf. v. 15.

she will lie in your bosom and my lord the king will be warm. Josephus (*Ant.* 7.343) ascribed the advice to the king's physicians, perhaps basing his interpretation on ancient medical prescriptions for hypothermia (see Montgomery and Gehman); see, too, the lengthy diagnosis of Abarbanel. The expression *škb bḥq* implies intimacy (cf. Gen 16:5; 2 Sam 12:3, 8), which in the present instance went unfulfilled; cf. v. 4 below.

3. *They found Abishag the Shunammite*. A town in the territory of the tribe of Issachar; cf. 2 Kgs 4:8. Many tales have been woven around the identification of the Shulammite in Song 7:1 with Abishag, on the assumption that the name of the town Shunem was changed to Shulem (the phonetic alteration of *n/r/l* is known). But all of them suffer from unfounded romantic speculation and can be set aside; see Pope 1977, 597–98, and the Note on 1 Kgs 2:17.

4. *yet the king did not have relations with her*. Literally, "he did not know her"; cf. the additional echo of David's "unawareness" in v. 18. The present remark is meant to confirm the decrepit state of David's old age; the vigor for which he was renowned had left him. But it is hardly because he "failed to pass the test of virility" (so Gray, 77) that the issue of a successor became urgent. It had been on the court agenda prior to the introduction of Abishag; the existence of the two rival parties vouches for that.

5. *Now Adonijah son of Haggith went about boasting: "I will be king."* The name Adonijah, "Yah is my lord," is written *ʾdnyh* in vv. 5, 7, 18; 2:28 and

'*dnyhw* in all other instances; this alteration bears no significance. The longer form '*dnyhw* (in accord with the standard spelling in preexilic inscriptions) is known from a number of Hebrew seals, see WSS, nos. 50, 403, 404, 423. Adonijah was David's fourth son, after Amnon, Chileab (or Daniel; cf. 1 Chr 3:2), and Absalom; cf. 2 Sam 3:3–4; he was born in Hebron and would have been in his mid-thirties. The mention of Haggith follows the Judean practice of recording the name of the king's mother; cf., e.g., 1 Kgs 14:21; 15:10, et al.

son of Haggith. Nothing further is known of Haggith. Nor should a rivalry between her and Bathsheba be posted simply on the basis of her repeated mention as mother of Adonijah.

went about boasting: "I will be king." As the king's eldest surviving son, Adonijah assumed that the throne would pass to him; cf. 1 Kgs 2:15. Amnon and Absalom had both been eliminated violently, and of Chileab, nothing more than his name is known. The use of the verb *htnś'* suggests criticism of Adonijah's self-exalting manner and reflects the attitude of the storyteller, who supported Solomon; cf. Num 16:3; Ezek 17:14; 29:15.

He acquired a chariot and horsemen and fifty outrunners. These ceremonial trappings had also been part of Absalom's display of rank and intention; cf. 2 Sam 15:1; also 1 Sam 8:11. Yet in conjuring up the earlier coup, the specific terms have been altered: in the case of Absalom, *merkābâ* and *sūsîm* are employed, while in the present passage *rekeb* and *pārāšîm*. The latter are the set terms used of Solomon's army (cf. 1 Kgs 9:19; 10:26) and were likely chosen to give the reader the idea that Adonijah "had made the decisive step toward rebellion by gathering a military force" (Ishida 1987, 173).

outrunners. The royal entourage included an escort of runners; cf. 1 Kgs 14:27; 2 Kgs 10:25; 11:11, 19 (where the "Outrunners Gate" is mentioned); who could be counted on as a loyal bodyguard (cf. 1 Sam 22:17); the NEB's "henchmen" implies unfounded disparagement. In addition, running by or in front of the king's chariot signified honor and obeisance to one's overlord; cf. 1 Kgs 18:46; and see the testimony of Barrakub, who "ran at the wheel of my lord, the king of Assyria" (i.e., Tiglath-pileser III; ANET, 655; KAI 215:12–13). In Esth 3:13, 15, *rāṣîm* are "couriers."

6. *Yet his father never once caused him displeasure.* The narrator's remark explains Adonijah's present behavior as due to his father's indulgence throughout "all his life" (*mymyw*).

He was, moreover, very handsome. Adonijah, like all previous kings and pretenders to the throne, was endowed with the physical qualities that seem to draw public attention in all ages; cf. 1 Sam 9:2 (Saul); 16:12 (David), 2 Sam 14:25 (Absalom); even a prophet can be seduced by such externals, cf. 1 Sam 16:7. Adonijah's good looks are mentioned here as reason for David's overlooking his son's presumptuousness.

and he was the one born after Absalom. Adonijah, David's fourth son (cf. 2 Sam 3:3–4), was his eldest living son. Accordingly, he could consider himself the rightful heir; cf. 1 Kgs 2:15.

7. *He conspired with Joab son of Zeruiah and with Abiathar the priest.* In the present context, the sense of *hyh dbr(ym)* ʿm is more than "talk with" (NEB) or "confer" (NJPSV); it conveys "private dealings" (Montgomery and Gehman) and plotting; cf. 2 Sam 3:17.

Joab son of Zeruiah. David's nephew and commander of the army (cf. 2 Sam 8:16; 20:23).

Abiathar the priest. A son of the priest Ahimelech; he survived the slaughter at Nob (cf. 1 Sam 22:20) and became a lifelong supporter of David.

they supported Adonijah. Literally, "they helped following Adonijah," a pregnant construction (Burney); cf. 1 Chr 12:21 (ʿzrw ʿm dwyd).

8. *Zadok the priest.* One of the two priests on David's staff (cf. 2 Sam 8:17; 20:25), who is first referred to in connection to the Ark (cf. 2 Sam 15:24–29). Zadok's conjectured foreign (Jebusite) ancestry has been neatly set aside by Cross (1973, 207–15), who argues for his origins among the priests of Hebron. See further the Note on 1 Kgs 2:35.

Benaiah son of Jehoiada. One of David's brave men (cf. 2 Sam 23:20–23), who was in charge of the Cherithite and Pelethite guard (cf. 20:23; and below, v. 44).

Nathan the prophet. Nathan is not referred to in the history of David after his censure of David in the Bathsheba affair (2 Sam 12); this may be just the happenstance of reportage, rather than a reflection on his position at court.

Shimei and Rei. Two otherwise unknown persons; because they do not play a role in the ensuing drama, commentators have resorted to emendation of MT (see Noth for a survey of suggested emendations and his hesitant retention of MT). It is not likely that Shimei is the Benjaminite Shimei son of Gera mentioned in 2 Sam 16:5; or Shimei, prefect of the district of Benjamin (1 Kgs 4:18). Lucianic recensions read the second name as *wrʿyw,* "and his friends" (so NAB); Josephus (*Ant.* 7.346) rendered: "David's friend Simueis." (On the title "friend of the king," cf. 1 Kgs 4:5 and Note there.)

David's warriors. A group of thirty brave souls had gathered around David during the period preceding his election to the kingship in Hebron; their names and the exploits of their commanders are given in 2 Sam 23:8–39. See B. Mazar 1986, 83–103. It is likely that, by this late stage in David's reign, some of their original number had passed on, and others had taken their place.

9. *Then Adonijah slaughtered sheep, oxen, and fatlings.* The occasion for this feast is not indicated; cf. 1 Sam 20:29; 2 Sam 15:7–8; the preceding verses suggest that Adonijah, having consolidated his camp, considered the time ripe to make a public move. From here on, all of the action through the end of the chapter takes place on a single day.

fatlings. An unspecified domesticated animal (cf. 2 Sam 6:13; Isa 1:11; Ezek 39:18), from **mrʾ,* "to fatten," attested verbally in MH and perhaps in BH in Isa 11:6 (according to 1QIsaᵃ: *ymrw* "will feed"); also Akk *marû* (CAD M/1, 307–8). The NEB, "buffaloes," follows a minority tradition, found in the Arabic translation of Saʿadia Gaon; see, too, Ibn-Janah: "large cattle."

by the stone Zoheleth near En-rogel. The spring En-rogel lay close to Jebusite Jerusalem and is noted as a border point between the tribal allotments of Judah and Benjamin; cf. Josh 15:7; 18:16. It is most likely to be identified with the major spring Bir Ayyub ("Job's Well"), some 500 meters south of the City of David, just beyond the confluence of the Kidron and Hinnom Valleys; see Mare 1992. The open area around the spring could easily have accommodated a gathering of the type here described; it also had served as the rendezvous point for David's informers during the rebellion of Absalom (cf. 2 Sam 17:17). The Zoheleth stone was a landmark at the time of the storyteller but is no longer identifiable. The site's putative cultic significance is found in its name, often rendered "Serpent's Stone," from *zḥl*, "to crawl, creep," and an association is sought with En-hattannin (Dragon's Spring or Jackal's Well) of Neh 2:13; there are those who prefer to connect it with a "slippery track" (Ar *az-zaḥweileh*) in the vicinity of Silwan (Gray, DeVries). In either case, the rock has been a magnet for tales, ancient and modern (see Mulder), none very credible.

he invited all his brothers, the king's sons, and all the men of Judah, the king's servants. The list of the guests included Joab and Abiathar; cf. vv. 19, 41. Besides the royal princes, Adonijah courted the influential circles from his native Judah, just as Absalom had done (cf. 2 Sam 15:9).

12. *Now let me give you advice, so that you may save your life and the life of your son Solomon.* Nathan's words assumed that, once Adonijah took over, the lives of Bathsheba and Solomon would be in danger, because they represented the potential of usurpation.

13. *Did not you my lord the king swear to your handmaid . . . ?* The direct quotation of David's oath is introduced by *kî*, as in v. 30; cf. 1 Kgs 11:22 and the Note there. That David had made such a solemn promise is nowhere mentioned before this verse, thus raising the suspicion of Nathan's having fabricated the matter; see further in Comment.

14. *While you are still talking there with the king, I will come in after you and confirm your words.* Nathan, in fact, says nothing about the oath given to Bathsheba concerning Solomon; he points out that Adonijah's actions can be either the elevation to the throne authorized by David or a coup (cf. below, vv. 24–27).

While you are still talking . . . I will come in. For other examples of this construction coordinating two simultaneous actions, cf. Gen 29:9; Num 11:33; 2 Kgs 6:33; Job 1:16, 17; Dan 9:19–20; see S. R. Driver 1892, §169.

15. *So Bathsheba came to the king in his chamber.* Bathsheba entered into the king's private chamber (cf. Judg 15:1) without ceremony; contrast the announcement of Nathan in v. 23. At the same time, she observed court etiquette by bowing (v. 16a) and waiting to be addressed (v. 16b) before speaking (v. 17). For the practice at the court of the Persian kings, cf. Esth 4:11.

Now the king was very old and Abishag the Shunammite was attending the king. It is not clear from the circumstantial nature of this sentence whether it serves as a reminder of the king's frail condition (so, e.g., Jones), or, as seems likely, it tells how "Bathsheba entered the chamber, even though the king was intimately in bed with Abishag, and no one was allowed to enter without permission, except her, for she was his wife" (Qimḥi). This reading makes Abishag a witness to the ensuing conversation.

18. *my lord the king, did not know.* Matters of utmost importance are going on behind the back of the king. He is indeed not in control. David's lack of knowledge (*lʾ ydʿt*) of Adonijah's actions echoes the loss of vitality (*lʾ ydʿh*) reported earlier (cf. v. 4).

21. *wrongdoers.* Or, "be held guilty"; for another nonritual use of **ḥṭʾ*, cf. 2 Kgs 18:14. Bathsheba implies that they would be in mortal danger if Adonijah acceded to the throne; it was just such a fate that overtook Adonijah and his close supporters at the hands of Solomon.

23. *They told the king: "Nathan the prophet is here"; and he came before the king.* Bathsheba exited after the announcement of Nathan's arrival; cf. below, v. 28.

24. *Nathan said: "My lord the king, did* you *say: 'Adonijah shall reign after me and he shall sit on my throne'?* The absence of the interrogative particle is not unusual; the question is in the intonation; see GKC, 150a.

25. *the officers of the army.* The Lucianic reading: "Joab, commander of the army," adopted by some commentators, NEB, and NRSV, levels the subtle differences in the various reports concerning the goings-on at En-rogel; MT is preferable (Montgomery and Gehman, Noth, Mulder).

they are now eating and drinking in his presence and saying. The use of the imperfect with *waw* after the present expresses the continuation of the action, as if the carousing led to the cry of the assembled: "May King Adonijah live!" See S. R. Driver 1892, §80.

'May King Adonijah live!' In the two previous descriptions of Adonijah's feast, the term "has become king" (vv. 9, 18) sufficed. Here, Nathan graphically employed the customary acclamation that was part of the succession ceremony; cf. v. 34 below and Note there.

27. *Has this matter come about by order of my lord the king . . . ?* The use of *ʾim* to introduce a single question is infrequent; cf. Isa 29:16; Job 6:12; see GKC, 150f. Nathan takes up the guise of the offended loyal servant.

28. *She came before the king and stood before the king.* Many find the second "before the king" tautologous (e.g., Gray: "an ugly repetition"); the versions show much variation and some translations follow LXX[BA], Vulg., "she stood before him" (e.g., NEB, NAB). Others concur with Montgomery and Gehman that "Semitic rhetoric is repetitive."

31. *"May my lord, King David, live forever!"* The blessing for the king's long life counters the implied end of his life spoken of in the preceding verse; it wards off, as it were, the "evil eye"; cf. similar preventive invocations in Deut 1:11; 2 Sam 24:3 (Ehrlich).

33. *Take your lord's servants with you.* They are specified in v. 38 as the Cherethites and the Pelethites, David's loyal guard (see Note there); cf., too, 2 Sam 20:6–7 for the terminology.

have Solomon my son ride my own mule. Riding the royal steed was a sign of favor (Esth 6:8); in the present instance, it sought to make Solomon's privileged position public.

mule. The *pered/pirdâ*, a hybrid animal that arrived in Israel through tribute and trade (cf. 1 Kgs 10:25; also Ezek 27:14), seems to have been favored by the upper class (2 Sam 13:29; 18:9), the ass (*ḥămôr*) being the common animal of transport (e.g., 1 Sam 25:42; 2 Sam 16:2; 1 Kgs 13:13).

bring him down to Gihon. Another name for the Siloam Spring in the Kidron Valley (Ar name: 'En Umm ed-Dereğ or 'En Sitti Maryam [= the Virgin's Spring]), the main water source of Jerusalem; cf. 2 Kgs 20:20; 2 Chr 32:30; 33:14. The Gihon is so named for the "gushing" or "breaking forth" (from *gyḥ) of its waters from an underground karstic cave, where the water collects before surfacing. There is nothing to suggest that the spring was endowed with a sacred character; rather, the Gihon was chosen as the site in order to give maximum publicity to the anointing, a counter to the private gathering at En-rogel. (The Gihon River, one of the four said to have flowed out of Eden [cf. Gen 2:13], is not related.)

34. *There Zadok the priest and Nathan the prophet shall anoint him as king over Israel.* For the rite of anointing, see Note to 2 Kgs 11:12. Both priest and prophet share the task (cf. v. 45), though only Zadok is mentioned in v. 39. It is arbitrary to eliminate as a gloss the reference to Nathan, as if he somehow encroaches upon "the priestly office" (as do Gray, Würthwein); note the prophetic anointment of Jehu in 2 Kgs 9:3, 6.

king over Israel. In the present instance, "Israel," rather than "Israel and Judah" (in v. 35, and read here by Luc.) is the preferable reading, because it refers to a solemn act of significance for the people of Israel as a whole.

then you shall blow the horn. The sound of the *šôpār* (a ram's horn; cf. Exod 19:13, 16; and Josh 6:5) warned of the approach of the enemy (cf. Hos 5:8) and summoned men to arms (cf., e.g., Judg 3:27; Neh 4:12). It was blown at the installation of Jehu (2 Kgs 9:13; cf. 2 Sam 15:10); for Joash, trumpets (the trumpet was exclusively a priestly instrument; see Milgrom 1990, 372–73) rather rams' horns, were used; cf. 2 Kgs 11:14.

and say: 'May King Solomon live!' Similar acclamations, wishing the new king health and long life, are recorded concerning Saul (1 Sam 10:24) and Joash (2 Kgs 11:12) and in the personal submission of Hushai before Absalom (2 Sam 16:16); for an interpretation of the jussive as indicative, meaning "the (new) king is alive and well," i.e., he reigns, see de Boer 1955.

35. *Go up after him, and he will come in and sit on my throne and he shall reign in my stead.* The new king's sitting on the throne is the final act in the rite of installation; cf. 2 Kgs 11:19.

for it is he that I have appointed to become ruler of Israel and Judah. The term *nāgîd* is used in Samuel–Kings of persons designated by YHWH for kingship, thus Saul (1 Sam 9:16; 10:1), David (1 Sam 25:30; 2 Sam 5:2; 6:21; 7:8), Solomon (1 Kgs 1:35), Jeroboam (14:7), Baasha (16:2), and Hezekiah (2 Kgs 20:5); these references indicate that the term is not restricted to the period of crown princeship but can be used also of a king's rule. In late usage, it acquires a broader sense, such as "prince" (e.g., Prov 28:16; Job 29:10) and "supervisor" (e.g., 2 Chr 31:13; 35:8). See Liver 1968a; Ishida 1977, 50–51; McCarter 1980, 178–79, 186–87. In this meaning, it seems similar to *ngd* in the Aramaic Sefire inscription (KAI 224:10); for an intepretation as "military commander," see Cross 1973, 220. The *qātîl* form of the profession is usually taken as a passive but might well be parsed as an active participle; see Speiser 1967, 118 n. 10.

Israel and Judah. The reference is to the two constituent political components of David's kingdom; cf. 2 Sam 5:5; 24:9; 1 Kgs 4:20.

36. *Amen.* "So be it" (Moffatt). This adverb, from **'mn*, "to be firm, true," expresses assent and trust in the fulfillment of the oath; cf. Num 5:22; Deut 27:15–26; Jer 28:6; Neh 5:13.

May YHWH the God of my lord the king so order. The MT is construable, taking **'mr* as "order, command" (cf. 1 Kgs 5:20; Esth 2:15); emendations follow one of several alternatives: three MSS read *y'śh*, "may he do," as in Jer 28:6 (so Šanda, BHS, Gray); Luc. and LXX seem to have read *y'mn*, "may he affirm" (so Skinner), but this is tautologous after "Amen."

YHWH the God of my lord the king. On the use of consonants without vocalization for the divine name, see the Note to 1 Kgs 22:53 (Cogan and Tadmor 1988, 21).

38. *the Cherethites and the Pelethites.* A unit of mercenaries under the command of Benaiah (2 Sam 8:18; 20:23); they remained loyal to David in the most adverse circumstances (cf. 2 Sam 15:17) and served him (cf. 20:7) until his death, after which they likely merged into the regular forces. Their origin from the Sea Peoples is suggested by relating the name Cherethite to the island of Crete (though it is referred to as *kaptōr* in BH; cf. Deut 2:23; Amos 9:7) and by taking Pelethite (*pĕlētî*), by analogy with Cherethite (*kĕrētî*), as Philistines (*pĕliští*); cf. the association of the two peoples in Ezek 25:16; Zeph 2:5. See Greenfield 1962.

39. *Zadok the priest took the horn of oil from the Tent and anointed Solomon.* Zadok must have taken the horn of oil before descending to the Gihon but is mentioned only at this juncture, since taking it was relative to the act of anointing forthwith described. A pluperfect, had it been available, would have served the narrator better (see Montgomery and Gehman).

the Tent. The Tent, referred to as the Tent of YHWH in 1 Kgs 2:28, was the tent prepared by David to receive the Ark (2 Sam 6:17); it was pitched somewhere within the City of David (hardly near the Gihon [so Robinson]).

40. *the people were playing pipes.* The festive atmosphere was marked by music and song; cf. the making of music during the transfer of the Ark to Jerusalem (2 Sam 6:5) and during festivals (Isa 30:29). The LXX reading, "dancing dances" (apparently reading *mḥllym bmḥlwt* fot MT *mḥllym bḥllym*), adopted by some (e.g., Skinner, Gray) is not preferable. "The stress seems to be made upon the *noise* [sic] which was made" (Burney).

so the earth was split by their sound. The joyful clamor is likened to the rumbling noise of an earthquake; cf. Num 16:31.

41. *Now Adonijah and all the invited who were with him heard (it) just as they finished eating.* The simultaneity of actions, expressed by the sequence *wyqtl–(w)qtl* (cf. Exod 9:23) is interpreted by Sutcliffe (1958) as if the commotion in the city put an end to the festivities.

"Why the sound of the city in uproar?" There is an elevated feel to Joab's remark in the use of *qiryâ*, a poetic word for "city," which is used only here and in Deut 2:36 in prose.

42. *Jonathan son of Abiathar the priest.* Jonathan appears as a bearer of news from the city, a role he had played during the Absalom rebellion, when he (together with Ahimaaz) had transferred information to David concerning developments within the rebel camp (cf. 2 Sam 15:27–28, 36; 17:17–21).

for you are a worthy man. Jonathan's "social and economic status" (Gray; also DeVries) would have been of no concern to Adonijah at this juncture. Often, Heb *'îš ḥayil* describes a "capable" person (Gen 47:6; Prov 31:10 [fem.]); hence, it suggests reliability and trust in adverse circumstances (2 Sam 2:7; 13:28); cf., too, v. 52, below.

43. *On the contrary.* The adversative force of adverb *'bl* is also present in Gen 17:19; for other asseverative uses, cf. 2 Kgs 4:14 ("still"); Gen 42:21 and 2 Sam 14:5 ("alas").

45. *the city was in an uproar.* An echo of the description in v. 41; there **hmh* is used; here the *Niphal* of **hwm*; cf. 1 Sam 4:5 for the "earth ringing with their shouts" (NEB).

46–48. *Furthermore, . . . and furthermore, . . . and furthermore.* Jonathan's words "tumble out and pile up" (Long, 39), as he excitedly adds one detail after another to his report; cf. 1 Sam 4:17.

46. *Furthermore, Solomon sat on the royal throne.* The narrator has exceeded the reasonable bounds of time and space in having Jonathan tell of the proceedings within the palace; he arrived at En-rogel just as Joab remarked on the horn and loud noise. He therefore could not have witnessed much more than the Gihon ceremony. But this modern, close reading does not disturb the flow of the narrative.

47. *May God.* The ketib "your God" is preferred by a number of commentators, noting the usage "YHWH your God" in v. 17 (cf. v. 36); but without the proper name of the deity, the generic *'lhym* (see above, Textual Note i) is preferable.

make the name of Solomon better than your name. A "good name" refers to one's fame and reputation, often gained by brave deeds; cf. 2 Sam 7:23 (of YHWH); 23:18, 22 (of David's heroes). For the Akk equivalent, *šumum damqum*, see CAD D, 69; Š/3, 293.

may he make his throne greater than your throne. The same blessing had been expressed by Benaiah in v. 37. Just as the first wish was for enhanced personal fame, this second one was for extended rule and dominion.

Then the king bowed low on the bed. David, bedridden, lowered his head in appreciation and acquiescence that YHWH had permitted him to see the peaceful transfer of the throne to his chosen successor; cf. the similar gesture of Jacob in his final days, Gen 47:31, and the comment of Speiser 1964, ad loc.

51. *Adonijah is in fear of King Solomon, and here he has taken hold of the horns of the altar.* Asylum at YHWH's altar was the accepted procedure by which a person suspected of manslaughter might save his life (until trial?; cf. Exod 21:14). The law of the cities of refuge offered permanent asylum; cf. Deut 19:1–10. In Adonijah's case, the altar offered him political asylum; see further below, on 1 Kgs 2:28.

the horns of the altar. Israelite altars were constructed with horn-shaped projections at each of their four upper corners (cf. Exod 27:2; 30:2); for examples of excavated horned altars, see A. Mazar 1990, nos. 11.21; 11.24. Their significance is nowhere stated, but it seems that, since the blood of sacrifices was daubed on the horns (e.g., Lev 4:7, 25), the horns were considered the most significant area of the altar (see Milgrom 1991, 236, 249–50). Note the symbolism of strength associated with animal horns in 1 Kgs 22:11 (see Note).

52. *but if he is caught in a wrongdoing.* Literally, "evil"; cf. 1 Sam 25:28. A single misstep would be his undoing; cf. 1 Kgs 2:13–25.

53. *Solomon said to him: "Go home."* Though formally still co-regent, Solomon seems to have had the authority to grant Adonijah amnesty. His former rival was free to return to his private affairs, having been warned to "stay out of trouble" (cf. v. 52), i.e. court business (Ehrlich); cf. David's handling of Absalom, 2 Sam 14:24.

COMMENT

Structure and Themes

The opening 8 verses of 1 Kgs 1 set the stage for the drama that unfolds in the following 45 (vv. 9–53), in which all the action takes place, on a single day in and around the court of King David. The reader is introduced to the enfeebled king, a mere shadow of the robust leader he once was, and to his upstart son Adonijah son of Haggith who, under the indulgent eyes of his father, has taken on the airs of royalty, behaving as if the throne were already his. But in fact, there are two rival parties in Jerusalem: one supports Adonijah; the other Solomon son of Bathsheba. On a fateful day, Adonijah moves to rouse his backers but, in the end, is outwitted by Nathan and Bathsheba, who see their man safely seated on the throne. This came about through the quick action of Nathan: at his instigation, Bathsheba reminded David of his promise to select Solomon as his successor, and both of them discredited Adonijah by reporting his unauthorized assumption of rule. David acted decisively in Solomon's favor, effectively putting an end to the question of succession. With the anointment of Solomon as king, support for Adonijah dissipated without a whimper; the would-be king sought refuge at the altar and was granted amnesty by the new monarch.

On the compositional level, 1 Kgs 1 is often singled out as one of the finest examples of early biblical narrative (so, e.g., Eissfeldt 1965, 50: "magnificent literary composition"), whatever its genre and purpose may have been (see further below). The action moves forward mainly through the use of speeches, with third-person descriptions kept to a minimum. Repetition serves as a prime narrative device. Thus, e.g., the scene at the Gihon is mentioned three times, twice in reported speech (vv. 9–10, 19, 25–26); Nathan's stated plan (vv. 11–14) is carried out (vv. 17–27); David's order to anoint Solomon (vv. 33–35) is twice repeated, in its implementation (vv. 38–40) and in a spoken report (vv. 43–48). Through the use of small nuanced differences in the repetitions, the narrator succeeds in characterizing the main protagonists (see Alter 1981, 97–100).

The first impression one receives upon reading 1 Kgs 1 is that this is "not the usual opening of a separate work" (i.e., the book of Kings; Long, 34). The narrator proceeds from the assumption that his reader is familiar with the main personalities of the story and with their roles in the previous history of David's reign; thus, he foregoes introducing them, preferring to launch directly into his tale. On this account, the prevailing consensus holds that 1 Kgs 1 (and parts of 1 Kgs 2) represents the concluding episodes of the Succession Narrative (2 Sam 9–20; 1 Kgs 1–2), which as its name suggests, relates the troubled history of the transfer of the throne to one of David's sons; the exposition of this thesis by Rost (1926) has served as the base line for all subsequent study. (The boundaries of this discrete unit in Samuel–Kings are disputed; see the survey of suggestions in Forshey 1992.)

The purpose and viewpoint of the narrator have been the subject of much critical debate. Rost's position that the Succession Narrative was basically a historical work, written "to the greater glory of Solomon" (Rost 1982, 104–5), was adopted by von Rad, who took it to be the "oldest specimen of ancient Israelite historical writing," the product of someone "who had an intimate knowledge of what went on at court," set down during the enlightened age of Solomon (von Rad 1966a, 176, 195, 203). More recent literary criticism has wrestled with the redefinition of the genre of the narrative; e.g., Whybray (1968) pointed to the wisdom themes common to Egypt and Israel that are at the base of this political pamphlet; Gunn (1978, 61) spoke of it "as a work of art and *serious* [sic] entertainment" that was dependent upon traditional oral motifs, which thus greatly reduced its historical character. Others have homed in on the questionably flattering portrayals of the main actors in the drama and have found antimonarchic and/or anti-Davidic themes that were later redacted in favor of the Davidids. Würthwein, for one, points to 1 Kgs 1:30, 35b, 46–48 as Dtr additions that are meant to cover up the serious doubts raised by the original narrative concerning the legitimacy of Solomon's accession. Van Seters finds this solution unsatisfactory, for he cannot conceive of Dtr having left the Court History so "unedited" that it still conveyed a perspective opposite to his own. Consequently, in Van Seters' view, this complex is an "antilegitimation story . . . a bitter attack upon the whole royal ideology of a 'sure house' for David" and represents "a post-Dtr addition to the history of David from the postexilic period" (Van Seters 1983, 289–90). Where others had found unadulterated natural characterizations of the actors, Van Seters finds criticism. (McCarter 1984, 9–16; Forshey 1992; Keys 1996, 14–42 offer brief reviews of these recent works.)

In the face of such a diversity of opinion, and given the restrictions of a commentary devoted solely to 1 Kings, the following appreciation of the opening chapter in the history of Solomon is tendered (to be amplified in the Comment on 1 Kgs 2). In the first place, the dependence of 1 Kgs 1 upon the earlier narratives in 2 Samuel is a chimera, because the material in 2 Samuel is much more dependent upon 1 Kgs 1 for the proffered unity of the Succession Narrative than is 1 Kgs 1 upon it. Rost found the theme of the Succession Narrative in 1 Kgs 1:20: "My lord the king, the eyes of all Israel are upon you, to tell them who will sit upon the throne of my lord the king after him." But nothing in the previous stories has prepared us for the rivalry and intrigue that are at the base of the drama during the days of David's decline. Though Adonijah's trappings of royal status recall those of Absalom (cf. 1 Kgs 1:5–6 and 2 Sam 14:25; 15:1), the plot development of 1 Kgs 1 is self-contained. In fact, the topic of succession is never raised in the so-called Succession Narrative before 1 Kgs 1. Nor are the main protagonists, Adonijah and Solomon, referred to in 2 Samuel, save for the reference to YHWH's approbation of Solomon in 2 Sam 12:24–25, which plays no part in the present drama. Bathsheba, for whose love David had gambled so heavily, vanishes after giving birth to Solomon, and no reference is made to David's promise to her concerning Solomon's future enthronement before 1 Kgs 1:13, 17 (a fact that serves the critics who take it as a fabrication). Moreover, allusion is made in 1 Kgs 1–2 to a number of incidents from the early history of David outside the bounds of the Succession Narrative: Abiathar's aid to David during his outlaw days and YHWH's punishment of the house of Eli (cf. 1 Kgs 2:26–27 and 1 Sam 3:11–14; 22:20); Joab's murder of Abner (cf. 1 Kgs 2:5, 32 and 2 Sam 3). In all, it appears that 1 Kgs 1 is an independent narrative that bridges the reigns of David and Solomon, whose author was familiar with much of David's life, but whose focus was the rise of the new king.[1] (This position was argued by Kaufmann 1957; Liver 1967, 88–89; and most thoroughly by Keys 1996, 54–70.)

By most modern definitions, 1 Kgs 1 cannot be classified as a historical report; the partisan position taken by the narrator disqualifies him as an objective witness to the process of succession to the throne of David. Solomon is David's choice, made in fulfillment of a solemn oath to Bathsheba, who also enjoyed the support of the prophet Nathan, who had earlier spoken of Solomon as the "Beloved of YHWH" (2 Sam 12:25). By contrast with Solomon, on whose behalf many acted but who himself remained in the wings, Adonijah is depicted as unworthy of the throne because of his presumptuous behavior, despite the fact

---

[1] The division of 1 Kings from 2 Samuel after 1 Kgs 2:11 that is indicated in Luc. by the title "3 Kings" is irrelevant to this discussion; see Introduction.

that he might have been considered the legitimate heir in some circles. When read in this way, the narrative may be seen as analogous to the compositions identified in ancient Near Eastern scholarship as "Royal Historical Writing of an Apologetic Nature" (Ishida 1987). Documents from the Hittite and Neo-Assyrian Empires, as well as the kingdom of YʾDY-Samʾal, show that the issue of the legitimation of the new king who had bested the person who stood in direct line of royal ascent was treated and promulgated in an official statement. Among the prominent elements in this genre, one finds the description of the rival's unworthiness and his rebellious attempt to wrest control against the will of the gods and the appointment made by the reigning king. While 1 Kgs 1 does not read like an official document or proclamation, its purpose surely sought to demonstrate the legitimacy of the accession of Solomon.

Finally, it ought to be pointed out that previous readings of 1 Kgs 1 have given insufficient consideration to a characteristic of biblical storytelling that was not adverse to describing the wily ways of heroes, showing how, against the odds, they outsmarted the competiton; cf., e.g., Jacob's behavior in securing the birthright from Esau and the blessing of his aged and sightless father (Gen 25:29–34; 27:1–40). Later editors, for example Dtr, included such revered traditions in their compilations to the consternation of postbiblical (and modern) readers who sought (and still seek) exemplary lessons in Scripture.[2] Read without such anachronistic encumbrances, the history of David's rise to the throne of Israel and Judah glorifies a hero who by dint of his wits founded the United Monarchy; the story of Solomon's accession complements this history—the son of the king's beloved wife was helped to the throne by the timely maneuvers of his supporters, a true heir indeed.

History

As argued above, 1 Kgs 1 is here understood to be a partisan, pro-Solomonic account, apologetic in tone; consequently, the course of Solomon's accession to the throne can only be described in broad outline, and this at some risk. Biblical sources nowhere present a statement concerning the procedure of royal succession. In ancient Near Eastern monarchies, the principle of primogeniture was generally recognized, though deviations from the rule, usually the result of favoritism, are known (Ishida 1977, 8, 16, 155). This principle seems to have been recognized during the earliest days of the Israelite monarchy (cf. 1 Sam 20:31), and it helps explain Adonijah's active claim to the throne and perhaps, as well, David's passivity to this show of ascendancy (1 Kgs 1:5–6; cf. 2:15). At the same time, the acquiescence of those who supported Adonijah to Solomon's designation, as well as the lack of any signs of rebellion against Solomon, seem

---

[2] This obviates the necessity of removing preexilic biblical writings to the postexilic period and reading them as free compositions with little or no basis in tradition, as Van Seters holds, here and at other points.

to indicate that the reigning king retained the prerogative to select another son, out of the order of succession. Concerning the position of the traditional elements in Israelite society and their role in the selection of the king, there is no indication that his accession was dependent upon the approval of tribal elders, especially elders from the Northern tribes; the manner of David's rise (cf. 2 Sam 2:4; 5:3) did not become constitutional (contra Alt 1966, 245).

The rivalry between the two parties at David's court—naturally "this is the way things happen in the atmosphere of a royal court" (Noth 1960, 202)—is often characterized as the attempt of the old guard, those who had been at David's side from the days of his flight from Saul until now (Joab, Abiathar) as well as the tribal leadership (the "men of Judah"), to protect their positions in the face of the intrusions of the younger Jerusalem circle (Benaiah, Zadok). In this struggle, Solomon threw in his lot with the new generation, which was only the first step among many that would alienate people from the Davidic dynasty.[3]

---

[3] The wisdom account in 1 Kgs 12 claims that Rehoboam made the same kind of choice with disastrous results for the United Monarchy.

II. SOLOMON TAKES CHARGE

(2:1–46)

2 [1]Now the time of David's death drew near, so he charged Solomon his son: [2]"I am going the way of all the earth; be strong and be a man! [3]Keep the mandate of YHWH your God, following his ways, keeping his statutes, his commands, and his laws and his warnings, as written in the Teaching of Moses, in order that you may be successful in all that you do and wherever you turn; [4]so that YHWH will fulfill his promise that he made concerning me: 'If your offspring watch their way to walk before me faithfully, with all their heart and all their soul, then no one of your line shall be cut off from the throne of Israel.'

[5]Furthermore, *you* know what Joab son of Zeruiah did to me, [a]what he did to two officers of the army of Israel, Abner son of Ner and Amasa son of Jether. He killed them and so brought about the blood of war in peacetime and put the blood of war on the girdle that is on his loins and the sandals that are on his feet.[b] [6]Act in accordance with your wisdom so that his white head does not go down in peace to Sheol. [7]But with the sons of Barzillai the Gileadite be loyal, and let them be among those that eat at your table, for they took me in when I fled from Absalom your brother. [8]Now you have with you Shimei son of Gera, a Benjaminite from Bahurim; *he* cursed me with a grievous curse on the day I was going to Mahanaim. But *he* came down to the Jordan to meet me and I swore by YHWH: 'I will not kill you by the sword.' [9]However now, [c]you should not clear him, for you are a wise man and you will know what to do to him, so as to bring down his white head in blood to Sheol."

[10]So David slept with his ancestors, and he was buried in the City of David. [11]The years that David reigned over Israel were forty years; in Hebron he reigned seven years, and in Jerusalem he reigned thirty-three years. [12]And Solomon sat on the throne of David his father, and his kingdom was firmly established.

[13]Then Adonijah son of Haggith came to Bathsheba mother of Solomon. She said: "Do you come in peace?" He said: "In peace." [14]He said: "I have something to say to you." She said: "Speak." [15]He said: "*You* know that to me the kingship belonged and that to me all Israel looked to rule, but the kingship turned away and became my brother's, for it was from YHWH that it became his. [16]And now, I have one request to ask of you. Do not refuse me." She said to him: "Speak." [17]He said: "Please talk to King Solomon—for he will not refuse you—to give me Abishag the Shunammite as wife." [18]Bathsheba said: "Very well. *I* will speak to the king on your behalf."

---

[a] A number of MSS, Luc., and Syr. add *waw*; see Note.

[b] Luc. and OL read: "my girdle on my loins and my sandals on my feet"; so NAB, NEB; see Note.

[c] Luc. "you," adopted by NAB, NEB equivocates; see Note.

[19]So Bathsheba came to King Solomon to speak to him about Adonijah. The king rose to greet her, and he bowed down to her. He sat on his throne, and he had a throne set for the king's mother, and she sat on his right. [20]Then she said: "I have one small request to ask of you. Do not refuse me." The king said to her: "Ask, my mother, for I will not refuse you." [21]She said: "Let Abishag the Shunammite be given to Adonijah your brother as wife." [22]King Solomon answered and said to his mother: "And why do you ask for Abishag the Shunammite for Adonijah? Ask the kingship for him! For he is my older brother! For him, for Abiathar[d] the priest, and for Joab[d] son of Zeruiah!" [23]Then King Solomon swore by YHWH: "So may God do to me and even more, for Adonijah spoke this way at the cost of his life. [24]Now, by the life of YHWH, who has established me and seated me[e] on the throne of David my father and who has made a house for me as he promised, this day Adonijah shall be put to death!" [25]King Solomon instructed Benaiah son of Jehoiada; he struck him down, and he died.

[26]To Abiathar the priest, the king said: "Go to Anathoth, to your fields; for though you are a man marked to die, I will not put you to death at this time, for you carried the Ark of the Lord YHWH before David my father and because you bore all the hardships that my father bore." [27]So Solomon ousted Abiathar from being priest of YHWH, in fulfillment of the word of YHWH that he had spoken concerning the house of Eli at Shiloh.

[28]When the news reached Joab—Joab had sided with Adonijah but had not sided with Absalom[f]—Joab fled to the Tent of YHWH and took hold of the horns of the altar. [29]Solomon was told that Joab had fled to the Tent of YHWH and that he was by the altar; so Solomon sent[g] Benaiah son of Jehoiada (with orders): "Go, strike him down!" [30]Benaiah came to the Tent of YHWH and he said to him: "Thus said the king: 'Come out!'" He said: "No, for here I will die!" Benaiah brought back word to the king: "This is how Joab spoke and how he answered me." [31]The king said to him: "Do as he spoke, and strike him down and bury him; so you will remove from me and my father's house (the guilt of) the innocent blood that Joab shed. [32]And YHWH will bring back his blood on his own head, for he fell upon two men more righteous and better than he, and he killed them with the sword—and my father did not know—Abner son of Ner, commander of the army of Israel, and Amasa son of Jether, commander of the army of Judah. [33](The guilt of) their blood will come back on the head of Joab and the heads of his offspring forever, but upon David and his offspring and his house and his throne there will peace forever from YHWH." [34]So Benaiah son of Jehoiada went up and struck him down and killed him; he was buried

---

[d] All versions read *'bytr* (for MT *wl'bytr*) and *wyw'b* (for MT *wlyw'b*); see Note.

[e] Read *wywšybny* for MT *wywšybyny*, with the additional *yod* (noted by Aleppo codex as *yatir*; Leningrad codex as qere-ketib).

[f] Luc., Vulg., Syr. read: "Solomon" (see Josephus, *Ant.* 8.13); see Note.

[g] Luc. and LXX add: "to Joab: 'What is the matter that you have fled to the altar?' Joab said: 'Because I was afraid of you, so I fled to YHWH.' So Solomon sent." See Note.

at his home in the steppe. [35]The king appointed Benaiah son of Jeohoiada over the army in his place; the king appointed Zadok the priest in place of Abiathar.

[36]Then the king sent and called for Shimei; he said to him: "Build yourself a house in Jerusalem and stay there, and do not go out from there anywhere else.[h] [37]For on the day that you go out and cross Wadi Kidron, know full well that you shall surely die. Your blood will be on your own head." [38]Shimei said to the king: "The matter is fine. As my lord the king has spoken, so shall your servant do." And so Shimei stayed in Jerusalem for a number of years. [39]Now three years later, two servants of Shimei ran away to Achish son of Maacah, king of Gath; Shimei was told: "Your servants are in Gath." [40]So Shimei immediately saddled his ass and went to Gath, to Achish, in search of his servants. Shimei went and brought his servants from Gath. [41]Solomon was told that Shimei had gone from Jerusalem to Gath and had returned. [42]The king sent and called for Shimei, and he said to him: "Did I not have you swear by YHWH and warned you: 'On the day that you leave and go anywhere, you know full well that you shall surely die.' And you said to me: 'The matter is fine. I accept.' [43]So why did you not keep the oath of YHWH and the order that I gave you?" [44]The king said to him: "*You* know all the wrong that you harbored in your heart, which you did to David my father; so YHWH has brought down your wrongdoing on your own head. [45]King Solomon is blessed, and the throne of David shall be established before YHWH forever." [46]Then the king ordered Benaiah son of Jehoiada; he went out and struck him down, and he died. Thus, the kingdom was firmly in Solomon's hand.

---

[h] Lit., "here and there."

Note on the Miscellanies in LXX in 1 Kings 2

Two sets of additions appear in LXX, the first in v. 35 (marked vv. 35[a–o] in Rahlfs edition), and the second in v. 46 (marked vv. 46[a–l]). The additions consist of (1) repetitions of Greek translations that appear in the main Greek text, (2) variant Greek translations of MT that sometimes appear in another position in the main Greek text or are missing altogether from that text, and (3) verses that have no counterpart in MT or the main Greek text. Montgomery's basic study (1932), complemented by Gooding's monographic investigation (1976) and Tov (1984), have greatly clarified the nature of these additions. "Misc. 1 deals with his [Solomon's] wisdom in building activities, while Misc. 2 deals with his wisdom in government, administration and supplies" (Gooding 1976, 7). Analysis of the particular verses chosen for repetition and their ordering suggested to Gooding that "the items have been carefully edited and worked up into themes" using proto-midrashic methods of interpretation (Gooding 1976, 106). Talshir took another tack: the miscellanies join together verses that are loosely connected to their context in MT in an attempt to give some order and sense to these scattered bits of information concerning Solomon's reign (Talshir 1990, 257–67). Whether there was a Hebrew *Vorlage* behind LXX (Tov, Talshir) or the editor(s) employed a Greek translation of Kings (Gooding) is a moot question. Thus, while the miscellanies are of interest for the study of the early exegesis of the book of Kings, they do not contribute to the textual history of MT.

NOTES

2   1. *Now the time of David's death drew near.* In Gen 47:29, this idiom sets the stage for the series of actions undertaken by Jacob before his demise.

so he charged Solomon his son. For the sense of *ṣwh* as drawing up one's last will and testament, see Note on 2 Kgs 20:2.

2. *"I am going the way of all the earth. . . ."* The same euphemism for dying is found in Joshua's first farewell address; cf. Josh 23:14.

be strong and be a man! The Philistine army was urged on to battle with Israel by this very phrase; cf. 1 Sam 4:9.

3. *Keep the mandate of YHWH your God.* The phrase *šmr mšmrt* is unusal in Dtr writing and is found only in Deut 11:1; it appears frequently in Priestly texts, in which it refers to "service," more specifically to "guard duty"—e.g.: Num 1:53; and "guarding against violation," Lev 8:35; see Milgrom 1970, 8–11. In the description of the installation of Joash, which draws upon priestly terminology, "guard duty" is also referred to; cf. 2 Kgs 11:5–7.

following his ways. A typical Dtr term; cf. 1 Kgs 3:13; 11:33, 38.

keeping his statutes, his commands, and his laws and his warnings. This string of terms appears innumerable times in Dtr writing; cf., e.g., Josh 22:5; 1 Kgs 3:14; 8:58, 61; 2 Kgs 17:13; 23:3.

as written in the Teaching of Moses. Also referred to as "this Book of Teaching" (Josh 1:8; 2 Kgs 22:8, 11) and the "Book of the Teaching of Moses" (2 Kgs 14:6).

in order that you may be successful in all that you do and wherever you turn. Success is also promised to the tribes of Transjordan (Deut 29:9) and to Joshua (Josh 1:9); and was enjoyed by Hezekiah (2 Kgs 18:7). The expresion seems to have roots in wisdom thought, cf. Prov 17:8 and Ps 111:10 (Weinfeld 1972, 346).

4. *so that YHWH will fulfill his promise that he made concerning me . . . then no one of your line shall be cut off from the throne of Israel.* So, too, 8:25; 9:5–7. But YHWH's promise to David through Nathan in 2 Sam 7:11–16 made no conditions on the continuation of the dynasty; those who would do wrong would be chastened, but no extended punishment is contemplated, certainly not the extinction of the eternal dynasty. On the question of the late origin of the conditionality of the Davidic covenant, see Comment.

to walk before me. The phrase means "to serve me." This Dtr idiom, *hlk* in *Qal*, is also employed in 3:6; 8:23, 25; 9:4, always with reference to the king; cf., too, *hthlk* in 2 Kgs 20:3 and Note there.

5. *Furthermore, you know what Joab son of Zeruiah did to me, what he did to two officers of the army of Israel.* Joab's acts of violence are viewed as having caused David personal harm but, though David roundly cursed Joab for the murder of Abner (cf. 2 Sam 3:29), he put up with his army commander until the end. The addition of *waw* to the second *'ašer* in MSS and some versions eases the asyndetic construction and, if accepted, is not to be taken as conjunctive but, rather, epexegetical (see Waltke and O'Connor 1990, 652–53), specifying Joab's wrong toward David.

Abner son of Ner. Abner, Saul's commander and the strongman behind his son Ishbaal, was set upon by Joab in revenge for the slaying of his brother Asahel; cf. 2 Sam 2:18–23 and 3:27.

Amasa son of Jether. Amasa was David's nephew (1 Chr 2:17), who had supported Absalom (2 Sam 17:25) but later was welcomed back by David and appointed army commander (19:14). Joab, another of the king's nephews, found an opportunity during the rebellion of Sheba to slay his rival, an act David never revenged but also never forgave (20:9–10).

He killed them and so brought about the blood of war in peacetime. Unlike blood shed during war, murder in peacetime was actionable, and Joab was thus guilty on two counts, since both Abner and Amasa were at peace with David at the time that they were struck down. The idiomatic *wyśm*, lit., "he set, placed," has the meaning "assign, impute, account as" in Deut 22:14, 17; 1 Sam 22:15; Job 4:18; cf. Deut 22:8 — the "bringing (**śym*) of bloodguilt upon a house." The struggle of the ancient versions to find a suitable rendition may be seen in their variety and does not suggest that emendation of MT is necessary (e.g., NAB "he took revenge" follows Luc., often retroverted to *wyqm*).

and put the blood of war on the girdle that is on his loins and the sandals that are on his feet. This clause explicates the preceding one, graphically describing the blood of Joab's victims as being spattered on his clothing. Still, some find this explication "colourless," because David's objection was that "the guilt [of the shedding of innocent blood] fell upon himself and his family as the responsible authority" (Montgomery and Gehman; so, too, Jones), and thus adopt the reading of Luc. and OL: "my girdle on my loins and my sandals on my feet." David is thus pictured as being driven to clear his name, even after his demise, of suspicion of collusion in these murders.

6. *Act in accordance with your wisdom.* This is rephrased in v. 9: "for you are a wise man and you will know what to do to him." Solomon's wisdom is the topic of praise and wonder throughout his long reign: in judgment (1 Kgs 3), statesmanship, and scholarly pursuits (1 Kgs 5, 10); here it is astuteness, even guile, that is being called for.

so that his white head does not go down in peace to Sheol. The abstract noun *śêbâ* is properly "grayness, old age"; the translation follows Speiser's remark that "in very advanced age the hair is white rather than gray" (1964, 323).

Sheol. The abode of the dead in the netherworld to which all descend after this life; see in detail, T. J. Lewis 1992b.

7. *But with the sons of Barzillai the Gileadite be loyal, and let them be among those that eat at your table, for they took me in when I fled from Absalom your brother.* During his stay in Transjordan, David had benefited from the support and hospitality of Barzillai, a wealthy Gileadite (2 Sam 17:27–29); in token of this kindness, David wished to reciprocate, but his offer was declined by the aged Barzillai. However, Barzillai's son Chimham joined David in Jerusalem (2 Sam 19:32–40), and it is the continuation of the favors that he apparently enjoyed at court that may be referred to here.

be loyal. For this idiom, see Note on 1 Kgs 3:6.

be among those that eat at your table. That is, to live off the royal dole; cf. 1 Kgs 18:19; 2 Sam 9:7; 19:29.

8. *Now you have with you Shimei son of Gera, a Benjaminite from Bahurim.* David had not forgotten or forgiven the humiliating scene he endured at the hands of Shimei during his abandonment of Jerusalem; cf. 2 Sam 16:5–13. This relative of Saul had an estate in Bahurim, perhaps to be found on the eastern slope of the Mount of Olives, at Rās et-Tmim near eṭ-Ṭur (with Avi-Yonah 1954).

he cursed me with a grievous curse. The singular expression *qllh nmrṣt* describes a harsh, bitter, and potentially harmful curse; from **mrṣ*, Niphal participle, the meaning of which is clarified by Akk *marāṣu* (cf. also Ar *mrḍ*), "to be sick, difficult, troublesome" (CAD M/1, 269–76), and note the description of curses: *arrat la napšuru maruštim*, "a grievous, indissoluble curse" (CAD M/1, 294). Note the similar adjectival construction using a passive participle, *mkh nḥlh*, "sore wound" in Jer 14:17(contra Noth).

But he came down to the Jordan to meet me, and I swore by YHWH: 'I will not kill you by the sword.' Many think that David's generous promise of pardon given at the moment of his return may have been a tactical move on his part, considering that Shimei showed up with a thousand Benjaminites in tow (cf. 2 Sam 19:16–24).

9. *However now, you should not clear him.* The reading in Luc., "but you," offers an emphatic contrast to the previous clause and is preferred by some (e.g., Montgomery and Gehman, Gray), though the summary "and now" may be original; cf. other examples of interchange of *'th* and *'th* in 1 Kgs 1:18, 20 and the Notes there.

you should not clear him. Hebrew **nqh*, "clean," often has the sense "to acquit, leave unpunished," as in Exod 20:7; Jer 30:11; Job 10:14; so also the adjective *nqy*, e.g., Exod 21:28; 2 Sam 14:9. Akkadian *zakû*, "to be clean," has a similar semantic range (CAD Z, 25–32), reflected, as well, in late Aram *zk'y*.

10–11. The notice of David's death and burial is followed by a summation of the years of his rule, an infrequent editorial procedure employed for the reigns that are not introduced by the standard Dtr formula; cf. 1 Kgs 11:42–43; 14:20 (in both cases, the elements appear in reverse order); 2 Kgs 10:35–36.

10. *So David slept with his ancestors.* This phrase means "to die peacefully" and does not refer to burial, as convincingly demonstrated by Alfrink 1943; see also Halpern and Vanderhooft 1991, 184–86. Of the kings who die a violent

death, only their interment is reported; cf., e.g., 2 Kgs 21:26; 23:30. On the problematic single exception of Ahab, see note on 1 Kgs 22:40; cf. also the Note on 2 Kgs 14:22 (and for a new suggestion on the identity of the king whose death is reported there as Joash, see Halpern and Vanderhooft 1990, 187–88). For confirming usage outside of Kings, cf. Gen 47:29–30; Deut 31:16.

he was buried in the City of David. The royal tombs of the Davidic dynasty were in use for close to three centuries, until days of Manasseh (see Note to 2 Kgs 21:18). The site was still known in the Persian period; according to Neh 3:16, it was located in the southeast part of the City of David. Josephus (*Ant.* 7.392–94; 13.249; 16.179) reports that these graves were robbed of their wealth by Hyrcanus and Herod (cf., too, the references in Acts 2:29). Despite these clues, modern exploration on the eastern hill south of the Ophel has not met with success in locating the tombs (see Ussishkin 1970, 46; 1993, 328–31), probably due to the continuous intensive urban settlement in this quarter of Jerusalem. The present-day site on Mount Zion in Jerusalem that bears the name "David's Tomb" is a medieval building built on the ruins of a Byzantine synagogue; it is far removed from the City of David, the hill south of the Temple Mount that descends to the Kidron Valley; for the history of the Mount Zion sepulcher, see Limor 1988.

11. *The years that David reigned over Israel were forty years; in Hebron he reigned seven years, and in Jerusalem he reigned thirty-three years.* This repetition of the datum given in 2 Sam 5:7 rounds off the length of David's seven and one-half years as king in Hebron to the typological number "seven."

12. *And Solomon sat on the throne of David his father and his kingdom was firmly established.* The Janus-like nature of this verse is reflected in the divergent divisions of the text in manuscripts and modern translations. The MT (by means of a *sĕtûmâ*) regards it as the concluding statement on David's reign, signaling the passing of the throne to the designated successor, as promised (cf. 2 Sam 7:12–13). A new narrative unit begins with v. 13. Contrariwise, Luc. inserts a heading before v. 12: "3 Kingdoms," taking the verse as the opening of a new book as well as a new reign. There is some literary justification for joining v. 12 with the following unit; v. 12, together with v. 46b, form an inclusio around the report of Solomon's execution of his rivals, setting it off from the other narratives concerning his rule in 1 Kgs 3–10. Indeed, only after the purge could it be said that Solomon's hold on the kingdom was secure (*mĕ'ōd*, v. 12). Less compelling is reading the verse as subordinate to v. 13: "When Solomon was seated . . ." (so, e.g., Montgomery and Gehman; NAB).

13. *Then Adonijah son of Haggith came to Bathsheba mother of Solomon.* The beginning of a new unit in the continuing saga of Solomon's accession did not require the full introduction of the actors employed here, following as it does 1 Kgs 1:5, 11; does this redundancy hint at rivalry between the two mothers (Walsh, 47)?

She said: "Do you come in peace?" He said: "In peace." The implication of the question is that the rivalry between the two parties had not dissipated, which suggests that this conversation took place not long after Solomon took the throne.

15. *He said: "You know that to me the kingship belonged. . . ."* Solomon as much as admits the correctness of Adonijah's words in v. 22.

that to me all Israel looked to rule. The idiom **śym pānîm*, lit., "to set the face," conveys intent, wish, and endeavor; cf. Lev 20:5; Jer 21:10, 44:11; Ezek 15:7, as does Akk *pānam šakānu* (CAD Š/1, 139–40). In other contexts, it means "to turn/proceed in a certain direction," as in Gen 31:21; 2 Kgs 12:18; Jer 42:15.

17. *He said: "Please talk to King Solomon—for he will not refuse you—to give me Abishag the Shunammite as wife."* Adonijah does not explain his request, leaving Bathsheba (and readers) to speculate on his motive. It was accepted practice for a new king to inherit the former king's harem (cf. 2 Sam 3:7–8; 16:21–22), and though David had not been intimate with Abishag, everyone at court knew that she had warmed his bed (1 Kgs 1:4). Was Adonijah plotting to gain the throne deviously, as Solomon interpreted this "one small request" (cf. further on v. 22)? Or did he move out of love for King David's former house-keeper (so Montgomery and Gehman)? In any case, to think that the desirable young woman could have served as a "sort of 'consolation prize'" for Adonijah after his having lost out to Solomon (Noth) attributes naïveté to the actors in this high-risk game.

18. *Bathsheba said: "Very well. I will speak to the king on your behalf."* The description of Bathsheba's conduct here and in the interview with Solomon that follows is artfully ambiguous. Was she meant to be portrayed as going along with Adonijah so as to lead him into Solomon's clutches? Or are we to imagine her as believing that there was nothing untoward in the request. The same mystery shrouds her earlier actions, in 1 Kgs 1.

19. *The king rose to greet her, and he bowed down to her.* The respect shown to Bathsheba by the king's bowing (*wysthw lh*) is softened somewhat by the reading "and he kissed her" (*wyšq lh*) in Luc. and LXX (adopted by NEB; cf. Josephus, *Ant.* 8.7: "he embraced her"); whether this is a true variant or the translator's finesse in accommodating the king's action to Greek court etiquette is hard to say.

he had a throne set for the king's mother, and she sat on his right. Bathsheba was given the seat of honor on the king's right; cf. Ps 45:10; 110:1.

the king's mother. The title *gĕbîrâ*, "Queen Mother" (cf. 1 Kgs 15:13 and Note there) is not used here; it is rather the personal relationship between mother and son, not her (purported) position at court, that is signaled here (as it is in the response "Ask, my mother" in v. 20).

22. *And why do you ask for Abishag the Shunammite for Adonijah? Ask the kingship for him as well!* Solomon's incensed response to this "small request" (v. 20) suggests that he suspected Adonijah of a larger goal, the kingdom itself; acquiring Abishag was a symbolic move toward the throne (see above, Note on v. 17).

Ask the kingship for him as well! The *waw* of *wš'ly* expresses the joining of the second clause to the preceding one, as if logically developing from it; cf. Ezek 18:32 (Joüon, 177m).

For he is my older brother! An echo of Adonijah's words in v. 15; for Adonijah's position among the sons of David born in Hebron, see Note on 1 Kgs 1:6. Even among those born in Jerusalem, Solomon was apparently not the oldest, cf. 2 Sam 5:15; 1 Chr 3:5; 14:5.

For him, for Abiathar the priest and for Joab son of Zeruiah! Masoretic Text *wlw wl'bytr* . . . picks up the "for him" (*lw*) of the first half of the verse; the versions (see above, Textual Note d) read a simpler text, omitting the second *wl*, thus obtaining "on his side are Abiathar . . ." (for this use of *lamed*, cf. Exod 32:26; Josh 5:13; 2 Kgs 10:6), and most all commentators and many translations follow suit.

23. *at the cost of his life.* For this sense of the *beth*, cf. 1 Kgs 16:34; also 2 Sam 23:17 ("at the risk of their lives").

24. *who has made a house for me as he promised.* Here, too, Solomon confirms Adonijah's words that the kingdom was his by the will of YHWH (cf. v. 15). It is pedantic and without textual warrant to correct MT "for me" (*ly*) to "for him" (*lw*), i.e., David (so, e.g., Stade and Schwally, Gray, NJPSV), because nowhere is there a specific reference to a promise by YHWH to Solomon. The MT represents the Deuteronomistic view that Solomon was the embodiment of the promise to David to establish an eternal dynasty (cf. 2 Sam 7:13); see Knoppers 1993, 70–71.

25. *King Solomon instructed Benaiah son of Jehoiada; he struck him down and he died.* Benaiah took on the role of the king's executioner; cf. also vv. 34, 46. Hebrew **pgʿ* often connotes a chance, unexpected meeting (e.g., Gen 28:11; Exod 23:4; 1 Sam 10:5; Amos 5:19), one that could be accompanied by a request (cf. Jer 7:16; Job 21:15); in the sense of a violent confrontation, it is markedly employed six times in the present chapter (vv. 25, 29, 31, 32, 34, 46), rather than the more common **nkh*, "to strike."

26. *Go to Anathoth.* This Levitical city within the territory of Benjamin (Josh 21:18) was on the road to Jerusalem (cf. Isa 10:30). Its identification with Rās el-Kharrubeh, just 5 km north and east of the City of David, has been called into question for lack of archaeological finds. Nearby Deir es-Sid may be the Anathoth of Jeremiah's day (cf. Jer 1:1), but the location of the tenth-century BCE town remains to be discovered; see Biran 1985.

to your fields. That Abiathar had land in Anathoth does not contradict the restriction on the Levites concerning the acquisition of territorial shares (*naḥălā*) in the Promised Land (cf. Num 18:23); in place of farmland, the Levites were to receive pasture land (*migrāš*) for their flocks outside the cities (cf. 35:1–8). According to Jer 32:7, there were still priestly families with holdings in Anathoth three and one-half centuries later.

for you carried the Ark of the Lord YHWH before David my father. No record of this activity is preserved; the oblique reference to returning the Ark to Jerusalem in 2 Sam 15:29 will hardly do. This lack has suggested to some that "Ark" (*'rwn*) should be corrected to read "ephod" (*'pwd*), the priestly vestment that Abiathar had available throughout his stay with David during his wanderings;

cf. 1 Sam 23:6, 9; 30:7 (so, e.g., originally Thenius, adopted by Montgomery and Gehman, Gray). But the uniqueness of MT speaks for its primacy; besides, all of the versions support MT.

and because you bore all the hardships that my father bore. Abiathar escaped from Nob and joined David (1 Sam 22:20–23), to whom he remained loyal for the next forty years. It is this faithfulness that earned him the amnesty granted by Solomon.

27. *So Solomon ousted Abiathar from being priest of YHWH, in fulfillment of the word of YHWH that he had spoken concerning the house of Eli at Shiloh.* Abiathar's banishment from Jerusalem was likely related to his having sided with Adonijah (cf. 1 Kgs 1:7), but Dtr has incorporated the act into the prophetic prediction-fulfillment theme that abounds in Kings; cf., e.g., 13:26; 14:18; 15:29; et al.; see Introduction.

the word of YHWH that he had spoken concerning the house of Eli at Shiloh. Abiathar son of Ahimelech, who had escaped from the slaughter at Nob (cf. 1 Sam 22:20; 23:6), was the last survivor of the Eliads, against whom a long-standing oracle (cf. 1 Sam 2:27–36) was now being fulfilled. On the problematic genealogy of this family, see Liver 1971; McCarter 1980, 349.

28. *Joab fled to the Tent of YHWH and took hold of the horns of the altar.* Joab is depicted as repeating the act that had won amnesty for Adonijah (1 Kgs 1:50–53), at least for the interim.

Joab had sided with Adonijah but had not sided with Absalom. This editorial aside seems superfluous and would be even more so if the reading of most versions, "Solomon" for MT "Absalom," were adopted. The comment reminds the reader of the personal tensions between Joab and Solomon and notes that, in similar circumstances, he had remained loyal to David, a point that might benefit him in the present crisis (see Walsh).

29. *so Solomon sent Benaiah son of Jehoiada (with orders).* The impact of Solomon's summary order of execution is softened by the short discourse between the king and Joab found in the long addition in Luc. and LXX (see above, Note g). Commentators are divided on the genuineness of what looks like an expression of Joab's "guilty conscience" (Montgomery and Gehman); still, it does not advance the story, since it would have been clear to both Solomon and Joab why he had fled to the altar. If the addition is original, it could have been lost in MT tradition through haplography, since both sentences begin with "So Solomon sent" (*wyšlḥ šmlh*).

31. *so you will remove from me and my father's house (the guilt of) the innocent blood that Joab shed.* The reference is to v. 5, as Solomon himself explicates in the following verse, v. 32. "Innocent" (*ḥinnām*) blood is properly blood shed "without a cause" (cf. 1 Sam 25:31), the adverb being used as a substantive; cf., too, Prov 24:28; 26:2; Ezek 30:16; see GKC, 128w.

34. *So Benaiah son of Jehoiada went up and struck him down and killed him.* The altar offered no sanctuary to the willful murderer; cf. Exod 21:12–14.

he was buried at his home in the steppe. Though he was executed on the charge of murder, Joab was given the honor due the long-term commander of

Israel's army and was interred on his estate. The family grave was in Bethlehem (cf. 2 Sam 2:32), which is located at the edge of the Judean steppe. On this rendering of *midbār*, see Note on 1 Kgs 19:4.

35. *the king appointed Zadok the priest in place of Abiathar.* If, as seems likely, both priests had served in some capacity in the pre-Temple Jerusalem cult (see Cross 1973, 207–13), this notice indicates that Zadok took over the duties of the ousted Abiathar (Ehrlich). Whether the promotion of Zadok is somehow related to the display of loyalty of this priestly clan from southern Judah to David during his days in Hebron, reported in 1 Chr 12:27–28 (see Olyan 1982), cannot be authenticated, due to the problematic nature of the lists (see Japhet 1993, 258–59). See further on 1 Kgs 4:2, 4.

37. *For on the day that you go out and cross Wadi Kidron, know full well that you shall surely die.* The Kidron is Jerusalem's eastern border, and to get to his property in Bahurim, Shimei would have had to cross it. But the point of Solomon's order was that Shimei was under house arrest within Jerusalem and all exits were closed to him, east as well as west (to Gath).

39. *Now three years later.* A literary topos, not a chronological datum; see Note on 1 Kgs 22:1.

Achish son of Maacah, king of Gath. David had found refuge at the court of Achish son of Maoch, king of Gath (cf. 1 Sam 21:11; 27:2), which would have made Achish a very senior statesman at the time of Shimei's trip to Gath. [DNF: "Probably papponymy is at work here, and this Achish is the grandson of David's patron."] The name Achish is now known from the seventh-century BCE inscription discovered at Ekron commemorating the erection of a temple by Ikausu (= Achish) son of Padi, ruler of Ekron; see Gitin, Dothan, and Naveh 1997, 9–11. On the probable identification of Gath with Tell eṣ-Ṣāfi (Zafit) in the northern Shephelah, see Seger 1992; NEAEHL 1522–24.

40. *So Shimei immediately saddled his ass and went to Gath, to Achish, in search of his servants. Shimei went and brought his servants from Gath.* Most ancient Near Eastern societies legislated against harboring runaway slaves, and the subject was sometimes included in state treaties; the law in Deut 23:16–17 is an exception to the rule (on fugitive slaves, see Mendelsohn 1962b, 386). From this single instance, however, there is no way of knowing whether an extradition agreement existed between Gath and Israel; whatever the case, Shimei succeeded in returning to Jerusalem with his property.

42. *And you said to me: 'The matter is fine. I accept.'* For this nuance of **šmʿ*, cf. Gen 37:27; Judg 11:17.

43. *So why did you not keep the oath of YHWH . . . ?* That is, an oath taken in YHWH's name; cf. 1 Sam 20:42.

45. *King Solomon is blessed, and the throne of David shall be established before YHWH forever.* With the elimination of Shimei, his curse on David (cf. v. 8) would lose its effectiveness and not be transferred to Solomon. A self-benediction such as this was meant to render ineffective whatever baleful effects the curse may still have retained; cf., too, the similar counterinvocation in v. 33b. Yaron (1958) has pointed to a similar pattern of speech in an Egyptian

legal papyrus, in which the crimes "come down upon the heads (of the guilty), whereas I (Ramses III) am privileged and immune until eternity" (ANET, 214b).

46. *Thus, the kingdom was firmly in Solomon's hand.* With the elimination of all potential usurpers, Solomon was now in full control. The present clause is a *Wiederaufnahme* that repeats v. 12b ("and his kingdom was firmly established") and together with it, brackets the stories of the king's political rivals.

COMMENT

Structure and Themes

In this second and concluding installment of the story of Solomon's accession to the throne, which began in 1 Kgs 1, the new monarch is depicted as coming out of the wings to center stage, where he now acts decisively against potential opponents.[1] The elimination of Adonijah had been foreshadowed in the king's warning to retire and to stay out of trouble (cf. 1 Kgs 1:52); it seemed, then, that it was just a question of time before Adonijah would be caught in wrongdoing. The pretext for his execution—his request for the maid Abishag—has always appeared flimsy to later readers; for example, to Cross, if Adonijah did ask for Abishag, "he deserved his speedy execution—for stupidity" (Cross 1998, 94). But to give credence to the depiction of Adonijah (and the others in his camp) in 1 Kgs 2 is to judge it through the eyes of Solomon's apologist, whose aim was to demonstrate that the king's opponents had behaved in a manner that led to their own doom. And, as if such conduct were insufficient cause for the king's action, there was David's testament, which authorized the dispatch of Joab and Shimei, both of whom had enjoyed royal good will that ran out with the demise of the old king. No matter which way one looks at it, the use of naked force to secure the throne cannot be disguised by Davidic warrant, concocted by a story-teller, however skillfully. Solomon eliminated his rivals under dubious circumstances and won. In a word, 1 Kgs 2 remains "a fairly sordid story of power politics thinly disguised as a morality tale" (Provan, 40).

Narrative techniques similar to those employed in 1 Kgs 1 are evident in 1 Kgs 2. Through the repetition of conversations, often with small nuanced alterations, the motives of the actors are exhibited; cf., e.g., vv. 16–17//20–21 (Adonijah and Bathsheba//Bathsheba and Solomon); 36–38//42 (Solomon and Shimei). On the other hand, note should be taken of the lack of symmetry within the narrative between the charge given in David's testament and its execution by Solomon. Thus, there is no report that the sons of Barzillai were treated to the king's benevolences (cf. v. 7); neither had David concerned himself with

---

[1] Once 1 Kgs 1 is freed from its cumbersome association with the "Succession Narrative" (see above, Comment on 1 Kgs 1), there is no need to question the association of 1 Kgs 2 with that composition, which according to most proposals ended with the accession of Solomon and the death of David. Noth's wrestlings are typical of most commentators.

the priest Abiathar, whom Solomon banished from Jerusalem (cf. vv. 26–27). In both of these cases, the terms contribute to the softening of the impression of both David's vengeful will and Solomon's bloody purge: David sought care for those who had cared for him, while Solomon spared Abiathar out of respect for the long years he had served at his father's side. Finally, concerning authorship, the continuity of story line between 1 Kgs 1 and 2 and the use of similar literary techniques suggest that they derive from a single storyteller. There is also just the hint of a connection with the following narratives in the history of Solomon's reign. In David's charge, Solomon was repeatedly urged to "act in accordance with your wisdom" (1 Kgs 2:6), "for you are a wise man and you will know what to do" (v. 9), and it is wisdom in all of its varied manifestations that is one of the defining features of Solomon's reign (cf. 1 Kgs 3:12, 28; 5:9, 10, 14, 21, 26; 10:4, 6, 8; 1 Kgs 11:41).

Dtr interposed himself into the narrative of 1 Kgs 2 more than in the previous chapter. Deuteronomistic passages are identifiable in: the stereotypical statement regarding the proper behavior expected of Israel's new king (vv. 2–4; v. 4 is a Dtr_2 expansion); the formulaic closing of David's reign—his death, a notation on the length of his rule, and his burial (vv. 10–11); and the *inclusio* emphasizing the firm establishment of Solomon's rule (vv. 12, 46b); perhaps, too, the allusions to the eternal peace to be enjoyed by the Davidids (vv. 24a, 33b, 45) should be included in this list (so Knoppers 1993, 71–76).[2] That Dtr could not have been pleased with the picture of his royal heroes in 1 Kgs 2— with that of David, who was the model of loyalty to YHWH for all generations (cf., e.g., 11:12–13, 32–34, 36, 38), and with that of Solomon, the wise and generous king—seems a reasonable assumption; at the same time, he did not rewrite or omit the unattractive material, as did the Chronicler, in whose presentation these idealized personalities could do no wrong.

History

Many have found cause to generalize that it was customary in ancient monarchies—perhaps even necessary—for a new king to eliminate political opponents in order to establish his rule, especially when he rose to the throne out of the established order of succession. In Solomon's case, nomination by David and formal enthronement apparently did not guarantee that his accession would remain unchallenged once David died. The resolution of the matter seems not to have been put off for too long. Upon becoming sole ruler, Solomon moved quickly against Adonijah and his supporters, who seem to have been caught unprepared for such decisiveness. Whether there was an immediate

---

[2] The conditionality of the promise to David as expressed in 1 Kgs 2:4 (and 8:25–26; 9:4–9) is a sign of lateness in Deuteronomistic thought (= Dtr_2)—i.e., the post-Josianic–early-exilic era, when the fall of the Davidic dynasty and the destruction of the Temple were accomplished facts. On these Dtr_2 passages, see Cross 1973, 287; Seeligmann 1992, 134–37; and Introduction. Composition, pp. 99–100 above.

cause for concern—the request for Abishag reads too much like a dramatic artifice, the work of the pro-Solomonic author, to be the whole story—is unknowable. In rapid sequence, the king's rivals were dispatched by Benaiah, commander of the mercenary guard, who personally had much to gain by the removal of Joab (cf. 1 Kgs 2:35).

III. THE KING'S VISIT TO GIBEON AND THE GRANT OF WISDOM

(3:1–15)

3 ¹Solomon became the son-in-law of Pharaoh king of Egypt; he married Pharaoh's daughter and brought her to the City of David until he completed building his house and the House of YHWH and the wall of Jerusalem round about. ²Only the people were sacrificing at the high places, because a house for the name of YHWH had not been built up to those days. ³Now Solomon loved YHWH, following the statutes of David his father; only he was sacrificing and making offerings at the high places.

⁴The king went to Gibeon to sacrifice there, for that was the great high place. Solomon used to sacrifice a thousand burnt offerings on that altar. ⁵At Gibeon, YHWH appeared to Solomon in a dream by night. God said: "Ask, what shall I give you?" ⁶Solomon said: "*You* have acted with great loyalty toward your servant David my father, as he walked before you in truth and in righteousness and integrity with you. You have kept this great loyalty toward him and given him a son sitting on his throne as it is today. ⁷Now then, YHWH, my God, *you* have made your servant king in place of David my father, yet I am a little child. I have no experience to lead. ⁸And your servant is among your people that you have chosen, a great people, so numerous they cannot be numbered and cannot be counted. ⁹So, give your servant an understanding heart to judge your people, to distinguish between good and bad; for who can judge this vast people of yours?" ¹⁰The Lord was pleased that Solomon had asked this thing. ¹¹God said to him: "Because you asked for this and did not ask for long life for yourself and you did not ask for riches for yourself, and you did not ask for the life of your enemies, but you asked for yourself understanding in hearing justice, ¹²now I do as you have spoken. I give you a heart of wisdom and understanding; there was no one like you before you, and there will not be anyone like you after you. ¹³And even though you did not ask, I give you both riches and honor, that there will not be any king like you during your lifetime. ¹⁴And if you follow my ways, keeping my statutes and commands as your father David did, I will give you long life." ¹⁵Solomon awoke and, indeed, it was a dream. When he came to Jerusalem, he stood before the Ark of the covenant of YHWH; he sacrificed burnt offerings and presented offerings of well-being and made a banquet for all his servants.

NOTES

3 1. *Solomon became the son-in-law of Pharaoh king of Egypt; he married Pharaoh's daughter and brought her to the City of David until he completed building his house and the House of YHWH and the wall of Jerusalem round about.* The king's marriage to the Egyptian princess is referred to again in 1 Kgs 7:8; 9:16, 24; 11:1. The placement of this verse in its present position is not immediately clear, because it is poorly connected to its context. Noth thought that its purpose was to highlight at the very outset the king's prominent international position, which the marriage surely indicated (Noth, 49). There is just the barest hint that the marriage took place early in Solomon's reign, perhaps before year 4, when he began work on the Temple (cf. 6:1, 37), and this would tie v. 1 to vv. 2–3, which also refer to the same early, pre-Temple period. There is no way to be more specific, since the "three years" of 2:39 are a literary device and have no chronological value (see Note there).

to the City of David. See Note at 2:10.

his house. For the king's palace, see the description in 7:1–12.

the House of YHWH. For this common locution referring to the Temple, see Note to 6:1. The construction of the Temple is set out in detail in 1 Kgs 6.

the wall of Jerusalem round about. Referred to again in 9:15 and 11:27.

2. *Only the people were sacrificing at the high places, because a house for the name of YHWH had not been built up to those days.* Notices concerning continued sacrifice at high places by the populace appear frequently in Kings, generally after a statement that the reigning king did what was pleasing to YHWH; cf. 1 Kgs 15:14; 22:44; 2 Kgs 12:4; 14:4; 15:4, 35. In the present instance, it clears the God-fearing Solomon of violating the altar law of Deut 12 by stating that the Temple had not yet been built. Considering the prevailing pattern of the editor and the opening word "only," v. 2 would read better after v. 3. Its present position may indicate that it was originally a marginal comment, mistakenly entered. Kaufmann's note (1964) that Heb *raq* may also be used affirmatively, in the sense "surely" (cf. 21:25; also Gen 20:11), does not alleviate the problem in Kings; Dtr's rhetoric overrides other considerations.

at the high places. Hebrew *bāmâ* is properly a cultic installation. The common translation "high place" goes back to LXX and Vulg. and seems to have been derived from the association of these cult sites with heights or mountain tops (e.g., 2 Kgs 16:4); but there were valley *bāmôt* as well (Jer 32:35). There is no textual reason to limit their distribution to the countryside, since cities also had their *bāmôt* (cf. 2 Kgs 23:8). In Amos 7:9, the term appears in parallelism to "sanctuaries," and thus *bāmâ* might better be rendered "shrine." Etymological attempts to clarify the meaning of what is obviously a technical term have not been wholly successful. A recent review (ABD 3:196) favors relating it to cognate Akk *bamtu, bamâtu* (CAD B, 76–79), which exhibit both the meaning "a part of the body" (chest?) and "open country, plain."

The overwhelming majority of references to *bāmôt* associate them with the illicit worship of YHWH, which continued after the Temple in Jerusalem was built. In the pre-Temple era, these installations were condoned, as Deut 12 set out (though the term *bāmôt* is not specifically used in Deuteronomy). Sacrifices were conducted at *bāmôt*, and the ensuing communal meals were consumed there (cf. 1 Sam 9:19). Some had buildings nearby, e.g., the room (*liškâ*, "hall"?) where Saul joined the other invited guests (v. 22), and note the term "*bāmôt*-houses" (1 Kgs 13:32). There is no textual evidence that *bāmôt* were Canaanite shrines taken over by the invading Israelites or that the term had an inherently pejorative meaning.

Many types of cultic installations uncovered in excavation have been styled *bāmôt* by archaeologists; and, considering that *bāmâ* seems to be a general term covering a wide range of sites built over the centuries, perhaps this is the best that can be done at present. See the thorough treatment of the philological and archaeological evidence by Vaughan 1974 and Barrick 1992, 195–200; 1996.

for the name of YHWH. A strictly Deuteronomic concept, discussed in the Note on 8:17.

3. *Now Solomon loved YHWH, following the statutes of David his father.* For this Deuteronomic phrase, cf. Deut 10:12; 11:22; 19:9; 30:16, with the unique turn of phrase "following the statutes of David" (rather than "the statutes of YHWH") that appears only in the present verse and is further explicated in 1 Kgs 3:14; cf. too 9:4.

only he was sacrificing and making offerings at the high places. The verbal forms in *Piel* are not correct, because *Piel* generally describes illicit worship at the high places; cf. 22:44 and the Note to 2 Kgs 16:4. In v. 4, where Solomon sacrifices to YHWH at Gibeon, the verb is correctly in *Qal*. To achieve consistency, *maqṭîr* in v. 3 would have to be pointed *mĕqaṭṭēr*.

4. *The king went to Gibeon to sacrifice there.* Gibeon has been identified with the village of el-Jib, 10 km northwest of Jerusalem, astride the major road leading from the Shephelah to the central hill country via Beth-horon. Israel spared the Hivite inhabitants of Gibeon and the cities in its vicinity (Chephirah, Beeroth, Kiriath-jearim) during the conquest of Canaan (Josh 9), enlisting them as Temple servants until late in the monarchy. Though Gibeon appears as a Levitical city in Josh 21:17, the present verse is the sole attestation of its role as a major cult site. A Davidic tradition claims that Saul violated the pact with the Gibeonites, and their consequent vengeance upon the king's descendants was royally sanctioned (2 Sam 21:1–6). Some have claimed that the city was Saul's capital and is referred to in 1 Samuel under the names Gibeah and Gibeah of Saul; see Blenkinsopp 1972; 1974, 1–7. For the archaeology of the site, see NEAEHL 511–14.

the great high place. That is, the largest in his realm; for the Hebrew superlative, cf. Gen 44:12. Other translations interpret this phrase "chief hill-shrine" (NEB); "the most renowned high place" (NAB); "leading country shrine" (DeVries). The Chronicler expands and explains its "greatness," i.e., its being important enough to attract a royal visitor, by noting that the desert Tabernacle as well as the bronze altar were in Gibeon; it was on this altar that Solomon sacrificed (2 Chr 1:3–6). On the Chronicler's rewriting of this verse, see Japhet 1993, 525–28.

Solomon used to sacrifice a thousand burnt offerings on that altar. The imperfect verb *ya'āleh* is frequentative; thus, there is no reason to think that on the occasion of the present visit such a large number of sacrifices was made. Besides, the number "a thousand" is not an exaggeration; rather, it is a typological expression for a great number, cf. Deut 1:11.

5. *At Gibeon, YHWH appeared to Solomon in a dream by night.* Dreams and night visions are a recognized means of divine revelation (cf. 1 Sam 28:6) and are frequently encountered in early literature (e.g., Gen 20:3 [Abimelech]; 28:12 [Jacob at Bethel]; 31:11 [Jacob in Haran]; 31:24 [Laban]; later prophecy looked askance at dreamers and saw them as self-deluded persons (Jer 23:25; cf. Num 12:6), and the Chronicler left out reference to the dream aspect of this revelation altogether (cf. 2 Chr 1:7).

God said: "Ask, what shall I give you?" Hebrew *mâ,* "what," properly in the indefinite use, as in 2 Kgs 2:9; cf. Gen 37:20; Mic 6:8. The generic term "God" rather than YHWH, appears here and again in v. 11.

6. *Solomon said: "You have acted with great loyalty toward your servant David my father. . . ."* Hebrew adds the pronoun *'attâ* for emphasis; cf. also v. 7, *"you have made . . . king."* YHWH's loyalty (Heb *ḥesed*) is the fulfillment of the promise to David of a son that would rule after him, as specifically stated in the second half of the verse. The study of *ḥesed* by Glueck (1967), with an introduction by Larue, remains fundamental to understanding the semantics of this biblical concept. Glueck showed that *ḥesed* is "conduct with a mutual relationship of rights and duties or conduct," whether between humans or between humans and God. In most cases, the older translation "faithfulness" can be rendered as "loyalty" or "mutual aid" and "reciprocal love."

as he walked before you in truth and in righteousness and integrity with you. That is, served you faithfully. For *hālak lipnê,* see Note on 1 Kgs 2:4. Hebrew *yišrat lēbāb,* lit., "uprightness of heart," only here in fem.; otherwise, *yōšer lēb(ab)*; cf. Deut 9:5; Job 33:3; Ps 119:7.

7. *Now then, YHWH, my God, you have made your servant king in place of David my father, yet I am a little child.*

a little child. A rhetorical phrase expressing inexperience, a sign of humility; cf. Jer 1:6. Rabbinic calculations made Solomon out to be 12 years old (cf. Rashi, Qimḥi, Seder Olam), but this hardly seems correct. Josephus gave his age as 14 (*Ant.* 8.211). On average, the Judahite kings acceded to the throne at the age of 22 (see Freedman 1993, 46*). Certainly, he was already a father when he assumed the throne (cf. 11:42 and 14:21). Yet all such reckonings are beyond the point and irrelevant to the story (Mulder 1989). By this phrase, Solomon means to point out that he is not up to the great task ahead.

I have no experience to lead. Literally, "to go out and to come in," as in Num 27:17, 21; Deut 31:2; Josh 14:11, expresses the discharge of public duties, especially in war; cf. 1 Sam 18:16; see van der Lingen 1992, 59–66. For a more general sense of "coming and going," cf. Ps 121:8. In Knoppers's view (1993, 82 n. 46), the negative use of the expression suggests that, with YHWH's gifts, Solomon will be able "to rule effectively without recourse to war."

8. *And your servant is among your people that you have chosen, a great people.* The promise to David that one of his offspring would succeed him was to be fulfilled within Israel, a people bound by a covenant with God (2 Sam 7:10, 12); these two ideas—the Davidic promise and the covenant with Israel—are seen as complementary in Deuteronomistic thought.

a great people. The idea of the greatness of the people of Israel is also inserted into Hiram's reply to Solomon; cf. below, 5:21.

so numerous they cannot be numbered and cannot be counted. The same terms are used with reference to the innumerable sacrifices offered up at the dedication of the Temple in 1 Kgs 8:5.

9. *So, give your servant an understanding heart to judge your people, to distinguish between good and bad; for who can judge this vast people of yours?* Moses also was not up to the task of judging Israel because of their number (so in the Deuteronomic depiction of the institution of judges in Deut 1:9–12); it is the fulfillment of YHWH's promise to the patriarchs (e.g., Gen 15:5; 28:14) that has brought about this difficulty.

an understanding heart. Literally, "a heart that listens" and considers; cf. 2 Sam 14:17. Skinner translated: "a discerning mind," the heart being the organ of comprehension in ancient Hebrew physiology. In Akkadian, wisdom is ascribed to the ear (*uznu*); cf. *ina uzni rapaštim ḫasisi palkê ša išruka apkal ilāni,* "with the great wisdom and wide understanding that the wisest of the gods presented me" (CAD Š/2, 46a). In Egyptian, the expression "hearing heart" refers to the agent for attaining understanding (see Shupak 1985). Throughout the ancient Near East, the ability to listen was seen as the source of wisdom. Note that Absalom incites against his father those who had come to the king's gate for justice by promising to give them what David had not: "You get no hearing from the king" (2 Sam 15:3).

to distinguish between good and bad. Because sound judgment is a godlike quality (cf. Deut 1:17), Solomon turns to YHWH for this trait. Cf. the words of the woman from Tekoa who complimented David on his ability "to discern (lit., 'to hear') good and bad," just like an angel of YHWH (2 Sam 14:17).

this vast people of yours. Hebrew *kābēd,* "heavy," here "numerous"; cf. Exod 12:38; with reference to a "large (army) force," cf. 2 Kgs 6:14; 18:17.

10. *The Lord was pleased that Solomon had asked this thing.* According to the oft-repeated evaluation of Dtr throughout the book of Kings, YHWH takes pleasure in the cultic loyalty of royal incumbents; here it is Solomon's humility that finds divine approval.

11. *God said to him: "Because you asked for this and did not ask for long life for yourself. . . ."* The preposition *lĕkâ,* "for yourself," conveys the potential benefit one might receive; cf. Deut 7:25; 1 Sam 12:17, 19; on this "dativus commodi," see Waltke and O'Connor 1990, 207–8. Only the third item, "did not ask for the life of your enemies," does not use this preposition; to have included it would have changed the meaning of the clause to asking for the persons of his enemies, i.e., taking them to be his slaves (with Ehrlich).

long life for yourself, and you did not ask for riches for yourself and did not ask for the life of your enemies. Wisdom, if achieved and properly used, can lead to long life, riches. and honor; cf. Prov 3:16. Of this triad, Solomon attained all, except a particularly long life.

the life of your enemies. This is the only item not picked up in vv. 12–14, where YHWH grants Solomon the unasked-for gifts. In light of Solomon's actions against present and future enemies reported in 2:13–46, the king is not portrayed as being in need of a divine endowment in this regard.

but you asked. The contrast is expressed by the simple *waw*; cf. 11:34.

12. *now I do as you have spoken. I give you a heart of wisdom and understanding; there was no one like you before, and there will not be anyone like you after you.* For the idea that the ability to judge is a God-given quality, cf. Deut 1:17; Ps 72:1–2. The words used here to describe the grant of wisdom are different from the ones in the request of v. 9, but this does not justify taking them as a second, nonjudicial class of wisdom that Solomon received (so Zalevsky 1973, 244–45). The root *špṭ,* "judge," sometimes conveys the sense of administrative ability (especially in the book of Judges); however, 1 Kgs 3 is wholly given over to judgment, as the case of the two women and the chapter's closing verses (vv. 16–28) prove. For wisdom in international affairs, cf. 5:26 and Note there.

13. *And even though you did not ask, I give you both riches and honor, that there will not be any king like you during your lifetime.* The Luc. and LXX omit "during your lifetime," as do most commentators. But the promise of unrivaled wealth throughout his reign does not sound "senseless" (Skinner) or in any way limiting. Later scribes may have wanted to make Solomon out to be the richest monarch that had ever lived and thus omitted the final phrase. Nor is this promise in conflict with the promise in v. 12, where he is made the wisest man of all time.

14. *And if you follow my ways, keeping my statutes and commands as your father David did, I will give you long life.* Length of days is not a gift given lightly; unlike riches, it is the reward for following YHWH's commands, a frequent Deuteronomic theme; cf., e.g., Deut 4:26; 5:30; 6:2; 11:9, and only here in Dtr.

15. *Solomon awoke and, indeed, it was a dream.* The verse is written from the point of view of Solomon who, upon awakening, realized (= *hinnēh*) he had had a vision; cf. the very same language concerning Pharaoh in Gen 41:7. See Berlin 1983, 62–63, 91–95; Kogut 1986.

For God's revelation classified as a dream, see above on v. 5. The pointing *wayyiqaṣ* (so Leningrad codex) is normal for this *primae yod* verb (cf. Judg 16:20; Ps 78:65), though many manuscripts have a *dagesh*-form (*wayyiqqaṣ*).

When he came to Jerusalem, he stood before the Ark of the covenant of YHWH; he sacrificed burnt offerings and presented offerings of well-being and made a banquet for all his servants. In public acknowledgment and thanks for YHWH's favor. This verse appears to be an attempt to correct the impression given of Solomon and his aberrant cultic behavior at Gibeon, especially as seen in Dtr circles. "The implication is that not only did Solomon receive wisdom, wealth, honor and long life at Gibeon, but he also realized the proper place for offering sacrifices to God" was in Jerusalem (Carr 1991, 80). Second Chronicles 1:5 makes it clear that it was upon the bronze altar built by Bezalel in the desert and installed by David in front of the Ark that Solomon offered.

COMMENT

Structure and Themes

The introductory unit (vv. 1–3) was constructed by Dtr and introduces the business of Solomon's reign, now that the king is unencumbered with rivals at home, his rule now firmly established (cf. 2:46). Not all of its elements, however, fit well together syntactically (especially vv. 2–3 with v. 1; see Note above).

If we take these three verses as a single editorial unit, the reference to Solomon's marriage to an Egyptian princess and to his worship at the high places may be contrasted to the description of his multiple liaisons with foreign women and their influence on his cultic habits in 11:1–8, which introduces the final Dtr evaluation of Solomon. Whatever the motive for his marriage to the Pharaoh's daughter may have been (see discussion at 9:16 for its political ramifications), vv. 1–3 stress that Solomon's love for YHWH is undiminished (cf. v. 3) and is, moreover, a source of blessing (vv. 4–15); in the later section, 11:1–2, it is Solomon's love of non-Israelite women that leads him away from YHWH toward disaster.

Some recent commentators have suggested that, even in 3:1–3, Dtr characterizes Solomon as bearing "the seeds of his own destruction," in his alliance with Egypt and his order of priorities, completing his own house before the Temple (Provan, 44–46; see also Walsh, 70, 85). Such readings, however, may be overreading, inasmuch as Dtr describes Solomon, and only him of all the kings of the Davidic dynasty, as "loving YHWH" (v. 3), so that his marriage to the Egyptian princess and his sacrifice outside Jerusalem are both understood and excused. Together, they serve as the counter to the decadence of the king's later years.

Though the marriage of Solomon to the Egyptian princess is mentioned no fewer than five times in 1 Kings, the significance of this union is nowhere discussed by the writer. Egyptian records show that rarely were daughters of the king married off to foreigners; thus, in certain circles in Jerusalem, this might have been considered more than just another political marriage, as were Solomon's other unions (11:1ff.). This unusual marriage was indicative of Solomon's major role in regional affairs and of diminishing Egyptian fortunes. See further in Comment on 9:16.

The suggestion to see the present unit as the first of two framing elements, 3:1–3//9:24–26, which mark off "Pro-Solomon" and "Anti-Solomon" evaluations (Porten 1967; Brettler 1991) calls attention to the difficult structural juxtapositions of the original materials in 1 Kgs 9–10 but does not satisfactorily solve their problem. The Deuteronomist's criticism of Solomon begins in 11:1 and not before. Nor does it help to point to the Law of the King in Deut 17:14–17 and its restrictions on amassing horses and wealth as proof that 1 Kgs 9:26–28 (horse trade) and 1 Kgs 10 (wealth) criticize Solomon for violation of Mosaic Law. On the contrary, wealth is YHWH's gift, in the view of 1 Kgs 3–10.

Besides serving as the formal introduction to and the first evaluation of Solomon's reign, items that Dtr included for every king who came to the throne in both Judah and Israel, vv. 1–3 foreshadow the following story, his visit to Gibeon, explaining how he came to sacrifice outside the chosen city.

Although all commentators agree that at the base of the account of Solomon's visit to Gibeon is a pre-Dtr account that has been edited by Dtr, the degree of editing recognized by each one differs greatly and, at times, seems somewhat arbitrary. Thus, e.g., Burney (28–32), followed by Montgomery and Gehman, noted Deuteronomistic phraseology in vv. 6, 8a, 12b, 14 and 15; Noth (44–45), who noted the difficulty in pinpointing the editorial phraseology, listed vv. 6–8, 13b, and 14 as Deuteronomistic; Weinfeld (1972, 246) claimed that Dtr's hands are to be felt "throughout the entire section . . . not only in its stylistic features but also in its thought" (so also Van Seters 1983, 307–8). Carr's extensive form-critical study (1991) identified the following verses as pre-Dtr: vv. 4, 5, 6aα, 7, 9a, 11aα1–3, 12abα, 13a, 13bβ, 14b. The unusual appearance of the generic *'ĕlōhîm* in vv. 5b and 11 instead of the tetragrammaton is a clue to the shape of the base story; the introduction of *'ădōnay* in vv. 10 and 15b seems to be from a later hand.

This most unorthodox tradition tells of the king's visit to the shrine at Gibeon, where he offers sacrifice and receives YHWH's gift of wisdom, all outside the sacred precinct of the Tent shrine in Jerusalem. As far as the story itself is concerned, Solomon is not portrayed as someone in need of exoneration; YHWH appears to him at Gibeon and responds to his request without reservation. An older, pre-Dtr level is at the base of this account, though it is presently heavily overladen with editorial phraseology.

Dreams are a favored means of divine communication in early biblical narratives (e.g., Gen 26:24; 28:11; 31:12, 46:2) and are recognized as a legitimate means for obtaining divine instruction (1 Sam 28:6). In this, Israel did not differ from other societies in the ancient Near East. On the basis of extrabiblical examples, it is often suggested that Solomon's dream at the sanctuary of Gibeon is to be classified as a "provoked incubation dream"—i.e., a purposeful overnight stay at a site where the divinity was believed to reside (Oppenheim 1956, 188–90). By this means, monarchs often sought support and endorsement for their endeavors. Solomon's coming to Gibeon has been compared to the case of the Sumerian king, Gudea of Lagash, whose desire to build a sanctuary for his god Ningirsu was confirmed in a dream; in like manner, Solomon sought YHWH's blessing for the construction of the Temple. The present wisdom focus of the story is, therefore, the result of rewriting (Kapelrud 1963). But one must admit that, if any such purpose was expressed in the original account, it can no longer be found in the received text.

A suggested parallel from Egyptian literature has often been pointed to in explication of the Gibeon dream. Several motifs taken up in the "royal novel" (*Königsnovelle*)—the divine selection of the future monarch and the request to repair his sanctuary, followed by sacrifices by the king-to-be at the god's sanctuary—remind some scholars of Solomon who, following his inaugural revelation at Gibeon during which he was granted the qualities needed to rule, returned to Jerusalem to sacrifice and feast with his staff (Herrmann 1953–54).

But in this proffered parallel, as well, the substance of the dream message in 1 Kgs 3 is unlike the Egyptian examples compared, especially the Thutmose IV dream episode (ANET, 449), in which the nomination of the king by the god is the main subject of the dream encounter. Besides, meeting the deity in a dream is not uncommon in the Bible (see Würthwein 1977, 32). Gray adopts and modifies Herrmann's suggestion; this passage (particularly vv. 6, 9, 11ff.), as well as "the so-called messianic passages" (in Isa 9 and 11), grant legitimation not only to Solomon's succession but to the Davidic ideology of kingship as well.

Stripped of its Deuteronomistic accretions, 1 Kgs 3:4–15, together with the royal Psalms 2:8; and 20:5–6; 21:3–10, have also been read as evidence for a ritual of royal investiture that was practiced in Israel, during which the new king was granted his initial wishes for a long rule of honor and success (Brekelmans 1982). In this view as well, literary motifs common to Israel and its neighbors have been detected.

But the biblical story of Solomon at Gibeon is *sui generis* in its wisdom emphasis and deserves to be read on its own terms. It serves as the introduction to a cycle of stories of the wise king's rule. It is not directly connected to Solomon's election to the Davidic throne, which he had already secured (1 Kgs 2), though reference to YHWH's promise on this score is made in vv. 6b–7a. Nor is it concerned with Temple construction, the validation for which was given in Nathan's instructions (2 Sam 7). The following story of Solomon's judgment (1 Kgs 3:15–27) and its coda (v. 28) show that wisdom is the predominant theme of the Gibeon pericope. Wisdom is of divine origin, a gift to the king, so that he may deal righteously with his people (cf. Ps. 72:1–2).

Solomon was warned by David that, in order for him to take firm hold of his throne, he would have to act wisely (cf. 1 Kgs 2:6, 9); this wisdom suggests shrewdness with respect to potential political enemies, a seemingly inborn trait. The wisdom that Solomon asks for at Gibeon is of another sort, though the same Hebrew term is used. YHWH grants him the gift of divine understanding needed to administer a great nation. In addition, Solomon's humility, in not asking for riches and honor and the power to defeat his enemies, is seen as the ground for these very gifts; they are the side benefits for following the ways of wisdom; cf. Prov 3:13–18.

History

The role of Gibeon as a major cult site is known only from the present account, and considering that the Deuteronomists delegitimized all sacrifice outside the chosen place and would have had no reason to invent such a story and to choose this unusual location, it seems safe to say that a reliable and, indeed, an old Gibeonite, i.e., Benjaminite tradition is at the base of the present account. According to Josh 9, the original Canaanite residents of Gibeon had been enlisted for cultic service, but just how and when the city's shrine achieved the high standing that elicited frequent royal visits (cf. 1 Kgs 3:4) remains unknown. In the Chronicler's retelling (2 Chr 1), the reader is reminded that, while the Ark of the Lord was in Jerusalem, the bronze altar was with the Tent of Meeting in Gibeon; but this is questionable evidence. (For suggestions that Gibeon was the capital of Saul's kingdom, see Note on v. 4.) One wonders whether, if in addition to the ancient sanctity associated with the site, political considerations did not lead Solomon to frequent Gibeon.

IV. The Judgment of a Wise King

(3:16–28)

3 [16]Then two prostitutes came to the king and stood before him. [17]One woman said: "If it please my lord, I and this woman live in the same house; and I gave birth while she was in the house. [18]On the third day after my delivery, this woman also gave birth; we were alone, no outsider was with us in the house, just the two of us in the house. [19]Now the son of this woman died during the night because she lay on him. [20]She got up in the middle of the night and took my son from beside me while your maidservant was sleeping, and she laid him in her bosom and she laid her dead son in my bosom. [21]When I got up in the morning to nurse my son, here he is, dead! But I looked carefully at him in the morning, and here he was not my son whom I had borne." [22]The other woman said: "No! For my son is the live one; your son is the dead one!" And this one was saying: "No! Your son is the dead one; my son is the live one!" Thus they argued before the king. [23]The king said: "This one says: 'This is my son, the live one; your son is the dead one.' And the other says: 'No! Your son is the dead one and my son the live one!'" [24]The king said: "Bring me a sword." They brought a sword before the king. [25]The king said: "Cut the live son in two! And give half to one and half to the other." [26]But the woman whose son was the live one said to the king, for she was overcome with compassion for her son: "Please, my lord, give her the live child, but by no means, don't kill him. And the other one was saying: "Neither I nor you shall have him! Cut him!" [27]The king replied: "Give her the live infant and by no means, don't kill him. She is his mother." [28]When all Israel heard of the judgment rendered by the king, they were in awe of the king, for they saw that God's wisdom was in him to do justice.

NOTES

3 16. *Then two prostitutes came to the king and stood before him.* Having just related the account of YHWH's grant of wisdom to Solomon, the editor presents an exemplary tale to illustrate how the wise king managed his realm.

Then. The introductory word "then" (Heb *ʾāz*) is a loose editorial phrase, frequent in Kings, used to tie together originally discrete literary units. Cf., e.g., 8:1, 12; 9:11b, 24b; 11:7; 16:21; 22:50; et al.; see further in the Note on 2 Kgs 16:5.

two prostitutes. Translating "inn-keepers" (so Wiseman; and as far back as Targum) is somewhat puritanical; the story line required that the two women not be living in their respective homes but together in some sort of shared residence. There is no expressed evaluation of the profession engaged in by these women, unless it is more implied than expressed; indeed, they are given their day in court the same as any other Israelite. After the initial introduction, the narrator proceeds to speak of "the woman," dropping the career designation altogether. Moreover, he describes the strong motherly feelings (v. 26) held by a woman of low social rank. On the biblical view of prostitution, see Goodfriend 1992.

two prostitutes came to the king and stood before him. Public access to the king for judgment was also implied in Absalom's provocative words that, were he king, the people would receive proper hearings, which they were not receiving with his father, David (2 Sam 15:3–4). Compare this with the attention given by David to the woman from Tekoa in 2 Sam 14:1–20 and by Joram to the plea made by the Shunammite woman later, in 2 Kgs 8:4–6.

17. *One woman said: "If it please my lord. . . ."* The form of Heb *bî*, here translated "please," has not been satisfactorily explained. Many adopt Honeyman's suggestion (1944) to relate it to **ʾby*, "need, want, desire," with the loss of the initial *ʾālep*; it always appears at the beginning of a sentence followed by *ʾădonî*, "sir," introducing a supplication; e.g., Gen 43:20; 44:18; Num 12:11; Judg 6:13; 1 Sam 1:26. KB, 120 views it as an elliptical expression: "upon me, my lord (shall come the harm our conversation could do)." It is also of interest that in the late Babylonian dialect of Akkadian, the particle *bî* is known, used only with the imperative of the verb *nadānu*, "to give" (CAD B, 216–17).

I and this woman live in the same house. Care should be taken not to introduce such modern terms as "house of ill repute" (*Dirnenhaus;* so Noth) into the ancient setting. The closest one might come to a permanent residence of sorts for these "professional" women was the tavern, which served as a place of refreshment and often a place to meet prostitutes. See provisionally, the remarks of Harris 1990, 222 n. 15; 224 n. 26.

while she was in the house. Without a conjunction in Hebrew; this resembles the late usage in Esth 7:8.

18. *On the third day after my delivery, this woman also gave birth.* An indefinite measure of time, an element common in storytelling, meaning "after a few days, shortly thereafter"; cf. Gen 22:4; 31:22; Josh 9:17; 1 Sam 30:1; 2 Sam 1:2; Esth 5:1.

we were alone, no outsider was with us in the house, just the two of us in the house. There were no witnesses, so it was her word against that of her housemate. Thus, the king would have to employ unconventional methods to determine the truth in this case. Some have found an allusion here to "clients" of the two women, recalling that the two spies who came to Jericho spent the night at the home of a prostitute (Josh 2:1).

19. *Now the son of this woman died during the night because she lay on him.* For this use of *ʾăšer*, cf. 8:33; 15:5; the fuller *ʿal ʾăšer* in 2 Sam 12:6; and *mippĕnê ʾăšer* in Exod 19:18.

20. *She got up in the middle of the night and took my son from beside me while your maidservant was sleeping, and she laid him in her bosom, and she laid her dead son in my bosom.* It is not clear how the sleeping woman learned that an exchange had been made.

21. *When I got up in the morning to nurse my son.* The twice-repeated notice in a single verse that morning had arrived is usually taken as a textual error

and the second one omitted; so already LXX; cf. Šanda, Noth, Gray, Würthwein. But perhaps the repetition refers to the difference between the ill-defined darkness of the early morning and the full morning light, when the recognition of the child's identity could be made. Note that, in vv. 19–20, "in the night" is also repeated. [DNF: "It could also reflect the agitation of the speaker."]

here he is, dead! See above, Note on v. 15.

But I looked carefully at him in the morning. If there were any telltale signs, such as clothing, that would have made the identification positive, she does not say. Moreover, how could she be believed, when she had slept so soundly through the claimed switch of infants?! Was this inconsistency a clue to the true mother? The verb **byn/bnn* in *Hithpolel* carries the iterative sense, i.e., of repeated or close scrutiny.

22. *The other woman said: "No! For my son is the live one; your son is the dead one!" And this one was saying: "No! Your son is the dead one; my son is the live one!" Thus they argued before the king.* The alternation between perfect and imperfect verbal forms conveys simultaneity; the scene had turned into a shouting match between the two women.

23. *The king said: "This one says: 'This is my son, the live one; your son is the dead one.' And the other says: 'No! Your son is the dead one and my son the live one!'"* The statements of the two women are given in chiastic construction. Were this a modern courtroom, one might interpret this verse as the judge's repeating the facts of the case before sentencing (Šanda).

This one says . . . and the other says. For this locution, cf. similarly 1 Kgs 22:21.

25. *The king said: "Cut the live son in two! . . ."* Hebrew **gāzōr* means "to cut, divide" and is here modified by *bišnayîm*, "in two," which is not repeated in v. 26. Its other uses are ambivalent and may simply mean "cut into parts," Ps 136:13 (of the Sea of Reeds) and 2 Kgs 6:4 (of wood).

And give half to one and half to the other. Literally, "half to one and half to one."

26. *But the woman whose son was the live one said to the king, for she was overcome with compassion for her son.* The storyteller reveals to the reader, for the first time, the identity of the true mother; it was "her son" who was alive. Yet we are not told whether she is the complainant or the respondent.

for she was overcome with compassion for her son. The *kî* has emphatic function, pointing to the "mental or sensory awareness of the character" (Van Wolde 1995, 635); see, too, Muilenburg 1961; Schoors 1981; Waltke and O'Connor 1990, 675.

overcome with compassion. Cf. Gen 43:30; Hos 11:8 (with *niḥûmāy*); Lam 5:10. Hebrew **kmr* is of questionable etymology; rather than a single root meaning "to become hot," Ibn-Janah and Qimḥi both suggest, in fact, two separate verbs: **kmr* in the present verse, meaning "arouse, bring about" (cf. Tg.: *itgôlalû*); with **kmr* in Lam 5:10, "dry up, shrivel," as it seems to mean in later MH and Aram.

the woman . . . said to the king. Hebrew repeats "said" after the long parenthetical description of the woman.

Please, my lord. See above on v. 17.

the live child. The pass. part. *yālûd* properly means "the born one."

And the other one was saying: "Neither I nor she will have him! Cut him!" She interrupted the speech of the first woman; cf. similar syntax in v. 22.

27. *The king replied: "Give her the live infant and by no means, don't kill him. She is his mother."* The threat to the child's life elicited compassionate motherly feelings and allowed the truth to be determined in what was otherwise an insolvable situation. The king's words were likely accompanied by a gesture, pointing to the woman who had spoken first. For the listener, her identity is further clarified by the king's quoting her words.

28. *When all Israel heard of the judgment rendered by the king, they were in awe of the king, for they saw that God's wisdom was in him to do justice.* YHWH's promise to the king at Gibeon had, indeed, been fulfilled (cf. vv. 11–12).

God's wisdom. Or "divine wisdom." The wisdom spoken of here is not the traditional lore of wise men, with which Solomon was also endowed (cf. 5:9–14), but the discernment necessary to render clever and difficult judgments. This quality was included in the list of judicial qualifications sought by Moses in Deut 1:15; cf. 16:19. The superlative use of *'ĕlōhîm* meaning "superior, extraordinary" (e.g., Gen 30:8) is inappropriate here.

COMMENT

Structure and Themes

There is much agreement among commentators that a folktale has been adopted by Dtr to show that YHWH's promise in the preceding section (vv. 4–15) of a grant of wisdom to Solomon to judge his people has indeed been fulfilled. The original oral quality of the tale is much in evidence; the narrative moves forward mostly by means of speeches, which also serve as a means to characterize the two protagonists and the king. Only the concluding v. 28 is from Dtr.

In the original folktale, the wisdom displayed by the king was likely to have been little different from the shrewd cunning and astuteness that had helped him secure the throne in the first place (cf. 1 Kgs 2:6, 9). By cleverly creating a threat to the child's life, the king forces one of the women to give up her claim, thus revealing her true identity. But Deuteronomistic wisdom, a godlike quality needed to judge between good and evil, was of another order; by inserting the tale after the dream episode at Gibeon, Dtr has led us to read the tale as the verification of YHWH's grant to Solomon of judicial wisdom.

Würthwein's adoption of the older Gressmann thesis (1907) that this tale made its way to Israel from distant India, where a large number of similar tales are attested, and was incorporated in a developed form into the Solomonic account in a post-Dtr stage (36–38) is not convincing; nor does taking 1 Kgs 4:1 as the original conclusion of the Gibeon dream episode support this view (see Note, ad loc.). Folkloristic parallels are not lacking, and one need not travel so far afield; Thenius brings a quote from Grotius, who quotes Diodorus, with a classical parallel.

Though the role of the king is central to the narrative, the women's role in bringing about the solution to the crisis should not be dismissed. Had one of the women not acted upon her motherly feelings and saved the king from carrying out his threat, a wholly other conclusion might be imagined. Yet this "saving" of the king from an injudicious decision does not justify including the true mother of the child among the Bible's "wise women," e.g., the woman of Tekoa (2 Sam 14:1–20) or the one from Abel Beth-Maacah (20:16; as suggested by Beuken 1989).

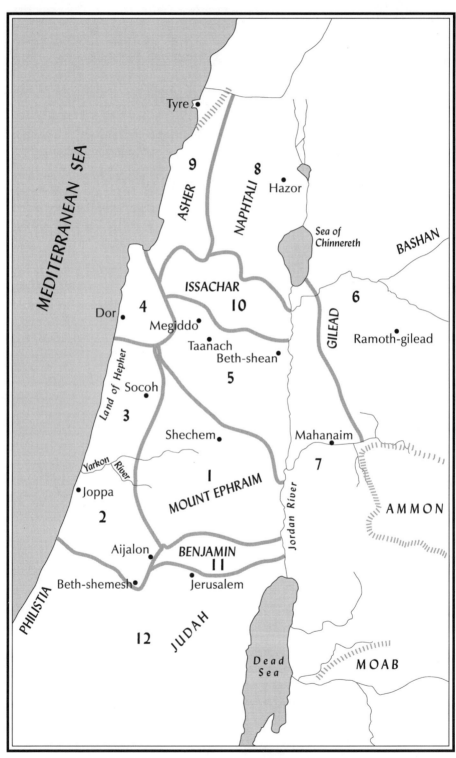

APPROXIMATE DISTRIBUTION OF SOLOMON'S DISTRICTS
(1 Kings 4:7–19)

V. THE ADMINISTRATION OF SOLOMON'S KINGDOM

(4:1–5:8)

4 ¹King Solomon was king over all Israel.
²These were his officers:

Azariah son of Zadok, the priest;
³Elihoreph and Ahijah sons of Shisha, scribes;
Jehoshaphat son of Ahilud, the recorder;
⁴and Benaiah son of Jehoiada, over the army;
and Zadok and Abiathar, priests;
⁵and Azariah son of Nathan, over the prefects;
and Zabud son of Nathan, priest (and) friend of the king;
⁶and Ahishar, over the household;
and Adoniram son of Abda, over the levy.

⁷Solomon had twelve prefects for all Israel, and they provided for the king and his household; each[a] had to provide for one month a year. ⁸These were their names:

Son of Hur in Mount Ephraim;
⁹Son of Deker in Makaz and in Shaalbim and Beth-shemesh and Elon-beth-hanan;
¹⁰Son of Hesed in Aruboth—in his charge were Socoh and all the land of Hepher;
¹¹Son of Abinadab—all the district of Dor. Taphath the daughter of Solomon was his wife;
¹²Baana son of Ahilud—Taanach and Megiddo and all of Beth-shean, near Zarethan, south of Jezreel, from Beth-shean to Abel-meholah up to the other side of Jokmeam;
¹³Son of Geber in Ramoth-gilead—in his charge were the villages of Jair son of Manasseh in the Gilead; in his charge was the region of Argob in the Bashan, sixty large cities with walls and bronze bars;
¹⁴Ahinadab son of Iddo—Mahanaim;
¹⁵Ahimaaz in Naphtali; he too married a daughter of Solomon, Basemath;
¹⁶Baana son of Hushai in Asher and Bealoth;
¹⁷Jehoshaphat son of Paruah in Issachar;
¹⁸Shimei son of Ela in Benjamin;
¹⁹Geber son of Uri in the land of Gilead, the land of Sihon king of the Amorites and Og king of Bashan;
and one prefect in the land ⟨of Judah⟩.[b]

---

[a] Ketib: *'ḥd*; qere: *h'ḥd*.
[b] Add *yhwdh*; lost through haplography. See Note.

[20]Judah and Israel were as many as the sand by the sea; eating, drinking, and making merry. 5 [1]Now Solomon ruled over all the kingdoms from the River, (through) the land of the Philistines to the border of Egypt; they brought tribute and served Solomon all his lifetime.

[2]Solomon's board for one day was thirty *kors* of fine flour, and sixty *kors* of flour, [3]ten fat oxen, and twenty pasture-fed oxen, and one hundred sheep, besides deer and gazelles, roebucks and fattened fowl.

[4]Indeed, he held sway over all "Beyond-the-River," from Tiphsah to Gaza, over all the kings of "Beyond-the-River." He enjoyed peace on all sides round about. [5]Judah and Israel dwelled securely, each person at the foot of his vine and at the foot of his fig tree, from Dan to Beer-sheba, all the days of Solomon.

[6]Solomon had forty thousand stalls for the horses of his chariot force and twelve thousand horsemen. [7]These prefects provided for King Solomon and all those who came to King Solomon's table, each one in his month; they let nothing be lacking. [8]They (also) brought the barley and straw for the horses and steeds to the appointed place, each according to his charge.

NOTES

4 1. *King Solomon was king over all Israel.* A similar statement introduces the list of officers who served David; cf. 2 Sam 8:15a.

2. *These were his officers.* The lists from David's reign do not have a similar heading; cf. 2 Sam 8:16; 20:23. The term *śar* appears here for the first time in the general sense of appointed civil officer. References in earlier contexts show that *śar* was also a military title: e.g., *śar ṣābā'*, "army commander." Rabin points out the phonological difficulty in the commonly-held view that the word is related etymologically to Akk *šarru*, "king," noting a suggested Egyptian borrowing (Rabin 1982a).

Azariah son of Zadok, the priest. That is, the high priest in Jerusalem, because there were countless priests scattered throughout the country. The mention of a priest at the head of an administrative list is unlike the lists from David's reign (cf. 2 Sam 8:16–18; 20:23–26); at most, it may reflect the interest of the list's composer, not necessarily the rank of the priest at Solomon's court. In the priestly genealogy in 1 Chr 5:35, Azariah is the son of Ahimaaz and grandson of Zadok, who is known from the account of Absalom's revolt (cf. 2 Sam 15:35–36). The mention of Zadok associates Azariah with this priestly line. The inclusion of the two older priests in the list in v. 4, both of whom ended their term of service early on in Solomon's reign, suggests a later editing of the list (see further, ad loc.).

3. *Elihoreph and Ahijah sons of Shisha, scribes.* The etymology of the title and the function of the scribe are much disputed, and the names of the individuals who held this position vary within MT and the translations. Many consider Shisha (Heb *šyš'*; in 1 Chr 18:16 *šwš'*) to be a textual variant of Seraiah (2 Sam 8:17) and/or Sheva (20:25), David's scribe. B. Mazar (1946–47) suggested that the common base of all of these forms was the Hurrian name *Šawa-*

šarri and that this person was a holdover from the old Jebusite administration that David had absorbed into his government after he took Jerusalem. Others have looked in the direction of Egypt for the source of David's administrative models and found the Egyptian scribal title *sšš ꜥt*, "dispatch writer" or "epistolary secretary" (Cody 1965) behind this name. Thus the two forms of the name represent a proper name (Seraiah) and a foreign title, mistaken as a proper name in the transmission of the text (see Mettinger 1971, 25–29).

Etymologically, Heb *sōpēr* seems to be derived from *sēper*, a "written" document, although the verb **spr* means "to count" not "to write." The major activity connected with the *sōpēr* is "writing" (Jer 32:4, 32; 1 Chr 24:6; cf. too Jer 8:8; Ps 45:2), which justifies the translation "scribe." Comparison with the Akk *šāpiru*, "overseer, provincial governor" (CAD Š/1, 453–58), which has sometimes been suggested, has not proved helpful in elucidating the functions of the Hebrew scribe. Mettinger concluded that "the royal secretariat [in Egypt], responsible for the royal foreign and domestic correspondence . . . (served as) the prototype of the Israelite office" (Mettinger 1971, 35–51, esp. 50). A few late texts refer to scribes, but there, too, little concerning the nature of the office can be deduced. During the reign of Josiah, Shaphan the scribe—he had an office in the royal precinct (cf. Jer 36:10)—acted as the king's emissary to the high priest (2 Kgs 22:3) and to Huldah the prophetess (v. 12). Similarly, Shebna the scribe took part in the official delegation sent by Hezekiah to negotiate with the Assyrians (2 Kgs 18:18).

Literacy was not a common skill in the ancient world, even among royalty; thus, the scribe filled a key, if not the central, position at court, as manifested by the oft-quoted footnote in a letter of Abdi-Ḫepa of Jerusalem to the scribe of the Egyptian Pharaoh (in the Amarna correspondence): "To the scribe of the king, my lord: Thus Abdi-Ḫepa, your servant. At your feet I fall. I am your servant. Present eloquent words to the king, my lord. I am a soldier of the king. I would surely die (?) for you! " (EA 287:64–70).

Within a growing state administration, more than one scribe may have been employed, which would explain the names of two scribes in the present verse. For the name *Elihoreph*, NEB reads: "in charge of the calendar." This is an adoption of Montgomery's suggestion to take the personal name *Elihoreph* as a title, with *ḥōrep* meaning "autumn," the season from which the new year was counted. Montgomery compared the office to that of the Assyrian eponym (*līmu*), after whom years were dated in Assyria. See Montgomery 1930; Montgomery and Gehman, ad loc. But there is no textual warrant whatsoever for the corrected reading. Other important discussions on this office include: Begrich 1933; 1940–41; Kitchen 1965, 17; de Vaux 1939.

For seals of scribes dating to the late monarchy, see Avigad 1986, 28–29; and Bordreuil 1975.

Jehoshaphat son of Ahilud, the recorder. Jehoshaphat had served under David; cf. 2 Sam 20:24. An official with this title took part in the team that negotiated with the Assyrian Rab-shakeh (2 Kgs 18:18), and a century later, another official with the same title appears as a member of the royal commission ordered to supervise king Josiah's Temple reform program (in the Chronicle's version of the story, 2 Chr 34:8). But from these few glimpses, little can be learned about the actual function of the officer.

On the basis of the verbal stem *zkr in the Hiphil, "to mention, to proclaim," and the existence of the office of herald in Egypt (whm.w, "speaker, herald") and Mesopotamia (nāgiru), whose duties included ceremonial and judicial reporting and announcing, similar functions have been suggested for the mazkîr in Israel; thus, NEB: "secretary of state"; NJB: "herald"; NAB: "chancellor"; Noth's "spokesman," who served as an intermediary between the king and people of Israel, gives a modern touch to this ancient office. The earlier renditions probably reflect the contemporary custom of their times; so, e.g., Tg., mmn' 'l dkrny', an archivist (?); Abarbanel described the mazkîr as the fiscal manager of the king's estate.

4. and Benaiah son of Jehoiada, over the army. Benaiah took control of the army after executing Joab (cf. 2:34). Under David, Benaiah had served as commander of "the Cherethites and the Pelethites," the foreign mercenaries who served the king loyally during the rebellion of Absalom (so 2 Sam 15:18; cf. 20:23) and the crisis concerning the passing of the throne to Solomon (1 Kgs 1:32, 36, 44). Because of his long service, which had begun in the previous administration, the old Benaiah may have been replaced by a younger commander before too long.

and Zadok and Abiathar, priests. Zadok had supported David in his appointment of Solomon; Abiathar had sided with Adonijah and was subsequently banished by Solomon (1 Kgs 2:26–27). But even though v. 2 indicated that Azariah son of Zadok was priest, there seems to be more than historic interest in listing the priests who had served only a short term at the start of Solomon's reign. In its present position, v. 4b follows the order of lists from the time of David in 2 Sam 8:18; 20:24. Skinner's comment that "4b is a particularly stupid interpolation" displays a modern insensitivity to ancient scribal practice, in which contradictions were left without any further comment.

5. and Azariah son of Nathan, over the prefects. That is to say, chief prefect. The list of prefects and the districts under their jurisdiction are detailed in the following list, vv. 7–19. Hebrew niṣṣāb, a Niphal part. from *nṣb, "to set up, post," in the present verse, 4:7; 5:7; and 22:48; the form něṣîb appears in v. 19, without any apparent difference in meaning (see ad loc.). Niṣṣāb is also used of other officials; cf. 5:30; 22:48. The Akk term šaknu from the verb šakānu, "to place, set," exhibits a similar variation in designating a variety of officials; in Neo-Assyrian titulary, šaknu is used of provincial governors and a host of subordinate officials (see CAD Š/1, 180–92).

and Zabud son of Nathan, priest (and) friend of the king. The LXX reads: Zakur, an alteration of consonants also known in the ketib/qere of Ezra 8:14. Lucianic recensions and LXXᴮ omit "priest," easing the anomalous conflation of a double title, which also obviates the need to deal with a non-Levitical priest. Montgomery and Gehman attribute a nonsacredotal meaning to the title "priest" (so, already Abarbanel, "a person of high rank"), comparing David's sons who were also priests (2 Sam 8:18); but such usage is unattested. A Zabad son of Nathan is known from the lineage of Judah (1 Chr 2:36).

The title "friend of the king" (Heb *rēʿēh hammelek*) is also borne by Hushai the Archite (2 Sam 15:37), "David's friend." The comment of Absalom—"Is this your loyalty to your friend? Why did you not go with your friend?" (16:17)—which puns on Hushai's title, confirms its meaning. Yet the function of the bearer of this title is far from certain. Targumic *šûšbîn*, "bridegroom's friend or best man," seems to be an ancient guess (cf. van Selms 1957). From Hushai's role during the rebellion of Absalom, it may be supposed that the "friend" was one of the king's trusted counselors (cf. 15:32–36), though as a formal position at court, it appears for the first and only time among Solomon's cabinet. It may be significant that in the Amarna correspondence, in a letter from the king of Jerusalem (EA 288:11), Abdi-Ḫepa calls himself the *ruḫi šarri* of the Pharaoh. This has been interpreted as either a transcription of a Canaanite term (which has its counterpart in the present Hebrew term) or as a transcription of the Eg *rḫ-nśw.t*, "king's acquaintance." The form *rēʿēh*, from *rʿ* with the added *heʾ* may be a Masoretic affectation, connecting the word with *rōʿeh*, "shepherd" (so B-L 465, d‴), yet preserving a distinction between the two words by the pointing with *ṣere*.

The title *mērēaʿ* in the Genesis narratives (cf. Gen 26:26) seems to be of different origin and related to the root *rʿh*, "to graze, shepherd"; see Safran 1985. For a similar term, see Note on *měyūddaʿ* in 2 Kgs 10:11.

6. *and Ahishar, over the household*. Ahishar is the only officer without a patronymic; this does not necessarily make him a foreigner (so Würthwein); cf. below, Note to v. 8. For conjectural reconstructions of the father's name based on the divergent LXX readings, see the early summary in Burney, ad loc., and Šanda; all are rejected by Montgomery and Gehman. The generality of the Heb *bayit* does not permit specification as to which "house" came under the purview of this officer, the royal household at court (thus making him a major-domo of sorts, the steward; translated in 2 Kgs 15:5; 18:18 as "royal steward"; cf. NEB "comptroller of the household") or the entire royal estate (so Noth). In the kingdom of Israel, the steward Obadiah was charged with finding fodder for the king's livestock (cf. 18:5); in Judah, Jotham son of King Azariah held this post during the period of his father's incapacity (2 Kgs 15:5); and the participation of the steward Eliakim in the delegation that met the Assyrian Rabshakeh by Jerusalem's walls (2 Kgs 18:18)—all point to the high rank of this official at court. The suggested derivation of the title from Egyptian or Mesopotamian prototypes is disputed (cf. Mettinger 1971, 70–79; Ahlström 1982, 32), though it was apparently in use in Canaanite Ugarit (in the form *ʿl. bt*); cf. Good 1979, 580–82.

More helpful is the Joseph narrative in which the hero twice finds himself "put in charge of his house," the entire household of his lord and master Potiphar (Gen 39:4, 5), and the entire royal household (41:40–45), where he is second only to Pharaoh. Taken together with Isaiah's fulmination against Shebna and his support of Eliakim, who as "over the household" holds "the key of David's palace" (Isa 22:15–24), the passage seems to indicate that this official was the highest in the land.

The title is known from a number of Hebrew epigraphical finds: (1) the grave inscription of "[ ]yahu, who was over the house" ([ ]*yhw 'šr 'l hbyt*); cf. Avigad 1953; (2–5) the seals of "Gedaliah, who was over the house." (For this seal and the identification of its owner, see Comment to 2 Kgs 25:22; for seals of the stewards Adoniyhu and Nathan, see Avigad 1986, 21–23; and of the officer whose name is not fully preserved, Avigad 1979, no. 1.)

and Adoniram son of Abda, over the levy. The Heb term *mas*, along with its cognate *massu* in the Canaanite dialects of Akkadian at Alalakh and Amarna (CAD M/1, 327), refers to "men enlisted in the levy, the corvée." See Biram 1953; Mendelsohn 1962a; Rainey 1970; Soggin 1982.

A corvée official appears for the first time in a list of David's ministers (2 Sam 20:24), and if this list postdates the one in 2 Sam 8:16–18, it may indicate that the levy was instituted relatively late in his reign. McCarter favors viewing the two lists as "deriving from a single source," duplicated because of editorial work on Samuel (McCarter 1984, 435); doubts are further raised by the fact that the same person held the post during both the reigns of David and Solomon (de Vaux 1961, 128–29; Würthwein). (Note that the same question is not raised with reference to Ahilud (v. 3), who served both kings as well!) The title appears on a seventh-century seal: *lpl'yhw 'šr 'l hms*, "Belonging to Pela'yahu, who is over the corvée" (Avigad 1980), and is evidence for the continuation of the call-up of Judeans for royal service during the late monarchy.

On those called up to do royal service, see below on 5:27–32 and 9:15–23. See also the alternate term, *sēbel*, in 11:28.

Adoniram. On the face of it, Adoniram held the office for a rather lengthy period, from sometime in David's reign through the accession of Solomon's son Rehoboam. Considering this very unlikely, many simply discount the text in 2 Sam 20:24 as secondary; besides, it is argued, only in Solomon's reign was it necessary to enlist a labor force for state service (de Vaux 1961, 129).

The name appears in several forms: Adoram (2 Sam 20:24; 1 Kgs 12:18); Adoniram (4:6; 5:28); Hadoram (2 Chr 10:18). Of these forms, the one in the present verse has been adjusted to conform to the patterns of Hebrew personal names; the other forms have sometimes been explained as containing the pagan theophoric element Hadad/Adad, god of the storm, which may indicate his non-Israelite origin (cf. the discussion of B. Mazar 1946–47, cited above, with reference to the sons of Shisha, the scribe, in v. 3).

Between vv. 6a and 6b, the LXX traditions have an insertion, preserved in a variety of forms; NJB renders: "Eliab son of Joab, commander of the army." Cf. most recently Barthélemy 1982, 338–39, for a reasoned statement rejecting the originality of this addition. Besides the textual issues, the LXX plus would have Solomon enlist a son of Joab as commander-in-chief, a highly questionable rehabilitation for the family of the rejected former army chief. [DNF: "The idea that Solomon would automatically reject any relative of Joab may seem reasonable, but in fact history tells us that enemies become friends and friends become enemies in the twinkling of an eye, and blood-ties play an important role in the parcelling out of offices and honors, in spite of past differences and bloody fights over the succession."]

7. *Solomon had twelve prefects for all Israel, and they provided for the king and his household; each had to provide for one month a year.* The main purpose of this twelve-part division of Solomon's kingdom was the provisioning of the royal household one month a year; in order to fulfill this assessment, each district would have had to be a viable economic unit. This seems to have required the partial abandonment of the tribal division (on the assumption that such a division was in force prior to Solomon), as the mixed territorial descriptions indicate. First Kings 5:7–8 offers a few details on the monthly due (see below), and it is these tax matters alone that define the responsibilities of the prefects. Other administrative matters, e.g., mobilization of the corvée, were given over to other royal appointees, perhaps on a tribal basis (cf. 5:30 and the example of Jeroboam, who was in charge of the labor force of the Joseph tribes; cf. 1 Kgs 11:28).

prefects. For the form, see above, Note on v. 5.

for all Israel. That is, both Judah and Israel, as in 3:28; 8:65; 11:42, and not just the Northern tribes. See further below on v. 20.

provided for. Hebrew *kilkēl,* "support, maintain," as in 17:4, 9; 18:4, 13; and Gen 45:11; 2 Sam 19:33–34.

each had to provide for one month a year. The article *he',* added in qere, is not strictly needed; cf. 1 Sam 13:17–18.

8. *These were their names.* An introductory phrase before lists; cf. Exod 1:1; 2 Sam 23:8; and in Cowley 1923, nos. 22, 34, 66.

Son of Hur in Mount Ephraim. **District One.** Not all of the allotment of the tribe of Ephraim is included in this district; according to Josh 16:3, 6, 8, Ephraim reached the sea coast. Mount Ephraim was allotted to both tribes of the House of Joseph (Josh 17:14–18), and some Manassite holdings (perhaps as far as Shechem; cf. 1 Kgs 12:25) were likely included in this first division. But the northern border depends on the demarcation of District Three (see below, v. 10).

Son of Hur. Five names in the list are of the form *ben* X, "son of X" (vv. 8, 9, 10, 11, 13). This unusual use of the patronymic instead of a full personal name was creatively explained away by Albright's suggestion that the upper right-hand corner of the original list was damaged when the editor of Kings came to incorporate it into his work (1925, 25–26; 1969a, 137; adopted by Montgomery and Gehman, 120; Gray, 134 note b; Noth, 59–60; NJB). Alt, noting the use of similar name-forms in earlier Ugaritic lists, took these officers to be of Canaanite origin, the form "son of X" indicating that they were descendants of families who had standing as state officials prior to the incorporation of these areas into Israel (Alt 1950; so Jones, 1:140; Würthwein, 44). But a recent study by Naveh (1990), based on name-lists from Ugarit through Talmudic times, shows that "there is no evidence that the omission of a person's personal name had any significance in terms of law, regulations, order or administrative rules." These shortened names were just informal, familiar nicknames. [DNF: "In poetic parallelism, the name and patronymic can be used for the same person, e.g., David//son of Jesse (e.g., 1 Kgs 12:16)."]

9. *Son of Deker in Makaz and in Shaalbim and Beth-shemesh and Elon-beth-hanan.* **District Two**. This district is demarcated by reference to cities assigned to the tribe of Dan (cf. Josh 19:41–43), partially recovered from the Amorites at a later period by the Joseph tribes (so Judg 1:35). For the identity and/or relationship of this district with Dannite territory (mostly inland), cf. Aharoni 1979, 311; B. Mazar 1960a; Rainey 1987–89; Strange 1966.

Makaz. A city mentioned only here; the present context suggests a location in the northern Shephelah, between Wadi Ayalon and Wadi Sorek. Many point to Kh. el-Muhezin, 17 km west-northwest of Beth-shemesh, as a possible candidate, but this name may be better connected with the Muhhazi mentioned in EA 298:25. The LXX reading *machemas/machmas* is not useful and looks like an attempt to identify Makaz with Michmas. An attractive suggestion by Pintore (1970, 190), and modified by Na'aman (1986, 114), would recover the common noun *mqṣ(h)*, "as far as," used in border descriptions; cf. Josh 15:2; 18:15.

Shaalbim. Probably Selbit, 3 mi. northwest of Aijalon.

Beth-shemesh. Beth-shemesh (Tell er-Rumeileh) is a border town, included in both Dan (Josh 19:41, as Ir-shemesh) and Judah (15:10); in Josh 21:16, it is listed as a Judahite Levitical city. See Tsafrir 1975, 44–45; NEAEHL 249–53.

Elon-beth-hanan. The first element of this toponym may be identical with Aijalon (cf. Josh 19:42), or it may be the Elon mentioned in the same verse; here it is specified that the town was the holding of the family of Hanan. The LXX separates the two by inserting "up to" Beth-hanan, otherwise unknown.

10. *Son of Hesed in Aruboth—in his charge were Socoh and all the land of Hepher.* **District Three**. Two major cities, Aruboth and Socoh, and the extended territory of the city of Hepher make up the Third District. The west-central territory of Manasseh, stretching in a band from the Sharon Plain to the central hill country, north of Districts One and Two, seems to be referred to.

Aruboth. The district center, mentioned only here, is of disputed location, dependent upon the position of the land of Hepher. Zertal's survey and excavation in the Manassite hills discovered the site Kh. el-Hamam in the rugged hills between the Dothan Valley and the Coastal Plain, which fits the historical picture, identifying Aruboth with Arbatta/Narbata of Second Temple sources (Zertal 1992).

Socoh. At least three cities carried this name (perhaps the name of a thorny bush?) in ancient Israel, two in Judah (Josh 15:35, 48) and one in the Sharon, mentioned only in the present verse. This Socoh is recorded in Egyptian documents from the mid–second millennium BCE and Shishak's campaign itinerary (e.g., ANET, 242; see Ahituv 1984, 178–79; Appendix 1, no. 1, 38) and is to be identified with Shuweiket er-Rās, 3 km north of Tul-Karm, an important junction on the *Via maris*.

all the land of Hepher. Hepher is both a royal Canaanite city (Josh 12:17) and a Manassite clan (17:3; cf. Num 26:32), indicating its (early?) incorporation into Israel; the names of two of the daughters (Noah and Hoglah) of Zelophehad son of Hepher appear as districts in the eighth-century Samaria ostraca, a fact that suggests that the land of Hepher should be located not too far from the capital city Samaria. Most identifications of Hepher in the west toward the Sharon (see ABD 3:138–39) fail in this regard; Tel Muḥaffar at the northern end of the Dothan Valley meets the historical and archaeological requirements (with Kallai 1986, 52–58; Wright 1967, 62*–64* took this site for Aruboth).

11. *Son of Abinadab—all the district of Dor. Taphath the daughter of Solomon was his wife.* **District Four.** A narrow strip of land on the seacoast, bounded on the north by the Carmel mountain range, and on its other sides by Districts One–Three. Its economic independence would have been based on the commercial wealth of Dor, a port city of some importance.

district. The translation "district" is a contextual guess, since Heb *nāpat* is of unknown derivation and is used only in association with Dor; cf., e.g., NJPSV: "Naphath-dor"; NJB: "the Slopes of Dor." For a recent suggestion to take it as a loanword from one of the languages of the Sea Peoples, meaning "wooded country," equivalent to Heb *šārôn*, see Ben-Dov 1976.

Dor. At Kh. el-Burj, by modern Tantura, about 14 km. north of Caesarea. Dor was occupied by the Tjekel, one of the Sea Peoples, during the last quarter of the second millennium (cf. ANET, 25–29) and remained a foreign enclave until Solomon's time (cf. Judg 1:27); it was under Israelite jurisdiction until its conquest by Tiglath-pileser III in 732. For the recent excavations at the site, see Stern 1994; ABD 2:223–25.

Taphath the daughter of Solomon was his wife. Many have commented on the fact that the king's son-in-law had been given a particularly wealthy district, as if it should have been otherwise.

12. *Baana son of Ahilud—Taanach and Megiddo and all of Beth-shean, near Zarethan, south of Jezreel, from Beth-shean to Abel-meholah up to the other side of Jokmeam.* **District Five.** Solomon's Fifth District included the Jezreel Valley and the northern half of the Jordan Valley on its western side down to Jokmeam and beyond. But, while this general orientation is manifest, the verse itself is most cumbersome and likely contains several glosses. The Jezreel Valley had been allotted to Manasseh in Josh 17:11–13; cf. Judg 1:27; but it remained an unsubdued Canaanite enclave until David's reign, despite the noted victories of Barak (Judg 4–5) and Gideon (Judg 6–7). The references to sites in Transjordan are for purposes of orientation and do not imply that the East Bank of the Jordan was part of this district (otherwise, Wright 1967, 66*; Ahlström 1982, 33).

Taanach. Tell Taʾannek, located 10 km southeast of Megiddo on the southern edge of the Jezreel Valley; for the history of the site and excavations there, cf. ABD 6:287–90; NEAEHL 1428–33.

Megiddo. The major city at the western extremity of the Jezreel Valley, Tell el-Mutesellim, guarding the *Via maris* highway as it exits the ʿIron Pass into the valley. For Solomonic constructions at Megiddo, see 1 Kgs 9:15; for the history of the site and excavations there, cf. ABD 4:666–79; NEAEHL 1003–24.

all of Beth-shean. The major city at the eastern end of the Jezreel Valley before the crossing of the Jordan, at Tell el-Ḥuṣn, and the lands under its jurisdiction.

Allotted to Manasseh (Josh 17:11), Beth-shean, like the other cities of the Jezreel Valley, was only brought under Israelite control in the days of the United Monarchy (cf. Judg 1:27–28). See ABD 1:693–96 and NEAEHL 214–23.

near Zarethan, south of Jezreel, from Beth-shean to Abel-meholah up to the other side of Jokmeam. A difficult geographical description. The territory of Beth-shean is here described by referring to other prominent border cities.

Zarethan. On the eastern bank of the Jordan; known for being the site where the casting of bronze vessels for the Temple took place (7:46), but this does not help in identifying the town with one of the many sites in the area; see the survey of opinions in ABD 6:1041–43. Its identification with Tell es-Saʿidiya, although popular, is not readily accepted by Pritchard, the site's excavator. Even the biblical tradition seems irreconcilable; the waters of the Jordan backed up, according to Josh 3:16, "at Adam [= Tell ed-Damiya], the city which is beside Zarethan," a distance of 12 miles! Zarethan is noted in the present verse to help delineate the borders of the Fifth District but was not part of it. The form of the name with the ending -*a(h)* may bear the locative sense of direction, "up to."

Jezreel. To the northwest of Zarethan, modern Zerin, part of the tribal allotment of Issachar (Josh 19:18); the Omride kings had holdings in Jezreel (cf. 1 Kgs 21:1), and the revolt of Jehu was centered in the town (2 Kgs 9). Jezreel is mentioned strictly for purposes of orientation, because the holdings of Issachar formed a separate district (cf. 1 Kgs 4:17).

Abel-meholah. Home of the prophet Elisha (19:16); among the suggested sites, many favor Tell Abū Sūs, on the western bank of the Jordan, some 15 km south of Beth-shean; cf. Zori 1967; ABD 1:11–12.

Jokmeam. Listed in 1 Chr 6:53 as an Ephraimite Levitical city, Jokmeam has been taken by many to be out of place in the present context; e.g., NJB rewrites the verse by exchanging the toponyms Jokmeam and Zarethan at the beginning of the verse. But according to B. Mazar (1960b, 198; cf. also Kallai 1986, 161–62), Jokmeam may have been near the northeastern border between Ephraim and Manasseh, at Tell el-Mazar, thus explaining its mention after Abel-meholah. This would have the Fifth District include most of the Jordan Valley. Taken this way, the various elements of the verse need not be rearranged (as suggested by Albright 1925, 26; followed by Naʾaman 1986), nor need Jokmeam be corrected to read Jokneam, at the western exit of the Jezreel Valley (cf. Josh 19:11; so, e.g., Noth).

13. *Son of Geber in Ramoth-gilead. In his charge were the villages of Jair son of Manasseh in the Gilead; in his charge was the region of Argob in the Bashan, sixty large cities with walls and bronze bars.* **District Six.** The northern Gilead and the Bashan up to the border with Aram–Damascus comprised this district. The first half of v. 13b agrees with Num 32:41 and Judg 10:4, in locating the villages of Jair in Gilead; the second half, absent in Luc., is based on an alternate tradition, which places these settlements in the Bashan, north of Gilead (i.e., above the Yarmuk River; cf. Deut 3:4, 14; and its derivative, Josh 13:30), in territory that was settled by Manasseh in a later stage of its expansion. For

the distribution of the texts reflecting these traditions and their analysis, see Kallai 1986, 248–59.

Ramoth-gilead. The Lucianic recensions read in all occurrences of the name Ramath-gilead; other LXX traditions alternate between Ramath- and Ramoth-gilead. In 2 Kgs 8:29, the town is simply Ramah, and in several instances the form "Ramoth in Gilead" appears (cf. Deut 4:43; Josh 20:8). These variations suggest that Gilead was added to the toponym Ramah to distinguish it from other towns of the same name (e.g., Ramah in Benjamin [Josh 18:25]; in Naphtali [19:36]; Ramath-Negev [19:8]).

Ramoth-gilead was identified by N. Glueck with Tell Ramith, south of the modern Syria–Jordan border; see NEAEHL 1291–93. At once a refuge city (Deut 4:43) and a Levitical city (Josh 21:36), Ramoth-gilead was the staging ground for several fateful encounters between the armies of Israel and Aram–Damascus (cf. 1 Kgs 22:29; 2 Kgs 8:28–29) because of its commanding position in the plateau of the northeastern Gilead.

the villages of Jair son of Manasseh. The encampments of Jair are also referred to in Num 32:41; Deut 3:14; Josh 13:30; Judg 10:4. This is a general territorial designation without specific towns in mind; the term *ḥawwâ* may have its cognate in Ug *ḥwt* and Ar *ḥiwa*, both meaning "stockade, circle of tents or houses"; see Rainey 1975a, 109.

in his charge was the region of Argob in the Bashan, sixty large cities with walls and bronze bars. A second region, delimited according to Deuteronomic traditions. The Argob region lay east of the Aramean kingdoms of Geshur and Maachah (cf. Deut 3:14), which occupied the high plateau between the Yarmuk River and Mt. Hermon. Just how far east the Argob extended—some suggest as far as el-Leja, that is, Mt. Druze (Tg.: *ṭĕrākôna*ʾ, Trachonitis)—is not clear; cf. ABD 1:376. The typological number "sixty" emphasizes the vastness of Jair's holdings in the Bashan.

14. *Ahinadab son of Iddo—Mahanaim.* **District Seven**. The very abbreviated description of the territory of this Trans-Jordanian district, with only the administrative center being mentioned, may be supplemented by what looks like a doublet in v. 19, on which, see below. Mahanaim was a city on the border between Manasseh and Gad (Josh 13:30), which suggests that this district encompassed the middle and southern settlements in Transjordan. The city served as the refuge for the Israelite forces who had escaped the rout at Mt. Gilboa (2 Sam 2:8) and later for David in his flight from Jerusalem (cf. 17:24). It had also served as administrative center during Eshbaal's short reign (2 Sam 2:9). For the site identification, either at Tulul edh-Dhahab or Tell Heğğağ, see ABD 4:472–73; Kallai 1986, 264 n. 345.

15. *Ahimaaz in Naphtali; he, too, married a daughter of Solomon, Basemath.* **District Eight**. According to Josh 19:33–34, the entire Upper Galilee, including the major royal fortress at Hazor (see 1 Kgs 9:15), was included in this district.

16. *Baana son of Hushai in Asher and Bealoth.* **District Nine** comprised the tribal territory of Asher in the western Galilee (cf. Josh 19:25–30). There is no

indication that the cities of the Cabul area had already been transferred to Tyre (cf. 9:10–13), which for some commentators provides a fixed point for dating the district list (e.g., Aharoni 1979; see further in Comment).

Bealoth. The inclusion of Bealoth further delimits the territory under Baana's jurisdiction. This toponym can hardly be identical with the Bealoth in Judah (Josh 15:24) although, by some rewriting, Albright maintained that a district in southern Simeon is referred to (1925, 36). Most commentators resort to some form of emendation: (1) following LXX[B]: *Maala*; and LXX[A]: *Maalot*; Thenius, Šanda, Gray, and others suggest that reference is to the Ladder of Tyre (*m'lh ṣwr*), the coastal area stretching north from the plain of Acre (cf. 1 Macc 11:59); (2) since only Zebulun of all the northern tribes is not listed in the district map, its name has been restored from the anomalous Bealoth by Klosterman; cf. Burney, Albright 1925, 35–36 and Wright 1967, 59*, who quotes Cross's explanation of the graphic corruption of the name Zebulun that produced Bealoth. But the difficult reading Bealoth seems preferable to a forced reconstructed name for a system that was not tribally based. As Kallai notes, "there is an allusion here to the expansion of the territory defined by the name of the tribe Asher" (Kallai 1986, 66), though we do not know what particular place is meant.

17. *Jehoshaphat son of Paruah in Issachar.* **District Ten.** Issachar's allotment in the Lower Galilee is outlined in Josh 19:18–22; it is squeezed in between Asher and Naphtali in the west and north, by Manasseh in the south, which had control of the Jezreel Valley (cf. above, v. 12), and the Jordan River on the east. The tribal territory of Zebulun may have been included in this district, which would have given Distirct Ten an allotment approximately the size of its two neighbors, Asher and Naphtali (Kallai 1986, 69).

18. *Shimei son of Ela in Benjamin.* **District Eleven.** A very small district (cf. Josh 18:11–20), the size of which raised the question of its ability to fulfill its share of the king's provisioning. Wright (1967, 67*) posited intense settlement and land use, together with the strategically placed city of Jericho and a dependence on Jerusalem as the factors that righted this perceived economic imbalance.

19. *Geber son of Uri in the Gilead, the land of Sihon king of the Amorites and Og king of Bashan.* Ostensibly this verse describes a twelfth district; but the opening of v. 19a looks suspiciously like a variant of v. 13a, "son of Geber in Ramoth-gilead," and the Bashan is also mentioned in v. 13bβ. Thus Albright (1925, 34–35) and Montgomery and Gehman properly discount the present half-verse as a doublet and count v. 19bβ ("and one prefect in the land") as the twelfth district (see further below). Creative reconstructions that, e.g., would have the "son of Geber" (v. 13) replace his father, who had been a Gileadite official that served before Solomon's division (v. 19; Ottosson 1969, 220), are too speculative to warrant acclamation.

Other solutions have been proffered. The Lucianic recensions and LXX[B] apparently resolved this duplication by reading "Gad" for "Gilead" (accepted by Kittel, Stade and Schwally, and Šanda). Yet the tribe of Gad was part of District

Seven (v. 14); Mahanaim, the district center, was a Gadite city (cf. Josh 21:36). Moreover, v. 19bα is a gloss, like the one in v. 13b, based on similar traditional Deuteronomistic statements; this is manifest by the inclusion of Og, king of Bashan.

Aharoni (1979, 314) reconstructed this district as the southernmost in Transjordan, including all of the Mishor from the Arnon to Heshbon. But the key location "Heshbon," needed for this reconstruction, is lacking in MT and is not to be found in any ancient translation. Kallai (1986, 69–72) maintains the text as is and offers the fact that the southern Gilead and the land of Sihon down to the Arnon are the district's borders. This, however, forces a meaning on the geographical term "Gilead" that is nowhere else attested and that disregards the nature of the Dtr gloss which mentions Sihon.

and one prefect in the land ⟨of Judah⟩. **District Twelve.** An old crux. The name of this last prefect is not given; the territory over which he had charge is also not preserved in MT. To take the phrase as referring to a super-governor over all of the others (as did Josephus, *Ant.* 8.2, 3; Vulg.; Rashi, Klostermann, Burney) means that Azariah son of Nathan mentioned in v. 5 is the referent; but this would still leave the list with only eleven districts and Judah conspicuously left out. To overcome these difficulties, "the land" has been taken as reflecting a "domestic" usage for "Judah" (Montgomery and Gehman); cf. "Tamar in the steppe in the land" in 9:18; in Neo-Assyrian usage, *māti*, "the land" refers to home territory. Better yet, is to read the first word of v. 20 with the end of v. 19, restoring the lost vocable "Judah." Perhaps "Judah" was originally written twice but one of the two words was lost through haplography; cf. Stade, Noth. Whatever the case, the name of the district prefect is lacking, unless Azariah had responsibility for Judah among his other duties (Mettinger 1971). The NAB's "in the king's own land" with the note "the royal territory of Judah had its own peculiar administration" is purely interpretive and lacks textual support.

one prefect. This term was discussed above in the Note on v. 5; the form *něṣîb* appears only here in Kings and, though it is favored in Chronicles (and so declared a late gloss by Noth), it is not suspect, because *něṣîb* does occur in earlier contexts, e.g., 2 Sam 8:6, 14; and Note to 1 Kgs 22:48.

20. *Judah and Israel were as many as the sand by the sea; eating, drinking, and making merry.* A proverbial picture of wealth and security. Many an ancient Near Eastern monarch boasted of the good times enjoyed by his subjects, e.g., Panamuwa, king of Samal (eighth century BCE): "in my days, Ja'udi (= Samal) ate and drank" (KAI 214:9). In 1 Kgs 5:9, the phrase is "as the sand on the seashore" (Heb *śĕpat hayyām*); *śĕpat* is inexplicably omitted in the present verse. For this image of plenitude, cf. Gen 41:49; of great population, Judg 7:12; Hos 2:1.

Judah and Israel. As argued in v. 19, the vocable "Judah" may have originally been written twice, with one lost by haplography; if only once, then its attachment to v. 19 is still preferable, with "Israel" in the sense of "all Israel" being the subject of v. 20. At some stage of transmission, "Judah" was mistakenly joined to "Israel" on the pattern of "Judah and Israel" in 5:5.

Closely following upon the present verse and complementing it is the statement in 5:1 concerning the rich tribute that Solomon received from his non-Israelite subjects. (Note that the Masoretic Text division of "open" and "closed" units connects 4:20 with 5:1 without a break.)

The LXX traditions preserve a variety of attempts at introducing some logical order into the material as preserved in MT, especially in what follows, e.g., in the matter concerning the provisioning required of the prefects in 5:7–8. The main LXX text presents: 4:20 (= MT 5:7); 4:21 (MT 5:8); 4:22 (= MT 5:2); 4:23 (MT 5:3); 4:24 (= MT 5:4). Several translations adopt this arrangement in whole or in part (NJB, NEB; NAB), even though many studies have concluded that the LXX texts are secondary rearrangements. See Montgomery and Gehman, 126; Gooding 1976, 40–49; and textual note on 1 Kgs 2 (above, pp. 171–72).

5 1. *Now Solomon ruled over all the kingdoms from the River, (through) the land of the Philistines to the border of Egypt.* The extent of Solomon's kingdom is related twice, in vv. 1 and 4. In v. 1, the terms are those of YHWH's promise to Abraham; cf. Gen 15:18. "The River," i.e., the Euphrates (cf., e.g., Gen 15:18; Deut 1:7), and "the border of Egypt," i.e., the northern Sinai Peninsula at the border of Canaan, apparently at the Wadi of Egypt (see on 8:65). The phrase "the land of the Philistines" is syntactically unconnected with the preceding "from" and looks like a gloss on "to the border of Egypt." Second Chronicles 9:26 (adopted by LXX at 1 Kgs 2:46k) reads: "and to the land of the Philistines, even to the border of Egypt."

they brought tribute and served Solomon all his lifetime. The lack of subject is a bit unusual, but is construable if the preceding "kingdoms" (Heb *mamlākôt*) is understood as "rulers" (and so read in 2 Chr 9:26); cf. v. 4 for the parallel "kings."

tribute. For this sense of Heb *minḥâ*, cf. 2 Kgs 17:3; Judg 3:15, 17; 2 Sam 8:2, 6.

2. *Solomon's board for one day was thirty* kors *of fine flour, and sixty* kors *of flour.* It has always been a challenge to try to crack the numbers given in this verse and to come up with a calculation of just how many enjoyed the king's largess. Abarbanel figured that 60,000 persons received their support from the royal coffers, not all of them necessarily residents of the capital; cf., earlier, *b. B. Meṣiʿa* 86b. For other suggestions, also in the tens of thousands, see, Kittel, Montgomergy and Gehman and Noth. Compare with Nehemiah's modest guest list in Neh 5:17–18. An unusal document from the reign of the Assyrian monarch Assurnasirpal II details the vast repast prepared for the 69,000 invited guests at the festivities held on the occasion of the inauguration of the king's palace in Calah; cf. ARI 2 §§676–82. Medieval tradition, perhaps based on a Greek source, told of the vast table set for the Persian king, which Lewis (1987) considers a "record of a special occasion . . . taken as normal."

kors. The *kōr* is properly a liquid measure, used of oil in Ezek 45:14, but is here the eqivalent of the dry measure "homer." The term is also known in Akk *kurru* (CAD K, 564–65). Calculation of its modern equivalent is problematic, and depends in large degree on the capacity of vessels found in excavation. Many figure the *kor* to be approximately 220 liters (Scott 1970, 52); others 360 liters (Powell 1992, 904).

3. *ten fat oxen*. I.e., stall-fed; literally, "fat, healthy," in contrast to the following.

twenty pasture-fed oxen. The vocalization *bāqār* "oxen" indicates that the noun *rĕ'î* (only attested in this verse, more common *mir'eh*) stands in apposition to "oxen."

deer and gazelles. This pair is mentioned in Deut 12:15 as examples of game animals not brought to the altar and therefore not requiring ritual cleanliness.

fattened fowl. Literally, "fowl of the stall, crib," cf. "stalled ox" (Prov 15:17). For the noun *'ēbûs*, cf. Isa 1:3; Prov 14:4; Job 39:9.

The identifaction of Heb *barbūr*, translated here by the neutral word "fowl," was lost early; Tg. already rendered "fowl" without specifying the kind. Qimḥi noted two rabbinic guesses: "capons" or birds from a country called "Barbur" (cf. *Qoh. Rab.* 2:10). Modern identifications include "cuckoos" (JB; Noth, comparing Ar *abū burbur*); "poultry" (NJB; G. R. Driver 1955, 133–34 points to Ar *birbir*), and "geese" (NJPSV). If the *barbūr* was indeed a rare species, its position at the end of the list of rather common animals conveys the sense "and even fine delicacies."

4. *Indeed, he held sway over all "Beyond-the-River," from Tiphsah to Gaza, over all the kings of "Beyond-the-River."* The verse looks like a gloss on v. 1, defining the territory under Solomon's rule in geopolitical terms, most of which are anachronistic, late designations. On the question of whether a "correct tradition" (Montgomery and Gehman) is nevertheless recalled, see Comment.

"Beyond-the-River." Hebrew *'ēber hannāhār*, lit., "across the River," is the Hebrew equivalent of a cuneiform administrative term (*eber nāri*) first used in the Neo-Assyrian period for the territory west of the Euphrates; it was later adopted by the Persians, as seen in Ezra 4:17; Neh 2:7. For a thorough discussion, see Rainey 1969.

Tiphsah. Tiphsah stands opposite Gaza in indicating the full extent of the Israelite domain. In terms of v. 1, the reference should be to a town on the Euphrates, but cuneiform sources do not mention any such place. Tiphsah, perhaps derived from **psḥ*, with the meaning "cross over," has been identified with Thapsacus, first mentioned as a ford on the Euphrates, at the great bend of the river, in Xenophon's *Anabasis* (I.4, 11, 17) with reference to Cyrus the Younger, and for this reason, its mention here is most often taken as a late gloss. No consensus regarding its location has been reached. Tiphsah in 2 Kgs 15:16 seems to be a different town (see ad loc.).

5. *Judah and Israel dwelled securely, each person at the foot of his vine and at the foot of his fig tree*. A proverbial image of security and peace; cf. Zech 3:10 and Mic 4:4, where it is completed by "with no one threatening (them)"; note the somewhat ironic use of the image in the promise of Rabshakeh in 2 Kgs 18:31 about the good times awaiting the exiles from Judah. Israel's prosperity described above in 4:20 is thus balanced by this statement on the lack of concern concerning foreign attack.

The traditional translation "*under* his vine and *under* his fig tree" has required commentators to posit that the vines were hung in trellis-like fashion on the fig trees; how else could one sit *under* the vine? But agricultural acrobatics is only necessary when the words are translated rigidly. Hebrew *taḥat* also means "at the foot of" (e.g., Exod 24:4; Deut 4:11).

from Dan to Beer-sheba. The conventional borders ascribed to Israel's settlement in the land, from north to south; cf. Judg 20:1; 1 Sam 3:20; 2 Sam 24:2, 15; from south to north, in 1 Chr 21:2; 2 Chr 30:5. This does not contradict the map of the full extent of Solomon's rule in v. 1, since only the home territories are meant here.

6. *Solomon had forty thousand stalls for the horses of his chariot force and twelve thousand horsemen.* The corresponding verse in 2 Chr 9:25 (and LXX at 1 Kgs 10:26) has "four thousand" for the impossibly high "forty thousand" in the present verse. The discordant numbers in the Kings–Chronicles traditions are harmonized in *b. Sanh.* 21b. In 10:26, Solomon's chariots number 1400, which would yield 2800 team-horses and 1200 reserves (so Šanda), a fact that indicates that "four thousand" is the better reading. Yet Provan (60) thinks that the "fantastic number" in Kings is what is to be expected from a writer who sought to portray Solomon as the prototypical multiplier of horses, warned against in Deut 17:16.

stalls. The translation of Heb *ʾūrwâ* is based on its use in Aramaic for Heb *ʾēbûs*, "crib," as in Isa 1:3; in 2 Chr 32:28, *ʾrwt* are shelters for animals. But this meaning is far from certain. In Akk, *urû* I is "stall" (AHw 1435a), alongside *urû* II, a "team" of horses (AHw 1435b), which may simply be an extension of the first term. The "four thousand" (revised reading) might be referring to teams of (chariot?) horses, each with a single replacement, thus explaining the ratio 4,000 team-horses : 12,000 riders (Davies 1986).

The inflated numbers employed here with reference to Solomon's horses and stalls, and later concerning the gold received as tribute (cf. 10:14), reflect a literary fashion similar to one employed in Assyrian royal inscriptions in which impossibly high numbers of booty and prisoners, as well as enemy dead, are recorded. Recent study of these texts has shown that stated quantities "need not be necessarily exact" but are expected to represent a "level of approximation" and often are an alternative to "non-numerical quantifications ('many,' 'several,' etc.)" (De Odorico 1995, 159).

Moreover, there is at present no archaeological evidence to confirm the vast number of structures that would have been needed to handle so many horses. The much-touted identification of the pillared buildings at Megiddo as Solomon's stables needs to be modified; archaeologists now date them to Ahab; see A. Mazar 1990, 476–78 (and further in Comment on 1 Kgs 20).

7. *These prefects provided for King Solomon and all those who came to King Solomon's table, each one in his month; they let nothing be lacking.* The verse picks up the thread of 4:19, expanding on the required tax transfers to the king (cf. 4:7).

all those who came to King Solomon's table. Hebrew *qārēb*, "approach, come near," appears only here with "table"; the more common usage is *ʾōkĕlê šulḥan*, "those that eat at the (royal) table"; cf. 2:7; 18:19; 2 Sam 9:11, 13; 19:29. Both expressions refer to persons who enjoyed the royal beneficence, e.g., the sons of Barzillai (cf. 1 Kgs 2:7).

be lacking. Hebrew *yĕʿaddĕrû*, only here in *Piel*; otherwise in *Niphal*.

8. *They (also) brought the barley and straw for the horses and steeds to the appointed place, each according to his charge.* In addition to the king's provisions (4:7), the prefects had a monthly quota that supported the vast military enterprise—in particular, the cavalry and chariot forces.

to the appointed place. Literally, "to the place where he would be," the subject not being indicated. One expects a plural verb (as the preceeding *yābi'û*), if the prefects are the subject; thus LXX adds: "the king"—they brought provender to wherever he, the king, happened to be on his journeys around the country (cf. Rashi).

steeds. Hebrew *rekeš*, also Mic 1:13; Esth 8:10, 14 is of unknown derivation, though Akk *rakāsu*, "to bind" is often pointed to in order to suggest the meaning "teams" (for chariots; so Noth), or bound during training (Wiseman); cf. NJB: "draught animals." The appearance of the term in Aram *rkšh* (G. R. Driver 1957, no. 6:4) and in late Egyptian *rkś* is not definitive. Ibn-Janah (1896) defined them as "good horses that had not seen long years of service"; the context of Esth 8:10 suggests swift riding horses.

COMMENT

Structure and Themes

Two administrative lists and a number of notes have been joined by editorial remarks to create a unit describing the administration of Solomon's realm.

I. *List One* (1 Kings 4:2–6)

This is the third list of royal officers ascribed to the days of the United Monarchy, two to David (2 Sam 8:16–18; 20:23–26), the present one to Solomon. Growth and change explain the differences, not only between the two Davidic lists themselves, but certainly between those of father and son. The increased complexity of the royal administration under Solomon reflects the needs of this master builder and entrepreneur, who seems to have lived in grand style at his subjects' expense.

The order of the lists may indicate the relative rank each official held within the administration. In the Davidic lists, the army commander is given precedence over the civilian officials, with the priests bringing up the rear. In the Solomonic list, the priest heads the list, followed by the civil and army officials respectively.

The list consists of personal names with a patronymic (except for Ahishar, v. 6), followed by a title with or without the article or by the area of service administered (*ʿal* + area). The article may have been used to distinguish this official from other lower-ranking ones of similar functions; thus, for example, Azariah, *the* priest—i.e., the high priest in the royal sanctuary. The title refers to the man first named, not his father, thus Azariah was the priest, not Zadok.

Long (1984, 72) classifies this list as a "literary text . . . deemed important for the author-editor" [Dtr], thus denying its status as an official register; contrast the view of Noth, who thought that we have "basically . . . authentic documents of Solomonic Age . . . from the royal chancellery in Jerusalem" (Noth, 62). From the formal perspective, the present list does not differ from the registers and lists of court personnel of varying lengths (from as few as six names to well over a hundred), known from the Neo-Assyrian archives at Nineveh (see SAA 7, nos. 1–7, 13–26). But this comparison does not explain what end the original Israelite registration served.

II. *List 2* (1 Kgs 4:7–19)

The district list is marked by what are perceived to be inconsistencies in matters of style, e.g., the manner in which the districts are presented: some are delineated by topographical markers (e.g., vv. 8, 13); others by cities (e.g., vv. 9, 12, 14) or tribal designations (e.g., vv. 15–18); and the amount of detail varies greatly (from a single word to a string of toponyms) — all of which suggests that the original list has been reworked, perhaps several times. Whether Dtr is responsible for its present shape, as might be suggested by the Deuteronomic glosses in vv. 13 and 19, or he was just one of several annotators cannot be determined with precision. Yet, for all this, the register-like quality of the document — introduction, personal-name entries followed by place-names — remains and, in this, it has affinities to administrative texts from Ugarit and Alalakh (see Hess 1996, 164; 1997); in no way does it now resemble "the form of ANNAL" (as proposed by Long 1984, 74).

III. *Miscellaneaous Notes* (1 Kgs 4:20–5:8)

The unit begins at 4:20 and continues through 5:8, as recognized by some translations that follow the Vulgate. It is composed of several subsections: (a) 4:20–5:5, chiastically arranged, 4:20//5:5; 5:1//5:4, surrounding 5:2–3; (b) 5:6 anticipates 5:8; (c) 5:7 (which may have at one time been related more closely to 4:7–19).

Dtr constructed a passage out of fragments of records that detailed the organization of the king's board (vv. 2–3), his military prowess (v. 6), the provisioning (v. 7), and the recognition he enjoyed throughout his vast realm, all of which brought peace and welfare to his subjects. These themes are found throughout the royal inscriptions of ancient Near Eastern monarchs, the particular biblical concatenation being unique (cf. Long, 75–76; earlier, Montgomery and Gehman, ad loc.).

History

I. *List One* (1 Kings 4:2–6)

The general nature of the titles ascribed to Solomon's officers does not always permit precision in determining their functions, nor is there much to indicate the date of the list. Only the mention of several holdovers from David's rule

(Jehoshaphat [v. 3] and Banaiah [v. 4]) points to the early years. But if the list has been editorially reworked (as is often suggested), then no single historical setting can be proposed.

On the other hand, comparison of the Hebrew titles to those in use in neighboring monarchies, especially Egypt, has led many commentators to suggest that the list reflects the bureaucratic setup first adopted by David and further developed under Solomon. Being a relative latecomer on the international scene, the Israelite monarchy did not have to resort to *de novo* invention of monarchic organization. And as has often been suggested, the posts created by David for his new kingdom were for the most part lifted wholly from Canaanite–Jebusite prototypes, then filled by officers who had been in the service of the last king of Jerusalem.

There is a tendency among commentators to tie many of the names together into family associations, even beyond the clear cases in which family relations are noted (as in the case of the king's sons-in-law, vv. 11, 15). Thus, for example, Nathan the prophet is seen as having been rewarded for his loyalty to Solomon by the king's assigning posts in his cabinet to his sons (v. 5). (This is also the case with the prefects in the second list. Baana [v. 16] is taken to be the son of Hushai, David's friend and confidant [2 Sam 15:37]). But this picture of widespread patronage in Solomon's administration remains a scholarly construct. At the same time, it should be remembered that, traditionally, the skills required for many professions were passed on from fathers to sons over the generations, until relatively recent times; the hereditary nature of the scribal craft is evidenced, not only in the appointment of Shisha's two sons (v. 3), but as late as the seventh century BCE, when members of the Shaphan family held influential posts at court (see Note on 2 Kgs 22:12).

II. *List Two* (1 Kings 4:7–19)

The radical conclusion that the district list is "virtually useless as a source of historical information" (Miller and Hayes 1986, 205–6), because it contains so many uncertainties, is a position even its exponents do not consistently follow. Nor is the polar claim, that the district list "provides a clear picture of the total extent and internal organisation of the kingdom of Israel, particularly as it shows very clearly the juxtaposition and the administrative division of tribal areas and city territories . . ." (Noth 1960, 213), wholly defensible. The recent assertion that records of this kind were not being produced in tenth-century Palestine (Ash 1995), making Solomon's court out to be an illiterate backwater, is here rejected as unnecessarily nihilistic. In the following discussion, allowance is made for the fact that only meager details are retrievable from the list, leaving many more questions open to scholarly speculation than perhaps one might like; its general scheme can, nevertheless, still be sketched.

a. *Date of List*

The Deuteronomist assigned the list to the reign of Solomon, but some have questioned whether it was not David who conquered and then incorporated the Canaanite enclaves into the kingdom, evidence for which is to be found in the comprehensive nature of the census described in 2 Sam 24. Yet the districting outlined in 1 Kgs 4 need not be "an outgrowth" of that census, "at the close of his life, after the consolidation of all of his conquests" (Kallai 1986, 41 n. 43; see also Ahlström 1982, 32 n. 29); military enlistment may have been David's major concern at the time. The district list looks like a new "political means of organizing the nation so that the king and the court could extract the most out of it" (Ahlström 1993a, 514), though a specific time slot during Solomon's reign is not ascertainable. Considerations vary. For example, the limits of District Nine, defined in very general terms as the territory of Asher, leave open the question of whether the cities of the Acco Plain were included or not; it would be useful to know whether they had already been ceded to Tyre, reported as taking place in Solomon's twentieth year (1 Kgs 9:10–13). The notations concerning the two prefects who were the king's sons-in-law (vv. 11, 15) could have been added editorially at any time, so calculating the age of Solomon's married daughters does not yield convincing results.

Albright (1925, 36) found what he thought to be clues to the Northern origin of the present version of the list: it begins with the area settled by Ephraim and Manasseh, which support at least five districts, at the same time that the southern territories are dealt with only briefly, if at all. The notations concerning sons-in-law of Solomon, also from Northern Israel, were handed down by families of these prefects, who claimed for themselves the status of old nobility.

b. *Organizing Principles*

The districts are identified either by traditional tribal designations (e.g., Naphtali, v. 15); or by topographical features (e.g., Mt. Ephraim, v. 8); or by city names, which, for the most part, were Canaanite centers only recently taken by Israel (e.g., Taanach and Megiddo, v. 12; cf. Judg 1:27–28). The order of districts proceeds from the central hill country to include all the land claimed by the House of Joseph (I, III–V) and Dan (II), to the Transjordanian holdings (VI–VII) and the Galilee (VIII–X), and concludes with Benjamin and Judah (XI–XII).

For a list of this sort to have had a functional, administrative use, it was likely to have been more detailed; and if so, when it was incorporated into the history of Solomon, it was probably curtailed by the editor, who may have thought that the map was known by his readers (e.g., the location of the tribe of Benjamin) well enough that a general orientation would suffice. One must also consider the possibility that the original list suffered in transmission and was not subsequently filled out. Modern readers need to complement their study with the use of other lists, particularly the ones in Josh 13–21.

As with Solomon's cabinet, the prototype for Solomon's district system has sometimes been traced to Egyptian models. Redford surveyed the many cases of dividing the responsibility for provisions of temple and palace on a calendaric basis in Egypt and its Asiatic territories from the mid–second millennium BCE until the Saite Dynasty; whether "directly inspired by contemporary Egyptian practice . . . or indirectly through the practice of the former Egyptian empire in Canaan is a moot point" (Redford 1972, 256; 1992, 372; see also Green 1979).

Much has been made of the fact that the district division seems to disregard certain tribal holdings, especially the holdings of Ephraim and Manasseh. Political considerations, "of repressive character, directed against the house of Joseph which was the political kernel of the northern tribes" (Mettinger 1971, 119), have been attributed to Solomon. But if these motivations were present, one wonders how the monarchy remained united through the end of Solomon's reign. For one thing, many of the nontribal districts had only recently been incorporated into the kingdom (cf. Judg 1:28, 30, 33, 35) and must have been still heavily Canaanite (cf. 1 Kgs 9:20–21), a fact that would have made it easy for the central administration to organize them as it saw fit. Besides, the need to create economically viable districts—in the matter of the king's table, each district had to supply one month's provisions a year—the district divisions had to take income and growth into consideration (as stressed repeatedly by Wright, who speaks of "equal economic units" [Wright 1967, 62*]).

Another issue often broached in discussions of Solomon's districts concerns their relation to the twelve-tribe system, as if the latter were "overlooked" or "disregarded" by Solomon in drawing up the administrative map presented here. But if the tribal system is a late historigraphic construct, as many argue, then the supposed inconsideration on the part of the royal bureaucracy becomes a superfluous proposal (Ahlström 1982, 33).

III. *Miscellaneous Notes* (1 Kings 4:20–5:8)

The vastness of Solomon's realm, recorded in anachronistic terms—from the Euphrates to the Sinai Peninsula—corresponds to the areas said to have been brought under Israelite control by David (cf. 2 Sam 8:1–14; 10); inasmuch as Solomon is never depicted as having waged war, he would have ruled these lands as an inheritance. Thus the question of historical reliability concerns the earlier data as much as it does the present verses. In general, the international picture at the beginning of the tenth century was such that Egypt and the northern (i.e., Hittite or Mesopotamian) powers that had fought during the second half of the second millennium for control of the Canaanite–Phoenician land bridge were all in eclipse. This permitted local states to try their hand at domination of their neighbors and unification of their conquests. In the contest between Aram-Zobah and Israel, David was victor, and in accepted parlance, he is thus considered to have been the founder of an empire, the one here ascribed to Solomon. Biblical sources only hint at the administrative structure set up by David in the conquered territories; governors were appointed in several lands adjacent to Israelite holdings (cf. 2 Sam 8:6, 14), but this may not have been the case in the distant Aramean states, where local dynasts who pledged fealty to David held on to their thrones (Malamat 1963a). There is little doubt that the idealistic, idyllic picture of Solomon's continuing in his father's footsteps as the region's most powerful monarch cannot stand; the attestation in 1 Kgs 11:14–25 tells of the outbreak of successful revolts against him at the start of his reign. See Comment, ad loc.

There is no real reason to discount the description of Solomon's daily board as a "sweeping editorial claim" that sought to enhance the picture of the king's wealth and influence (Miller and Hayes 1986, 195). Solomon's menu seems modest when compared to some from Egypt and Mesoptamian centers (Millard 1994a, 47).

VI. SOLOMON'S WISDOM

(5:9–14)

5 ⁹God granted Solomon wisdom and exceedingly much understanding, and breadth of heart, as the sand on the seashore. ¹⁰Solomon's wisdom was greater than the wisdom of all the Kedemites and all the wisdom of Egypt. ¹¹He was wiser than all men, than Ethan the Ezrahite, and Heman and Chalkol and Darda, the sons of Mahol; and his fame was in all the nations round about. ¹²He uttered three thousand proverbs, and his songs were a thousand and five. ¹³He spoke of trees, from the cedar that is in Lebanon to the hyssop that grows out of the wall; he spoke of beasts and of birds and of creeping things and of fish. ¹⁴They came from all peoples to hear Solomon's wisdom, (sent) by all the kings of the earth who had heard of his wisdom.

NOTES

5 9. *God granted Solomon wisdom and exceedingly much understanding.* The same description appears in 3:12. But in contrast to the judicial wisdom granted him there, in the present context, Solomon is endowed with analytical and practical wisdom of the kind that could be found in many quarters of the Near East.

breadth of heart. The limited examples of the Hebrew idiom *rōḥab lēb* do not help pinpoint the image; cf. Ps 119:32; Isa 60:5, where the verbal forms mean "thrill, rejoice." The heart often signifies the seat of intelligence; cf. Jer 4:9; Job 12:3; and it is this quality that appears in the semantic parallel in Akkadian: *uznu rapaštu u libbi rapšu*, "great wisdom and a wide heart" (ABL 878:7); cf., too, *libbu rapšu la kāṣir ikki*, "magnanimous and forbearing" (VAB 7, 194:14; cf. CAD I, 59b). This suggests the sense "breadth of mind."

as the sand on the seashore. Generally, this figure conveys the sense of uncountable numbers (cf. above, 4:20); here, the king's great understanding is compared to the seemingly endless expanse of the seacoast, stretching to the horizon.

10. *Solomon's wisdom was greater than the wisdom of all the Kedemites.* Literally, "sons of Kedem," i.e., the easterners, in general. From the names that follow in v. 11, the reference seems to be to the Arab tribes in the eastern deserts (cf. Judg 6:3, 33; Isa 11:14; Ezek 25:4), rather than to residents of the north Syrian steppe (cf. Gen 29:1). The book of Proverbs quotes teachings ascribed to Agur (Prov 30:1) and Lemuel (31:1), both from the Arab tribe of Massa, in the vicinity of Tema in northwest Arabia (cf. Gen 25:15; 1 Chr 1:30).

and all the wisdom of Egypt. Compare with Gen 41:8; Isa 19:11 for the picture of Egyptian pharaohs surrounded by wise advisers. The impact of Egyptian wisdom on Israel is especially pointed in Proverbs, where an entire literary unit, 22:17–23:11, exhibits close affinity to the Instruction of Amenemope; cf. Scott 1965, 20–21, 135–36.

11. *He was wiser than all men.* The suggestion to read: *hā'ĕdomîm*, "the Edomites" for MT *hā'ādām*, "men"—based on several biblical verses that seem to intimate the existence of an Edomite circle of wise men, e.g., Jer 49:7; Obad 8; and noting that Zerah (= Ezrah) appears in the Edomite genealogy in Gen 36:13; also Eliphaz the Temanite (Job 2:11; for Teman in Edom, cf. Gen 36:11)— has attracted several followers (Šanda, Montgomery and Gehman, Gray, Noth), but it is without textual support.

than Ethan the Ezrahite, and Heman and Chalkol and Darda, the sons of Mahol. Famed wise men, unattested outside of this verse. The context suggests that they were non-Israelites, but by the time of the Chronicler, they were given Israelite ancestry, as grandsons of Judah, taking "the Ezrahite" to refer to Zerah son of Judah and Tamar (1 Chr 2:6); this is hardly evidence for "their antiquity" (so Gray). In another late genealogy, Ethan and Heman are made over into Temple singers of Levitical pedigree (cf. 1 Chr 15:17, 19), and two Psalm titles credit them as being composers (cf. Ps 88:1: Heman the Ezrahite; Ps 89:1: Ethan the Ezrahite). Albright (1969b, 210 n. 95) translated *'ezrah* as "native" (cf., e.g., Num 9:14), thus making Ethan a Canaanite, famed for his wisdom (adopted by NJB). (For a new suggestion to take *'ezrah* as a loanword from Akk *um/nzarhu*, "homeborn," used of persons and animals, see Deller 1984.)

and Heman and Chalkol and Darda, the sons of Mahol. Here Albright (1969b, 123) also took the paternal name as a common noun, "members of the orchestral guild," from *māhôl*, "circle dance." See also de Vaux 1961, 382.

Chalkol. The name has supposedly been found in the Late Bronze Age Megiddo ivories (**Kulkul*) as the name of a female singer in the temple of Ptah in Ashkelon (so Albright 1969b, 123 and others), but this says nothing about the present passage.

Darda. In 1 Chr 2:6, the name appears as Dara, but this variant does not aid in its interpretation.

and his fame was in all the nations round about. Literally, "his name"; cf. Gen 6:4: "men of renown" (*haššēm*).

12. *He uttered three thousand proverbs, and his songs were a thousand and five.* "Proverbs" (*māšāl*) and "songs" (*šîr*) represent two major categories of ancient poetic composition. Hebrew regularly uses nouns in the singular in enumerations, in small and large numbers; cf. Waltke and O'Connor 1990, §7.2.2b. Both "three thousand" and "a thousand and five" are meant to convey the idea of very large numbers and then some, like "a thousand and one nights." On round numbers in inscriptions, see above, Note on 5:6. For some, this verse served as the proof text verifying the ascription of Song of Songs to Solomon; cf. Pope 1977, 22, 295–97.

13. *He spoke of trees, from the cedar that is in Lebanon to the hyssop that grows out of the wall.* Many medieval commentators, reflecting contemporary conceptions of wise men, pictured Solomon as the *Ur*-scientist who produced scientific works on the nature of all living things in the plant and animal world, including a study of their usefulness to man as food and medicine; cf., e.g.,

Qimḥi and Gersonides. The book of Proverbs, however, opens another avenue of interpretation: the natural world served as an object lesson from which
mankind could derive beneficial lessons for the conduct of human affairs; e.g.,
Prov 6:6–7; 30:24–28.

He spoke of trees. From the impressive tall trees of the north to the insignificant hyssop. Jotham's parable in Judg 9:8–15 is probably the best-known biblical
example of a wisdom teaching in which trees are the subject; cf., too, the parable concerning the cedar and the thorn bush cited in a diplomatic exchange
between Amaziah and Jehoash in 2 Kgs 14:9.

from the cedar that is in Lebanon. See below on 1 Kgs 5:22.

to the hyssop that grows out of the wall. The identification of *'ēzôb* as "hyssop"
is based on LXX, although this is not altogether accurate. The plant in question
is often mentioned in rituals, as in the marking with blood of the dwellings of
the Israelites in Egypt (Exod 12:22), sprinkling the leper and leperous house (Lev
14:4–7, 49–51) and the preparation and sprinkling in the red heifer rite (Num
19:6, 18); cf. Ps 51:9. Rabbinic descriptions point to *Majorana syriaca*, still
used in the ceremonial Passover sprinkling as performed by the Samaritans.
Yet this shrub, while plentiful in Israel, and used as a popular spice (Ar *za'atar*),
does not grow out of walls but only on stony ground. See Zohary 1982, 96–97.

he spoke of beasts and of birds and of creeping things and of fish. Wisdom
based on observation of animal behavior is well represented in Proverbs (see
Forti 1996) and is summarized in Job 12:7–8: "But ask the beasts, and they will
teach you; the birds of the sky, they will tell you. Or speak to the earth, it will
teach you; the fish of the seas, they will inform you."

14. *They came from all peoples to hear Solomon's wisdom, (sent) by all the
kings of the earth who had heard of his wisdom.* Verse 14b contains a strange
construction: Heb *mē'ēt*, "from," has no antecedent. The Luc. and Syr. resolve
the unevenness (on the basis of 2 Chr 9:23–24?) by adding "he received gifts,"
which is adopted by many commentators, NEB, and NJB. Burney compares 2 Sam
15:3 and translates: "deputed by all the kings . . ."; so NAB, NJPSV.

Solomon's wisdom spread by word of mouth, not necessarily in writing, and
it was to hear the master firsthand that foreign dignitaries went to Jerusalem.
The visit of the Queen of Sheba (cf. below, 1 Kgs 10:1–13) exemplifies this
worldwide interest in Solomon's special gift. Later tradition elaborated on this
theme; e.g., Josephus quoted a Phoenician source that told of a contest of wits
between Solomon and Hiram (*Ag. Ap.* 1.113–15); further elaborations can be
found in Ginzberg 1928, 4:130–42.

COMMENT

Structure and Themes

This is a loosely constructed unit of single statements, moving from YHWH's
gift of wisdom (v. 9, resuming 3:2) to its incomparability (v. 10) and Solomon's

outranking of all of the world's wise men (v. 11) to a description of the prodigious product of his wisdom (v. 12) and its subject matter (v. 13), which brought him an audience from the entire world (v. 14).

The subject of Solomon's wisdom, already treated extensively in 1 Kgs 3, is here taken up once again (cf. also below, 5:26 and 10:1). The aspect of the present passage is not the practical wisdom needed to govern; rather, it is Solomon's extensive knowledge of the ways of the world that brought him international praise. The suggestion that Solomon was dependent on the onomastic tradition preserved in the extensive encyclopedic lists of the animal kingdom produced in the learned circles of Babylonia and Egypt (Alt 1951a) is less apt than it seemed when originally put forward. "The science of lists" (*Listenwissenschaft*) was a didactic undertaking and not an encyclopedic enterprise (M. Fox 1986). It was not related in any way to wisdom circles and misconstrues the nature of Solomon's wisdom (Day 1995, 61–62), which was expressed through proverb and song, not onomastics. The animal and plant proverbs in Prov 6:6–8; 30:15, 17–19, 24–31 are examples of the kind of wisdom that Solomon may have contributed to the field.

We are told that Solomon's ability was world renowned and that Solomon could compete with the best of Egypt and the desert Arabs. Surprisingly, the wise scholars of Mesopotamia (known by their professions to the author of Dan 4:4) are absent from the listing in vv. 10–11, which may mean only that the immediate, nearby circle of countries is mentioned. (For a recent overview of ancient Near Eastern wisdom, see ABD 6:928–30.)

History

It is commonly held that this encomium is an expression of the esteem in which Solomon was held by later tradition and should not be taken in any way as a contemporary report. The earliest hint at Solomon's connection with Israelite wisdom outside of the book of Kings is the title in Prov 25:1, a witness to the fact that, by the late eighth century, collections of proverbs were being associated with the wise king. The origins of other ascriptions, such as his being the author of Song of Songs and Qoheleth (cf. above to v. 12) are unretrievable. Yet even without such determinations, it would not have been unusual for contemporary court circles to ascribe wisdom to their monarch, the ruler of a vast kingdom and builder of the nation's Temple; many a Near Eastern ruler was similarly praised. On such a base, later tradents could have fashioned the current description of Solomon's wisdom as his recollected image developed.

VII. Negotiations with Hiram

(5:15–32)

5 ¹⁵Hiram king of Tyre sent his servants to Solomon when he heard that he had been anointed king in place of his father, for Hiram had always loved David. ¹⁶Solomon sent (in reply) to Hiram: ¹⁷"You knew that my father David could not build a house for the name of YHWH his God because of the wars that surrounded him, until YHWH made them subject to him.[a] ¹⁸Now YHWH my God has given me rest all around; there is no adversary and no misfortune. ¹⁹And so I intend to build a house for the name of YHWH my God, as YHWH promised David my father: 'Your son, whom I shall set upon your throne in your place, *he* will build the house for my name.' ²⁰Now, then, give orders to cut cedars in the Lebanon for me; my servants will be beside your servants, and I will pay you for your servants whatever you say. *You* know that we have no one who knows how to cut trees like the Sidonians."

²¹When Hiram heard Solomon's words, he was greatly pleased; he said: "Blessed be YHWH today, who has given David a wise son over this great people." ²²Hiram sent (in reply) to Solomon: "I have heard what you sent to me. *I* will do all that you wish in the matter of the cedar trees and juniper trees. ²³My servants will bring (the trees) down from the Lebanon to the sea and *I* will make them into rafts in the sea (and deliver them) to the place you shall send to me; there I will have them broken up and *you* can transport them. You, for your part, will fulfill my wish by providing food for my household." ²⁴So it was (that) Hiram would provide Solomon with all the cedar and juniper trees he wished, ²⁵and Solomon provided Hiram with twenty thousand *kors* of wheat as food for his household and twenty *kors* of beaten oil. These Solomon provided Hiram yearly. ²⁶YHWH granted Solomon wisdom, as he had promised him; and there was peace between Hiram and Solomon, and the two of them concluded a treaty.

²⁷King Solomon raised a levy from all Israel, and the levy was thirty thousand men. ²⁸He sent them to the Lebanon, ten thousand a month in rotation; one month they would be in the Lebanon and two months at home. Adoniram was Over-the-levy.

²⁹Solomon had seventy thousand basket carriers and eighty thousand quarriers in the mountains, ³⁰excluding the officers of Solomon's prefects who were in charge of the work, three thousand three hundred, who oversaw the people doing the work. ³¹The king gave orders to quarry large stones, quality stone, in order to lay the foundation of the house with hewn stone. ³²Solomon's builders and Hiram's builders and the Gebalites fashioned (them); thus they prepared the timber and the stone to build the house.

---

[a] Lit., "his (i.e., David's) feet" (with ketib: *rglw*); "my (i.e., Solomon's) feet" (qere: *rgly*).

NOTES

5   15. *Hiram king of Tyre sent his servants to Solomon when he heard that he had been anointed king in place of his father, for Hiram had always loved David.* The accession of a king was the occasion for a diplomatic exchange between courts; cf. 2 Sam 10:2; in Amarna letter 33:9–18, a greeting sent upon accession is accompanied by a request for a shipment of copper.

Hiram. Hiram I reigned ca. 970–636 BCE, having ascended the throne after the death of his father, Abibaal (Katzenstein 1997, 82). The name Hiram (*ḥyrm*) is the abbreviated form of Ahiram, "my (divine) brother is exalted" (Heb ʾ*ḥyrm*; Phoen ʾ*ḥrm*; so, on the tenth-century BCE coffin inscription from Byblos; see Z. S. Harris 1936, 75); cf. the Hebrew name Ahiram in Num 26:38. In 1 Kgs 5:24 and 32, the alternate form, Hirom, appears, which represents the late Phoenician pronunciation (transcribed in NA inscriptions of Tiglath-Pileser III as *Ḥirumu*). The same form occurs in the name of the Phoenician craftsman who supervised the Temple construction; cf. 7:13, 40.

had always loved David. Not an expression of endearment but a term for the treaty relationship between the two kingdoms. The same sense is attested for Akk *râmu*, "to love"; cf. Moran 1963, 80–81. This statement may contain a bit of diplomatic exaggeration, considering that David's contacts with Hiram (cf. 2 Sam 5:11) were likely established toward the end of his reign; otherwise, an exceptionally long rule for Hiram must be posited (see McCarter 1984, 145–46; also Green 1983; and Comment below).

16. *Solomon sent (in reply) to Hiram.* The message that follows draws on 2 Sam 7 and is correctly seen by critics to be a free composition by Dtr. The correspondences are noted below.

17. *"You knew that my father David could not build a house for the name of YHWH his God because of the wars that surrounded him, until YHWH made them subject to him. . . ."* That David did not build the Temple was of particular concern to biblical writers. In 2 Sam 7:4–7, Nathan directs that the project be delayed for a generation, since a temple was seen as not being consistent with the accepted mode of worship in early Israel. In the present verse, it was David's preoccupation with war that prevented him from building the Temple. In 1 Chr 22:8, these wars are interpreted as having disqualified David ("you have spilled much blood") from the noble undertaking.

build a house for the name of YHWH his God. Compare with 2 Sam 7:13; 1 Kgs 3:2.

because of the wars that surrounded him. The subject *milḥāmâ* in the singular followed by the plural *sĕbābûhû*; cf. Exod 1:10, also with "war" in the singular, and GKC, 145e for feminine collective nouns with plural verbs. The NJPSV circumvents by translating: "enemies." Alternately, Targum, later Kittel, Šanda, and Noth render: "the hostility with which they (the enemies) surrounded me."

made them subject to him. Literally, "placed them under his feet," the image being of the victor placing his foot on the neck of the subdued in total submission; cf. Josh 10:24; similarly, "make your enemies your footstool" in Ps 110:1.

The same figure of speech was used by Shalmaneser III, "who put his feet on all the countries as if they were a footstool" (CAD K, 7). For visual representations of this act, cf. ANEP 393 (Egyptian king, Thutmose IV); Barnett and Falkner 1962, 146 (Tiglath-pileser III).

18. *Now YHWH my God has given me rest all around.* Cf. 2 Sam 7:1, 11.

there is no adversary and no misfortune. For Heb *śātān*, "adversary," see at 11:14. "Misfortune," lit., "evil encounter" (*pegaʿ rāʿ*); Heb *pegaʿ* is a chance, unplanned meeting; cf. the use of the verb in 1 Sam 10:5; Amos 5:19. A more realistic picture of the difficult political situations that Solomon faced, even at the very beginning of his reign, is reported in 1 Kgs 11:14–25; see Comment there.

19. *And so I intend to build a house for the name of YHWH my God.* Hebrew *ʾomēr*, lit., "say," implies here "intend, purpose"; cf. Exod 2:14; 1 Sam 30:6. The time had arrived to set to work for, according to Deuteronomic regulation, the single sanctuary was to be built when Israel achieved rest and settled the land; cf. Deut 12:9–10.

as YHWH promised David my father. A reference to 2 Sam 7:12–13.

20. *Now.* A syntactic marker; after all the formalities and preliminaries are concluded, the substance of the letter is introduced by *wĕʿattâ*; see Note on 2 Kgs 5:6.

give orders to cut cedars. For the use of the voluntative with the weak *waw*, see S. R. Driver 1892, §62.

in the Lebanon. The double range of mountains separated by *el Beqaʿ* ("the Valley"), running parallel to the Mediterranean coast for about 170 km, from the Litanni River in the south to the el-Kebir. The name, documented in all ancient sources, likely means "the white(-capped) one," due to the permanent snow in its upper reaches.

my servants will be beside your servants. That is, will provide the physical labor under the supervision of the skilled loggers.

You know that we have no one who knows how to cut trees like the Sidonians. Nor did any nation in the near East have the skill needed for the task. This rich source of timber is reported from as early as the mid–third millenium BCE in Egyptian sources (ANET, 227) until classical times; see references collected in Šanda, Montgomery and Gehman, to which may be added the use of cedars of Lebanon for Baal's palace in the mythology of Ugarit (ANET, 134a). A late eighth-century administrative letter from an Assyrian official in Tyre contains a report to the king about the trouble he has had enforcing the restrictions on sales of wood brought down from the Lebanon through the port of Sidon (Saggs 1955, 127–28).

the Sidonians. "Sidonians" is used here as a term for "Phoenicians" in general, even though Hiram is styled the "king of Tyre" (v. 14). Somewhat later, at least by the reign of Ethbaal, Tyre had gained supremacy over Sidon, and the king took the title "king of Sidon"; see Note on 16:31.

21. *When Hiram heard Solomon's words, he was greatly pleased; he said: "Blessed be YHWH today, who has given David a wise son over this great people."* All versions, except Luc., read "God." But it is no more unusual for the

foreign king to invoke the name of Solomon's God than it is for the Assyrian Rab-shakeh to speak of YHWH as having commissioned the Assyrian attack on Jerusalem; cf. 2 Kgs 18:25.

22. *I will do all that you wish.* Compare with 9:11. The expression *ʿāśô ḥēpeṣ* is favored by Second Isaiah; cf. Isa 46:10; 48:14; 58:13, where it means "following/ fulfilling one's desire."

in the matter of the cedar trees. Hebrew *'erez* is identifed as *Cedrus libani*, renowned for its beauty and impressive height, which in some instances has reached as much as thirty meters; cf. Ezek 31:3–7 for a hymn of praise to this mighty cedar, "the envy of all the trees"; cf., too, 2 Kgs 14:9; 19:23; Isa 2:13; 10:34; the cedar was also desired for its fragrance; cf. Hos 14:7; Song 4:11. Its wood was in demand throughout the Near East for construction of ships, buildings, and furniture because of its superior quality (Koehler's doubts [1937, 163–65], followed by Noth, nothwithstanding). M. Weippert has surveyed the ancient Near Eastern references to the cedar and the other timbers of the Lebanon (1980–83, 642–45).

juniper trees. Hebrew *běrôš*, traditionally translated "cypress," is the *Juniperus excelsa*; also in Akk *burāšu* (CAD B, 326–28). See Feliks 1957, 79–81; Zohary (1982, 106–7) considers it a collective name for three species of firs.

23. *My servants will bring (the trees) down from the Lebanon to the sea and I will make them into rafts in the sea (and deliver them) to the place you shall send to me.* Hiram's counters with his own proposal: his countrymen will fell the trees and see that they are delivered to a port in Israel; from there, Solomon's men will take over. Was this a sign of generosity or a wish to keep close watch over the Phoenician monopoly in forestry (see Ikeda 1991, 116)?

rafts. The hapax legomenon Heb *dōbĕrôt*, "rafts," from **dbr*, "to lead, drive"; in 2 Chr 2:15, it is replaced with *rapsōdôt*, another unique word (but more familiar to the Chronicler's audience?), and the Chronicler adds that the rafts reached Jaffo, from where the logs were transferred overland to Jerusalem, a procedure associated with the building of the postexilic Temple; cf. Ezra 3:7. Sea transportation of this kind, "the only possible method for such huge timbers," is known from Egyptian and Mesopotamian sources (see references in Montgomery and Gehman, 135–36). The "pregnant construction" in the present verse is extended unnecessarily in 2 Chr 2:15 by adding the word *nĕbî'ēm*, "we will bring."

there I will have them broken up and you can transport them. After being towed to their destination as single crafts, the rafts were to be disassembled in order to be moved to the construction site inland.

You, for your part, will fulfill my wish by providing food for my household. In payment for the timber, Solomon was to supply Hiram's need for foodstuffs.

24. *So it was (that) Hiram would provide Solomon with all the cedar and juniper trees he wished,* 5:25. *and Solomon provided Hiram with twenty thousand* kors *of wheat as food for his household and twenty* kors *of beaten oil.* The inversion of subject and verb in v. 25, compared with v. 24, gives the meaning: "Solomon, for his part"; see S. R. Driver 1892, §160, Obs. The quantity of grain given here is almost twice Solomon's yearly receipt (cf. v. 2) and thus seems

suspect. Could ancient Israel have been so fruitful as to provide for the needs of two royal houses, in addition to the common consumption? This is unlikely, given the statement in 9:11 concerning the large debt accumulated over the years, which had to be paid for by the transfer of land to Hiram; see further, ad loc. Many have adopted Šanda's suggestion that Hiram profited greatly from the surplus supplies, exported through his trading links throughout the Mediterranean.

twenty thousand kors *of wheat.* For the *kor* measure, see above, Note on 1 Kgs 5:2.

as food. Hebrew *makkōlet* for *ma'ăkōlet* (Isa 9:4, 18), with elision of *'alep*; similarly, *māsoret* for *ma'ăsōret* in Ezek 20:37.

twenty kors *of beaten oil.* Twenty *kors* of oil seems too little, unless this extra-fine oil was exclusively for Hiram's household; the reading in Luc. and LXX, represented in 2 Chr 2:9: "twenty thousand baths of oil," looks much too high. "Beaten oil" refers to the process by which fine olive oil was obtained. As observable in Near Eastern villages to this day, small amounts of olives are carefully pounded (so as not to crush the bitter pits) into a mash, which is then boiled until the oil begins to float to the top. The cooled oil is of exceptional quality. Beaten oil was used in lighting the lamp in the Tabernacle (Exod 27:20) and in the preparation of the flour offerings (cf., e.g., Exod 29:40; Num 28:5).

These Solomon provided Hiram yearly. So, at least, at the beginning of their alliance; see further at 9:11.

26. *YHWH granted Solomon wisdom, as he had promised him.* The editorial conclusion of the pericope. In v. 26a, the reference is to YHWH's promise made at Gibeon to give Solomon a "heart of wisdom and understanding" (3:12); in v. 26b, the alliance between the two kings is a fulfillment of the additional grant of "riches and honor" unlike any ever enjoyed by kings (3:13). All the phraseology is Deuteronomic; "as he had promised"; cf. Deut 1:21; 6:3; 9:3; 1 Kgs 8:20, 53, 56.

and there was peace between Hiram and Solomon, and the two of them concluded a treaty. The term *šālôm* suggests that the treaty covered more than just the Temple construction and its payment. Amicable commercial relations (covered by a separate treaty?) were in the interest of both kingdoms, details of which can be gathered from 9:26–28; 10:11, 22. Late legend has Solomon marrying a daughter of Hiram in order to cement the ties with Tyre (Katzenstein, 1997, 88 n. 59), but such tales are of no contemporary worth, since they probably developed out of a reading of 11:1, where Sidonian women are mentioned as part of Solomon's harem.

27. *King Solomon raised a levy from all Israel, and the levy was thirty thousand men.* On the technical terms for the levy, see above, Note on 4:6. The additional report in 9:15, 20–22, according to which only the remaining Canaanites were forced to render labor to the state is at odds with the present one. No amount of philological fine-tuning, e.g., suggesting a distinction between *mas* and *mas 'ōbēd* (so Gray) will do; comparison of Josh 16:10 with Judg 1:30, 33, 35 and 1 Kgs 9:21 with 2 Chr 8:8 shows that the two are equivalent. Nor will

interpreting "from all Israel" as Canaanites "drawn from throughout Israel" (Provan) do for an expression whose meaning is well attested. Soggin (1982, 265) correctly rejects Noth's suggestion to take this as a late post-Dtr addition that construed "all Israel" in 1 Kgs 4:1 narrowly, rather than as referring to all of Solomon's empire. The reference to state work undertaken by Ephraimites (11:28) is sufficient to support the correctness — and early date — of this datum.

28. *He sent them to Lebanon, ten thousand a month in rotation; one month they would be in Lebanon and two months at home.* The present note contradicts Hiram's explicit statement that his servants would fell the trees (v. 23), obviating the need for Israelites to serve in Lebanon, unless one adopts the view of Montgomery and Gehman that the Israelites provided the raw labor for the skilled Phoenicians.

in rotation. Literally, "exchanges, replacements," from *ḥlp; cf. Job 10:17; 14:14 for use in the context of an army.

and two months at home. Literally, "in his (i.e., the worker's) house," and not "in his (i.e., Solomon's) house," as if referring to work on the king's palace. The syntax is eased if the suffixed *waw* is taken as dittography of the following *w'dnyrm*.

Adoniram was Over-the-levy. This officer was introduced in 1 Kgs 4:6.

29. *Solomon had seventy thousand basket carriers and eighty thousand quarriers in the mountains.* Reference is to quarry work done close to the construction site, since there was no need for importing stone to the mountanous land of Israel.

basket carriers. Hebrew *nōśē' sābbal,* lit., "bearer of a burden," is related to the term *sēbel,* which like *mas,* refers to a type of state service. The etymologically similar term *sablum,* "levy" is attested in texts from Mari (see CAD S, 4, perhaps of West-Semitic etymology; on the relation to the cognate Akk *zubbulu,* see Held 1968). This service cannot be limited to "aliens" (so Rainey 1970, 201–2), since Israelites from the House of Jospeh were subject to *sēbel,* as well; cf. 11:28; 12:4.

30. *excluding the officers of Solomon's prefects who were in charge of the work, three thousand three hundred, who oversaw the people doing the work.* Great confusion reigns concerning the identification of these officers and their exact number. Their title suggests that they were responsible to the district prefects (cf. 9:23), and if this is so, then the number of persons called up for state service was likely divided among the twelve prefectures. As to the number of officers involved, a parallel tradition in 9:23 gives their number as 550, and the context there makes them out to be Israelite officers who supervised the Canaanite corvée. In the present verse, they seem to have been in charge of the Israelites who were called up for state service; cf. 5:27–28, where 30,000 is the number given for the corvée workers. The Chronicler has another set of numbers; in 2 Chr 2:16–17, there are 3,600 foremen over the Canaanite levy; cf. 2:2; and in 8:10, there were 250 who oversaw the work. Montgomery and Gehman offer an ingenious solution to the Kings discrepancy: a late editor added 30,000 (the original Israelite levy, v. 27) and 150,000 (the Canaanite levy,

v. 29 and 2 Chr 8:8–10) = 180,000; then on the basis of the ratio 550 : 30,000 he calculated that 3,300 overseers would be necesssary for 180,000 workers.

On the alternation between *šlš*, "three," in Kings and *šš*, "six," in Chronicles as the result of an abbreviation using the single letter *š*, see G. R. Driver 1960, 125.

31. *The king gave orders to quarry large stones, quality stone, in order to lay the foundation of the house with hewn stone.* This information corresponds to the description in 7:10–11 and may have been drawn from there.

to quarry. Literally, "they transported"; Tg.: *w῾qrw*, "they uprooted." In Qoh 10:9, the verb is used parallel to "split (wood)," which will suit the present context; cf. 1 Kgs. 6:7, *'eben massā῾*, "quarried stone."

quality stone. Literally, "costly" (NJPSV: "choice"). In LBH, *yāqār* has the sense "weighty" (cf. Qoh 10:1), but in early contexts, it is used of precious materials (otherwise, all medieval commentators). Montgomery and Gehman, followed by Gray, noted what looks like an Arab cognate with the meaning "split," thus "dressed stones."

32. *Solomon's builders and Hiram's builders and the Gebalites fashioned (them); thus they prepared the timber and the stone to build the house.* The specification of the Gebalites, skilled workers from the Phoenician port city of Byblos (also referred to in Josh 13:5 and Ezek 27:9), gave early translators (LXX[B]) and some modern translators difficulty, leading them to suggest numerous emended readings, mostly as a verbal form: *wygblwm*, "they bordered them with grooved edges" for MT *whgblym* (see the summary in Burney, Šanda, adopted by Gray). For some unexplained reason, the plain sense of the text, as expounded by Rashi, among other medievals, was not adopted: "They were expert in stone masonry for construction as in Ezek 27:9," which refers to the skills of the Byblian shipwrights; see, too, Montgomery and Gehman. Furthermore, this single word adds a significant historical datum to the little that is known concerning the north Phoenician coast in the tenth century BCE; Byblos was an independent city, with which Solomon may have negotiated separately. On Byblos, see ABD 2:922–23.

COMMENT

Structure and Themes

This section is a major Dtr composition with attached notes, perhaps by a later hand. It divides into: vv. 15–26—a unified literary piece depicting the negotiations between Solomon and Hiram; vv. 27–28a—enumeration of the labor force sent to Lebanon as corvée; v. 28b—a footnote naming the commander of the national corvée; vv. 29–30—the work roster; vv. 31–32—quarry work for the Temple. Deuteronomistic language is particularly visible in vv. 17–19 (cf. 2 Sam 7:11, 13); vv. 21, 26 (cf. 1 Kgs 3:4–28, esp. vv. 12–13).

The shift from the wisdom theme, with which the preceding section closes, to the Hiram pericope and Temple-building is bridged by v. 15, in which Hiram serves as an example of a foreign king who admired (cf. v. 14) and acclaimed (v. 21) Solomon's wisdom.

The diplomatic correspondence between Hiram and Solomon reconstructed in these verses follows the accepted norms of ancient Near Eastern rhetoric. On the one hand, the writer utilizes the occasion of the accession of a new king to send personal greetings, referring to previous agreements between the two monarchies, and thus hinting at his desire for continued alliance. On the other hand, his counterpart thanks the sender directly, while openly asking for a favor.

There is a bit of irony in Solomon's boasting of the good times that are his lot (v. 18). The term for misfortune (Heb *pega'*), which he claims is absent from his realm, is the same one used for the removal of his political enemies in 2:25, 29, 34, 46, which he himself carried out. Moreover, 11:14–28 exposes the adversity that was present all through his reign.

History

Because of the heavy editing, "only the outlines of this section can be regarded as authentic history" (so Montgomery and Gehman, 136; Noth [88] misrepresents this position); still, the verisimilitude of the diplomatic negotiations between the two kings and the terms of the treaty do breathe the air of the period. Records from Tyre have reached us circuitously in the quotations by Josephus from Greek translations of Tyrian annals found in the histories of Dius and Menander. These secondhand reports mention Solomon, "king (or: tyrant) of Jerusalem," who competed with Hiram in solving riddles (*Ant.* 8.143, 146–49; *Ag. Ap.* 1.113–15, 120). But these extrabiblical sources do not give details concerning the relations between the two kingdoms, though description of Hiram's building of temples in Tyre does echo the theme of the present chapter. (For the use of the biblical story in the polemics concerning the relationship between Phoenicia and the Hasmonean kings during the second century BCE, see Mendels 1987.)

If Hiram's letter was sent close to the time when Solomon ascended the throne in Jerusalem, then the negotiations between the two monarchs continued for a number of years, until Solomon's fourth year, when work began on the Temple (cf. 6:1). It would have been in the interest of both monarchs to establish "brotherly" relations (cf. 9:13). Solomon's kingdom sat astride several major trade routes (the westward-bearing road from Eilat through the Negev to the Mediterranean coast, and the King's Highway running north through Transjordan to Damascus and beyond). Their accessibility was a principal factor in Hiram's recognition of Israel's new king, for Tyre was *the* major player in international commerce in that age. Solomon, in turn, benefited from the tax and custom duties generated by the use of these roads. The Tyrian hinterland, the Lebanon in particular, was a source of supreme building timber, and this was another enticement for Solomon to join in treaty with Hiram. In return, Hiram acquired the foodstuffs that Israel could supply. At some later time, Solomon signed on with the Tyrian ruler as partner in overseas mercantile ventures (cf. 9:26–28); in this, it is doubtful that he would have been on an equal footing with Hiram, considering that Phoenician seamanship was unmatched. All this is not a claim for viewing the relations between Tyre and Jerusalem as being solely based upon economics. The two kingdoms were bound by a treaty between equals (9:13), between monarchs who had established peace (5:26) and cooperation between their kingdoms, undisturbed by outside powers to the south or northeast (Fensham 1969).

Regarding the reference to amity between Hiram and David in 1 Kgs 5:15, supported in part by 2 Sam 5:11, questions of chronology and circumstance complicate drawing a picture of this early contact between the two. Hiram I ascended the throne ca. 970 BCE (following the sequence of Tyrian kings established by Katzenstein 1997, 80–84). He was nineteen years old and reigned for thirty-four years; this corresponded with the last five years of David's reign. It may be that Abibaal, Hiram's father, had already opened discussions with David, if we consider David's extension of Israelite influence into Syria, among Tyre's near neighbors.

VIII. THE CONSTRUCTION OF THE TEMPLE

(6:1–38)

6 ¹It was in the four hundred and eightieth year after the departure of the Israelites from the land of Egypt, in the fourth year ªof the reign of Solomon over Israel,ª in the month of Ziv, that is the second month, he built the House for YHWH.

²The House that King Solomon built for YHWH was sixty cubits long, twenty ⟨cubits⟩ᵇ wide, and thirty cubits high. ³The porch in front of the main hall was twenty cubits long along the width of the House, ten cubits deep in front of the House. ⁴He made windows for the House, splayed and latticed. ⁵He built an extensionᶜ on the walls of the House, that is, the walls of the House around the main hall and the shrine; he made side-chambers all around. ⁶The lowest side-chamberᵈ was five cubits wide, the middle one was six cubits wide, the third one, seven cubits wide; for he made recesses in the House on the outside all around, so as not to fasten onto the walls of the House. ⁷Concerning the building of the House, it was built of undressed stone from the quarry; no hammers or ax or any iron tool was heard in the House during its building. ⁸The opening of the lowestᵉ (side-chamber) was on the right side of the House; spiral stairs went up to the middle (side-chamber) and from the middle to the third.ᶠ ⁹So he built the House and completed it; he roofed the House with coffers in rows of cedar wood. ¹⁰He built the extensionᵈ along the entire House, (each story) five cubits in height; he paneled the House with cedar wood.

¹¹The word of YHWH came to Solomon: ¹²"As to this House that you are building, if you will follow my statutes and obey my rules and keep my commands, following them, then I will fulfill my promise to you that I made to David your father. ¹³I will dwell among the Israelites and I will not forsake my people Israel."

¹⁴Solomon built the House and he completed it. ¹⁵He built the walls of the House on the inside with cedar planks from the floor of the House upᵍ to the beamsʰ of the roof; he overlaid (them) with wood on the inside. He overlaid the floor of the House with juniper planks. ¹⁶He built twenty cubits in the rearⁱ of the House with cedar planks from the floor up to the beams;ʲ he built it on

---

ᵃ⁻ᵃ Moved up in translation.

ᵇ Add 'ammâ with several MSS, Luc., LXX, Vulg., Syr.

ᶜ Ketib: yṣwˤ; qere: yṣyˤ.

ᵈ Ketib: hyṣwˤ; qere: hyṣyˤ. Read with LXX: ṣlˤ; see Note.

ᵉ Read tḥtnh with Luc., LXX, and Tg. for MT tyknh, "middle."

ᶠ Perhaps read hšlyšyt, as in v. 6; so several MSS; see Note.

ᵍ Many MSS read wˤd for MT ˤd.

ʰ Read qwrwt for MT qyrwt; Luc. and LXX have a double reading; see Note.

ⁱ Ketib: myrkwty, with excessive waw.

ʲ Read hqwrwt with LXX for MT hqyrwt; see Textual Note h.

the inside as a shrine, the Holy of Holies. [17]The House was forty cubits (long), that is, the main hall in front of it.[k] [18]The cedar for the House on the inside was carved with gourds and open flowers; everything was of cedar; no stone was seen.

[19]He prepared a shrine in the House in the innermost part to place there the Ark of YHWH's covenant. [20]The interior of the shrine was twenty cubits long and twenty cubits wide and twenty cubits high; he overlaid it with refined gold; he (also) overlaid the cedar altar. [21]Solomon overlaid the House on the inside with refined gold; he drew chains[l] in front of the shrine, and he overlaid it with gold. [22]He overlaid the entire House with gold, until completing the entire House; and the entire altar belonging to the shrine he overlaid with gold. [23]In the shrine, he made two cherubs of pinewood; it was ten cubits high. [24]One wing of the cherub was five cubits, and the other wing of the cherub was five cubits; it was ten cubits from wing tip to wing tip.[m] [25]The other cherub was ten cubits; the two cherubs had the same size and the same shape. [26]The height of one cherub was ten cubits, and so was that of the other cherub. [27]He placed the cherubs in the inner House; and the wings of the cherubs were spread out so that the wing of one touched the wall, and the wing of the second cherub touched the second wall, and their wings that were toward the inside touched each other.[n] [28]He overlaid the cherubs with gold.

[29]He carved round all the walls of the House carved figures of cherubs, palmettes, and open flowers, (both) on the inside and out; [30]and he overlaid the floor of the House with gold, (both) inside and out. [31]As for the entrance to the shrine, he made doors of pinewood; the jamb (and) the doorposts were a fifth (of the wall). [32]As for the two doors of pinewood, he carved on them carved figures of cherubs, palmettes, and open flowers, and he overlaid (them) with gold and hammered out the gold on the cherubs and the palmettes. [33]Similarly, for the entrance to the main hall, he made doorposts of pinewood, a fourth (of the wall), [34]and two doors of juniper wood, with two folding leaves for one door and two folding leaves[o] for the other door. [35]He carved cherubs, palmettes, and open flowers (on them) and overlaid (them) with gold, applied evenly on the engravings.

[36]He built the inner court with three courses of hewn stone and a course of cedar beams.

[37]In the fourth year, in the month of Ziv, the House of YHWH was founded; [38]and in the eleventh year, in the month of Bul, that is the eighth month, the House was completed according to all its details and all its specifications.[p] It took seven years to build it.

---

[k] For MT *lpny*, " before me," read perhaps *lpnyw*, with *waw* lost through haplography.
[l] Ketib *brtyqwt*; qere: *brtwqwt*.
[m] Lit., "from the tips of the wings to the tips of the wings."
[n] Lit., "wing to wing."
[o] Read *ṣlʿym* for MT *qlʿym*; see Note.
[p] Read with qere *mšptyw* for ketib *mšptw*.

NOTES

6   1. *It was in the four hundred and eightieth year after the departure of the Isra-*
elites from the land of Egypt, in the fourth year of the reign of Solomon over
Israel, in the month of Ziv, that is the second month, he built the House for
YHWH. The Luc. and LXX rearrange the chronological notices: 6:1 precedes
5:31, 32; followed by 6:37, 38. But the framing of the building account in 1 Kgs 6
achieved by the positioning in MT is thus lost; besides, the date of completion
in v. 38 is a fitting closure and contrasts well with 7:1 (see Note, ad loc.)

the four hundred and eightieth year after the departure of the Israelites from
the land of Egypt. This is an artificial number based on a calculation of twelve
generations of forty years; LXX reads 440, perhaps counting only eleven generations of priests between Aaron and Zadok (cf. 1 Chr 5:29–34). In any case, no
historical value can be assigned to the date, either for the Exodus or for any
event that preceded Solomon. For the attempts to date the event by means of
the Hiram–Solomon correspondence, see above in Note on 1 Kgs 5:15. (A similar span of four hundred and eighty years has been suggested as separating the
building of the Temple and the founding of the altar by the returnees from
Babylon; but this is nowhere stated and requires some manipulation of the figures; see Introduction, Chronology.) The use of a fixed past date for reckoning
purposes (= era) is not attested before the Hellenistic age in Phoenician inscriptions, which has led to the suggestion that this verse is a late addition; but see
the Neo-Babylonian evidence discussed by Hallo 1988.

in the fourth year of the reign of Solomon over Israel. The date could have
been reported in a royal chronicle (see Note on 1 Kgs 14:25). The indication of
the starting date of the project seems to follow Phoenician rather than Mesopotamian custom, in which the Mesopotamians simply record in general fashion that the building was begun "in a propitious month on a suitable day." The
elements recorded in the present verse — date, object built, dedication — appear
(in various combinations) in Phoenician inscriptions, suggesting to Hurowitz
(1992, 229–31) that a building or votive text, "written by one of the Tyrian or
Byblian workmen involved in the project," was available to Dtr in composing the
date. The synchronism of Solomon's fourth year with the eleventh year of Hiram
recorded by Josephus (*Ant.* 8.62; "twelfth year" in *Ag. Ap.* 1.126) is highly questionable (Katzenstein 1997, 82–83), and so internal biblical calculations must
suffice for fixing an absolute date. Allowing for a short co-regency of Solomon
with his father, David (see Introduction, Chronology), the project may have
been started close to Solomon's assuming full independent rule; this has led
Hurowitz (1992, 226–27) to suggest that the date has been purposefully moved
up in order to credit Solomon with the pious first act of Temple-building.

the month of Ziv. This is one of several month names from the old Phoenician calendar to be found in this unit describing the Temple's construction; cf.
6:37–38; 8:2. The concentration of these names here — and nowhere else in the
Bible — has suggested to some that the building report stems from an old Isra-

elite record of the project influenced by the contacts with the Phoenicians responsible for the construction; see Cassuto 1975, 223–24 nn. 44–45.

month. In the present verse, Heb *hōdeš* is the term for month, unlike v. 38, where (the older?) *yeraḥ*, lit., "moon," is employed (as in the tenth century BCE Gezer Calendar [ANET, 320a]).

that is the second month. A gloss, identifying the Phoenician month name by the signification used in Israelite reckoning, which employed ordinal numbers from one to twelve. This is the month *'Iyyar* (= April/May) in the postbiblical and current Jewish calendar.

he built the House for YHWH. The Temple is most often styled *byt yhwh*, "the House of YHWH" (cf., e.g., 1 Kgs 3:1; 6:37; 7:12, 40, 45, 48, 51; 8:10, 11, 63, 64 et al.); on this basis, *byt yhwh* in Arad inscription no. 18, line 9 (ANET, 569) looks like a reference to the Jerusalem Temple, not to a country shrine. Compare also the inscription on the small ivory pomegranate thought to be a Temple artifact (Avigad 1989; see Note on 7:18). The term "House of YHWH" recalls the common ancient Near Eastern conception that the deity resided within the Temple, which was considered his earthly dwelling; for this view in Egypt, see H. N. Nelson 1944, 44; and in Mesopotamia, see Oppenheim 1944, 59. See also comment to 1 Kgs 8:12–13.

2. *The House that King Solomon built for YHWH was sixty cubits long, twenty ⟨cubits⟩ wide, and thirty cubits high.* These are interior dimensions and do not take into consideration the thickness of either the exterior walls or those that separated the Temple's three rooms. The total of sixty cubits included the main hall and shrine; the porch was measured separately (cf. v. 3). The common cubit (Heb *'ammâ*; for its relation to Akk *ammatu*, see Powell 1992, 6:899–900) was approximately 17.5 inches (Scott 1970, 346–49). Toward the end of the monarchic period, a larger cubit measure was adopted, "a cubit plus one handbreadth," about 20 inches (cf. Ezek 40:5; 43:13); cf. 2 Chr 3:3 for the notation that the dimensions were given according to "the former measure."

3. *The porch.* Others render "portico" (NJPSV, NJB); "vestibule" (NEB, NRSV); but in 7:6–8, some suggest "hall." The MT is inconsistent in regard to spelling; *'wlm* and *'lm* appear in 1 Kgs 6 and 7, 1 and 2 Chr, and Ezek 40–41 passim; *'ylm* in Ezek 40:16–36. Hebrew *'ûlām* is of unknown derivation (cf. Akk *ellamu*, "front" [CAD E, 101], used only adverbially). There were no doors that led to the porch, nor is it stated that it had sidewalls, which leaves open the possibility that it may have been unroofed. The porch was set off by two free-standing columns (cf. 1 Kgs 7:21). In Ezekiel's temple, one reached the porch by ascending stairs (cf. Ezek 40:49), because the entire building was on a raised platform (41:8).

in front of the main hall. Hebrew *hêkal*, a loanword from Sum é.gal, "great house," through Akk *ekallu*, "royal palace, property" (CAD E, 52–61), is used primarily to designate the Temple, though in 1 Kgs 21:1, it refers to a palace.

twenty cubits long along the width of the House, ten cubits deep in front of the House. Since the height of the porch is not given, the porch was most likely open to the sky; the notice in 2 Chr 3:4 that its height was "one hundred and twenty cubits" is absurd.

4. *He made windows for the House, splayed and latticed.* The terms for the window design are obscure, nor are they any clearer in reference to the palace in 1 Kgs 7:4. The versions thought in terms of fortification embrasures, "open inside and closed outside" (Tg.; cf. Vulg., Syr.), but such a precautionary procedure would not have been needed for windows high up toward the ceiling of the main hall (as required by the location of the surrounding enclosure on the outside of the hall; cf. v. 5); additionally, the windows were for providing light to the main hall of the Temple. Hebrew *mašqôp*, "lintel" (cf. Exod 12:7), as well as LH *šqwp/šqwph* and Akk *askuppu/askuppatu*, "doorsill, threshold" (CAD A/2, 333–35), suggest that **šqp* is used with reference to frames. Artistic representations of window frames preserved on ancient ivories indicate the use of indented splaying; see ANEP 131. Latticed windows (lit., "closed," from **ʾṭm*; cf. Prov 17:28; 21:13) are to be found in the gate structure (Ezek 40:16) and Temple hall (41:16, 26) of Ezekiel's vision of rebuilt Jerusalem; see ANEP 334 for similar windows in the fortress of Ashkelon. For the use of the genitive construction (*ḥallônê*) to express an attribute, cf., e.g., Isa 17:10 (GKC, 128p). (The suggestion to see behind the vocable *ḥallônê* the architectural term *bît ḥilāni*, used in Akkadian to describe a Syrian-type structure [so Ouellette 1969], can be dismissed, since the plan of the Temple, unlike the king's palace, was of a different design; see Note on 7:6.)

5. *He built an extension on the walls of the House, that is, the walls of the House around the main hall and the shrine.* Hebrew *yāṣûʿa*, "bed, couch" (cf. Gen 49:4; Ps 63:7; Job 17:13), is derived from **yṣʿ*, "to lay, spread out"; but this is hardly appropriate here (nor is Ouellette's suggestion "bedroom"; cf. Ezek 41:9 [1972, 188–89]). The qere *yāṣîʿa* here and in vv. 6, 10 may be an attempt to distinguish between two related, yet different, terms. An extended surface seems to be spoken of, though the exact architectural referent cannot be fixed. Talmudic tradition, followed by medieval commentators, held *yāṣîʿa* to be synonymous with the terms *ṣelaʿ* and *tāʾ* (b. B. Bat. 61a), probably due to what seems to be an erroneous reading in v. 6, where *yāṣîʿa* appears instead of *ṣelaʿ* (see Note on v. 6 for correction). Noth guessed that this "layer" was used to level off the roof; Mulder took it to be a "vertical" (!) layer "to give the temple both greater sturdiness and greater beauty."

he made side-chambers all around. Hebrew *ṣelaʿ*, "rib" (cf. Gen 2:21), is also the "side of a hill" (2 Sam 16:13); like Heb, the cognate Akk *ṣēlu* can refer to a side structure, the "wing" of a building (CAD Ṣ, 126). Haran (1984, 212) interprets the present verse differently: the Temple's exterior was covered by upright planks (for *ṣelaʿ* as "planks," cf. vv. 15–16) and, together with horizontal boards (*yāṣîʿa*), created a box-like structure, whose purpose was to cover up the building's rough-hewn stone (see, too, Hurowitz 1994, 31–32). However, unlike vv. 15–16, in which the type of wood is specified, in the present verse, this specification is absent and the verb *ʿāśô* suggests that an architectural feature is the object (cf. v. 4). Furthermore, the complicated three-story construction seems superfluous if the goal was simply adornment, for the planks could be applied directly to the walls, as they were inside the House without the additional structure. Noth sought a connection between these "ribs" and the planks in vv. 15–16 and, since nowhere is the material of the extension stated, he suggested that the extension was of wood, rather than stone.

The sanctuary at ʿAin Dara in northern Syria now provides an example of side-chambers constructed on three sides of the main building, putting to rest the objection that this feature was not known in Solomon's Age (see Abu Assaf 1990, 11–20; Monson 1996). The side-chambers were likely used for the storage of equipment, as well as for the stock of supplies needed for the daily operation of the cult; sacred dedications (cf. Note on 7:51) could also have been kept there. Excavated temples from many areas of the ancient Near East show that storage rooms were common in cultic complexes, in many of which, the floor space of the annexes exceeded that of the main sanctuary (Kitchen 1989).

the shrine. See Note on v. 15.

6. *The lowest side-chamber was five cubits wide.* The versions support the correction of *yāṣîʿa* to *ṣelaʿ*, which is the term used in v. 8 for the storage rooms, *yāṣîʿa* being the name of the entire structure; besides, *yāṣîʿa* is masculine, and the adjective here is feminine, as expected for *ṣelaʿ*.

five cubits wide. In addition to the numeration x ʾammâ, "x cubits," the form x bāʾammâ, "x by the cubit (measure)" is frequently attested; cf. 1 Kgs 6:6, 17, 25, 26; 7:23, 24, 27, 38; also, e.g., in Exod 26:2, 8; Ezek 40:5, 21. No difference in meaning can be detected. (DeVries's suggestion to view this alteration "as a stylistic characteristic of the specific underlying documents" requires rewriting too many verses in MT according to LXX to be convincing.)

for he made recesses in the House on the outside all around, so as not to fasten onto the walls of the House. The extension, while seen as integral to the Temple, was not tied into the structure of the main building; its ceiling and roof-beams rested on "recesses" (*mgrʿwt* from **grʿ*, "to diminish, withdraw," only here of construction; NEB: "rebates") and were not set into the walls of the Temple. The stepped, recessed sidewalls gave strength to the structure, allowing it to carry the high walls and cross-beams of the roof.

7. *it was built of undressed stone from the quarry.* Rough-hewn stone, lit., "whole stone," was transported from the quarry site (cf. 1 Kgs 5:31 for **nsʾ* in the sense of "lift up/out, quarry"). But the present description is contradicted in Chronicles, where David prepares "hewn (i.e., dressed) stone" for the Temple (1 Chr 22:2), apparently following 1 Kgs 5:32. Some medieval commentators (and NAB "dressed," NJPSV "finished," NJB "quarry-dressed") adopt the latter interpretation.

no hammers or ax or any iron tool was heard in the House during its building. This note (by Dtr?) emphasizes that only whole stone was used in the Temple; the stones were set in place, with no further preparation beyond what had been done at the time of removal (cf. Josephus, *Ant.* 8.60, 69). This procedure echoes the requirement that Israelite altars were to be built of natural, unworked stone (Exod 20:25); the altar on Mount Ebal was so erected (Josh 8:31;

cf. Deut 27:5). The significance of this act was expounded in *m. Mid.* 3:4: "Iron was created to shorten man's days, and the altar was created to lengthen man's days; it is not proper that what shortens be lifted against what lengthens."

no hammers or ax. Hebrew *maqqebet* is a mallet (used in tenting; cf. Judg 4:21), as well as a craftsman's hammer (Isa 44:12; Jer 10:4). With the ax (Heb *garzen*), trees could be felled (Deut 19:5; 20:19), and tunnels dug (see Siloam inscription, line 4; see translation in Cogan and Tadmor 1988, 337).

8. *The opening of the lowest (side-chamber) was on the right side of the House.* The MT *htyknh*, "middle," is a copyist's error; the versions reflect the required "lower" (*hthtnh*; Tg. "ground") floor entrance to the side-building. There is no way to decide from the description whether the entrance was inside the main hall, allowing easy access to the side-chambers, or was on the outside of the building.

the right side. Facing the Temple, the entrance would have been on the north side; but if a point on the compass is meant, then on the "south side" (Moffatt, NRSV). Hebrew *ketep*, "shoulder," is used, by extension, in topographic descriptions as "slope, side"; cf. Num 34:11; Josh 15:8, 10, 11; and as an architectural term for the flank of a structure from the entrance to the corner; cf., e.g., 1 Kgs 7:39; 2 Kgs 11:11; Ezek 40:18 (see Haak 1983).

spiral stairs went up. Hebrew *lûl* is a hapax legomenon understood by most ancient versions as a "winding stairway." The same root may be related to the noun *lūlā'ôt*, the "loops" on the edges of the cloth sides of the Tabernacle (cf. Exod 26:4). In the Herodian Temple, workmen entered the Holy of Holies from the upper story by being lowered in boxes through a *lwl*, usually taken to be a small "passageway" or "trapdoor" (*m. Mid.* 4:5); on the basis of superior Mishnaic MSS, the word is better read *blwl*, with the *beth* as radical, suggesting that this is the reading in MT as well (so Qimron 1974); in both cases the meaning remains the same: a spiral construction (cf. *šblwl*, "snail" [Ps 58:9]). Targum *mĕsibbātā'* is likely influenced by the *mĕssibâ* of the Herodian Temple by which one ascended to the upper chamber (cf. *m. Mid.* 4:5); on this roofed (stepped?) corridor, see Patrich 1986.

from the middle to the third. The unexpected plural *šlšym* (cf. Gen 6:16) might be better read as *šlyšyt* as in v. 6, unless the third-story rooms are meant (Qara).

9. *So he built the House and completed it.* The completion of work is duly noted, using the same verb **klh* as in Gen 1–2:4a, where it describes divine inspection and approval of the work of creation (see Speiser 1964, ad Gen 2:2). This half-verse is repeated as a *Wiederaufnahme* in v. 14, thus setting off the unit describing the outer shell (vv. 2–8) from the unit describing the building's interior work (vv. 15–35); two interpolations, vv. 9b–10, 11–13, have found their way to this spot.

he roofed the House. For Heb **spn*, cf. 1 Kgs 7:3, 7; Jer 22:14; Hag 1:4.

with coffers in rows of cedar wood. A conjecture, based on Heb *gēb*, "hollow, depression"; cf., e.g., 2 Kgs 3:16; Jer 14:3 (in both instances, where water collects); here it may be a reference to the "coffers" (= hollow squares) formed by the crossing of the cedar roof beams (Montgomery and Gehman; earlier, Geršonides). Mulder's "drain pipes and eavestroughs" are, by his own admission, "only a conjecture." For examples of roofing palaces and temples with *gušūrē erēni ṣirūti* , "immense cedar logs" and "sweet-smelling" wood in Mesopotamian royal inscriptions, see CAD G, 145; Ṣ, 239.

10. *He built the extension along the entire House, (each story) five cubits in height.* The three-storied extension (cf. v. 5) can hardly have been only five cubits high, so this probably is a reference to each of the three stories. Many emend *ḥmš*, "five," to read *ḥmš ʿsrh*, "fifteen," since the entire structure seems to be referred to by use of the singular *yāṣîʿa* (Stade and Schwally; Burney).

he paneled the House with cedar wood. Hebrew *ʾḥz*, "to hold, grasp," used in the sense "to fasten" in v. 6, here means "to mount, panel"; so also does the cognate Akk *aḥāzu* (in D stem), "to mount an object (in precious materials)," e.g., "edged (*uḫḫuzu*) with ivory and boxwood" (CAD A/1, 179–80). Perhaps the Heb verb should also be read in *Piel* (so Šanda, Noth), otherwise attested only in Job 26:9. A collection of references to woodwork and decoration in extrabiblical sources is given by Montgomery and Gehman, ad loc.

12–13. *"As to this House that you are building, if you will follow my statutes and obey my rules and keep my commands, following them, then I will fulfill my promise to you that I made to David your father. I will dwell among the Israelites and I will not forsake my people Israel."* This interpolated divine word draws from both Dtr and P terminology and is lacking in OG; many, therefore, consider it a very late addition. Following Burney, for the Dtr phrases: "keep my commands," cf., e.g., 1 Kgs 2:3; 9:6; 11:34; "fulfill my promise," cf. 1 Kgs 2:4; 12:15; the P phrases, "if you will follow my statutes and obey my rules," cf. Lev 26:3; "I will dwell among the Israelites," cf. Exod 25:8; 29:45; Num 5:3; 35:34 (see the Note on 1 Kgs 8:12 for YHWH's indwelling).

14. *Solomon built the House and he completed it.* See above on v. 9.

15. *He built the walls of the House on the inside with cedar planks.* The noun *ṣelaʿ* (cf. v. 5) seems to carry the extended meaning "ribbing," i.e., "planks, boards." Noth thinks this is a reference to a special construction technique.

from the floor of the House up to the beams of the roof. The double reading in Luc. and LXX "up to the beams (*qwrwt*) and up to the walls (*qyrwt*)" reflects the frequent graphic interchange of *waw* and *yod* in the Herodian script. "Beams" is to be preferred here and in v. 16.

he overlaid (them) with wood on the inside. The perfect verb, set between two *waw*-consecutive forms, suggests that this clause is a gloss.

16. *He built twenty cubits in the rear of the House with cedar planks from the floor up to the beams.* The description is from the point of view of someone standing in the main hall who observed that there was a chamber of wood built up against the back of the hall; in Ezek 41:3, a [stone?] wall of two cubits separated the hall and the shrine. On the cube-like shape of the shrine, see below, v. 20.

he built it on the inside as a shrine, the Holy of Holies. The translation hides the problematic *lô*; perhaps it is accusative, in advance of the following *lidĕbîr* (so Tg.).

a shrine. The term *děbîr* refers to the innermost chamber of the Temple, the adytum; it appears only in the section of Kings and its parallel in 2 Chronicles that describe the Temple construction, and once more in Ps 28:2. There is no resolution concerning the root meaning: LXX transliterates, and older etymologies followed Vulg. "oraculum" as if it derived from **dbr*, "to speak" (so KJV); most others posit **dbr*, "to be behind" (cf. Ar **dbr*) — therefore, "the innermost room"; it is arguable whether *dbr* is a Semitic loanword in Egyptian (so Noth) or an Egyptian term borrowed into Canaanite (Tvedtnes 1982, 217).

the Holy of Holies. Or "the most holy." This phrase, also in 1 Kgs 7:50; 8:6, is borrowed from priestly descriptions of the area curtained off for the Ark in the Tabernacle; cf. Exod 26:33, 34; Num 4:4, 19.

17. *The House was forty cubits (long), that is, the main hall in front of it*. A confused verse. The "house" usually refers to the entire building, which explains the gloss "that is, the main hall" (absent from Luc., LXX). This was the largest room in the Temple, forty by twenty cubits, i.e., approximately 1740 sq. ft., the main place of cultic ceremonies (after the altar in the forecourt).

in front of it. The last word in MT *lpny*, "in front of me," is contextually impossible. Emendation yields: "and forty cubits was the main hall in front of the shrine (*lpny hdbyr*)," supposing an "original" connection between vv. 17 and 20, before being separated by vv. 18–19; see Burney, Skinner, Montgomery and Gehman, and others, and the immediately following Note. A minimalist emendation of *lpny* to *lpnyw* (with *waw* lost through haplography), "in front of it," affords some sense to MT.

18. *The cedar for the House on the inside was carved with gourds and open flowers; everything was of cedar; no stone was seen*. This verse and "he prepared a shrine" in v. 19 are lacking in Luc. and LXX; they interrupt the description of the shrine by relating to the decoration of the main hall, suggesting secondariness. This "afterthought" might have been induced by the mention of the hall in the immediately preceding reference, in v. 17.

carved with gourds and open flowers. The verb **qlʿ*, "to carve," is used only in verses relating to Temple decoration, vv. 29, 32, 35; 7:31. In 2 Chr 3:5, *miqlaʿat* seems to have been replaced by *šaršěrôt*, "chains, garlands" (n.b., the Chronicles verse reflects 1 Kgs 6:29); this substitution is evidence for the MH meaning of **qlʿ* as "to twist, braid." Hebrew *pěqāʿîm* (also 7:24) seems to be a variant of *paqquʿôt*, translated "bitter apples" in 2 Kgs 4:39. Targum translated "eggs," descriptive of the round shape of the design. The motif of flowers was also used to decorate the Temple doors; cf. vv. 32, 35; the motif of the gourds was cast on the bronze Sea; cf. 7:24.

19. *He prepared a shrine in the House in the innermost part to place there the Ark of YHWH's covenant*. The verse picks up v. 16, noting that the shrine served as the repository for the Ark; cf. 8:6.

to place. Hebrew *lttn* is an anomalous form of the infinitive; it looks like a combination of BH *ltt* and MH *l(y)tn*; cf. the form *ttn* in 1 Kgs 17:14, where the qere suggests *tt*.

the Ark of YHWH's covenant. The Ark had been referred to in 1 Kgs 2:26 and 3:15, prior to its placement in the Temple; on its function, see Note on 8:9.

20. *The interior of the shrine was twenty cubits long and twenty cubits wide and twenty cubits high.* For the possible connection of this verse with v. 17, see above; if read together, the harsh opening words *lpny hdbyr* are tenable. The dimensions describe a cube-like shrine, twenty cubits on all sides, ten cubits lower than the height of the main hall. This differential is variously accounted for: (1) the shrine was raised above the floor of the hall, accessible by a short flight of stairs (e.g., de Vaux 1961, 314; Galling 1937, 518); in this regard, note is sometimes taken of the raised podium or pedestal in non-Israelite sanctuaries, upon which the cult object was set; (2) the roof over the shrine was lower by ten cubits, in the manner of Egyptian structures with slanted roofs (Vincent 1956, fig. 112); (3) the presence of unutilized space between the ceiling of the shrine and the roof (Noth; Busink 1970, 209).

he overlaid it with refined gold. This term also appears in v. 21; 7:49, 50; 10:21. The adjective *sāgûr* is cognate with Akk *sakru*, "refined," from *sekēru*, "to heat, treat (gold)" (CAD S, 81b, 213–14); cf. Job 28:15, where *sĕgôr* stands parallel to *kesep* ("silver"). (The profession *msgr* in 2 Kgs 24:14 may be related to this root; amend Note there accordingly.) Its meaning may have been unknown to the Chronicler, who rendered it "good/fine (*ṭwb*) gold" (2 Chr 3:8; so, too, Targum to the present verse).

he (also) overlaid the cedar altar. The MT has the repetitive "and the entire altar belonging to the shrine, he overlaid with gold" in v. 22b, which favors the emendation of v. 19, based upon Luc., LXX, to read: "He made an altar," followed by the last four words of v. 21: "in front of the Debir and overlaid it with gold" (so Burney, Montgomery and Gehman). The gold appointments of the shrine probably attracted this reference to the altar, since it most naturally belongs in the list of cultic appurtenances reported in 1 Kgs 7:48–50. Assuming that Solomon's Temple served as the model for many of the descriptions of the desert cult, the gold-plated altar before the shrine was the altar of incense; cf. Exod 30:1–3; it is also dubbed "the altar of gold" in 1 Kgs 7:48. (The older scholarly theory on the late introduction of incense into the cult has been laid to rest by archaeological finds; see Haran 1978, 229–45.) Ezekiel's association of this altar with the table of showbread (41:22) is confused, as 1 Kgs 7:48 makes clear; there is no substantive reason to identify the two objects, as is sometimes suggested (see Busink 1970, 288–93; on which, see further the Note on 7:48).

21. *Solomon overlaid the House on the inside with refined gold; he drew chains in front of the shrine, and he overlaid it with gold.* The "house" refers to the inner shrine, unlike the use in the rest of the chapter. If the chains were to cordon off the holy area from general access, then they compete for that function with the two pine doors (cf. v. 31); a decorative function seems less likely. In 2 Chr 3:14, a "curtain" is associated with the shrine, as it was in the desert Tabernacle, there hung on four posts (cf. Exod 26:31–33). This has led to the

speculative emendation of 1 Kgs 6:21: "(Solomon) drew a Veil with golden chains across in front of the inner shrine" (NEB; cf. Thenius, Burney).

he drew. A singular instance of **br,* "to pass," in *Piel.*

chains. The rare Heb *rattôq* is derived from **rtq,* "to bind" (Nah 3:10); also Ezek 7:23; cf. Isa 40:19.

22. *He overlaid the entire House with gold, until completing the entire House; and the entire altar belonging to the shrine he overlaid with gold.* This verse supplies no further information on the gold appliqué to the walls of the shrine (cf. vv. 20a, 21a) or to the altar in front of it (cf. v. 20b).

the entire altar belonging to the shrine he overlaid with gold. Though not defined, the altar inside the Temple was for the offering of incense, on the analogy of the altar in the desert tabernacle; cf. Exod 30:1–10; 1 Chr 28:18. See above, in Note on v. 20.

23. *he made two cherubs of pinewood.* The cherubs were fabulous creatures that served in the divine retinue; e.g., YHWH moved about on a cherub (Ps 18:11 [= 2 Sam 22:11]; Ezek 10:18–19) and was depicted as seated on a cherub throne (cf., e.g., 2 Kgs 19:15; Ps 80:2; hence the epithet "who sits [= is enthroned] on the cherubs"); legend told of a cherub assigned to guard the way to Eden (Gen 3:24; cf. Ezek 28:14). Ezekiel's inaugural vision (Ezek 1) offers a singular image of the cherubs, whose ultimate inspiration may have been the colossal images of "winged sphinxes" that stood watch at the portals of Mesopotamian temples and palaces (see Greenberg 1983b, 54–57). Examples of cherub figures incorporated in royal thrones are known from the Phoenician arena already in the late second millennium BCE and could have served as models for the cherubs in Solomon's Temple; see examples in ANEP 644, 646–47, 649; also the ivory decorations in ANEP 128, 332. The relationship between Heb *kĕrûb* and Akk *kurību,* "protective genius" (CAD K, 559), from *karābu,* "to make a gesture of adoration" (CAD K, 197), often cited, is far from transparent; the term appears only in late cuneiform texts and is used of beings functionally different from the biblical cherubs. See also Mulder; Freedman and O'Connor 1983; Mettinger 1995.

pinewood. The identification of *'ēṣ šemen* is still disputed, as the inconsistencies represented in modern translations show: e.g., NEB, "wild olive"; NJPSV, "olive"; but in Isa 41:19, "oleasters"; Neh 8:15, "pine" (noting "Heb. uncertain"). The gathering of assorted branches in Neh 8:15, listing *zayit,* "olive," and *šemen* is sufficient to indicate their distinctness. The *pinus halepensis* (Aleppo pine), from which a resinous pitch and oil can be extracted, fits the requirements both of environment and size (e.g., for carving large figures) of all citations; see Zohary 1982, 114; earlier, Qimḥi, Gersonides, ad loc.).

it was ten cubits high. The massive cherub figures were half as high as the entire inner shrine. The awkward reference to a single cherub (rather than the plural "cherubs" immediately preceding) is blurred in most translations by "each one was"; the syntax is improved by transferring the dislocated v. 26 to this place (see Stade, who is followed by most commentators).

24. *One wing of the cherub was five cubits, and the other wing of the cherub was five cubits; it was ten cubits from wing tip to wing tip.* Taken together with the following verses, the picture is of the four outstretched wings of the two cherubs, their outer wings touching the side-walls of the shrine, their two inner wings touching each other.

25. *the same size and the same shape.* Hebrew *qeṣeb*, "cut, shape," appears again only in 1 Kgs 7:37.

27. *He placed the cherubs in the inner House.* In the present verse and in vv. 29–30, the shrine is called the "inner House"; cf. 1 Kgs 7:50. To make the positioning of the cherubs perfectly clear, the Chronicler adds: "their face was toward the House (= main hall)" (2 Chr 3:13).

the wings of the cherubs were spread out. A rephrasing of the puzzling plural verb in MT, where a singular form is expected; Luc. and LXX read: "they [i.e., the cherubs] spread their wings"; cf. Exod 25:20; 37:9. The positioning of the Ark (cf. 19) beneath the outstretched wings of the cherubs is not related until 8:7; see note there.

29. *He carved round all the walls of the House.* The reference is to the shrine, styled the "inner House" in v. 27; cf. 7:50; cf. Ezek 41:17. Hebrew **ptḥ*, in the sense "to engrave" (cf. 1 Kgs 7:36; Exod 28:36; Zech 3:9), is often compared to Akk *patāḫu*, "to break through, bore" (AHw 846–47), even though the cognate is not used to describe the production of artwork. Little engraved wood has survived from the ancient world (see, e.g., the side of the throne of Thutmose IV, ANEP 393), but its high quality might be judged by the ivory pieces that have been recovered; see Barnett 1982, pl. 48f; 49b, e; 50a, c; 51. Noth thinks that separate engraved strips of wood were fastened to the plank-covered walls. For an example of the composition of motifs, from the painted walls at Khorsabad, see Busink 1970, pl. ix.

round. The noun *mēsab* ("environs" in 2 Kgs 23:5) is here used adverbially; some suggest correcting to the easier reading: *(mi)sābîb* (Stade; Burney).

carved figures of cherubs, palmettes, and open flowers. The walls of the shrine were decorated more elaborately than the side-walls of the main hall (cf. v. 18), with the cherub figures evoking the cherubs within.

palmettes. Hebrew *timōrâ* is probably the technical term for the "palm tree" (*tāmār*) ornamentation, known in Mesopotamia and Syria–Palestine from as early as the third millennium BCE, and used to decorate a variety of cult objects; for this, as well as the suggestion to use *timōrâ* as the term for the specific Israelite column design, see Shiloh 1977.

(both) on the inside and out. Though not specifically noted in v. 19, there seems to have been a separation between the hall and shrine; both sides of this partition (?) were decorated with carved figures.

30. *and he overlaid the floor of the House with gold, (both) inside and out.* The subject is the inner House, the Holy of Holies. The last two words, "inside and out," conflict with v. 15, which tells of the juniper flooring of the main hall. Perhaps this phrase is a vertical dittography of the end of v. 29 (so Hurowitz

1994, 35; cf. Noth), rather than a purposeful late "exaggeration" to make Solomon's undertakings more splendid than they were in reality (Mulder).

31. *As for the entrance to the shrine, he made doors of pinewood, the jamb (and) the doorposts were a fifth (of the wall).* That a doorway led into the shrine means that there was a built separation (a wall of stone? or a partition of wood?), not mentioned above in describing the interior divisions. The doorway was four cubits wide, one-fifth of the twenty-cubit width of the Temple building (so KJV). As Millard (1989a, 137*) points out, the width of the doorways would have been a significant item to specify, since doorways "control access to the interior and its visibility to those outside." Earlier, Thenius envisioned a two-piece lintel, together with the two doorposts and lintel, adding up to a pentagonal doorway. But *ḥămiššît* is mostly taken as a pentagonal door jamb, a strange structural feature indeed. The suggested recessed frame (Noth; cf. NJB: "five indented sections") is based on an unsupported textual emendation, though archaeological examples of such frames have been pointed out (see, e.g., ANEP 131). For the construction with *'et*, cf. Exod 26:1 (S. R. Driver 1892, §195, 1).

jamb. Hebrew *'ayîl* is difficult; it appears again in Ezek 40:9; 41:3, but with no further clarification. It is lacking in some LXX MSS, perhaps because it was taken as identical to the following *mĕzûzâ*, "doorpost." Because of its asyndetic syntax, Montgomery and Gehman considered it a gloss; see also Rashi: "doorpost"; Qimḥi rendered: "lintel"; Gersonides: "threshold"; all of which are guesses. The current translation "pilasters" (NAB, NEB) is difficult to accommodate architecturally. The jamb refers to the support (of different thickness and material) behind the doorpost (so Yeivin [1968, 339]).

32. *As for the two doors of pinewood, he carved on them carved figures of cherubs, palmettes, and open flowers, and he overlaid (them) with gold and hammered out the gold on the cherubs and the palmettes.* For the construction, with a casus pendens and the perfect with consecutive, cf. S. R. Driver 1892, §133, 2. Mesopotamian building-texts from many periods describe the making of doors, their fragrant wood and precious mountings and decorations of gold, silver, bronze, and ivory; see CAD D, 54–55.

hammered out. In order for the cherubs and palmettes to be seen through the overlay, the gold leaf was beaten thin. This shows that the gold was applied to specific areas of the doors (as well as of the inner walls). The verb **rdd* in *Hiphil* appears only here; it is used in the Targum to translate Heb **rq'*, "beat, spread out," in Exod 39:3; Num 17:4.

33. *Similarly, for the entrance to the main hall, he made doorposts of pinewood, a fourth (of the wall).* The set of doors opening into the main hall were larger than those between the hall and the shrine; cf. v. 31.

34. *and two doors of juniper wood, with two folding leaves for one door and two folding leaves for the other door.* The exchange between *qĕlā'îm*, "hangings, curtains," and *ṣĕlā'îm*, "ribs" (here translated "leaves" in both cases; also see above on v. 5), while explainable as the derivation of both *qop* and *ṣade* from an original *d* (see Qimḥi and Montgomery and Gehman), is not expected in the

same verse; it is probably a transcriptional error (caused by the opening word [*qelaʿ*] of v. 35?).

juniper wood. The choice of wood for the doors, pine for the shrine (cf. v. 31) and juniper for the main hall, may reflect the comparative worth of these materials, pinewood considered the more luxurious; note that the cherubs were fashioned from pinewood (cf. v. 23).

folding leaves. If Ezek 41:24 is taken as an explication of the present verse, *gĕlîlîm* describes the turning or revolving of one panel on the other (here translated "folding"). But it could also be a reference to the "hinges" (Tg.) or "swivel-pins" (NEB) of the doors or even the sockets (Wiseman) upon which they revolved.

35. *He carved cherubs, palmettes, and open flowers (on them) and overlaid (them) with gold.* The doors that opened into the main hall were as elaborately decorated as the doors to the shrine, if not more so; cf. vv. 29, 32. Note that over three hundred years later, Hezekiah stripped the Temple doors of their gold in payment of indemnity to his Assyrian overlord (cf. 2 Kgs 18:16).

applied evenly on the engravings. An explanation, for the first time in the chapter, that the gold was inlaid upon the incised figures. The term for "graving" is **hqh* (// **hqq*; see Ezek 23:14), a *Pual* passive participle.

36. *He built the inner court with three courses of hewn stone and a course of cedar beams.* The height of the wall is not indicated, merely the manner of its construction: one course of wood to three of stone. The term *kĕrūtôt*, "beams," is derived from **krt*, "to hew" (cf. 1 Kgs 7:2). Other courts were similarly built (cf. 7:12); note, too, the like construction of the Temple as described in Ezra 6:4. The introduction of wood beams at regular intervals added to the strength of the stone wall, a precaution against collapse due to earthquakes; there is no indication that above the level of beams, the wall was completed by brickwork (so de Vaux 1961, 316; also Thomson 1960; see further the Note on 7:9).

hewn stone. Used also in the foundations of the Temple (cf. 5:31), without the restrictions of sanctity noted in v. 7 above.

the inner court. A wall enclosed the Temple and separated it from the king's palace; an outer wall created the Great Court (cf. 7:9, 12) that encompassed both the sacred and secular buildings. The position of a second court, referred to in 2 Kgs 21:5 and 23:12, cannot be determined (see Notes there); it may have been added to the Temple precinct after Solomon's era (at the expense of the Great Court?); cf. the reference to the "new court" in 2 Chr 20:5. Two gateways opened into the inner court, the Sur Gate (cf. 2 Kgs 11:6) and the Gate of the Outrunners (11:19); the latter led to the king's palace.

37. *In the fourth year, in the month of Ziv.* The common Canaanite term *yerah*, which appears in the Gezer calendar and Phoenician, is used instead of Heb *hōdeš*, as also in v. 1; see Note, ad loc.

38. *in the eleventh year, in the month of Bul, that is the eighth month.* Another Phoenician month name, glossed by the reckoning in the Israelite calendar; cf. above, vv. 1, 37. The name Bul is attested in Phoenician inscriptions; see KAI 14:1; 32:1; 38:2. This is the month (Mar)Heš wān (= September–October).

according to all its details and all its specifications. Targum translates: "to all its orders (plans?) and everything befitting it"; the last phrase recalls a phrase used in Mesopotamian inscriptions relating that the building (of both temples and palace) was carried out "as appropriate" (Hurowitz 1992, 234–35).

It took seven years to build it. Seven years represents an ideal number; the extra six months (cf. vv. 1 and 38) have been rounded off.

COMMENT

Structure and Themes

At the center of the history of Solomon's reign stands the Temple. Following the account of the successful completion of the negotiations between Solomon and Hiram for its construction (1 Kgs 5:15–32), Dtr introduced a report of the building, its layout and prominent architectural features and ornamentation. In comparison with the scant outline regarding the nearby royal buildings in 7:1–12, the detailed description of the Temple attests to the significance it held for the author, not merely as Israel's central sanctuary at which all worship was to be conducted, but as testimony to Solomon's loyalty to YHWH upon whose House he expended great wealth.[1]

The description in 1 Kgs 6 generally follows the path that a visitor to the building might take and notes items observable on such a tour. First to be described is the overall structure, from the entrance porch to the main hall, the annex, the stonework, and the roofing (vv. 2–10); this is complemented by a description of the decor and appointments, especially those of the inner shrine (vv. 15–30). Turning to leave, one would notice the doors leading out to the courtyard (vv. 31–36). Looked at in detail, the Temple was a rectangular structure, approximately 105 feet long, 30 feet wide, and 45 feet high (not including the inside and outside walls and the extension), set on a straight, east–west axis (cf. Ezek 40:6; 43:4). The approach to the Temple was from the east, and after passing through an open porch (*'ûlām*) that was set off right and left by two massive bronze columns (cf. 7:15–22), one entered into the main hall (*hêkal*). Light entered the hall through splayed windows close to the ceiling; the roof was of interlacing cedar beams. Beyond this hall, in which most of the cultic ceremonies were held, was the shrine (*dĕbîr*), the holiest space in the Temple, the abode of the Ark of the Covenant. Two wood-carved cherubs with outstretched wings protected the Ark. A three-storied extension, built on the offsets of the main building, encompassed the Temple on its two sides and back. The rooms of the extension varied in size from floor to floor in the manner of an inverted pyramid, the larger ones on the top story; they were used to store equipment and gifts dedicated to the Temple. The walls of the main hall were paneled in juniper wood, carved in floral and fruit designs, and overlaid with gold; its floor

---

[1] This assumes that the preexilic Dtr could have provided more details concerning the palace complex from personal observation; but he chose to limit himself to a trim, short report.

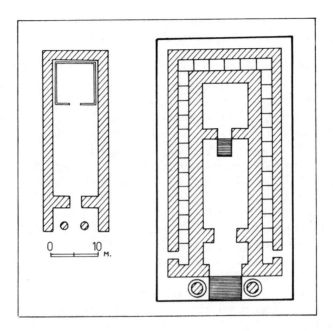

Fig. 1. Two suggested floor plans for the Temple of Solomon (cf. I Kings 6), from A. Mazar, *Archaeology of the Land of the Bible*, 376, fig. 9.4. *Reproduced courtesy of A. Mazar.*

was covered with juniper planks. The shrine was even more elaborately decorated; it was entirely of gold overlay, both its floor and carved walls, competing in splendor with the golden pinewood cherubs. In all, none of the structural stonework was left uncovered. Large decorated wooden doors were hung at the entrance to the main hall and the entrance to the shrine. Outside, the inner courtyard, surrounded by a wall of stone and cedar beams, marked off the Temple precinct from the other buildings on the mount.

When studied in detail, this description presents an interpretive challenge.[2] Many of its unique architectural terms were not understood even in antiquity, as attested by the variety of ancient translations; lack of comprehension may be behind some of the scribal slips of the pen (e.g., *yṣwʿ* written for *ṣlʿ* [v. 6]; *qyrwt* for *qwrwt* [v. 16]). One must also bear in mind that alterations to Solomon's Temple were made during the close to four hundred years of its existence (cf., e.g., 2 Kgs 16:10–18), further obfuscating the original plans for later readers. Thus, in a number of instances, the basic description was glossed in

---

[2] Care should be exercised when utilizing the descriptions of the Temple in Ezek 40–42 and 2 Chr 3:1–14; both are late texts, the first a visionary's dream of restoration (though probably laced with a good measure of realism, stemming from the prophet's familiarity with the Temple prior to his exile to Babylon), and the second a late, interpretive reading of 1 Kings.

successive attempts to clarify terms, or perhaps even to fill out a seemingly defi-
cient text; e.g., vv. 7, 18–19. Gaps are also in evidence; e.g., the overall dimensions in v. 3 overlook the measurements of the thickness of the walls, both of the
shell and of the inner partitions between the Temple's three areas. Not a word
is said about the building's foundations; this is another indication that only
what met the eye was described. Finally, upon incorporation of the description
into Kings by Dtr, editorial interpolations were made—e.g., the dates in vv. 1,
37–38; the oracle in vv. 11–13. Because this text is evidently multilayered, the
suggestion to take the description as the embellished "recollections" of Dtr in
exile (Van Seters 1983, 310) seems inadequate. At the same time, it is hard to
imagine that at the base of the description lies an "oral tradition of instructions
to the various craftsmen" (so Gray, following Noth); one could hardly raise the
rafters of the Temple, let alone its walls, using just 1 Kgs 6. The opinion that
"this report stemmed from archival sources kept by priests (and/or scribes?) in
the Jerusalemite royal establishment" (Long 1984, 88; see also Wiseman) is
also hard to endorse; there is nothing particularly "archival" or "priestly" about
1 Kgs 6 (see Van Seters 1997; otherwise Zwickel 1999, 57).

Recent study of the building accounts in cuneiform royal inscriptions
(Hurowitz 1992) has opened new avenues to understanding the constituent
elements and composition of 1 Kgs 5–8. These inscriptions include the report
of a divine call or sanction to construct (or reconstruct) a temple, the prepara-
tions by the monarch for the undertaking, a general description of the building,[3] the dedication, rounded off with blessings for the builder and his progeny.
It may be assumed that the interests of Judah's kings were not much different
from those of their Mesopotamian counterparts: the desire to broadcast now
and for posterity their devotion to the gods as demonstrated in the construction
and repair of sanctuaries. Though the chapters describing the Temple's construction cannot be classified as a royal inscription, many of their basic components may reach back to monarchic circles. The involvement of Davidic kings
in the affairs of the Temple was a subject that engaged royal scribes (cf., e.g.,
2 Kgs 12:7–17; 16:10–16). The factual description of the building in 1 Kgs 6
may have been written for an administrative survey or study purposes. In analogous fashion, a number of Mesopotamian texts of undefined genre record
building plans in detail, a few written on the reverse side of drawings of structures (Hurowitz 1992, 250–56). At the same time, it does not seem likely that
1 Kgs 6 was ever incorporated into the *Book of the Deeds of Solomon* (1 Kgs
11:41), as suggested by Liver 1967, 87–88 (so, too, DeVries); the wisdom themes
of this near-contemporary courtly composition are totally lacking in these technical chapters (see further, Note on 7:14), and architectural plans would have
been extraneous to that work.

The Deuteronomist was not interested in the particulars of the priestly ritual
that was performed in the Temple, nor was the religious symbolism of the build-

---

[3] Sennacherib's descriptions of his extensive projects at Nineveh do record a number of specific, detailed measurements, e.g., of the land reclaimed; see Luckenbill 1924, 103–16.

ing of concern (though it is a topic of interest in modern research; see Meyers 1992b, 359–60). In the few places where the editorial hand is felt, the interpolations serve to integrate the architectural description into the overall reading of Solomon's reign: vv. 1, 37–38 provide the chronology of construction; vv. 11–13 present a divine oracle. Calendric notations outside the regnal formulas are uncommon in Kings (cf. 1 Kgs 14:25; 2 Kgs 12:7; 18:13; 22:3); it is not surprising to find them with reference to the central sanctuary of the realm. The placement of the oracle (vv. 11–13), after the completion of the outer shell of the Temple building and before detailing the building's interior (for the editorial *Wiederaufnahme* in vv. 9 and 14, see Note on v. 9), was seen as the appropriate moment for YHWH to inform Solomon of the conditions under which the indwelling of the deity in Israel would be assured; these conditions are reiterated in 9:1–9, an oracular reply to Solomon's prayer at the Temple's dedication. Note that both divine words use the verbs "follow, walk" (*hālak*), "obey, do" (*ʿāśâ*), and "keep" (*šāmar*; cf. 6:12 and 9:4). The two oracles frame large blocks of material detailing the Temple interior and its furnishings (1 Kgs 6:15–35; 7:15–50) and the dedication ceremonies (1 Kgs 8). Noting the absence of this passage from all Greek texts and on the basis of the use of several typically Priestly terms, Burney argued for a Priestly redactor as the interpolator; at the same time, Deuteronomistic phraseology is not lacking, especially the reference to the promise to David (v. 12), suggesting that the statement may be from a late writer familiar with both Deuteronomistic and Priestly styles (see Skinner).

History

The Temple of YHWH occupied the highest elevation within the royal complex erected by Solomon on the mountain to the north of the City of David (cf. 2 Kgs 11:19; 12:11; 23:4). Considering the urban landscape of the City of David, this choice was well conceived. The small, compact city of about fifty dunams (approx. 12 acres) was ill suited to house a temple and a palace (most likely contemplated as a single complex, though the building of the latter was delayed in deference to the former [according to 1 Kgs 7:1]). The Temple Mount (including the Ophel) tripled the dimension of the capital city. Moreover, the location of the Temple on the height above the city accorded the House of YHWH the prominence and the sense of awe and inspiration worthy of the dwelling of the national deity. Though the site is not specified in 1 Kgs 6, its location on the Temple Mount (the present day *Ḥaram eš-Šarif*) is universally acknowledged.[4] Jewish tradition associates this site with Mount Moriah, an identification first recorded in 2 Chr 3:1. Two prominent Israelite traditions, the near-sacrifice of Isaac (Gen 22:1–14) and the saving of Jerusalem from a

---

[4] Lacking archaeological remains and textual evidence, there is no way to fix the exact spot on the Temple Mount where the building stood; see Busink 1970, 1–20 for a review and rejection of the oft-made suggestion that the inner shrine was set atop the sacred rock *es-sakhra*.

divine plague during the reign of David (2 Sam 24:10–16), are here joined in endowing the Temple Mount with ancient chosenness: it was here that YHWH had exhibited his quality of mercy to two of Israel's most prominent ancestors. The Chronistic identification is not necessarily a late view, a response to the sectarian tensions of the Persian period; it had likely developed in preexilic Judah in the attempt to grant Jerusalem and its Temple legitimacy in its struggle for recognition (see Cogan 1986).[5]

The Temple erected by Solomon is lost for all time, except for its description in 1 Kgs 6.[6] Most modern attempts at reconstruction have given considerable attention to comparative study of the archaeological finds from Israel and neighboring lands; see the surveys of Stinespring 1962, 542–47; Busink 1970, 44–58 (to which add: Yeivin 1968; Ouellette 1976). The tripartite building had its roots in the architectural traditions of Phoenicia, more specifically, north Syria, as would be expected of a project executed with major support from Hiram of Tyre (Ussishkin 1966a; Davey 1980, 142–43; for a dissenting view of the Temple as an Israelite creation, see Ahlström 1982, 34–36; 1993a, 531; earlier, Busink 1970, 617). The ninth-century sanctuary excavated at Tell Tainat (or: Taʿjinat) on the lower Orontes and the somewhat later one at nearby ʿAin Dara on the River Afin, offer evidence of floor plans laid out in a manner resembling Solomon's Temple (see ANEP 739); the building at ʿAin Dara has a wraparound structure similar to the extension of the Jerusalem Temple, until now unexemplified. But, considering the dates of these foreign structures and the indeterminable date of the base text of 1 Kgs 6 and its subsequent glosses (see above), the extent of Solomon's part in the enterprise remains unknown.

The same judgment holds with regard to the description of the lavish use of gold on the walls of the Temple and the floor of the shrine ascribed to Solomon: that such "enhancement . . . is entirely compatible with ancient practice" (Millard 1997, 36) does not affirm the contemporaneity of the description with Solomon.

---

[5] To state that the location was "familiar" to the audience addressed by Kings and so could be skipped over (so Kalimi 1990, 362) misses the point of the Moriah identification.

[6] Rupprecht's highly speculative thesis (1977) that Solomon rebuilt and extended an existing Jebusite sanctuary that had been taken over by his father, David, discounts the unanimous view of all biblical texts concerning the originality of Solomon's undertaking.

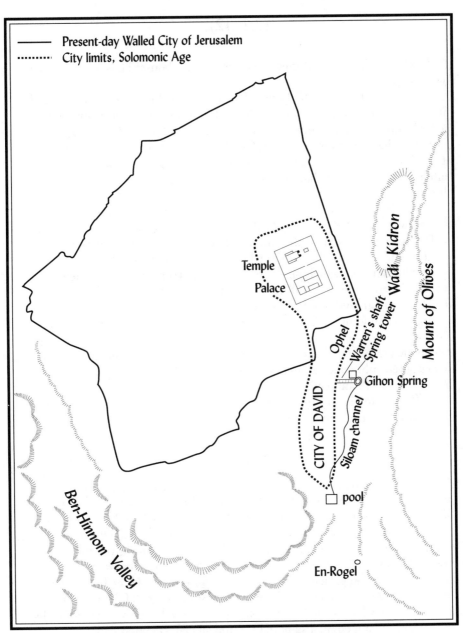

JERUSALEM IN THE 10TH CENTURY B.C.E.

IX. THE PALACE COMPLEX

(7:1–12)

7 ¹And it took Solomon thirteen years to build his house. Thus he completed his entire house.

²He built the House of the Forest of Lebanon, one hundred cubits long and fifty cubits wide and thirty cubits high, with four rows of cedar columns, and cedar beams on the columns; ³and it was roofed with cedar from above, over the planks that were on the columns, forty-five (in number), fifteen to a row; ⁴and splayed (windows), (in) three rows, facing each other, three times; ⁵and all the entrances and doorposts had squared frames, and opposite, facing each other, three times.

⁶He made the porch of columns, fifty cubits long and thirty cubits wide, and a porch was in front of them, and columns with a canopy was in front of them.

⁷He made the porch of the throne where he was to give judgment—the porch of judgment, and it was roofed with cedar from floor to beams.[a]

⁸And his house in which he was to reside, the other court within the porch, was of like construction; and he made a house like this porch for Pharaoh's daughter, whom Solomon had married.

⁹All these buildings were of quality stone, hewn to measure, smoothed with a smoothing tool, inside and out, from the foundation to the coping, from outside to the great court; ¹⁰and it was founded (upon) quality stone, large stones, stones of ten cubits and stones of eight cubits, ¹¹and above were quality stones, hewn to measure and cedar wood. ¹²And the great court, round about, three rows of hewn stone and a row of cedar beams; and (likewise) the inner court of the House of YHWH and the porch of the house.

NOTES

7 1. *And it took Solomon thirteen years to build his house. Thus he completed his entire house.* In 1 Kgs 9:10, the "thirteen years" are added to the "seven years" of 6:38 and summed up as "twenty years"; by this calculation, Dtr determined that Solomon did not turn to his private needs until completing the Temple.

2. *He built the House of the Forest of Lebanon.* The name given to this hall was likely prompted by the large number of cedar columns and roof beams. Its function within the palace complex can only be guessed. Three hundred gold bucklers as well as the king's gold service were stored there (cf. 10:17, 21; cf. Isa 22:8); but it may have served as more than just the royal armory and treasury. Its size suggests that it could also have been the official reception hall.

---

[a] Read *hqwrwt* for MT *hqrqʿ*; see Note.

one hundred cubits long and fifty cubits wide and thirty cubits high, with four rows of cedar columns, and cedar beams on the columns. It was the largest of the buildings on the mountain, even greater than the Temple; cf. 6:2–3. The use of column construction allowed for the wide span of fifty cubits.

3. *and it was roofed with cedar from above, over the planks that were on the columns, forty-five (in number), fifteen to a row.* The term *ṣĕlāʿôt* presents an interpretational difficulty, having been used in a number of senses with reference to the Temple. In 6:5, 8, they were "side-chambers," while in 6:15, "planks," the latter adopted in the present verse. A number of commentators (Benzinger, DeVries, Würthwein) prefer "rooms, chambers" and reconstruct a two- or three-storied Forest House. But this seems unlikely, since the verse speaks of the roofing; in addition, no stairs to the upper floors are reported (as in 6:8) for what would have been a very large number (45!) of rooms.

4. *and splayed (windows), (in) three rows.* The term *šāqūp* is used with reference to the windows of the main hall of the Temple; see the Note on 1 Kgs 6:4.

facing each other. Or, "window toward window." This seems to describe the positioning of the windows, set in opposite walls, parallel to one another.

5. *and all the entrances and doorposts had squared frames.* Similar phraseology was employed to describe the doorways in the Temple (cf. 6:31, 33). except that there, the size and positioning of the doorways vis-à-vis the two side-walls was described. On the term *šeqep*, cf. Note on 6:4.

and opposite, facing each other, three times. Unfathomable; perhaps a dittography from the preceding v. 4b. The LXX reads: "from entrance to entrance, three times"; see, at length, Montgomery and Gehman; also Noth.

6. *He made the porch of columns, fifty cubits long and thirty cubits wide, and a porch was in front of them.* A new structure is described. The relation between the two porches is unclear, especially in view of the third vestibule described forthwith in v. 7. This difficulty is eased by omitting v. 6bα as a garbled repetition of parts of v. 6a (Šanda, Noth); NAB saves the half-verse: "the porch extended the width of the columned hall," taking "in front of them" as referring to the columns.

and columns with a canopy was in front of them. Hebrew *ʿāb* appears again in Ezek 41:25, where it is made of wood; in both instances, its meaning is unclear. Etymologically, it should mean something like "thick"; cf. 1 Kgs 12:10; Deut 32:15; and below, the Note on v. 46; thus "beam" (Qimḥi); most modern scholars picture an overhanging roof; NEB: "cornice." Galling guesses (1955, ad Ezek 41:25) that this was a "railing" separating the hall from the rest (followed by Noth, Würthwein).

7. *He made the porch of the throne where he was to give judgment—the porch of judgment.* The dimensions of this hall are not given; the golden throne upon which the king sat when he held court is described in 10:18–20. Syntactically, "the porch of judgment" is intrusive. Is it a gloss?

and it was roofed with cedar from floor to beams. The MT, "from floor to floor," is hard to sustain and should be corrected with Vulg. and Syr.; see Note to 6:15;

Montgomery and Gehman's "= from bottom to top" is hard to derive from the text without emendation. A subordinate clause, as in v. 7b, is rarely introduced by *waw*; cf. S. R. Driver 1892, §161, 2. On the basis of this verse, the term *sāpūn* (cf. 6:9) may have the extended meaning "paneled."

8. *the other court within the porch*. For other instances of a noun followed by an adjective defined by the article, cf. v. 12; 2 Kgs 20:4 (qere); see S. R. Driver 1892, §209. Though the floor plan of the palace is not restorable, comparison with *ḥilāni*-buildings suggests that this court was actually in the back, behind the others; see further in Comment. For other examples of *mibbêt* indicating direction, cf. 2 Kgs 11:15; Exod 26:33; Lev 16:2.

was of like construction. The shortened description has left the referent unclear.

and he made a house like this porch for Pharaoh's daughter, whom Solomon had married. This is the second of five references to this marriage in 1 Kings; cf. 3:1; 9:16, 24; 11:1; in the present context, it interrupts the account of the building's layout. That special quarters were built for Pharaoh's daughter points to her privileged position among the king's other wives.

9. *All these buildings were of quality stone, hewn to measure*. These terms appear in 5:31; see Note, ad loc. The standard measure of hewn stone in use is not given; in later times, hewn stone for walls between properties was set at "five handbreadths" (*m. B. Bat*. 1:1).

smoothed with a smoothing tool. The tool *mĕgērâ*, otherwise unknown except for its use by captives from Ammon (2 Sam 12:31), was dragged or pulled (< *grr*) across the face of the stone block to give it a smooth, polished look (following Barkai 1997). There is no archaeological evidence that "saws" (the common translation) were used in stonework. Examples of smooth-dressed ashlar masonry have been uncovered at a number of sites dating to the ninth century; see A. Mazar 1990, 472.

from the foundation to the coping. Hebrew *ṭōpaḥ/ṭepaḥ*, "handbreadth" (cf. 1 Kgs 7:26; Exod 25:25; Ezek 40:5), is difficult to accommodate in the present context, the upper part of a wall. The suggested Akk cognate (de Vaux 1961, 316; followed by Noth) is unrelated; see AHw 1321, s.v. *tappātu*, "companion" (A4). If, in the end, the term is derived from "handbreadth," then perhaps it refers to the width of the overhanging margin or trim at the ceiling (so Barkai 1997).

from outside to the great court. This phrase is often corrected (see Montgomery and Gehman for several emendations); it looks ahead to v. 12, which treats the outside courts, and perhaps v. 12 was its original location.

12. *And the great court, round about, three rows of hewn stone and a row of cedar beams*. The court surrounding the entire complex was constructed in the same manner as the inner court; cf. 6:36.

and (likewise) the inner court of the House of YHWH and the porch of the house. The first half of this clause refers back to 6:36; the second half does not specify the house, the House of YHWH or the king's palace, but if the former, it is redundant. The whole is lacking in Luc. and LXX, which seem to have another version of the clause attached to 6:36; see Burney for discussion and a corrected retroversion into Hebrew.

COMMENT

Structure and Themes

This unit and the next are textually no better preserved than 1 Kgs 6, with which they are related; problems of understanding unique technical terminology as well as glosses that both clarify and update the descriptions seem to have confounded later copyists and led to many corruptions. Comparison of several sections of 1 Kgs 7 that are duplicated in other biblical books shows that MT in 1 Kgs 7 represents a very poor manuscript (see the hyperbole of Stade and Schwally ["the worst preserved of OT texts"]; Montgomery and Gehman).

The indications "seven years" and "thirteen years" for the length of time of the Temple and palace constructions respectively (6:38; 7:1) need not be read as a criticism of Solomon (as proposed by Walsh, Provan). In Dtr's view, Solomon did "have his priorities straight"; first he built the Temple; only then did he attend to his own interests. This is shown by the total "twenty years" given for the two projects (cf. 9:10), proof that they were construed as having been consecutive enterprises that occupied Solomon during half of his reign, despite the fact that they were probably executed simultaneously (Noth). This reading may have spurred the rearrangement in Luc. and LXX^B, in which vv. 1–12 appear after v. 51; cf. Josephus (*Ant.* 8.130–40) who placed the description of the palace after the Temple dedication (in MT 1 Kgs 9:10). Otherwise, see Trebolle Barrera (1982, 24–28), who considers LXX preferable: MT has inserted 7:1–11, along with 6:37–38, by means of *Wideraufnahme* (cf. 6:36 // 7:12).

The descriptions of the porches and halls of the palace complex are considerably less detailed than the descriptions given for the Temple. Except for the House of the Forest of Lebanon (vv. 2–5), which was apparently a most impressive building, the others are dismissed with a single verse—the king's private quarters with even less, a simple "ditto" (cf. v. 8)—leaving the reader uncertain as to their configuration. For Dtr, it was not important to expand on these secular buildings, and so he returned in vv. 13–51 to matters of the Temple.

History

As remarked previously with reference to the Temple, the lack of archaeological remains and, in this instance, the scant verbal description make reconstruction of the palace complex highly speculative. Despite this, the Syrian *bit ḫilāni* seems to be the most reasonable model for Solomon's palace. A typical *ḫilāni* building included a pillared porch that led into a number of halls and open inner courts surrounded by smaller rooms (see Hrouda 1972–1975). The ground plans of several tenth–ninth century BCE buildings at Megiddo resemble the

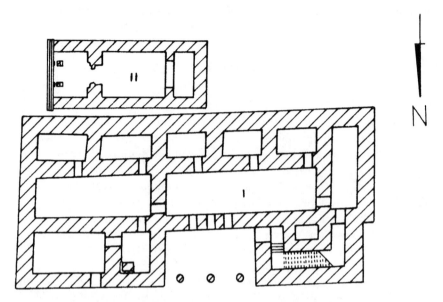

N

Fig. 2. The plan of the *bit ḥilāni*–type palace (I) and attached temple (II) at Tell Tainat (northern Syria, eighth century BCE), from A. Mazar, *Archaeology of the Land of the Bible*, 377, fig. 9.5 C. *Reproduced courtesy of A. Mazar.*

ḥilāni-palaces excavated at Zincirli, strengthening the suggestion that this was also the plan of the Jerusalem palace (Ussishkin 1966b).[1] If so, the number of separate buildings described in 1 Kgs 7 is two, the House of the Forest of Lebanon and the Palace. They were located on the Temple Mount, south of the Temple, separated from it by the wall of the Inner Court, with all three enclosed by the wall of the Great Court.[2] See Map 2.

---

[1] It has been argued from the recent discovery of a *bit ḥilāni* dated to the mid–tenth century BCE (Iron II) at Bethsaida, just north of the Sea of Galilee, that the Aramean kingdoms, Israel's neighbors to the east and north, were the mediators of this type of palace architecture; see Arav and Bernett 2000.

[2] Some ruins of the palace were apparently visible a century and a half after its destruction, when Nehemiah undertook the reconstruction of Jerusalem's walls; cf. Neh 3:25; after this, reference to the structure ends.

X. The Furnishings of the Temple

(7:13–51)

7 [13]King Solomon sent to bring Hiram from Tyre; [14]he was the son of a widow of the tribe of Naphtali, and his father was a Tyrian, a coppersmith. He was endowed with wisdom, understanding, and knowledge to perform all work in bronze. He came to King Solomon and did all his work.
[15]He fashioned the two columns of bronze; eighteen cubits, the height of one column; a cord of twelve cubits could encompass the one column ᵃ<and its thickness was four fingers, (it was) hollow; and so was>ᵃ the second column. [16]He made two capitals to put on top of the columns, cast in bronze; five cubits, the height of one capital; five cubits, the height of the second capital; [17]lattices, latticework, festoons, chainwork for the capitals on top of the columns—seven for the one capital and seven for the second capital. [18]He made the pomegranates,ᵇ two rows around the one lattice to cover the capitals that were on top of the columns;ᶜ and so he made for the second capital. [19]And (the) capitals that were on top of the columns, lilywork, in the main hall, four cubits, [20]and (the) capitals on the two columns, even above, close by the belly that was opposite the latticeᵈ and the pomegranates, two hundred in rows around the second capital. [21]He set up the columns for the porch of the main hall. He set up the right-hand column and named it Jachin, and he set up the left-hand column and named it Boaz; [22]and on top of the columns, lilywork. The work of the columns was finished.
[23]He made the Sea, cast (of metal), ten cubits from rim to rim, circular, five cubits high and thirty cubits its lineᵉ all around; [24]and gourds under its rim encircling it all around for ten cubits, encompassing the Sea round about, two rows of gourds, cast during its casting; [25]standing on twelve oxen, three facing north and three facing west and three facing south and three facing east, with the Sea on them from above and their hind quarters (turned) inward; [26]its thickness (was) a hand's breadth, and its rim was like the rim of a cup, (like) a lily flower; it could hold two thousand *baths*.
[27]He (Hiram) made the stands, ten (of) bronze; the length of one stand four cubits, its width four cubits, and its height three cubits. [28]This was the construction of the stand(s). They had frames and frames between the crosspieces; [29]and on the frames between the crosspieces, lions, oxen, and cherubs, and so on the

---

ᵃ⁻ᵃ Restored with Jer 52:21; Luc.; LXX: *h'ḥd w'byw 'rb' 'ṣb'wt nbwb wkn h'm(w)d*; lost in MT through haplography.
ᵇ So with 2 MSS; MT reads "columns"; see Note.
ᶜ So with many MSS; MT reads "pomegranates"; see Note.
ᵈ Read with qere *hśbkh* for ketib *śbkh*.
ᵉ Read with qere *wqw* for ketib *wqwh*; so also Jer 31:38; Zech 1:16.

frames. Above[f] and below the lions and the oxen, spirals of hammered work. [30]Each stand had four bronze wheels and bronze axles, and its four legs had shoulder pieces under the laver; the shoulder pieces were cast with spirals at each end. [31]Its mouth[g] within the crown and above (it) for one cubit; its mouth was round like the construction of a pedestal, one and one-half cubits, and there were carvings even on its mouth. Now their frames were square, not round. [32]There were four wheels under the frames, and the axletrees of the wheels were in the stand; the height of each wheel was one and one-half cubits. [33]The construction of the wheels was like the construction of a chariot wheel: their axletrees and their rims and their spokes and their hubs were all cast. [34]There were four shoulder pieces at the four corners of each stand; its shoulder pieces were part of the stand. [35]At the top of the stand, a half-cubit high, (the mouth) was circular; at the top of the stand, its supports and its frames were part of it. [36]He engraved on the panels « »[h] cherubs, lions, and palms, with spirals at each end[i] round about. [37]In this manner, he made the ten stands, a single casting, one measure and[j] one form for all of them.

[38]He made ten bronze lavers; each laver contained forty *baths*, each laver being four cubits; there was one laver on each stand for the ten stands. [39]He placed five stands on the right side of the House and five on the left side of the House, and he placed the Sea at the right side of the House toward the southeast.

[40]Hiram[k] made the pots[l] and the shovels and the sprinkling bowls.

Thus, Hiram brought to a close all the work that he did for King Solomon (on) the House of YHWH:

[41]Columns—two;
  the bowls of the capitals that were on top of the columns—two;
  the latticework—two—to cover the two bowls of the capital that were on top of the columns;
[42]the pomegranates—four hundred—for the two latticeworks, two rows of pomegranates for each latticework to cover the two bowls that were over the columns;[m]
[43]the stands—ten;
  the lavers—ten—(those) on the stands;

[44]the Sea—one;
  the cattle—twelve—beneath the Sea;

---

[f] MT reads "from above" with preceding clause; Luc., LXX join to the following "and above" (*wmm'l*); see Note.

[g] Read *pyh*, lit., "her mouth," for MT *pyhw*, "his mouth," as immediately following.

[h] MT adds: "its supports and on its frames" (*ydtyh w'l wmsgrtyh* [qere: *msgrtyh*]); see Note.

[i] Read *m'br 'yš* for *km'r 'yš*; cf. v. 30. 4QKgs: *mm'r*.

[j] Read *wqṣb* with 4QKgs; Vulg.; Syr.; and some Heb MSS; MT: *qṣb*.

[k] Many MSS read *ḥyrm* for MT *ḥyrwm*, "Hirom"; see Note on v. 13.

[l] Read *hsyrwt* with 4QKgs, Luc., LXX, and many Heb MSS for MT *hkyrwt*, "the lavers"; cf. v. 45.

[m] Perhaps read with Luc., LXX: *šny* for MT *pny*.

[45] the pots, the shovels, and the sprinkling bowls—

all these[n] vessels that Hiram made for King Solomon for the House of YHWH were of burnished bronze. [46] In the plain of the Jordan, the king cast them in the thick earth, between Succoth and Zarethan. [47] Solomon left all the vessels out of account because of their very great number; the weight of the bronze was not ascertained.

[48] Solomon made all the vessels of the House of YHWH:

the altar, of gold;

the table upon which was the showbread, of gold;

[49] the lampstands, five on the right and five on the left, in front of the shrine, of refined gold;

the flowers, the lamps, and the tongs, of gold;

[50] the basins, the snuffers, the bowls, the ladles, and the firepans, of refined gold;

and the hinges of the doors to the inner house, the Holy of Holies, (and) the doors of the house, of the main hall, of gold.

[51] Thus, all the work that King Solomon did for the House of YHWH was finished. Solomon brought the votive objects of his father, David, the silver, the gold, and the vessels (and) deposited (them) in the treasury of the House of YHWH.

---

[n] Read with qere *h'lh* for ketib *h'hl*.

NOTES

7 13. *King Solomon sent to bring Hiram from Tyre.* For the verb pair **šlḥ* + **lqḥ*, cf. 2 Kgs 6:13. Hebrew **lqḥ*, "to take," also has the sense "to acquire, to buy"; cf. Prov 31:16; Neh 5:2 (as does its Akk cognate *leqû* [see CAD L, 139–40]); hence, perhaps the translation should be: "sent to hire Hiram of Tyre." In the Chronicler's retelling, Solomon had procured the services of Hiram during the negotiations with King Hiram; cf. 2 Chr 2:6, 12–13.

Hiram of Tyre. The craftsman's name, Hiram, is the same as the name of the king of Tyre (for its meaning, see Note on 5:15); it appears as Huram-abi in 2 Chr 2:12 (cf. 4:16; once as Hiram, 4:11); for various suggestions regarding the meaning of the problematic addition *-abi*, lit., "my father," see Japhet 1993, 544. (Note the rendering of NEB: "master Huram," taking *'āb* as a title.)

14. *the son of a widow of the tribe of Naphtali.* In 2 Chr 2:13, she is a Danite woman. The change of tribal affiliation seems to be connected with the Chronicler's association of Hiram with the desert artisan Bezalel, who was assisted by Oholiab of the tribe of Dan (cf. Exod 35:34); see Williamson 1982, 201.

and his father was a Tyrian, a coppersmith. The mixed marriage went unremarked, but the father's patently foreign pedigree was explained away by the medieval commentators through the suggestion that he was an Israelite from Naphtali, married to a Danite woman, who resided in Tyre. Those who take the reference to Hiram's Israelite mother as a late remark born of the anti-Phoenician attitude of the postexilic age (e.g., Würthwein) confirm by this approach the historical veracity of Solomon's Tyrian connection. Montgomery and Gehman note instances of hiring of foreign craftsmen for work in distant courts.

He was endowed with wisdom, understanding, and knowledge to perform all work in bronze. This standard triad, "wisdom, understanding, and knowledge," is applied to Bezalel, the fashioner of the Tabernacle in the desert (Exod 31:3); to God, as creator of heaven and earth (Prov 3:19–20); and to the future Davidic king (cf. Isa 11:2, somewhat expanded). A further sense of Heb *ḥokmâ*, in addition to meanings exhibited in 3:12 and 5:9, 26, is its use with reference to skilled persons, e.g., seafarers (Ps 107:27), weavers (Exod 28:3), and even warrior-kings (Isa 10:13). Translations range from "a man of great skill and ingenuity" (NEB; cf. NJPSV) to "artistry, intelligence, skill" (Montgomery and Gehman).

bronze. Hebrew *nĕḥōšet* is "copper" ore (Deut 8:9; Job 28:2) but mostly refers to the "bronze" alloy that had come into widespread use in the ancient Near East and Palestine by the second millennium BCE (see Muhly 1973, 256–60).

15. *He fashioned the two columns of bronze; eighteen cubits, the height of one column; a cord of twelve cubits could encompass the one column ⟨and its thickness was four fingers, (it was) hollow; and so was⟩ the second column.* The parallel text in Jer 52:21 and Luc. and LXX help restore MT here (see above, Note[a–a]), which has lost a long passage due to haplography (skipping from *hʿmd* to *hʿmd*). (This obviates the need to view the description in Jeremiah as referring to a later replacement of the original columns, either pillaged or renovated; so Yeivin 1959.)

He fashioned. Most critics (Noth is the exception) correct MT *wayyāṣar* to read *wayyiṣṣōq*, "he cast," following Luc. and LXX. Hebrew **yṣq* is used throughout in reference to the metalwork of the Tabernacle; cf., e.g., Exod 25:12; 26:37; 36:36; 37:3, 13; 38:5, 27; and in the ensuing description of Temple utensils; cf. 1 Kgs 7:24, 30, 46. But the minting of bullion in 2 Kgs 12:11 (*wyṣrw*) speaks against the emendation; see Note, ad loc.

(it was) hollow. The hollowness decreased the weight of the column considerably. For Heb *nābôb*, "hollow," cf. Exod 27:8; 38:7 (referring to the acacia wood altar), and Job 11:12 (of a hollow, empty person).

a cord of twelve cubits could encompass the one column. Biblical Hebrew lacked a term for circumference. (There is no textual warrant for correcting "twelve" to "two," as did Albright 1969b, 143.)

16. *He made two capitals to put on top of the columns.* The term *kōteret* <*ktr*, "to surround," appears only with reference to these columns; was it coined to suggest their majestic "crown"-like cap (for *keter*, cf. Esth 1:11; 2:17; 6:8)?

17. *lattices, latticework, festoons, chainwork for the capitals on top of the columns.* The terms "lattice" (cf. 2 Kgs 1:2) and "festoons" are glossed by the phrases following them (Ehrlich).

festoons. The term *gĕdilîm* appears again as the "twisted" fringes of garments (Deut 22:12); the cognate Akk *gidlu* (CAD G, 66) is attested only in late texts and may be a loanword from Aram *gĕdiltā'*.

seven for the one capital and seven for the second capital. The LXX reads *sĕbākâ*, "lattice," for MT *šibʿā*, "seven," adopted by many commentators, NEB, NAB; this brings v. 17 into line with the description in v. 42. But this may be an unnecessary correction, because the latter verse is part of a list that could easily have had different notations (see Noth, ad v. 42).

18. *He made the pomegranates, two rows around the one lattice to cover the capitals that were on top of the columns.* The verse is perplexing as it stands in MT, but the perplexity is relieved somewhat by assuming that the term ʿammûdîm ("columns") has been exchanged for *rimmōnîm* ("pomegranates"); v. 41b confirms this in the note that the proper place of the capitals (not pomegranates) was on top of the columns. After "two rows," LXX adds "bronze pomegranates"; cf. v. 42; the clause "to cover the capitals that were on top of the columns" is missing in LXX and is found in v. 17 (adopted by many commentators as its original location; see Stade).

the pomegranates. The abundance of the *Punica granatum* and its popularity are attested by its inclusion among the seven species with which the land of Israel was blessed (Deut 8:8; cf. also Num 13:23); this is also shown by the many toponyms composed with the element *rimmôn*—e.g., Gath-rimmon (Josh 21:24), ʿEn-rimmon (Neh 11:29). In the decorative arts, pomegranates are found embroidered on the hem of the ephod of the high priest (Exod 28:33–34; 39:24–26). See also the miniature ivory pomegranate bearing the inscription: "To the house [of YHWH (?)] , holy to the priests" (Avigad 1989) and the pomegranate pendants on the stand from Ugarit (ANEP 588).

two rows. The *waw* before "two" is explicative, "that is," two rows of pomegranates.

19. *And (the) capitals that were on top of the columns, lilywork, in the main hall, four cubits.* In addition to syntactical problems, the verse duplicates v. 16 in part, contradicts the measurement given there ("five cubits," the height of each capital), and adds that the whole resembled the lily. Perhaps this is a variant, preserved because of the information concerning the lilywork; yet this is repeated in v. 22 without seeming reason. A variant form of v. 19 (and v. 20a) appears in LXX after v. 21.

lilywork. It is now generally acknowledged that Heb *šôšan/šûšan/šôšannâ* is the white lily (*lilium candidum*), a wild flower of Israel's rocky hills, now limited mostly to the north of the country (Feliks 1957, 234–40; Zohary 1982, 176–77); the identification with the lotus plant, i.e., water lily (and Egyptian *sššn*), so NAB, is inappropriate to the descriptions of the flower's dissemination; cf., e.g., Song 2:1–2; 6:2–3 (unless *šôšan* is a loanword in Semitic used with reference to a native plant with a calyx and flower similar to the lotus).

20. *and (the) capitals on the two columns, even above, close by the belly that was opposite the lattice and the pomegranates.*

close by the belly. Incomprehensible. No satisfactory suggestion has been made to identify the "belly" of the capital. If one may connect this with the equally opaque "bowls" in v. 42, then the belly might be the bulge at the lower part of the capital.

even above. For the preposition *lĕ'ummat*, "by the side, corresponding," cf. Exod 25:27; 38:18; with *mem*, it appears only here.

two hundred in rows. The total number of pomegranates is "one hundred" in Jer 52:23, but cf. below, v. 42.

around the second capital. The context suggests that a slip of the pen has occurred; the most natural reading would be "around the capitals" (or "the one capital"; so Stade), which was filled out by copying the end of v. 17. NEB: "the two capitals."

21. *He set up the right-hand column and named it Jachin, and he set up the left-hand column and named it Boaz*. The most reasonable suggestion is to take these names as the catchwords of sentences that had been inscribed on the columns, one on each; the first: *ykyn* (= Jachin) *ks' dwd wmmlktw lzr'w 'd 'wlm*, "He will establish the throne of David and his kingdom for his offspring forever"; and the second: *b'z* (Boaz) *yhwh yśmḥ mlk*, "In the strength of YHWH shall the king rejoice" (originally proposed by Scott 1939). In Mesopotamia, doors and gates bore festive names that implored the gods for blessings and protection; in these instances, the entire sentence was the name—e.g., a gate at Nineveh named: "Enlil (is the) establisher of my (Sennacherib) reign" (see Hurowitz 1992, 257 n. 2). See also Yeivin 1959; Albright 1969b, 140–44; Meyers 1983.

22. *and on top of the columns, lilywork*. A duplicate of v. 19a.

23. *He made the Sea, cast (of metal), ten cubits from rim to rim, circular, five cubits high and thirty cubits its line all around*. The enormous size of the Sea has led some to doubt the figures given (Bagnani [1954] branded them preposterous) and to redraw the vessel to meet individual imaginings. The circumference of thirty cubits (LXX: "thirty-three" may be a dittography) is an approximation, *pi* (3.14+) being unknown. Whether the Sea was cylindrical or a hemisphere cannot be determined.

its line all around. Another locution for circumference; cf. above, v. 15.

24. *and gourds under its rim encircling it all around for ten cubits, encompassing the Sea round about, two rows of gourds*. Decorative gourds were carved on the Temple walls; cf. 6:18.

for ten cubits. This looks erroneous, since the circumference of the Sea was thirty cubits; NEB corrects to "thirty" (with Burney). The suggestion to read "ten to a cubit" (NAB, NJPSV) goes against usage and grammar (the number would have to be masc.). Perhaps the words are a repetition of the measurement given in v. 23bα (so Noth).

cast during its casting. The ornamentation of the Sea was "cast in one piece with it" (NJPSV).

25. *standing on twelve oxen, three facing north and three facing west and three facing south and three facing east, with the Sea on them from above and their hind quarters (turned) inward*. Twelve oxen, the main work animals in ancient economies (cf. 1 Sam 11:7) and thus symbols of strength, were fashioned and distributed equally around the base of the Sea. The practicality of bearing the

weight of the large vessel (even more when filled) may have required resting the base of the Sea on a stone socle, in which case, the oxen served more of a decorative function (so Busink 1970, 331; Würthwein); yet the alterations made by Ahaz, who set the Sea on the stone ground (cf. 2 Kgs 16:17), would seem to negate this suggestion (as well as the suggestion by Bagnani 1954 that this was its original position).

26. *its thickness (was) a hand's breadth, and its rim was like the rim of a cup, (like) a lily flower.* For the terms, see vv. 22 and 23.

it could hold two thousand baths. The measure of the *bath*, based on an approximation of a jug inscribed *bt lmlk*, "bath of the king," is ca. 22 liters (Scott 1970, 350–51), yielding a volume of 44,000 liters! See also Powell 1992, 902.

27. *He (Hiram) made the stands, ten (of) bronze; the length of one stand four cubits, its width four cubits, and its height three cubits.* Many find that the stand discovered in Larnaca, Cyprus, though of much smaller dimensions (23 cm on each side and 39 cm high) than the stands here described, offers the closest parallel in concept and design; see photograph in Burney, opp. p. 91. A recent find at Ekron of three bronze wheels, a frame fragment, a bud pendant, and a linchpin, all from a wheeled stand, point to Canaanite contacts with the Cypriote tradition during the Late Bronze Age (see Dothan 1992).

28. *This was the construction of the stand.* Beyond the general agreement concerning the Larnaca artifact, no consensus exists concerning the details of the description given in MT. For a sampling of reconstructions, see Busink 1970, 342, 345, 347, 348.

They had frames and frames between the crosspieces. The translation "frames" derives from the root sense of **sgr* for *msgrt* as being an enclosure of some sort; cf. the frame around the table of showbread in Exod 25:25; NAB; NEB: "panels"; NJPSV: "insets." Hebrew *šĕlābîm*, from **šlb*, "to join" (cf. Exod 26:17; 36:22), is understood in the sense of MH *šĕlibāʾ*, "rung" of a ladder. Burney would emend (without textual support) the first "border frames" to "supports," i.e., the crosspieces (cf. NJPSV note, ad loc.).

29. *and on the frames between the crosspieces, lions, oxen, and cherubs, and so on the frames.* The final clause of v. 29a contains the word *kēn*, translated in v. 31 "pedestal, stand"; but, inasmuch as the present verse describes the decorative pieces affixed to the sides of the stand, *kēn* is taken adverbially; cf. v. 18. Otherwise, NJPSV, following medieval commentators ("above the frames was a stand").

Above and below the lions and the oxen. Read with Luc. and LXX, against MT, which has "above" marked with the disjunctive *ʾatnaḥ*.

spirals of hammered work. A guess; two unfathomable terms. Hebrew *lōyôt* (also vv. 30, 36) might be derived from **lwh*, "to encircle, twist" (cf. Akk *lam/wû*, "to move in a circle," used for arranging decorations in a circular form; see CAD L, 72). Burney arbitrarily corrects to read: "cherubs," and NEB adds this word, maintaining "spiral design." The other crux, *môrād*, seems as though it should be related to **yrd*; hence, "beveled work" (NRSV; with Burney); most others relate to **rdd*, "to hammer" (Rashi, Qimḥi, Kittel, Šanda); cf. 6:32.

30. *bronze axles.* Hebrew *seren* is a hapax; Tg. and medieval commentators interpreted as if it were metathesized *neser*, "board, plate"; modern scholars relate it to Syr. *srn*ʾ, "axle."

with spirals at each end. The MT *mʿbr ʾyš lywt* looks like the parallel of *kmʿr ʾyš wlywt sbyb* in v. 36b; both are obscure.

and its four legs had shoulder pieces under the laver. The shoulder pieces may have been "the brackets" (so NJPSV) in the four corners of the stand that held the feet.

31. *Its mouth within the crown and above (it) for one cubit; its mouth was round like the construction of a pedestal, one and one-half cubits, and there were carvings even on its mouth.* Hebrew *kōteret*, translated "capital" in vv. 16–20, is here "the crown" (cf. Esth 1:11), a figurative reference to the upper circular piece into which the laver was set, as within a mouth.

carvings. The term *miqlāʿôt* referred to wood carvings on the walls and doors in the Temple in 1 Kgs 6:18, 29, 32; here they are the engravings on the metal framework.

Now their frames were square, not round. The description returns to the bottom of the stand.

32. *There were four wheels under the frames, and the axletrees of the wheels were in the stand; the height of each wheel was one and one-half cubits.* Further details on the wheels of v. 28. The translation "axletrees" for Heb *yādôt*, lit., "hands," follows Vulg. and many commentators; Tg. renders "supports"; see also Burney and Skinner.

33. *their rims and their spokes and their hubs were all cast.* Of the three technical terms, only *gab* appears again in Ezekiel's vision in 1:18, though it is of little help in defining these "brows" (cf. Lev 14:9). The translation of the other terms, *ḥiššûq* from *ḥšq, "to tie, bind," and *ḥiššûr*, of otherwise unattested etymology, are approximations.

34. *There were four shoulder pieces at the four corners of each stand; its shoulder pieces were part of the stand.* The brackets (cf. v. 30) were of one piece with the frame.

35. *At the top of the stand, a half-cubit high, (the mouth) was circular; at the top of the stand, its supports and its frames were part of it.* The verse repeats, in garbled fashion, vv. 31a and 33. The subject is missing at the opening, and if the mouth is referred to, it was one and one-half cubits high (and so corrected by many); NAB rearranges the verses, so that v. 31 follows v. 35.

its supports. Hebrew *yād* (pl. *yādôt*) is used in vv. 32–33 to describe the wheel mechanism of the stands, perhaps the "axletrees." Here, the upper part of the stand is spoken of; hence the translation "support, stay"; in 1 Kgs 10:19, the word refers to the "armrests" of the throne. Others suggest "handles."

36. *He engraved on the panels cherubs, lions, and palms, with spirals at each end round about.* The MT has the additional "its supports and on its frames" between the words "panels" and "cherubs," a dittography from v. 35. The remainder of the verse describes the decorative elements on the four sides of the

stands, a duplicate of v. 29. In the present verse, the figures are engraved (?) on panels, rather than being fixed between the struts (as in v. 29), and "palms" substitute for the "oxen."

37. *one measure and one form for all of them.* "Measure" and "form" were used with reference to the cherubs in 6:25. The rare suffixed form (*lĕkūl-lāhĕnâ*) appears again (also in pause) in Ezek 16:53; see GKC, 91f.

38. *He made ten bronze lavers.* Hebrew *kiyyôr* is a loanword; in Akk *kiūru* is also a foreign word that appears in reference to "cauldrons" taken by Sargon II as booty from Urartu (CAD K, 476b). The Sumerian etymology suggested by Albright (1969b, 149, 217 n. 63) remains unproved; it may be of Urartian derivation (< *kiri*; see AHw 496a). The lavers contained the water for the priestly ablutions prior to the performance of the ritual acts in the Tabernacle; cf. Exod 30:17–21; while in 2 Chr 4:6, with reference to the Temple, they were the source for the rinsing of the burnt offerings. In the Second Temple, a single laver was installed (*m. Mid.* 3:6), which the Qumran sectarians thought would be placed in the House of the Laver in the New Jerusalem (see Schiffman 1999).

each laver contained forty baths, *each laver being four cubits; there was one laver on each stand for the ten stands.* Each laver contained 880 liters of water (cf. above, Note on v. 26).

39. *He placed five stands on the right side of the house and five on the left side of the house, and he placed the Sea at the right side of the house toward the southeast.* From the description of the position of the Sea, it follows that "right" and "left" refer to "south" and "north" respectively; see Note on 6:8. The weight of the stands and the lavers filled with water made their mobility less than practical.

40. *Hiram made the pots and the shovels and the sprinkling bowls.* For the form of the name *Hirom*, see Note on v. 13. All three utensils are listed in Exod 27:3 and 38:3.

the pots. The copying slipup in MT *kyrwt* for *syrwt* is easy to explain: *kywr* was the subject in v. 38. (Note, as well, the single use of *kywr* as "pot" in 1 Sam 2:14.) In the present case, the pots were used for carrying away the suet from the altar; cf. Exod 27:3; 38:3 (not for cooking sacrificial meat; so Wiseman).

the shovels. Employed in sweeping up the ashes from the altar; cf. the verbal use of **y'h* in Isa 28:17.

the sprinkling bowls. The blood of the sacrifice was collected in these utensils and then dashed (from **zrq*, hence *mizrāq*) against the altar; for the rite, cf. Exod 24:6. They might also have served in libation rituals, since the word is a "drinking bowl" in Amos 6:6; cf. Zech 9:15.

Thus, Hiram brought to a close all the work that he did for King Solomon (on) the House of YHWH. Similar concluding statements were written for the work on the Temple; cf. 6:9, 14; see Note, ad loc.

41. *the bowls of the capitals that were on top of the columns.* The term *gūllâ* (cf. Zech 4:2, 3) was not previously used in describing the capitals; cf. the term

"belly" in v. 20. What appears to be the cognate Akk *gullatu* is a "column base" (CAD G, 128b; note that the citation from correspondence to Sargon reports the casting of four *gullāte* of bronze for two *ḫilāni*-palaces). The suggestion that the two terms "belly" and "bowls" refer to the two parts of a double capital (Yeivin 1959) has not won many adherents.

45. *all these vessels that Hiram made for King Solomon for the House of YHWH were of burnished bronze.* Before the summarizing statement, Luc. and LXX add: "and the forty-eight columns of the king's house and the House of YHWH, all the works of the king Hiram made." Such a large number of columns, introduced as an afterthought, nowhere else referred to, raises the question of the originality of this addition; its source remains unknown. Was it appended for the greater glory of Solomon (Noth)? [DNF: "This looks like a massive haplography in MT. LXX shows that the passage ends with the same words as the preceding: *lbyt yhwh*."]

all these vessels. The qere is the preferred reading; the ketib is probably a simple metathesis. Qimḥi explained the error as produced by a scribe whose mind wandered to the Tabernacle, where the implements were in service, causing him to write *h'hl*, "the tent" for *h'lh*, "these."

burnished bronze. Hebrew **mrṭ* is properly the act of making bald, bare, or smooth, as in pulling out hair (Ezra 9:3; Neh 13:25; also Ezek 29:18); cf. "tall and smooth-skinned" (Isa 18:2). In the present instance, it describes the smoothing away of imperfections; cf. the polished sword in Ezek 21:14.

46. *In the plain of the Jordan.* Literally, "circle of the Jordan," the valley on either side of the River Jordan; cf. Gen 13:12; 19:29. The towns mentioned are on the East Bank, on the road taken by Gideon in his pursuit of the fleeing Midianites; cf. Judg 7:22ff.

the king cast them in the thick earth. The translation follows 2 Chr 4:17: *b'by* "in the thickness of" the ground. From early on, it was understood that Heb *bm'bh h'dmh* referred to the clay ground (Vulg. *in terra argillosa*) of the Jordan Valley used for molds in the casting of the metal objects; so Ibn Janah: "the thickest and richest of them"—i.e., made of the finest of clay. The NJPSV offers "earthen molds"; NAB: "in the clayey ground"; NEB: "in the foundry." Some critics needlessly corrected the text; e.g., "at the ford of Adamah" (Moore 1895, 212–13; Benzinger, Skinner [for the town name Adam, cf. Josh 3:16]); or "in the foundries of Succoth, between Adamah and Zarethan" (Albright 1925, 33 n. 37). On the dependence of such suggestions on the disputed geography of the middle Jordan Valley, see following Note.

between Succoth and Zarethan. Succoth is identified by many with Tell Deir ʿAlla (ABD 6:217–18), an identification rejected by the excavator of the site (ABD 2:126–29). On Zarethan, see Notes on 4:12 and 11:26 (for "Zeredah," the reading in 2 Chr 4:17 for "Zarethan").

47. *Solomon left all the vessels out of account because of their very great number; the weight of the bronze was not ascertained.* The verse is read according to Masoretic accentuation, with the verb taken in the sense of LH, "set

aside, leave out" (so Rashi, Qimḥi). Others divide after v. 47aα: "Solomon put all these objects in their places" (NEB); note the imaginative "Solomon put all these objects (on a scale)" (Mulder).

the weight of the bronze was not ascertained. A rhetorical statement, like "so numerous they cannot be numbered and cannot be counted" (1 Kgs 3:8), indicating an extremely large quantity.

48. *Solomon made all the vessels of the House of YHWH.* With regard to the equipment of gold for the inner service, their production is accredited to Solomon, not to a foreigner, though the king himself was certainly not the craftsman. All was produced by executive order.

the altar, of gold; the table upon which was the showbread, of gold. These items are not listed among the booty carried off by Nebuchadnezzar in 2 Kgs 25:13–17 (cf. Jer 52:17–23), because they were part of the earlier spoliation of Jerusalem; cf. 2 Kgs 24:13.

the altar, of gold. There is no textual warrant for identifying the altar and the table as a single object; for the use of the altar for the burning of incense, see Note on 6:20.

the table upon which was the showbread, of gold. The dimensions and construction of the table in the Tabernacle (cf. Exod 25:23–28) may reflect the table of the Temple. Note the abbreviated form "table of show" (Num 4:7). For the weekly rite of setting out twelve loaves on this golden table, cf. Lev 24:5–9.

the showbread. This familiar translation is found already in KJV and is retained in NAB; others suggest: "Bread of the Presence" (NEB, NRSV); "bread of display" (NJPSV). David's acquisition of "showbread" at Nob (cf. 1 Sam 21:2–7) is the earliest reference to this rite.

49. *the lampstands, five on the right and five on the left, in front of the shrine, of refined gold.* The lampstands were arrayed on either side of the entrance into the shrine along the back wall of the main hall of the Temple, from where they gave light to the inner recesses of the building (cf. Num 4:9, where the *mĕnōrâ* in the Tabernacle is called "the lampstand for lighting"). The single lampstand of the Tabernacle, detailed in Exod 25:31–37, may have been modeled on the Temple candelabrum (contra Meyers 1976, 35–36; 1992a, 142–43, who places much weight on the term "refined gold" that is no different from the "pure gold" [cf. 1 Kgs 6:20 and 2 Chr 3:4]).

refined gold. See Note on 6:20.

the flowers. A floral motif is also mentioned in connection with the Tabernacle lampstand; cf. Exod 25:31, 33; Num 8:4.

the lamps. The oil receptacles that served as lamps were of both the open and the closed variety, as the archaeological remains have shown, but the textual descriptions make no such distinction.

the tongs. These implements are associated with the lamps, perhaps for adjusting the wicks (Hurowitz 1995a, 154).

50. *the basins.* Hebrew *sap* is a container for liquids, a "bowl, basin" for blood in Exod 12:22; for poison in Zech 12:2; cf. also 2 Sam 17:28.

the snuffers. The implement referred to by Heb *mězammĕrôt* is disputed; it appears again only in 2 Kgs 12:14. Etymology plays the major role in the interpretation: derivation from **zmr*, "to make music," led medieval commentators, as one, to translate "musical instruments"; modern scholars prefer **zmr*, "to trim, prune," and therefore, "snuffers," a tool for trimming the wicks of the lamps.

the bowls. In v. 40, this term was translated "sprinkling bowl," since there it referred to the bronze implements used in the rites of the sacrificial altar; the golden bowls served some other purpose within the Temple.

the ladles. The spoon-shaped (Heb *kap*, "palm of the hand") implements were used in censing; cf. Num 7:14; cf. also Exod 25:29; 37:16; Num 4:7.

the firepans. These firepans are associated with the incense altar, not the bronze sacrificial altar (Exod 27:3) or the lampstand (Exod 25:38); incense was carried into the shrine in firepans as part of the Yom Kippur rite (cf. Lev 16:12); note the description of coals brought in firepans from the outside altar to the inner sanctuary in *m. Yoma* 4:4. See also the contest of the firepans in Num 16.

and the hinges of the doors to the inner house, the Holy of Holies, (and) the doors of the house, of the main hall. Two glosses clarify the references to "inner house" and "house."

the hinges of the doors. A crux. Besides being out of place in a list of cultic implements, gold hinges lack practicality, since they could not have carried the weight of the doors; were bronze hinges (or better, "hinge sockets" [cf. *m. Kelim* 11:2]) thought to be covered with goldleaf? This translation of Heb *pōt(â)* is a contextual guess (cf. Vulg., Syr.); the rendering "panels" in NEB, follows G. R. Driver (1937, 38) in associating the word with Akk *pūtu*, "forehead." The other occurrence of *pōt(â)*, in Isa 3:17, is no less problematic; the traditional association with pudenda has led to many fanciful etymologies that are better abandoned for the reading *p'thn*, "their heads" (so NJPSV). Another probe seems to have its roots in the parallel listing in 2 Chr 4:22, where the "entrance" (*pth*) of the House and its doors are mentioned; this may have prompted taking *pōtôt* as golden "keys" (*mpthwt*) (so Rashi, Qara); see most recently Hurowitz (1995a, 161), who thinks of some sort of latching device that played a part in a ritual at the Temple doorway.

51. *Thus, all the work that King Solomon did for the House of YHWH was finished*. A final summary statement, suggesting successful closure, more so than the verb **klh*, "to complete," used to mark various stages of construction; cf. 6:9, 14, 38; 7:1, 40.

Solomon brought the votive objects of his father, David, the silver, the gold, and the vessels. David's dedications to YHWH of spoil and tribute are reported in 2 Sam 8:9–12; for other royal dedications, cf. 1 Kgs 14:26; 15:15.

(and) deposited (them). For another example of asyndetic use of the perfect, cf. 13:18; Montgomery and Gehman omit the clause as a gloss referring to Solomon's gifts.

COMMENT

Structure and Themes

The enumeration of the bronzework crafted by Hiram (vv. 15–40) is ordered, from the large display items to the small handheld utensils: two columns (vv. 15–22); the Sea (vv. 23–26); ten stands and basins (vv. 27–39); cultic utensils (v. 40).[1] The somewhat detailed construction plans are occasionally interrupted by verbs ("he fashioned" [v. 15]; "he made" [vv. 18, 23, 27, 38, 40] in an editorial attempt to create a narrative ascribing the fashioning to the Tyrian craftsman, Hiram. An inventory list (vv. 41–45) is appended; the use of the terms gullâ (v. 41–42) and nĕḥōšet mĕmōrāṭ (v. 45) points to the independence of this list from the preceding verses. Finally, mention is made, in list-like fashion, of the golden objects made by Solomon (vv. 48–50); the implication seems to be that these most precious implements, which were to be used in the service within the Temple, were made by an Israelite, not a foreign craftsman.

The Columns (vv. 15–22)

The two columns that stood to the right and the left, as one passed through the porch of the Temple, and bore the names Jachin and Boaz, respectively, have been the subject of repeated study; see Albright 1969b, 135, 140–44. Their absence from the description of the building plan of the Temple in 1 Kgs 6 would seem to confirm the suggestion that they were free-standing columns, not integrated structurally into the building; see the pottery model of a shrine from Tell el-Faraʿah (north; A. Mazar 1990, 378); and the drawing of the Melqart temple in Tyre on a relief from the palace of Sennacherib (Barnett 1956, fig. 9, opp. p. 93). They were too tall—18 cubits (27 ft.)—to have served as cressets; nor is there any feature that suggests that they were originally "phallic symbols . . . that as stylized pomegranate trees the pillars symbolized fertility" (Mulder, 321). Rather, the columns functioned more as symbolic markers of the passage from the profane to the holy, as the gateway into the abode of YHWH (Meyers 1983). They bore inscriptions that expressed the deity's support for the Davidic kings, the endowers of the Temple, who ruled with YHWH's blessing (Scott 1939; see above on v. 21).

The Sea (vv. 23–26)

This huge reservoir that stood to the southeast of the Temple building must have been wondrous to behold. That "the Sea" had "cosmic significance" in Israelite thought, as is so often put forward (Albright 1969b, 144–45), is nowhere stated; comparison with Akk apsû, "deep water, sea," used very rarely and late as "water basin" (CAD A/2, 197), seems forced. In this regard, the absence of the Sea from the new Temple of Ezekiel is telling; the mythical, life-giving waters issue from beneath the threshold of YHWH's House (Ezek 47:1)—that is, from the deity himself in his dwelling. The largeness of "the Sea" would have been

---

[1] The list in 2 Chr 4:1 includes the casting of the bronze altar, but this is nowhere mentioned in the work of Hiram in 1 Kgs 7. See further the Note on 1 Kgs 8:64.

sufficient to earn its name, since its main function seems to have been as a private pool for priestly ablutions (2 Chr 4:6); because of its size, access to it would have been difficult without a ladder or a stepped stool.

The Stands (vv. 27–37)

There are numerous proposals for the disentanglement of this description, which is repetitive as well as expansive. Solutions include the elimination of vv. 31 and 35 as "additions" (Würthwein); viewing vv. 32–36 as a "secondary" presentation (Montgomery and Gehman; Burney restricts this to vv. 34–36). The contradictory descriptions of the decorated sidepieces are hard to harmonize; perhaps stands from different periods are being depicted (say, after the removal of the original stands by Ahaz [2 Kgs 16:17] and their subsequent replacement).

The practical use of these wheeled stands with their water basins is hard to imagine. If the water was for rinsing the sacrifices (so 2 Chr 4:6), a means was necessary for carrying the water from the stands (were they equipped with a spigot?) to the altar area, since the weight of a filled stand was upwards of 2520 kg (so Busink 1970, 349; Kittel calculated 3400 kg), not an easily transportable wagon. (n.b.: Neither with respect to the stands nor to the Sea is any indication given of the source or the means for filling it.)

Two Lists (vv. 41–45, 48–50)

The first of these lists, vv. 41–45, summarizes the bronzework fashioned by Hiram for use in the cultic activities in the inner court of the Temple; its independence from vv. 15–39 has already been noted. (In detail and style, it does not resemble the "colophons" known from the priestly material in the Pentateuch—e.g., Lev 7:37–38; 11:46–47; et al. [contra Long].) The list resembles an inventory, suggesting that its original provenance may have been the Temple treasury or storehouse; at the same time, the Temple's royal benefactor would also have had an interest in documenting his contributions. (Affinities to this biblical list can be seen in the inventories and memoranda of precious metals and stones from Sargonid Assyria; see Fales and Postgate 1992, 72–105.)

The second list, vv. 48–50, enumerates the golden vessels made by Solomon for service in the Temple; it is not preceded by detailed plans for their fashioning (nor for that matter are there plans for the small bronze vessels in v. 40). (For the arrangement of the information in columnar fashion [item-use-material], see Hurowitz 1995a, 153–54). Early critics branded these verses late and dependent on the Tabernacle account in Exod 25 and 30; the rearrangement in Luc. and LXX added to the suspicion of nonoriginality (e.g., Stade; Burney, who presents an extensive rewriting; Skinner). But here, too, the independence of the unit can be seen in the listing of ten lampstands (rather than the single one in the Tabernacle) and the use of terminology distinctive of the Temple (hêkal, děbîr)—e.g., "snuffers." Furthermore, that the Temple was equipped with golden vessels is confirmed by 2 Kgs 25:14–15; Jer 52:18–19.[2]

---

[2] Japhet (1993, 569–70) speculates on the basis of the data given concerning the altar in 2 Chr 4:1 that the Kings chapter has undergone a thorough editing; the details of the gold items were

As with the description of the Temple construction in 1 Kgs 6, the basic units of 1 Kgs 7:13–51 are of indeterminable date; in this regard, the absence of Dtr's distinctive phraseology is a drawback. Even the assumption (of Noth and many others) that the description was part of the *Book of the Deeds of Solomon* (cf. 11:41) does not secure its attribution to Solomon's reign. A mid-eighth-century BCE date may be considered for at least part of the description in 1 Kgs 7, considering that Ahaz undertook major alterations to the Temple in order to pay the indemnity imposed by Tiglath-pileser III (cf. 2 Kgs 16:17–18); Van Seters' late (= exilic) writer, remembering what the Temple looked like, would not have seen the bronze oxen (cf. 1 Kgs 7:25, 44), which had been shipped to Assyria a century and a half earlier.

History

Most surveys of Solomon's reign incorporate the data from 1 Kgs 7:13–51 in their discussions of the king's furnishing of the Temple, without tackling the question of the date of the lists at the base of the description. At whatever stage the Temple was fully equipped, the source of the copper, especially in the immense ("immeasurable," cf. v. 46) quantities described, should be considered. The mines at Timnaʿ north of Elath were not in use during the monarchic period (see Manor 1992, 554; contra Gray). It could not compete with the major site at Feinan in southern Jordan, where evidence of copper smelting on an industrial scale from the ninth century onward has been discovered (see Hauptmann et al. 1992). Northern supplies might still have been available as well (cf. 2 Sam 8:8 for the "import" by David of copper from Tebah and Berothai). The practical questions of fashioning (even by the "lost wax" method) the large objects and their transfer from the Jordan Valley require adoption of the suggestion that the casting was done in sections that were later assembled on site in Jerusalem.

---

omitted in Kings so as not to appear contradictory to the Tabernacle tradition in Exodus, because "they were so different from their counterparts." But perhaps it was their very similarity to the Tabernacle utensils that made a repetition in Kings superfluous.

XI. THE INAUGURATION OF THE TEMPLE

(8:1–66)

8 ¹Then Solomon assembled ᵃthe elders of Israel—all the heads of the tribes, the ancestral chieftains of the Israelites to King Solomon—in Jerusalem, to bring up the Ark of YHWH's covenant from the City of David, that is, Zion. ²All the men of Israel assembled before King Solomon in the month of Ethanim—at the Festival—that is, the seventh month. ³When all the elders of Israel had come, the priests carried the Ark, ⁴and they brought up the Ark of YHWH and the Tent of Meeting and all the holy vessels that were in the Tent; the priests and the Levites brought them up. ⁵(All the while) King Solomon and the whole assembly of Israel who were present with him before the Ark were sacrificing sheep and oxen, so numerous that they could not be numbered or be counted. ⁶The priests brought the Ark of YHWH's covenant to its place, to the shrine of the House, to the Holy of Holies, beneath the wings of the cherubs; ⁷for the cherubs spread wings over the place of the Ark; and the cherubs formed a canopy over the Ark and its poles from above. ⁸The poles were so long that the ends of the poles could be seen from the sanctuary in front of the shrine; but they could not be seen outside. They are there until this day. ⁹There is nothing in the Ark save the two tablets of stone that Moses placed there at Horeb, when YHWH made a covenant with the Israelites when they left the land of Egypt.

¹⁰As the priests left the sanctuary, the cloud filled the House of YHWH; ¹¹the priests could not stand in attendance because of the cloud, for the presence of YHWH had filled the House of YHWH. ¹²Then Solomon said:

> YHWH intended to dwell in thick cloud.
> ¹³I have indeed built a princely House for you,
> a place for your dwelling forever.

¹⁴Then the king turned around and blessed all the congregation of Israel; all the congregation of Israel was standing. ¹⁵He said: "Blessed be YHWH, God of Israel, who with his own mouth promised David my father and with his own hand fulfilled (his promise): ¹⁶'From the day I brought my people Israel out from Egypt, I have not chosen a city out of all the tribes of Israel to build a house for my name to be there; but I chose David to be over my people Israel.' ¹⁷Now my father David had in mind to build a house for the name of YHWH, God of Israel. ¹⁸But YHWH said to David my father: 'Whereas you had in mind to build a house for my name, you have done well by these thoughts. ¹⁹However, *you* shall not build the house, but your son who shall issue from your loins, *he*

ᵃ The LXX, Syr., and many Heb MSS add "all"; cf. v. 3.

shall build the house for my name.' [20]YHWH has fulfilled the promise he made, and I have succeeded my father David and sat on the throne of Israel as YHWH promised; and I have built the House for the name of YHWH, God of Israel. [21]I have set a place there for the Ark in which is YHWH's covenant that he made with our ancestors when he brought them out from the land of Egypt."

[22]Solomon stood before the altar of YHWH opposite all the congregation of Israel; he spread his palms heavenward [23]and said: "YHWH, God of Israel, there is no god like you, in heaven above or on earth below, keeping with loyalty the covenant with your servants who serve you wholeheartedly, [24]who kept your promise to your servant David my father; with your own mouth you promised and with your own hands you fulfilled, as it is today. [25]So, now, YHWH, God of Israel, keep your promise to your servant, David my father: 'No one of your line sitting on the throne of Israel shall be cut off at my instance, if your sons watch their way to serve me as you served me.' [26]Now, then, ⟨YHWH,⟩[b] God of Israel, may the promise[c] that you made to David my father be confirmed.

[27]But, indeed, can God dwell on earth? Here the heavens and the highest heavens cannot contain you; how much less this House that I have built? [28]Yet, turn to the prayer and the supplication of your servant, O YHWH, my God, to listen to the praise and the prayer that your servant offers before you this day, [29]that your eyes may be open toward this House night and day, to the place of which you said: 'My name shall be there'; that you might listen to the prayer that your servant offers toward this place. [30]Listen to the supplication of your servant and your people Israel, which they will pray toward this place. *You* shall listen in your dwelling in heaven, listen and forgive.

[31]If a man wrongs his neighbor, and the latter utters an imprecation against him to curse him, and the curse is taken before your altar in this House; [32]then *you* shall listen in heaven and act; judge your servants, condemning the wicked by bringing his way on his head and acquitting the righteous by rewarding him according to his innocence.

[33]When your people Israel are defeated by an enemy because they have sinned against you and then return to you and praise your name and pray and make supplication to you in this House, [34]then *you* shall listen in heaven; forgive the sin of your people Israel and restore them to the land you gave to their ancestors.

[35]When the heavens are shut up and there is no rain, because they have sinned against you, and they pray to this place and praise your name, turning from their sin so that you answer them; [36]then *you* shall listen in heaven; forgive the sin of your servants, your people Israel, so that you teach them the good way that they should follow. Grant rain to your land that you gave to your people as an inheritance.

[37]If there is famine in the land; if there be pestilence; if there be blight, mildew, locusts, hoppers; if their enemy presses upon them in one of their cities[d]—

---

[b] Add "YHWH" with many MSS, LXX; cf. vv. 15, 20, 23, 25, and 2 Chr 6:17.

[c] With qere: *dbrk*; ketib: *dbryk*; so, too, LXX and Syr.

[d] Read with Luc., LXX, Syr.: *b'ḥd š'ryw* for MT: *b'rṣ š'ryw*; see Note.

whatever the plague or the sickness (may be)—[38]every prayer (and) every supplication that any one of your people Israel shall have, each of whom knows his own affliction, when he spreads his palms to this house, [39]then *you* shall listen in heaven, your dwelling place, and forgive and act. Render to each man according to his ways as you will know his heart, for you alone know the hearts of all men, [40]so that they may fear you all the days that they live on the land that you gave to our ancestors.

[41]Moreover, to the foreigner, who is not of your people Israel, who shall come from a distant land because of your name—[42]for they shall hear of your great name and your strong hand and your outstretched arm—who shall come and pray toward this House, [43]*you* shall listen in heaven, your dwelling place, and act in accord with all that the foreigner asks of you, so that the peoples of the earth may know your name, to fear you as do your people Israel and know that your name is proclaimed over this House that I have built.

[44]When your people go out to war against their enemy, wherever you shall send them, and they pray to YHWH in the direction of the city that you have chosen and the House that I have built for your name, [45]listen in heaven to their prayer and their supplication and act justly toward them.

[46]When they sin against you—for there is no person who does not sin—and you are angry at them and deliver them to an enemy who carries them off as captives to his country,[e] far or near, [47]and then they take it to heart in the land of their captivity, they repent, and make supplication to you in the land of their captors: 'We have sinned and we have acted perversely ⟨and⟩[f] we have acted wickedly.' [48]If they return to you with all their heart and with all their soul in the land of their enemies who captured them, and if they pray to you in the direction of their land that you gave their ancestors, the city that you chose and the House that I have built[g] for your name, [49]listen in heaven, your dwelling place, to their prayer and their supplication and act justly toward them, [50]forgive your people who have sinned against you, for all their transgressions by which they transgressed against you, and cause their captors to have mercy upon them so that they will show them mercy. [51]For they are your people and your inheritance, whom you brought out from Egypt, from the midst of the iron furnace, [52]so may your eyes be open to the supplication of your servant and the supplication of your people Israel, to listen to them whenever they call out to you. [53]For *you* have set them apart for yourself as an inheritance out of all the peoples of the earth, as you promised through Moses your servant when you brought our ancestors out from Egypt, O Lord YHWH."

[54]When Solomon finished offering all this prayer and supplication to YHWH, he rose from before the altar of YHWH, from kneeling with his palms spread heavenward; [55]he stood and blessed all the congregation of Israel in a loud voice:

---

[e] Lit. "the country of the enemy." LXX omits "the enemy," cf. 2 Chr 6:36; see Note.

[f] Add *waw* with 2 Chr 6:37, LXX, Vulg.; see Note.

[g] Read with qere: *bnyty*; ketib: *bnyt*, "you built."

[56]"Blessed be YHWH who has given rest to his people Israel according to all he promised. Not one word of all the good things that he promised through his servant Moses has gone unfulfilled. [57]May YHWH our God be with us as he was with our ancestors. May he not abandon us and not forsake us. [58]May he turn our hearts toward him, to follow all his ways and keep his commands and his statutes and his laws that he commanded our ancestors. [59]And may these my words that I have made in supplication before YHWH be close to YHWH our God day and night, that he do justice with his servant and with his people Israel, as each day requires; [60]that all the peoples of the earth shall know that YHWH, he is God; there is no other. [61]May your heart be fully with YHWH our God, following his statutes, and keeping his commands, as on this day."

[62]Now the King and all Israel with him offered sacrifice before YHWH. [63]Solomon offered the sacrifice of well-being, in which he offered to YHWH twenty-two thousand oxen and one hundred twenty thousand sheep. Thus, the king and all the Israelites inaugurated the House of YHWH. [64]On that day, the king consecrated the center of the court that was in front of the House of YHWH; for it was there that he made the burnt offerings and the meal offerings and the fat of the offerings of well-being—the bronze altar that was before YHWH was too small to hold (all) the burnt offerings and the meal offerings and the fat of the offerings of well-being.

[65]At that time, Solomon celebrated the Festival; all Israel was with him, a great assembly from Lebo-hamath to the Wadi of Egypt, before YHWH our God for seven days and seven days, fourteen days. [66]On the eighth day, he dismissed the people and they blessed the king. They went home[h] happy and glad at heart for all the good that YHWH had done for David his servant and Israel his people.

---

[h] Lit., "to their tents."

NOTES

8   1. *Then Solomon assembled the elders of Israel.* For the editorial term "then," which bears no chronological significance, see the earlier remarks, on 3:16. Commentators are taken by what they perceive to be conflicting dates concerning the Temple's inauguration: according to 6:38, the construction was completed in the eighth month but, according to 8:2, 65, the ceremonies were held in the seventh month. Some explain this as an eleven-month delay due to the need to finish casting the bronze cult vessels (e.g., Stade and Schwally, Skinner, Šanda); others suggest that the fall Festival was originally celebrated in the eighth month (cf. 12:32) and was later changed in Judah (see Montgomery and Gehman, following Morgenstern). For Noth, Gray, and Würthwein, the opening *'āz*, "then," glosses over the discrepancy. If we had an indication of the year of the ceremonies, apparently suppressed by "then," it would be easier to understand these incongruous traditions.

all the heads of the tribes, the ancestral chieftains of the Israelites. The dignitaries are described in terms known from the Priestly source of the Pentateuch; for *r'šy ḥmṭwt*, cf. Num 30:2; 32:28; for *nśy'y h'bwt lbny yśr'l*, cf. Num 7:2; also Josh 14:1; 19:51.

to King Solomon—in Jerusalem, to bring up the Ark of YHWH's covenant from the City of David, that is, Zion. The Ark had been housed in a tent since its transfer by David from Kiriath-jearim, in stages, to the City of David; cf. 2 Sam 6.

the City of David, that is, Zion. Zion is name of the Jebusite stronghold taken by David (2 Sam 5:7). Archaeologically, it has been sought in the saddle of the hill, south of the Temple Mount, overlooking the Kidron Valley. See NEAEHL 2:698–704. In its developed usage, in Psalms (e.g., Ps 2:6; 48:13) and prophetic literature (e.g., Isa 1:27; Jer 26:18), Zion stands for the city of Jerusalem as a whole, and Mount Zion is the sobriquet for the dwelling place of YHWH.

2. *All of the men of Israel assembled before King Solomon.* At first glance, this verse looks like a contradiction of vv. 1, 3, which report the tribal leaders as the main invitees, while in v. 2, the "men of Israel," i.e., the army (so, quite often in 2 Sam 15–20, following Tadmor 1968, 49–57) assembled for the ceremonies. For this and other signs of multiple sources in this unit, see discussion in Comment below.

in the month of Ethanim—at the Festival—that is, the seventh month. The placement of the Festival notice is secondary, because it interrupts the identification of the month name with its counted number; cf. the proper order in 6:1, 38.

the month of Ethanim. Another example of a Phoenician month name; cf. 6:1, 38, and Notes there; for inscriptional attestations of Ethanim, see KAI 37:1, 2; 41:4. From the date in 6:38, it would appear that it took the king an additional eleven months to organize the Temple and prepare for the dedication ceremonies.

the Festival. That is, Sukkoth, the major pilgrimage festival at the end of the harvest season, at which time the Israelite farmer, having completed the ingathering, could make the pilgrimage to Jerusalem and stay the required week in the capital city without concern for his fields or their crops; cf. Deut 16:13–15; Lev 23:33–43. On the coordination of the dedication ceremonies with Sukkoth, see below on 8:65.

3–4. *When all the elders of Israel had come, the priests carried the Ark, and they brought up the Ark of YHWH and the Tent of Meeting and all the holy vessels that were in the Tent.* The Tent of Meeting associated with Moses and the desert wandering, accorded a prominent position in Priestly tradition (cf. Exod 26; 36:8–38), appears here for the first time in a Deuteronomistic context, not having been referred to after the scandal involving Eli's sons (1 Sam 2:22); the Tent referred to in 1 Kgs 1:39 is of different origin; see Note, ad loc. The reference in 2 Chr 1:3 to the location of the Tent of Meeting in Gibeon is without historical foundation, being a legitimizing note added to the story of Solomon's visit. On the source of the present notice, see Comment. The disposal of the Tent and the holy vessels, once having been brought into the Temple, is not reported. Rabbinic tradition spoke of their being stored away (*b. Soṭah* 9a), and this was a reasonable surmise, since these vessels comprised an almost duplicate set with the ones fashioned by Solomon. Recent scholarly debate has focused on the extraordinary suggestion of Friedman (1987, 183) that the Tabernacle was erected in the Holy of Holies; see the stinging criticism of this view by Hurowitz 1995b, 142–44.

the priests and the Levites brought them up. The distinction between the two classes within the tribe of Levi is a mark of P (cf., e.g., Num 3:5–10); in D, "the levitical priests, the whole tribe of Levi" are qualified to serve (cf. Deut 18:1–8).

5. *(All the while) King Solomon and the whole assembly of Israel who were present with him before the Ark were sacrificing sheep and oxen.* The offerings made at this juncture (cf. v. 62 for further sacrifices) marked the removal of the Ark from the City of David and its entrance into its permanent abode; cf. David's offerings when the Ark first entered the City in 2 Sam 6:17. Comparison to the "stages" of that earlier pericope (2 Sam 6:13; Skinner, Gray) and taking the sacrifices to be "precautionary" offerings (Provan) are not particularly apt, especially when one considers the very short distance that the Ark was actually carried, from the City of David up the hill to the Temple.

the whole assembly of Israel who were present with him. Another Priestly phrase; cf., e.g., Num 14:35; 16:11; 27:3.

so numerous that they could not be numbered or be counted. Cf. the similar turn of phrase in 1 Kgs 7:47.

6. *The priests brought the Ark of YHWH's covenant to its place.* Hebrew *'rwn hbryt / bryt yhwh* is the D locution for the Ark; cf. Deut 10:8; 31:9, 25, 26; Josh 3:3; 8:33; 1 Kgs 3:15; 6:19; in P, it is *'rwn h'dwt*, "the Ark of the Pact/Testimony"; cf. Exod 25:22; Num 7:89. The Ark was constructed according to the divine model brought by Moses from Sinai (Exod 37:1–9) and, as the divine seat, it symbolized the Deity's presence among Israel and led them on their march through the desert (Num 10:35–36) and in battle (14:44); see Haran 1959.

to the shrine of the House, to the Holy of Holies. A Priestly term; see Note on 1 Kgs 6:16.

beneath the wings of the cherubs. See Note on 6:23–28.

7. *for the cherubs spread wings over the place of the Ark.* Each cherub spread just one wing toward the center of the inner chamber, its other wing spread out toward the wall; cf. 6:27. For the symbolism of the outstretched wings as the seat of YHWH's throne and the Ark as His footstool, see Haran 1959; 1978, 254–57.

and the cherubs formed a canopy. The MT: *wyyskkw*, from **skk*, "cover, screen"; cf. Exod 25:20 (*skkym*); the reading in 2 Chr 5:8 *wyykssw*, from **ksh*, looks like a transcriptional inversion (cf. 1 Chr 28:18) and is not preferable. The verb **skk* is used of the "shielding cherub" in Ezekiel's dirge over the king of Tyre (Ezek 28:14, 16).

over the Ark and its poles from above. Or "staves"; cf. Exod 25:13–15. The only function of the poles was for transporting the ark, and they could have been removed once the ark was installed in its permanent place in the shrine;

cf. Num 4:6; see further in v. 8. Hebrew *baddîm*, from **bdd*, meaning "part, separation, extension," is also used of branches of a tree; cf. Ezek 17:6.

8. *The poles were so long that the ends of the poles could be seen from the sanctuary in front of the shrine; but they could not be seen outside.* According to the description in Exod 26:31–33, a veil was to be hung in front of the Ark, preventing the viewer standing in the sanctuary from gazing directly into the Holy of Holies and at the Ark; a veil is not mentioned in the present verse; thus, the ends of the poles of the Ark could be seen. From this description it may be determined that the Ark was placed on an east–west orientation.

the sanctuary in front of the shrine. Hebrew *hqdš* refers to the outer sanctuary, usually called the *hykl*, the main hall of the Temple (1 Kgs 6:17, 33; 7:21); cf. the similar Priestly usage in Exod 26:33.

They are there until this day. The phrase seems to confirm the directive in Exod 25:15 that the transport poles were not to be removed. Noth, following a long line of commentators, would transfer v. 8b to v. 9 as a reference to the covenant tablets within the Ark, rather than to the insignificant curiosity of the extended staves. For the phrase "until this day" in etiological contexts, see Note on 2 Kgs 2:22. The present day referred to need not always mean the era of Dtr but, rather, the time of the underlying tradition; here, a pre-586 date is plausible.

9. *There is nothing in the Ark save the two tablets of stone that Moses placed there at Horeb.* According to Deut 10:1–5, Moses followed the divine instruction to place the second set of tablets in the Ark. In contrast to the JE and P traditions that spoke of the Ark as YHWH's throne, D saw it as the repository of the covenant document; see Weinfeld 1972, 417–18. A late tradition (Heb 9:4) told of the jar of manna (cf. Exod 16:33) and Aaron's staff (cf. Num 17:25) also being in the Ark, in contrast to the earlier statements; see, too, Gersonides. Was there a question regarding what exactly was stored in the Ark that the present statement was countering? Qimḥi comments: "This is proof that neither the fragments of the (first) tablets nor the Book of the Covenant were in the Ark."

at Horeb. The toponym, favored by D, for Sinai; cf. Deut 1:2, 19; 5:2; and 1 Kgs 19:8.

when YHWH made a covenant with the Israelites when they left the land of Egypt. There is no need to add to MT (following Lucianic and LXX) *lḥwt hbryt*; Tg. also eased the syntax by adding *dʿlyhwn ktybyn ʿsrʾ ptgmyʾ qymʾ*, "upon which are inscribed the ten commandments of the covenant." For a similar ellipse, omitting the object, cf. 1 Sam 20:16; 22:8.

10. *As the priests left the sanctuary, the cloud filled the House of YHWH.* The cloud is the Priestly term for YHWH's physical appearance; cf. Exod 16:10; 33:9. Its amorphousness afforded a numinous quality fit for representing "the perceptible Presence [*kābôd*] of Deity" (Montgomery and Gehman).

11. *the priests could not stand in attendance because of the cloud, for the presence of YHWH had filled the House of YHWH.* Most others translate *kābôd*, "the Glory" (NAB, NEB, NRSV); but Heb *kābôd* is "essence, being, presence," whether used of the deity or a person (cf. Gen 49:6; see Speiser 1964, 365; Milgrom 1991, 588–89; Greenberg 1983b, 51 suggests "majesty"). According to

Priestly tradition, which is at the base of the present description, YHWH revealed himself in fire and cloud (Exod 24:17; Num 17:7). In the pericope describing the installation of the desert Tabernacle, the resting of the cloud upon it was the signal that YHWH had taken up residence in the newly completed Tent; cf. Exod 40:34. And Moses, like the priests in the present instance, was unable to enter the Tent of Meeting when the deity alighted thereupon; cf. 40:35. In all, it was felt that YHWH had exhibited his pleasure with the completed enterprise.

12. *Then Solomon said.* The editorial "then" introduces the insertion of a poetic quotation from an unnamed source; cf. the similar usages in Num 21:17; Josh 10:12. In LXX, vv. 12–13 appear after vv. 14–53, thus giving precedence to the king's prayer. The divergent and expanded reading of LXX is considered by many "superior to MT" (Burney) and "appears to be original" (Montgomery and Gehman). The retroverted text begins with an additional half-line: "The sun did YHWH make known (or, with Luc.: 'set') in heaven." Read together with MT, the poem declares: Though YHWH created the sun, he chose deep darkness as his dwelling, in the Temple prepared for him by Solomon. Still, the loss of this stich from MT has not been convincingly explained. For recent treatments, see Albright 1969a, 231; Görg 1974; Loretz 1974; Knauf 1997, 82–86.

In LXX, the poem ends with the notation: "At the dedication. Is it not written in the Book of Song?" This appears to be a reference to the source of the composition, similar to the notations in Josh 10:13 and 2 Sam 1:18 that credit their poetic lines to the *Book of Jashar* (*spr hyšr*). On this basis, Wellhausen (1899, 269; followed by many; note stricture of Montgomery and Gehman) corrected 1 Kgs 8:13 (LXX) "song" (*hšyr*) to read "Jashar" (*hyšr*).

YHWH intended. Hebrew *'āmar lĕ-* means "intend to" (cf. 1 Kgs 5:19); "promise" (2 Kgs 8:19).

thick cloud. Along with the fire and cloud, Heb *'ărāpel* is one of the expressions for the numinous quality of the divine presence; cf. Exod 20:21; Deut 4:11; 5:19; 2 Sam 22:10 // Ps 18:10; Job 22:13.

13. *I have indeed built a princely House for you.* Hebrew *zĕbûl* appears again in Isa 63:15 and Hab 3:11. The translation follows the usage in Ug in which *zbl*, "prince," is synonymous with "ruler" and is used in titles of deities: *zbl bʿl ʾrṣ*, "Prince Baal of the Earth," and *zbl ym*, "Prince Yam" (Albright 1936, 17–18); the translation "elevated, exalted" derives from the basic meaning of **zbl*, "to lift, carry, bear"; cf. Akk *zabālu*, "to carry, transport" (CAD Z, 1–6; see Held 1968, 90–92). See also the Note on 2 Kgs 1:2.

a place for your dwelling. Here, unlike Exod 15:17, the reference is to an earthly abode; this is in direct contrast to vv. 39, 43, 49; Ps 33:14, where the phrase refers to God's dwelling in the heavens. The reference to YHWH's abode in Exod 15:17 is to his heavenly home, which he made with his own hands. Cross and Freedman (1955, 240, 250) translate "dias for your throne," and compare the Ugaritic mythological motif of temple-building by the gods; see the later view of Cross (1973, 142–43). Note also that in Akk *parakku*, "dias, sanctuary" (AHw 827–28), refers to the dwelling place of the gods, the cella of

Mesopotamian shrines where the cult statue resided. Is the biblical phrase "a place for your dwelling" an allusion to a kindred concept, a reference to the Ark and the cherubs on which YHWH sat enthroned?

15. *He said: "Blessed be YHWH, God of Israel, who with his own mouth promised David my father and with his own hand fulfilled (his promise).* Solomon praises YHWH for having kept his promise, given by Nathan to David in 2 Sam 7; cf. 1 Kgs 8:16a and 2 Sam 7:6a; 1 Kgs 8:16b and 2 Sam 7:8–9.

Blessed be YHWH. Rather than calling down blessing upon YHWH, a somewhat presumptuous idea, the passive *bārûk* may be construed, like *rāḥûm* and *ḥannûn*, as epithets of the deity, acknowledging that He is the source and dispenser of all blessing. For a singular view on the development of the *bārûk*-formula through the various stages of Israelite religion, see Greenberg 1983a, 30–36.

16. *'From the day I brought my people Israel out from Egypt, I have not chosen a city out of all the tribes of Israel to build a house for my name to be there. . . .'* The statement echoes 2 Sam 7:6–7 but modifies it by noting YHWH's delay in choosing a city for his dwelling (and not his objection to a permanent habitation).

a house for my name. So, too, 1 Kgs 3:2; 5:18; 9:3 and throughout Dtr. See Note on v. 17 below.

but I chose David to be over my people Israel. The LXX[B] adds at the head of this clause: "but I have chosen Jerusalem that my name might be there"; cf. 2 Chr 6:6. This clause "corrects" history by giving precedence to the choosing of Jerusalem, while the earlier tradition (cf. 2 Sam 5:6–9) spoke of David's choice of the city. The LXX reading is accepted by many, but it is rejected by Stade, Montgomery and Gehman, Noth; recently, on the basis of a very small fragment, 4QKgs, which read the addition of Chronicles as part of Kings, Trebolle Barrera (1995, 171) opted for the originality of the addition, lost in MT due to homoioteleuton. If restored as original in Kings, it would be the only statement in the Dtr history to quote YHWH as declaring His choice of Jerusalem (cf. Ps 78:68; 132:13–14), indeed an ideological tenet missing from that writing.

17. *Now my father David had in mind to build a house for the name of YHWH, God of Israel.* Hebrew *hāyâ ʿim lĕbab*, lit., "be with the heart"; cf. also v. 18; 10:2; Deut 15:9; Josh 14:7; similarly *ʾăšer bilĕbab*, lit., "what is in the heart," cf. Deut 8:2; 1 Sam 9:19; 14:7; 2 Sam 7:3; 2 Kgs 10:30. For another perspective on David's plan to build the Temple, see Note on 1 Kgs 5:17.

for the name of YHWH, God of Israel. Inasmuch as Deuteronomy and the Deuteronomistic literature it inspired conceived of the deity in abstract terms, the Temple was the place solely for "the name of YHWH"; this contrasted with priestly conceptions of His "presence," represented by the cloud and fire that were the physical signs of His dwelling among men. See von Rad 1953, 37–44; Weinfeld 1972, 191–209; and further in Comment below.

19. *However, you shall not build the house, but your son who shall issue from your loins, he shall build the house for my name.* Further echoes of Nathan's prophecy; cf. 2 Sam 7:12–13.

who shall issue from your loins. That is, whom you shall father; cf. 2 Sam 7:12, "who issues from your body (*mm'yk*)."

21. *I have set a place there for the Ark in which is YHWH's covenant.* For the tablets of the covenant stored in the Ark, see above on v. 9.

22. *Solomon stood before the altar of YHWH opposite all the congregation of Israel.* Solomon assumed a posture of prayer; cf. the use of "stand before" in Jer 15:1; 18:20; Ps 106:30–31; Neh 9:2. The gesture and idiom apparently derive from "a court ceremony of showing deference to the king by standing in his presence"; see Gruber 1980, 146–51. See, too, the Note on 1 Kgs 1:2.

before the altar of YHWH. See Note below, on v. 64.

he spread his palms heavenward. A gesture expressive of need and help that takes on the sense of prayer and supplication; cf. Exod 9:29; Isa 1:15. Note, too, the equivalent phrases **nś² kpym*, lit., "raise the palms," in Lam 2:19; 3:41; **prś ydym*, "spread the hands," in Isa 65:2; Lam 1:17; **šṭḥ ydym*, "stretch forth the palms," Ps 88:10. The cognate Akkadian terms used in descriptions of Mesopotamians at prayer—*upnī petû*, "open fists"; *idī petû*, "open hands"; *qāta našû*, "lift up hand"—are studied by Gruber 1980, 50–89.

23. *and said: "YHWH, God of Israel, there is no god like you. . . ."* For the idea of the exclusivity of YHWH in Deuteronomic writing, cf. Deut 4:39; Josh 2:11; for the earlier idea that spoke of YHWH's superiority over the other gods, cf. Exod 15:11; Ps. 86:8.

keeping with loyalty the covenant. Literally, "the covenant and the loyalty" (*hbryt whhsd*); for *hesed* as the term for the steadfastness and constancy of a relationship, see Note on 1 Kgs 3:6. This Deuteronomic expression (cf. Deut 7:9, 12) seems to be attested on the large amulet from Ketef Hinnom in Jerusalem; see Barkai 1989, 52, lines 3–4, preceded by the word "love(r)," a term that connotes steadfastness.

who serve you wholeheartedly. Literally, "who walk before"; cf. 2:4; 3:6; 9:4.

24. *who kept your promise to your servant David my father; with your own mouth you promised and with your own hands you fulfilled, as it is today.* Solomon acknowledges that the promise of a son who would build a Temple has indeed come to pass; the promise of an everlasting dynasty was yet to be fulfilled.

25. *So, now, YHWH, God of Israel, keep your promise to your servant, David my father: 'No one of your line sitting on the throne of Israel shall be cut off at my instance, if your sons watch their way to serve me as you served me.'* A Deuteronomistic thought expressed earlier in David's testament; cf. 2:4 and Note there.

at my instance. Literally, "in front of me"; for this idiomatic sense expressing approval, cf. Gen 6:11 (and the remarks of Speiser 1964, ad loc.); Num 32:20–22.

26. *Now, then, ⟨YHWH,⟩ God of Israel.* The tetragram is added before "God of Israel," with LXX, as is common in many of the opening sections of this prayer (cf. vv. 15, 20, 23, 25).

27. *But, indeed, can God dwell on earth? Here the heavens and the highest heavens cannot contain you; how much less this House that I have built?* The Deuteronomistic conception in this verse contrasts with the anthropomorphic

idea of YHWH dwelling on earth, as declared in v. 13. Compare, too, the rejection of YHWH's earthly dwelling in Isa 66:1.

the highest heavens. Or, "the heavens of heavens"; cf. Deut 10:14; Ps 148:4; Neh 9:6; expressing the superlative, similar to *šyr hšyrym*, "the song of songs," i.e., the finest of songs. On the Mesopotamian conception of a three-tiered heaven and the residence of the gods in specific levels, see Lambert 1972–1975; Horowitz 1998, 243–67.

28. *the praise.* Hebrew *rinnâ*, from **rnn*, "a strong raising of the voice" (Ibn-Janah); it is both a "cry" of fright, as in 1 Kgs 22:36, and of joy, as in Isa 35:10 (// *śmḥh*, "happiness"); Ps 105:43 (// *śśwn*, "joy"); 126:2 (// *ṣhwq*, "laughter"); also in the Deuteronomistic passages in Jer 7:16; 11:14; 14:12. Praise suits the present context best; the opening of Solomon's prayer, as befitting of all the ensuing requests, began with praise of YHWH's incomparability (v. 23).

29. *that your eyes may be open toward this House night and day.* LXX and 2 Chr 6:20 have the reverse order "day and night," as does 1 Kgs 8:59 below. The present verse preserves the order of the ancient day, cf. Gen 1:5.

to the place of which you said: 'My name shall be there.' See note on v. 16.

30. *listen in your dwelling in heaven.* Literally, "at the place of your dwelling in heaven"; cf. the use of *'el* in 6:18 (Gray).

31. *If a man wrongs his neighbor.* The translation of the opening words in Hebrew *'ēt 'ăšer* (in 2 Chr 6:22: *'im*) by "if" simplifies a difficult construction. In other cases, *'ēt 'ăšer* introduces an object clause *after* the main clause (cf. Gen 30:29; Deut 9:7; 29:15; Josh 2:10).

and the latter utters an imprecation against him to curse him. The offended person requires of his fellow an exculpatory oath, the curse becoming operative only if he is not cleared. The MT (both Leningrad and Aleppo MSS) reads *wĕnāšā' bô 'ālâ lĕhaʾălōtô*, from **nšʾ/lh*, "exact, require"; though this verb is used with reference to monetary claims (cf. Deut 15:2; 24:10) and is unattested with other objects, it can be construed to mean: the wronged person forces an oath upon his fellow in order to prove his claimed innocence (so Rashi, Qimḥi; NAB, NEB). Other Heb MSS vocalize as if from **nśʾ*, "to carry, lift, utter," giving a more natural idiom; cf. *nśʾ 'l śptym* (Ps 16:4; also 50:16 [with *ph*]); so NJPSV.

an imprecation. Hebrew *'ālâ* is "curse, imprecation, adjuration" and in conjunction with *bĕrît*, "treaty, pact, oath," represents the sanctions that accompany and guarantee the terms of the agreement; cf. Deut 29:11, 13. See Brichto 1963, 22–76, esp. 53–55.

the curse is taken. The MT can hardly stand as is. If *wbʾ 'lh* is not a dittography of the preceding, then one of the following emendations may be adopted: *ûbāʾ bāʾālâ*, "he takes the oath" (cf. Neh 10:30), and *lĕhaʾălōtô bĕʾālâ* (Ehrlich, followed by Noth) are the easiest to construe.

before your altar in this House. Medieval commentators took the imprecation here as referring to the ordeal required of the suspect wife (Num 5:11–31); the term *'ālâ* appears in both cases. But in the instance projected by Solomon, there is no specification of the wrong by the first party or for YHWH's decision to be arrived at by means of an ordeal. Appeal was made directly to YHWH by prayer and, through a means unspecified (an oracle by the Urim and Thummim?), the parties came to know his decision.

32. *judge your servants, condemning the wicked . . . and acquitting the righteous.* The same ability to render just decisions is desirable in mortal judges; cf. Deut 25:1.

by bringing his way on his head. The idiom appears many times in Ezekiel; cf. Ezek 9:10; 11:21; 16:43; 22:31. See also 1 Kgs 2:44.

33. *When your people Israel are defeated by an enemy because they have sinned against you.* The common Near Eastern theology ascribed defeat to the national god; see, e.g., the Mesha Inscription (Cogan and Tadmor 1988, Appendix 1, no. 1); in Israel, this punishment was the result of abandoning YHWH's ways.

and then return to you and praise your name and pray and make supplication to you in this House. The "returning" in repentance to YHWH by Israel's routed army must be from the place of their detention outside the land, since v. 34 speaks of restoration to the land. In this regard, the final clause "in this House" is somewhat misleading because the supplicants are captives abroad; this might be better read *'el habbayit / hammāqôm hazzeh,* "to this House/place"; cf. vv. 29, 35, 38, 42.

35. *When the heavens are shut up and there is no rain, because they have sinned against you.* The promise of seasonal rains and the threat of drought as contingent upon Israel's loyalty to YHWH were expressed in the Mosaic oration in Deut 11:13–17; cf. also 28:24.

turning from their sin so that you answer them. The MT vocalizes *tā'ănēm;* so Tg., Syr.; Luc. and LXX vocalize *tĕ'annēm,* "when you humble them," followed by many modern scholars. This may be preferable, considering that "answer them" precedes the call on YHWH to pardon. Gersonides sought a third way, taking **'nh* in the sense of "testify, bear witness," as in Ps 55:20 (which is better rendered "chastise").

37. *if there be blight, mildew.* This pair of agricultural calamities also appears in Deut 28:22; Amos 4:9; Hag 2:17. Hebrew *šiddāpôn* is properly "blasting," the withering result of the scorching east wind (cf. Gen 41:6; 2 Kgs 19:26). Its opposite is Heb *yērāqôn,* lit., "greenness, yellowness," a crop condition caused by the overabundance of rain, hence mildew (following Hareuveni 1929). In Jer 30:6, the same term is used for "jaundice" in humans.

locusts. Hebrew *'arbeh* is the general term for locusts; cf. the vivid description in Joel 1 of one such onslaught and its destructive consequences; also Exod 10:13–15. See discussion in Cogan 1994, 25–28.

hoppers. Hebrew *ḥāsîl,* so named because it "consumes, liquidates" (< **ḥsl*) everything in its path, probably represents one of the growth stages of the locust; other stages are indicated by the terms *gāzām,* lit., "cutter," and *yeleq,* "grub;" cf. Joel 1:4. On the inter-Semitic semantics of **ḥsl,* see Held 1965, 398–401.

if their enemy presses upon them. Hebrew *yāṣar,* imperfect *Hiphil* of **ṣrr,* "to press, restrict"; cf. Deut 28:52; Neh 9:27; 2 Chr 28:20 (and not from **ṣwr,* "besiege").

in one of their cities. The MT: "in the land of their cities" is indeed "very forced and unnatural" (Burney). The Deuteronomic expression "in one of their cities" (cf. Deut 15:7; 16:5; 17:2; 23:17) is read in Luc., LXX, Syr.

38. *each of whom knows his own affliction.* Literally, "the plague of his heart." Whatever the particular "personal" (Qimḥi) illness may be, the person turns to YHWH out of the realization that his affliction is from him. The pl. verb *ydʿwn* would better be read as a sg. in line with the following sg. *prś;* the pl. may have been influenced by the pl. verbs in the following vv. 42, 43 (also *ydʿwn*).

39–40. *forgive and act. Render to each man according to his ways as you will know his heart, for you alone know the hearts of all men, so that they may fear you all the days that they live on the land that you gave to our ancestors.* Cure in response to prayer will prove to the supplicant that his affliction was God-sent and that YHWH is indeed the source of forgiveness (Qimḥi).

41. *Moreover, to the foreigner.* The non-Israelite is here the *nokrî,* the occasional visitor to Israel or one who dwells abroad, in contrast to the "alien" (Heb *gēr*), who resides with the Israelites in their land.

who is not of your people Israel, who shall come from a distant land because of your name. The Naaman tale (2 Kgs 5, especially v. 17) exemplifies the spread of YHWH's fame; cf. the acknowledgment of YHWH by the queen of Sheba (1 Kgs 10:9) and the sailors of Jonah's ship (Jonah 1:16).

42. *for they shall hear of your great name and your strong hand and your outstretched arm.* These images of YHWH's mighty acts, either singly or in combination, appear often in Deuteronomy and later Deuteronomistic writing; cf. Deut 4:34; 5:15; 7:19; 11:2; 26:8; Jer 21:5 (note the reversal of adjectives!); a "strong arm" alone occurs in JE; cf. Exod 6:1; 32:11.

who shall come and pray toward this House. Presence in the Temple was not required of the Israelite or of the foreigner.

43. *your name is proclaimed over this House that I have built.* Proclaiming the name over a structure indicated possession and ownership; cf. the act of conquest at Rabbath-Ammon in 2 Sam 12:27–28; the Ark of YHWH in 2 Sam 6:2; with reference to a person or people, cf. Deut 28:10; Isa 4:1; Amos 9:12. For the related phrase "to place his name," see Note on v. 17 above, and Weinfeld 1972, 193.

44. *When your people go out to war against their enemy, wherever you shall send them.* Before setting out to battle, the approval of the deity was sought (cf. Num 27:21); thus war became an act undertaken at the instance of YHWH — as, for example, the wars of Canaan; cf. Deut 2:24.

in the direction of the city. Literally, "way"; cf. 1 Kgs 18:43.

45. *and act justly toward them.* Also vv. 49, 59; cf. Deut 10:18; Mic 7:9; Ps 9:5. The translation "maintain their cause" (KJV, NRSV) suggests "partiality to Israel" (Gray), but this misrepresents YHWH, who was known for his "just" behavior (cf. Deut 32:4; Isa 61:8).

46. *When they sin against you — for there is no person who does not sin.* An idea expressed again in Qoh 7:20.

and you are angry at them. The *Hithpael* of **'np* is more frequent in Deuteronomy and Dtr writing; cf. Deut 1:37; 4:21; 9:8, 20; 1 Kgs 11:9; 2 Kgs 17:18. *Qal* is the preferred form in Psalms; cf. Ps 60:3; 79:5; 85:6; also Isa 12:1.

and deliver them to an enemy who carries them off as captives to his country, far or near. Note the paronomasia in the choice of verbs in this verse and the following two: *wšbwm, šbyhm, whšybw, nšbw, šm, wšbw, šbyhm, wšbw, npšm, šbw.*

Exiles were usually carried off to distant lands, yet at times they were taken to locations close to their original homes. For example, the settlers brought to Samaria came from Hamath in Syria, as well as from Babylon and Susa (see Note on 2 Kgs 17:24).

to his country, far or near. Literally, "to the land of the enemy." The omission of "the enemy" in LXX and 2 Chr 6:36 eases the grammar of MT, the definite followed by two undefined adjectives.

47. *and then they take it to heart.* Or "reflect," lit., "bring back to their heart"; cf. Deut 4:39; 30:1; Lam 3:21; in Isa 44:19, the idiom is parallel to "know" (*yd'w*) and "understand" (*ybynw*).

We have sinned and we have acted perversely ⟨and⟩ we have acted wickedly. In Ps 106:6 and Dan 9:15 a similar string of verbs stands asyndetically.

48. *If they return to you with all their heart and with all their soul.* Deuteronomic phraseology; cf. Deut 4:29–30; 30:10; 2 Kgs 23:25.

if they pray to you in the direction of their land that you gave their ancestors, the city that you chose and the House that I have built for your name. Daniel's prayer (Dan 6:11) is an early example of turning toward the land of Israel and Jerusalem during prayer; cf. also 1 Esd 4:58; Tob 3:11.

50. *cause their captors to have mercy upon them so that they will show them mercy.* Though not explicitly expressed, the ultimate mercy would be a speedy return to their land; cf. Ps 106:46–47; Neh 1:11.

51. *For they are your people and your inheritance.* The idea that the people of Israel were YHWH's portion is well rooted in Deuteronomic thought; cf. Deut 4:20; 9:26, 29; and is related to the redemptive act of the Exodus; cf. also Deut 32:9; below v. 53; see Loewenstamm 1986. "People" and "inheritance" appear as a word pair in parallelism; cf. Isa 47:6; Joel 2:17; 4:2; Mic 7:14; Ps 28:9; 78:62, 71; 94:5, 14; 106:4–5, 40.

iron furnace. Egypt, mostly known as a "slave house," was compared in Deuteronomic circles to a blast furnace used for smelting iron ore, so harsh were the conditions of life; cf. Deut 4:20; Jer 11:4.

52. *so may your eyes be open.* The opening infinitive verb does not connect with the preceding verse or verses; 2 Chr 6:40 and LXX ease this by reading *yhyw.*

53. *For you have set them apart for yourself as an inheritance out of all the peoples of the earth.* Israel's selection is spoken of in these terms in Lev 20:24, 26; cf. also Exod 19:5.

54. *When Solomon finished offering all this prayer and supplication to YHWH, he rose from before the altar of YHWH, from kneeling with his hands spread heavenward.* Kneeling suggests humility and obeisance; it mostly appears

with reference to praying (e.g., 1 Kgs 19:18; Ps 95:6; Ezra 9:5) but also is an act acknowledging superiors (e.g., 2 Kgs 1:13; Esth 3:2 [without "knees"]). Examples of prostration in Mesopotamian rituals are rife; see CAD Š/3, 215 (s.v. *šukênu*); in submission to royalty, CAD Š/3, 315–16 (s.v. *šupālu*). Solomon's upright position in v. 22 seems to contradict the present description and has been taken as a sign of the composite nature of the chapter. But standing and kneeling are orientations appropriate to different moments of prayer; cf. Neh 9:2–5; see Ap-Thomas 1956; Levenson 1981, 156. See also the depiction on a cult socle of the Middle Assyrian king Tukulti-Ninurta I (1243–1207 BCE) as both standing and kneeling before the symbol of the god Nusku in ANEP 576. Considering this, the Chronicler's developed portrayal (2 Chr 6:13) may only be an amplification (otherwise Japhet 1993, 590).

he rose. The MT *qām* in the perfect is hardly good grammar; *wyqm* is expected.

55. *he stood and blessed all the congregation of Israel in a loud voice.* Solomon calls for YHWH's blessing upon the assembled.

56. *who has given rest to his people Israel.* According to the Deuteronomic view, the era of "rest" was to have begun with the completion of Israel's wars of conquest, cf. Deut 12:9; Josh 21:42; in the revised Dtr vision, it was ushered in during Solomon's days, cf. 1 Kgs 5:18.

Not one word of all the good things that he promised through his servant Moses has gone unfulfilled. For this Dtr phrase, cf. Josh 21:43; 23:14; 2 Kgs 10:10.

58. *May he turn our hearts toward him, to follow all his ways and keep his commands and his statutes and his laws that he commanded our ancestors.* An admission that God's gracious support will be needed in the future in order to ensure Israel's obedience to His law; cf. Ps 119:36.

59. *as each day requires.* This idiom is used of "daily allowance" in 2 Kgs 25:30.

60. *so that all the peoples of the earth shall know that YHWH, he is God; there is no other.* YHWH's fame in the world would be broadcast by his just dealing with Israel.

YHWH, he is God; there is no other. So too Deut 4:35, 39; 7:9. Because the affirmation "there is no other (beside him)" is so frequent in the polemics of Second Isaiah (Isa 45:5, 6, 14, 18, 21, 22; 46:9), Weinfeld sees this as evidence for late (i.e., exilic) origin (1972, 212). But the use of this phrase in the spontaneous outcry of the people at Mt. Carmel (cf. 1 Kgs 18:39) suggests that it may have been a traditional creedal exclamation.

61. *May your heart be fully with YHWH our God.* Or "wholehearted." Also in 1 Kgs 11:4; 15:3, 14; see Note on 2 Kgs 20:3.

62. *Now the king and all Israel with him offered sacrifice before YHWH.* At first glance, the present verse may look like a resumptive repetition of v. 5, bracketing all of the material in between (so, Long, 106; also Noth; Mulder); but the terms used in the two verses are not strictly equivalent, one of the signs of resumptive structures; *mĕzabbĕḥîm* (v. 5) versus *zōbĕḥîm* (v. 62); *ṣō'n ûbāqār* (v. 5) versus *zebaḥ* (v. 62); *hammelek šĕlōmōh wĕkol 'ădat yiśrā'ēl* (v. 5) versus *hammelek*

wĕkol yiśrā'ēl (v. 62). The sacrifices referred to in v. 5 were offered in honor of the Ark; in v. 62, they marked the inauguration of the House of YHWH. Furthermore, the focus on sacrifice, a topic lacking from the lengthy Dtr prayer just completed, suggests that the source of this description is the pre-Dtr source; see Comment.

63. *Solomon offered the sacrifice of well-being, in which he offered to YHWH twenty-two thousand oxen and one hundred twenty thousand sheep.* Most commentators discount the figures as editorial imaginings, an amplification for the greater glory of the king. The comparisons sometimes made with large gatherings in Assyria (e.g., Wiseman), aimed at bearing out Solomon's feast, are irreconcilable with the reality of early Israel as presently reconstructible.

Solomon offered the sacrifice. The active participation of the king in the cultic ritual (cf. below, v. 64) does not make him a priest; his part is no different from that of David (2 Sam 6:18), Jeroboam (1 Kgs 12:32), and Ahaz (2 Kgs 16:12–15), all of whom officiated, by dint of their rank, on special occasions (see de Vaux 1961, 113–14).

Thus, the king and all the Israelites inaugurated the house of YHWH. Others translate "dedicated." But Heb **ḥnk* refers to beginnings, e.g., the early education of a child, its "first" steps (cf. Prov 22:6); to the "start" of living in a new house (cf. Deut 20:5); and to the "inauguration" of the Tabernacle (cf. Num 7:10), the Temple (1 Kgs 8:63), and the wall of Jerusalem (Neh 12:27); this meaning was recognized by Rashi; Qimḥi; see Reif 1972.

64. *On that day, the king consecrated the center of the court that was in front of the House of YHWH.* A onetime sanctification of the rock surface surrounding the altar was needed to overcome the pressure of the multitudes who are described as having been in attendance at the ceremonies.

the bronze altar that was before YHWH. This altar was not noted among the items fashioned by Hiram in 1 Kgs 7; it appears in the list in 2 Chr 4:1 between the two bronze columns (2 Chr 3:15–17 // 1 Kgs 7:15–22) and the Sea (2 Chr 4:2–5 // 1 Kgs 7:23–26). The omission in Kings is striking, since the altar is again mentioned in 9:25; furthermore, a story concerning its replacement is prominently included in 2 Kgs 16:10–16 (where the altar's small size is also at issue). It is hard to imagine that Dtr thought that David's altar (cf. 2 Sam 24:25) was somehow incorporated into Solomon's Temple but chose not to include one word about its deposition (Montgomery and Gehman speculate that this was David's altar, refurbished by Solomon). See, at length, Mulder, 454–55. The simplest solution to this conundrum is to assume a textual omission in 1 Kgs 7. [DNF: "The best solution is whole-word haplography. Note that in 2 Chr 4:1–2 each verse begins with the same word *wayya'aś*. The scribe's eye simply jumped from the first *wy'ś* to the second *wy'ś*, thus leaving out a whole sentence."]

65. *At that time.* On this editorial phrase, loosely joining units, see the Note on 1 Kgs 3:16.

Solomon celebrated the Festival. That is, Sukkoth, the Festival of Tabernacles, as noted earlier in v. 2; cf. Neh 8:14. The inaugural celebration may have been coordinated with Sukkoth for the pratical purposes noted above in v. 2; in later times, this festive season of pilgrimage to the Temple city was turned to use for public convocations; cf. Deut 31:10–13; Neh 9:1.

from Lebo-hamath to the Wadi of Egypt. For the identification of Lebo-hamath in the northern Lebanese Beqa', see Note on 2 Kgs 14:25 (to which add: Röllig 1980–1983); for the "Wadi of Egypt" as the "border of Egypt," see Note on 1 Kgs 5:1; and, on its identification with Wadi el-Arish, see Note on 2 Kgs 24:7. Another set of borders is given in 1 Kgs 5:1.

before YHWH our God. Though the phrase is typical of Dtr (cf. vv. 57, 59, 61), it is most unusual for the narrator to speak in the first person. The addition in Luc. and LXX, though accepted by many, is probably superfluous: *bbyt 'šr bnh 'kl wšth wśmḥ* (Luc. adds: *wmhll*) *lpny yhwh 'lhynw,* "in the house that he built, eating and drinking, rejoicing (and praising) YHWH our God."

seven days and seven days. The following verse, in which the people are sent home on the eighth day, indicates that the second "seven days" in the present verse is secondary; indeed, Luc. and LXX have only "seven days." The addition may be an intrusion from 2 Chr 7:9, which reported a fourteen-day celebration, a week for the inauguration of the altar (!), which was followed by the week of Sukkoth. (The Chronicler reports a similar extension of the Passover celebration during Hezekiah's reign; cf. 2 Chr 30:23; comparison to Solomon's festivities is specifically noted in v. 26.)

66. *On the eighth day, he dismissed the people.* The Deuteronomic festal law (Deut 16:13, 15) did not know of the solemn gathering prescribed for the eighth day of Sukkoth (cf. Lev 23:36; Num 29:35); the matter is rectified in 2 Chr 7:9–10. Medieval commentators adopted the Chronicles calendar and masked the dismissal on the final day of the festival.

they blessed the king. In the LXX: "he blessed it" (the people?); cf. 2 Sam 6:18.

They went home. Literally, "to the tents"; cf. 1 Kgs 12:16.

happy and glad at heart. The combination appears again in Esth 5:9. Hebrew *ṭôb lēb* refers to cheer and lightheartedness, such as comes from drinking (Qoh 9:7; Esth 1:10; Ruth 3:7) and constant partying (Prov 15:15), as well as pleasure over an accomplishment (Judg 16:25; 18:20). See also 1 Kgs 21:7. In Deut 28:47, the picture of satiety as YHWH's gift to his followers stands in contrast to hunger and thirst, the lot of people taken captive by their enemies.

COMMENT

Structure and Themes

The presentation of the inauguration of the Temple in 1 Kgs 8 is a parade example in M. Noth's classic thesis of the periodization of history as seen by the Deuteronomist. Deuteronomistic historiography directed attention to major turning points in Israel's history by the address of the generation's leader, who surveyed the past and pointed to the new era about to open. In the present instance, Solomon is depicted as offering praise to YHWH for fulfilling His promise to David, as he, the king, fulfilled his destiny to build a House for YHWH, which was now to become the focus for Israel's worship (Noth 1981, 9).

The overall structure of 1 Kgs 8 is easily discernible and follows an agenda typical of such ceremonies (in view of similar celebrations in Mesopotamia, as shown by Hurowitz 1992, 260–77). Three acts are played out: (1) the Temple is formally inaugurated by the introduction of the Ark in the Holy of Holies (vv. 1–13); (2) the king offers blessings for the assembled and a prayer to YHWH concerning the role of the Temple (vv. 14–61); (3) celebration (vv. 62–66).

Act 1. The opening unit (vv. 1–11) recounts the ceremonial transfer of the Ark of the Covenant from the City of David, where it had resided since the reign of David, to the Holy of Holies of the Temple. Through the image of the divine presence in the cloud, YHWH is depicted as taking up residence in his House (vv. 10–11), an appropriate foreshadowing of Solomon's Presentation Prayer in vv. 12–13, in which he states YHWH's preference for dwelling in thick darkness (Ehrlich). These short poetic lines preserve a pre-Dtr view of the Temple as YHWH's earthly home (contrast vv. 13 and 27), in terms that are part of the oldest biblical poetry. A rich scholarly debate regarding the genre of this prayer—"a Canaanite poetic tradition . . . or even a song book in Israel . . . or perhaps a typical household dedicatory speech . . . or even a type of praise song with analogues in Egyptian literature . . ." (Long 1984, 97)—has not led to a consensus.

Considering that the inauguration of the Temple was a foundational moment in the history of the Israelite cult, it is not surprising to find that several traditions converge at this juncture, each underscoring its particular perspective on the event. From the overloaded descriptions (e.g., the diversity of designations for those in attendance: "the elders of Israel—all the heads of the tribes, the ancestral chieftains" [v. 1]; "the men of Israel" [v. 2]; "the whole assembly of Israel" [v. 5]) and an examination of the language, it seems that an older text (from the *Book of the Deeds of Solomon*? [so Noth]) had been worked up by Dtr, which was later glossed by a Priestly writer. Contrary to older opinion that the shortened text of Luc. and LXX preserved the pre-Priestly redaction (see Burney, at length), it has been shown (Hurowitz 1992, 262–66) that the Greek text shortens both Dtr and P elements; therefore, it is not a witness to an earlier Hebrew version of these verses. It is possible, however, to speak of a one-time Priestly revision, whose purpose was to point up the legitimacy of the Solomonic Temple as heir to the desert Tabernacle by reference to the Tent of Meeting and its sacred vessels. The Temple ceremony became, as it were, a second inauguration, parallel to the one described in Num 7:1–2, in which all of the tribal leadership (*kwl r'šy hmṭwt*) participated (see Knoppers 1995, 240–42).

Act 2. Solomon's prayer (vv. 27–53) is crafted for maximum effect on the listener; in reality, there is a dual audience: YHWH, the ostensive addressee, and the community of Israel, those in attendance at the inauguration and those who would later hear/read this composition. A hymn of praise, thanking YHWH for fulfilling His promise to David (vv. 15–21), precedes the prayer and is

complemented by a personal petition imploring YHWH to keep His promise
with respect to dynasty (vv. 23–26). Surprisingly, Solomon's words lack a votive,
quid pro quo feature; inasmuch as the Temple is not the residence of YHWH,
the king cannot expect reciprocal blessing for his good deed. He must rely on
YHWH's remaining faithful to the promise made to David. Moving from here
to the prayer's central theme, Solomon avers the incompatibility of the two
conceptions of YHWH's absolute transcendence and His dwelling on earth.
The solution: the Temple will serve as the focal point for Israel's prayers, to which
YHWH will direct His attention (vv. 27–30). Just as YHWH need not inhabit
the House in order for Him to hear these appeals, all people, *in imitatio dei*,
will be able to turn to Him under all circumstances and from all locations and
feel assured that they will be answered.

Following this creedal statement, seven hypothetical occasions that may
prompt persons' turning to YHWH through the Temple are outlined: (1) dis-
putes among Israelites that require an oath at the Temple's altar (vv. 31–32);
(2) defeat and capture of Israel's forces by an enemy (vv. 33–34); (3) drought
(vv. 35–36); (4) miscellaneous natural disasters (vv. 37–40); (5) prayer by foreign admirers of YHWH (vv. 41–43); (6) prayer for victory before battle (vv. 44–
45); (7) prayer by repentant exiles (vv. 46–51). In each case, the worshiper is
assured that YHWH will hear his or her case and act justly, for Israel enjoys a
special relationship with YHWH, reaching back to its selection and deliverance from Egypt (vv. 52–53). A large number of the situations envisioned are
reminiscent of the covenant curses spelled out in Deut 28; cf. e.g., 1 Kgs 8:33
// Deut 28:25; 1 Kgs 8:35 // Deut 28:23–24; 1 Kgs 8:37 // Deut 28:21, 22, 27, 35,
38, 39, 42, 59–61; 1 Kgs 8:46 // Deut 28:36–37, 64–68, further evidence of the
prayer's Deuteronomistic composition.

The scholarly disagreement on the date of composition of Solomon's prayer
(vv. 22–53) revolves around the question of a single or multiple edition of the
Dtr history.[1] The reference to exiles' praying toward the Temple (vv. 44–51) is
considered proof of an exilic date by those who argue for a single exilic edition
of Kings (Noth). Those who hold that Kings is basically a preexilic work by
Dtr$_1$ view these references as stemming from the hand of the exilic Dtr$_2$ (Cross
1973, 287; Levenson [1981] accepts the double redaction of Kings but argues
that the prayer is a single exilic [Dtr$_2$] composition[2]). Others contend that the
threat of exile was a fact of life in Israel throughout the days of the resurgent
Neo-Assyrian Empire, and so the Exile is not a usable marker for the date of

---

[1] Kaufmann (1960, 268 n. 1), alone of all modern critics, denied the Deuteronomistic nature
of Solomon's prayer, since it does not refer to the centralization of worship. Besides overlooking
the Dtr idiom that pervades the composition (see Weinfeld 1972, 36 n. 2), Kaufmann did not consider the implication of the repeated statement that all prayer is to be directed toward the one
Temple in Jerusalem, taking for granted that, with its inauguration, all other sanctuaries had
become null and void.

[2] First Kings 8:44–53 cannot easily be classed with other Dtr$_2$ passages; cf., e.g., Deut 4:25–31
and 30:1–10, which project a different basis for exile and return: Israel, scattered among the
nations, repents of the idolatrous ways it had led and returns to a forgiving YHWH.

composition.[3] Strengthening the preexilic position is the absence of even the slightest hint that prayer was to be directed to a Temple that lay in ruins, that vast numbers of Israelites languish in exile, or that the Davidic dynasty had been effectively terminated. Absent, as well, is reference to the sacrificial cult that was practiced in this central sanctuary. Consequently, Solomon's prayer might well be viewed as the composition of the preexilic Dtr_1, containing the prescription for a reconstituted cult in which prayer replaced the ubiquitous sacrifices in Josiah's reforms. Sacrifices had been outlawed by Josiah for Judeans who lived outside the Temple city (see Weinfeld 1972, 44–45).

Solomon's closing blessing of the people (vv. 54–61) is in effect a further call upon YHWH to grant them the mind to live by His ways.[4] In terms of formal structure, the pattern of two blessings of the people (vv. 14, 55), with an intervening personal prayer, is also reported during the Tabernacle inaugural; cf. Lev 9:22–23 (see Milgrom 1991, 588 ad Lev 9:23; Hurowitz 1992, 287–88).

Act 3. Sacrifice and rejoicing by the multitudes who had assembled for the ceremonies and the week of the Festival of Sukkoth conclude the report.

History

Because the major part of 1 Kgs 8 stems from Dtr and later annotators, and only a few verses seem to reach back to the early days of the monarchy (particularly vv. 12–13), only the barest outline of the inauguration of the Jerusalem Temple is retrievable. Solomon's central role in the ceremonies is not an editorial creation *de novo*; it is in line with the well-established ancient Near Eastern tradition in which the monarch, after the completion of the construction of a temple, offered sacrifice and prayers to the deity for his personal as well as the national welfare (Hurowitz 1992, 291–300; also Weinfeld 1972, 35–37). In this final act, Solomon brought to fulfillment the transformation of Israel's cult that had begun under David by the transfer of the Ark of the Covenant to Jerusalem (2 Sam 6). Though the Temple is customarily referred to as a "royal chapel," due both to its relatively small size and its proximity to the palace, the installation of the Ark within its confines gave it an all-Israel character. By this move, whatever Canaanite-Phoenician features the physical building may have incorporated were henceforth associated exclusively with YHWH. At the same time, centralization of the cult and pilgrimage to the Holy Mountain in Deuteronomistic terms were still generations away.

---

[3] On this basis, Gray (214) observed that the deportation in v. 34 could refer to Israelite exiles from Samaria; vv. 44–53 are an expansion of the theme by a later redactor.

[4] This blessing is lacking in 2 Chr 6, an omission that is commonly taken as a sign that the Chronicler took exception to the king's blessing the people, a task assigned to the priests in the postexilic Temple (so, e.g., Burney; Montgomery, and Gehman). But Solomon's first blessing of them is reported as it was in Kings (cf. 2 Chr 6:3; also 1 Chr 16:2), and thus, another explanation for this absence (e.g., textual accident such as haplography [DNF]) ought to be sought.

XII. YHWH'S SECOND APPEARANCE TO SOLOMON

(9:1–9)

9 ¹Now when Solomon had completed building the House of YHWH and the king's house and everything that Solomon's desire wished to do, ²YHWH appeared to Solomon a second time, as he had appeared to him in Gibeon. ³YHWH said to him: "I have heard your prayer and your supplication that you have made before me. I have consecrated this House that you have built to place my name there forever, and my eyes and my heart shall be there for all time. ⁴As for you, if you will walk before me as David your father walked with integrity and with uprightness, doing all that I commanded you, keep ᵃmy statutes and my rules, ⁵then I will establish your royal throne over Israel forever, as I promised concerning David your father: 'No one of your line shall be cut off from the throne of Israel.' ⁶But if you turn from me, you and your children, and do not keep my commands (and)ᵇ my statutes that I have given you, and you go and worship other gods and bow down to them, ⁷then I will cut Israel off the land that I have given them, and I will dismiss this House that I have consecrated for my name. Israel shall become a proverb and a byword among all the peoples. ⁸And this House will be a ruin;ᶜ everyone who passes by will be appalled and whistle. And when they say: 'Why did YHWH do this to this land and to this House?' ⁹they will be told: 'Because they forsook YHWH their God, who brought their fathers out of the land of Egypt, and embraced other gods and bowed to themᵈ and worshiped them. Therefore YHWH brought all this evil upon them.'"

ᵃ Second Chronicles 7:17 and versions read *wḥqy*, "and my statues"; see Note.
ᵇ Some MSS and versions read *wḥqty*; cf. 2 Chr 7:19 (*ḥqwty wmṣwty*).
ᶜ Read *'yyn* for MT *'lywn*; see Note.
ᵈ Qere: *wyšthww* (pl.); ketib: *wyšthw* (sg.).

NOTES

9 1. *Now when Solomon had completed building the House of YHWH and the king's house.* Though this introductory clause places the ensuing revelation after the completion of all of Solomon's projects (close to midway in his reign; cf. the dates in 6:38 and 7:1), contextually, YHWH's word is in reply to Solomon's prayer at the dedication of the Temple; note especially 9:2 and 8:54.

and everything that Solomon's desire wished to do. There is no merit in emending Heb *ḥēšeq*, "desire" to *ḥēpeṣ* so that it complements the verb *ḥāpēṣ*, "wished," or vice versa, correcting *ḥāpēṣ* to *ḥāšaq* (cf. v. 19). While *ḥšq* is not a common verb, it is known; cf. Isa 21:4.

2. *YHWH appeared to Solomon a second time, as he had appeared to him in Gibeon.* In response to Solomon's sacrifice and prayer at Gibeon, YHWH granted the king wisdom and honor for the successful rule of his kingdom (1 Kgs 3:4–15); in the present instance, YHWH responds to his prayer and sacrifice with a warning, rather than a further gift.

in Gibeon. The site of revelation is not specified, but there is no reason to suppose that it was Gibeon (so DeVries) rather than Jerusalem.

3. *YHWH said to him: "I have heard your prayer and your supplication that you have made before me. . . ."* See 8:54 and the numerous instances throughout the dedication prayer that refer to YHWH's receipt of prayer directed to Him (vv. 28, 34, 39, 45, 49). The addition in Luc. and LXX: "Now I do for you according to all your prayer" is seen as genuine by some (Skinner, Burney) and secondary by others (Noth); cf. 2 Chr 7:15–16 for a different sort of expansion.

I have consecrated this House that you have built to place my name there forever. A unique idea. It is usually a human who dedicates (Heb *hiqdîš*) gifts to God (cf., e.g., 2 Sam 8:11); here it is God who endows the gift presented to Him with holiness (the same Hebrew verb), apparently meaning that He has agreed to receive Solomon's gift and take up residence in the Temple (cf. 1 Kgs 8:10–11).

and my eyes and my heart shall be there for all time. Unlike 8:29, 52, where YHWH is asked to be awake ("open-eyed") to Israel's prayers, here He promises not to stray after other concerns but to be continually focused on His dwelling; cf. Num 15:39 for eyes and heart as the cause of improper turning from YHWH.

4. *As for you, if you will walk before me as David your father walked with integrity and with uprightness.* The behavior of David, founder of the dynasty and recipient of YHWH's promise, served as the yardstick by which all of his successors were measured; for a singular reservation of this approbation, cf. 15:5.

walk before me. That is, serve me; cf. 8:23.

with integrity and with uprightness. A wisdom expression used of David in Ps 78:72; it is also used of Job in 1:1, 8 (without *lēb*).

keep my statutes. The addition of *waw* in 2 Chr 7:17 and the versions eases the asyndetic construction, but other examples of its use are found in this section; cf. vv. 3a and 6 (Noth).

5. *then I will establish your royal throne over Israel forever, as I promised concerning David your father.* The promise of an eternal dynasty was delivered by Nathan in 2 Sam 7:13, repeated by David in his deathbed will in 1 Kgs 2:4, referred to by Solomon in his dedication prayer in 8:25, and is here reinforced by God in a warning, soon to be violated. On the question of the conditionality of the promise, see Comment to 2:4.

concerning David. Hebrew ʿal, as in 2:4; correction to ʾel (with many MSS) is pedantic.

'No one of your line shall be cut off from the throne of Israel.' Cf. Note on 2:4; 8:25; Jer 33:17, 18; 35:19.

the throne of Israel. The Deuteronomist uses this term with reference, not only to kings of the United Monarchy but, after the secession of Israel, to kings of the Northern Kingdom (cf. 2 Kgs 10:30; 15:12), though here it can only be the Davidic dynasty that he has in mind.

6. *my commands (and) my statutes.* The asyndetic construction of MT is eased in the versions and some MSS; if original, the *waw* could easily have been lost through haplography, since *yod* (in the previous word) and *waw* are all but identical in the square script; cf. also Gen 26:5 and 2 Kgs 17:13.

7. *then I will cut Israel off the land that I have given them.* That is, send them into exile, as the next clause explains. Not a common Dtr phrase; cf. 1 Sam 20:15; Zeph 1:3.

I will dismiss this House that I have consecrated for my name. Or "renounce, disown." Literally, "I will send away," a most unusual locution, in which the Temple, and not Israel as would be expected, is the object of *šillaḥ* (e.g., Jer 15:1). In 2 Chr 7:20, the verb *hišlîk* replaces *šalaḥ*, in line with the expression as it appears in other Deuternomistic verses; cf. 2 Kgs 13:23; 17:20; 24:20.

a proverb and a byword. A Deuteronomic expression; cf. Deut 28:37; Jer 24:9. Hebrew *šĕnînâ*, "a byword," is properly a sharp, pointed remark; cf. the verbal use in Deut 6:7, with the sense "to incise"; hence, "Drill them into your children" (NAB); "Impress them upon your children" (NJPSV). Others take **šnn* as an alternate form of **šnh*, "teach, repeat"; thus, "an object of repeated discussion" (Tigay 1996, 266).

8. *And this House will be a ruin.* Reading *ʿyyn* for MT *ʿlywn* "will be high (*ʿelyôn*)," which is contextually impossible. Second Chronicles 7:21 reads, "and this House that was high," which is not much better; nor is "as for this high House" (cf. Luc.). Targum "and this house that was high shall be a ruin" may preserve a double reading, *hyh ʿlywn* and *yhyh lʿyyn*. For Heb *ʿyyn/m*, "ruin," used in descriptions of destruction, cf. Mic 3:12 and Jer 26:18.

everyone who passes by will be appalled and whistle. A proverbial image favored by Jeremiah; cf. Jer 18:16; 19:8—with reference to Israel; 49:17—to Edom; 50:13—to Babylon; cf. Zeph 2:15, referring to Nineveh; cf. also Ezek 27:36; Lam 2:15. The passersby in the present verse are foreigners (see v. 9), because Israel has been sent away from the land into Exile; cf. also Deut 29:23. This figure also appears in the inscriptions of Ashurbanipal (the same age as most of the biblical references) regarding Arabia, which is the cause of wonderment to all who observe its destruction; cf. ANET, 300.

will whistle. Rather than take this act as intending "to ward off a like fate" (NJPSV), the astonished observer seems to be expressing his consternation, further shown by shaking the head and clapping the hands in Lam 2:15; see Greenberg 1997, 564 ad Ezek 27:36. "The horrific wounds inflicted on Jerusalem will appal those who see them, and a sharp expelling of the breath, indicative of the terror which the sight inspires, will issue as a kind of whistling" (McKane 1986, 453).

And when they say: 'Why did YHWH do this to this land and to this House?' Compare with Deut 29:23–27; Jer 22:8–9. The question-and-answer sequence as it appears in the Assyrian text cited above (ANET, 300) explains the destruction as divine punishment for nonobservance of treaty obligations, there in regard to the Assyrian monarch; in Deuteronomic writing, it regards the breach of YHWH's covenant.

9. *and embraced other gods.* Literally, "held fast"; only here and in its parallel, 2 Chr 7:22.

COMMENT

Structure and Themes

The vision of YHWH appears as a reply to Solomon's inaugural prayer in 1 Kgs 8:22–53; it is the second such appearance, parallel to the earlier encounter at Gibeon (3:5–14). Both visions speak of loyalty to YHWH's law as the condition for the continued rule of the House of David, except that in the present instance there is an explicit reference to destruction and exile, the punishment for disobedience. While this in itself does not represent sufficient warrant to posit an exilic date for the entire unit, the change in address from Solomon (vv. 3–5) to the entire nation (vv. 6–9) does point to the secondary nature of these latter verses—from the hands of Dtr$_2$. (On the question of reference to the Exile in preexilic contexts, see Comment to 1 Kgs 8.) The outlook is Deuteronomistic throughout, as indicated by the terms used; see discussion in the Notes.

It has sometimes been held that, with this vision, Dtr begins his criticism of Solomon; in 1 Kgs 9–11, in which a number of themes treated earlier (1 Kgs 3–5) are repeated, Solomon is no longer the favored king but is depicted in a hostile manner as he proceeds down the road to the ultimate apostasy of idolatry (Noth 1981, 60–62; cf. also Parker 1988; Provan speaks of the king's foolish behavior, "heading . . . for a fall."). A refinement of this view suggests postponing the start of the critique to 9:26, where the clustering of wealth and honor (10:1–13) as well as the amassing of horses (vv. 26–29) attest to Solomon's having violated the law of the king in Deut 17:14–17 (Brettler 1991). All in all, however, the repeated elements in 1 Kgs 9–10 have a "cumulative effect," explicating and expanding upon what has already been told of Solomon's good works and his honored position (Knoppers 1993, 124). In this part of the history, wealth and fame are not culpable.

XIII. THE FURTHER WORKS OF SOLOMON

(9:10–28)

9 [10]Now at the end of the twenty years it had taken Solomon to build the two houses, the House of YHWH and the king's house—[11]Hiram king of Tyre had supplied Solomon with cedar and juniper trees and gold, as much as he wished—then King Solomon gave Hiram twenty cities in the land of the Galilee. [12]But when Hiram went from Tyre to see the cities that Solomon had given him, they did not please him. [13]He said: "What are these cities that you have given me, my brother?" He named them The Land of Cabul, (their name) until this day. [14]Hiram sent the king one hundred and twenty talents of gold.

[15]This is the matter of the levy that King Solomon raised to build the House of YHWH, his house, the Millo, the wall of Jerusalem, Hazor, Megiddo, and Gezer.—[16]Pharaoh king of Egypt had come up and captured Gezer; he burned it down and killed the Canaanites who lived in the city. Then he gave it as a marriage gift to his daughter, Solomon's wife.—[17]Solomon built Gezer, Lower Beth-horon, [18]Baalath, Tamar[a] in the Steppe, in the land, [19]and all the store-cities that belonged to Solomon and the chariot cities and the cavalry cities—all Solomon's desire that he had for building in Jerusalem and in Lebanon and in all the territory of his rule. [20]All the people who remained from the Amorites, the Hittites, the Perizzites, the Hivites, the Jebusites, who were not Israelite,[21]—their children who remained in the land after them, whom the Israelites could not doom to destruction—Solomon imposed corvée upon them until this day. [22]But Solomon did not enslave the Israelites, for they were the armed force, his servants, his officers, his adjutants, his chariot officers, and his horsemen.

[23]These were the officers of prefects who were in charge of Solomon's work, five hundred and fifty who oversaw the people doing the work.

[24]But the daughter of Pharaoh went up from the City of David to her house, which he built for her. Then he built the Millo.

[25]Solomon used to sacrifice burnt offerings and offerings of well-being three times a year on the altar that he built for YHWH, and used to offer incense with it that was before YHWH. Thus he set up the House (of YHWH).

[26]King Solomon built a fleet at Ezion-geber, which is near Eloth on the shore of the Red Sea, in the land of Edom. [27]Hiram sent his servants in the fleet, shipmen who were experienced on the sea, with Solomon's servants. [28]They came to Ophir; there they acquired gold: four hundred and twenty talents that they delivered to King Solomon.

---

[a] Qere: *tdmr* (Tadmor) for ketib: *tmr* (Tamar).

NOTES

9 **10.** *Now, at the end of the twenty years it had taken Solomon to build the two houses, the House of YHWH and the king's house.* That is, the seven years of building the Temple (6:38) and the thirteen years of the king's palace (7:1).

11. *Hiram king of Tyre had supplied Solomon.* Hebrew *niśśa'*, Piel of **nś'*, "to support, bear," financially. The punctuation is that of tertie *he'* verbs; cf. 2 Sam 5:12 for the alternate *niśśē'*. Syntactically, the perfect tense in v. 11a does not follow the protasis in v. 10 easily; nor can v. 11b beginning with "then" be the apodosis. These are signs of the compositeness of the unit vv. 10–14.

with cedar and and juniper trees and gold. Gold was not part of the original agreement between the two kings (cf. 5:24–25) and may have been added here from the notice in v. 14.

as much as he wished. As has been agreed upon earlier, in 5:24.

then King Solomon gave Hiram twenty cities in the land of the Galilee. On "then" as an editorial term, lacking chronological significance, see comment at 2 Kgs 16:5.

in the land of the Galilee. Hebrew *gālil* is a general term for "district" (cf. Josh 13:2; 22:10–11); it became associated mostly with the northern region of the Promised Land, from the Jezreel Valley northward (cf. Josh 20:7; 21:32; 2 Kgs 15:29; Isa 8:23), and is not restricted to its eastern portions (contra Alt 1937, 52–64).

12. *But when Hiram went from Tyre to see the cities . . . , they did not please him.* In Num 23:27, the same expression is used, except there it is with reference to a place as being agreeable.

13. *He said: "What are these cities that you have given me, my brother?"* Hiram's reaction may not have been delivered at a face-to-face meeting of the personages; the words could have been part of an exchange of letters similar to the one described in 5:15–24.

my brother. A term common in diplomatic parlance, expressing the relationship between parties of equal status, often formalized in treaty; cf. also 20:32–33; Amos 1:9. For the ancient Near Eastern equivalent (*aḫḫūtu*, "brotherhood"), see Munn-Rankin 1956, 76–84; Liverani 1990, 197–202.

He named them The Land of Cabul, (their name) until this day. Hebrew *wayyiqrā'* may also be taken as the 3d masc. sg. impersonal and translated "it was called, they are called," thus dissociating Hiram from the naming. But this would sever the implied connection between Hiram's disappointment with the gift of land and the name Cabul. Unlike the typical name-etiology, in which the name is usually etymologized (cf. Exod 2:10; 1 Sam 1:20; 4:21–22), in the present instance, Cabul is not explained and remains unexplicable (see further below). Perhaps the name was originally unrelated to the incident recorded here and only subsequently associated with it.

them. For the masc. instead of the fem. suffix, explained as colloquial interference, cf. the examples collected in GKC, 135o.

The Land of Cabul. The name is still preserved by the village of Kabul, some 8 km southeast of Acco. Cabul appears as a border town of the tribe of Asher in Josh 19:27; and in the Roman period, it still demarcated the boundary between the plain of Acco and the western Galilee and was fought over during the Jewish uprising (Josephus, *Life* 212–15). Since early times, the name has been variously explained. Josephus (*Ant.* 8.142) interpreted it from Phoenician *ke + bal*, "good for nothing, worthless" (cf. Ewald, Burney, Moffatt; NEB: note ad loc.: "That is Sterile Land"). The LXX rendered: "boundary"; favored by Montgomery and Gehman: "a march-land" (based on a reading *gĕbûl*, "border"?). Rabbinic exegetes, following *b. Sabb.* 54a, connected the name with **kbl*, "to tie, bind," a land of binding, in which one's feet sink because of its mud and sand (so Rashi, Qimḥi). Iron Age ruins have been excavated at Kh. Ras ez-Zeitun, 1.5 km NE of Kabul (Gal 1985). Still, there is no good reason for the transfer of the name of the small town Cabul to the entire district (cf. Noth).

14. *Hiram sent the king one hundred and twenty talents of gold.* A footnote referring back to v. 11a, where an unspecified amount of gold is first mentioned; the Cabul story, introduced by "then" in v. 11b, has severed the connection between the two, creating the illusion that the gold is somehow related to the transfer of the cities and payment for them (cf. Stade and Schwally). For other examples of such footnoting, several verses removed, cf. 2 Kgs 16:17–18, detailing 16:8. (Long misunderstands the workings of this editorial practice and overreads the text; he would see in v. 14a "delayed climax," contrasting the "grandness of Hiram's contribution to Solomon's building program . . ." with "the meanness of Solomon's payment in kind . . . twenty cities which were mere villages" [Long, 112].)

one hundred and twenty talents of gold. The talent (Heb. *kikkar*) was the largest unit of weight in ancient Israel and was divided into sixty shekels (cf. Exod 38:25–26). Based on the evidence of actual weights archaeologically discovered, the shekel has been calculated at 11.4 gms (ABD 6:906), which would make the talent about 35 kgs. Note that the gift of the queen of Sheba was also 120 talents of gold (cf. 10:10).

15. *This is the matter of the levy that King Solomon raised.* Hebrew *wĕzeh dĕbar X* is a "detailing formula" used in various original and secondary contexts to specify a particular aspect of a preceding notice and is introduced by a *waw-*explicative. This formula also appears with reference to the fallow year (Deut 15:1–2); the cities of refuge (Deut 19:4–6); the circumcision of the Israelites (Josh 5:4–7); and the installation ritual of the priesthood (Exod 29:1). From these examples, it appears that, in the present verse, the introductory statement on which the formula depends is missing, something like: Solomon raised a levy . . . "This is the account of the levy. . . ." Moreover, the unit is broken up by v. 16, concerning Pharaoh's daughter. Its placement in 1 Kgs 9 is hard to comprehend, because it might better have been attached to the first mention of the levy in 5:27. The formula is also known from the extrabiblical Siloam Inscription (Cogan and Tadmor 1988, 337); cf. also 1 Kgs 11:27. See Talshir 1981–1982 for a thorough investigation.

the levy. See above, 4:6 and 5:27ff., and the discussions there.

Millo. Literally, "the filled-in" area. Now generally taken to be the terrace system built on the eastern flank of the City of David, overlooking the Kidron Valley, as originally suggested by Kenyon after the excavations of the area in the 1960s; see Kenyon 1971, 33–35; Shiloh 1984, 26. Topography required the Millo to be shored up periodically; cf. David's activity there in 2 Sam 5:9; and further details on the work undertaken during Solomon's reign in 1 Kgs 11:27. For the use of an etymologically similar word in late Aramaic (*ml'*), see Steiner 1989.

the wall of Jerusalem. Already mentioned in 3:1 and, for a fuller reference, see Note on 11:27.

Hazor, Megiddo, and Gezer. The three major fortresses are listed from north to south, Hazor in the Upper Galilee, Megiddo at the entrance to the Jezreel Valley from the coast, and Gezer in the northern Shephelah. Six-chambered gateways and casemate walls unearthed at all three sites were pointed to as evidence of Solomonic construction (Yadin 1958); criticized by Ussishkin 1980; cf. also Aharoni 1982, 195–97; Milson 1986. For current opinion, see further in Comment.

Hazor. See the Note at 2 Kgs 15:29, to which add NEAEHL 594–606 and ABD 5, 578–81.

Megiddo. See Note at 4:12.

Gezer. See Note in the following verse.

16. *Pharaoh king of Egypt had come up and captured Gezer; he burned it down and killed the Canaanites who lived in the city.* This parenthetical note explains how Gezer became part of Solomon's realm. Though only meager information is available from Egyptian sources, it is widely accepted that the Pharaoh is to be identified with Siamun, the penultimate king of the 21st dynasty (ca. 978–959 BCE), this based mainly on the assumption that the marriage took place early in Solomon's reign (cf. 3:1); see the full survey of suggestions in Green 1979. A relief fragment from Tanis depicting the smiting of prisoners by Siamun has been identified with the campaign against the Philistines reported in the present verse; see, among others, Goldwasser 1949; disputed by Lance 1976.

Gezer. From this major city in the northern Shephelah just west of the Aijalon Valley, all inland traffic from the sea coast to the hill country could be controlled. It had been assigned to the tribe of Ephraim (according to Josh 16:3) but was not taken during the settlement (Judg 1:29). Nor was it occupied during the Davidic expansion (see Lance 1967). For the identification of Stratum 7 at Gezer with the destruction described in the present verse, see Dever et al. 1970, 60–63; 1971, 110; and the general survey of the archaeological history of the site in NEAEHL 496–506.

the Canaanites who lived in the city. Though on the border of Philistia and encompassed by the Philistine centers at Ekron, Gath, and Ashkelon, Gezer was still considered a Canaanite city.

Then he gave it as a marriage gift to his daughter, Solomon's wife. The marriage of Solomon to the Pharaoh's daughter was already mentioned in 3:1 and in 9:4a. The fact of the marriage was the source of much discomfort to rabbinic exegetes for, on the face of it, Solomon seems flagrantly to have disregarded Mosaic Law, which forbade taking foreign women; cf. Deut 7:3 and specifically 23:8–9. The Greek texts and especially the Greek Miscellanies at 1 Kgs 2:46 deal with the marriage in much the same manner as did rabbinic midrash, excusing the king for his trespass; see Gooding 1976, 18–23, 66–73.

marriage gift. Literally, "send-off" or parting gift, given to the bride-to-be when she left her father's house, and something that became part of her dowry. Cf. the figurative use in Mic 1:14.

17. *Solomon built Gezer, Lower Beth-horon.* The first words of the verse resume (by *Wiederaufnahme*) the thread of the account in v. 15, broken off by v. 16, by repeating information given there concerning the construction at Gezer (Anbar 1988, 391), then continuing the list of fortified sites. These forts were not all equally important, judging from their location and their archaeological remains.

Lower Beth-horon. Second Chronicles 8:5 adds: "Upper Beth-horon"; LXX reads only: "Upper Beth-horon." The two Beth-horons are located on the main road from the northern Shephelah (via Gezer) to the central mountain range and are commonly identified with Beit ʿUr et-taḥta and Beit ʿUr el-Foqa, just 4 km apart. Joshua pursued the Canaanite coalition that had attacked Gibeon down this route (cf. Josh 10:10), and the towns served as a border point between the tribes of Ephraim and Benjamin (16:5; 18:13–14).

18. *Baalath.* The identification of this fort is problematic, because a number of sites bear this name. There is a Baalath in Danite territory (Josh 19:44), probably identical with Mt. Baalah on the western border of Judah (15:11); it has been identified at a site situated on the Mugar Ridge on Wadi Sorek (Kallai 1986, 369). Another candidate is the Baalah, that is, Kiriath-jearim (Josh 15:9) in the Judean hills, and a further Baalath can be found in the Negev of Simeon (Josh 19:8; cf. 15:29). Most geographers hold for the Danite Baalath, as did Josephus, *Ant.* 8.152.

Tamar in the Steppe, in the land. Qere reads *tdmr*, "Tadmor," for *tmr*, as do most versions, as well as 2 Chr 8:4. A reference to Tadmor, the major caravan center in north Syria, identified with the ruins at Palmyra, is reasonable within the context of Chronicles, which also tells of Solomon's overpowering Hamath-zobah (8:3). (For two contrary evaluations of the Chronicles verse, see Williamson 1982, 228–30; Japhet 1993, 622–23.) But within Kings, Tadmor is incongruous with the geographically sound list, with the north–south orientation of sites, all within the land of Israel. Taking the specification "in the Steppe, in the land" as referring to the land of Judah (cf. 4:19), Tamar is the preferred reading. Tamar was indeed a significant point on the southern border of the Promised Land; cf. Ezek 47:19; 48:28. Eusebius (*Onamasticon* 8) located (Hazazon-) Tamar (Gen 14:7) a day's journey from Kurnub. For the identification of Tamar at ʿAin Ḥuṣb in the Arava Valley, see Aharoni 1963; 1979, s.v.

19. *and all the store-cities that belonged to Solomon and the chariot cities and the cavalry cities.* A further expansion on the previous list of named cities,

explaining their character and function, though there is no way to tell whether each of them served multiple purposes.

all the store-cities. Or "garrison cities"; used only here and Exod 1:11, and the late (derivative?) 2 Chr 8:4, 6; 16:4; 17:12; 32:28. The versions suggest that they were centers for the storing of supplies, as already implied by 2 Chr 32:28. Two etymologies for Heb *miskĕnôt* from Akkadian have been suggested: (1) *maškanu* (CAD M/1, 369–73), "threshing floor, agricultural settlement"; (2) *muškēnu* (CAD M/2, 272–76), "commoner, poor, destitute," that is, "cities (built) by forced labor" (so Speiser 1958, 27). In both instances, the *š* > *s* is accounted for by assuming a loan into Hebrew. Yet, West-Semitic **škn*, "to see to, care for," offers a sufficient etymology for this technical term without recourse to distant borrowings. See further the Note on 1 Kgs 1:4.

the chariot cities and the cavalry cities. Referred to again in 10:26.

all Solomon's desire that he had for building in Jerusalem and in Lebanon and in all the territory of his rule. This is the only reference in the Solomonic traditions to construction in Lebanon; the word is lacking in Luc. and LXX[B], and some consider that it was added late on the basis of 5:28. But the following clause, "in all the territory of his rule," which echoes the wide borders of 5:1, may be the ultimate source of this general statement. Moreover, it is hard to comprehend under what circumstances this building could have been accomplished, since the Lebanon was not being included in the Israelite domain.

20. *All the people who remained from the Amorites, the Hittites, the Perizzites, the Hivites, the Jebusites, who were not Israelite.* Biblical sources relate the names of as many as ten peoples (Gen 15:19–21) living in Canaan on the eve of the Israelite entry. A stereotyped list of "seven" is widely used (cf. e.g., Deut 7:1), which is sometimes cut down to "six" (e.g., Exod 23:23), and to "five," as in the present verse. Missing from the present list: Canaanites and Girgashites; these are supplied by late LXX MSS.

21. *their children who remained in the land after them, whom the Israelites could not doom to destruction — Solomon imposed corvée upon them until this day.* For other examples of the object (introduced by *waw*) prefixed to the main *waw*-consecutive construction, cf. 12:17; 15:13; 2 Kgs 16:14; 25:22; see S. R. Driver 1892, §127a.

corvée. The technical term *mas* (see Note to 4:6) is here glossed by *ʿōbēd*, "work, service" (at a time when *mas* had come to mean more generally "tax"?); and though not all instances are so glossed, no distinction of meaning should be drawn (as suggested by Mendelsohn 1962b).

until this day. In other words, as is still the case; cf. 8:8. In complementary fashion, the first introduction to the book of Judges notes that the Canaanites continued to reside in the land alongside the Israelites in numerous fortified cities until such time as Israel acquired sufficient strength to enslave them (rather than their being proscribed, as Deut 7 would have it); cf. Judg 1:28, 30, 33, 35. Solomon's practice was at variance with the terms of Deuteronomic Law as set out in Deut 20:10–18, where only the residents of distant cities outside the bounds of the Promised Land could be impressed into state service. It is remarkable that he was not criticized within Deuteronomistic circles for this breach of law. The need for manpower to maintain an empire would seem to have dictated this adjustment of the ideal.

The present verse suggests that the enslaved Canaanites were not assimilated into the Israelite community even centuries later, and evidence for this has sometimes been sought in the reference to "sons of Solomon's servants" listed in the census lists in Ezra 2:58, though in that context they were Temple attendants.

22. *But Solomon did not enslave the Israelites.* The Hebrew seems contradictory at first, as v. 22a speaks of nonenslavement (*lōʾ nātan ʿebed*) of Israelites, while 22b notes their being the king's servants (*ʿăbādîm*); but the nuanced use of the noun *ʿebed* for both "bondman" and "court attendant" can be maintained without emendation. The use of *nātan lĕ-*, "to make," with *ʿebed* is attested only here.

for they were the armed force, his servants, his officers, his adjutants, his chariot officers, and his horsemen. In contradiction to 5:27, which states that Israelites were required to do service on state projects; see Note, ad loc.

his adjutants. Literally, "third-men"; for the present translation, see Note at 2 Kgs 7:2.

23. *These were the officers of prefects who were in charge of Solomon's work, five hundred and fifty who oversaw the people doing the work.* The formula "these were . . ." (cf. 4:2 and Note) suggests that the original source from which this item was taken contained a list of the 550 supervisors, probably cut short by the editor at this point because of its length. For the duplicate of the present verse, with an alternate number of supervisors, see discussion at Note on 5:30.

24. *But the daughter of Pharaoh went up from the City of David to her house, which he built for her.* This verse and the following one are footnotes to v. 15, adding particulars connected with constructions in Jerusalem.

But. The restrictive sense of the conjuction *ʾak*, "but," is hard to reconcile in the context (despite the examples sometimes brought from Gen 27:30 and Judg 7:19); see Burney for older attempts at rewriting the verse. It is perhaps better to read with LXX *ʾaz*, "then." This would produce two consecutive clauses introduced by particles of time (*ʾaz, bāʿēt hahîʾ*), for which, cf. 2 Kgs 16:5, 6.

to her house, which he built for her. For its construction, cf. 1 Kgs 7:8b.

Then he built the Millo. See above, v. 15. From the collocation with v. 24a, medieval exegetes deduced that the house built for Pharaoh's daughter was located in the Millo, outside the city. But, at most, only a sequential relationship is implied by the positioning of these two half-verses.

25. *Solomon used to sacrifice burnt offerings and offerings of well-being three times a year on the altar that he built for YHWH.* A peculiar verse with several ungrammatical features, only loosely connected to the preceding verses. It credits Solomon with initiating the pilgrimage cycle of sacrifice (on what seems to be the bronze altar; see Note at 8:64) and constant maintenance of the Temple.

used to sacrifice. Heb *wĕheʿĕlâ*, perfect with the conjunction in frequentative sense.

three times a year on the altar. Likely a reference to the three pilgrimage festivals (Exod 23:14–27; Deut 16:1–17), spelled out in 2 Chr 8:13.

on the altar that he built. This is the only reference in all of Kings to Solomon's building an altar for animal sacrifice; it is not included in the list of constructions by Hiram although at the Temple dedication, the altar was in place, despite its remaining unutilized (cf. 8:64). That omission may have prompted the insertion of the present half-verse, perhaps by a late annotator.

and used to offer incense with it that was before YHWH. An old crux. If parsed "used to offer incense along with it (i.e., the animal offerings) on the altar that stood before YHWH," the reference could be to the incense altar that stood in the Temple's main hall (Rashi, Qimḥi). But the syntax remains inexplicable because "with it" has no referent. Klostermann's emedation *'et 'iššô*, "his fire offering," has almost universally been adopted.

Thus he set up the House (of YHWH). Hebrew *šillam*, with the sense of "putting everything in order" (Ehrlich). But the completion of the construction was already noted above in 6:14 and 38; therefore, if this is not a "useless repetition" (Montgomery and Gehman), some other matter is referred to here. "Paying (*šlm*) vows" (cf. Ps 76:12; 116:14; so Gray) does not help much. As interpreted by 2 Chr 8:12–16, Solomon saw to the festival sacrifices and the priestly work in the Temple, thus bringing his grand project to a successful fulfillment. In the present context, however, *šillam* (perfect) follows descriptions of the king's repeated attention to the Temple and not to a one-time action; perhaps, therefore, the sense is "he kept the Temple in repair," which would accord with royal obligation as understood throughout the ancient world. Taken in this fashion, the final clause would be a late gloss, because it would exhibit late Hebrew usage.

26. *King Solomon built a fleet at Ezion-geber, which is near Eloth on the shore of the Red Sea, in the land of Edom.* The scarcity of timber in this desert area raises serious questions concerning the possibility of building a fleet on location. Gray suggests that it could have been obtained from the nearby Edomite highlands, "tolerably well-wooded until the Turks devastated the woods for fuel for the engines on the Hejaz railway." On the other hand, the ships could have been constructed on the Mediterranean coast at Tyrian shipyards, dismantled and transported, to be rebuilt at Eilat; an admittedly difficult logistical operation (proposed by Ikeda 1991, 114–15; see evidence for such activity in Egypt and in classical traditions collected by Casson 1971, 136).

a fleet. Hebrew *'ŏnî*, properly "ship," masc. sg. used as a collective; also fem., as in next verse.

Ezion-geber. The identification of Ezion-geber with Tell-el-Kheleifeh, a small mound on the northern coast of the Gulf of Elath between modern Aqaba and Elath, popularized by Glueck (last, revised survey, Glueck 1965 and NEAEHL 867–70) and defended by Meshel 1975, seems less likely after the restudy of the excavated material by Pratico 1986. Kheleifeh is rather a small caravanserai, a half km from the coast, where no port or natural conditions for one were found. Ezion-geber may be sought on Jazirat Faraun (= "Pharaoh's Island," popularly known as Coral Island) in the Gulf, south of Elath, where a suitable anchorage and medieval ruins are visible. See Rothenberg 1962; ABD 2:724–25; NEAEHL 964. It would not have been unusual to utilize an offshore island as a port, as was the custom at several Phoenician cities — e.g., Tyre and Arwad; further Raban 1998, 432–33.

which is near Eloth on the shore of the Red Sea. Hebrew *'et*, with the meaning "near"; cf. 2 Kgs 9:27; Judg 3:19; 4:11.

Eloth. Otherwise, Elath; cf. 2 Kgs 16:6. It is generally agreed that the Iron Age ruins, if any survived the harsh conditions of desert flooding, may lie buried beneath the modern city of Aqabah.

Red Sea. Literally, "the Sea of Reeds" (Heb *yam sûp*); also Num 21:4, not to be confused with the Sea of Reeds in the Exodus account, Exod 13:18; 14:2, which was not far from Goshen in the area of the Nile Delta.

in the land of Edom. The designation "Edom" refers to the southern part of the Negev, below a line running from the tip of the Dead Sea to Kadesh (cf. Num 34:3–4). On whether the mention of Edom here has political as well as geographical implications, see Comment.

27. *Hiram sent his servants in the fleet, shipmen who were experienced on the sea, with Solomon's servants*. Solomon made use of Phoenician sailors and ship-builders, as did Egyptian kings before him (Montgomery and Gehman).

28. *They came to Ophir*. Ophir is of problematic identification. Renowned as a source of gold (cf. Job 28:16; Ps 45:10), Ophir developed the secondary meaning of fine-quality gold; cf., e.g., Isa 13:12; Job 22:24. The words *zhb 'pr*, "Ophir gold," appear incised on an 8th-century BC Hebrew (?) ostracon discovered at Tell Qasile (today in north Tel-Aviv) (B. Mazar 1950). But this find is of little help in determining Ophir's geographical location. The Luc. and LXX reading *Sopheir* (repeated in Josephus, *Ant.* 8.164) has been explained as an inner-Greek transcriptional error (the repetition of the preceding *sigma*) and has nothing to do with sites with similar-sounding names in India and East Africa, which are often claimed to be the site of Ophir. (Note that in Gen 10:30 the toponym *Sephar* appears in connection with Ophir, which might have influenced the Greek tradition.) The inclusion of Ophir among the Arab sons of Shem in the Table of Nations in Gen 10:29 and the gold brought to Solomon by the queen of Sheba (1 Kgs 10:10) have drawn many to conclude that Ophir "doubtless lay in Arabia" (Montgomery and Gehman). Albright (1969b, 130–31) identified Ophir with the general region of the Somali coast of Africa by taking this verse together with 10:22 and the trade items listed there and comparing them to the products brought back by the Egyptians from their voyages to Punt. Such African trade does not preclude the Arabian identification; several of the Arab Semites are also recorded as sons of the African Cush in Gen 10:7, reflecting the trade between the Horn of Africa and South Arabia, which could well have served as a transshipment point for the items lised in 1 Kings. See the exhaustive survey of suggestions in North 1967; also ABD 5:26–27.

there they acquired gold: four hundred and twenty talents that they delivered to King Solomon. Universally considered to be an exaggerated number, even larger in 2 Chr 8:18: "450"; LXX[B] reads "120" (favored by many as more reasonable). But the latter reading looks like an assimilation to the number that appears in 1 Kgs 9:14 and 10:10 and is not preferable.

COMMENT

Structure and Themes

Unraveling the sense of the composite editorial unit on the ceding of Cabul (vv. 10–14) remains problematic. On first reading, it appears that the transfer of Cabul is in partial payment for the help extended by Hiram to Solomon during his lengthy, two-decade building spree. Solomon could have fallen into arrears in the payments to Tyre, due on a yearly basis (cf. 5:25); at least this is the implication of the collocation of the present verses. The debt would have been paid, then, by the transfer to Hiram of Israelite territory (cf. 2 Sam 24:6–7, where the western Galilee was counted in Joab's census), adjacent to Tyre. But there is no indication that Solomon defaulted on his contract, and so some suggest that the land transfer may simply have been a separate transaction bent on filling Solomon's empty treasury. Cabul was pawned for 120 talents of gold (so Skinner, Montgomery and Gehman, Gray, Wiseman; see further on the syntax of v. 11b and the clause beginning with *'āz*).

Hiram's dissatisfaction with the conveyance is inexplicable for, whatever the root meaning of the name *Cabul* may be, the district can hardly be considered to have been poor, with its cities and the fertile agricultural land of the plain of Acco; thus, if offered to Hiram, it would have likely been annexed to Tyre without further ado. Perhaps the deprecatory remark may be taken as the editor's intending "to counteract (or at least soften) the negative political implications of the loss of Israelite territory to Hiram" (ABD 1:797).

The entire Cabul passage is rewritten in 2 Chr 8:1–2, where it is Hiram who transfers the cities to Solomon; but this is a face-saving measure conceived by the Chronicler, for whom it was inconceivable that Solomon would have pawned part of the Promised Land. Wiseman's harmonization—imagining Solomon's mortgage and subsequent redemption of Cabul—is just that—imagination; so is that of Aharoni (1965; 1979, 307–8), who thinks of a compromise, Hiram's keeping the Acco Plain, Solomon's getting back inland Cabul. (For other earlier rewritings, cf. Montgomery and Gehman, who correctly reject them all.)

The following unit (vv. 15–28) is a miscellaneous collection of short notices under the broad rubric of Solomon's construction projects, the labor force and its supervisors, and appended remarks. The juxtaposition of these notes of various genres follows the associative principle of editing. Thus, the matter of the corvée raised for building and fortifications holds many pieces together; the mention of Gezer in v. 15 attracts the item on the transfer of Gezer to Solomon as a wedding gift in v. 16; this is followed by the completion of the construction list in vv. 17–19. The matter of the corvée is complemented by details on those enlisted and those who held supervisory posts in vv. 20–22. Following are two notes very loosely connected with the preceding account of the levy and barely connected within themselves: the number of supervisors (v. 23) and the transfer of Pharaoh's daughter to her palace (v. 24; the note on Solomon's yearly sacrifices in v. 25 creates a subunit, parallel in substance to 3:1–3). Solomon's maritime activity in association with Hiram in vv. 26–28 rounds off this miscellany, looking back to vv. 11–14, especially to the "gold" mentioned in v. 14 and taken up again in v. 28. These verses can also be read as an introduction to the story of the visit of the queen of Sheba (10:1–13), a monarch from the Red Sea area, the ever-ready source of gold for Solomon (cf. v. 10).

For the most part, the substantive material would seem to derive from "archival records" (Long, 114) or "official records" (Van Seters 1983, 302), though the hand of the editor is unmistakably felt in vv. 19–22, 25.

History

The issue of the authenticity of the present section is central to its use as one of the key building blocks in reconstructing the extent of Solomon's kingdom and its management. The verses describe a vigorous, active monarch in control of the affairs of state, but there is no way to date the various endeavors. Major construction was undertaken at key locations throughout the kingdom, from Hazor in the Upper Galilee to Gezer in the Shephelah, down to Tamar in the eastern Negev. Established sites were strengthened, while others that had been either abandoned or destroyed were rebuilt. All of them may have served multiple functions, whether as military depots or administrative centers; some may have housed the residences of the district prefects (e.g., Hazor or Megiddo). Despite the fact that some archaeologists have argued for a reevaluation of the dating of many excavated sites earlier assigned to the tenth century (notably that of Stratum IV at Megiddo, assigned to the time of Ahab), which if accepted would reduce considerably the evidence for Solomon's building activities, to others it remains clear that a mixture of fortification and public construction did take place during Solomon's reign (see A. Mazar 1990, 380–87, 469; Fritz 1996; Dever 1997).

At the same time, many areas outside the boundaries of the Promised Land that had been inherited from David probably had by now regained their independence completely or became semiautonomous (see Comment to 11:14–25). Nevertheless, the port of Eloth within the rebellious region of Edom still served as the home terminal for the joint sea ventures of Israel and Tyre. The Philistine coastal cities are nowhere referred to, because they seem not to have been part of the kingdom; and Gezer became a royal estate only after its transfer by Egypt to Israel (see further below). The Aramean kingdoms, which had engaged and then succumbed to David (2 Sam 8:3–12), also go unmentioned, except for the revolt and defection in Damascus (1 Kgs 11:23–25). Consequently, Solomon's kingdom looks as though it comprised essentially the Land of Israel, whose extent is reflected in the traditional phrase "from Dan to Beersheba" (cf. 5:5). (The reference in 2 Chr 8:3–4 to battles in the vicinity of

Hamath and the fortifying of Tadmor is of disputed nature and best set aside; see above, Note to v. 18.)

It is an open question whether the valley of Acco, between Mount Carmel and the kingdom of Tyre, was ever wholly under Israelite control. The literary evidence is equivocal. Though included in the inheritance of the tribe of Asher (Josh 19:24–31), it does not appear among David's conquests (despite the note on the border point "stronghold of Tyre" in 2 Sam 24:7); and even if it had passed into his hands, this dominance was short-lived. Tradition attributed its final loss to Solomon's dealings with Hiram.

Explicit reference to military encounters is lacking in the account of Solomon's reign, yet the king's attention to security and continued development of Israel's international position is much in evidence; behind a number of incidents, the presence of a strong army can be detected. Thus, Siamun's raid in Philistia. While Siamun sought to reassert Egyptian commercial ties to the area and probably moved so as to take advantage of the uncertainties over the transfer of rule from David to Solomon, he was caught short by capturing Gezer, which lay on Solomon's front doorstep; he overstepped the limits of his power, so to speak. The "gift" of Gezer and the marriage of the Egyptian princess to a foreigner went a long way in defusing a potential Egypt–Israel flareup. It was indeed unusual for Egyptian kings during the New Kingdom or Empire to marry their daughters to outsiders (Schulman 1979a), but the days of Solomon were "humbler days" (Kitchen 1973, 280–83; earlier, Malamat 1963a, 9–10; note, too, the other out-marriage, that of Hadad the Edomite in 1 Kgs 11:19). The diplomatic relations thus established between the two monarchs were advantageous to both parties; Siamun acquired a recognized foothold in Philistia and its trade centers and, for Solomon, the annexation of Gezer and the subsequent fortification of the destroyed (!) city opened a sure corridor to the coast through an area that David had inexplicably failed to take.

Incorporation in the Israelite Kingdom of the areas populated by the indigenous Canaanite population was already inferred from the analysis of the Prefects' List in 1 Kgs 4:7–19; in the present section, these peoples are depicted as supplying the major share of the work force mobilized for the royal building enterprise. Their subjugation was likely completed during David's reign (cf. the map of David's census in 2 Sam 24) and, under Solomon, they were forcibly mobilized for state service. Though the late editor (Dtr) would have us believe that the Israelites were spared this burden and served solely in the military (1 Kgs 9:22), the imposition of the corvée upon Israel is recorded in 5:27–30. Considering the extent of the building undertaken by Solomon throughout his realm, this report of universal service does not seem mistaken. And this counterindication is closer to the historical picture, for the heavy yoke of the corvée was one of the factors in the revolt of the Northern tribes, both during Solomon's reign (11:27–28) and after his death (12:4).

Solomon's overseas commercial expeditions in association with Hiram are treated together in the Comment to 1 Kgs 10:22.

XIV. The Visit of the Queen of Sheba

(10:1–13)

10 ¹Now the queen of Sheba had been hearing of Solomon's fame for the sake of the name of YHWH, so she came to test him with hard questions. ²She came to Jerusalem with a very large force, camels bearing spices, a very great amount of gold, and precious stones. When she came to Solomon, she told him everything she had in her mind, ³and Solomon replied to all her questions;ᵃ there was nothing hidden from the king that he could not tell her. ⁴When the queen of Sheba saw all of Solomon's wisdom, the house that he built, ⁵the food of his table, the seating of his servants, the post of his attendantsᵇ and their dress, his cupbearers, and the burnt offerings that he brought to the House of YHWH, she was left breathless. ⁶She said to the king: "It was true what I heard in my country about your affairs and your wisdom. ⁷But I did not believe the things until I came and my own eyes saw; indeed, they did not tell me half of it. You have more wisdom and wealth than the report I heard. ⁸Happy are your people. Happy are these your servants, who wait upon you continuously, who can hear your wisdom. ⁹Blessed be YHWH your God who has delighted in you, setting you on the throne of Israel; because of YHWH's love of Israel forever, he made you king to do justice and righteousness." ¹⁰Then she gave the king one hundred twenty talents of gold and a very large quantity of spices and precious stones. There was never again such a large quantity of spices as that which the queen of Sheba gave King Solomon. — ¹¹Moreover, Hiram's fleet, which carried gold from Ophir, brought from Ophir a very large amount of *almug* wood and precious stones. ¹²The king made supports from the *almug* wood for the House of YHWH and the king's house, and harps and lyres for the singers. Such *almug* wood has not come or been seen to this day. — ¹³King Solomon gave the queen of Sheba all she desired, whatever she asked, besides what he gave her as befitted King Solomon. Then she and her servants left and returned to her country.

ᵃ Lit., "words."
ᵇ Read with qere: *mšrtyw*; ketib: *mšrtw*.

NOTES

10 1. *Now the queen of Sheba had been hearing of Solomon's fame.* The verb in participle may be used to indicate a past state of affairs, the circumstances behind the principal action being described; cf. Gen 27:5; see Waltke and O'Connor, §37.6b–c.

the queen of Sheba. Sheba is apparently to be located in the area of modern-day Yemen, in the southwestern part of the Arabian Peninsula (and not in the northern deserts as in Gen 25:3; Job 1:15 [contra Montgomery and Gehman], although all of the Sabeans may ultimately be related). The name appears as one of the sons of Yoktan in Gen 10:28, along with other South Arabian toponyms, e.g., Hazarmaveth and Ophir (Eph'al 1982, 227–29). Assyrian inscriptions from the late eighth and the seventh centuries BCE record the names of several Arabian queens in the north Arabian Desert (Eph'al 1982, 63–64), but there are no records from as early as the tenth century from either area. Late biblical texts regularly associate the land of Sheba with gold and spices (e.g., Isa 60:6; Jer 6:20; Ezek 27:22).

for the sake of the name of YHWH. Or: "through the name of YHWH," apparently referring to YHWH's grant of wisdom and great fortune to Solomon (3:13); similar to the praise for YHWH in Josh 9:9; cf. also Jer 3:17. But, while some sense can be made of the phrase, commentators have found it syntactically harsh and noted its absence from the parallel verse, 2 Chr 9:1. Conjectural rewriting, such as moving it to 9:25 or introducing a reference to the Temple, which has supposedly dropped out (see summary in Burney), are solutions that do not command much confidence.

so she came to test him with hard questions. Hebrew *ḥîdâ* is sometimes more than a "riddle" (as it is in Judg 14:12–20); it may be an incisive teaching of wise elders (cf. Prov 1:6; Ps 78:2). The accepted etymology from Aramaic *'hydh* is challenged by Held (1985, 93–96), who notes the semantically equivalent Akk *ḥiādu.* Examples of the queen's probing queries are left for the listener/reader to supply; see further in Comment.

2. *She came to Jerusalem with a very large force.* Hebrew *ḥayil* often refers to an army "force" (cf., e.g., 2 Kgs 6:15; 18:17) and, though the queen must have been accompanied by an armed escort, a nonmilitary sense, such as "wealth," may have been intended here; cf. Isa 60:5–6 for the "riches" (*ḥyl*) that flow to Jerusalem, "gold and frankincense" from Sheba. Read this way, v. 2aβ explicates 2aα.

camels bearing spices. In 2 Chr 9:1, the added conjunction "and" (*wĕ-*) smooths the asyndetic construction of Kings.

spices. Hebrew *bōśem* is the general term for spices and aromatics; it is specifically "balsam," a fragrant local resin (cf. Song 5:1; *Commiphora opobalsamum*; in MH *'ăparsĕmôn*). The Arabian *bōśem* (cf. Ezek 27:22), as an imported luxury product, was worthy of a king (Ps 45:9), a prized part of the royal treasury (cf. 2 Kgs 20:13). On the identification, see ABD 1:573–74. According to Josephus, the queen actually brought balsam shrubs, thus introducing this source of the Dead Sea perfumes to the Holy Land (*Ant.* 8.174).

a very great amount of gold, and precious stones. She proceeded to present these treasures to the king in an exchange of gifts; cf. v. 10.

she had in her mind. See Note on 8:17.

3. *and Solomon replied to all her questions.* Literally, "he told her all her words." She plied him with riddles, and he solved them (cf. Judg 14:12); nothing was too difficult for him.

4. *When the queen of Sheba saw all of Solomon's wisdom, the house that he built.* Namely, the royal palace, which she could observe as she moved about; cf. the following verse.

5. *the food of his table, the seating of his servants.* The queen was wined and dined at the king's table, at which other courtiers were seated.

the post of his attendants and their dress. For Heb *ma'ămad*, cf. the expression *'amôd lipnê*, "be in attendance" (cf. 1 Kgs 1:2); for *malbūš*, "dress" or "garments," cf. 2 Kgs 10:22. The LXX reads "his dress," a reference to the king's splendid wardrobe, rather than to that of his servants; this reading is also alluded to in Matt 6:29; Luke 12:27.

his cupbearers. Hebrew *mšqyw* is both "his drinks" and "his cupbearers"; the reference to drinking cups in v. 21 suggested this meaning also in the present verse for some commentators (so Gersonides, Qara, Stade and Schwally). But all modern translations follow the ancient ones and 2 Chr 9:4 (which moves the word up to join "waiters"), interpreting *mšqyw* as the king's butlers.

his burnt offerings that he brought to the House of YHWH. Solomon's attention to the cult, his generous and frequent offerings, was remarked on in 8:62 and 9:25. The reading in 2 Chr 9:4, *'lytw*, "his ascent," may refer to a particularly impressive architectural feature of the palace by which Solomon ascended to the House of YHWH. Montgomery and Gehman repoint to read *'ălōtô*, "his going up," i.e., his processional, the pomp with which the king entered the Temple; so Ehrlich, comparing Ezek 40:26.

breathless. Literally, "there was no more spirit in her." She was overwhelmed by the display of wealth and wisdom; not that she lost "courage" to compete any further with him (Burney). Compare the loss of "spirit" for lack of food (1 Sam 30:12), equivalent to fainting away.

6. *She said to the king: "It was true what I heard in my country about your affairs and your wisdom. . . ."* The placement of the substantive (rather than an adjective) at the head of the sentence emphasizes the verity of the preceding description.

about your affairs. The NEB and NJPSV translate "about you," apparently adopting the LXX reading *dbrk* (sg.) for MT *dbryk* (pl.); for *'l dbr* meaning "concerning, about," cf. 2 Sam 18:5.

7. *You have more wisdom and wealth than the report I heard.* "Wisdom" is omitted in Luc. and other LXX MSS; "prosperity" is missing from 2 Chr 9:6. Considering the items detailed in vv. 4b and 5, the "prosperity" (Heb *ṭôb*, "good") is likely a reference to the king's wealth.

8. *Happy are your people. Happy are these your servants, who wait upon you continuously, who can hear your wisdom.* The exclamation *'ašrê* is most often parsed as a "petrified plural noun found only in construct phrases or with suffixes" (Waltke and O'Connor, §40.2.3a; also GKC, 93 l; otherwise Joüon, §89k [rare fem. ending]), used mostly in psalms and wisdom pieces (see TDOT 1:445–48).

your people. The Luc., LXX, Syr., read "your wives" (*nšyk*), preferred by many commentators and NEB and NJB. Invoked in support of this emendation of MT is the supposed "feminine psychology . . . it is good Oriental etiquette for a lady to ask after a gentleman's wife, not for a gentleman to do so" (Montgomery and Gehman, 217), a comment out of step with end-of-the-century tastes and understanding. The foregoing description, in vv. 5–6, leaves the reader unprepared for such a comment on the part of the queen. The subject of the king's wives is introduced again in 11:1–13.

who wait upon you. For this idiom, see Note on 1 Kgs 1:2.

9. *Blessed be YHWH your God who has delighted in you, setting you on the throne of Israel; because of YHWH's love of Israel forever, he made you king to do justice and righteousness.* An encomium that praises YHWH for his choice of Solomon (also expressed earlier by Hiram, in 5:21) and for his everlasting love of Israel (often in Deuteronomy: 4:37; 7:8, 13; 10:15; 23:6).

10. *Then she gave the king one hundred and twenty talents of gold.* The same amount of gold was given by Hiram; cf. 9:14. Rather than being a fixed sum deemed the correct amount to be delivered to a great sovereign, the number is typological, standing for completeness.

11. *Moreover, Hiram's fleet, which carried gold from Ophir, brought from Ophir a very large amount of almug wood and precious stones.* A parenthetical note on luxury items that arrived via the Red Sea, suggested by the itemization in v. 10. In contrast to 9:26–28, in which the fleet is Solomon's, and Hiram appears as partner to an Israelite enterprise, the present verse speaks only of Hiram's voyage to Ophir. The two are joined again, on an equal basis, in v. 22. Considering that 1 Kgs 10 emphasizes the contributions of foreign monarchs to Solomon's riches (cf. vv. 10, 15, 25), the reference to Hiram alone is in order.

from Ophir. See above at 9:28. The second "from Ophir" is lacking in LXX and 2 Chr 9:10 and is at odds with the identification of *almug.*

almug *wood.* Hebrew *'almūggîm*, a hapax; 2 Chr 2:7 has the transposed form *'algûmmîm*; KJV: "sandal-wood;" NAB: "cabinet wood"; NEB, NJB, NJPSV: "almug wood." From ancient times, the identification of this wood has been problematic; the proffered "sandalwood" derived from Sanskrit is "extremely unlikely" (Greenfield and Mayerhoffer 1967, 83–85). Though the present verse seems to indicate that the wood was imported from a tropical source, 2 Chr 2:7 suggests that the *almug* was native to the Mediterranean coast and Lebanon. Distinction between the two sources for *almug* wood led to positing two separate timbers and one Talmudic tradition, which is alive in Modern Hebrew, identified the Red Sea *almug* with "coral" (b. *Roš Haš.* 23a). In Ug, *almg* appears among other native trees; in Akk, the *elammakku* was a tree whose wood was prized by Mesopotamian kings from the days of Yaḫdunlim, king of Mari, down to Sennacherib; for references to its use for doors, tables, and beds, see CAD E, 75–76; cf. Malamat 1965b, 368. Accepting this identification, the second *m'pyr* "from Ophir," indeed looks like a dittograph.

12. *The king made supports from the* almug *wood for the House of YHWH and the king's house, and harps and lyres for the singers.* A second footnote, expounding on the use of *almug* wood, referred to in v. 11.

supports. Hebrew *misʿād* is a hapax. From its root meaning, "supports" of some kind may be suspected but, beyond this, nothing specific can be said. The early translations offer "pillars"; "railings" or balustrades; so also the medieval commentators. The NJPSV "decorations" follows Syr., and NEB "stools" looks like guesswork, although Akk *nēmedu*, a kind of armchair or footstool (CAD N/2,156), derives from *emēdu*, "to lean against, stand by, place, support." Second Chronicles 9:11 has *mĕsillôt*, unidentifiable "ramps" (?); on this reading, see R. Weiss 1968, 130.

harps and lyres. This commonly accepted translation is based on mere guesswork, since the instruments designated by Heb *kinnôr* and *nēbel* are far from clear. Both were handheld instruments, the former plucked "by hand" (cf. 1 Sam 16:16), the latter perhaps by a plectrum. See ABD 4:937 for a summary of the evidence, which suggests that "lyre and lute (?)" might be a better rendition.

for the singers. Part of the court staff; cf. 2 Sam 19:36; 2 Chr 35:25; as well as the Temple; cf. Ezek 40:44. Sennacherib's Prism Inscription from his Third Campaign records that "male and female singers" were among the people deported from Judah (see translation in Cogan and Tadmor 1988, 339).

13. *King Solomon gave the queen of Sheba all she desired, whatever she asked.* This clause has served as the point of departure for those who interpret the visit as a diplomatic mission, during which negotiations between the two royal personages were held; see further in Comment.

besides what he gave her as befitted King Solomon. Hebrew *kĕyad hammelek*, lit., "according to the king's hand" (= power), refers to the king's largesse, as in Esth 1:7; 2:18. He was reciprocating the gifts received at her hands (v. 2).

Then she and her servants left and returned to her country. A typical closing of a narrative; cf. 1 Sam 28:25.

COMMENT

Structure and Theme

The theme of Solomon's great wisdom and wealth, especially as recognized by a foreign monarch, ties the story of the queen of Sheba into the overall context of the Solomonic history. This unit is bracketed by references to gold, beginning with the note on the enormous quantity of gold brought from Ophir (9:28), mentioned again in the footnote in v. 11, and followed up by further gold accountings scattered throughout vv. 14–25. The unparalleled luxury of those days is further underscored by editorial notes in vv. 10b, 12b.

By some accounts, the story interrupts the series of notes begun in 9:26–28, which continues in 10:16ff., evidence for its secondary introduction into the present context; many of these "fantastic" notes about the king's riches are themselves "young," and show no particular Dtr signs (e.g., Eissfeldt, Würthwein). But such a reading, which posits gloss upon gloss, misses the associative technique by which materials of diverse genres were originally interwoven.

Though the ostensive purpose of the queen's visit was to verify the rumors concerning Solomon (by her own admission in v. 6), Dtr refrained from giving the details of the contest that took place between the host and his guest. Apposite tales probably were not lacking by the time of the composition of Kings (as seen in the "harlots' judgment" in 3:16–27, a testimony to the king's wisdom) and, if this is true, they must have been judged extrinsic to the current context, in which praise of Solomon and his God take center stage. It was for later tradition to take up the slack and more so. For example, Josephus knew the queen by name, Nikaule, who ruled "Egypt and Ethiopia" (*Ant.* 8.158–59). A series of suggestive riddles, typical entertainment at a wedding feast, were later associated with Sheba's queries (*Midrash Mishle*; Stein 1993). The post-Talmudic *Targum Sheni* to the book of Esther relates a story that had developed around the theme of Solomon's unique throne; other tales told of their love-making, while the Qu'ran emphasizes the conversion of the queen to the true faith (see the surveys in these traditions by Silberman 1974 and Watt 1974; Lassner 1993 analyzes the social setting of the Jewish and Muslim embellishments); the Ethiopian royal line took pride in its ancestor, the son of Solomon and Sheba (for the late Ethiopic lore, see Ullendorff 1974; and that of medieval Christian Europe, Watson 1974).

History

Our knowledge of the history of Sheba and its neighbors is still scanty, and archaeological investigation has only begun to uncover the civilizations of south Arabia (Van Beek 1974). Nothing in the way of architecture or documentation attests to a tenth-century BCE Sabean Kingdom over which the unnamed queen who visited Jerusalem might have reigned. But while the possibility of such a visit cannot a priori be ruled out, a number of details in the account point to the end of the eighth or the beginning of the seventh century as providing a likely setting for the creation of this fabulous tale. This was the age when trade with South Arabia flourished; Assyria's kings received gifts and tribute of gold, precious stones, spices, and camels from sundry Arab tribes, over whom queens often ruled, though none of these desert denizens can be directly traced to Sheba (cf., e.g., ANET, 284a, 286a, 292a; Eph'al 1982, 82–87; 118–23). Likewise, it is reported that Hezekiah of Judah boasted of his stores of "silver and gold, spices and fine oil" (2 Kgs 20:13), the same Hezekiah under whose auspices the proverbs of Solomon were "copied" and studied (cf. Prov. 25:1). Wisdom circles in Jerusalem, then, in developing the image of the all-wise and wealthy Solomon, may well have recounted that an Arabian queen came from afar, centuries earlier, during the heyday of Israel's imperial age, bearing rich gifts, as was the contemporary protocol. Granted this reconstruction, many of the critical readings of this legendary account have missed the intended mark of the storyteller: e.g., taking the queen's visit as a "trade mission" (Wiseman), writing that one of the hard questions put to Solomon (cf. v. 3) concerned the caravan routes running through his realm (Ahlström 1993a, 518–19); saying that she left for home after having gained a commercial agreement with Solomon (Bright 1981, 215); all after the king's 24th year (Malamat 1982, 203); all such historical speculations stray far from the discernible facts.

XV. CONCLUDING NOTES ON SOLOMON'S WEALTH AND TRADE

(10:14–29)

10 [14]Now the weight of the gold that was received by Solomon in a single year was six hundred sixty-six gold talents, [15]besides (what came) from traders and the business of merchants and all the Arab kings and the governors of the land.

[16]King Solomon made two hundred large shields of beaten gold; six hundred (shekels) of gold went into one large shield; [17]three hundred bucklers of beaten gold, three minas of gold went into one buckler. The king put them in the House of the Forest of Lebanon.

[18]The king made a great ivory throne and overlaid it with pure gold. [19]The throne[a] had six steps; the back of the throne[a] had a rounded top. There were arms on each side of the seat, with two lions standing beside the arms. [20]And twelve lions were standing there on the six steps on each side. There was nothing like it ever made in any kingdom.

[21]All King Solomon's drinking vessels were of gold; all the vessels in the House of the Forest of Lebanon were of refined gold; there were none of silver, (for) it was considered of no value in Solomon's days. [22]For the king had a Tarshish fleet on the sea with Hiram's fleet. Once every three years, the Tarshish fleet would arrive carrying gold and silver, ivories, apes, and peacocks.

[23]Thus, King Solomon exceeded all the kings of the earth in wealth and wisdom. [24]All the world sought an audience with Solomon in order to hear his wisdom, which God had put in his heart. [25]And each one brought his tribute: silver vessels, gold vessels, garments, arms, spices, horses, and mules, according to the yearly due.

[26]Solomon assembled chariots and horsemen; he had one thousand four hundred chariots and twelve thousand horsemen. He stationed them[b] in the chariot cities and with the king in Jerusalem. [27]Solomon made silver (as plentiful) in Jerusalem as stones, and he made the cedars as plentiful as the sycamores in the Shephelah. [28]The source of Solomon's horses was Egypt and Cilicia; the king's merchants purchased them in Cilicia. [29]A chariot exported from Egypt cost six hundred shekels of silver and a horse one hundred fifty; and similarly, they exported (them) to all the kings of the Hittites and the kings of Aram.

---

[a] Ketib: *ksh*; qere: *ks'*.
[b] Vocalize: *wayyanniḥēm*; see Note.

NOTES

10 14. *Now the weight of the gold that was received by Solomon in a single year was six hundred sixty-six gold talents.* An extraordinary amount, perhaps the

approximate summary of 120 (in 1 Kgs 9:14) + 420 (in 9:28) + 120 (in 10:10); so Šanda, who suggests that "in a single year" refers to one particular year of unprecedented income, not to every year. Comparison of this figure (over 25 tons!) with the wealth claimed to have been amassed by Egyptian and Mesopotamian conquerors does not make it more "feasible," as Millard (1989b) would have it; the reconstructed picture of the Davidic-Solomonic monarchy supports taking the high number as a literary coinage, meant to impress the reader/listener; see Note to 5:6.

15. *besides (what came) from traders and the business of merchants, and all the Arab kings, and the governors of the land.* Only the general sense of this additional note on the king's income from trade duties can be gotten from the very difficult Hebrew.

traders. Hebrew *'anšê hattārîm*, seemingly from **twr*, "to explore, scout," after goods and merchandise (so medieval commentators), but in this sense, only in the present verse. The Tg.: *mē'ăgar 'ûmānayā'*, "from the tariff of the artisans"; similarly LXX: *phoron*, translating Heb *'onšê* (as in 2 Kgs 23:33), and adopted by all moderns: "besides the tolls of the traders." The proposed emendation to *taggar*, from Akk *tamkāru* through Aram, "merchant," one involved in international business (as opposed to *rōkēl*, the small businessman of the local market [see next Note]) (so, e.g., Šanda; Landsberger 1967, 176, 187) remains an attractive guess based on a LH lexeme.

the business of merchants. Hebrew *misḥar hārōkĕlîm*, from **rkl*, "to trade"; cf. Ezek 27:13; Neh 13:20; on the basis of Song 3:6, the medieval commentators conjectured that they were spice traders. As used in Ezek 27, *rōkēl* is synonymous with *sōḥēr* and does not connote the "peddler" as it can in LH; cf., too, Nah 3:16. This may explain the substitution in 2 Chr 9:14 of *hārōkĕlîm* by *hassōḥărîm* (Elat 1977, 202–3 elaborates on the international position of these traders under royal patronage).

As for the disputed meaning of **sḥr*, "to move about," as well as "trade," see Speiser 1961. Perhaps it is best to repoint the first word as *missaḥar*, rather than create an unattested noun; for *saḥar*, cf. Isa 23:3, 18.

all the Arab kings. The punctuation erroneously gives *'ereb* "mixed unit" for *'ărāb*, "Arab." For "mixed" groups, cf. Exod 12:38; Ezek 30:5; Neh 13:3; note that Jer 25:24 preserves a doublet. See, too, the comment on Ezek 30:5 in Greenberg 1997, ad loc.

governors of the land. The district administrators of home territories (1 Kgs 4:7–19) are designated by the term *niṣṣābîm*, "prefects"; consequently, the "governors" (*paḥôt*) referred to here may be the administrators of foreign lands. On this relatively late term, see 20:24.

16. *King Solomon made two hundred large shields.* Hebrew *ṣinnâ*; a shield of body length to protect the entire person, perhaps on three sides; cf. the image in Ps 5:13: "Envelop us with your favor as with a large shield." In 1 Sam 17:7, an attendant carried such a shield for Goliath. See the illustration in ANEP 372.

of beaten gold. Hebrew *šāḥûṭ* is of uncertain etymology. The Luc., LXX, and later Talmudic tradition (*b. Ḥul.* 30b; followed by Rashi, Qimḥi) offer "beaten" or "stretched out" (metathesis of *šṭḥ?). This means that the shields were not of solid gold, but their wooden frame was covered with a hammered overlay. Others, e.g., Tg.: "fine gold"; Vulg.: "pure gold."

six hundred (shekels) of gold went into one large shield. Literally, "went up upon," i.e., it took six hundred shekels of gold to cover each shield.

17. *three hundred bucklers of beaten gold.* Hebrew *māgēn* denotes a small, round, hand-held shield.

three minas of gold went into one buckler. There were fifty shekels in a mina, making the buckler one-quarter as expensive as a shield.

The king put them in the House of the Forest of Lebanon. The shields were, for the most part, used in royal ceremonies; cf. 14:26 on their pillaging by Shishak. For the shields of the Temple guard, cf. 2 Kgs 11:10. The archaeological and extrabiblical textual references to gold (and bronze) shields collected by Millard (1994c) point up their analogous use in many ancient cultures. In the depiction of the temple of Muṣaṣir (Urartu) on a relief from Khorsabad, round shields can be seen hung above either side of the entrance (ANEP 370); in the booty taken from that temple were "six golden shields, which were suspended to the right and left of his (the god's) cella" (CAD A/2, 269a). On the House of the Forest of Lebanon, see Note on 7:2.

18. *The king made a great ivory throne and overlaid it with pure gold.* Hebrew *mûpāz* is a hapax, interpreted in 2 Chr 9:17 as *ṭāhôr*, "pure" gold; so Luc., LXX, Tg. Perhaps related to this puzzling word is 'ûpāz-gold in Jer 10:9 and Dan 10:5, which looks like a place-name (Tg. offers "Ophir"). The plain sense requires the gold appliqué to have been separate from the ivory inlay and not covering it. Compare the beds and armchairs inlaid with ivory sent as tribute by Hezekiah to Sennacherib (see Cogan and Tadmor 1988, 339).

19. *The throne had six steps.* Ketib: *ksh*; qere: *ks'*; also Job 26:9.

the back of the throne had a rounded top. For "a rounded top," many commentators (e.g., Šanda, Montgomery and Gehman, Gray) and some translations (NEB) adopt LXX and read: "had a calf's head" (*r'š 'ēgel* for MT: *r'š 'āgôl*); cf. Josephus, *Ant.* 8.140. The interchange is explained as a Masoretic alteration to avoid associating Solomon with the "sinful" calf symbolism, later known from Jeroboam's kingdom (cf. 12:28–30). However, depictions of thrones from the ancient Near East show straight-back chairs with rounded tops as the conventional style; e.g., ANEP 332, 458; and see the survey of Canciani and Pettinato 1965.

There were arms on each side of the seat. The use of *šebet* for the throne seat is otherwise unattested.

with two lions standing beside the arms. Animal figures are known to have been worked into chair armrests (cf. ANEP 332, 458); here the lions are described as freestanding alongside the throne. For "lion" imagery with reference to the tribe of Judah (i.e., the House of David), cf. Gen 49:9; and, in general, as symbolic of strength, though used ironically, cf. Ezek 19:1–9; Nah 2:12–14.

20. *And twelve lions were standing there on the six steps on each side.* The pl. 'ryym, only here, after the regular 'rywt in the preceding verse may just be

an error, rather than an artificial form distinguishing the throne lions from the real ones (GKC, 87o, followed by Montgomery and Gehman).

There was nothing like it ever made in any kingdom. The enthusiasm of the Israelite writer can easily be countered by numerous examples of grand thrones built for foreign monarchs; see, e.g., the listing in Montgomery and Gehman, ad loc.; see also ANEP 415–17, 458, 460, 463. The only feature unexampled in ancient Near Eastern representations of thrones is the six-stepped approach to the throne's platform.

21. *All King Solomon's drinking vessels were of gold; all the vessels in the House of the Forest of Lebanon were of refined gold.* In addition to the shields (vv. 16–17), the royal "museum" had other gold pieces on display. For "refined gold," see Note to 6:20.

there were none of silver, (for) it was considered of no value in Solomon's days. The first negative (*'ên*) should not be omitted (GKC, 152y footnote 1; Stade, following 2 Chr 9:20); good sense can be obtained by dividing the verse into two separate clauses (so LXX and all medieval commentators).

22. *For the king had a Tarshish fleet on the sea with Hiram's fleet.* Tarshish is mentioned as a port of call for the Phoenician merchant fleet; cf. Isa 23:1, 6; Jer 10:9; Ezek 27:12; Jonah 1:3; and 2 Chr 9:21, in which the present verse is read: "For the king had ships that sailed to Tarshish" (cf. 20:36–37). An argument in favor of the identification of Tarshish with the Iberian Tartessos on the Atlantic Coast is its being the source of metals (cf. Ezek 27:12) not available in Asia Minor; see Elat 1982. But association with Tarsus in Anatolia seems better founded. Tarshish appears together with "the descendants of Javan [= Greece]: Elishah [= Cyprus] and Tarshish, Kittim [= Kition] and Dodanim [= Rhodes]" in Gen 10:4; a similar listing is given in an Assyrian text of Esarhaddon: "from Cyprus to Tarsus (Akk *Tarsisi*)" (ANET, 290a). Moreover, upland from Tarsus, important ore deposits are known from the Taurus Mountain range. See, in full, Lemaire 2000.

The designation "Tarshish fleet" in no way implies that Solomon was involved in Tyre's Mediterranean trade. Most agree that in the present context, the reference is to a type of ship, rather than to a particular destination — thus, a large oceangoing vessel. Influencing this judgment is the cargo of monkeys and peacocks, pointing in the direction of Africa rather than the Mediterranean. Barnett (1956, 91–92) detected a Tarshish-ship in a relief fragment depicting the escape of Luli, king of Sidon, from Sennacherib's army aboard a ship equipped with oars (Gk *tarsos*) rather than sails; see illustration, Barnett 1977, 42.

Once every three years. Denotes a very long voyage, similar to a storyteller's "three-day journey," and should not be read as an attempt to indicate its exact length. Thus, referring to Herodotus's report of the three-year circumnavigation of Africa by Phoenician sailors, from a Red Sea port, returning through the Pillars of Heracles (Gibraltar), at the instigation of Neco of Egypt (Herodotus 4.42) is extraneous to the present datum.

Given the realities of such a journey, its length was due as much to the rigors of ancient seafaring as it was to the distance to the final port of call. Navigating the Red Sea down to Aden and then through the Straights of Mandab into the Indian Ocean required great skill, with particular attention given to seasonal winds and currents. Long layover periods likely account for much of the "three years" mentioned.

the Tarshish fleet would arrive carrying gold and silver, ivories. The Heb hapax *šenhāb* may be a compound word—*šēn*, "tooth," plus *hb*, "elephant" (derived from Egyptian). Otherwise, "ivory" is simply *šēn*, as in 22:39, which prompts some to prefer the older emendation *šēn* (*wĕ*)*hobnîm*, "ivory and ebony," as in Ezek 27:15 (BDB 1042a). The history of ivory use and trade in the ancient world is surveyed by Barnett 1982.

apes. Hebrew *qôp* is a *Kulturwort* that appears in late Akk as *uqupu* and may ultimately have arrived in Semitic-speaking areas through Egyptian *gf* (see Albright 1969b, 212–13). Just what species of monkey is referred to is indeterminable. Note that Sumerian UGU.BI$_4$ = Akk *pagû* is not the source of this etymon; see Klein 1979. For monkeys brought as gifts to Ashurnasirpal II, see Barnett 1977, 43, and as tribute to Shalmaneser III, see ANET, 353–54. See also ARI 2 §§248, 426, 597–98.

peacocks. Hebrew *tūkkî* may be a loanword from Tamil (*tokai*); see Rabin 1982b; so NJPSV. This would imply trade with India or at least with an intermediate port through which these impressive creatures would have been available. Others suggest some form of ape; NAB, NEB: "monkeys"; NJB: "baboons" (based on a derivation from Egyptian *ky* with a prefixed feminine *t*; so Albright 1969b, 213; cf. G. R. Driver 1955, 134 n. 5). The ancient translators were no more decisive; Tg. and Syr.: *ṭawwāsîn*, "peacocks"; Luc. transliterates, and other LXX versions are suspect.

23–24. *Thus, King Solomon exceeded all the kings of the earth in wealth and wisdom. All the world sought an audience with Solomon.* The reading in 2 Chr 9:23, "all the kings of the world" (so Luc., LXX, Syr. in present verse), assimilates MT 1 Kgs 9:23. Though "all the world" seems elliptical, note that a similar pair— "all peoples" and "all the kings of the earth"—appears in 1 Kgs 5:14.

sought an audience. The idiom also appears in Ps 24:6; Prov 29:25.

wisdom which God had put in his heart. Cf. 1 Kgs 3:12.

25. *And each one brought his tribute: silver vessels, gold vessels, garments, arms, spices, horses, and mules, according to the yearly due.* The presentation of gifts was anticipated by LXX in its reading of 5:14; see Note there.

arms. Hebrew *nešeq* is regularly "weapons" (cf. 2 Kgs 10:2) and is so translated by all except LXX, which offers *stakten*, "myrrh," a unique rendering (favored by Montgomery and Gehman and several others) explained as having been influenced by the following "spices" and derived from a root with an Ar cognate; but all this is unnecessary. Presentations of weapons are perfectly in order; note, e.g., the weapons sent by Tushratta of Mitanni as gifts to Amenhotep III (EA 22).

spices. See Note on 10:2.

26. *Solomon assembled chariots and horsemen; he had one thousand four hundred chariots.* This "reasonable" number of chariots was the basis for discounting the exaggerated figure in 5:6; see ad loc.

twelve thousand horsemen. The same number as given in 5:6.

He stationed them in the chariot cities and with the king in Jerusalem. The MT: *wayyanḥēm,* "he led them," better vocalized (as in 2 Chr 9:25) *wayyanni-ḥēm.* Cf. similar mispointing in 2 Kgs 18:11. Some of the chariot cities were listed above, in 9:15, 17–18. Two toponyms in the central Negev, Beth-marcaboth ("House of Chariots") and Hazarsusah ("Horse-fold"; Josh 19:5), may have been royal establishments.

27. *Solomon made silver (as plentiful) in Jerusalem as stones.* Echoing v. 21, which spoke of the deflated value of silver. In its present position, the verse interrupts the associative linking of the "chariot cities" (v. 26) and the horse trade (vv. 28–30); Montgomery and Gehman: "a late intrusion . . . probably introduced from Ch[ronicles]."

and he made the cedars as plentiful as the sycamores in the Shephelah. Hebrew *šiqmâ* is the *Ficus sycomorus,* a tree common to the lowlands of Israel, suitable for roofing (cf. *b. Meṣiʿa* 117b); its fig-like fruits were "dressed" (cf. Amos 7:14) to make them edible; see Feliks 1981, 56–60. That costly cedars, imported from Lebanon, were plenteous is here proclaimed as another sign of Solomon's being flush with gold.

28. *The source of Solomon's horses was Egypt and Cilicia.* The Masoretic punctuation did not recognize that *qwh* is the toponym Que (in cuneiform sources *Qua/Que*), later Cilicia; Luc., LXX, and Vulg. (*Coa;* so Eusebius; still NEB) seem to have preserved some recollection of a proper noun, but it was not until the late nineteenth century, with the aid of newly-deciphered inscriptions, that it was rediscovered. Singularly, Abarbanel had reasoned that it "was the name of a place or a locale of plentiful good horses." Neighboring Togarmah was a recognized source for equestrian needs; cf. Ezek 27:14.

Egypt. Much controversy reigns over this vocable, whether it is to be read *miṣrayîm,* "Egypt," as it is throughout the Bible, or *muṣri,* "Musri," a toponym in Cappadocia known from Assyrian texts down to the tenth century (see Tadmor 1961; somewhat different, RlA 8.497), and unattested in MT. In favor of the reading "Musri" is its location in a well-attested horse-rearing area (unlike Egypt) and, taken together, Que and Musri would represent the major Anatolian depots for horse trading (so Montgomery and Gehman, Noth, DeVries, Jones, NJB, et al.). The biblical references to Judah's dependence on Egypt for horses and chariots (e.g., Isa 31:1–3) referring to military aid and the occasional gift of horses from Egypt to Assyria (e.g., ANET, 286b), though several centuries later than the Solomonic era, are small in number compared with the quantity of horses—hundreds and sometimes thousands of animals—that the mountain kingdoms north and east of Assyria surrendered to the Empire as tax and tribute (e.g., ARI 2 §§574; Lie 1929, 31, line 193; see Elat 1977, 69–82). Might "Egypt" be, after all, a gloss or dittography from the following verse, and so omitted (with NAB)?

the king's merchants purchased them in Cilicia. Or: "obtained them by purchase" (NEB). For the derivation of *mĕḥîr* from Akk *maḥiru* (CAD M/1, 92–98, "market place, tariff, purchase price"), see Landsberger 1967, 184 n. 2.

29. *A chariot exported from Egypt cost six hundred shekels of silver.* Literally, "came up and went out"; the verb *ʿlh* is often used for leaving Egypt; cf. Gen 13:1; Exod 1:10; 12:38; 13:18. Many modern translations transpose as "imported." The long form of the verb plus *waw*-consecutive (*wtʿlh*), rather than the jussive, appears many times in Kings and seems to be preferred before a guttural; e.g., 1 Kgs 16:25; 18:32; 2 Kgs 3:2; 13:11; see Joüon, §79m.

from Egypt. A problem exists concerning the identification of the toponym *mṣrym* as Egypt similar to the problem raised in v. 28; Egypt is not a land of timber and is not known to have exported chariots. The northern timber reserves are well known; and perhaps "Musri" was the original reading here as well. Emendation of the initial particle *mem* to *lamed*, "to Egypt" (so Mowinckel 1962, 282 n. 11) would place Egypt on the receiving end of the transaction, as are the Hittite and Aramean kings mentioned at the end of the verse. Ikeda (1982, 221–27) argues that the reference here is to a single chariot, "first and foremost for ceremonial and processional use," its very high price being another example of Solomon's great wealth.

six hundred shekels of silver. An inflated figure; see the Note on similar large numbers at 1 Kgs 5:6. The LXX reads 100.

and a horse one hundred fifty. The LXX, 50. According to the figures in MT, the price of a horse was a quarter of that of a chariot; in LXX, with its lower figures, it was half as expensive. Lacking evidence for contemporary market prices, one would be foolish to prefer the lower set as "more probable" (Stade and Schwally) or to judge them as "probably a correction to meet later proportions of value" (Montgomery and Gehman).

similarly, they exported (them) to all the kings of the Hittites and the kings of Aram. Solomon's merchants (mentioned in v. 28) are the only antecedent for "they."

kings of the Hittites. For their identification as the rulers of the neo-Hittite kingdoms in north Syria, see Note to 11:1.

COMMENT

Structure and Themes

The first unit consists of a series of short notes, vv. 14–15, 16–17, 18–20, 21, 22, associatively connected by the repeated mention of gold, acquired through trade and tribute. The theme of incomparability ties them all to the previous unit on the visit of the queen of Sheba (vv. 10, 12, 20). Everything is wrapped up by the summary in vv. 23–25, somewhat of an *inclusio*, paralleling the distant 3:13; 5:9, 14. The "superabundant exaggeration" of this closing section has sometimes been compared to extrabiblical texts: "V. 25 appears to be phrased after the pompous lists of booty in Ass. inscriptions" (Montgomery and Gehman, 225). But, whereas those lists have a foothold in the rapacious pillaging actually undertaken by Assyria's monarchs, the biblical hyperbole is of another sort. The descriptions of Solomon's "accruing of bullion, vessels, and other valuable artifacts in Jerusalem is not intended to be credible, but incredible" (Knoppers 1993, 130–31). Thus, the fashioning of so many shields and the king's stepped throne are but examples of the extravagant display to which this enormous wealth was put.

A second unit, vv. 26–29, stands outside the summary statement in vv. 23–25; it is a report concerning horses and chariots ("much like a business memorandum," Montgomery and Gehman), but it is more than an afterthought or a tag to v. 25. Reading these verses together with the condemnation of Solomon, which follows immediately in 1 Kgs 11, suggests that behind the collocation stands the prohibition in the Deuteronomic law of the king's amassing horses and silver and taking many wives (Deut 17:16–17). (This connection was made by R. Isaac in *b. Sanh.* 21b and adopted by Qara, ad loc.)

History

Pride of place among Solomon's commercial endeavors must be given to his alliance with Tyre, which served as Israel's major trading partner, in reciprocal import-export (5:15–25), as well as in international markets (9:26–28; 10:11–22). In both sectors, the Phoenicians could have dictated the terms of this relationship, considering their recognized position as "merchant of the peoples" (Ezek 27:3). The Israelites' contribution to the partnership was access to the inland routes that crisscrossed the Palestinian land-bridge as well as manpower for joint ventures. It does not seem likely that Solomon took part in Mediterranean trade, almost exclusively a Phoenician venue. But voyages originating at the southern Red Sea port of Ezion-geber were a different story.

Only the trade items recorded in 9:28 and 10:11, 22 can provide some indication of the direction taken by the Israelite-Phoenician vessels once the open seas were reached; both passage to the east—the Persian Gulf and India—and to the west—the Horn of Africa and south—were options. The Egyptian "Tale of the Shipwrecked Sailor" (Simpson 1973, 50–56) refers to the cargo brought from Punt (see Note on 9:28), which included various spices and cosmetics, "giraffe tails, large cakes of incense, elephant tusks, hounds, apes, baboons and every kind of precious thing." This striking similarity speaks for an African itinerary of the combined fleet. Trade in this region would have brought Israel and Tyre into competition with Egypt, and Solomon's treaty with Siamun may have regulated the terms by which the northern "newcomers" entered what had been for centuries an Egyptian bailiwick (Yeivin 1959–60; Kitchen 1971; Ikeda 1991, 125–28).

A piquant detail on the luxury items seen at Solomon's court, part of the receipts of the African trade, is recorded in the reference to monkeys and peacocks (v. 22). Ancient Near Eastern monarchs delighted in exotic pets (Barnett 1973; Ikeda 1982, 219–20; 1991, 121–22), and the presence of these animals in Jerusalem supported the claim that Israel's king equaled or even surpassed the others.

A sure picture of the role of Solomon's traders in the international horse-and-chariot trade is unattainable, let alone the claimed "royal monopoly" of these middlemen (so Bright 1981, 217, among others, and rightly rejected by Schley 1987), given the disputed topographical names in these verses. For one thing, the neo-Hittite and Aramean kings would not have had need for their services in markets so close to home in Anatolia. Reason requires that for Israelite tradesmen to have done business on the supposed scale given here would have meant recognition in upper Syria of Israelite control of the major north–south roadways, as well as Israel's harmonious relations with the Phoenician maritime powers and with Egypt. Such a situation may have existed for a short while during the early years of Solomon's reign, before the final breakaway of Damascus (cf. 11:23–25). But perhaps the reference is, after all, to the role of the Israelite merchants as middlemen or Egyptian agents for the marketing of luxury items (see above, Notes to vv. 28–29).

XVI. SOLOMON'S APOSTASY

(11:1–13)

11 ¹Now King Solomon loved many foreign women; besides Pharaoh's daughter, (there were) women from the Moabites, Ammonites, Edomites, Sidonians, Hittites, ²from the nations of which YHWH said to the Israelites: "You should not join with them and *they* should not join with you, for they surely will entice you after their gods." To such (women) Solomon held fast out of love. ³He had seven hundred wives of royal rank and three hundred concubines; and his wives enticed him. ⁴In Solomon's old age, his wives enticed him after other gods, and his heart was not fully with YHWH his God as was the heart of David his father. ⁵Solomon followed Ashtoreth, god of the Sidonians, and Milcom the abomination of the Ammonites.ª ⁶Solomon did what was displeasing to YHWH and was not loyal to YHWH as David his father. ⁷Then Solomon built a high place for Chemosh, the abomination of Moab on the mountain east of Jerusalem, and for Molech, the abomination of the Ammonites.ᵇ ⁸Thus he did for all of his foreign wives, who sacrificed and offered to their gods.

⁹YHWH was incensed at Solomon, for he had turned away from YHWH God of Israel, who had appeared to him twice ¹⁰and had commanded him about this matter of not following other gods; but he did not keep what YHWH commanded. ¹¹YHWH said to Solomon: "Because this was your will, and you did not keep my covenant and my statutes which I commanded you, I most certainly will tear the kingdom away from you and give it to your servant. ¹²But I will not do it during your days, for the sake of David your father, but I will tear it away from your son. ¹³Still, I will not tear away the whole kingdom; I will give your son one tribe for the sake of David my servant and for the sake of Jerusalem, which I have chosen."

ª Syr. adds (from v. 7?): "and after Chemosh, the abomination of the Moabites."
ᵇ LXX adds: "and for Ashtoreth, the abomination of the Sidonians" (so 2 Kgs 23:13).

NOTES

11   1. *Now King Solomon loved many foreign women; besides Pharaoh's daughter, (there were) women from the Moabites, Ammonites, Edomites, Sidonians, Hittites.* Strictly speaking, these nations were not part of the autochthonous population of Canaan forbidden to the Israelites in Deut 7. The LXX extends the list by adding "Arameans" before "the Moabites," and "Amorites" after "the Hittites," at the same time omitting "Sidonians." [DNF: "The original total was no doubt seven, which can be recovered by combining the two lists."]

besides Pharaoh's daughter. The translation smooths over difficult syntax, which has led all commentators to declare the present phrase a late gloss inserted for completeness; LXX removed it to the end of the verse. Note that, in contrast to all of the other women, it is nowhere stated that Solomon built an Egyptian shrine for Pharaoh's daughter in Jerusalem (see 9:16).

Ammonites. Naamah, the mother of Rehoboam, was an Ammonite; cf. 14:21.

Sidonians. Late legend told of Solomon's marrying a daughter of Hiram; see Katzenstein 1997, 88 n. 59. Note the erroneous MT punctuation *ṣēdnîyōt* for the expected *ṣidōnîyōt*.

Hittites. A number of biblical sources utilize the Hebrew term *Ḥittî* in a manner similar to the Neo-Assyrian usage of KUR *Ḥattu*, which originally signified the Hittite Empire and the geographical sphere under Hittite rule and later came to serve as the name for the "Neo-Hittite" states of Anatolia and upper Syria that were the political and cultural heirs of the imperial Hittites (Cogan forthcoming a). Besides the present verse, see, e.g., "the land of the Hittites" in the Euphrates Valley (Josh 1:4); "kings of the Hittites" (1 Kgs 10:29; cf. 2 Kgs 7:6). These latter-day Hittites should be distinguished from "the Hittite," who was part of the autochthonous population of Canaan whom Israel encountered when they entered the land (cf. e.g., Gen 15:20; Num 13:29; Josh 11:3). Note that these "early" Hittites are always referred to in the collective singular, *Ḥittî*, while the first-millennium Hittites appear in the plural, *Ḥittîm*.

2. *from the nations of which YHWH said to the Israelites: "You should not join with them and they should not join with you. . . ."* Hebrew **bw' bĕ-*, as in Josh 23:7, 12, with the sense of associating with, mixing with; interpreted as "intermarry" by NAB, NEB; erroneously "have sexual relationship" (e.g., Jones, Knoppers), which in BH is *bw' 'l*; cf. 2 Sam 16:22. The reference is to the divine command in Deut 7, which lays out the rules for Israel's treatment of the inhabitants of Canaan, specifically, the *ḥērem* regulations: "Do not marry them; do not give your daughter to his son and do not take his daughter for your son, for he will turn away your son from me and worship other gods . . ." (Deut 7:3–4).

for they surely will entice you after their gods. Hebrew *nṭh lb (Qal and Hiphil; vv. 2, 3, 9), "turn the heart," replaces the regular Deuteronomic term **swr mĕ-* (Qal and Hiphil) "turn from (following YHWH)"; cf., e.g., Deut 7:4; 17:17. The LXX reads: "lest"; though favored by some critics, the emphatic *'āken* in MT is construable; cf. Waltke and O'Connor §39.3.5d.

to such (women) Solomon held fast out of love. Hebrew *dabāq bĕ-*, "stick, cling to, hold fast"; cf. 2 Kgs 3:3 for "holding onto" the sins of Jeroboam. Solomon's behavior contrasts with the Deuteronomic plea to love God and to cling to Him; cf. Deut 30:20; Josh 22:5; cf. also Deut 10:20; 11:22; 13:5. For clinging to foreign nations, cf. Josh 23:12.

3. *He had seven hundred wives of royal rank and three hundred concubines; and his wives enticed him.* This sweeping statement describes Solomon's legendary harem. The suggestion is often made that the women were princesses of foreign monarchs who were in league with Solomon, apparently comparing Heb *śārôt* to masc. sg. *śar*, "prince." But *śārôt* describes the present

position of the women vis-à-vis Solomon, as "queens" (cf. Isa 49:23//"kings"), and not necessarily their noble pedigree. See the remarks of Noth, ad loc.; on the royal harem, de Vaux 1961, 115–17. The number of his women adds up to the typological 1000 (700 + 300); cf. also the poetic line in Song 6:8, in which 60 wives, 80 concubines, and countless maidens are lavished upon the king. Later sources use more down-to-earth figures for Rehoboam's (2 Chr 11:21) and Abijah's (13:21) harems.

4. *In Solomon's old age, his wives enticed him after other gods.* In Deut 17:17, the corresponding phrase is construed actively: "so that his heart not go astray."

and his heart was not fully with YHWH his God as was the heart of David his father. Or "wholehearted"; see Note on 8:61.

5. *Solomon followed Ashtoreth, god of the Sidonians.* Somehow, perhaps by scribal oversight, only Ashtoreth, of all the foreign gods mentioned in this passage, "escaped" being referred to by the pejorative appellation "abomination" (cf. Ehrlich).

Ashtoreth, god of the Sidonians. Closely associated in Ugaritic texts with Baal (as one of his consorts?) and attested in later Phoenician texts, this Canaanite goddess is referred to by the singular form (11:33; 2 Kgs 23:13); in all other citations (e.g., Judg 2:13), the plural Ashtaroth is used, perhaps standing for a general term "goddesses" or implying multiple local manifestations of the deity; see DDD cols. 203–13. Some have thought that the vocalization is an example of purposeful defamation on the pattern of the noun *bōšet*, "shame," considering that the original form was *'aštart* (cf. the Mesopotamian Ishtar). See also ABD 1:491–94.

and Milcom, the abomination of the Ammonites. A purposeful alteration of "god of the Ammonites"; so also of Chemosh and Milcom in v. 7. But cf. v. 33 for the unaltered text. Hebrew *šiqqūṣ* denotes a detestable, loathsome object, mostly said of idols, and is often used in Deuteronomy, Dtr, and late prophecy, e.g., Deut 7:26 (**šqṣ* // **tʿb*, "abhor"); 29:16; Isa 66:3; Ezek 5:11.

Milcom. Besides the current context, the name of this Ammonite deity is known from extrabiblical inscriptions; see DDD cols. 1076–80. In a number of instances in MT, it is misvocalized as *malkām*, "their king," as in 2 Sam 12:30; Jer 49:3; Zeph 1:5.

6. *Solomon . . . was not loyal to YHWH as David his father.* Hebrew *millē' 'aḥărê*, lit., "be fully behind," support; earlier, in Num 32:11–12; Deut 1:36; Josh 14:8, 9, 14.

7. *Then Solomon built a high place for Chemosh, the abomination of Moab.* The chief god of the Moabites; cf. Num 21:29; Jer 48:46; known from the Mesha Inscription (Cogan and Tadmor 1988, Appendix 1, no. 1) and the names of Moabite kings and private persons; see DDD cols. 356–62.

on the mountain east of Jerusalem. Namely, the Mount of Olives, a venerable cult site (cf. 2 Sam 15:32), as made clear by 2 Kgs 23:13 (see Note there), where it is remarked that the altar was still standing over three centuries later.

and for Molech, the abomination of the Ammonites. That is, Milcom, as in v. 5 (and so read by Luc.); there is no reason to identify the two; see Note on 2 Kgs 23:10. A (willful?) slip of the pen.

8. *Thus he did for all of his foreign wives, who sacrificed and offered to their gods.* For further examples of participial clauses in which the subject/personal pronoun is omitted, cf. 5:1; Gen 24:30; 37:15; 1 Sam 20:1; cf. GKC, 116s. The *Hiphil* of **qṭr* usually indicates licit worship, the *Piel* idolatry; cf. 1 Kgs 22:44 and Note to 2 Kgs 16:4. A similar anomalous form appears in Jer 48:35.

9. *YHWH was incensed at Solomon.* The verb **'np* in *Hitpael* is used only in Deuteronomy (Deut 1:37; 4:21; 9:8, 20) and Dtr (2 Kgs 17:18). In other biblical passages (and the Moabite Mesha Inscription, line 5), *Qal* forms are common.

for he had turned away from YHWH God of Israel, who had appeared to him twice. The article used as a relative pronoun is a feature of LBH; cf. GKC, 138k and Burney, ad loc.

twice. See above, 1 Kgs 3:5ff.; 9:2ff.

10. *and had commanded him about this matter.* For waw + perfect in narrations of past time as indicating pluperfect, cf. Waltke and O'Connor §32.3e.

of not following other gods. The warning was specifically stated once, in 9:6.

11. *YHWH said to Solomon: "Because this was your will. . . ."* Because the present divine word echoes the prophecy of Ahijah, Qimḥi attributes it to him. The preposition *ʿim* taken as expressing volition and purpose (BDB 768b, 4b); cf. Job 10:13; 15:9; 23:10. More than old age was behind Solomon's apostasy; a willful abandonment of the covenant brings down upon him the harshest of punishments, the sundering of the kingdom.

and you did not keep my covenant and my statutes which I commanded you. The term "covenant" (*běrît*) is known in Kings (e.g., 19:10, 14; 2 Kgs 17:15, 35; 18:12; 23:2, 3, 21) but is not as widely used as are *torâ, miṣwâ, ḥôq,* and *ʿēdūt.* It can also refer to political "treaties" (as in 1 Kgs 5:26; 15:19; 20:34).

I most certainly will tear the kingdom away from you and give it to your servant. Literally fulfilled by the choice of Jeroboam, "Solomon's servant" (cf. v. 26), and symbolically enacted by Ahijah in vv. 29–31; see Note there.

12. *But I will not do it during your days, for the sake of David your father, but I will tear it away from your son.* The delay until after Solomon's death reflects the events as they developed, here presented as a lasting favor to David.

13. *Still, I will not tear away the whole kingdom; I will give your son one tribe.* Specified in v. 32 and 12:20: "Only the tribe of Judah followed the House of David." Otherwise, see 11:31 and 35, which speak of "ten tribes"; see Note there.

for the sake of David my servant and for the sake of Jerusalem, which I have chosen. Another softening of the punishment: though the kingdom founded upon the Davidic covenant and the chosen city will be diminished, they will survive the rupture.

COMMENT

Structure and Themes

The critique of Solomon for his apostate behavior is undisputedly Deuterono-mistic in language and ideology, and it prepares the reader for the choosing of Jeroboam and the secession of the North (cf. especially v. 33). The root of Sol-omon's downfall was his many foreign wives, the very danger of which Israel was warned by Moses in Deut 7:1–4. But unlike that passage, 1 Kgs 11 enumer-ates women from nations not of the seven Canaanite peoples, reminding one of the inclusiveness of Ezra's law against foreign marriages. According to Ezra 9:1–2, 12, the nations with whom Israel was forbidden to marry included those restricted from joining the cult community spoken of in Deut 23:2–9. This "intentional exegetical attempt to extend older pentateuchal provisions to the new times" (so Fishbane 1985, 116, with reference to Ezra) is the innovation of Deuteronomistic historiography.

Parts of the unit may have belonged to a pre-Dtr tradition. Thus, the de-scription of the royal harem in v. 3 does not speak of "foreign" women and their idolatrous influence on the king; rather, like the "Law of the King" in Deut 17:16–17, it is the accumulation of gold, silver, horses, and women that leads to Solomon's overbearing haughtiness (cf. Talshir 1990, 268–71). And though the service of the gods at the high places built by Solomon in vv. 7–8 was by his wives, not the king, still the context of these verses implicates Solomon in active idol-atry. (See the explication of Gersonides at 11:4–9 of Solomon's sin as the license he granted his wives to erect sites for the practice of idolatry in Jerusalem.)

YHWH's promise of punishment is delivered to Solomon by unspecified means (vv. 11–13), its terms echoing the words of Ahijah in his selection of Jeroboam (vv. 11//30–31; 12//34; 13//36).

History

Given his international position, it would have been quite natural for Solomon to have married foreign princesses, as had his father, David, in his time (cf. 2 Sam 3:3). But little beyond this can be said about the king's one thousand women (cf. v. 3); the listing in v. 1 is too general and, except for the repeated reference to his marriage with Pharaoh's daughter and to the fact that the mother of Rehoboam was an Ammonitess (14:21), nothing else is known of Solomon's political unions.

XVII. THE REBELLIONS OF HADAD AND REZON

(11:14–25)

11 [14]So YHWH raised up an adversary for Solomon, Hadad the Edomite; he was of the royal line in Edom. [15]Now, when David was fighting[a] Edom—at the time that Joab the army commander went to bury the slain, having killed every male in Edom, [16]for Joab and all Israel stayed there for six months until they wiped out all males in Edom—[17]Hadad[b] together with some Edomite men, his father's servants, fled in the direction of Egypt. Hadad was still a young lad. [18]They set out from Midian and came to Paran; they took some men with them from Paran and they came to Egypt, to Pharaoh, king of Egypt, who gave him a house, arranged for his maintenance, and gave him land. [19]Hadad found very much favor with Pharaoh, and so he gave him in marriage his wife's sister, the sister of the *Tahpenes*, (that is) the queen mother. [20]The sister of the *Tahpenes* bore him a son, Genubath; the *Tahpenes* weaned him in Pharaoh's house, and Genubath remained in Pharaoh's house with Pharaoh's children. [21]When Hadad heard in Egypt that David slept with his ancestors and that Joab the army commander was dead, Hadad said to Pharaoh: "Permit me to leave, so that I can go to my own country." [22]Pharaoh said to him: "But what are you lacking with me that you want to go to your own country?" He said: "Nothing, but do let me leave."

[23]God raised up an adversary for him, Rezon son of Eliada, who had fled from Hadadezer, king of Zobah, his lord. [24]He gathered men about him and became a leader of a band, when David slew them. They went to Damascus and lived there, and he[c] became king in Damascus. [25]He was an adversary of Israel all the days of Solomon, together with the harm that Hadad (caused); he was hostile toward Israel and became king over Aram.

---

[a] Read with LXX, *bhkwt*, for MT, *bhywt*; see Note.
[b] Heb: "Adad."
[c] Heb: "They."

NOTES

11 14. *YHWH raised up an adversary for Solomon.* The reference is to a human foe, opponent, as in 5:18; cf. also Num 22:22, 32; 1 Sam 29:4; 2 Sam 19:23; Ps 109:6 (// "wicked man"). In LBH, *śāṭān* developed the meaning "prosecutor" (cf. Zech 3:1–2; Job 1:6) and eventually became the name for the one who incites to sinful acts (cf. 1 Chr 21:1); see M. Weiss 1987, 352–62.

Hadad the Edomite. Hadad is likely a hypocoristicon in which only the divine name is retained, an uncommon circumstance, since it is the theophoric element that is usually omitted. The storm god Hadad was revered throughout the ancient Near East, not only in Aramean areas; cf. DDD cols. 716–26. Hadad appears as an element in an Edomite personal name (Gen 36:35) and is attested in the Amarna name Yaptiḫ-Hadda, king of Moresheth-Gath (?) (EA 288:45; 335:10), which obviates the suggestion (Lemaire 1988) to transfer Hadad to Aram and rewrite the whole story (correctly seen by Na'aman 1992, 75).

he was of the royal line in Edom. He may have been a prince, not necessarily in line for the throne (Bartlett 1989, 108); for the suggestion to identify him with the last king (corrected *hdd* for *hdr*) in the Edomite King List in Gen 36:39 (so Montgomery and Gehman), see Comment.

15. *Now, when David was fighting Edom.* Reading (as do most commentators) with LXX *bhkwt* for MT *bhywt*, as in 2 Sam 8:13, and as suggested by the particle *'et.* But the text there reads "Aram" for "Edom" (the alternation between *'d[w]m* and *'rm* occurs frequently in MT, cf. 2 Kgs 16:6; cf. also the prose title to Ps 60:2) which, if adopted, would seem to suggest that Joab, not David was the perpetrator of the slaughter in Edom, David being occupied with battles in Syria.

at the time that Joab the army commander went to bury the slain, having killed every male in Edom. These details, especially the noble act of burying the dead, have given rise to speculative alterations of the text (e.g., Šanda, followed by Gray); Tg. *lhls' qtyly'*, "to strip the slain" (of their gear), may be answering to the propriety of burying foreign dead by skirting the act altogether. Were the dead fallen Israelites after all? (so Ehrlich, Noth).

to bury. The infrequently attested *Piel* form *qibbēr* is intensive, buried "in masses" (BDB 868b); cf. also Num 33:4; Ezek 39:14.

16. *for Joab and all Israel stayed there for six months until they wiped out all males in Edom.* Reference to the war waged against Edom is made in 2 Sam 8:13; Ps 60:2; cf. 1 Chr 18:12, where Abishai, the brother of Joab (1 Sam 26:6), is credited with the victory. There is nothing to support the suggestion that this detail is a Dtr expansion in accord with the *ḥērem* law (Vanoni 1984, 48, 94–95).

17. *Hadad, together with some Edomite men, his father's servants, fled in the direction of Egypt. Hadad was still a young lad.* The name Hadad is anomalously written *'dd*, substituting the East-Semitic form for the Aramaic *hdd*.

18. *They set out from Midian and came to Paran.* Midian is sometimes associated with Transjordan, e.g., with Moab in the Baalam episode (Num 22–23); with Amalek and Qedemite raiders (Judg 6–8); a different Midianite clan joined Moses and Israel in their desert wanderings (Exod 18).

they took some men with them from Paran and they came to Egypt. A realistic detail; guides familiar with the territory were hired to help them cross the desert. Only the general direction of the escape route can be sketched. From Midian in the east (where they had hidden?), the party headed west through the Sinai to Egypt (Bartlett 1976, 210–11; also Rothenberg 1970, 18–19). Their first stop was Paran. Though known from the stories of Israel's wanderings in Sinai, Paran cannot be pinpointed with any accuracy; it may be the general name for the southern deserts, i.e., the Sinai Peninsula (see Aharoni 1979, 199).

to Pharaoh, king of Egypt. Based on the assumption that Hadad was an infant when he arrived and that he married and had a son by the time David died, the time was ca. 990, and the reigning Pharaoh was Amenemope.

who gave him a house, arranged for his maintenance, and gave him land. For a similar grant of an estate as upkeep, cf. the story of Sinuhe, ANET, 22a. The LXX lacks "gave him land," judged by some to be a gloss (Stade, Gray, Würthwein); but these words may have been lost through haplography (leaving everything out between *lw* and *lw*).

arranged for his maintenance. That is, gave orders (Heb *'āmar*) to provide him with a royal allowance; cf. 2 Chr 29:24.

19. *Hadad found very much favor with Pharaoh.* A later Pharaoh, not Solomon's "father-in-law"; perhaps Siamun.

and so he gave him in marriage his wife's sister, the sister of the Tahpenes, *(that is) the queen mother.* Tahpenes is not to be confused with the city-name Tahpanhes (Jer 43:7) or Tehaphnehes (Ezek 30:18), as in some older commentaries. The word seems to be the Hebrew transcription of Egyptian *t3-ḥ(mt)-p3-nsw*, "wife of the king," as pointed out by Grdseloff 1947, 88–90; cf. Kitchen 1973, 273–75 n. 183. In Hittite cuneiform, the term is also transliterated *dahamunzu* (cf. Federn 1960, 33). For the less likely suggestion that the word is a proper name, see Albright 1955, 32.

(that is) the queen mother. The Egyptian term is glossed by the Heb *gĕbîrâ*, literally the "chief or main wife"; see Note on 15:13. Generally, a pronoun *hû'/hî'* introduces the gloss, as in 6:38; 8:2; and especially in geographic identifications; cf., e.g., Gen 14:17; Josh 18:13. But asyndetic translations are known, e.g., Ezek 19:9 (*sûgar//haḥîm*); Prov 22:21 (*qōšt//'imrê 'emet*). See Fishbane 1985, 44–46.

20. *The sister of the* Tahpenes *bore him a son, Genubath.* Other masculine names with the *-at* suffix include Ahuzzath (Gen 26:26), Becorath (1 Sam 9:1), Shimeath (2 Kgs 12:22), but the present name is likely Egyptian or even Edomite.

the Tahpenes *weaned him in Pharaoh's house, and Genubath remained in Pharaoh's house with Pharaoh's children.* The foreign child was raised at court as one of Pharaoh's own, not unlike the young Moses.

22. *Pharaoh said to him: "What are you lacking with me that you want to go to your own country?" He said: "Nothing, but do let me leave."* Two distinct uses of the particle *kî* can be noted. In the first instance, *kî* introduces the direct quotation; cf. Gen 29:34; 1 Kgs 1:13; GKC, 157b; the second one, following the negative, is "but, rather," as in 2:20; 3:22; Gen 18:15.

Nothing. Heb *lō'* should not be corrected to *lô* "to him" (with Burney and supposed qere). Cf. similarly Gen 19:2.

23. *God raised up an adversary for him.* God, rather than YHWH, as in v. 14; can this be taken as indicating the original source of the account, or is this merely a stylistic variant? Noth's correction to YHWH is in either case gratuitous.

In LXX, the entire episode, vv. 23–25aα, has been inserted between v. 14a and 14b, where it is hardly original. The similarity of the opening phrase, "YHWH/God raised up an adversary," may be behind this dislocation.

Rezon son of Eliada. The name means "ruler, potentate" (cf. Judg 5:3; Isa 40:23; Prov 8:15; 31:4) and is attested with the same meaning in Phoenician (KAI 26: A III 2). On this basis, B. Mazar (1986, 157) proposed taking Rezon as a royal title, his personal name being Hezion (preserved in 1 Kgs 15:18). For the suggestion to identify the two as variant forms of a single name, see Note on 15:18.

who had fled from Hadadezer, king of Zobah, his lord. The Aramean kingdom of Zobah ruled over by Hadadezer was named after its capital-center, Ṣupite (so later Assyrian texts; perhaps Baalbek in the upper Beqaʿ Valley of Lebanon). David had conducted a series of wars against Hadadezer, whose sphere of influence stretched from the Euphrates to Ammon in Transjordan; cf. 2 Sam 8:3–8; 10:6–13. Hadadezer is unknown in extrabiblical sources but has been identified with the Aramean king who captured territory just south of Carchemish during the reign of Ashur-rabi II, a contemporary of David (cf. Albright 1975, 533–34; Malamat 1973, 141–42; note the reservations of Pitard 1987, 91).

24. *He gathered men about him and became a leader of a band.* On *gĕdûd*, see Note on 2 Kgs 5:2.

when David slew them. The clause, like v. 15, coordinates the events with David's reign. It is lacking in Luc. and judged a gloss by most critics, based on 2 Sam 8:5, many arguing on supposed historical grounds that the rebellion of Rezon took place only with the weakening of Israel's hold on the Aramean kingdoms; Noth suggested that it fits better at the end of v. 23. But the clause signifies nothing more than that Rezon broke away from under Hadadezer's rule to become a freebooter as a result of David's victory.

They went to Damascus and lived there, and he became king in Damascus. The outline of Rezon's rise to kingship is very much like that of David in his day (cf. 1 Sam 22). The plural *wymlkw* in MT cannot be maintained and may have been so written because of the preceding plural verbs; perhaps restore *wayyamlikûhû*, "they installed him as king."

25. *together with the harm that Hadad (caused).* The present translation follows MT (so NJPSV and partly NAB), but the unexpected reintroduction of Hadad at this point is a bit harsh, and it hints at details not included in the rendition given in vv. 14–22. This has led to innumerable rewritings of this passage. Most transfer it, following the larger alteration in LXX, to be placed after v. 22 and read: "Hence the harm which Hadad caused; he loathed Israel and ruled Edom" (NJB; cf. also NEB). But LXX may be an attempt to smooth a difficult Hebrew text, especially *ʾrm* (MT) read as *ʾdm*. If the clause is not secondary altogether (Noth), might the name Hadad be a shortened form of the Aramaic name Hadadezer, which makes it identical with the Edomite Hadad?

he was hostile toward Israel. If the verse is left in its present location, the subject would most naturally be Rezon. For Heb *wayyāqoṣ bĕ-* in the sense "dislike, loathe," cf. Gen 27:46; with *mipnê*, "be in dread of," cf. Exod 1:12 (not at all "racial hostility" [Burney]); Num 22:3; in Prov 3:11, **qwṣ* is parallel to **mʾs*. The Tg. *ûmĕrîd*, "he rebelled," cannot be used to justify an emendation to *wyysq* "he oppressed" (Kittel); it is, rather, the translator's sense of the active hostility felt toward Israel; cf. other modern attempts—NJPSV: "he repudiated [the author-ity] of Israel"; NEB: "he maintained a stranglehold on Israel." Emendation to *wyqm bĕ-* (so Joüon; cf. Mic 7:6; Ps 27:12) will not work; the idiom deals with false witnessing.

and became king over Aram. If this passage is removed to follow v. 22 it is nec-essary to read *'dm* for *'rm*.

COMMENT

Structure and Themes

Two independent stories (vv. 14–22; 23–25), the first somewhat fuller than its fellow, have been joined by Dtr under the rubric "God raised up an adversary" against Solomon (vv. 14, 23). Their placement following the reprimand of So-lomon in vv. 11–13 suggests that the punishment actually began during his life-time, rather than being delayed until after his death (as promised in v. 12). This idea has been judged foreign to Dtr, inasmuch as Deuteronomistic theology in Kings is linear rather than cyclical, as in Judges (so, e.g., von Rad 1962, 347). Likewise, the internal chronology of the two traditions contradicts the present setting of the king's old age (see Glatt 1993, 162–67 for the suggestion that the chronological displacement can be reconciled if we assume that the seeds of rebellion planted early on "only fully blossomed toward the end of Solomon's reign." For earlier attempts at harmonization, see Qimḥi, Gersonides). These considerations have suggested to some that the entire unit is a post-Dtr addition (e.g., Würthwein, Jones; Edelman 1995). Despite these arguments, stylistic con-siderations (see Note to v. 14) and the juxtaposition of Solomon's remark to Hiram of his enjoying a peaceful rule (5:18) and the present description of ad-versaries who rose against him (both using the verb *pāgôʻa*) give the impression of a single editorial hand, not necessarily of very late date. Moreover, Dtr had good reason to alter his general scheme at this juncture; the kingdom was rent asunder after Solomon's death, and a historiography that foresaw a final cli-mactic judgment of the House of David in the destruction of Jerusalem just would not do. The two tales of rebellion by foreigners who tore at the kingdom from without introduce and amplify the rebellion of Jeroboam, who eventually succeeded in rending it from within.

The source of the stories cannot easily be fixed. To consider the Hadad tale derived from "Edomite annals . . . accessible to a Judaean writer in the reign of Jehoshaphat" (Gray) goes beyond what we know of the Edomite Kingdom and its literary activity. Both stories might have been better placed in a history of David, inasmuch as their relation to the history of Solomon's reign is meager indeed. If they once spelled out the disturbances that Hadad and Rezon caused Israel, then Dtr cut short the accounts of rebellion. For example, the tale of Hadad now appears to lack an ending and, except for its extraneous reap-pearance in v. 25, the reader does not know if or when Hadad rebelled against Solomon. Perhaps the reworking sought to preserve something of the idyllic picture of Solomon's reign; after all, Dtr had claimed that there was "peace on all sides; there [was] neither adversary nor misfortune" (5:18).

The changes exhibited by LXX in this unit are a rewriting of the two stories, which eases the incongruences in MT by providing an ending to the Hadad affair and locating Rezon in a reasonable setting. Whether these alterations were found in a Hebrew manuscript used by a Greek translator (Talshir 1990, 293) or are the work of a late, Greek-speaking scribe (Gooding 1967b) is not clear.

History

In contrast to biblical tradition, which speaks of a kingdom of Edom prior to establishment of the Israelite monarchy (cf. Gen 36:31–39), the archaeological record attests to scattered villages to the east of the Arabah Valley in the eleventh to tenth centuries BCE; to the west, in the Negev highlands, there is evidence for a more extensive "enclosed settlement" ("fortress") pattern. It is this area, which bordered the tribe of Judah, that may have suffered cruel treatment at the hands of David and Joab (Na'aman 1992, 72–74; otherwise Bartlett 1989, 106–7). Just how extensive the slaughter was is unascertainable, since the claim that all Edomite males were slaughtered (11:16) sounds like hyperbole, a piece of propaganda that could have been advanced by either side in the conflict. Administrators and garrisons were stationed by David in the western part of Edom (2 Sam 8:14), and Israelite rule continued for well over a century (cf. 1 Kgs 22:48), a fact that raises doubts about the restoration of a hereditary monarchy in Edom during Solomon's reign (Bartlett 1989, 110–13). The return of Hadad to Edom, besides being "politically embarrassing for Siamun," who was allied with Solomon, seemingly inflicted little real harm on Israel (above, v. 25); the trade conducted by Solomon and Hiram through the Red Sea port of Ezion-geber/Eilat (cf. 9:26–28; 10:22) continued unaffected.

Damascus was another story. It, like the other Aramean kingdoms that were formerly submissive to Hadadezer of Aram-Zobah, had recognized David's hegemony (2 Sam 10:19); but unlike the more distant Aramean kingdoms that maintained their autonomy, Damascus had come under direct Israelite administration (8:6). If, as the present notice indicates, Rezon abandoned Hadadezer after the latter's defeat in order to establish himself in Damascus, he may have gained and maintained a foothold in the city as a servant of David. Whatever his troubling Israel "all the days of Solomon" may have meant, there is no report of military action taken against him. (For that matter, no engagements at all are recorded for Solomon.) The fortification of Hazor in the Upper Galilee (1 Kgs 9:15) can be understood as a response to this new threat to Israel's northern border. Solomon may have lost Damascus, but lacking details, we may be too rash to speak of a rapid diminution of David's empire. Israel's position in important international circles (Egypt and Phoenicia) remained firm for at least a quarter of a century.

XVIII. JEROBOAM—INTIMATIONS OF KINGSHIP; SOLOMON'S DEATH

(11:26–43)

11 [26]Now Jeroboam son of Nebat, an Ephraimite from Zeredah—the name of his widowed mother was Zeruah—was a servant of Solomon; he raised his hand against the king. [27]This is the account of his raising his hand against the king. Solomon built the Millo (and) closed the breach in the City of David, his father. [28]Now the man Jeroboam was a capable man. Solomon took note of how the young man performed his task, and so he put him in charge of all the corvée of the House of Joseph.

[29]At that time, Jeroboam had left Jerusalem, and the prophet Ahijah the Shilonite met him on the road;[a] he[b] was wearing a new robe. When the two of them were alone in the open country, [30]Ahijah took hold of the new robe he had on and tore it into twelve pieces. [31]He said to Jeroboam: "Take ten pieces for yourself, for thus says YHWH, God of Israel: 'I am about to tear the kingdom out of Solomon's hands, and I will give you ten tribes. [32]But one tribe shall be his for the sake of David, my servant, and for the sake of Jerusalem, the city I have chosen out of all the tribes of Israel. [33]For he[c] has forsaken me and bowed down[c] to Ashtoreth, the goddess of the Sidonians,[d] Chemosh, the god of Moab, and Milcom, the god of the Ammonites, and has not followed[c] my ways to do what was pleasing to me and (keep) my statutes and rules, as David his father. [34]But I will not take all the kingdom away from him, for I will keep him a ruler[e] as long as he lives, for the sake of David, my servant, whom I chose and who kept my commandments and my statutes. [35]But I will take the kingdom away from his son and give it to you—the ten tribes. [36]To his son will I give one tribe, so that there be a lamp for David my servant forever before me in Jerusalem, the city that I have chosen for myself to establish my name there. [37]But it is you that I will take, and you shall reign over all you desire, and you shall be king over Israel. [38]If you obey all that I command you and follow my ways and do what is pleasing to me, keeping my statutes and commandments as David my servant did, then I will be with you and I will build a lasting dynasty for you as I did for David.[f] I will give Israel to you [39]and, in view of this, I will humble David's descendants, but not forever.' "[f]

---

[a] LXX adds: *wysyrhw mn hdrk*, "and he took him aside."
[b] LXX reads: "Ahijah" for MT "he."
[c] So with Luc., LXX, Vulg., Syr.; MT reads: "they"; see Note.
[d] MT: *ṣydwnyn*; 15 MSS: *ṣydwnym*.
[e] So MT; LXX apparently reads: *nś' 'ś' l'*, "I will oppose him"; see Note.
[f-f] Lacking in LXX.

[40]Solomon sought to kill Jeroboam, but Jeroboam promptly fled to Egypt to Shishak, king of Egypt; he stayed in Egypt until Solomon's death.

[41]The rest of the history of Solomon and all that he did and his wisdom are indeed recorded in the Book of the Deeds of Solomon. [42]The length of Solomon's reign in Jerusalem over all Israel was forty years. [43]So Solomon slept with his ancestors and was buried in the City of David, his father. Rehoboam his son succeeded him.

NOTES

11   26. *Now Jeroboam son of Nebat.* The name means "May the kin increase" (following Noth 1928, 206–7; for *ʿam* as a kinship term, see Speiser 1960).

an Ephraimite from Zeredah. "Ephraimite," as in Judg 12:5; 1 Sam 1:1. Confusion abounds concerning the identity of Zeredah, due to the readings in Luc. and LXX that transcribe the name as *Sareira* and the appearance in 2 Chr 4:17 of Zarethan (cf. 1 Kgs 4:12; 7:46) instead of Zeredah. Zarethan is located east of the Jordan in the vicinity of Succoth (see above, Note to 4:12), and there is nothing to suggest that it is identical with the town in the present verse. If Zeredah was situated in the Ephraimite hills, as seems most likely, then its name may have been preserved at the spring ʿEin-Sarida, 25 km southwest of Shechem, near Deir Ghassaneh (as suggested by Albright 1933, 26–28). Recent archaeological surveys of the area discovered Iron Age ruins at Kh. Banat-Bar, a site overlooking the spring and valley and, as Kochavi (1989, 198–201) proffers, fits a place whose name means "dry, exposed land" (cf. *Ben Yehuda Thesaurus*, 11.5618–19). (The town Zererah referred to in Judg 7:22 may be a miswritten Zarethan; see Boling 1975, 148.)

the name of his widowed mother was Zeruah. It is unusual for the mother's name to follow the patronym though, in the formula of the kings of Judah, the mother's name is often recorded (e.g., 2 Kgs 14:2; 15:2, 33; 18:2; 21:1, 19; 22:1; 23:36; 24:8, 18); Noth speculates that she was a widow who raised Jeroboam and is thus specifically mentioned. Zeruah apparently means a woman afflicted with a "skin disease" (not necessarily leprosy; see Comment to 2 Kgs 5:1) and should not be taken as a "Jewish perversion" of an original Zeruiah intended to "vilify the rival house of Israel" (so Gray, 290 note a, 293; cf. Skinner, Würthwein); if this were the case, the formulation would have been *ben ʾiššâ ṣĕrûʿâ*, "son of a leprous woman"; cf. Jephtah, *ben ʾiššâ zônâ*, "son of a prostitute" (Judg 11:1). (Indeed, the LXX 12:24b makes her out to be a harlot, to the denigration of Jeroboam.) Nor is the late omission of the phrase in the Hexapla evidence for its being secondary; the remaining words leave an awkward Hebrew construction. Names describing such ailments are known in Hebrew—e.g., *Gārēb* (2 Sam 23:38) and in Akk *Garasu* (Kwasman 1988, 58 [= ADD 487:1′, 5′]), in both languages with the meaning "leper" (cf. Stamm 1967, 324–25). Ephʿal (forthcoming) now points out that a similar expression appears in Akkadian omen literature in which an unfit person who seizes the throne is called "a widow's son." In this case, the note on Jeroboam's lineage turns out to be a literary expression bereft of biographical significance.

servant of Solomon. This designation seems to echo the phrase "and I will give it to your servant" (v. 11, above) in the promised sundering of Solomon's kingdom.

he raised his hand against the king. Hebrew *hērîm yad* is attested only here. Its semantic equivalent *nāśā' yad* appears in the Davidic narratives in descriptions of the uprisings of Absalom (2 Sam 18:28) and Sheba (20:21). (Note that Tg. to the Samuel passages translates *nś' yd* by *hrym yd.*) Both idioms use the prepositional particle *bĕ-*, conveying the hostile sense of the act performed, which the KJV caught in the translation "lifted his hand against." Modern translations opt for "rebel" or "revolt" (NAB, NEB, JB), replacing the figurative language with a word that has a clear political connotation. Note that the Akk idiom *qātam dekû*, "to raise a hand," expresses rejection and unfriendliness — e.g., *minamma qātka ana muḫḫija tadka*, "Why do you behave in an unfriendly way towards me?" (cf. CAD D, 127a).

Rabbinic exegesis circumscribed Jeroboam's rebellious act as inciting the public against Solomon, especially concerning the harsh levy of the king (cf. *b. Sanh.* 101b). The exact nature of the uprising cannot, however, be retrieved, since details are lacking in MT. The alternate story in LXX suggests that he had begun to assume regal-like prerogatives (12:24b: "he had 300 horse-drawn chariots") within Ephraim; but this detail comes from a late expansion. See further in the Excursus.

27. *This is the account of his raising his hand against the king.* The introduction to Jeroboam's rebellion, by means of the *wĕzeh dĕbar ha-* formula (see above, Note on 9:15), is not followed by the expected details of that act (Talshir 1981–1982, 32–33). The full story of his rebellion seems to have been cut short by the insertion of the Ahijah prophecy (vv. 29–39), since the conclusion in v. 40 hints at a fuller account of the planned and/or actually staged uprising. It is not likely that a newfound arrogance on the part of Jeroboam stemming from Ahijah's support was all that the revolt was about (so Qimḥi; cf. Gooding 1967b, 183ff.). The LXX and the Greek Supplement contain additional details on Jeroboam's activities, but these are of disputed originality; see Excursus.

Solomon built the Millo (and) closed the breach in the City of David, his father. Neither the location of these two constructions nor whether there was any relation between them is stated. B. Mazar suggested that the city wall at the Ophel (from the period of the Jebusite settlement of Jerusalem) had been breached during the expansion of the city northwards by David and that Solomon rectified this situation by the establishment of the royal center on the Temple Mount and its fortification (E. Mazar and B. Mazar 1989, 58). For the Millo construction, see above on 9:15 and 24; on the City of David, see 3:1.

28. *Now the man Jeroboam was a capable man.* For another instance of the construction *wĕhā'iš* PN plus adjective, cf. Num 12:3.

a capable man. Hebrew *gibbôr ḥayil*, here as in 1 Kgs 1:42, appears in its basic meaning "man of valor," "of great energy" (NEB, NJB), and cf. 2 Kgs 5:1, the valorous Aramean commander Naaman. The developed sense of "men of high economic status" appears in 2 Kgs 15:20 (see Note there), but there is nothing that suggests that Jeroboam was appointed to his post because he was "a man of property" (Gray; cf. Würthwein) or a "man of means" (NAB).

how the young man performed his task. He was "efficient," a description that complements the preceding "capable" (so Montgomery and Gehman).

so he put him in charge of all the corvée of the House of Joseph. The terms *mas, sēbel/sabbāl, mĕlā'kâ,* all indicating compulsory state service, are discussed above, in Notes on 5:27, 29, 30.

House of Joseph. If the state corvée was organized on the basis of the twelve-district system, as were the other taxes (cf. 5:7), then the term "House of Joseph" refers to Mt. Ephraim (4:8) and not to the dispersed Joseph tribes as a whole.

29. *At that time.* A formulaic expression, only loosely connecting the two units.

the prophet Ahijah the Shilonite. The name Ahijah, "Yah (= YHWH) is my (divine) brother," is also known from the Ophel ostracon (*'ḥyhw*; KAI 190:2) and Lachish letter no. 3 (KAI 193:17).

Shiloh, the town of Ahijah's residence (cf. 1 Kgs 14:2), had been the major priestly center during the days of Samuel (cf. 1 Sam 1:3; 3:3), until its destruction by the Philistines (implied by Jer 7:12–14 and Ps 78:60). Excavations at Kh. Seilun, 30 km north of Jerusalem to the east of the main highway leading to Shechem (cf. Judg 21:19), found evidence of the resettlement of Shiloh after the Philistine attack; cf. Shiloh's review (1971) of the excavation reports at the site of ancient Shiloh by Buhl and Holm-Nielsen; also NEAEHL 1364–70.

Ahijah the Shilonite met him on the road. The LXX addition: *wysyrhw mn hdrk,* "and he took him aside," seems to explain how, at the end of the verse, they are said to have been "in the open country" (lit., "field"); but this may be a pedantic expansion (otherwise Burney, Šanda, Noth). A secluded, unobserved spot was appropriate for talk of secession; cf. 2 Kgs 9:1–10.

he was wearing a new robe. Jeroboam was wearing the cloak. The wording of the succeeding clause, "took hold of, grabbed" (*wayyitpoś*), solves the ambiguousness of this clause (noted by Qimḥi), because this action is inappropriate on one's own garment; rather, the action was performed on a garment worn by a second party (cf. Gen 39:12). Thus, Ahijah seized Jeroboam's cloak! The LXX reads "Ahijah," removing the ambiguity, but this interpretation is erroneous; cf. its adoption by NAB: "Ahijah took off his new cloak"; JB: "Ahijah was wearing a new cloak."

a new robe. The fact of "newness" is twice stressed (vv. 29, 30) and is an essential element in the performance of the symbolic act that follows (cf. Skinner, Noth). Note the new devices used by Elisha: the "new flask" in 2 Kgs 2:20 and the floating ax head in the 6:1–7; see the Comment at 2:20.

30. *and tore it into twelve pieces.* A comparison is almost universally made between this scene and the one in 1 Sam 15:27–28, which describes how Saul took hold of and tore the edge of Samuel's cloak, interpreted by the prophet as symbolic of the tearing of the kingdom from Saul. Reference is also made to the use of the "edge/hem of a garment," Akk *qaran ṣubātu,* and "lap/loin gar-

ment," *sissiktu/sikku*, in Mesopotamian tradition, where the hem was a "symbolic extension of one's personality" and consequently applied as a legally binding "signature" to clay documents as a pledge (Speiser 1965, 393); it also conveys the sense of submission in supplication to a superior (for which, cf. Zech 8:23; see Brauner 1974, 35–38; and the reinvestigation of these terms and their legal function by Mallul 1986, 20–36).

Yet the comparison is at best only partially apt. The tearing of the hem by Saul was fit symbolism for divesting him of his kingdom. In the present instance, however, it is not Solomon's cloak that is rent but Jeroboam's; the meaning of the act was that YHWH (through his prophet) was dividing anew the rule over the twelve tribes. What holds for both acts is the use by a prophet of imitative magic, giving force to a prediction made in YHWH's name.

31. *I am about to tear the kingdom out of Solomon's hands.* Echoing the punishment announced in vv. 11, 13 and in the summary sermon in 2 Kgs 17:21.

ten tribes. The MT *ʿśrh hšbṭym* would be better read *ʿśrt hšbṭym*, as in v. 35. This is the locus classicus for the concept "ten tribes"; it appears only here and in v. 35 in the entire Bible. If this verse is part of the original kernel of the Ahijah tradition, as it seems to be, then Benjamin was included within that number, despite later developments (cf. 12:21). Inasmuch as the Levites were landless, the two tribes of Judah and Simeon would complete the counting of twelve tribes. For a different tradition, see immediately, v. 32.

32. *But one tribe shall be his.* The one tribe can only be the tribe of Judah, and the presence of Deuteronomistic terminology in this verse and v. 36 marks the phrase as late preexilic, from the era when David's kingdom consisted of Judah alone. The reading "two tribes" in LXX, here and in v. 36, may be an attempt to accommodate the numbers to the "ten tribes" referred to in vv. 31, 35, and actual history. [DNF: "The one tribe here is the additional tribe given to Judah—namely Simeon—consistent with the 10 tribes to the north."]

33. *For he has forsaken me and bowed down . . . and has not followed.* Continuing v. 31, supplying the ground for the promised action. The end of the verse, "as David his father," as well as the preceding v. 31 and the following v. 34 require that the subject throughout v. 33 be Solomon; consequently the verbs should be read in the singular (as in most versions). The plural verbal forms in MT may have derived from one of several causes: the description of Solomon's apostasy was disturbing to a late scribe-annotator who, unlike the Chronicler, excluded the entire unit from his work and rewrote the verse to include the people in the falling away from YHWH (cf. a similar alteration in 9:6). Or, perhaps such passages as 14:22–24 and especially the long sermon in 2 Kgs 17:15–16 were in the mind of the copyist. In those passages the nation, rather than the king, is branded idolatrous. In either case, the original text no doubt read with verbs in the singular.

Ashtoreth, the goddess of the Sidonians, Chemosh, the god of Moab, and Milcom, the god of the Ammonites. For these deities, see above on vv. 5, 7. The LXX reads here, as does MT in v. 7, the tendentious "abomination" (*šiqqūṣ*) for "god" and "goddess"; MT preserves the original reading in this case.

and (keep) my statutes and rules. A clumsy phrase, not in LXX; cf. v. 38.

34. *But I will not take all the kingdom away from him.* Noth conjectures, without textual warrant, that "all" should be struck as an unreasonable gloss (NJB omits), inasmuch as the verse speaks of postponing the division of the kingdom; NAB translates "any of the kingdom."

for I will keep him a ruler as long as he lives. Hebrew *nāśî*', "ruler" (not "prince"; cf. Speiser 1963, 111–17), is the usual term for the premonarchic tribal leadership of Israel in the Priestly narration of the Pentateuch and Joshua and influences Ezekiel's use of the term for Israel's future ruler; in Deuteronomistic literature, it occurs only here (on the "chieftains" in 1 Kgs 8:1, see there). Contrasted with the promise of kingship to Jeroboam in v. 37, this statement might imply that Solomon was to be demoted to the status of chief over Judah. But the continuation of the verse, "for the sake of David . . .," upon which this statement rests, shows that this can hardly be its intention. Rather, *nāśî*' seems to be the term for the Davidic king preferred in certain preexilic circles (cf., e.g., Ezek 12:10, 12; 21:30; 34:24), perhaps as an expression of "opposition to absolute kingship . . . with an undertone of longing for the tribal rule" of Israel's early days (Liver 1968b, 981–82). And if this is the meaning of its use in v. 34, it is unique in all of Deuteronomistic literature.

For the MT, LXX has *antitassomenos antitaxomai autō,* "I will oppose him," which appears again as the translation of MT Hos 1:6: *kî nāśō' 'eśśa' lāhem.* Contextually, the passage in Hosea seems to mean: "(nor) will I forgive/pardon them." (For this rendering, cf. Qimḥi, ad loc., and for **nāśô',* "forgive," cf., e.g., Num 14:18; Ps 99:8.) Burney, on the basis of LXX and the verse in Hosea, suggested that the original reading in 1 Kgs 11:34 was *nāśō' 'eśśa' lô,* "for I will surely forgive him"; and some have adopted it (e.g., Gray, who considers MT a "singularly inept remark"!). But this retroversion is unsatisfactory in the context. Nowhere is it suggested that Solomon was to be pardoned for, according to the Deuteronomists, it was his sinful behavior that brought about the sundering of David's kingdom.

35. *But I will take the kingdom away from his son and give it to you.* The legal formula *lqḥ-ntn* used for the conveyance of property (cf., e.g., Gen 20:14; 21:27), as well as its confiscation and granting to another party (1 Sam 8:14), is employed here in the description of YHWH's transfer of the kingdom. The equivalent formula that appears in Akk is *našû-nadānu* and Aram *nṣl-ntn;* see Labuschagne 1974 and Greenfield 1977.

36. *so that there be a lamp for David my servant.* On Heb *nîr,* here and in 1 Kgs 15:4, see Note to 2 Kgs 8:19.

37. *But it is you that I will take.* The emphatic position of the accusative pronoun *'ōtkâ,* "you," contrasts with "his son" in v. 36.

and you shall reign over all you desire and you shall be king over Israel. That is, over the Northern tribes; cf. 4:20. Hebrew *'iwwâ,* "desire, long for," with *nepeš,* "person, self," as subject appears frequently in Deuteronomic passages; with reference to physical desires, cf. Deut 12:20; 14:26; to kingship, cf. 2 Sam 3:21.

38. *If you obey all that I command you . . . then I will be with you and I will build a lasting dynasty for you as I did for David.* The phraseology of Nathan's prophecy to David (cf. 2 Sam 7:9a, 16a) is here strikingly adapted to Jeroboam, legitimizing the founding of a rival kingdom in the North. But unlike that promise, which was given in perpetuity—viz., the sinful behavior of individual future dynasts would not bring down the House of David—Ahijah's remarks speak of a House of Jeroboam contingent on its founder's untarnished service of YHWH (as underscored by Caquot 1961, 18–19). This verse is the strongest case for an original, pre-Dtr prophecy, of Northern origin, legitimizing Jeroboam's rule; see further in Comment.

39. *and, in view of this, I will humble David's descendants, but not forever.* The phrase "in view of this" (moved up from the end of the clause in translation) has no clear antecedent and, because vv. 38bβ–39 are lacking in LXX, the entire sentence is often seen as "the interpolation of a late reader" (so Skinner; cf., too, Stade, Burney, Noth). But the ideas expressed here need not be altogether secondary. Just as Nathan's promise is reflected in v. 38a–bα, so in the present verse, a reflex of that same promise may be seen. There David is told that his offspring will be chastised for their wrongs, but YHWH's favor will not be withdrawn from them as it was from Saul (cf. 2 Sam 7:14–15); here the humbling of his descendants is an interim setback. Note also that the term *zeraʿ*, "seed, descendant" (as well as "house") appears in both prophecies (2 Sam 7:12; 1 Kgs 11:39).

On the pointing of *w' ʿnh*, with the *'alep* retained orthographically without a vowel, as noted in qere, see GKC, 23d.

40. *Jeroboam promptly fled to Egypt to Shishak, king of Egypt.* That Jeroboam found refuge in Egypt at the court of Shishak, the first king of the 22d (Libyan) dynasty (ca. 945–924 BCE), is indicative of a change in Egyptian policy toward Solomon; the stable relations between Egypt and Israel under Siamun would not have allowed for Jeroboam's stay; cf. above on 3:1; 9:16; and further in Comment.

Shishak, king of Egypt. He is the first Egyptian monarch referred to by name; all of the others up to this point were known by the honorific "pharaoh" ("great house"). The name is transcribed in two forms, *šyšq* in the present verse and *šwšq* in 14:25 (ketib), and apparently reflects two stages in the pronunciation of the king's name. The Eg *Shoshenq* is preserved in Heb as *šušaq* and the Akk transcription *š/su-š/si-in-qu* (Streck, VAB 7.720; note that this does not refer to King Shoshenq!), while the LXX *sousakim* is typical of late transcriptions, e.g., in Manetho and Josephus. See Kitchen 1973, 73 n. 356; Rainey 1971, 655–56.

he stayed in Egypt until Solomon's death. The length of Jeroboam's exile cannot be determined. Kitchen fixes his flight to "soon after 945 B.C." and reckons that the "potential 'government in exile'" had to wait fifteen years to make its next move (Kitchen 1973, 294); but such conjecture is not without its drawbacks.

41. *The rest of the history of Solomon and all that he did and his wisdom are indeed recorded in the Book of the Deeds of Solomon.* This is the first appear-

ance in Kings of an editorial statement summing up the reign of a Judean (or Israelite) king. The reference to other written works is generally taken to mean that the sources mentioned were used by the editor in the composition of Kings and that they were accessible to his readers. Most often cited are *The History of the Kings of Judah* and *The History of the Kings of Israel* (for this translation, see the Introduction. Composition). *The Book of the Deeds of Solomon*, evidently a separate work that surveyed Solomon's long reign, is referred to only in the present verse. Considering the varied and unusual collection of materials that make up the Solomonic history and the particular emphasis on the king's wisdom, Liver surmised (1967, 75–101) that *The Book of the Deeds of Solomon* was the product of the wisdom circles at the court of Jerusalem. On the relatively late date of this book, see the Introduction.

42. *The length of Solomon's reign in Jerusalem over all Israel was forty years.* As in the case of David (cf. 1 Kgs 2:11), so also with Solomon, the typological number "forty" is used to express the successful completion of a full reign. With reference to the succeeding kings, in both kingdoms, the length of their reign is as a rule given in the opening formula, but this procedure was forfeited for Solomon, who was introduced by the lengthy tale of his accession.

43. *So Solomon slept with his ancestors and was buried in the City of David, his father.* For the burial formula and the location of the royal sepulcher, see Note on 2:10.

Rehoboam his son succeeded him. The standard Dtr introduction to the reign of Rehoboam and its evaluation comes in 14:21ff.; for now, the story of the secession of the Northern tribes is the center of attention. The name Rehoboam can be parsed to mean "The kin have expanded" and, like the name *Jeroboam* in which *'am* also appears (see above, v. 26), expresses the spirit of national well-being experienced during the Solomonic age. It is of interest to note that the Ammorite name *Hammurapi*, of similar etymology, was translated into Akkadian as *kimta rapaštum*, "extensive family" (cf. CAD K, 377b).

COMMENT

Structure and Themes

The unit, composed of two distinct members, (1) vv. 26–28, 40; (2) vv. 29–39, is not attached to the preceding stories by the introductory phrase "God raised up an adversary for him," as in the cases of Hadad and Rezon in vv. 14, 23, though Dtr surely took Jeroboam as the third, most successful, of these three trouble-makers. The Ahijah pericope (2) is introduced by the report of Jeroboam's rebellion (1), which is now truncated, giving prominence to the word of the man of God.

Despite the fact that most commentators grant that the prophecy of Ahijah originated in an "older," i.e., pre-Dtr, "Northern source" or "prophetic cycle," there is no agreement on the division of the verses between the two (or as many as four) redactional levels and their original scope; see Knoppers 1993, 191–97, for a concise survey of the main critical positions. Such detailed source analysis, into fragments of verses assigned to sundry hands, seems inadvisable when dealing with traditional literature that can grow and develop undetected within the same circle of tradents. Thus, it seems best to speak of the kernel of the Ahijah prophecy (vv. 29–31 are all that is left unretouched) and its Dtr reworking, the two detectable levels within the present text.

Ahijah and Jeroboam figured in the original Northern tale, in which the prophet is represented as instrumental in appointing the king and initiating dynastic change (cf. the Samuel traditions in 1 Sam 8–10; 15–16; Jehu son of Hanani in 1 Kgs 16:1–4; Elisha in 2 Kgs 9:1–3). The promise of kingship to Jeroboam in terms that resemble YHWH's covenant with David (see above on vv. 37–38), despite their Deuteronomistic echo, may stem from an oracle of legitimation upon which the Northern monarchy was founded. The whole was thoroughly redacted by Dtr, tying it into the history of Solomon and his backsliding ways, set out in 11:1–13.[1]

History

The circumstances surrounding Jeroboam's rebellion against Solomon cannot be ascertained. The note concerning Jeroboam's discovery by Solomon and his appointment as the corvée supervisor of the House of Joseph (vv. 27–28) might be read as alluding to issues that were to come to the fore years later at the Shechem assembly (1 Kgs 12)—viz., the feeling of the Northern tribes that the royal burden was unjustly allocated. Furthermore, the core of the Ahijah prophecy suggests that Jeroboam's act was more than a personal mutiny; he had support from the veteran leadership of the Ephraimite tribes. Shiloh, the home of YHWH's Ark of the Covenant in pre-Davidic days, was likely a symbol of Northern Israel's former glory, now eclipsed by the Jerusalemite establishment, both royal and priestly. But how widespread Jeroboam's insurrection was cannot be said, and its date can be set only in the most general terms. Since he found refuge at Shishak's court, it took place sometime after Shishak had ascended the throne in Egypt—i. e., after 945 BCE; the length of Jeroboam's "exile" in Egypt is unknown.

---

[1] An engaging attempt to reconstruct a positive portrait of the Israelite king from the Judean critique of Jeroboam is presented by Zakovitch 1991, 87–97. He finds that Jeroboam was held to be "a second Moses who liberated them from the burden of the second Pharaoh, the king of Judah."

HISTORY OF THE DIVIDED KINGDOM

◆

XIX. REHOBOAM'S ABORTED CORONATION

(12:1–19)

12 ¹Rehoboam went to Shechem, for all Israel had come to Shechem to make him king. ²When Jeroboam son of Nebat learned of this—he was still in Egypt where he had fled from King Solomon—Jeroboam returned from Egypt.ᵃ ³They sent for him and Jeroboam and the whole assembly of Israel cameᵇ and spoke to Rehoboam: ⁴"Your father made our yoke heavy. You, then, lighten the hard labor of your father and the heavy yoke which he imposed upon us and we shall serve you." ⁵He said to them: "Go away for three days and then come back to me." So the people went away.

⁶King Rehoboam then took counsel with the elders who had served Solomon his father during his lifetime: "How do you advise answering this people?" ⁷They spokeᶜ to him: "If you become a servant of this people today and serve them and answer them by speaking kind words, then they will be your servants forever." ⁸But he rejected the advice that the elders gave him and took counsel with the youngsters who had grown up with him, those who were serving him. ⁹He said to them: "What do you advise that we answer this people who spoke to me: 'Lighten the yoke that your father imposed upon us'"? ¹⁰Then the youngsters who had grown up with him said: "Thus you should say to this people who spoke to you: 'Your father made our yoke heavy; and you, lighten it for us!' Thus you should speak to them: 'My little thing is thicker than my father's loins. ¹¹Now my father burdened you with a heavy yoke, and I will add to your yoke; my father disciplined you with whips, and I will discipline you with scourges.'"

¹²Jeroboam and all the people cameᵈ to Rehoboam on the third day, as the king had said: "Come back to me on the third day." ¹³The king answered the people harshly, and he rejected the advice that the elders had given him. ¹⁴He spoke with them in accordance with the youngsters' advice: "My father made

---

ᵃ Read with 2 Chr 10:2, "Jeroboam returned from (*wayyāšob mi-*) Egypt," for MT "Jeroboam remained in (*wayyēšeb bě-*) Egypt"; see Note.

ᵇ Read with qere: *wyb'*; ketib and many MSS: *wybw'*; see Note.

ᶜ Read with qere *waydabběrû*; ketib sg.

ᵈ Read with qere *wybw'* (Leningrad); ketib *wybw*. LXX: pl.

your yoke heavy, and I will add to your yoke. My father disciplined you with whips, and I will discipline you with scourges."

[15]The king did not listen to the people, for YHWH had brought this about in order to fulfill the promise that YHWH had spoken through Ahijah the Shilonite to Jeroboam son of Nebat. [16]When all Israel saw that the king had not listened to them, the people answered the king:

What share have we in David?
No lot in the son of Jesse!
To your tents, O Israel,
Now look to your own house, O David!

So the Israelites went to their homes.[e] [17]But as for the Israelites who lived in the towns of Judah, Rehoboam ruled over them.

[18]King Rehoboam dispatched Adoram, who was in charge of the corvée, but all Israel stoned him to death. With effort, King Rehoboam had mounted his chariot to flee to Jerusalem. [19]Thus Israel has been in rebellion against the House of David until this day.

---

[e] Lit., "their tents."

NOTES

12   1. *for all Israel had come to Shechem.* In contrast to 11:42, in which "all Israel" of Solomon's rule is the late, comprehensive term for the twelve tribes, here and in what follows the term refers to the Northern tribes (contra Provan), as it does in the traditions concerning David's election—i.e., "all of the tribes of Israel" (2 Sam 5:1).

Shechem. As a site known for its early cultic importance (cf., e.g., Gen 12:6–7), with a significant record in Israelite tradition (cf. Gen 34; Josh 24; Judg 9), Shechem held a special place among the Northern tribes, enough so that Rehoboam journeyed there to be hailed king. Some have speculated that it was the district center of Mt. Ephraim (cf. 1 Kgs 4:8; so Würthwein, following Wright). The city later served as the first residence of Jeroboam (cf. v. 25). For the problematic archaeological record of tenth-century Shechem, see NEAEHL 1345–54.

2. *Jeroboam returned from Egypt.* The MT preserves a contextually impossible reading, the correct version of which can be retrieved from 2 Chr 10:2: "Jeroboam returned from Egypt." It would make little sense to note his remaining in Egypt and then immediately describe his presence in Shechem. There is still some tension between vv. 3, 12 and v. 20, which seems to imply a later return. In fact, the negotiations take place between Rehoboam and the people, suggesting that perhaps Jeroboam was secondarily added to the text. These discrepancies are not felt in LXX, which has Jeroboam return home to Zererah

(11:43 LXX; cf. 12:24–25), where he remains until called to the assembly in v. 20. The suggestion to invert vv. 1 and 2 (Stade) eases the difficulty slightly, but has no textual basis. See Trebolle Barrera 1982, 12–19. Another solution would be to take v. 20 as originating in another rendition of Jeroboam's appointment (see Note there).

3. *Jeroboam and the whole assembly of Israel came.* Read the verb with qere, also in v. 12; Heb often prefers the sg. verb with compound subjects; see GKC, 145o, p; 146f.

the whole assembly of Israel. In the main body of the tale, *qāhāl* is the term for "assembly." Its equivalent, *ʿēdâ*, is used only in v. 20. From the general sense of "meeting, gathering" in preexilic texts, it has the more specific meaning of a societal institution with regulatory responsibilities in Ezra–Nehemiah (Liver 1979, 69–70).

4. *Your father made our yoke heavy.* The figure of a "yoke" (*ʿōl*) is frequently used when speaking of burdens and service imposed by a superior—e.g., Gen 27:40; Deut 28:48; Isa 14:25; 47:6; Jer 27:8; Ezek 34:27. In Mesopotamian texts, *nīru*, "yoke," is the common term signifying dominion and rule, especially in Neo-Assyrian royal inscriptions; cf. CAD N/2, 262–63.

You, then. For this emphatic usage, cf. Gen 26:29; 1 Kgs 18:11, 14; 21:7.

lighten the hard labor of your father. The request is not for cancellation of their duties or even exemption (as supposedly enjoyed by Judah on the basis of 1 Kgs 4:19; see Note there) but merely a moderation of their burden.

5. *Go away for three days.* A common literary phrase meant to indicate "short period of time"; cf., e.g., 3:18; 2 Kgs 20:5, 8; Gen 22:4; 34:25; Esth 5:1. It is not necessary to repoint MT *ʿôd* to *ʿad* (apparently so LXX), as if "a *previous* postponement had taken place" (Burney); for this Heb usage, cf. Jonah 3:4. The parallel in 2 Chr 10:5 has simply "Come back in three days," which suggested to Ehrlich that the present verse should be parsed in similar fashion.

6. *took counsel.* The pointing of the verb *wayyiwwāʿaṣ* with final *pataḥ* instead of *segol* is unexpected but is consistently so in this verb; so v. 28; cf. GKC, 64b.

with the elders. The identity of this group has been debated vigorously following the suggestion to see them as an "advisory council" with roots reaching back to the premonarchic period; they were "patriarchal notables" who "served in an advisory capacity" (Malamat 1965a, 171–81; his 1963 work included a comparison to Sumerian epic tradition and a proposed "bicameral" system of administration, which he toned down in the 1965 discussion). Without denying the societal function of the "elders" in the towns and cities of early Israel, whose role was formally recognized in the legal tradition (Reviv 1989b, 35–101) and continued to function as such during the monarchy (cf. 1 Kgs 21:8; also 20:7–8), there is no evidence for a permanent body of elders at Solomon's court (contrast Lipiński 1974). Considering the contrast with the "youngsters" (v. 8) and the genre of the account as a whole, the elders refer to "elder statesmen," unofficial advisors to whom the king could turn for seasoned advice (so Noth; Debus 1967, 30).

who had served Solomon his father. Hebrew *ʿōmēd ʾet pĕnê* for the more frequent *ʿōmēd lipnê*, "to be in attendance," e.g., v. 8; 1 Kgs 1:2; 10:8; 17:1.

How do you advise? The Niphal of **yʿṣ* is properly reciprocal, "take counsel among yourselves," from which emerges the advice delivered to the king.

7. *answer them by speaking kind words.* They advised that he answer them in a conciliatory manner, which the Chronicler specifically added to his rendition in 2 Chr 10:7; *ûrĕṣîtām,* "and you would appease them."

kind words. For this sense of the Heb *dĕbārîm ṭôbîm,* cf. Zech 1:13; Prov 12:25 (sg.). It has been put forward that the phrase implies more than just offering the people a pleasing response and, in fact, should be rendered "set good conditions," formally grant them relief (so Weinfeld 1982, comparing Mesopotamian royal grants). While the phrase "good thing(s)/word(s)" appears in both Akkadian and Aramaic within covenantal settings (see Note on 2 Kgs 25:28), these are always portrayed as acts of grace granted by a superior to his servants. *Mišarum-*acts, on the other hand, are general acts of amnesty to the whole population, remissions of debt, not concerned with taxes. In the present case, negotiations are conducted over an agreement that would offer relief from perceived oppressive imposts; therefore, the elders suggest that he respond with "appeasing" words. Furthermore, there is no hint that the issue concerns the restoration of an exemption from certain taxes previously enjoyed by Shechem or other Northern cities (on the Mesopotamian model of *kiddinūtu,* "privileged status of a city or temple personnel"; CAD K, 344–45).

8. *But he rejected the advice that the elders gave him.* The clause is repeated verbatim in v. 13a; its present position anticipates the decision.

the youngsters who had grown up with him. That is, raised at court, educated in court etiquette; cf. Dan 1:3–5. N. Fox (1996) suggests taking the word "youngsters" as a technical term for a special group of youngsters raised at court, the sons of officials and courtiers, on the analogy of the *ḥrdw n kʒp* in Egypt. Whatever the case, the expression should not be taken literally, since the king himself was 41 years old (cf. 14:21); but this is not a sign of derogation (so Gray). The word "youngsters" is most apt in describing the essence of the contest between them and the rival "elders."

those who were serving him. For similar syntax after the relative *ʾăšer,* cf. 1 Kgs 21:11; 2 Chr 10:8 eases the construction by omitting the second *ʾăšer.*

9. *What do you advise that we answer this people?* Having rejected out of hand the elders' advice (cf. v. 8), the king is portrayed as ready to adopt the youngsters' counsel even before he hears what they have to say.

10. *My little thing is thicker than my father's loins.* This pithy remark has the ring of a known proverb (so Wiseman) or, at least, makes use of imagery that usually accompanies proverbial sayings.

My little thing. Most translations and commentators understand the word as referring to the "little finger," while Qimḥi, with a feel for the manly talk among Rehoboam's companions, took it for the penis, thus further accentuating the strength with which Rehoboam was advised to act (cf. Targum). The use of a rude expression would have been appropriate in the setting of a private audience of the "youngsters" with the king (Noth); in the following meeting with the Northerners, Rehoboam astutely omits repeating these insulting words (Weisman 1996, 214–15). The pointing of both the noun and the adjective is problematic. The MT (Aleppo codex) points: *qoṭonî*, from an otherwise unattested *qoṭen*, modified by the feminine *ʿābâ*, "thick."

11. *scourges.* Hebrew *ʿaqrabbîm*, lit., "scorpions." An apt term for a barbed whip, considering the thorny nature of the "scorpion-plant" (cf. Ezek 2:6). Akkadian usage also knows of a "thorny whip" (*qinnaz zaqtum*; CAD Q, 256) and barbs likened to the "sting of a scorpion" (CAD Z, 132, 166, s. v. *zuqaqīpu*). See the recent discussion by Garfinkel 1987.

12. *Jeroboam and all the people came.* On reading the verb with qere, see Note to v. 3.

13. *The king answered the people harshly.* For *qāšâ*, "severe word," as a substantive used adverbially following *dabbēr*, "speak," cf. Gen 42:7, 30 (in plural); following *ʿānô*, "answer, respond," cf. 1 Sam 20:10; 1 Kgs 14:6; cf. also Ps 60:5.

15. *The king did not listen to the people, for YHWH had brought this about in order to fulfill the promise that YHWH had spoken through Ahijah the Shilonite to Jeroboam son of Nebat.* A Dtr remark inserted into the narrative in order to bring it in line with the Ahijah prophecy in 11:29–39. Compare a similar editorial insertion in 2 Sam 17:14.

for YHWH had brought this about. Literally, "the turn of affairs (issued) from YHWH." For *sibbâ*, 2 Chr 10:15 substitutes *nĕsibâ* (Modern Heb, "circumstance, cause").

16. *What share have we in David? No lot in the son of Jesse!* An echo of the rallying call of the rebel Sheba son of Bichri in 2 Sam 20:1, with rhetorically negative *mâ* replacing *ʾên* (BDB 553a). The terms "share" and "lot" echo the theme of inheritance legally protected under the Law but abrogated by the House of David. Any earlier feeling of consanguinity between the North and Judah (cf. 2 Sam 5:1) had since dissipated.

To your tents, O Israel. "Home!" The assembly was hereby disbanded. The text in 2 Chr 10:16, which reads: "Each man to your tent . . ." is closer to 2 Sam 20:1; this may be a case of purposeful accommodation in Chronicles to the earlier text than a textual accident in Kings (Kalimi 1995, 191–92). For the time-honored term "tents" in the sense of "dwellings," cf. 1 Kgs 8:66; Judg 20:8 (where it is parallel to "house"); it had no current significance (such as tents erected for the tribal representatives during the Shechem assembly).

Now look to your own house, O David! For the sense of *rʾh*, "care for, attend to," cf. Gen 39:23. But it can also be construed ironically: "Look who is left with you and over what sort of house you will rule, now that you will not rule over the house of Israel!" (Qimḥi; similarly Noth). The LXX seems to have read *rʿh*; Tg. translates *mĕlôk*: "Rule!"

So the Israelites went to their homes. Šanda took the clause as proleptic, inasmuch as the assembly had not yet chosen Jeroboam, but he did not consider the independent features of v. 20 (see below).

17. *But as for the Israelites who lived in the towns of Judah, Rehoboam ruled over them.* For the syntax, see the Note on 9:21. Just who these Israelites were is unclear; nor is there any previous mention of such settlement of Northerners in Judah, unless one considers 2 Chr 11:16–17 a complimentary indication (Jones). This, taken together with the marginal nature of the verse at this juncture, suggests that the verse might be a late gloss, providing a reason that the Benjaminites came to join Rehoboam in the aborted campaign against Jeroboam; cf. v. 20. Šanda would move v. 17 to follow v. 20, leaving its present location unexplained.

18. *King Rehoboam dispatched Adoram, who was in charge of the corvée.* This looks like a variant form of the name *Adoniram* given in 4:6; 1 Chr 10:18 has Hadoram. If it is the same person, Adoniram would have been an old man by this time, since he had already held this post under David (cf. 2 Sam 20:24), a fact that leads many to doubt the integrity of the notice. Most readers note the lack of political sensitivity in the choice of Adoniram as the person to negotiate with the rebel tribes: "how little Rehoboam and his youthful advisers understood the gravity of the situation" (Skinner); but such evaluations represent, at best, after-the-fact wisdom, reading back from the historical developments.

but all Israel stoned him to death. As it now stands, "all Israel" would seem to refer to the Israelites assembled at Shechem, an indication that the conclave had not yet dispersed (cf. v. 16). On the other hand, if this was a later meeting, it could refer to the Israelite representatives at those later negotiations. For **rgm b-*, cf. Lev 24:16. In most other cases, the verb is followed by the accusative, where *beth* is instrumental, e.g., Num 14:10.

With effort, King Rehoboam had mounted his chariot to flee to Jerusalem. It is unlikely that Rehoboam had accompanied Adoram on the renewed mission to the North (if this was indeed a second one). The use of the simple perfect indicates that the action is not consequential (as in all translations); it introduces a parenthetical remark describing how, at the previous assembly in Shechem, the king himself had been forced to beat a quick retreat after the Israelites had rejected his terms for rule (Ehrlich).

With effort. In Ruth 1:18, the verb expresses determination.

19. *Thus Israel has been in rebellion against the House of David until this day.* An editorial Dtr summary, formulated as an etiological closure to the preceding account.

has been in rebellion. For **pš'* in the sense of "to violate a political obligation, to rebel," see Note to 2 Kgs 1:1.

until this day. See above, Note to 1 Kgs 8:8.

COMMENT

Structure and Themes

A main unit, telling of the failed negotiations between Rehoboam and the Northern tribes, has been glossed in several critical spots, creating some confusion.

The insertions revolve around the question of Jeroboam's participation in the proceedings; inasmuch as he goes unmentioned throughout most of the narration, the verses that introduce him are in all likelihood secondary (vv. 3, 12). Moreover, v. 20 suggests that Jeroboam was indeed not present at the assembly. The unit is tied to the preceding Ahijah prophecy (11:29–39) by the editorial v. 15, emphasizing YHWH's "behind the scenes" management of the affairs of men (as, for example, in Exod 14:1–8).

The account is a "wisdom" tale written in praise of Solomon's trusted advisers (Liver 1967), whose position in the court of Rehoboam, his successor, may have come into jeopardy. Groups of court advisers or single individuals with whom monarchs take counsel are a common phenomenon; differences of opinion and contradictory recommendations leave the king to decide the course of action (cf. 2 Sam 16:20–17:14). In the present case, the storyteller, perhaps one of the old king's wise men, claims that rejection of their experienced counsel led to the breakup of the United Monarchy. He contrasts two groups of advisers, both of which vied for the king's ear and heart. The tenor of his story is critical of the "youngsters" for their intemperate advice as opposed to the wise counsel of his comrades, the "elders." These paradigmatic characters act out a drama in which didactic exposition takes precedence over historical detail. This analysis of the text curbs the suggestion of other commentators that the terms "old" and "young" are a reflex of actual court titles; rather, they are part of the storyteller's polemic. Finally, the tale's implied sympathy for the demand of the Northern tribes to ease their tax burdens is insufficient grounds for considering it to be of Israelite origin (so Würthwein).

The meeting at Shechem was ostensibly called to crown Rehoboam as successor to Solomon on the throne of the United Kingdom. It is nowhere stated that public acclamation was a necessary feature for the transfer of rule. The only other instance of such an act, in 2 Kgs 11, was during a time of crisis, as in 1 Kgs 12. Rehoboam journeyed to Shechem for the ceremonies in an obvious gesture to the Northern tribes (Tadmor 1982, 253–54). At the same time, it must have been known that the continued rule by a scion of the House of David would not be automatic. David's agreement with the North (2 Sam 5:1–3) does not seem to have come up for discussion at the time of the accession of Solomon, but events prior to Solomon's death certainly put the issue on the political agenda (cf. 1 Kgs 11:27). Thus, Rehoboam could certainly have expected that the topic of the onerous corvée would be raised.

History

Only the barest outline of the historical circumstances surrounding the secession of the North is obtainable from this wisdom tale. Relaxation of the corvée is the main demand of the Northern tribes for continued association with the House of David. Scholarly speculation has raised auxiliary issues that may have fostered alienation from Judah, among them a deteriorating security situation with the rise of Damascus, the selling off of Cabul to finance projects in Judah, itself a continuation of Davidic nepotism (Halpern 1974). Given their geographic and demographic superiority as compared with Judah, the Northern tribes may have felt that they were shouldering a disproportionate share of the tax burden but enjoying few benefits from the association with the United Monarchy. Jeroboam's failed insurgency and exile in Egypt (1 Kgs 11:26–28, 40) did not detract from his position as representative of Israel's desire for independence. Rehoboam, on his part, was unable to stem the tide of rebellion, but the polemics of the wisdom tale, which depict him as coarse and rough-hewn, do not provide further information on the weaknesses of the kingdom he had inherited.

XX. An independent Israel

(12:20–24)

12 ²⁰All Israel heard that Jeroboam had returned; they summoned him to the assembly and made him king over all Israel. Only the tribe of Judah followed the House of David.

²¹Rehoboam came[a] to Jerusalem and assembled all the House of Judah and the tribe of Benjamin—one hundred eighty thousand select soldiers—to fight against the House of Israel in order to restore the kingship to Rehoboam son of Solomon. ²²But the word of God came to Shemaiah, the man of God: ²³"Say to Rehoboam son of Solomon, king of Judah, and to all the House of Judah and Benjamin and the rest of the people:

²⁴Thus said YHWH: 'You shall not set out to make war against your kinsmen, the Israelites. Let each man return home, for this matter has been brought about by Me.'" They heeded the word of YHWH and turned back in accordance with the word of YHWH.

---

[a] Read with qere *wyb'*; ketib *wybw*.

NOTES

12 20. *All Israel heard that Jeroboam had returned.* It is difficult to consider this verse to be the continuation of the previous scene (cf. vv. 3, 12); rather, it is a separate, very succinct notice concerning Jeroboam's return from his self-imposed exile in Egypt and his enthronement. The use of alternate terminology (*'ēdâ* instead of *qāhāl*) points in this direction (cf. Note on 12:3).

All Israel. As in the first unit, vv. 1–19, the reference can only be to the ten tribes.

they summoned him to the assembly. The term *'ēdâ*, most frequent in the Pentateuch and favored by P, is employed here; it is replaced in LBH by *qāhāl* (cf. v. 3; see Hurvitz 1970; 1982, 65–67). The assembly, whether elders, princes, or chiefs, acted as "a political body invested with legislative and judicial" duties; see Milgrom 1978, 65–76. The scene in the text, as such, confers legitimacy on Jeroboam's rule.

Only the tribe of Judah followed the House of David. For **hāyâ 'aḥarê* signifying political allegiance, cf. 16:21; 2 Sam 2:10. The LXX adds the harmonizing statement "and Benjamin" from the next verse, contradicting the opening "only."

21. *all the House of Judah and the tribe of Benjamin.* The tribe of Benjamin is mentioned explicitly for the first time. The two tribes' being joined together in a single phrase is most prevalent in late writing; cf., e.g., Ezra 1:5; 4:1; 10:9; 2 Chr 15:2, 8, 9; 25:5; 31:1; 34:9.

one hundred eighty thousand select soldiers. An incredible number, pointing up the lateness of the narrated episode. The reading in LXX, 120,000, does not ease matters.

select soldiers. As in Judg 20:15–16, 34; 1 Sam 24:2. The verb *bḥr entered the late Akkadian lexicon, under Aramaic influence, with the nuance of "to levy, recruit" soldiers; see CAD B, 186, s.v. *beḫēru.*

22. *But the word of God came to Shemaiah, the man of God.* Shemaiah is unknown in Kings outside of the present context; in Chronicles, he figures in the reworked Shishak incident (2 Chr 12:5), where again he teaches obedience to YHWH. (In the LXX addition, Shemaiah replaces Ahijah in its rewriting of 11:29–39.) The general title "man of God" is borne in Kings by men otherwise known as prophets, e.g., Elijah (17:18); Elisha (2 Kgs 4:9); and unnamed messengers of YHWH (e.g., 1 Kgs 13:1ff.); in 2 Chr 12:5, Shemaiah is indeed dubbed "prophet."

the word of God. "The word of YHWH" is read in 2 Chr 11:3 and here by LXX, Syr., Tg.

23. *and the rest of the people.* It is not at all clear to whom "the rest of the people" refers.

24. *You shall not set out to make war.* The verb *ʿlh alone can convey hostile approach and attack—e.g., Judg 1:4; 1 Sam 7:7; 1 Kgs 14:25; 2 Kgs 17:5; sometimes the object of ʿlh, "set out" or "go up," is the noun "war," as in Judg 20:18; sometimes, as in the present case, it is a second verb, "to make war"; cf. Judg 1:1.

for this matter has been brought about by Me. The fact of YHWH's workings is expressed in the same fashion in 1:27.

turned back. Or "returned"; cf. 13:17.

COMMENT

Structure and Themes

This incident is likely a late addition to the Rehoboam-Jeroboam cycle, since it recalls other prophetic tales introduced into the tradition through the book of Chronicles (e.g., 2 Chr 12:5–8; 15:1–7; 16:7–10; 25:14–16; esp. 28:7–15). A number of considerations point to the didactic, unhistoric nature of these verses: the unrealistically large number of men mustered to fight against the North; the appearance of an otherwise unknown "man of God," who warns Rehoboam to desist from military action because the rebellion of Israel is YHWH's will. Its relative lateness can be seen in the attachment of Benjamin to Judah, a matter of some ambiguity in other materials (e.g., v. 20 immediately preceding; cf. also 11:31, as contrasted with 11:32, 36). The goal of this late, midrash-like story (so Kittel) seems to have been to exculpate Rehoboam for not having brought Israel back under the House of David, enlisting once again the theme of YHWH's predetermination of the course of history.

History

The joining of Benjamin with Judah and the House of David is never explained in Kings. Benjamin's desertion of the Northern cause is even more puzzling when it is remembered that Saul was a Benjaminite and that Sheba son of Bichri, a Benjaminite, had led a rebellion against David (2 Sam 20:1–22). Most historians have argued that, because of the proximity of Jerusalem to the Benjaminite border, it was necessary for Judah's kings to occupy Benjaminite territory as a security buffer against attacks on the capital city. In the long run, this situation may have been interpreted as Benjamin's having linked its fortunes with Judah from the start.

Full-scale war does not appear to have broken out between Judah and the Northern tribes over their secession. Rather, border clashes between the two seem to have continued over a number of years (cf. 14:30), probably before and after the raid of Shishak.

EXCURSUS

The Alternative Story of the Rise of Jeroboam: LXX 1 Kgs 12:24a–z

The most extensive of the Greek additions to 1 Kings is the unit that appears after MT 1 Kgs 12:24 and is numbered 12:24a–z. Unlike the other instances of LXX pluses, this addition is a unified composition, a coherent story that parallels and duplicates events already related in 1 Kgs 11 and 12, except for the narrative of the sick child, which follows in 1 Kgs 14. Many verses have a parallel in MT, while there are an equally large number of items that are exclusive to this story, which presents another reading concerning the rise of Jeroboam.

After a notice about the accession of Rehoboam—he was only sixteen when he took the throne (12:24a)—Jeroboam is introduced. He, the son of a whore, is the official in charge of the levy under Solomon (12:24b). He has his eyes on the throne, and his manner provokes Solomon to seek his death, whereupon he flees to Egypt (12:24c). There he marries into the royal family (12:24e), but after hearing of Solomon's death (12:24d), forsakes all to return home (12:24f). The son born to him in Egypt soon falls ill and dies, in accord with the prophecy of Ahijah to the mother of the child (12:24g–n^a). At this point, the scene shifts abruptly to Shechem, where a meeting between the tribes of Israel and King Rehoboam takes place (12:24n^b). A prophecy by Shemaiah concerning Jeroboam's future rule over Israel (12:24o) is seen to be fulfilled as the negotiations between the two sides fail (12:24p–t), even though it is nowhere stated that Jeroboam took the throne. Rehoboam thought to recover Israel by force, but he backed off on the advice of Shemaiah, for it is the word of YHWH that the kingdom be divided (12:24x–z).

Scholarly study has focused on the evolution of this story, questioning whether it represents a recension of MT Kings—i.e., a purposeful reworking of the text ("midrashic" [Montgomery and Gehman, 254]; "strange and arbitrarily ordered compilation" [Noth, 270]) — or an earlier (pre-Dtr) version of the Jeroboam story that preserves traditions rejected in the development of MT ("an independent Northern tradition . . . worked over by a Judean editor" [Gray, 311]?). However, Talshir's exhaustive analysis (1990) has shown that the author of the addition fashioned the story out of ready-made components, freely adding and arranging them with great skill. He created a coherent retrospective that is critical of both the protagonist (Rehoboam) and the antagonist (Jeroboam).

A few items in the addition suggest that at its base was the narration now preserved in MT. For example, the prophecy of doom tendered by Ahijah to the wife of Jeroboam concerning her sick child is suited more to a royal personage than to the child (v. 24m), yet according to the order of events in the story, Jeroboam has not yet become king. This item has been repositioned from its natural context attested to in MT (14:10–11). Or, if the Shemaiah episode (12:21–24) is a post-Dtr addition to Kings, as seems likely, the writer of the alternative story used it and its prophetic spokesman creatively in his new-spun tale. Talshir's suggestion is that the story was written in translation Greek from a Hebrew *Vorlage* (that can be sensed, for one thing, by a number of wordplays stemming from similar-sounding words in the reconstructed Hebrew; e.g., 12:24f: *mṣrym, ṣrrh, mṣwr*). It is a "historical midrash," not unlike what may be found in the work of the biblical Chronicler; yet because of its shortness, the date and home of the story are difficult to set. The writer's anti-Jeroboam stance — the compounding of his sinful acts, while at the same time avoiding any mention of Solomon's sins — may mean that he lived at the time of the strife between the Jerusalem community and the Samaritans.

XXI. THE REIGN OF JEROBOAM (ISRAEL)

(12:25–32)

12 ²⁵Jeroboam built Shechem in the hill country of Ephraim and dwelled there. Then he went out from there and built Penuel.

²⁶Jeroboam said to himself: "Now the kingdom will revert to the House of David. ²⁷If this people (continues) to go up to offer sacrifice in the House of YHWH in Jerusalem, the heart of this people will turn back to their lord, to Rehoboam, king of Judah; they will kill me and return to Rehoboam, king of Judah." ²⁸So the king took counsel. He made two golden calves and he said to them:ᵃ "Enough going up to Jerusalem! Here are your gods,ᵇ O Israel, who brought you up from the land of Egypt." ²⁹He set up one in Bethel, and the other he assigned to Dan. — ³⁰This matter was indeed sinful. — The people went ahead of that one as far as Dan. ³¹He made a shrine of the high place and he appointed some of the people priests who were not Levites. ³²Jeroboam established a festival in the eighth month on the fifteenth day of the month, like the Festival in Judah, and he ascended the altar. This he did in Bethel, sacrificing to the calves that he made; and he stationed in Bethel the priests of the high places that he had appointed.

ᵃ LXX, Vulg. read *ʾl hʿm*, "to the people," for MT *ʾlhm*, "to them."

ᵇ So according to MT vocalization of following verb; see Note.

NOTES

12 25. *Jeroboam built Shechem in the hill country of Ephraim.* No signs of this activity have been uncovered in the excavations at Tell Balâṭah — only the poor settlement of Shechem X. On the other hand, if its destruction is attributable to Shishak, the following rebuilding of Shechem IX might be associated with Jeroboam; cf. NEAEHL 1345–54.

and dwelled there. Shechem was the king's first residence but was later replaced by Tirzah (14:17), which served all of Israel's rulers until the construction of Samaria under Omri (cf. 15:33; 16:8, 15, 23). Perhaps *wayyēšeb bāh* should be rendered: "he ruled from there"; the semantic range of Heb *ʾyšb* includes "sitting (upon the throne)," therefore "rule"; cf. Exod 15:14–15; Deut 1:4; 3:2; Amos 1:5, 8 (// "bearer of the scepter"); Ps 2:4. For similar usages in Akk, Aram, Ug, see Paul 1991, 52.

Then he went out from there and built Penuel. Penuel is the town in Transjordan in Wadi Jabbok, in the neighborhood of Mahanaim and Succoth, known from the Jacob traditions (Gen 32:31–32) and the route of Gideon's pursuit of the Midianites back to the desert (Judg 8:8–9). The time and circumstances behind Jeroboam's fortification of Penuel are unrecorded; see further the

Comment. If this move preceded Shishak's campaign, it provided little refuge; Penuel is apparently the reading of no. 53 in Shishak's list. Several sites have been identified as ancient Penuel, including: Tulul ʾed-Dahab esh-Sherqiyeh (on the southern bank of the Jabbok) (Aharoni 1979, 34) and Tell ʾel-Ḥammah (Kallai 1986, 264 n. 345). Translating wayyēṣēʾ as "he left" (NAB) or "moved out" (NJPSV) implies that Jeroboam transferred his residence to Transjordan, but there is nothing to suggest that Penuel, far removed from the Israelite heartland, became his capital. In fact, the royal residence was moved to Tirzah, just north of Shechem (cf. 14:17).

27. the heart of this people will turn back to their lord, to Rehoboam, king of Judah. That is, "revive their allegiance" (NEB). The Deuteronomist has Jeroboam acknowledge the rightful rule of Rehoboam.

28. So the king took counsel. The verb is the same as in v. 6 and, though it is not followed by an object, parsing it as reflexive (e.g., "after giving thought to the matter," NEB; cf. Noth) seems subjective.

He made two golden calves. The iconography of the ancient Near East has clarified the position of these much-maligned cult objects. A variety of animals is attested as serving as stands and pedestals for the gods, who appear in human form astride the backs of their brutish servants; cf. ANEP 470–74, 486, 500–501, 522, 531, 534, 537. In Canaanite mythology, the bull is associated with the chief deities, El and Baal, and bull figurines have been recovered in cultic contexts (A. Mazar 1982; note should be taken of the difficulty in distinguishing between bull and calf figurines and in specifying the deity represented; Fleming [1999] has explored the issue of the association of the head of the pantheon with the adult bull and the second-generation deity with the calf). Yet Jeroboam's choice of a calf (n.b.: it has become fashionable in some circles to translate "young bull" on the basis [?] of Ps 106:19) is likely linked to Israelite tradition and the calf built by Aaron (related in Exod 32), both in its form and function. In the desert tale, the calf was meant to attract YHWH to a new resting place within the camp, luring the deity back after the long absence of Moses, which broke off the communication between YHWH and Israel. This tradition, though denigrated in the present Pentateuchal rendition, may well have been known in Northern Israelite circles in a positive form and thus have served Jeroboam in promoting a cult independent of the Jerusalem Temple and its cherub figures. In 2 Kgs 17:16, the calves are described as "molten images," as is the calf in Exod 32:4, 8; cf. also 1 Kgs 14:9.

he said to them. The reading ʾl hʿm, "to the people," in LXX, Vulg., for MT ʾlhm, seems to be more explicative than an original reading, the reference to the people being repeated from the preceding verse for clarity.

Enough going up to Jerusalem! For the comparative use of mem with an infinitive, cf. Gen 4:13; 36:7; 1 Kgs 8:64; though sometimes the preposition is omitted, e.g., in Deut 1:6; 2:3; cf. GKC, 133c.

who brought you up from the land of Egypt. The plural verb heʿelûkā is a tendentious vocalization, stressing the polytheistic nature of Jeroboam's cult; this same stance is reflected in Exod 32:4; otherwise, this verb appears in the singular, as in Neh 9:18 (favored by many in 1 Kgs 12:28, though without textual warrant). The question of whether the plural is original or reflects late Masoretic sensitivity is much debated. See further in the Comment.

29. *He set up one in Bethel, and the other he assigned to Dan.* For the contrasting order of the words in 29b, cf. similarly in 5:25; 10:10, 13; 18:42; 22:20. The location of the two sites at the extreme borders of the new kingdom is sometimes thought to have played a part in their choice as royal cult centers, yet ideological considerations may have been the dominant consideration, as remarked by Qimḥi: "He (Jeroboam) said to them: 'This place (Bethel) is also chosen, like Jerusalem, for Jacob had said of this very place: "It will be a house of God"' (Gen 28:22)." Dan, too, could claim a worthy ancestor in its "founding father," the grandson of Moses (cf. Judg 18:30). But, in contrast to Bethel, which is referred to as a state sanctuary in Amos 7:13 and Hos 10:5, Dan goes unmentioned in the later literature; this has led some critics to consider the calf at Dan a Dtr embellishment in order to make sure that Jeroboam's cult was understood as being polytheistic (Motzki 1975, 475; followed by Würthwein, Jones). But the rich polemic in Judg 18 against the Danite shrine points to its being more than just another high place. See further in the Comment.

Bethel. For the archaeology of Bethel, see NEAEHL 192–94.

Dan. For the archaeology of Dan, see NEAEHL 323–32 and, more fully, Biran 1994.

30. *This matter was indeed sinful.* This clause is expanded in Luc. by the additional phrase "for Israel"; other versions reflect MT. In either case, it interrupts the recital of Jeroboam's cultic reform and reflects the evaluation in 13:34 (see Note there).

The people went ahead of that one as far as Dan. This awkward sentence is often corrected by adding, before the reference to Dan, the putative original: "the one (calf) to/at Bethel" (which Luc. exhibits after MT), producing the Heb construction *lipnê hā'eḥād ... wĕlipnê hā'eḥād*, "before the one ... before the other" (so NEB, NAB). Noth pictured a simple scenario: Jeroboam himself took part in the dedication of the calf in Bethel, but the other one was accompanied to its shrine by popular entourage all the way to Israel's northern border (see also de Vaux 1971a, 98–99). If this is correct, this half-verse may be pointing out the excessiveness of Israel's sin: in their enthusiasm for calf-worship, these idolaters journeyed ("went in procession," NJB) as far as Dan.

Finally, considering that the polemic in Exod 32 is related to the polemic in 1 Kgs 12, one wonders whether an echo of that account cannot be heard in the present verse. In Exod 32:1, it is the calf (with YHWH enthroned) which "was to go before" (i.e., lead) the people; in 1 Kgs 12:30, the people lead the calf.

31. *He made a shrine of the high place.* The singular may be referring specifically to the shrine at Bethel, the object of the king's concern (with Barrick 1996, 624–25); most construe as plural (Montgomery and Gehman, citing GKC, 124r) or correct to *bāttê habbāmôt*, with 13:32. The other *bāmôt*-shrines

are not ascribed to Jeroboam in particular; cf. 2 Kgs 23:19. The very limited number of references to these shrines are all to Israelite practice (e.g., 13:32; 2 Kgs 17:29, 32; 23:19); if these structures were in use in Judah, they went unnoted.

The excavation report of Dan (Biran 1994, 165–83) describes a "sacred precinct," whose foundations date back to the end of the tenth–early ninth centuries BCE and can be assigned to Jeroboam (Stratum IV). No *bāmâ* or hint of a golden calf was found: *pithoi*, some with snake decorations, Phoenician vessels, an incense stand, and a water pool are all that remain of this "earliest" cult site in Dan. It was apparently destroyed after a generation or two and rebuilt in the ninth century (by Ahab?).

he appointed some of the people priests who were not Levites. An ironic statement, inasmuch as the Law of Moses does not require the appointment of Levitical priests in idolatrous cults, which the writer considers Jeroboam's cultic innovations to have been.

he appointed. For the suggestion that Heb ʿāśô, "to do, make," had become a calque, acquiring extended meanings through Aramaic, see Note on 2 Kgs 17:29, where the present expression appears with reference to priests appointed by the foreigners in Samaria.

who were not Levites. Priests were required by Deut 18:1–8 to be Levites.

some of the people. As pointed out in the Note on 2 Kgs 17:32, the sense is not that the priests were low-class persons (so KJV) but that they were of the wrong class. The ones chosen were of necessity trained in cultic matters. On qĕṣēh/qĕṣôt, see Speiser 1964, ad Gen 47:2; Greenberg 1997, ad Ezek 33:2.

32. *Jeroboam established a festival in the eighth month on the fifteenth day of the month, like the Festival in Judah.* The Festival of Sukkoth was celebrated in the seventh month (cf. 1 Kgs 8:2 and discussion there). The impression given in the present verse that the holy day proclaimed by Jeroboam was the same as the one in Judah is corrected in v. 33; Jeroboam had, in fact, invented a new festival.

in the eighth month. The most frequent explanation for the move of the Festival to the eighth month is that the Northern calendar differed from the calendar of Judah; Jeroboam's act was another facet of his program to restore older Israelite tradition. The one-month difference in the celebration has been sought in "actual climatic and agricultural conditions prevalent in the north of Palestine," where crops ripened later than in the South (Talmon 1958, 56–57). By allowing that the date in Lev 23:34 ("P") for Sukkoth was set only in a relatively late period (in contrast to the open-endedness of Deut 16:13), the accusation against Jeroboam would be limited to the active role he played in the idolatrous cult (Würthwein).

and he ascended the altar. As part of the inaugural ceremony of the Bethel sanctuary and the new holiday. The participation of the king at the altar, though here noted critically because it was in violation of strict Levitical law (Num 18:7), may not be as heterodox as it first seems. Solomon is described as taking

Fig. 3. A bronze figurine of a bull from a site in the hills of Samaria (cf. 1 Kings 12:28). *Reproduced courtesy of Israel Exploration Society.*

an active role in the dedication ceremonies of the Temple (cf. 1 Kgs 8:64); Ahaz also ascended and sacrificed on the new altar built at his behest (2 Kgs 16:12–13). In the present case, Jeroboam was following Jerusalemite precedent, which called for the king to officiate at temple inaugurations.

This he did in Bethel, sacrificing to the calves that he made. The phrase emphasizes the idolatrous nature of Jeroboam's cultic innovations.

COMMENT

Structure and Themes

The only "factual" item seemingly free of polemic in this section is v. 25; but what interest Jeroboam's building activities held for Dtr is unclear. Matters of this sort are usually noted, if at all, in the closing summaries of reigns (cf., e.g., 1 Kgs 22:39; 2 Kgs 14:22; 20:20). This juxtaposition of the item to the reference to Jerusalem in the following verse (v. 26) has suggested that these two cities, Shechem and Penuel, served in succession as capitals (see further below).

The remainder of this unit is written from a Judean point of view and is highly polemical, reflecting Dtr dogma on Jerusalem's centrality. Jeroboam's cultic activities are portrayed as innovations that sought to win the people's hearts; but such a concern is anachronistic, for worship outside of Jerusalem at rural

Fig. 4. Several fire pans at the foot of an altar, Tel Dan (cf. 1 Kings 12:31). *Reproduced courtesy of Israel Exploration Society.*

shrines was the norm in both kingdoms, and the cycle of pilgrimage festivals to the chosen site (cf. Deut 16:1–17) was a later development. The royal shrines at Bethel and Dan, the calf images and the new priesthood, and the new festival are all explained as measures taken to counter the Solomonic Temple; continued attendance at its festivities would lead to political reunification.

Jeroboam's acts are presented as idolatrous, yet not in the commonsense use of the term. Inasmuch as Pentateuchal law prohibited the use of all images in the worship of YHWH, any breach of orthodox practice was branded idolatry, whatever the intention of the worshiper may have been. Thus, the original form and function of the calves, as pedestals (Obbink 1929; Albright 1969a, 197–98), atop cult standards (Eissfeldt 1940–1941) or divine escorts (Weippert 1961), mattered little; Dtr went out of his way to present them as actual "gods." Such critique was not new to Dtr and is found earlier, in Hos 8:4–6; 10:5–6. These verses, despite the prophet's polemics, raise the question of whether, on the popular level, a distinction between a pedestal for YHWH's presence and his godhead was always maintained.

The three constitutive elements of Jeroboam's reform—image, shrine, and celebration—should be read alongside Exod 32, the "original" calf story, in which Aaron is involved in the same three activities. Aaron oversees the construction of a molten calf (vv. 2–4a); he announces: "These are your gods, O Israel, who brought you up from the land of Egypt" in front of the calf (v. 4b); and he constructs an altar and proclaims a feast (v. 5), at which sacrifices were offered (v. 6). Whether one takes Jeroboam as an innovator or merely a reviver of alternate Israelite cultic practice, it is hard not to read Exod 32, in its present redaction, as a Judean polemic against Jeroboam and his calves (Aberbach and Smolar 1967). At the base of Exod 32, one senses the presence of alternative priestly traditions in which Aaron is portrayed at the side of Moses and, like him, is subject to divine revelations; this explains the glossing over of whatever punishment he may have merited or received for the leading role he took in the making of the calf. Bethel was the probable home of such traditions where, among the Aaronide priests (cf. Judg 20:26–28), tales and ritual associated with the revered ancestor would have found refuge and support until renewed by the first Israelite king. (In this regard, the significance of the names borne by Jeroboam's sons, Nadab and Abijah, echoing the names of Aaron's sons, Nadab and Abihu, should not be underestimated.)

History

Jeroboam's cultic reforms were an essential part of the establishment of an independent political entity. Their aim: the consolidation and strengthening of the new kingdom. Some of the reforms had, in all likelihood, deep roots in traditional Northern practice—e.g., the veneration of YHWH through the calf symbol. The sacred sites chosen to become royal sanctuaries had served their tribes for generations. Other items may have been newly introduced—e.g., the new date of the fall Festival (v. 32). Purposeful calendric alteration is typical of schismatics. The position of Jerusalem may have worried him far less than stated here for, after all, the secession was supported by a cry for Israelite "rights" that had found little expression under the Davidide rule.

The fortification of Penuel remains clouded. Perhaps Jeroboam sought to increase Israel's hold on the territories on the eastern bank of the Jordan; it will be remembered that during the Absalom uprising, David found refuge among some of the Gileadites, who may have maintained sympathy with Judah (Gray). Just how long or effective such efforts were cannot be said, since Transjordan was later raided by Shishak.

XXII. THE MAN OF GOD FROM JUDAH

(12:33–13:34)

12 ³³So he ascended the altar that he made in Bethel on the fifteenth day of the eighth month, the month in which he invented on his own^a to establish a festival for the Israelites. As he ascended the altar to offer sacrifice, **13** ¹there came a man of God from Judah to Bethel by YHWH's word. Just as Jeroboam was standing on the altar to offer sacrifice, ²he called out against the altar by YHWH's word: "O altar, altar! Thus said YHWH: 'A son shall be born to the House of David, Josiah by name, and he shall slaughter upon you the priests of the high places who offer sacrifices upon you, and human bones shall be burned^b upon you.'" ³On that day, he gave a portent: "This is the portent that YHWH has foretold: 'The altar shall break apart, and the ashes upon it shall be spilled.'" ⁴When the king heard the word of the man of God that he called out against the altar in Bethel, Jeroboam stretched out his hand from the top of the altar and said: "Seize him!" But the hand that he stretched out against him withered, and he could not draw it back to himself.

⁵The altar broke apart, and the ashes were spilled from the altar, in accordance with the portent the man of God had given by YHWH's word. ⁶Then the king addressed the man of God: "Please entreat YHWH your God and pray on my behalf that my hand may be restored to me." The man of God entreated YHWH, and the hand of the king was restored to him and became as at first. ⁷Then the king spoke to the man of God: "Come home with me and take some food,^c and I shall give you a gift." ⁸But the man of God said to the king: "If you were to give me half your house, I would not come with you, nor will I eat bread, nor will I drink water in this place, ⁹for thus he has ordered me by the word of YHWH: 'You shall not eat bread or drink water, nor shall you return by the road you came.'" ¹⁰So he left by a different road and did not return by the road he had come to Bethel.

¹¹There was a certain old prophet living in Bethel. His son came and told^d him all the things that the man of God had performed that day in Bethel; (and) the words that he had spoken to the king, they told them to their father. ¹²Their father said to them:^e "Which road did he take?" His sons had seen^f the road that the man of God who came from Judah had taken. ¹³He said to his sons: "Saddle an ass for me!" They saddled an ass for him and he mounted it ¹⁴and

---

^a Read with qere, *mlbw*, for ketib, *mlbd*.

^b MT: *yśrpw*; LXX, Vulg., Syr. *yśrp*.

^c MT Leningrad vocalizes: *ûsĕ'ādâ*; Aleppo: *ûsă'ādâ*; see Note.

^d For MT sg., LXX, Vulg., Syr. read pl. subject (cf. vv. 11b, 12); also 2 MSS.

^e Luc. adds: *l'mr*.

^f MT: *wayyir'û*; Luc., LXX, Vulg., Syr., Tg.: *wayyar'ûhû*; see Note.

set out after the man of God. He found him sitting under a terebinth and said to him: "Are you the man of God who came from Judah?" He said: "I am."

[15]He said to him: "Come home with me and eat some bread." [16]He said: "I cannot go back with you or enter your home; I cannot eat bread or drink water with you in this place. [17]For the order I have by YHWH's word is: 'You shall not eat bread or drink water there; nor shall you[g] return by the road you came.'"
[18]He said to him: "I, too, am a prophet like you, and an angel spoke to me by YHWH's word: 'Bring him back with you to your house; let him eat bread and drink water.'" He was lying to him. [19]So he went back with him, and he ate bread and drank water in his house.

[20]While they were sitting at the table,[h] the word of YHWH came to the prophet who had brought him back. [21]He announced to the man of God who had come from Judah: "Thus said YHWH: 'Because you rebelled against the order of YHWH and have not obeyed the command that YHWH your God gave you [22]but have gone back and eaten bread and drunk water in the place of which He spoke: "Do not eat bread and do not drink water," your corpse shall not come to the grave of your ancestors.'" [23]After he had eaten bread and had drunk, he saddled the ass for him—belonging to the prophet who had brought him back[i]—[24]and he set out. On the way, a lion came upon him and killed him. His corpse was left lying on the road, with the ass standing by it and the lion standing by the corpse. [25]Now some people were passing by, and they saw the corpse lying on the road and the lion standing by the corpse; they came and told it in the town where the old prophet lived. [26]When the prophet who had brought him back from the road heard it, he said: "It is the man of God who rebelled against the order of YHWH! YHWH handed him over to the lion who mauled him to death, in accordance with the word of YHWH that he foretold to him." [27]Then he spoke to his sons: "Saddle the ass for me!" and they saddled (it). [28]He set out and found his corpse lying on the road; the ass[j] and the lion were standing by the corpse; the lion had not eaten the corpse, nor had it mauled the ass. [29]The prophet lifted the corpse of the man of God, laid it on the ass, and brought it back; the old prophet[k] came back to the town to mourn over him[l] and to bury him. [30]He laid the corpse in his own grave, and they mourned over him: "Alas, my brother!" [31]After he had buried him, he said to his sons: "When I die, bury me in the grave where the man of God is buried; lay my bones next to his bones,[m] [32]for the word that he announced by YHWH's word against the altar in Bethel and against all the shrines of the high places in the towns of Samaria shall surely come about."

---

[g] Many MSS read: *wlʾ*.

[h] MT has the notation *pisqāʾ běʿemṣaʾ pāsûq*; see Note on 2 Kgs 1:17.

[i] LXX omits the clause and reads: *wyšb*, "he went back."

[j] Read with many MSS: *whḥmwr* for MT *wḥmwr*.

[k] Elements reordered; cf. Luc. and see Note.

[l] Read: *lspdw*; *waw* lost through haplography.

[m] LXX assimilates text of 2 Kgs 23:18; see Note.

³³After this incident, Jeroboam did not turn back from his evil way. He kept on appointing some of the people as priests of the high places; anyone who so desired, he would install as priestⁿ at the high places. ³⁴By this matter it became a sin for the House of Jeroboam to its utter destruction from the face of the earth.

ⁿ Read with LXX, Vulg., Syr. *khn*; MT: *khny*.

NOTES

12 **33.** *So he ascended the altar that he made in Bethel on the fifteenth day of the eighth month.* This verse is basically a repetition of the preceding verse, and it adds nothing substantial to the description there. Its purpose is to serve as a transition to the following tale, noting the occasion of the altercation between Jeroboam and the man of God. Thus, it looks as though the editor considered this ascending of the altar to have taken place during the inaugural sacrifice (otherwise Noth, who reads it as if it said: 'On one such occasion, when the king ascended the altar . . .'). Only the matter of the altar, of all the cultic reforms that Jeroboam instituted, was necessary to carry the story forward. His other "sins" come in for criticism in the *Wiederaufnahme* in 13:33–34.

which he invented on his own. The verb **bd'* appears again in Neh 6:8, in both instances with the negative sense "to fabricate." This remark probably reflects the seriousness with which Jeroboam's innovation was viewed and was not merely said "to mock . . . a liturgical ignoramus" (so Robinson).

13 **1.** *there came a man of God from Judah to Bethel.* The opening word *wĕhinneh* cannot be the beginning of the tale and is dependent on some preceding statement that is no longer retrievable.

a man of God. A common designation for a person who is regarded a messenger of YHWH, including men such as Moses (Deut 33:1) and Elijah (1 Kgs 17:18) and the anonymous man who appeared to the parents of Samson (Judg 13:6, 8). Later in the present story, the term is equated with "prophet" (v. 18).

by YHWH's word. The term appears seven times in this chapter (vv. 1, 2, 5, 9, 17, 18, 32), pointing to the tale's central theme; cf. also 20:35.

2. *O altar, altar!* The repetition directs the attention of the attendants to the object addressed; it is also used to arrest an actor in his footsteps; cf. Gen 22:11; 46:2; Exod 3:4 (Qimḥi).

human bones shall be burned upon you. Not only out of disrespect for the dead, but also for the ultimate defilement of the altar.

shall be burned. In MT: *yśrpw*, the impersonal plural; read as *yśrp* singular by LXX, Vulg., Syr.

3. *he gave a portent.* The unusual syntax, with the verb in perfect tense, indicates that the verse along with its complement in v. 5 are not original to the story. In the present context, the syntax produces a foreshadowing effect referring to another act associated with Josiah. Far-off signs are not entirely unusual, as seen by YHWH's sign to Moses concerning the assured success of his mission in Exod 3:12 fulfilled later at Mt. Sinai. But in the present instance, the sign is almost immediately realized (v. 5).

a portent. Hebrew *môpēt* is a miraculous sign performed by a man of God or prophet that validates the divine word; cf. Exod 7:9; Deut 13:2. It is often paired with the word *'ôt*, "sign," especially in descriptions of YHWH's mighty acts in Egypt (e.g., Deut 4:34; 6:22; 7:19).

the ashes upon it shall be spilled. Hebrew *dešen* is properly "fatness," also used of the olive tree (Judg 9:9) and the "luxuriance" of the land (Ps 65:12). In cultic contexts, it is the burned suet on the altar, a mixture of fat and ashes; cf. Lev 1:16; 4:12; 6:3, 4. Unlike the ashes of legitimate sacrifices that are disposed of in a "clean place" (Lev 1:16), the ashes on the Bethel altar are to be unceremoniously scattered.

4. *Jeroboam stretched out his hand.* That is, he pointed in the direction of the man of God, indicating whom he wanted imprisoned, while he himself was standing on the altar. Still, a hostile or harmful intent is implied; cf. Gen 22:12; 2 Sam 18:12.

But the hand that he stretched out against him withered, and he could not draw it back to himself. The man of God is protected by an unsolicited divine act. To rationalize the withered arm as "a muscular spasm or nervous rigidity . . . the result of a cerebral hemorrhage or embolism" (Wiseman; cf. Gray) is to misconstrue the sign, besides distracting from the movement of the story. Jeroboam has not taken sick; he has been punished for his intent to harm YHWH's messenger.

withered. Literally, "dried up"; cf. Zech 11:17. The threatening hand had become inoperable.

5. *The altar broke apart, and the ashes were spilled from the altar.* The realization of the sign given in v. 3 is completely unexpected and disturbing, for the king was still standing on the altar. Furthermore, the following conversation disregards the altar's ruin, concerning itself solely with the king's immobilized hand. On this addition to the original story, see Comment.

6. *Then the king addressed the man of God: "Please entreat YHWH your God. . . ."* Though the man of God had not called down the punishment upon Jeroboam, the king asked him to intercede on his behalf, thus acknowledging his affront to YHWH's agent. Moses, the archetypical man of God, came under YHWH's protection when attacked (verbally) by his siblings (cf. Num 12:9–10); he, too, was called upon to pray for the cure of the punished (vv. 11–13).

entreat. The sense of the idiom **ḥlh pĕnê*, only in *Piel*, is established by context; in Zech 8:21–22, it is glossed by **bqš 't yhwh* and, in Mal 1:9, the hoped-for response is God's graciousness. Perhaps the root meaning is "to weaken, soften" anger; therefore, "to mollify."

7. *Come home with me.* There is no need to think that the king had invited the man of God to accompany him home (to Shechem?) or that he had a home in Bethel. The Bethel sanctuary, like most, had a hall for dining; cf. 1 Sam 9:22.

take some food. The MT (Leningrad): *ûsĕ'ādâ*; (Aleppo): *ûsă'ādâ*; both punctuations are noted in *Minḥat Shay*. The first form is the common lengthened imperative; the second, with the *ḥatep-qameṣ* may have developed because of the opening *waw* and the guttural; cf. Jer 22:20. The idiom *s'd lb(b)*, lit., "to sustain, support the heart" (Gen 18:5; Judg 19:5, 8; Ps 104:15), is here curtailed; in like fashion, MH uses simply *sĕ'ûdâ* for "meal."

I shall give you a gift. In recognition of the man of God's status, validated by the two signs, Jeroboam responds with the offer of a gift, as was customary when calling upon a prophet; cf., e.g., 14:3; 1 Sam 9:7–8. Hebrew *mattāt* is employed here for the more usual *mattānâ*; also Ezek 46:5, 11; Prov 25:14; Qoh 3:13; 5:18.

8. *If you were to give me half your house, I would not come with you*. Nothing could entice the man of God to disobey the instructions he had been given by YHWH, a pronouncement that he would soon forsake (cf. vv. 15–19). Balaam uses the same idiom in refusing to contravene the divine word; cf. Num 22:18; 24:13; also Esth 5:3, 6; 7:2.

9. *You shall not eat bread or drink water, nor shall you return by the road you came*. These puzzling restrictions draw attention to the total rejection of Bethel; neither fraternization with the king nor repeated use of the roads of this doomed place was allowed. Nothing suggests that the restrictions were undertaken because the man of God faced danger as a result of his words (as interpreted by Skinner: "to avoid pursuit"; Gray: "to avoid molestation"). Perhaps the man of God's returning by the same way that he had come would somehow symbolically suggest that he was in retreat from his prophecy of doom (so Simon 1976, 90–91). Though they may suffer personal discomfort, men of God were occasionally asked to act out in their lives the inherent sense of the messages they delivered; e.g., Jer 16:2, 5; Ezek 4.

10. *So he left by a different road and did not return by the road he had come to Bethel*. Both masc. and fem. gender of the noun *derek* in a single verse; for another case (*maḥăneh*), cf. Gen 32:9.

11. *a certain old prophet*. The terminological distinction between the "man of God" from Judah and the "old prophet" from Bethel is carefully maintained by the narrator; in v. 18, the identity of the two designations is claimed by the old prophet. There is no ground for taking "prophet" as a disparaging title (Skinner); to do that, it would have been necessary for the text to brand him a "false prophet" (as does Tg.). Rabbinic homiletics rescue the prophet from anonymity (cf. Qimḥi) but destroy the literary quality of the tale.

His son came and told him. It is not necessary to read "his sons" with the versions; the text relates the words of one of the sons and then continues in the plural to indicate the participation of all of the sons in the conversation. No reason is given for the old man's nonattendance at the sacrifice, though incapacity is not indicated, given his activeness in seeking out the man of God twice in a single day (vv. 12–14; 27–29).

that day. Literally, "today," from the son's point of view.

12. *His sons had seen the road.* The MT punctuation *wayyir'û* in *Qal* is one of "the strongest (cases) that can be urged in favor of the pluperfect" (S. R. Driver 1892, 87); cf. Qimḥi. The versions all read (*lectio facilior?*) *wayyar'ûhû*, "they showed him" (in *Hiphil*).

14. *under a terebinth.* On the use of the definite article in Hebrew (*hā'ēlâ*) indicating that the object was the one known and recognized, where in English the indefinite article is used, cf., e.g., Gen 14:13; 42:23; 1 Kgs 19:9; see GKC, 126,4. Consequently, it is misguided to look for a specific tree in the vicinity of Bethel (e.g., Gen 35:8, as does Skinner) under which the man rested. Moreover, the tree in Gen 35:8 is an oak (*'ālôn*), not a terebinth (with which it is sometimes confused, as in De Vries).

terebinth. Two types of terebinth (*'ēlâ*) were prevalent in ancient Israel, *pistacia palestina* and *pistacia atlantica*, the latter filling an ecological niche in semi-arid places and reaching great height and age; it is most likely the species referred to in most biblical references (Zohary 1982, 110–11).

18. *I, too, am a prophet like you.* The generic "man of God" is here determined by the title "prophet." The two interchange in the Elijah and Elisha traditions without apparent significance, e.g., 17:18 ("man of God"); 18:22 ("prophet"); 20:13, 22 ("prophet"), 28 ("man of God"); 2 Kgs 5:8, 14, 20 ("man of God"); 5:3, 13 ("prophet").

and an angel spoke to me by YHWH's word. This explanation by the old prophet was not a signal, missed by the man of God, that he was lying, for it would not have been considered unusual for an angel to do YHWH's bidding, even when a man of God was the recipient of the act or message (e.g., 1 Kgs 19:5–7). There is nothing "anti-angelological" in this innocent statement (contra Rofé 1988a, 180).

He was lying to him. For other examples of a circumstantial clause, asyndetically attached, cf., e.g., 7:51; 18:6; Gen 21:14; see S. R. Driver 1892, §163. This aside was intended for the reader; had the author wished to express the point of view of the subject, he could have chosen the locution, *wykḥš lw l'mr* "He lied . . . ," set at the head of the verse; cf. Gen 18:15. The lie was not that he claimed to be a prophet, for he later does receive YHWH's word (v. 20); it was, rather, the purported message. What the old prophet sought to gain by his prevarication is not elucidated in the text and has been the subject of continuing speculation. Josephus thought that he feared for his position and honor with Jeroboam (*Ant.* 8.236–37); attached to the shrine of Bethel, the prophet had an interest in the doom oracle spoken against its cult (Gray). DeVries frees the old prophet of responsibility altogether, because he was the instrument of a divine test of the man of God, the words "he lied" being a late rationalization.

19. *So he went back with him.* The MT *wyšb 'tw* was read by Luc. and LXX as *wayyāšeb 'ôtô*, "he brought him back."

20. *While they were sitting at the table.* Two idioms describe dining, *yšb 'l šlḥn*, "sit at the table," and *'kl ('l) šlḥn*, "eat (from) the table" (cf. 2 Sam 9:7; 1 Kgs 2:7; 18:19); correction of the first *'el* to *'al* (Montgomery and Gehman; BH³)

misses the point. For similar instances of a participial clause at the head of a sentence, cf. 2 Kgs 2:11; 8:5.

21. *you rebelled against the order of YHWH.* The verb **mrh* with *pî YHWH* is used of Moses and Aaron, who disobeyed YHWH's command at Meribah (cf. Num 20:24; 27:14); and of all the Israelites in Nehemiah's prayer (Neh 9:17 [*mry*], 26 [**mrh*//**mrd*]).

22. *your corpse shall not come to the grave of your ancestors.* For the desire to be buried with one's ancestors, cf. Gen 47:30; 50:25. Yet more seems to be meant than not being brought home for a proper burial. The description in vv. 24–25 of the carcass "left lying" abandoned on the road suggests that the punishment of the man of God was that his body would be cast out, treated as unwanted carrion.

23. *After he had eaten bread and had drunk.* As above in v. 18, so also here the man of God is depicted as unresponsive; he receives the word of YHWH with equanimity. He finishes his meal and is prepared to meet his fate.

he saddled the ass for him. The old prophet is the subject of this clause, saddling the ass for his guest. As in vv. 13, 27, *lô* is not "for himself" but "for another." When the rider saddles up, the preposition *lě-* is not used; cf. Gen 22:3; Num 22:21; 2 Sam 17:23; 1 Kgs 2:40; 2 Kgs 4:24 (with the possible exception of the problematic 2 Sam 19:27).

belonging to the prophet who had brought him back. A somewhat clumsy clause, lacking in LXX, which might have been added at a later stage in order to clarify for the reader whose donkey was saddled. Up to the present scene, the man of God has always been depicted as proceeding on foot. For the preposition *lě-*, meaning "belonging to," cf. 2 Kgs 5:9 and 1 Sam 14:16 (with Ehrlich).

24. *a lion came upon him and killed him.* The motif of the devouring lion as an instrument of divine punishment is associated with Bethel in particular, e.g., 2 Kgs 17:25–26. Evidence for this folk belief can also be found in the treaty of Esarhaddon with Baal of Tyre, in which the gods Bethel (*^dBaiati-ili*) and Anath-Bethel (*^dAnati-Baiati-ili*) are invoked to punish the violator of the pact by delivering him "to a man-eating lion" (ANET, 534a; on these gods, see DDD cols. 331–34). See also 1 Kgs 20:36; 2 Kgs 17:25. (That the image of the fearful roar of the lion in Amos 3:6, where it is likened to a prophet's mission, gave rise to the present tradition [so Gray, 323] requires a stretch of one's imagination.)

a lion came upon him. For Heb *mṣ'* in the sense of "chance upon, meet (unexpectedly)," cf. Gen 37:15; 1 Kgs 20:36, 37; 2 Kgs 4:29; 10:13, 15.

His corpse was left lying on the road. For the term "to cast out, abandon" (*hšlyk*) concerning a corpse, cf. Isa 14:19; Jer 22:19.

with the ass standing by it and the lion standing by the corpse. To make the point that the lion was fulfilling a divine order, the carnivore did not devour the dead man or the donkey, in departure from its natural behavior. Indeed, the donkey watched over its rider; the lion stood guard over both of them.

the corpse. While Heb *něbēlâ* can be used for both human and animal dead, the term does suggest the disparaging sense "carcass," since it is frequently associated with unwanted bodies (e.g., 2 Kgs 9:37; Josh 8:29; Jer 26:23; 36:30), cast out on the rubbish heap (in contrast to more dignified gĕwiyyâ; cf. Gen 47:18; 1 Sam 31:10); cf. the first option in Qimḥi.

25. *Now some people were passing by.* The spectacle of a fearsome lion standing guard, as it were, over a corpse was so unusual that the townspeople who observed the scene recounted it at home. Its portentous nature is recorded three times, in vv. 24, 25, and 28.

26. *who mauled him to death.* Here and in v. 29, the verb *šbr,* "to break," refers to injury; it is often applied to animals that have suffered a fatal blow; cf. Exod 22:9, 13; Lev 22:22; Ezek 34:4, 16; Zech 11:16. Akkadian *šebēru* has a similar semantic range (CAD Š/2, 249–50).

in accordance with the word of YHWH that he foretold to him. A frequent refrain in Kings, underscoring the fulfillment of a prophecy previously proclaimed; cf., e.g., 14:18; 15:29; 16:12, 34; 17:16; 22:38. See further in Introduction. Composition.

29. *and brought it back.* An ironic note. The man of God who had betrayed his mission by returning with the old prophet (cf. vv. 16–19) is returned once more to the scene of his downfall, this time to be given final honors.

the old prophet came back to the town. The MT looks overloaded with additional words, and if Luc. is followed, "the old prophet" and "came back" may be omitted (so, many commentators).

to mourn over him. Hebrew *spd,* like Akk *sapādu,* seems to have had the primary sense of "beating one's breast" in a public gesture of grief and may still be sensed in Isa 32:12 (Gruber 1980, 436–56).

30. *He laid the corpse in his own grave.* In the family sepulchre.

they mourned over him: "Alas, my brother!" For this and other formulaic phrases that served in funeral laments, cf. Jer 22:18; 34:5 (where the formula for a royal personage is given as: "Alas, lord. Alas, his honor"); also Amos 5:16. Cries of woe in Heb include: *hôy, hô, hah, ʾăbôy, ʾôy, ʾay, ʾahāh, ʾoyâ,* all variants on the basic outpouring of the soul (which seems to have been universal; cf. Akk [*ina muḫḫi bī*]*ti isappid uʾi iqabbīma,* "he mourns [for the tem]ple and says, 'Woe!'" [CAD S, 150–51]).

31. *When I die, bury me.* Waw-consecutive with perfect after an indication of time, as in, e.g., Exod 16:6–7; 17:4; 2 Kgs 20:17 (S. R. Driver 1892, §163b; Waltke and O'Connor 1990, §32.2.6b).

lay my bones next to his bones. In this manner, it would be impossible to distinguish bone from bone. The LXX adds: "so that my bones may escape with his bones," an obvious reference to the prediction in v. 2 and its fulfillment described in 2 Kgs 23:16–18. Several commentators object to the old prophet's referring to "my bones," "considering that a living man would hardly have used" such an expression (Montgomery and Gehman); LXX "lay me" is preferred. But the words of Joseph (Gen 50:25) are enough to discount such delicacies.

32. *for the word that he announced . . . shall surely come about.* An inclusio of sorts, tying the lengthy second scene of the tale to the opening scene and the prophecy declared against the altar.

and against all the shrines of the high places in the towns of Samaria shall surely come about. Strictly speaking, the city of Samaria had not yet been founded (cf. 16:24), and its mention here points to the lateness of the final editing of the story. Many date this to sometime after the Assyrian conquest (post-720 BCE), when the hill country of Israel was officially annexed and named *Samerina*.

33. *After this incident.* An editorial phrase, more common in the plural (*haddĕbārîm hā'ēlleh*; cf., e.g., 1 Kgs 17:17; 21:1), joining originally discrete literary units. In the present case, what follows is a short Dtr passage, taking up the theme broken off at 12:32. See further in Comment.

He kept on appointing. In this repetition of 12:31, the elements appear in reverse order, a sign that reference is being made to the earlier verse. The verb **šwb* in the sense of repetition appears twice in this verse and may have been suggested to the editor by its repeated use in the preceding narration, vv. 9, 16, 17, 18, 19, 22, 23, 26, 29.

he would install as priest. The idiom *millē' yad*, lit., "fill the hand," is used for investiture and ordination (e.g., Judg 17:5, 12; Num 3:3). Its Akk equivalent, *qātam mullû*, "to hand over," can include objects as diverse as prisoners and enemies, as well as the abstract concepts "rule" and "the four winds" (CAD M/1,187). See also 2 Kgs 9:24.

34. *By this matter it became a sin for the House of Jeroboam.* Compare with 12:30. Though promised to Jeroboam by Ahijah (cf. 11:38), a dynasty was never achieved. Jeroboam's son Nadab reigned for only two years and was assassinated by Baasha (15:25–32).

to its utter destruction from the face of the earth. The verb *lhšmyd*, "to destroy," is frequent in Deuteronomy in descriptions of YHWH's punishment of Israel (e.g., 6:15; 7:4; 9:8, 19, 25; 28:48, et al.); its association with *lhkhyd*, "to annihilate," is not otherwise known (cf. Exod 23:23).

COMMENT

Structure and Themes

A two-act prophetic tale concerning a man of God from Judah and his mission to Bethel (13:1–32) has been set into the history of Jeroboam; the literary frame (12:33 and 13:33–34), which criticizes Jeroboam's cultic acts, is wholly Deuteronomistic. The tale's two scenes, vv. 1–10, 11–32, are closely related: the man of God from Judah is the main actor in both, and his explanation for his rejection of Bethel—an explicit command from YHWH (vv. 7–9, 15–17; cf. vv. 18–22)—moves the action forward from one scene to the other. Further joining of the scenes is observable in the specific mention of Josiah and the future defilement of the altar (v. 2; cf. v. 32 and 2 Kgs 23:15–16) and the request of the old prophet to be buried alongside the man of God, foreshadowing Josiah's sparing of their joint grave (v. 31; cf. 2 Kgs 23:17–18). Finally, the sevenfold repetition of the phrase "the word of YHWH" (see Note on v. 1) unites the various elements into a single whole and serves as its motto. (Würthwein [1973] analyzes the chapter as two distinct, unrelated legends, later combined and rewritten by Dtr$_2$, which requires heavy-handed excisions of much of the story. What is left is a general threat against an anonymous king of Israel and an almost meaningless "grave tradition" of a few lines that told of two prophets, one from Judah and one from Israel, buried together. But because the shape of tradition in its preliterary stage is ultimately unascertainable, the arbitrariness of Würthwein's dissection has not won over many adherents.)

This north Israelite prophetic tale (with Noth), though critical of Jeroboam's cult reform (see further in Comment on 1 Kgs 14), contained another focus: the "word of YHWH," its lasting force, and the role of its carriers. YHWH's word, once pronounced, has a life of its own; it will be fulfilled, even though centuries lapse. The deliverer of YHWH's word is similarly goal-directed; he does not operate independently but is commissioned by the command of YHWH, and any deviation is punishable. The word of YHWH as delivered to a prophet is amendable, but only through a new revelation to the prophet himself (cf. Abarbanel). Thus, as in the case of Jeremiah when confronted with a YHWH-word contradictory to his own, surface signs of the truthfulness of the new message must be questioned; only a new word of YHWH to the prophet himself can verify the truth (Jer 28). The severe punishment of the man of God from Judah taught the lesson of obedience to one's mission and, at the same time, reiterated the isolation of Bethel.

Readers concerned with theology and moral teaching have had a difficult time with 1 Kgs 13. A man of God who strays from his mission and a lying old prophet, the former punished summarily, the later going scot-free, to be rescued in due time from oblivion by the dead man's bones—this is a perplexing concoction indeed! Morality aside (a new study has tried to vindicate YHWH by attributing venal motives to the man of God; see Reis 1994), these matters, like the lying spirit sent by YHWH (1 Kgs 22:21–22), do not seem to have been of concern to the biblical storyteller, in seeming acknowledgment of the devious ways of divine justice.

Despite this unitary reading of the tale, a number of small items, especially in the first scene, create some roughness and are likely to be late accretions. Throughout, the main actors remain anonymous: the man of God, the king, the old prophet; only in v. 1 is Jeroboam specified by name. Yet, even if this identification is an editorial addition, it is particularly apt, considering that Jeroboam was the acknowledged founder of the Bethel sanctuary. What other king of Israel might have been criticized for his acts at the Bethel altar? Verses 3 and 5 seem to interrupt the narrative; v. 6 follows naturally after v. 4. Moreover, if the king was standing on the altar (or its steps/ramp), he would most likely have fallen over with its collapse. If it is allowed that v. 3 can be read as predicting a second action to be taken against the altar in the distant future, then only v. 5 remains intrusive, inserted by an annotator who could not wait for Josiah to tear down the sinful installation (for the suggestion that this addition foreshadowed Josiah's action, see Simon 1976).

The Deuteronomistic elements in 1 Kgs 13 appear in the frame verses 12:33 and 13:33–34 and in the *ex eventum* Josianic references in vv. 2 and 32b. The editor underscores the image of Jeroboam as an unrepentant sinner; the matter of the prophetic prediction against the altar and the temporary punishment that he himself experiences (vv. 1–6) make no impression on this arch-heretic. Even the conversion of the old prophet from Bethel who ackowledges the truth of the warning pronounced against the altar goes unheeded. An epilogue to the tale of the man of God from Judah, also Deuteronomistic in composition, has been inserted into the history of Josiah in 2 Kgs 23:15–20. It is the concluding act of the drama that took place at Bethel on the day of the altar's inauguration, complementing and accentuating the lesson of 1 Kgs 13: the word of YHWH is trustworthy. Josiah's actions in Samaria are motivated by his zealousness for cleansing the land, but the specific attention given to the Bethel installation, which had stood in competition with the Jerusalem Temple for generations, was of particular interest to Dtr. Indeed, a later Davidide had arisen to eradicate the stain of Jeroboam's sins. Josiah is unaware of the prophecy of the man of God, of which he is informed after the fact (2 Kgs 23:17). Yet the word of YHWH needs no reminder, because it is self-fulfilling; even centuries later, it finds its object (Simon 1976, 110–11).

Because of the Deuteronomistic affinity with the prophets as forewarners of YHWH's judgment (cf. 2 Kgs 17:13), Dtr incorporated prophetic tales into his discourse on Israel's history, the present one serving him in his criticism of Jeroboam. (A second prophetic critique by Ahijah, Jeroboam's original supporter, follows in 1 Kgs 14:1–18.) Thus, rather than being "secondary . . . perhaps linked with Amos' appearance in Bethel" (Eissfeldt 1965, 290) or "post-Deuteronomistic" (Jepsen 1971), the tale of the man of God "fits admirably into the larger scheme of prophecy and fulfillment observable throughout the Deuteronomistic History" (Lemke 1976, 317 [for whom 1 Kgs 13 is nevertheless an insertion]; cf. Knoppers 1994, 50–64).

XXIII. A PROPHETIC ORACLE OF DOOM AGAINST JEROBOAM

(14:1–20)

14 ¹At that time, Abijah son of Jeroboam fell ill. ²Jeroboam said to his wife: "Come now, disguise yourself so that no one will recognize that you[a] are the wife of Jeroboam and go to Shiloh. Ahijah the prophet is there,[b] the one who foretold that I would be king[c] over this people. ³Take with you ten (loaves of) bread, some wafers, and a flask of honey and go to him. He will tell you what will happen to the lad." ⁴The wife of Jeroboam did so. She set out to go to Shiloh, and she came to the house of Ahijah. Now Ahijah[d] could not see, for his eyes had grown dim with old age.

⁵YHWH had said to Ahijah: "The wife of Jeroboam is coming to inquire (of YHWH) through you about her son who is ill. Thus and thus you shall speak to her. And when she comes, she will be hiding her identity." ⁶When Ahijah heard the sound of her footsteps as she came in the doorway, he said: "Come in, wife of Jeroboam. Why is it that you are hiding your identity? I have been sent with a harsh message for you. ⁷Go, say to Jeroboam: 'Thus said YHWH, the god of Israel: "Because I elevated you from among the people and made you ruler over my people Israel, ⁸and I tore the kingdom from the House of David and gave it to you, yet you have not been like my servant David, who kept my commandments and who followed me with all his heart, doing only what pleased me; ⁹you have acted worse than all who preceded you. You have gone and made for yourself other gods, molten images to anger me, and me you cast off behind your back.

¹⁰Therefore, I will bring disaster upon the House of Jeroboam, and I will cut off every male belonging to Jeroboam, even the restricted and the abandoned in Israel. I will stamp out the House of Jeroboam as one burns dung completely.

¹¹Those of Jeroboam('s kin) who die in the city, the dogs will eat; those who die in the field, the birds of heaven will eat."' For YHWH has spoken. ¹²As for you, hurry back to your home; as soon as you set foot in the town, the child will die. ¹³And all Israel will lament him and bury him, for he alone of (the House of) Jeroboam shall be brought to burial, for in him alone of all the House of Jeroboam has some good been found by YHWH, the god of Israel. ¹⁴Then YHWH will raise up for himself a king over Israel who will destroy the House of Jeroboam this very day, even right now! ¹⁵YHWH will strike Israel like a reed that sways in water and will uproot Israel from this good land that he gave to

---

[a] Ketib: *'ty*; qere *'t*.

[b] Many MSS read *whnh*; MT *hnh*.

[c] The MT: *lĕmelek*; LXXᴬ; Syr., Vulg. read as if pointed *limlōk*; see Note.

[d] Written: Ahijahu; see Note.

their ancestors; he will scatter them beyond the River (Euphrates), because they made their poles of Asherah, angering YHWH; [16]and he will hand Israel over because of the sins of Jeroboam which he committed and because he caused Israel to sin."

[17]The wife of Jeroboam set out immediately and came to Tirzah. As soon as she set foot on the threshold of her house,[e] the lad died. [18]They buried him, and all Israel mourned over him, in accord with the word of YHWH, which he had spoken through his servant, Ahijah the prophet.

[19]The rest of the history of Jeroboam, how he fought and how he reigned, are indeed recorded in the History of the Kings of Israel. [20]Jeroboam had reigned twenty-two years, and he slept with his ancestors. Nadab his son succeeded him.

---

[e] Lit., "the house."

NOTES

14 1. *At that time*. A loose editorial connective, with no chronological significance; cf. 11:29.

Abijah son of Jeroboam. The theophoric element *yh* in the name Ahijah is evidence for Jeroboam's acknowledging the national deity (however else one evaluates the editorial charge of apostasy). Abijah is only mentioned in the present tale and his age cannot be determined; he is referred to both as "lad" (vv. 3, 17) and "child" (v. 12).

2. *Come now*. For **qwm* used as an auxiliary verb indicating the start of an action, see Note to 2 Kgs 8:1.

disguise yourself. **Šnh*, "to change," appears only here in *Hithpael* in the sense "to change one's appearance."

that you are. The ketib *'ty* preserves the older form of the 2d fem. sg. (cf. 2 Kgs 4:16, 23; 8:1) and is dialectical in these Northern stories; see Introduction. Composition. The need for a masquerade suggests that Ahijah had become critical of Jeroboam and that the only way to obtain a neutral, untainted prophecy concerning the lad was by some means unconnected with his father. The charade did not, could not, work.

that I would be king. It is not necessary to repoint MT following the versions (so Gray, with many earlier commentators); cf. 15:13: *miggĕbirâ*, "from (being) queen mother." Jeroboam thought: Ahijah's prophecies are true; after all, he did predict that I would become king. Now, he surely knows what will happen to the child. But oddly, at the same time, Jeroboam believed that the prophet would not penetrate the woman's disguise (Ehrlich).

3. *Take with you*. It was common practice to offer a gratuity (*tĕšûrâ*, "present," according to 1 Sam 9:7) to a prophet when seeking advice or intercession; cf. 2 Kgs 5:15; 8:8. The nature of the gift was not to betray its royal bestower.

some wafers. Hebrew *niqqūdîm* occurs again in Josh 9:5, 12, where the context suggests the meaning "hard or dried cakes" (BDB 666a; cf. Tg. *kĕsānîn*, "roasted kernels," "that one nibbles at the tavern" [Qimḥi]). The translation "mouldy" in NEB at Josh 9:5, suggested by *nāqōd*, "spotted" (cf. Gen 30:32), is not suitable for the present verse, since the gift brought by the king's wife, though modest, was certainly respectable. The NEB's "raisins" seems to contain an etymological jump, from "spotted" to "baked goods covered with seeds or raisins" (Walsh).

a flask of honey. Honey was one of the emblematic signs of the bounty of the land of Israel, frequently referred to as "a land flowing with milk and honey" (cf. e.g., Exod 3:8; 13:5; Num 13:27; Deut 6:3), and was an appreciated gift at home (2 Sam 17:29) and abroad (Gen 43:11). Honey was hunted in the wild (cf. Deut 32:13; Judg 14:8–9; 1 Sam 14:25–27), yet bee-keeping is not referred to in the Bible. Therefore, some writers question whether apiculture, practiced from earliest times in Egypt, was known in Israel before the Hellenistic age (Neufield 1978). Fruit syrup, especially of dates, is often thought to be the "honey" referred to (cf., e.g., Šanda; Montgomery and Gehman).

He will tell you what will happen to the lad. Recovery from illness is also the subject of the inquiries recounted in 2 Kgs 1:2ff.; 8:8ff.

4. *Ahijah could not see.* The prophet's name is written in its full form, Ahijahu, here and in vv. 5–6, its only appearances in the entire collection of stories concerning Jeroboam; it is hard to ascribe literary-critical significance to this spelling. [DNF: "The long full form of such names was the standard spelling in all preexilic inscriptions, whereas the short form turns up in postexilic inscriptions."]

had grown dim with old age. Loss of sight is expressed by several idioms: *qāmû 'ēnāyw*, lit., "his eyes became fixed" (1 Sam 4:15); *wattikheynā 'ēnāyw*, "his eyes dimmed" (Gen 27:1; Deut 34:7); *'ēnê X kabdû*, "X's eyes were heavy" (Gen 48:10); *kālû 'ēnāyim*, "the eyes fail" (Jer 14:6, with Ibn-Janaḥ; cf. Tg.).

with old age. That is, many years have passed since he had first met Jeroboam and announced to him that he would be king. The masc. form *śyb*, rather than the usual fem. *śybh*, appears only here.

5. *YHWH had said to Ahijah.* YHWH informed the prophet of the upcoming visitor and instructed him concerning the reply he was to give her; cf. 1 Sam 9:15–16.

to inquire (of YHWH) through you. Taking the phrase to be elliptical for **drš dbr yhwh*, "to seek the word of YHWH," as in 1 Kgs 22:5; see also 2 Kgs 1:16; 22:18.

Thus and thus you shall speak to her. For this idiom, cf. 2 Kgs 5:4. The divine message is hidden from the reader, heightening the drama and expectation of the following encounter between the woman and the blind prophet.

And when she comes. The MT has the jussive form *wîhî*, "let it be," where *wĕhāyâ* is expected. If not a copyist's error (so Joüon 1923, §119z; cf. S. R. Driver 1892, §121 Obs. 3), then some sense of the conditional must be meant (cf. Montgomery and Gehman). In either case, the LXX vocalization *wayyĕhî* adopted by many commentators does not recommend itself; the clause is part of the divine message to the blind Ahijah preparing him for his initial encounter with the woman (v. 6b), in which he confronts her directly (cf. Haupt). The clause would read well were it placed before the preceding "thus and thus you shall say to her."

she will be hiding her identity. Rather than repeting the verb used in v. 2, the writer uses another verb here. Hebrew *nkr in *Hithpael*, lit., "to act as a stranger"; cf. Gen 42:7, where it probably has the same hostile overtones as its Akk cognate *nakāru* (CAD N/1, 159–71). In the present verse, its only other appearance, the verb conveys changing one's own appearance.

6. *the sound of her footsteps as she came in the doorway.* The verb agrees with the suffix of *"her"* footsteps," an accusative of state or manner (GKC, 118p); cf. 1:41.

Why is it that you are hiding your identity? For the pronoun *zeh*, used enclitically with adverbial force, see Burney. A translation "Why, then" does not do justice to this idiomatic usage.

I have been sent. That is, commissioned, the verb *šlḥ commonly used of prophetic messengers; for example, Exod 3:12; 2 Kgs 2:2; Isa 6:8.

with a harsh message. See Note on 1 Kgs 12:13.

7. *Because I elevated you from among the people and made you ruler over my people Israel.* The allusion is to Ahijah's earlier prophecy of appointment in 11:29–39. For the Davidic term "ruler," see Note on 1 Kgs 1:35.

8. *like my servant David, who kept my commandments and who followed me with all his heart, doing only what pleased me.* For David's ways, a constant yardstick for loyal behavior, cf. 3:6; 9:4; 11:4, et al.; only in 15:5 is a blemish noted.

9. *You have acted worse than all who preceded you.* This stereotypical Dtr evaluation (cf. e.g, 16:25, 30) is irrelevant in the present instance of Israel's first king.

You have gone and made for yourself other gods. An allusion to the accusation made in 12:28. See also 2 Kgs 17:29.

molten images. The initial *waw* is explicative. The term *massēkâ*, first used of Aaron's calf in Exod 32:4, 8; Deut 9:12, 16, refers to the golden calves introduced in the shrines of Bethel and Dan (cf. 1 Kgs 12:28; 2 Kgs 17:16).

and me you cast off behind your back. The emphatic syntax is not always reflected in modern translations. The NEB and NJB "turn your back on me" (a different idiom than the one here, *ntn/*pnh ʿrp) misses the image of casting out something unwanted; also in Ezek 23:35; Neh 9:26.

10. *I will cut off every male . . . even the restricted and the abandoned.* These phrases recur in 1 Kgs 16:11; 21:21; 2 Kgs 9:8; 14:26. For an explication of these aphoristic images, see the Note to 2 Kgs 9:8, to which add: Talmon and Fields 1989.

I will stamp out the House of Jeroboam as one burns dung completely. Also 1 Kgs 16:3; 21:21. Behind the translation "stamp out" and "burn" is a single verb in Hebrew, *bāʿēr, "to light or kindle (a fire), burn, consume completely"; hence, "stamp/root/sweep out." It is used frequently in Deuteronomic writing in exhortations when referring to eliminating evil(doers) from Israel; cf. Deut 13:6; 17:7, 12; 19:13, 19; 21:21; 22:21, 22, 24; 24:7; cf. 2 Kgs 23:24. The figure of burning dung down to ash appears only in the present verse. For dung used as fuel, see Ezek 4:12 and comment ad loc. in Greenberg 1983b, 107. (If the noun *bĕʿîr*, "beast, animal" [e.g., Exod 22:4; Num 20:11], is derived from this same root, it ascribes the ruin of the pasture to the overgrazing of these animals.)

11. *Those of Jeroboam('s kin) who die in the city, the dogs will eat; those who die in the field, the birds of heaven will eat.* The formulation is repeated again in 16:4 and 21:24 with reference to Baasha and Ahab respectively. The fact that the same punishment is promised the violator of YHWH's covenant (Deut 28:26) may elucidate the prophet's view that the king had indeed violated the terms of his divine appointment (cf. 1 Kgs 11:38). There is a common Near Eastern background to this curse as demonstrated by its use in the loyalty treaty of Esarhaddon (ANET, 538, lines 426–27, 451–52; see Hillers 1964, 68–69). Dogs, as a rule, scavenged city streets (as well as outside its walls; cf. 2 Kgs 9:10, 35–36), while birds cleared the open fields of unwanted corpses. For other uses of this image, see 1 Sam 17:46; Jer 15:3; Ezek 29:5; 39:17; Ps 79:2. In all of these passages, nonburial meant that the dead would be denied rest in the afterworld.

For YHWH has spoken. A phrase that marks the closing of the divine word (cf., e.g., with some variation, Isa 1:20; 21:17; 24:3; 40:5; Mic 4:4), adding a sense of solemnity and finality.

12. *as soon as you set foot.* In MT *bbʾh*, the *heh* is inexplicable; it is best to read the simple infinitive *bbʾ*.

13. *for in him alone . . . has some good been found.* Abijah's proper burial (cf. v 18) clashed with the preceding prophecy concerning the violent end of the House of Jeroboam. This prompted the editorial rationale that "some good" had been found in the child before he died. Hebrew *dābār ṭôb*, "a good thing," often connotes YHWH's promise of favor and fortune (e.g., Josh 21:43; 23:15; 1 Kgs 8:56; Jer 29:10; 33:14). It can also refer to proper cultic behavior on the part of a worshiper; cf. 2 Chr 19:3. Rabbinic exegesis took this to be the sense of "good" here: against his father's order, Abijah made a pilgrimage to the Temple in Jerusalem (*b. Moʾed Qaṭ.* 28b; quoted by many medieval commentators, Thenius, and Skinner; see further, Cogan, forthcoming b).

14. *a king over Israel who will destroy the House of Jeroboam.* Baasha later assassinated Nadab, fulfilling this prophecy (cf. 15:27–30).

this very day. The demonstrative *zeh* preceding *hayyôm* adds determination to the noun, as in 2 Kgs 6:33; Josh 9:12; Isa 23:13.

even right now. If MT is textually intact, *ûmeh gam ʾattâ* presents a crux. It might be parsed: "And what? Even now!" Compare Gen 44:10; 1 Sam 12:16; Joel 2:12; Job 16:19. Perhaps this is an allusion to the oncoming death of the queen's son. But if it is taken as introducing the following prediction of the nation's punishment (v. 15), the phrase may mean "and what is moreover"; compare with the Targumic paraphrase "and even those who will be born from now and further on" (so Qimḥi, Gersonides); note NEB's "This first; and what next?"

15. *YHWH will strike Israel.* Up until this point, the focus of Ahijah's prophecy has been the personal misconduct of Jeroboam for which he will be punished; now the sinful ways of the entire nation will bring about their scattering

beyond the Euphrates. A similar double indictment is found in the concluding peroration on Israel's downfall in 2 Kgs 17:7–23, but in that passage, national responsibility (vv. 7–17) outweighs the blotted record of Jeroboam (v. 21). See further in Comment to 2 Kgs 17:7–23.

like a reed that sways in water. Perhaps an oblique reference to the political upheavals in Northern Israel during the decades that preceded its downfall (Eissfeldt). The instability and unreliability of reeds are proverbial; cf. 2 Kgs 18:21; Ezek 29:6; for like use in Akk comparisons, see CAD Q, 88, e.g., "the kings hostile to me bend like reeds (*qanê*) in a storm." Mention of the Euphrates in the second half of the verse may have drawn the speaker to refer to quivering reeds.

and will uproot Israel from this good land that he gave to their ancestors. Compare with Deut 29:27; Jer 12:14.

he will scatter them beyond the River (Euphrates). A prophecy fulfilled with the conquest of the kingdom by Assyria; cf. 2 Kgs 17:6.

because they made their poles of Asherah, angering YHWH. For these poles, see Note on 2 Kgs 21:7.

16. *he will hand Israel over.* This clause is foreshortened; its sequence may be supplied from the Deuteronomistic expression referring to Israel's chastisement: "deliver them to their enemies" (cf. Judg 2:14; 2 Kgs 17:20; also 1 Kgs 8:46).

because of the sins of Jeroboam. Both forms of the noun, sg. *ḥṭ't* (15:26, 34; 16:19, 26) and pl. *ḥṭ'wt* (15:30; 2 Kgs 10:31; 13:2, 11; 14:24; 15:18, 28; 17:22) are attested, alternating without pattern.

17. *Tirzah.* Not mentioned earlier in the story. A move from Shechem had taken place under unrecorded circumstances; on Tirzah as the royal residence, see the Note on 15:21.

18. *They buried him, and all Israel mourned over him.* The standard terminology for interment and lament, as in 13:29–30.

in accord with the word of YHWH, which he had spoken through his servant, Ahijah the prophet. The editorial formula of verification; the word of YHWH had been fulfilled as prophesied. (Cf. 13:26; 15:29; 16:12, 34; 17:16; 22:38.)

19. *The rest of the history of Jeroboam, how he fought and how he reigned, are indeed recorded in the History of the Kings of Israel.* The standard closing formula for all the kings of Israel and Judah (cf. above 11:41).

how he fought. The previous tales did not tell of the king's military adventures, having concentrated upon cultic matters; from the notice in 14:30 (= 15:6), one also learns of the continued war waged between Jeroboam and Rehoboam.

how he reigned. A singular turn of phrase not used of any other king of Israel, and it may be a reference to his having established the independent kingdom of Israel.

History of the Kings of Israel. This translation replaces "the annals of the kings of Israel," the name used throughout 2 *Kings* (Cogan and Tadmor 1988); it reflects more accurately the sense of this featureless term. See, at length, in Introduction. Composition.

20. *Jeroboam had reigned for twenty-two years.* Jeroboam reigned from 928 to 907 BCE. As in the case of Solomon (cf. 11:42), the closing formula in 14:20

includes the length of Jeroboam's reign. Since no formal introduction to his reign had been given, his rise having been presented in the wisdom account in 1 Kgs 12, the chronological note was appended at this point; similar editorial considerations removed the data on the reign of Jehu to the end of the account of his reign (cf. 2 Kgs 10:36). A new archaeological discussion of the find-spot of the seal of "Shema, servant of Jeroboam" found at Megiddo (ANEP 276; Cogan and Tadmor 1988: Illustration 12a) dates the seal to Jeroboam son of Nebat rather than Jeroboam son of Joash, as held by many (see Ussishkin 1994; earlier Yeivin 1960).

COMMENT

Structure and Themes

A consensus concerning the nature of this story has developed: a prophetic tale of Northern origin, which told of an inquiry through the prophet Ahijah concerning the welfare of the king's son, is now "overshadowed by the two prophetic speeches" (Long), the work of the Dtr editor. The first address (vv. 7–11), formally a direct oracle from YHWH, is an indictment directed at the House of Jeroboam; the second (vv. 14–16), Ahijah's speech, elaborates on the former, as it moves from the imminent overthrow of Jeroboam to the exile of Israel as punishment for their following Jeroboam. The prediction of exile, fulfilled centuries later, as well as the singling out of the behavior of the entire nation (though ensnared by Jeroboam) as angering YHWH are thematic elements that are associated with Dtr_1. (The specificity of exile beyond the Euphrates [v. 15] is no more jarring than the mention of Josiah by name [13:2].) The reader also senses that, in the story elements that remain of the original tale (vv. 1–6, 12[–13?], 17–18), expression of Ahijah's rejection of Jeroboam can be found, particularly in the prediction that his son was at the point of death, as punishment for his father's sins. Likewise, the disguise of Jeroboam's wife, however misguided, suggests tension between the king and his former mentor. It is this that the Deuteronomist has extended, using the prophecy of Ahijah in 11:29–39 (especially vv. 31, 33–35 in 14:8). The reign of Jeroboam has thus come full circle and is brought to a close; its rise was prefigured by a prophecy (11:29–39), and its downfall was likewise predicted by a word of YHWH (14:7–16).[1]

Note may be taken of the literary imagery used in describing the punishment promised to the House of Jeroboam in vv. 10–11. These verses seem to contain a tinge of coarseness to the modern ear (especially v. 10a), considering the frequent remarks of twentieth-century commentators on this account (e.g., "two scurrilous ditties . . . the first ribald and flagrantly offensive" [DeVries]); but they are dependent upon traditional themes reflecting ancient life; their use is

---

[1] Cohn (1985) strived to read the entire Jeroboam narrative (11:26–14:20) as an artistic composition; but all of the varied elements utilized by Dtr to tell the story of Jeroboam do not fit neatly into the proposed "chiastic shape."

restricted to prophecies concerning the early dynasties of Israel (cf. 16:3–4, [11]; 21:21–24), which may justify supposing their Israelite origin.

This entire unit is lacking in pre-Hexaplaric texts of the LXX, because the story had been incorporated in the addition, at 12:24g–n; see Excursus: The Alternative Story of the Rise of Jeroboam.

History

The putative falling-out between Jeroboam and Ahijah, stripped of its Deuteronomistic elaborations, could have had several sources. The prophet's support of Jeroboam's rise to the kingship in the North (11:29–39) had been based on the hope for the revival of local customs and institutions, which had been displaced by the upstart Jerusalemite establishment under Solomon. In addition, as a son of Shiloh, Ahijah would likely have favored a return of the town to its former position as a revered cult center. Yet Jeroboam's reforms favored other sites and thus turned the prophet into a virulent critic of his reign (cf. Evans 1983, 118–19).

THE CAMPAIGN OF SHISHAK, KING OF EGYPT
(1 Kings 14:25–26;
Egyptian Itinerary: Appendix 1, No.1)

XXIV. THE REIGN OF REHOBOAM (JUDAH)

(14:21–31)

14 [21]Now Rehoboam son of Solomon became king in Judah. Rehoboam was forty-one years old when he became king, and he reigned seventeen years in Jerusalem, the city that YHWH chose to place his name there out of all of the tribes of Israel. His mother's name was Naamah, the Ammonitess. [22]Judah did what was displeasing to YHWH; they incensed him more than their ancestors had done by their sins that they committed. [23]They, too, built for themselves high places and pillars and poles of Asherah on every lofty hill and under every fresh tree. [24]There were even male prostitutes in the land; they practiced all of the abominations of the nations whom YHWH dispossessed before the Israelites.

[25]In the fifth year of King Rehoboam, Shishak[a] king of Egypt marched against Jerusalem. [26]He carried off the treasures of the House of YHWH and the treasures of the royal palace; he carried off everything. He (even) took the golden bucklers that Solomon had made. [27]King Rehoboam had bronze bucklers made to replace them, and he would entrust them to the officers of the outrunners who guard the entrance to the royal palace. [28]Whenever the king went to the House of YHWH, the outrunners would carry them and then return them to the guardroom of the outrunners.

[29]The rest of the history of Rehoboam and all that he did are indeed recorded in the History of the Kings of Judah. [30]There was war between Rehoboam and Jeroboam all the years. [31]Rehoboam slept with his ancestors, and he was buried with his ancestors[b] in the City of David, and the name of his mother was Naamah the Ammonitess. Abijam[c] his son succeeded him.

---

[a] Ketib: *šwšq*; qere: *šyšq*. Cf. 11:40.
[b] LXX and 2 Chr 12:16 omit *ʿm ʾbtyw*.
[c] Some MSS, Chr, and LXX read: Abijah.

NOTES

14 21. *Now Rehoboam son of Solomon became king in Judah.* The Lucianic recension adds "and Benjamin," a late plus never represented in the opening rubric of Judah's kings. Though the formulaic *mlk ʿl*, "became king over," appears here in the anomalous *mlk b-*, "became king in," it is hard to describe this change as "purposeful . . . (meaning) 'only in Judah'" (Noth).

Rehoboam was forty-one years old when he became king. Rehoboam's age is supported by 2 Chr 12:13; in 2 Chr 13:7, he is described as being "a young lad," but this is a rhetorical phrase, probably based on the term "the youngsters," with whom he grew up (cf. 1 Kgs 12:8).

he reigned seventeen years. Rehoboam reigned between 928 and 911 BCE.

Jerusalem, the city that YHWH chose to place his name there out of all of the tribes of Israel. Jerusalem's chosenness is exalted in this singular instance of an intrusive gloss in the regnal formula of Judah's kings. Noth wondered whether Dtr meant to point to the city's uniqueness specifically with reference to the first king of Judah alone. On the other hand, it is questionable whether "a theology of Jerusalem . . . to support the dynastic pretensions of the House of David" (so Gray) was already in place at time of Rehoboam. For the explication of the phrase, see 8:16.

His mother's name was Naamah, the Ammonitess. The mother of a king is noted only for the kings of the Davidic dynasty, as a matter of honor and prestige. On the role of the queen at court, see Note to 15:13. It is tempting to identify Naamah as one of Solomon's foreign wives (cf. 11:1), but Rehoboam was forty-one when he took the throne, which means that Solomon married Naamah while he was still a prince at his father's court. (Had David arranged this diplomatic union? See Malamat 1999.) There is nothing to suggest that Naamah was the source of her son's "evil ways" (so Provan; both of these items are read into the text by the commentator-preacher). Nor can the early elaboration in the LXX at 12:24a, that she was the daughter of Hanun son of Nahash, king of Ammon (cf. 2 Sam 10:1–2), be credited as based on information deleted by Dtr or unknown to him.

22. *Judah did what was displeasing to YHWH; they incensed him more than their ancestors had done by their sins that they committed.* The subject in the LXX is Rehoboam, and all verbs are read in sg.; 2 Chr 12:14 omits the independent subject altogether, reading: "He did." The Chronicler's reading is the one expected; as a rule, the editorial evaluations open with a statement concerning the king's behavior (unnamed after his introduction in the preceding verse), not that of the nation. See further in Comment.

they incensed him. As seen from the word pair in Deut 32:21, **qn'* (in *Piel*) implied anger (**k's*), especially when one's prerogatives were usurped by another; so, with Joseph's brothers (Gen 37:11) and the husband whose wife has strayed (Num 5:14). In Exod 20:5, YHWH is described as "impassioned" (*qannā'*) because of Israel's misdirected worship of other gods (cf. Luzzatto, ad loc.). With the preposition *lamed, qinnē'* is "to be zealous" on behalf of someone (cf. Num 25:13; 1 Kgs 19:10). Modern English "to be jealous" misses the mark.

more than their ancestors had done. This phrase may have been the incentive for specifying "Judah" as the subject at the head of the verse. If said of Rehoboam, the present clause would imply that both David and Solomon had been sinners.

23. *They, too, built for themselves.* Like Jeroboam and the Israelites; cf. above, v. 15.

high places. See Note on 3:2.

and pillars and poles of Asherah. These appurtenances were typical of the Canaanite cult; cf. Deut 12:3. Anyone who has seen the excavated stone pillars

(ANEP 871, 872) could not speak of them as "phallic symbols" associated with a fertility cult (contra Provan). For the "poles of Asherah," see Note to 2 Kgs 21:7; on the goddess Asherah, see Note to 1 Kgs 15:13.

on every lofty hill and under every fresh tree. The standard phrase for locating Canaanite cult sites (e.g., Deut 12:2–3; Jer 2:20; 3:6; 17:2; Ezek 6:13; 20:28). The choice of these sites is most frequently explained as associated with fertility rites and the symbolic association of the green tree with nature's birth and rebirth. Older explanations sought the residence of minor gods in these sacred groves (W. R. Smith 1956 [1894], 133, 185–91) or otherwise deified trees (Albright 1969a, 189–91). Yet all of this remains highly conjectural. Hosea (4:13) offers a more natural understanding of these pleasant country surroundings, where the feasting that followed the offering of sacrifices led to licentiousness, unrelated to worship. Taken as a merism, it might simply have the sense of "everywhere," high and low (Walsh).

under every fresh tree. The sense of the adjective *ra'ănān*, used of the olive tree (Ps 52:10), trees in general (Deut 12:2), oil (Ps 92:11), and a bed (Song 1:16), is "freshness, moistness" (Ibn-Janah; variously rendered: NAB, RSV: "green tree"; NEB, NJB: "spreading tree"; Moffatt: "leafy"; NJPSV: "luxuriant"). [The translations offered in Cogan and Tadmor 1988 ad 2 Kgs 16:4 and 17:10 should be corrected accordingly.]

24. *There were even male prostitutes in the land.* This translation of Heb *qādēš*, lit., "sacred, consecrated person," is based on the contextual understanding of its use in Deut 23:18–19, where prostitution by both sexes is prohibited. The four references to *qādēš/qĕdēšîm* in Kings (1 Kgs 14:24; 15:12; 22:47; 2 Kgs 23:7) offer no insight into the cultic role of these "consecrated" persons, and just what was found abhorrent in their behavior. They were banned by Asa (15:12) and rounded up one last time by Jehoshaphat (22:47); cf., too, the note that there were "houses of sacred males" in the Temple precinct, likely introduced during the reign of Manasseh (2 Kgs 23:7). The almost universal understanding that the term refers to cult personnel who engaged in sexual acts (undertaken out of oath or obligation) has not stood up to the scrutiny of scholarly investigation, which concludes that there is no evidence for ritual prostitution (i.e., sexual intercourse performed within the context of a fertility cult) in Israel, Canaan, or any other area of the ancient Near East; rather the references seem to be speaking about licentious behavior and debauchery (see Gruber 1983; Frymer-Kensky 1992, 199–202; van der Toorn 1992b; Tigay 1996, 480–81, 540–41; Bird 1997).

they practiced all of the abominations of the nations. The ungrammatical MT *'św kkl ht' bt hgwym* should probably be read *wy'św kt'bt hgwym* as in 2 Kgs 21:2.

25. *In the fifth year of King Rehoboam.* Dated political and/or military events are rarely, if ever, recorded in Kings (cf. the exceptional notice in 2 Kgs 18:13 and the Note there); most items of this sort are simply attached to the narrative by a formulaic phrase: "then," "at that time," "in his days," and so on. The present notice may have derived from an extract from a royal or Temple chronicle. See

Introduction. Because Egyptian documentation does not permit setting absolute dates for the twenty-one-year reign of Shishak, the date for Shishak's action
can be calculated on the basis of the biblical data alone; Rehoboam's fifth
year was 923 BCE. Kitchen explains the uncompleted state of the monuments
of Shishak at Karnak, of which the relief of his Palestinian campaign is part, as
due to the king's death; thus, the campaign occurred at most a year or so before
(Kitchen 1973, 72–74; note that he dates the accession of Rehoboam to 931/
930, following Thiele; accordingly, his dates for Shishak, 945–924, are a bit
high. See Introduction. Chronology). For the less likely date of "fairly early" in
Shishak's reign, see Redford 1973, 10.

Shishak. On the form of the king's name, see the Note on 11:40.

26. *he carried off everything.* Taking the *waw* as explicative.

the golden bucklers that Solomon had made. These costly, ceremonial shields
had been deposited in the House of the Lebanon Forest for safekeeping; cf.
1 Kgs 10:17. According to later tradition, the "golden quivers" that David took
from Hadadezer (2 Sam 8:7) were also despoiled by Shishak; cf. Josephus, *Ant.*
7.105; LXX to 2 Sam 8:7 and 4QSamᵃ; but see 2 Kgs 11:10 and the Note there.

27. *King Rehoboam had bronze bucklers made to replace them.* The extrava-
gances of Solomon's days were over.

and he would entrust them. The perfect with *waw*-consecutive, perhaps influenced by the following description of the recurrent practice.

to the officers of the outrunners. For *rāṣîm*, see Note on 1:5 and 2 Kgs 11:11.
For "entrust to," lit., "into the hand of" (*ʿl yd*), compare "Give him over into
my care" (Gen 42:37).

28. *Whenever the king went to the House of YHWH, the outrunners would
carry them.* During the coronation ceremony of Jehoash, David's quivers were
carried by the captains of the hundreds, while the outrunners appeared with
"their weapons" (their bucklers?); cf. 2 Kgs 11:10–11.

and then return them to the guardroom of the outrunners. Unlike the golden
bucklers, which had been (on display?) in the House of the Forest of Lebanon,
the less valuable bronze replacements were kept by the outrunners.

guardroom. Hebrew *tāʾ* appears again in Ezek 40:10, 12 as the architectural
term for "gate-chamber." For its Akk equivalent, *tāʾu*, see von Soden 1950.

30. *There was war between Rehoboam and Jeroboam all the years.* An additional "historical" footnote, formulated by Dtr; details were deemed dispensable.
The placement of the footnote after the closing summary (v. 29) and before the
burial notice (v. 31) is not an unusual editorial practice; cf., e.g., 1 Kgs 15:23,
32; 22:47–50; 2 Kgs 15:16, 37.

31. *the name of his mother was Naamah the Ammonitess.* An erroneous duplication, as the name of the king's mother had already been given in v. 21.

Abijam his son. So, always in Kings; "Abijah" in Luc. and Chronicles (1 Chr
3:10; 2 Chr 12:16; 13:1; et al.). See Note on 15:1.

COMMENT

Structure and Themes

The reportorial shift from Israel to Judah (from Jeroboam to Rehoboam) is in accord with the chronological framework developed by Dtr for presenting the history of the divided monarchy. The reign of Rehoboam is the first for a king of Judah to be recorded in standard formulaic fashion: name of monarch, age at accession, length of reign, mother's name (v. 21); Deuteronomistic evaluation (vv. 22–24); reference to sources (v. 29); death and burial, name of successor (v. 31; see, in detail, Introduction. Composition). The item concerning the threat to Jerusalem and the bribe paid to obtain relief from the threat (vv. 25–29) is an example of an additional report, in some detail, which was occasionally introduced by the author because of its particular interest.

The evaluation of Rehoboam is rather moderate, considering that the earlier account attributed the loss of much of the kingdom to his arrogance (1 Kgs 12). In MT, the focus has shifted from royal misbehavior to the idolatry of the people of Judah, seen as a copy of Canaanite ways (vv. 22–24). This approach, which seems to exonerate the Davidic king, is also to be found with respect to other reigns; cf. 1 Kgs 22:43–44; 2 Kgs 12:3–4; 14:3–4; 15:3–4, 34–35, except that in these cases, the kings of Judah are specifically said to have been faithful to YHWH. Can this, by extension, have been Dtr's evaluation of Rehoboam as well? Nowhere is he accused of personal sinning (despite the stereotype in 1 Kgs 15:3). All of the particulars of Judah's sin are standard Deuteronomistic phraseology and appear (in a decidedly extended form) in the lesson on Israel's downfall in 2 Kgs 17:8–11.

The report of Shishak's campaign (vv. 25–26) is presented in the formulaic "threat and relief" pattern (see Introduction. Composition), and much has been made by recent critics of the fact that Dtr shows no sign of knowing the extent and exact nature of the campaign. At most, it is argued, a Temple record ("chronicle"?) of the delivery of the golden shields was all that was available to the editor (e.g., Van Seters 1983, 301). But what specific information Dtr may have had on the event is unknowable, since the short note in vv. 25–26 reflects only his focused interest in Jerusalem. At the same time, the inclusion of an exact date ("the fifth year"), a most unusual practice for Dtr who typically joins items of this sort to his regnal surveys by general formulas (e.g., "in those days," "at that time"), speaks for the authenticity and the reliability of this datum cited from a contemporary Judahite source. There is a hint of criticism of Rehoboam in the statement concerning the gold shields and their replacement by ones made of inferior bronze, but this is not clearly stated. Nor does Dtr offer any explanation for Shishak's advance against Jerusalem, though the juxtaposition of the Deuteronomistic evaluation (vv. 22–24) and the report of Shishak may imply a causal relationship. For the Chronicler, by contrast, the answer is at hand: Shishak was the instrument for YHWH's punishment of Rehoboam for having thrown off YHWH's law (2 Chr 12:1–12).

History

Shishak's raid on Palestine is one of the rare instances in which an event recorded in Kings is complemented by a contemporary extrabiblical document. The many questions raised by the terse statement of the bribe paid by Rehoboam to the Egyptian king in order to save Jerusalem (v. 25) are not solved by the monumental Egyptian inscription; at best, this source broadens the military perspective, at the same time adding new queries.[1] The wall relief in the temple of Amun at Karnak commemorating Shishak's campaign originally recorded over 150 Palestinian toponyms, close to a third of which are now missing or are of disputed reading (see the translation of a section of the text in Appendix 1, no. 1). In literary terms, it copies the itinerary style known from the pharaonic inscriptions of the late New Kingdom. Neither Jerusalem nor any other city in Judah is mentioned; and however one reconstructs the route of the Egyptian advance through Palestine, it emerges that Judah was spared. Indeed, Rehoboam had paid for its deliverance (cf. 14:25–26). Israelite cities on the coastal plain and in the Jezreel and Jordan Valleys (excluding the central hill country) as well as settlements in the Negev fared far less well, having borne the brunt of the attack. Archaeologists have been quick to identify destructions levels in late tenth-century BCE levels of excavated sites with Shishak (A. Mazar 1990, 395–98), though the recent dispute on the dating of tenth- and ninth-century finds has called this approach into question (Naʾaman 1998, 274–75). If the entire campaign was a super-razzia, with no intent of reestablishing an Egyptian presence, then the ravages of war may well have been minimal, making their imprint harder to find *in situ*. The stele erected by Shishak at Megiddo (see Fig. 5), like all such monuments set up in the course of a military campaign, was a symbolic reminder to the local population of the "true" master of the vital commercial links that crisscrossed Palestine. Shishak seems to have satisfied himself with having made a successful "demonstration and a plundering expedition" (Noth 1960, 240). Then he withdrew, leaving Israel and Judah to their own devices.[2]

Recalling that Jeroboam found refuge at Shishak's court some years earlier (1 Kgs 11:40), one wonders just what it was that led to the political break between the pharaoh and his protégé that allowed for a campaign of this sort; some breach of understanding between Jeroboam and Shishak may have been perceived as unpardonable, unless one ascribes underhandedness to the Egyptian monarch. Whatever the case, relations between Judah and Israel did not

---

[1] Among the significant studies (including bibliographies) of the Shishak inscription: Noth 1938; B. Mazar 1957; Herrmann 1964; Kitchen 1973, 293–300, 432–47; Redford 1973; Aharoni 1979, 323–30; Ahlström 1993b; recently surveyed by Naʾaman 1998.

[2] The report in 2 Chr 11:5–12 on Rehoboam's construction of store cities in the Shephelah and parts of the hill country of Judah bristles with difficulties; the validity of the notice itself is in question (Japhet 1993, 665–66). Therefore, it seems ill-advised to speculate on whether this fortification plan was carried out prior to Shishak's campaign (Kallai 1986, 79–83) or represents a strengthening of Judah's defenses with an eye to the future after its conclusion (Aharoni 1979, 330–32).

Fig. 5. Fragment of stele erected by Shishak, king of Egypt, excavated at Megiddo, after R. S. Lamon and G. M. Shipton, *Megiddo I*, fig. 70.

improve after Shishak's campaign; rather than having stood together against the common enemy, each had taken an independent course, likely increasing the bad blood between them.

As seen earlier, Rehoboam had chosen not to attempt holding the United Monarchy together by arms (cf. 1 Kgs 12:21–24), yet an independent Israelite Kingdom that included the territory of Benjamin would have posed a constant threat to Jerusalem. It is, therefore, reasonable to understand the clashes reported during the reigns of Rehoboam (14:30), Abijam (15:6), and Asa (15:16) as being mostly concerned with the defense of Judah's capital; they all took place within Benjamin, at times as close as 5 km to Jerusalem.

XXV. The Reign of Abijam (Judah)

(15:1–8)

15 [1]In the eighteenth year of King Jeroboam son of Nebat, Abijam became king over Judah. [2]He reigned three years in Jerusalem; his mother's name was Maacah, daughter of Abishalom. [3]He followed all the sinful ways[a] of his father that he practiced before him, and his heart was not fully with YHWH his God as was the heart of David his ancestor. [4]For the sake of David, YHWH his God gave him a lamp in Jerusalem by establishing his son[b] after him and by maintaining Jerusalem.

[5]For David had done what was pleasing to YHWH and did not stray from all that he commanded him all the days of his life, except in the matter of Uriah the Hittite. [6c]Now there was war between Rehoboam[d] and Jeroboam all his days.[c] [7]The rest of the history of Abijam and all that he did are indeed recorded in the History of the Kings of Judah. There was war between Abijam and Jeroboam. [8]Abijam slept with his ancestors, and they buried him in the City of David. Asa his son[e] succeeded him.

---

[a] MT: *ḥṭ'wt*, pl.; many MSS *ḥṭ't*, sg.

[b] LXX: "his sons" (so Stade and Schwally, Burney, BH[3]).

[c] Luc. and LXX lack this repetition of 14:30; see Note.

[d] Some MSS read "Abijam."

[e] Often emended: "his brother"; see Note.

NOTES

15 1. *In the eighteenth year of King Jeroboam son of Nebat, Abijam became king over Judah.* This date looks like a contradiction to the one given in 14:21, which attributes a reign of "seventeen years" to Rehoboam, and if we take into consideration the fact that Rehoboam and Jeroboam began to reign in the same year. The difference of a half-year in the counting of regnal years between the two kingdoms is behind this "optical" discrepancy. See Introduction. Chronology. Abijam may not have been first in line to succeed to the throne; his choice may have been due to his mother's being the favorite wife of Rehoboam (cf. 2 Chr 11:21–22) and, if so, it is one of many indications that this woman had garnered political power for herself at court (see further on v. 13).

In the eighteenth year. The MT reads *wbšnt* for the usual *bšnt*; it is used again in this exceptional fashion in 15:9; 2 Kgs 8:16; 9:29.

Abijam. In contrast to Kings, the name appears in Chronicles as "Abjiah," with the Israelite theophoric element clearly expressed (cf. 2 Chr 11:22 et al.).

2. *He reigned three years.* Abijam reigned between 911 and 908 BCE.

His mother's name was Maacah, daughter of Abishalom. The king's lineage was preserved in conflicting traditions: in the present verse: "Maacah, daughter of Abishalom"; and in 2 Chr 13:2: "Micaiah, daughter of Uriel of Gibeah." Moreover, Maacah is also said to have been the mother of Asa (1 Kgs 15:10), which would make Asa the brother of Abijam, not his son (as in v. 8). Some commentators view this discord as stemming from a misunderstanding of the nature of Maacah's position as Queen Mother (see below, Note to v. 13), which led a late writer to regard her mistakenly as the mother of both Abijam and Asa. According to the unverifiable genealogy given by Josephus (*Ant.* 8.249), the mother of Maacah was Tamar, daughter of Absalom, son of David; cf. Luc. and some LXX MSS at 2 Sam 14:27 (thus NEB's: "granddaughter of Abishalom"; NJB: "descendant of Absalom"). Accordingly, Maacah bore the name of her great-grandmother (cf. 2 Sam 3:3; cf. Burney). That the first Maacah was of Aramean descent—she was the daughter of King Talmai of Geshur—does not bear on the worship of Asherah by the later Maacah (see below, v. 13).

3. *He followed all the sinful ways of his father that he practiced before him.* Nothing specific is indicated beyond his not having taken action against his father's idolatrous practices; cf. 14:22–24.

4. *YHWH his God gave him a lamp in Jerusalem.* Cf. 11:36 and the Note to 2 Kgs 8:19.

by establishing his son after him and by maintaining Jerusalem. Late semantics may be behind this unique clause. In LBH *$^{\zeta}md$ replaces *qwm in BH; this produces two half-verses in synonymous parallelism: "establish" ($hqym$)//"set up" ($h^{\zeta}myd$).

by maintaining Jerusalem. This phrase appears only here. For this sense of Heb *lĕha$^{\zeta}$ămîd*, "to cause to stand firm," cf. Exod 9:16 and Prov 29:4, where it appears as an antonym to *$hāros$, "to destroy."

5. *except in the matter of Uriah the Hittite.* This qualification of David's righteousness by reference to his involvement in Uriah's death (cf. 2 Sam 11:15–17) is not noted in any other instance of Dtr's praise of David (cf., e.g., 3:6; 9:4; 11:38); and because it is lacking in LXX, it is universally taken to be a post-Dtr expansion.

6. *Now there was war between Rehoboam and Jeroboam all his days.* A dittography of 14:30, correctly missing from Luc. and LXX; the similarity of this verse with v. 7b, the apposite notation, likely contributed to this scribal error. The NRSV's rewriting, "The war begun between Rehoboam and Jeroboam continued all the days of his life," is unsupportable.

7. *There was war between Abijam and Jeroboam.* As in 1 Kgs 14:30, Dtr chose not to elaborate on this point.

COMMENT

Structure and Themes

This tightly constructed unit is a Dtr creation, utilizing the standard formulas of regnal reportage. From this point forward in Kings, the accession of a king in one kingdom is synchronized with the reigning king in the sister kingdom (until the fall of Samaria); the working out of this intricate system of alternation between Israel and Judah was likely done by Dtr (see Introduction. Chronology).

Abijam is criticized for not conforming to the standard of loyalty to YHWH set by David, yet no particular misdeed is mentioned;[1] thus, the basis for Dtr's evaluation remains unexaminable, leading one to consider it as deriving from a need to set up Abijam as a foil for the reforming King Asa who followed him.

History

The tensions between Israel and Judah noted for the reigns of Jeroboam and Rehoboam continued into the next generation. If the threat to Jerusalem during the reign of Asa (15:16–17) is taken as paradigmatic of this early period, then the wars noted for Abijam's short, three-year reign (15:7) focused upon the attempt to protect the Judean capital by establishing a defensible border between the two kingdoms.

---

[1] The diametrically opposed, positive picture of Abijam presented by the Chronicler in 2 Chr 13 cannot be explained as a development of the account in 1 Kgs 15. Most commentators consider that at the base of 2 Chr 13 lay a historically reliable source (not available or not utilized by Dtr) that told of the victory of Abijam over Jeroboam and the occupation of the Benjaminite cities, Bethel, Jeshanah, and Ephron (v. 19; Williamson 1982, 250, 254; Japhet 1993, 687–88); this was developed by the Chronicler into the present account in accord with the writer's theological tenets.

XXVI. The Reign of Asa (Judah)

(15:9–24)

15 ⁹In the twentieth year of Jeroboam, Asa became king over Judah. ¹⁰And he reigned forty-one years in Jerusalem, and his mother's name was Maacah, daughter of Abishalom. ¹¹Asa did what was pleasing to YHWH like David his ancestor. ¹²He expelled the male prostitutes from the land and removed all the idols that his ancestors had made. ¹³He even deposed his mother, Maacah, from (serving as) queen mother, because she had made a horrid object for Asherah. Asa cut down her horrid object and burned (it) in Wadi Kidron. ¹⁴But the high places were not removed; yet Asa was loyal to YHWH throughout his life. ¹⁵He brought his father's sacred objects and his own sacred objects[a] into the House of YHWH—silver, gold, and vessels.

¹⁶There was war between Asa and Baasha king of Israel all their days. ¹⁷Baasha king of Israel marched against Judah, and he built Ramah so as to prevent anyone from going out and coming in to Asa king of Judah. ¹⁸So Asa took all the remaining silver and gold in the treasuries of the House of YHWH and the treasuries of the royal palace,[b] and he handed them over to his servants. King Asa sent them to Ben-hadad son of Tabrimmon son of Hezion, king of Aram, who reigned in Damascus (with this message): ¹⁹"There is a treaty between me and you (as there was) between my father and your father. Now I am sending you a bribe of silver and gold. Go, break your treaty with Baasha king of Israel so that he may withdraw from me." ²⁰Ben-hadad acceded to King Asa and sent his army officers against the towns of Israel; he attacked Ijon, Dan, Abel-beth-maacah, and all Chinneroth—all the land of Naphtali. ²¹When Baasha heard (about this), he stopped building Ramah and stayed in Tirzah. ²²Then King Asa mustered all Judah, with no exemptions; they carried away the stones and the timber of Ramah, which Baasha had built, and King Asa built Geba of Benjamin and Mizpah with them.

²³The rest of ≪ ≫[c] the history of Asa and all his exploits and all that he did and the cities that he built are indeed recorded in the History of the Kings of Judah. But in his old age, he became ill with a foot ailment. ²⁴Asa slept with his ancestors and he was buried with his ancestors in the City of David, his ancestor. Jehoshaphat his son succeeded him.

---

[a] Read with ketib: *qdšw*; qere: *qdšy*.

[b] Ketib: *byt mlk*; qere: *byt hmlk*.

[c] MT has the additional *kl*, "all."

INCURSION OF BEN-HADAD I, KING OF ARAM–DAMASCUS
(*1 Kings 15:20*)

NOTES

15 9. *In the twentieth year of Jeroboam.* Abijam's third year (see v. 2) ended in the spring of 908, in time for Asa to begin counting his first full year—both occurring in the twentieth year of Jeroboam.

In the twentieth year. For the expendable *waw* in *wbšnt*, see Note on 1 Kgs 15:1.

10. *he reigned forty-one years.* Asa reigned between 908 and 867 BCE.

his mother's name was Maacah, daughter of Abishalom. Many emend v. 8 from "son" to "brother" in order to solve its contradiction with the present verse. Otherwise, his "mother" would have to have been his "grandmother" (so NAB, NEB); and if so, she "retained her office and rank" as queen mother during her grandson's reign (Jones). A novel reading suggests that there is substance to this notation as transmitted by MT—namely, Dtr intended to suggest that "Asa was the product of an incestuous relationship between Abijam and Maacah," adding to Abijam's flawed record (Provan); yet this smacks of harmonizing exegesis. Or might the woman Micaiah referred to in 2 Chr 13:2 have been Asa's mother (Yeivin 1942–1944)? The consonantal similarity of the names *mˁkh* and *mykyhw* could have contributed to such confusion. [DNF: "It is possible that the same name, *Maachah*, was involved, but a different woman."]

12. *He expelled the male prostitutes.* For these hierodules, see Note on 14:24. Concerning a much later period, it is reported that female devotees of Asherah were engaged in work at the quarters of male prostitutes (2 Kgs 23:7); and if the association is not accidental, perhaps the persons expelled by Asa were also devotees of the same goddess, whose cult the king banished from Jerusalem (cf. below, v. 13).

from the land. This reform act extended beyond the capital (cf. 1 Kgs 14:24); the others were centered on the royal cult.

removed all the idols. Hebrew *gillūlîm* (always pl.) is by context a pejorative term for idols, one favored by late preexilic writers (Dtr, Jeremiah, and especially Ezekiel—thirty-nine times!). No consensus on its etymology has been reached; see BDB 1122a for what might be the cognate Aram (Palymyrene), *gllˀ*, "stone"; see Greenberg 1983b, 132. At the same time, the biblical term etymologically resembles Akk *gillatu*, "crime, misdeed" (CAD G, 72) from the verb *gullulu*, "to commit a sin" (CAD G, 131–32), often used of moral or cultic crimes (H. Tadmor, private communication).

13. *He even deposed his mother, Maacah, from (serving as) queen mother.* For Heb *hēsîr*, "remove (from office)," cf. Judg 9:29; 2 Chr 36:3; Job 34:20; the same verb, **swr*, in *Qal* appears in vv. 12 and 14, and its tripling in these verses reechoes the theme of cult reform. On the syntax, cf. Notes on 1 Kgs 9:21 and 14:2.

queen mother. Though the meaning of the royal title *gĕbîrâ*, lit. "lady," is clear—it appears again in 11:19; 2 Kgs 10:13; Jer 13:18; 29:2 (cf. "the king's mother" in 2 Kgs 24:15)—the function of the women who served in that position is disputed. Both state and cultic functions have been attributed to them, with nothing decisive available from Israelite sources except the present verse. Much has been made of Hittite practice, in which the *tawananna*, "queen mother," was active in both of these spheres of court life, and sometimes she continued to exercise influence after the death her husband (see de Vaux 1961, 117–19; Bin-Nun 1975); by analogy, Maacah's position during the reign of her grand-son Asa has been so explained. Her patronage of the Asherah cult is taken as one aspect of her responsibility in representing the goddess at court, which included legitimizing her son's rule in the name of YHWH's consort (Acker-man 1993; cf, earlier Ahlström 1963, 57–63). But such highly speculative pro-posals (acknowledged by Ackerman) go beyond the evidence. It is just as reasonable to understand the activity of the few queen mothers whose names are known as highly ambitious women whose personal drive (and political con-nections?) led them to positions of exceptional influence (Ben-Barak 1991; also Spanier 1994).

because she had made a horrid object for Asherah. Etymologically, *mplṣt* is something that causes one to "shake, shudder, quake"; cf. Isa 21:4; Ezek 7:18; Job 9:6; hence "horrid" thing. Older commentaries sought to specify its shock-ing nature, guessing that it was "phallic-like" (Rashi; cf. Vulg.), perhaps the reasoning behind NAB: "obscene object."

for Asherah. The term *'ăšērâ* has a number of meanings, distinguishable by context. (1) Asherah is the name of the Canaanite goddess, consort of El, known from Ugaritic myths as one of the major divinities in the pantheon. In this sense, she is referred in the present verse and in 18:19; 2 Kgs 21:7; 23:4. (2) Asherah (in sg. and mostly masc. pl.) is a tree or wooden object associated with the cult of the goddess; cf., e.g., Deut 16:21; Judg 6:25–26; 1 Kgs 16:33; 2 Kgs 13:6. The attraction of Asherah and the warning against her veneration by many biblical writers is a moot question; the devotion of Maacah, the queen mother, to Ashe-rah, "Great Lady," has been seen as pariculary apt. On these issues and whether Asherah served as YHWH's consort (as proposed by the readings of the ʿAjrud inscriptions), see Note on 2 Kgs 21:7 and the surveys of Day 1992; Wyatt 1995; Binger 1997.

and burned (it) in Wadi Kidron. The horrid object was likely made of wood; cf. the trees associated with the cult of Asherah, Deut 16:21. The Kidron ran east of the City of David, and after its juncture at En-rogel with Wadi er-Rababi coming from the west, continued its course to the Dead Sea. Since part of the wadi opposite the city was developed as "the king's garden" (cf. 2 Kgs 25:4), the refuse would have been strewn at some distant point, from which the winter rains could wash it away. Compare the similar cleansing activity at this location by Josiah in 2 Kgs 23:4–6.

14. *But the high places were not removed; yet Asa was loyal to YHWH throughout his life.* The Deuteronomist's positive appraisal of Asa is marred by the king's not having banned worship at the high places; cf. 22:44; 2 Kgs 12:4; 14:4; 15:4, 35 for examples of similar deviations from cultic rigorism, all of which

include the exculpation of the king: "the people continued to sacrifice . . . at the high places."

15. *his own sacred objects.* The ketib is the preferred reading, as shown by 2 Chr 15:18; the incomplete construct of qere is inadmissible. For other dedications to the Temple, see 1 Kgs 7:51 and 2 Kgs 12:19. The implication of this notice (based on a pre-Dtr source?) is that these unspecified items had been dedicated and stored in some other shrine; it was to Asa's credit that he deposited them in the Temple (Montgomery and Gehman). Šanda speculated that the reference is to booty taken from the battles with Israel enumerated in 2 Chr 13:19.

16. *There was war between Asa and Baasha king of Israel all their days.* The insertion of this note at this juncture, in the formulaic terms known elsewhere (cf. 1 Kgs 14:30; 15:7), serves to introduce Baasha's hostile moves in v. 17 (Montgomery and Gehman read it as the protasis of that verse).

Baasha king of Israel. Baasha has not yet been introduced formally; the notes on his rebellion against Nadab (below, v. 27) and ascent to the throne of Israel (v. 33) are reported in accordance with the synchronic method of presentation of the two kingdoms; see further in Introduction. Chronology.

17. *he built Ramah so as to prevent anyone from going out and coming in to Asa king of Judah.* Thus, he effectively blockaded Asa in his capital. For the same terms used with reference to the siege of Jericho, see Josh 6:1. The date of this belligerency reported in 2 Chr 16:1, "in the thirty-sixth year of Asa," cannot be reconciled with the chronological data in Kings, according to which Baasha reigned until the twenty-sixth year of Asa (cf. 1 Kgs 15:33 and 16:8); it is either erroneous or resulted from the Chronicler's theological structuring of the reign of Asa (see Japhet 1993:704–5).

Ramah. This Benjaminite city (Josh 18:25) is identified with er-Ram, 8 km north of Jerusalem, at the juncture of the east–west road through Beth-horon and the north–south road through the Jerusalem hills. Ramathaim-zophim, the home of Samuel (1 Sam 1:1) is likely identical with Ramah (following B. Mazar 1975a, 81; cf. Kallai 1960, 44–45, 48–51, 59–63). During the period of the Judges, Ramah was a border city between Ephraim and Benjamin (cf. Judg 4:5).

18. *the remaining silver and gold.* That is, what had not been handed over to Shishak (cf. 1 Kgs 14:26), as well as the votive offerings he himself had delivered to the Temple (cf. above v. 15).

Ben-hadad son of Tabrimmon son of Hezion, king of Aram. Ben-hadad, "son of (the god) Hadad," is the title of several kings of Aram-Damascus (cf. Notes to 20:1; 2 Kgs 6:24); the present Ben-hadad is the first with this name; see the Note on 2 Kgs 6:24. His identity has a tortured scholarly history. Albright (1942b) read the king's name and his ancestry as given in the present verse in the very worn lines of the Melqart stele (ANET, 501); but this now seems highly unlikely (for a review of the scholarly discussion, cf. Dearman and Miller 1983; Pitard 1987, 138–44). Early suggestions identified his grandfather Hezion with the brigand Rezon who founded a dynasty in Damascus (1 Kgs 11:23–25), basing themselves on a supposed corruption of an original *Hezron (e.g., Thenius, Klostermann, Burney). For the suggestion to take Rezon as the royal title of Hezion, see the above Note on 11:23; and for the identity of both names, Heb *rzn* = Akk *ḫazan(n)u*, "mayor, potentate," see Malamat 1973, 151 n. 23, following Landsberger 1964, 60 (but cf. Pitard 1987, 104–7). The name *Hezion* is now known in an Akkadian transcription (*Ḫadianu*) on the Pazarcik stela, a name borne by a later king of Damascus in the early eighth century BCE (Grayson 1996, 239–40). *Tabrimmon* is otherwise unknown. It is an Aramean name, meaning "(the god) Ramman is good"; Ramman was a manifestation of the storm god, Hadad, and in this form is referred to in 2 Kgs 5:18 (see Note there).

19. *"There is a treaty between me and you (as there was) between my father and your father. . . ."* This noun sentence is parsed as describing the present relationship between Judah and Damascus; they were allied kingdoms, under an agreement dating from the reigns of their fathers (a fact not noted elsewhere). However, it cannot be ruled out that this declaration represents the initial contact between Asa and Ben-hadad, with Asa proposing a renewal of his father's treaty. The sending of a rich offering would have been called for in either case, considering the fact that Asa was asking Ben-hadad to break an existing alliance and turn against a treaty-brother.

Now I am sending you a bribe of silver and gold. The basic meaning of Heb *šōḥad*, "bribe," has been maintained, rather than "present" (NAB, NEB, NRSV) or "gift" (NJPSV, NJB). As in the case of Ahaz and his payment to Tiglath-pileser III in 2 Kgs 16:8, the term used is not original to the message but is one inserted by Dtr in order to taint Asa's act. For similar usage of the equivalant term in Mesopotamian historical texts, see the Note to 2 Kgs 16:8 and Tadmor and Cogan 1979, 499–503.

Go, break your treaty with Baasha king of Israel so that he may withdraw from me. Compare with 2 Kgs 12:19.

20. *his army officers.* The term appears here and again in the later Gedaliah episode (Jer 40:7, 13; 41:11, 13); it is remarkable that, after so many generations, King Asa was remembered in connection with the fortifications he built at Mizpah (Jer 41:9).

He attacked Ijon, Dan, Abel-beth-maacah, and all Chinneroth — all the land of Naphtali. The entire Upper Galilee down to the Sea of Galilee was attacked; the towns are listed in a north–south direction. A somewhat longer list of cities in the Galilee taken during the campaign of Tiglath-pileser III appears in 2 Kgs 15:29. But unlike that instance, in which the territory was annexed to Assyria, in this instance it was plundered but not cut off from Israel. See Comment.

Ijon. Identified with Tell ed-Dibin (cf. 2 Kgs 15:29 and Note there).

Dan. On the site and excavations at Tel Dan, see Note on 1 Kgs 12:29.

Abel-beth-maacah. Located south of Ijon at Abil el-Qamḥ (cf. 2 Kgs 15:29 and Note there).

all Chinneroth. In the plural, as in Josh 11:2; for the sg., Chinnereth, one of the cities of Naphtali, see Deut 3:17; Josh 19:35. The identification of Chinnereth with Tell el-ʿOreimeh, some 9 km north of Tiberias, on the northwestern shore of the Sea of Galilee, is generally acknowledged (see Aharoni 1979, s.v.; Aḥituv 1984, 126; NEAEHL 299–301). In the present verse, the additional "all" and the plural "Chinneroth" refer to the town and the surrounding plain that bears the same name; this is the area known as Genesar/Gennesaret in the postbiblical period.

21. *When Baasha heard (about this), he stopped building Ramah.* The Aramean thrust into Israel forced Baasha to give up plans on the Israel–Judah border and divert his forces to the north.

and stayed in Tirzah. Lucianic recensions and LXX read as if vocalized *way-yāšob tirṣātâ*, "he returned to Tirzah" (adopted by NEB and NJB); MT seems contextually preferable: Baasha remained in Tirzah and did not continue to pressure Asa. Tirzah is reasonably identified with Tell el-Farʿah (north), 11 km northeast of Shechem, just off the highway through Wadi Farʿah that leads from the hill country to Beth-shean; see Aharoni 1979, s.v.; Aḥituv 1984, 190. Canaanite Tirzah (Josh 12:24) was settled by the tribe of Manasseh (17:3) and has sometimes been read among the cities attacked by Shishak (see Appendix 1, no. 59). Jeroboam's rule had begun in Shechem (1 Kgs 12:25), but under unknown circumstances he removed to Tirzah (cf. 14:17). The city apparently survived Shishak's campaign and continued as capital of the Northern Kingdom until the founding of Samaria by Omri (15:33; 16:8, 15). Excavations at Farʿah uncovered evidence for the occupation of Stratum 3, stretching from the end of the Late Bronze city until the beginning of the ninth century, in seeming coordination with the scant historical notes in Kings; see NEAEHL 433–40. And, somewhat surprisingly, Tirzah is associated with beauty in Song 6:4.

22. *Then King Asa mustered all Judah.* Not only in ancient Israel was the call to perform state service done by public proclamation (Heb *lĕhašmîʿa*; cf. 1 Sam 15:4; 23:8 [in *Piel*]); this was also the practice in ancient Mesopotamia. The terms *šišīt nāgiri*, "the proclamation of the herald," and *dikut māti*, "the call-up of the land," often appear synonymously in Neo-Assyrian texts in referring to the corvée; cf. Postgate 1974, 78, 132, 227.

with no exemptions. Hebrew *nāqî*, usually "clean, innocent," here refers to a person's being freed from state obligations; cf. Deut 24:5. The semantic equivalent in Akkadian, *zakû*, "to be free," is the common term in Assyrian royal grants for the freeing of land from various taxes, foremost among them the performance of the royal corvée; cf. Postgate 1974, 238–44. The term for exemption from corvée in the Akkadian documents from Ugarit was also *zakû*; e.g., *uzakkišu šarru bēlšu ištu šipri ekallim*, "the king, his lord, freed him from work for the palace" (cf. CAD Z, 31a). On this basis, Rainey (1975b, 104) argues cogently that Heb *ḥopšî* in 1 Sam 17:25 falls into the same semantic range and means "exempt" (and is unlike Akk *ḥupšu* and Ug *ḥpt/ḥbt* [CAD Ḥ, 241–42], which indicate members of low social orders).

King Asa built Geba of Benjamin and Mizpah. Geba is located at Tel el-Ful, 5½ km north of Jerusalem, astride the strategic north–south mountain road and, together with Mizpah, it guarded the approaches to Jerusalem. Geba of

Benjamin or Gibeah (Judg 20:4, 5) may also have been known as Gibeath-elohim (1 Sam 10:5) and even Gibeah of Saul (1 Sam 11:4; so B. Mazar 1944; for a dissenting view, see Demsky 1973, 26–31; also Aharoni 1979, s.v.). Though closer to the capital than Ramah, a fortress at Geba and another at Mizpah would have provided security and control over the territory between them.

Mizpah. Mizpah (vocalized Mizpeh in Josh 18:26) was a major center in the pre-monarchic period (Judg 20:1; 1 Sam 7:5, 16) close to the northern frontier of Benjamin; it is identified with Tell en-Nasbeh, 12 km north of Jerusalem. For the remains of the fortifications said to reflect Asa's initiative, see NEAEHL 1098–1102. On the later history of Mizpah, see the Note on 2 Kgs 25:23.

23. *the cities that he built.* See v. 22.

But in his old age, he became ill with a foot ailment. As a rule, Dtr did not note royal illnesses; the only other instances recorded in Kings concerns the leprosy of Azariah (2 Kgs 15:5), which led to his quarantine and removal from office, and Hezekiah's disease (2 Kgs 20). Concerning Asa, the implication seems to be that his foot ailment led to his death. The Luc. has the additional phrase "he did evil" after "but in his old age," thus explaining the king's affliction. The Chronicler found room to criticize Asa in his personal plight; he sought help from doctors (a pun on the name Asa and the Aram *'asyā'*, "doctor") rather than YHWH (2 Chr 16:12).

Talmudic sages (*b. Sanh.* 48b) discussed the nature of the disease and identified it as *pôdagrā'*, "gout of the feet"; modern guesses (e.g., "a peripheral obstructive vascular disease with ensuing gangrene" [Wiseman, Jones]) are not more provable. Perhaps it was the unusualness of the occurrence that prompted its recording; that seems to have been the rationale behind the allusions to the strange deaths noted in Old Babylonian omen texts; e.g., King Amar-Sin died of *nišik šēni*, "the bite of a shoe" (whatever that is?!) (CAD N/2, 282a).

24. *Jehoshaphat his son succeeded him.* The reign of Jehoshaphat is not treated until 22:41–51, after the demise of Ahab.

COMMENT

Structure and Themes

After the introductory formula for the new reign, Asa is evaluated as having behaved positively with respect to the cult of YHWH. Few kings of Judah are so described (Jehoshaphat [22:43], Joash [2 Kgs 12:3], Amaziah [14:3], Azariah [15:3], Hezekiah [18:3], and Josiah [22:2]), and only with reference to Asa, Hezekiah, and Josiah, are specific reform acts reported. Besides ridding the cult of idolatrous appurtenances (1 Kgs 15:12–13), Asa was noted for dedicating items to the Temple (v. 15), only later to be removed and dispatched to Ben-hadad as a bribe (v. 18); this last incident was likely viewed negatively by Dtr, though this is not specifically stated (contrast 2 Chr 16:7–10). Asa's conflict with Baasha was one stage, perhaps even a particularly serious stage, in the protracted wars between Israel and Judah. The relatively lengthy report given over to it

(1 Kgs 15:17–21) was due to Dtr's interest in the payment to Ben-hadad that was commandeered from the temple and the palace (see above on v. 19).

Asa's illness is recorded in a casual manner (15:23) and joins the notes on the illnesses of two other kings of Judah: Azariah (2 Kgs 15:5) and Hezekiah (20:1–11). In no case are the afflictions interpreted as divine visitations, as was customary in much ancient writing.

History

A generation of hostilities between Judah and Israel reached new heights during the reign of Asa,[1] with Baasha's approach to Jerusalem; the latter's fortification of Ramah gave him control over Judah's commercial life and posed a continual threat to the security of the Southern capital (1 Kgs 15:17). In an open admission of weakness, Asa turned to Ben-hadad I of Aram-Damascus, and asked that he violate his non-aggression treaty with Israel in favor of the one with Judah, smoothing the way for this treachery with a heavy payment (v. 19). It thus seems that the earlier hostility between Jerusalem and Damascus that followed upon the Aramean move for independence during the reign of Solomon (11:23–25) had evolved into a treaty relationship between the two, perhaps urged upon Jerusalem by the breakaway of the North. Asa's hoped-for relief was not long in coming; as a result of the Aramean incursions into Israel's Galilee, Baasha withdrew from the southern border with Judah to defend his Northern district. There is no way of knowing how successful he was against Ben-hadad, and just how long Ben-hadad was free to move about Galilee at will; the destruction levels at several key Northern sites and their rebuilding suggest that Israel regained its foothold in the territory within a short time.[2] As for Asa, his political machinations having paid off, he moved to fortify Judah's border; he tore down Baasha's constructions at Ramah and pushed the border a few miles farther north into Benjamin, to Mizpah and Geba (15:22).

---

[1] The reign of Asa in 2 Chr 14–16 is a presented in a fully developed narrative, based upon material not found in the 25 verses of 1 Kgs 15. Besides an additional war (with Zerah the Cushite, 2 Chr 14:8–14) and the admonitions of two prophets, the Chronicles' version provides dates for all of the major events during Asa's reign. Of interest to the present commentary are the data that Baasha moved against Judah "in the thirty-sixth year of Asa" (2 Chr 16:1) and that Asa fell ill in his "thirty-ninth year" (16:12). These dates contradict the chronology of Kings, in which Baasha reigned twenty-four years (1 Kgs 15:33; cf. 16:8), beginning in the Asa's third year, some ten years earlier. Because theological considerations seem to have been behind the Chronicler's scheme—Asa's evil deeds all appear in the last years of his reign (see Japhet 1993, 703–5; otherwise Williamson 1982, 255–58)—they were not included in the 1 Kgs summary. As for Asa's connivance with Ben-hadad, no date, early or late, can be reasonably suggested.

[2] Though their city names are not recorded in 15:20, destruction levels at Tel Dan (Stratum IV; Biran 1994, 181–83) and Hazor (Stratum IXA and IXB; Yadin 1972, 142–46; confirmed by Ben-Tor and Ben-Ami 1998) have been associated by their excavators with the Aramean thrust under Ben-hadad I; so, too, the fortress at ʿEn Gev on the eastern side of Lake Kinneret (stratum V; Ahlström 1985).

Asa was also active in strengthening the position of the cult of YHWH; he increased the Temple endowment by transfers to its treasury and took measures against the cult of Asherah, which had infiltrated Judah. Despite the fact that this traditional Canaanite cult had the support of Maacah, the queen mother, Asa destroyed the cult image, ousted the personnel, and even sent Maacah packing.

XXVII. The Reign of Nadab (Israel)

(15:25–32)

15 ²⁵Nadab son of Jeroboam became king over Israel in the second year of Asa king of Judah, and he reigned over Israel for two years. ²⁶He did what was displeasing to YHWH and followed the way of his father and the sin that he caused Israel to commit. ²⁷Baasha son of Ahijah of the House of Issachar conspired against him. Baasha struck him down at Gibbethon of the Philistines, while Nadab and all Israel were besieging Gibbethon. ²⁸Baasha killed him in the third year of Asa king of Judah, and he succeeded him. ²⁹As soon as he became king, he struck down all the House of Jeroboam; he did not leave a soul belonging to Jeroboam until he destroyed it, just as YHWH had promised through his servant Ahijah the Shilonite, ³⁰because of the sins that Jeroboam committed and by which he caused Israel to sin, thereby angering YHWH, God of Israel. ³¹The rest of the history of Nadab and all that he did are indeed recorded in the History of the Kings of Israel. ³²ᵃThere was war between Asa and Baasha king of Israel all their days.ᵃ

ᵃ LXX omits the repetition of v. 16 in MT.

NOTES

15 25. *he reigned over Israel for two years.* Nadab reigned between 907 and 906 BCE. His two-year reign was less than full term; cf. vv. 25 and 32.

27. *Baasha son of Ahijah of the House of Issachar.* The name *Baasha* was also known in Aramaic-speaking areas; in the Kurkh monolith inscription of Shalmaneser III (see Appendix 1, no. 2), Baasha was the name of the king of Rehob, a small Aramaic kingdom, allied with Adad-idri of Damascus. The identification of a usurper by his tribal affiliation is unattested elsewhere; cf. 2 Kgs 15:13, 17 and Notes there for the suggestion that the names *Jabesh* and *Gadi* refer to the home districts of the conspirators. The LXX traditions (Luc.: of Beth *Beddama*; LXXᴮ: Beth *Belaan*) may reflect an otherwise unknown place-name in Isaachar (so Gray).

Baasha struck him down. Seizing the throne is usually related with the set formula *wayyakkēhû/wayyak*, followed by *waymîtēhû* (v. 28); cf. 16:10; 2 Kgs 15:14, 25, 30. And as is generally the case, no motive is given for the assassination (see below, Comment).

at Gibbethon of the Philistines. Gibbethon was a Levitical city of the tribe of Dan (Josh 19:44; 21:23); it is apparently referred to in two extrabiblical sources, the itinerary of Thutmose III (Aḥituv 1984, 101, s.v. Gebath) and a relief of Sargon II (reproduced in Albenda 1986, plate 95). If the identification of Gibbethon with Tell Melat (Malat) is correct, the town was overshadowed by Gezer, its prominent neighbor just a few miles to the east. Gezer had become part of the Northern Kingdom at the time of the division of the kingdom, and was likely raided by Shishak (see Appendix 1, no. 11), so the siege at Gibbethon indicates that the Philistines had pushed their way to Israel's border, from which they were not to be easily dislodged; cf. 16:15.

while Nadab and all Israel were besieging Gibbethon. The same description is repeated in 16:15, where the term "the people" is substituted for "all Israel" in the present verse. In 16:16, both terms appear synonymously (see also v. 17), showing that they refer to Israel's fighting force, not the general population. See Note on 2 Kgs 13:7.

29. *he struck down all the House of Jeroboam.* For similar acts of bloody removal of political rivals, see 16:12 and 2 Kgs 10:1–11.

just as YHWH had promised through his servant Ahijah the Shilonite. Punishment of the House of Jeroboam was in fulfillment of Ahijah's prophecy given in 14:14. For another view of Baasha's actions, see 16:7.

32. *There was war between Asa and Baasha king of Israel all their days.* A repeat of v. 16, where it serves to introduce the tale of Ben-hadad's betrayal of Baasha; despite the editorial regularity that can be observed in the positioning of such notes at the close of a reign (cf. 14:30; 15:7; 2 Kgs 15:16), it still seems redundant.

COMMENT

Structure and Themes

The narrative returns to the history of the Northern Kingdom, and not until 22:41–51 is the reign of a Judean monarch taken up as such. Following the negative evaluation of Nadab, who followed his father's ways, the insurrection of Baasha against Nadab is presented, using the formulaic terms of conspiracy and seizure of the throne employed elsewhere (cf. 2 Kgs 15:10, 14 [somewhat shortened], 25, 30; see also 1 Kgs 16:16).

The revolt against Nadab obviates need here of a death and burial notice, as is also the case with other usurpations throughout Kings.

History

There is nothing to suggest that kingship in Israel was viewed differently than in Judah, that it was based on a charismatic ideal that "militated against any continuing link between the occupant of the throne at any time and his successors" (Alt 1966, 247). Hereditary monarchies were a fact of life throughout the ancient Near East, and the kingdom of Israel was no exception (Ishida 1977, 6–25). Therefore, the ground for the overthrow of the House of Jeroboam (and for the seemingly endless rise and fall of dynasties in Israel) should be sought in other areas of societal organization. For one thing, ten competing tribes and a large native Canaanite base could not have made for an easy monarchic union (see Würthwein). It is also clear that, over the centuries, a conspicuous number of adventurers (e.g., Omri, Jehu, Pekah) emerged from the ranks of the Israelite army; with the support of their forces, these usurpers succeeded in wresting the throne from the incumbents. Thus, on the analogy of Zimri's revolt (16:8–9; though he was a generation removed), one suspects that Baasha's seizure of the throne from Nadab stemmed from a similar group and like circumstances (Tadmor 1968, 62–64; also Reviv 1993, 101–4). The source of the military's discontent is an open question, though concern over security matters would naturally have been high on its list. The war with Judah was still unresolved a generation after secession (15:7, 16) and, at Israel's southwestern border, the Philistines had pushed into the territory that had once been Solomon's second district (15:27). But whatever the case, the army had the support of the traditionalists in Israelite society, for whom Ahijah and other prophetic figures were a mouthpiece.

XXVIII. The Reign of Baasha (Israel)

(15:33–16:7)

15   ³³In the third year of Asa king of Judah, Baasha son of Ahijah became king over all[a] Israel in Tirzah for twenty-four years. ³⁴He did what was displeasing to YHWH; he followed the way of Jeroboam and the sin that he caused Israel to commit. 16 ¹The word of YHWH came to Jehu son of Hanani concerning Baasha: ²"Since I have elevated you from the dust and have made you ruler over my people Israel, but you followed the way of Jeroboam and caused my people Israel to sin, angering me with their sins,[b] ³I am going to stamp out[c] Baasha and his House. I will make your House[d] like the House of Jeroboam son of Nebat. ⁴Those of Baasha('s kin) who die in the city the dogs will eat; those of his (kin) who die in the field the birds of heaven will eat. ⁵The rest of the history of Baasha and what he did and his exploits are indeed recorded in the History of the Kings of Israel. ⁶Baasha slept with his ancestors and was buried in Tirzah. Elah his son succeeded him. ⁷Moreover, there was the word of YHWH concerning Baasha and his House through Jehu son of Hanani the prophet, because of all the evil that he did in displeasing YHWH, angering him by his actions and becoming like the House of Jeroboam, and because he struck it down.

------

[a] LXX and a few MSS omit *kl* in MT; see Note.

[b] Luc. and LXX read *bhblyhm*, "their emptiness," for MT *bḥṭ'tm*; see Note.

[c] MT: *mab'îr* (Hiphil); several MSS read: *mĕbā'ēr* (Piel); see Note.

[d] LXX: "his house" (cf. NEB).

NOTES

15   33. *In the third year of Asa king of Judah, Baasha son of Ahijah became king over all Israel in Tirzah for twenty-four years.* Baasha reigned between 906 and 883 BCE. This is the only instance in MT in which the introductory formula of rule has the adjective "all"; it is omitted by LXX. Was it meant to be a foreshadowing of the division of "all Israel" into two warring camps shortly after Baasha's death?

in Tirzah. This is the first reference to Tirzah as Israel's capital in an introductory formula, though it seems to have served as such from the time of Jeroboam's reign (cf. 14:17; 15:21).

16   1. *The word of YHWH came to Jehu son of Hanani concerning Baasha.* Jehu plays no further role in Kings beyond uttering the present warning and condemnation of Baasha. The Chronicler, on the other hand, has his father, Hanani, speak harsh words against Asa (2 Chr 16:7) and reports that Jehu criticized Jehoshaphat (2 Chr 19:2–3) and that he authored a work now included

in the *History of the Kings* (2 Chr 20:34); all of these elaborative items are historically dubious.

2. "*Since I have elevated you from the dust and have made you ruler over my people Israel. . . .*" There is no preceding prophecy concerning the selection of Baasha, yet these words of divine sanction suggest that there had been prophetic support for Baasha's seizure of the throne. The words of the present denunciation copy in large measure the words uttered against Jeroboam in 1 Kgs 14:7–11.

angering me with their sins. The LXX reads "with their emptiness" (*hblyhm*), as in 16:13 and 26 and Deut 32:21 (the prototype of this idiom?), which may be preferable inasmuch as the locution in MT is otherwise unexampled; see further in 16:13.

3. *I am going to stamp out Baasha and his House.* The verb in this idiom is regularly in *Piel* (cf. Note on 14:10) and should be pointed in *Piel*.

4. *Those of Baasha('s kin) who die in the city the dogs will eat; those of his (kin) who die in the field the birds of heaven will eat.* Repeating part of the traditional curse; cf. 14:11; 21:24; 2 Kgs 9:10.

5. *The rest of the history of Baasha and what he did and his exploits are indeed recorded in the History of the Kings of Israel.* The exploits of Baasha's 23-year reign were recounted in reference to Asa of Judah (cf. 1 Kgs 15:16–21) and there from a Judean perspective.

6. *Baasha slept with his fathers and was buried in Tirzah.* The burial site of Israelite kings is not regularly given; cf. 16:28; 22:37; 2 Kgs 10:35; 13:9, 13; 14:16.

7. *Moreover, there was the word of YHWH concerning Baasha and his house through Jehu son of Hanani the prophet, because of all the evil that he did in displeasing YHWH, angering him by his actions and becoming like the House of Jeroboam, and because he struck it down.* An alternate version of Jehu's prophecy against Baasha to the one in vv. 1–4. It is placed, in the most unusual manner, after the closing of Baasha's reign. The point of the insertion may have been that this tradition included the extirpation of Jeroboam's line as part of Baasha's sins, in a manner similar to Hosea's denunciation of Jehu's bloody revolt against the House of Omri (Hos 1:4; cf. Qimḥi, Skinner); this explication was considered and rejected by Montgomery and Gehman as "ethical moralizing." That Baasha's rebellion, in fulfillment of an earlier prophecy, should be accounted as a sin is indeed out of place in Kings. The second *wĕ'al* ("and because") might be parsed as a conjunctive phrase, "despite that"; cf. Job 16:17; Isa 53:9 (BDB 758b). The *waw* ("and") of the first *wĕ'al* looks like a dittography and may be omitted.

through Jehu son of Hanani the prophet. Hebrew *bĕyad*, "by the hand of," "though," alternates with *'el*, "to," in 16:1 and 21:28.

because of all the evil. The MT has *w'l* ("and because of"); the *waw* ("and") is lacking in LXX and a number of MSS, and the form without *waw* is preferable.

because he struck it down. He, Baasha, had struck down the House of Jeroboam; cf. 15:27–28.

COMMENT

Structure and Themes

The relatively lengthy reign of Baasha is presented succinctly; the report consists of the standard editorial formulas (15:33–34; 16:5–6) and a prophetic condemnation, preserved in two versions (16:1–4//16:7). No historical notices are recorded, since the items relating to Baasha's "exploits" (v. 5) that were of interest to Dtr had already been utilized in the unit on Asa (15:16–22) and the unit on the revolt against Nadab (15:27–29). The word of Jehu (16:2–4) resembles the earlier prophecy of Ahijah against Jeroboam (cf. 14:7, 10b–11a); the terms used in both were part of the conventional rhetoric of curse. The rationale behind the repetition in 16:7, however, is unclear; the introductory wĕgam, "moreover," points to its secondariness. The short clause (four words!) in v. 7b condemning Baasha for his slaughter of the House of Jeroboam, although unique, seems scant reason for including Jehu's prophecy once again. Perhaps a textual variant of the former condemnation is at the base of v. 7.

History

The impression that the short text leaves concerning Baasha's two-decade rule is that it was one of continuous strife. It began in a bloody revolt against the House of Jeroboam, while the army was engaged in the northern Shephelah fighting the Philistines (15:27); the lack of success on that front is notable, because a quarter of a century later the same adversaries still stared at each other across the same battle line (16:15). Nor did Baasha's moves against Judah meet with much success: Baasha was outmaneuvered by Asa's renewal of the treaty between Damascus and Jerusalem, which brought Aramean troops to the Israelite Galilee (15:17–21). This dismal record may have instigated the military revolt against Baasha's son Elah within a year of his assuming the throne.

XXIX. THE REIGN OF ELAH (ISRAEL)

(16:8–14)

16 ⁸In the twenty-sixth year of Asa king of Judah, Elah son of Baasha became king over Israel in Tirzah for two years. ⁹His servant Zimri, commander of half the chariotry, conspired against him. While he was in Tirzah, drinking himself drunk in the house of Arza, "Over the Household" at Tirzah, ¹⁰Zimri came, attacked him, and killed him in the twenty-seventh year of Asa king of Judah. He succeeded him as king. ¹¹At his accession, as soon as he took the throne, he struck down all the House of Baasha, ᵃnot leaving a single male, neither kinsmen nor friends. ¹²Zimri destroyed all the House of Baashaᵃ in accordance with the word of YHWH, which he spoke againstᵇ Baasha through Jehu the prophet, ¹³becauseᶜ of all the sins of Baasha and the sins of Elah his son that they committed and caused Israel to commit, angering YHWH the God of Israel with their emptiness. ¹⁴The rest of the history of Elah and all that he did are indeed recorded in the History of the Kings of Israel.

ᵃ⁻ᵃ LXX omits due to homoioteleuton.

ᵇ Read ʿl with MSS.

ᶜ Read ʿl with LXX.

NOTES

16 8. *In the twenty-sixth year of Asa king of Judah, Elah son of Baasha became king over Israel in Tirzah for two years.* Elah reigned between 883 and 882 BCE; but, though credited with two years (cf. 16:15, the synchronism of Zimri with Asa), his rule was far less.

9. *His servant Zimri.* Zimri is introduced without a patronymic, perhaps an indication of his lowly lineage. The name looks like a hypocoristicon, whose verbal element *zmr* may mean "strength, might," from the common Semitic root *dmr* (Cross and Freedman 1955, 243); compare with the well-known Amorite name Zimri-Lim; for a critique of this view and other suggestions, see Loewenstamm 1969.

commander of half the chariotry. The title hints at the organization of the Israelite chariot forces, nothing more. New administrative texts from the reign of Sargon II offer a glimpse into the organization of the Neo-Assyrian equestrian and chariot units; cf. Dalley and Postgate 1984, 27–47.

drinking himself drunk. A similar colorful note appears in 20:16.

in the house of Arza, "Over the Household" at Tirzah. On the title of the royal steward, see the Note on 4:6. If "at Tirzah" is taken as part of Arza's title (so Noth), then his stewardship was over only the royal residence and not all royal lands.

10. *Zimri came, attacked him, and killed him.* For this formula, see 15:27 and the Note there.

11. *not leaving a single male, neither kinsmen nor friends.* A repetition of the phrase appearing in 14:10, explicated by the additional "neither kinsmen nor friends." For the other examples of such use of the double *waw* ("neither . . . nor"), see Gen 34:28; Num 9:14; Josh 9:23 (with Burney).

neither kinsmen. Literally, "redeemer," i.e., a near relative whose duty it was to avenge the murder of a family member.

nor friends. Hebrew *rēʿēhû*, plural with the *yod* omitted (see GKC, 91k), as in 1 Sam 30:26; Job 42:10.

12. *Zimri destroyed all the House of Baasha in accordance with the word of YHWH, which he spoke against Baasha through Jehu the prophet.* The fulfillment of prophecy is duly noted; cf. 15:29.

13. *angering YHWH the God of Israel with their emptiness.* The phrase occurs again in v. 26; 2 Kgs 17:15; and Deut 32:21; from the last phrase, the sin of idolatry can be inferred. Besides this general statement, no indication is given of the specific grievous wrongs committed by Baasha and Elah.

COMMENT

Structure and Themes

This unit is similar to the one concerning Nadab (15:25–31). Inasmuch as both Elah and Nadab were the sons of kings who had risen to the throne under rebellious circumstances and both were assassinated after a short reign, Dtr used a single model in noting their reigns. The formulaic terminology for reporting a revolt appears once again (16:9–10). In conclusion, Dtr noted that the prophecy of Jehu condemning the attempt to establish a new dynasty in Israel was indeed actualized (16:12–13).

History

The standardized report of Zimri's coup is uninformative about the perpetrator's motives. Zimri, likely with the support of his cohort at Tirzah, may have taken advantage of the engagement of the army at Gibbethon to stage his coup. It was initiated by an attack on Elah at a private party, and it was this breach of personal trust that lived on in popular memory—even the likes of Jezebel made reference to Zimri's act of treachery (2 Kgs 9:31). However, he was soon challenged by an army officer more popular than himself.

XXX. THE REIGN OF ZIMRI (ISRAEL)

(16:15–20)

16   [15]In the twenty-seventh year of Asa king of Judah, Zimri became king in Tirzah for seven days; it was while the army was encamped against Gibbethon of the Philistines. [16]When the encamped army heard that Zimri had conspired and had even killed the king, all Israel made Omri, the commander of the army, king over Israel that very day in the camp. [17]Then Omri together with all Israel withdrew from Gibbethon and laid siege to Tirzah. [18]When Zimri saw that the city had been captured, he went into the citadel of the palace and burned down the palace over him, and he died; [19]because of the sins that he committed, by doing what was displeasing to YHWH, by following the way of Jeroboam, and the sin that he committed[a] by causing Israel to sin. [20]The rest of the history of Zimri and the conspiracy that he formed are indeed recorded in the History of the Kings of Israel.

---

[a] Luc. and LXX omit *ʿāśâ* (MT); see Note.

NOTES

16   15. *In the twenty-seventh year of Asa king of Judah, Zimri became king in Tirzah for seven days.* The year was 882 BCE.

it was while the army was encamped against Gibbethon of the Philistines. A campaign in the northern Shephelah was again being waged; cf. 15:27. In that verse, the term used to describe the army was "all Israel"; here it is *hāʿām*, lit., "the people." For the meaning of *ʿam* as "army," cf. 20:15; 2 Kgs 8:21; 13:7, and the Note there.

16. *all Israel made Omri, the commander of the army, king over Israel.* Within context, "all Israel" can only refer to Israel's fighting force, as the repetition in v. 17 shows. This is different from the use of the term "all Israel" in 15:33.

17. *Then Omri together with all Israel withdrew from Gibbethon.* The siege on Gibbethon was lifted and a new one set against Tirzah.

18. *he went into the citadel of the palace.* The royal residence had not yet fallen into the hands of the attacking forces who had breached the city's defenses. For the suggested etymology of *ʾarmôn*, see the Note to 2 Kgs 15:25, where the citadel was the site of the assassination of Pekahiah.

burned down the palace over him, and he died. A hero-like end for one whose deeds lived on in folk memory (cf. 2 Kgs 9:31). Late classical tradition told of Sin-shar-ishkun, the last Assyrian king (mistakenly named Sardanapalus), who, seeing that Nineveh was about to fall to the barbarians, threw himself into the fire of his burning palace, a portrayal likely derived from the fiery demise of Shamash-shum-ukin in Babylon in 648 BCE; see, at length, Streck 1916, ccxcix n. 1.

the palace. Hebrew *byt mlk*, a construct unit without the article; cf. the qere and ketib of 15:18; 2 Kgs 11:20; 15:25; it may have been taken as definite (Burney; cf. Amos 7:13) or as "a kind of title" (Noth). The Moabite Mesha Inscription (line 23) uses the same undetermined construction (*bt mlk*).

19. *because of the sins that he committed.* The whole verse is a rather clumsy appendage to the tale of Zimri's suicide, but there is no firm reason for viewing it as a post-Dtr addition (as do Noth, Jones).

the sin that he committed by causing Israel to sin. The MT *ʿāśâ* is unidiomatic, perhaps having entered the text from the phrase *ḥṭʾ lʿśwt* at the beginning of the verse; it is best omitted, with LXX.

COMMENT

Structure and Themes

This section illustrates the editorial commitment to the overall structure of the regnal framework. The short, seven-day reign of Zimri, taken up solely with defending his coup, is evaluated by Dtr as sinful; like all of the other kings of Israel who preceded him, Zimri is said to have adhered to the sinful ways of Jeroboam (v. 19), for which he was removed. In a reign as short as this, what wrong could Zimri have done?

History

Whatever support Zimri may have had in Tirzah, it was no match for the forces under Omri. These troops interrupted their siege of Gibbethon to hurry to the capital, where, in a week's time, they overwhelmed Zimri. Rather than be taken captive, he took his own life in the flames of his burning palace.

XXXI. THE REIGN OF OMRI (ISRAEL)

(16:21–28)

16   ²¹Then the people Israel were divided into two;ᵃ half of the people followed Tibni son of Ginath to make him king; the (other) half followed Omri. ²²The people who followed Omri prevailed over the people who followed Tibni son of Ginath. Tibni died,ᵇ and Omri became king.ᶜ

²³In the thirty-first year of Asa king of Judah, Omri became king over Israel for twelve years; in Tirzah he was king for six years. ²⁴He bought the hill Samaria from Shemer for two talents of silver. He built (on) the hill and named the city that he built Samaria, after Shemer, the owner of the hill. ²⁵Omri did what was displeasing to YHWH; he was worse than all who preceded him. ²⁶He followed all the way of Jeroboam son of Nebat and his sinᵈ that he caused Israel to commit, angering YHWH the God of Israel with their emptiness. ²⁷The rest of the history of Omri, what he did and the exploits he undertook, are indeed recorded in the History of the kings of Israel. ²⁸Omri slept with his ancestors and was buried in Samaria. Ahab his son succeeded him.

ᵃ Lit., "into half." Luc. and LXX omit; see Note.
ᵇ Luc. and LXX add: *kai Ioram o adelphos autou en to kairo ekeino*, "and Joram his brother at that time"; see Note.
ᶜ LXX adds: *meta Thamnei*, "after Tibni"; cf. Luc.; *ton Thabennei*; see Note.
ᵈ Qere *wbḥṭ'tw*, "his sin," for ketib *wbḥṭ'tyw*, "his sins."

NOTES

16   21. *Then.* The editorial "then" (cf. 9:11) may have suppressed a chronological note fixing the date of the struggle between Tibni and Omri.

the people Israel. An appositional construction comparable to "the hill Samaria" in v. 24; cf. Judg 20:22. Noth takes the phrase as a reference to a broad spectrum of the population rather than just the "army" in v. 16; this in turn supports his understanding of the rival camps: a contest between the native Israelite civilian population and military elements led by the foreigner Omri (for Soggin [1975], Tibni was the popularly designated king). But these speculations do not account for "all Israel," who supported Omri (v. 17).

were divided into two. With Luc., many commentaries (and NAB) omit *laḥēṣî*, lit., "into half," as "clumsy" (Noth), explaining it as a dittography of the following *ḥăṣî*; but a verb plus *laḥēṣî* is not altogether unidiomatic (cf. 2 Sam 10:4), and haplography, which "is much more common in the Bible" [DNF], may account for its absence in Luc.

half of the people followed Tibni son of Ginath to make him king; the (other) half followed Omri. For Heb *hāyâ 'aḥarê*, "followed," cf. 2 Sam 2:10; 1 Kgs 12:20.

Tibni son of Ginath. The LXX and Josephus vocalize the name as Tabni. No further information is available on the identity and background of this new competitor for the throne. The name *Ginath* has been taken by some (Gray; Yeivin 1979a, 333 n. 51) to be derived from the place-name *Gina*, the Ginna of EA 250:17, 22, perhaps Beth-haggan of 2 Kgs 9:27 in the territory of Manasseh.

22. *The people who followed Omri prevailed over the people who followed Tibni son of Ginath.* Hebrew *ḥāzāq*, "be strong," is also transitive, meaning "prevail against, be stronger than, overpower" with the accusative particle "*'et*," as here; cf. Jer 20:7; 2 Chr 28:20; with *min*, cf. 1 Kgs 20:23, 25; 2 Sam 10:11; and with *ʿal*, cf. 2 Chr 8:3; 27:5.

Tibni died. The addition in LXX "and Joram his brother at that time" might be considered an original detail, because it lacks tendentiousness. The death of the two brothers at one time hints at their falling in battle rather than succumbing to natural causes; cf. Josephus's statement that Tibni was killed (*Ant.* 8.311). It is unlikely that Heb *wayyāmot*, "he died," has the meaning "dethroned" as does the parallel word in Hittite (so Miller 1968), or serves as evidence that Tibni was in fact the recognized monarch.

Omri became king. The LXX addition "after Tibni" regards Tibni as having been recognized as king; calculated according to the synchronisms in MT, Tibni reigned four years, see the Note on v. 23.

23. *In the thirty-first year of Asa king of Judah, Omri became king over Israel for twelve years.* Omri was king between 882 and 871 BCE. Counting from the date of Zimri's insurrection given in 16:15, the civil war that followed his death lasted four years; at the same time, the synchronism in v. 29 shows that the twelve years credited to Omri included the war years.

Omri. The uncertain derivation of the name *Omri* has led many to consider him to have been "of Canaanite extraction" (Gray) or a foreign mercenary (Montgomery and Gehman; Noth); others assign him to the tribe of Issachar, considering the fact that the royal house had landholdings in Jezreel; cf. 21:2 (Šanda). This might be further supported by the reference to the (town) name *Shimron* associated with Issachar (1 Chr 7:1) and the reference to Omri son of Michael of Issachar (1 Chr 27:18; cf. 7:3), perhaps an ancestor of King Omri (so B. Mazar 1989, 216). The name *Omri* is recorded in extrabiblical texts: in Moabite, *ʿmry* (Mesha Inscription, lines 4–5); and in Assyrian, *Ḥumri*. As founder of the first lasting dynasty in Israel, whose rulers were the first Israelite kings that Assyria encountered, Israel became known as *bīt Ḥumri*, "the house of Omri," in Neo-Assyrian inscriptions until the fall of Samaria in the late eighth century.

in Tirzah he was king for six years. Omri had captured Tirzah from Zimri (v. 18); thus these six years included the four years of Tibni's insurrection plus two additional years.

24. *He bought the hill Samaria from Shemer for two talents of silver.* Excavations at Samaria/Sebaste have uncovered the architectural remains of the Omri dynasty, whose first kings developed the site. The archaeological evidence shows that it was occupied between the eleventh and ninth centuries BCE; the relatively large number of wine and oil installations is indicative of intensive agricultural

activity in the area (Stager 1988). For the finds and the scholarly differences over their interpretation, see Kenyon 1971, 71–89; Aharoni 1982, 203–4; NEAEHL 1300–1310.

the hill Samaria. Hebrew *hhr šmrwn*, an appositional construction; cf. *hmlk dwd* (2 Sam 3:31); *hnhr prt* (1 Chr 5:9). The site, a high hill (430 m above sea level) some 10 km northwest of Shechem, is well situated on the road network connecting the coastal plain and the hill country.

Samaria. The etiology of the name is surprising, because there is no reason to think that Omri would have named his city after the original owner of the hill. It is more likely that site was already known as *Šōmrôn* when purchased (note other mountain names with the same -*ôn* ending: *Şion, Hermon, Lebanon*), and the association with the name *Šemer* is a secondary etymology (so Noth). In regard to the form of the name, NA texts from the reign of Adad-nirari III onward (early eighth century BCE) use *Samerina* (see partial listing in Parpola 1970, 302–3; Ephʿal 1991), and in NB, it is *Šamaraʾin*. Both of these cuneiform transcriptions reflect an alternative form, *Šamrayîn*, known in later Aramaic (cf. Ezra 4:10 and Cowley 1923, 113, 30:29); see Tadmor 1958, 40.

Shemer. An Israelite name; cf. 1 Chr 6:31; 7:34; perhaps a hypocoristicon (e.g., the name *šmryhw*). There is nothing to suggest that he was other than a local landowner (contra Gray, who posits that Shemer was "a Canaanite community").

27. *The rest of the history of Omri, what he did and the exploits he undertook.* The LXX omits "he undertook" (the second *ʾšr ʿśh*), and reads "and all (*wkl*) that he did." While the term "the exploits" is never followed by a relative clause in MT, the dozens of variations in these closing formulas in the LXX tradition throughout Kings make reconstruction of an *Urtext* next to impossible and attest to scribal carelessness.

28. *Omri slept with his ancestors and was buried in Samaria.* The verse does not imply that the ancestral graves were moved to Samaria. The phrase **škb ʿm ʾbwt* indicates peaceful death (see Note on 2:10), making Omri the first king to be interred in the new capital.

COMMENT

Structure and Themes

Tibni was not given a separate entry in the Dtr scheme because it was very likely that, in the official register of the kings of Israel, the one controlled by the Omrides, he was treated as a rival claimant to the throne. In some quarters, however, he was apparently recognized as king (see Note to v. 22), and he was able to fend off Omri's attacks for a protracted period.

Omri is judged to have been worse than any of the kings who had preceded him on the throne of Israel, yet Dtr did not bring a particular charge (contrast the infidelities of Ahab in 16:31–33). The item concerning the purchase and construction of Samaria is introduced, somewhat unusually, ahead of the editorial evaluation in v. 26 (but cf. the placement of 16:9 and 16), probably to help explain how it was that Omri reigned only six years in Tirzah and the rest of his twelve years in Samaria (but this is not explicitly said; contrast 2 Sam 5:5). The founding of a new capital cannot have been regarded as meritorious, especially since Omri was roundly criticized. Rather, inasmuch as Samaria served from here on out as the capital of the Northern Kingdom, v. 24 is a footnote to history for the reader's sake; Dtr included occasional marginal notes concerning engaging constructions: e.g., Ahab's "Ivory House" (22:39); Hezekiah's conduit (2 Kgs 20:20). In the present instance, Israel's legal claim to the site is confirmed by the record of its purchase; cf. similar documented acquisitions in Gen 23:3–20 (Cave of Machpelah); 33:18–20 (the parcel of land in Shechem); 2 Sam 24:18–25 (Araunah's threshing floor); see Zakovitch 1979.

History

Omri's accession to the throne of Israel was not supported by the entire army. Though he had taken Tirzah in quick order, leading to Zimri's suicide, some of the Israelite army (perhaps stationed on the northern front facing Damascus) elevated Tibni son of Ginath as king. It appears that at the start the rival military factions were equally pitted and, according to the chronological reckoning in 1 Kgs 16:15, 23, the struggle between the two "kings" was fought for close to four years.[1] That other elements joined the contending sides cannot be gainsaid; but it is overdone to make Omri out to be a foreigner (Canaanite?) simply on the basis of a name etymology (see Note on v. 23) or to see him as having triumphed over the legitimate king designated by the popular assembly (so Soggin 1975). Other options are just as likely; the contest may have been waged between the military and civil authorities or between competing Israelite tribes, factors that shaped the history of the kingdom of Israel more than once. In the end, Omri succeeded in founding Israel's first dynasty, whose strength and wealth became especially prominent during the reign of his son Ahab.

The military aspects and foreign dealings of Omri's reign, though curtailed in the entry in the book of Kings, are partially recoverable; they convey the picture of a distinctly new turn in Israelite history. The extrabiblical Moabite Stone (see translation in Cogan and Tadmor 1988, appendix 1, no. 1) of Mesha, king of Moab, reports that "Omri, king of Israel, oppressed Moab many years." It is not clear how Aram-Damascus responded to these moves into territory through which international trade in Transjordan moved; no military encounters between Omri and Ben-hadad are known.[2] But this sign of military vitality on the part of Israel probably fostered the alliance between Israel and Tyre, sealed with the marriage of Ahab to Jezebel (cf. 16:31). Both Israel and Tyre benefited from the new agreement: new markets were gained for Israel's produce. The products

---

[1] The histories of both Noth (1960, 229) and Bright (1981, 239) omit mention of Tibni by name in their description of the interregnum.

[2] On the problematic statement in 20:34, implying hostilities and capitulation, see the Note there.

of Phoenicia's skilled artisans and imported wares found a welcome home in Samaria and beyond. As for relations with Judah, Israel under Omri (and his successors) ceased trying to recover the Benjaminite territory lost to Asa, and evidently a treaty with Jerusalem respecting the legitimacy of each dynasty was concluded, as the marriage between the two royal houses indicates (cf. 2 Kgs 8:26). At the same time, all parties must have been aware that, just over the horizon, a militarily active Assyria under Ashurnasirpal II had begun periodic campaigning against the Aramean states in northern Syria up to the Mediterranean coast.[3] A united effort to stem that advance, however, was yet to be organized.

Nowhere is it stated what motivated Omri to establish a new capital at Samaria. Its location and topographical features speak for the wisdom of his choice. The palace at Tirzah may have been damaged during the abortive coup of Zimri (cf. v. 18) and perhaps also during the long struggle with Tibni. But in this matter Omri resembles many other ambitious Near Eastern monarchs who left their mark in stone and mortar as signs of valor and dynastic stability. The example of the Davidic capture and establishment in Jerusalem was near at hand. The archaeological remains uncovered at Samaria attest to the impressive city constructed on the site; the design of the palace and its workmanship are evidence that Phoenician masons were employed in this project, just as they had been in Jerusalem in the days of Solomon. And considering that a good part of Omri's "official" reign was spent in overcoming internal opposition, much of the work probably fell to Ahab.

---

[3] Ashurnasirpal II (883–859 BCE) reached the Mediterranean coast during the course of a second campaign to the area, the date of which is not preserved (and not during his expedition to Carchemish; with Brinkman 1968, 393–94; Grayson 1976, 138–40). He stated: "I reached the Great Sea of the land of Amurru. I washed my weapons in the Great Sea and brought sacrifices to the gods" (ANET, 276).

XXXII. The Reign of Ahab (Israel)— INTRODUCTION

(16:29–34)

16 ^{29}Ahab son of Omri became king over Israel in the thirty-eighth year of Asa king of Judah. Ahab son of Omri reigned over Israel in Samaria for twenty-two years. ^{30}Ahab son of Omri did what was displeasing to YHWH,[a] more than all who preceded him. ^{31}Now, as if it had been a slight thing to follow the sins of Jeroboam, he took as wife Jezebel daughter of Ethbaal king of the Sidonians, and he went and served Baal and bowed down to him. ^{32}He erected an altar for Baal (in the) House of Baal that he built in Samaria. ^{33}Ahab (also) made the pole of Asherah. Ahab did more to anger YHWH God of Israel than all the kings of Israel who preceded him.

^{34b}In his days, Hiel[c] of Bethel built Jericho. At the cost of Abiram his eldest son he laid its foundation, and with Segub[d] his youngest son he set its doors, in accordance with the word of YHWH, which he spoke through Joshua son of Nun.[b]

---

[a] Luc. adds "he was worse" (cf. v. 25).
[b-b] Luc. omits.
[c] LXX reads this name as "Achiel."
[d] Read with qere: *śgwb*; ketib: *śgyb*.

NOTES

16 29. *Ahab son of Omri became king over Israel.* Ahab reigned between 873 and 852 BCE. He is the first Israelite king to be mentioned in a cuneiform inscription; *Aḫabu Sirilāya*, "Ahab the Israelite," made a significant contribution in military personnel to the anti-Assyrian league that had organized in the west against Shalmaneser III in 853 (see appendix 1, no. 2; and Note on 22:1 and Comment).

in the thirty-eighth year of Asa king of Judah. This date synchronizes with 16:15 and, unlike v. 23, grants Omri the entire twelve-year period following Zimri's demise. This reckoning may be the official Omride date for the dynasty, which considered the Tibni affair an uprising against Omri, the legitimate king.

31. *Now, as if it had been a slight thing to follow the sins of Jeroboam.* The parallel construction in Ezek 8:17, the interrogative *hănāqēl* (strictly rhetorical) followed by a finite verb, obviates previous suggestions to repoint (cf. Burney, Ehrlich).

Jezebel daughter of Ethbaal king of the Sidonians. The name of this Tyrian princess may be parsed **yš zbl* (> *yzbl* > *'yzbl*), "Zebul exists," with Zebul taken as an epithet of Baal; see Note on 8:13 and the discussion of the ninth-century

Phoenician seal on which the name is inscribed in Avigad 1964 and WSS no. 740.

Ethbaal king of the Sidonians. Ethbaal reigned ca. 887–856 BCE (with Katzenstein 1997, 129). Items concerning the rise and the vigorous rule of Ethbaal (*Ithobalos* in Josephus; *Tuba'il* in later cuneiform) can be garnered from Josephus, extracted from Menander's *History*, based on native Phoenician sources; cf. Josephus, *Ag. Ap.* 1.123; *Ant.* 8.317, 324; 9.138. The title "king of the Sidonians" reflects the expansion and supremacy of Tyre over its northern neighbor. In Josephus, the title is "king of Tyre and Sidon" (also used in the contemporary inscriptions of Shalmaneser III; see, e.g., ANET 281a).

he went and served Baal. For the auxiliary use of *hālak* with the sense "proceed," cf. the Note on 2 Kgs 3:7. Not very likely is a literal interpretation, in which Ahab is pictured as having journeyed to Tyre to worship his new god (so Šanda).

32. *He erected an altar for Baal (in the) House of Baal that he built in Samaria.* Ahab's introduction of the cult of Baal in Samaria is hardly different from Solomon's installation of various high places in Jerusalem (cf. 11:7); both monarchs honored their wives by supporting the worship of their native gods.

an altar for Baal (in the) House of Baal. The long-standing identification of Baal with the Tyrian Baal known as Melqart ("king of the city"; for the god and his cult, see, at length, de Vaux 1971b, 238–51) is now questioned, since it is based on a late, second-century BCE equation of that god with Baal.

Considering the nature of the Baal in 1 Kgs 18 (see further at 18:21), the Baal in question is more likely to have been Baal-Shamem, "Lord of the Heavens," another Phoenician god venerated as a weather god (ABD 1:548; *DDD* cols. 348–53, 1053–58). This Baal cult was not extirpated until Jehu's rise; cf. 2 Kgs 10:18–28. For the later history of the Temple of Baal in Samaria, see 2 Kgs 10:21–29 and Note on v. 25 there.

33. *Ahab (also) made the pole of Asherah.* This is apparently a reference to the well-known Asherah symbol in Samaria, which survived into the post-Jehu age (cf. 2 Kgs 13:6). On the goddess Asherah, see Note on 1 Kgs 15:13.

Ahab did more to anger YHWH God of Israel. A summary statement and not necessarily a reference to other sins (as NJB suggests: "and committed other crimes as well").

34. *In his days.* On this editorial connective, see Notes on 2 Kgs 8:20 and 15:19. While it may be admitted that Dtr used this formula to introduce short items from his sources (both oral and written), it remains a question whether he quoted verbatim or rephrased them.

Hiel of Bethel. The LXX reading, *Achiel*, preserves the full original element *'aḥî*, "my brother," common in Phoenician names; a similar short name is Hiram for Ahiram. For other examples of the gentilic form of compound names, cf. Judg 3:15 (*ben-haymînî*); 6:11 (*'abî-ha'ezrî*); 1 Sam 6:14 (*bêt-haššimšî*); 16:1 (*bêt-hallaḥmî*).

built Jericho. The writing of Jericho with final *he'* is unique and reflects the oldest stage in the use of letters as vowel markers in Hebrew orthography. In all other appearances, the name is written *yr(y)ḥw*. See also *glh* (Josh 15:51; 2 Sam 15:12); *š(y)lh* (Gen 49:10; Josh 18:1). The city is reported to have been utterly destroyed by Joshua (Josh 6:24) and a curse put upon it against its resettlement (v. 26). Scattered references seem to suggest that it was, nevertheless, inhabited at various times before the rebuilding in this passage (cf. Judg 3:13; 2 Sam 10:5). Nevertheless, archaeological excavations have recovered only scant evidence of Iron Age settlement from fill on the slopes of the site; see NEAEHL 674–81.

At the cost of. For this usage, see Note on 2:23.

he laid its foundation, and . . . he set its doors. The two end points of the construction process.

Segub his youngest son. The name *Segub* appears again in 1 Chr 2:21. For the alteration between *yod* and *waw* caused by their similarity in late script, cf. *pʿw* (Gen 36:39) and *pʿy* (1 Chr 1:50); *ʿlwn* (Gen 36:23) and *ʿlyn* (1 Chr 1:40).

in accordance with the word of YHWH, which he spoke through Joshua son of Nun. Compare with Josh 6:26. The Greek of the book of Joshua preserves significant variants of the names of the protagonists in this tradition and its connection with Jericho. On these grounds, Mazor (1988) argues for the primacy of the LXX tradition that was reworked in several stages in MT, suggesting that Luc. of 1 Kgs 16 (in which it is lacking) reflects a stage before the tradition was included in Kings.

COMMENT

Structure and Themes

The reign of Ahab is introduced in typical fashion, with synchronism and length of reign.[1] The critical evaluation of the king as being the worst to have come to Israel's throne is supported by the notice of his having taken the Phoenician princess Jezebel to wife and his worship of Baal and Asherah; the juxtaposition is evidently meant to intimate the corrupt influence of this marriage. In this, Ahab's apostasy follows that of Solomon (cf. 11:1–10); both monarchs were led astray by their foreign wives. Such evaluations are typical of Deuteronomic thought, which saw outmarriage as the root of all sin against YHWH (cf. Deut 7:3–4; cf. Josh 23:12). The formulaic conclusion to Ahab's reign is not given until 1 Kgs 22:39–40, because Dtr has introduced a lengthy series of prophetic stories of varied origin and interest; in most of them, Ahab plays a leading role in his opposition to the heaven-sent men of God.

The single verse (v. 34) concerning the rebuilding of Jericho at the cost of the children of Hiel of Bethel is only loosely associated with the reign of Ahab; perhaps we are meant to understand that the king was the royal sponsor of the

---

[1] LXX (Luc.) reproduces 22:41–51 at the head of this section (as well as in the corresponding location in MT), basing itself on an alternate chronology, which dated the accession of Jehoshaphat to the 11th year of Omri. See Introduction. Chronology for a discussion and evaluation of this alteration.

project. While it is conceivable that a notice concerning the Jericho project was recorded in an official source (as were other royal and public works; cf. 22:39),[2] the present verse is a piece of traditional lore touching on the efficacy of the curse uttered against the site by Joshua in Josh 6:26; contrast Long 1984, 173–74, who speaks of "a commemorative style . . . found in royal building inscriptions." Was it meant to be another example of the rebellious ways of Ahab, coming after the idolatrous constructions recorded in vv. 32–33? The formulaic "in accordance with the word of YHWH that he spoke through PN" joins this story to the many other cases of prophecy fulfilled that were of interest to Dtr and reported throughout Kings (cf., e.g., 13:26; 14:18; 15:29; 16:12; et al.; see further in Introduction. Composition). The nexus between the construction at Jericho and the death of Hiel's children ascribed to the curse of Joshua has spawned any number of rationalistic explanations, from the children's having been offered up as "threshold sacrifices" (DeVries; cf. Würthwein) to their succumbing to the contaminated waters of the Jericho oasis (cf. Gray; Hulse 1971); most simply acknowledge "that some tragic fate actually overtook Hiel's sons, and that the common opinion recognized in this the operation of the ancient curse pronounced by Joshua" (Skinner; so also Montgomery and Gehman).

History

An outline of the political affairs of Ahab's reign can be traced from a few of the prophetic stories in the following chapters, especially 1 Kgs 20 and 22. Regarding his cultic allegiances, it would seem on the face of it that Ahab's construction of a Baal Temple in Samaria was no different from Solomon's construction of sundry high places in Jerusalem (cf. 11:7–8), a courtesy to his foreign wife in accord with the accepted norms of international diplomacy. Whether he was a "true believer" in Baal cannot be ascertained; such a claim is often countered by pointing to his honoring the national deity YHWH, evidence for which is found in the Israelite names of his sons, Ahaziah and Jehoram.

---

[2] Because the only archaeological evidence for building at Jericho during the Iron Age dates from the 7th century BCE (see works cited in Note on v. 34), Würthwein suggested that a featureless folk tradition was wrongly attributed to Ahab by Dtr; contrast Noth, who on the basis of the same evidence thought that Hiel's construction must have been "very modest."

XXXIII. ELIJAH AND THE GREAT DROUGHT

(17:1–24)

17 ¹Elijah the Tishbite, one of the residents of Gilead,ᵃ said to Ahab: "By the life of YHWH, God of Israel, whom I serve, there will be no dew or rain these years, except by my word."

²The word of YHWH came to him: ³"Go away from here; turn eastward and hide in Wadi Cherith, east of the Jordan. ⁴You will drink from the wadi, and I have ordered the ravens to feed you there." ⁵So he proceeded to do according to the word of YHWH. He went and stayed in Wadi Cherith, east of the Jordan.

⁶The ravens would bring him bread and meat in the morning and bread and meat in the evening,ᵇ and he would drink from the wadi. ⁷After some time, the wadi dried up because there was no rain in the land.

⁸Then the word of YHWH came to him: ⁹"Up, go to Zarephath of Sidon and stay there. Now I have ordered a certain widow there to feed you." ¹⁰So he set right out for Zarephath. When he came to the entrance of the town, there was a widow gathering wood. He called to her: "Please bring me a little water in a vessel so I can drink." ¹¹As she went to bring (it), he called to her: "Please bring me a bit of bread in your hand." ¹²She said: "By the life of YHWH, your God, I have nothing baked, only a handful of flour in the jug and a little oil in the flask. Here I am gathering a few sticks, so that I can go in and prepare it for myself and my son. We shall it eat and then we shall die." ¹³Elijah said to her: "Have no fear. Come, do as you have said. But first make me a small cake from it and bring it out to me, and afterwards make (something) for yourself and your son. ¹⁴For thus said YHWH, the God of Israel: 'The jug of flour shall not give out and the flask of oil shall not fail, until the day that YHWH givesᶜ rain on the face of the earth.'" ¹⁵She went and did according to Elijah's word. She ate, she and heᵈ and her household for some time. ¹⁶For the jug of flour did not give out and the flask of oil did not fail, according to the word of YHWH that he spoke through Elijah.

¹⁷Sometime afterward, the son of the woman, the mistress of the house, fell ill; his illness became so severe that he had no breath left in him. ¹⁸She said to Elijah: "What have I to do with you, man of God?ᵉ Did you come to me to call attention to my sin and kill my son?" ¹⁹He said to her: "Give me your son!" He took him from her bosom and brought him up to the roof chamber where he was staying and laid him on his bed. ²⁰He called to YHWH: "YHWH, my God,

---

ᵃ Luc., LXX read: "of Tishbe in Gilead"; see Note.

ᵇ LXX reads: "bread in the morning and meat in the evening."

ᶜ Ketib: *ttn*; qere: *tt*.

ᵈ Read with qere, *hyʾ whwʾ*, for ketib, *hwʾ whyʾ*.

ᵉ A number of MSS add *kî*; see Note.

will you bring harm even to the widow with whom I lodge by killing her son?" [21]He stretched out on the child three times; he called to YHWH: "YHWH my God. Let the child's life return to his body." [22]YHWH heard Elijah's call; the child's life returned to his body and he revived. [23]Then Elijah took the child and brought him down from the roof chamber into the house and gave him to his mother. Elijah said: "See, your son is alive." [24]The woman said to Elijah: "Now indeed I know that you are a man of God and that the word of YHWH in your mouth is true."

NOTES

17   1. *Elijah the Tishbite, one of the residents of Gilead.* The name of the prophet is followed by the gentilic in 21:17, 28; 2 Kgs 1:3, 8; 9:36. Other prophets, as well, are identified by their hometowns; e.g., Ahijah the Shilonite (11:29); see also 19:16; 2 Kgs 14:25. The MT reading "one of the residents" is difficult, since Heb *twšb*, "resident," is a term that appears in legal contexts with reference to foreigners who sojourn in the land of Israel; e.g., Lev 25:23, 35, 45; also Gen 23:4. On this basis, Elijah has sometimes been seen as a non-Israelite who converted to the faith of YHWH (Keil) or just an "immigrant" to Gilead (Walsh). Preferable is the LXX reading "of Tishbe (Thesbon) in Gilead," adopted by NEB, NAB, NJB. A Thisbe in Galilee (of the tribe of Naphtali) is mentioned in Tob 1:2, and this toponym may have influenced the present gloss specifying Tishbe in Gilead; cf. "Beer-sheba of Judah" (1 Kgs 19:3), "Beth-shemesh of Judah" (2 Kgs 14:11). However, no town of Tishbe in Gilead is attested in ancient sources. Early Christian tradition sanctified the site of el-Istib, 13 km north of the Jabbok on Jebel Ajlun, in the vicinity of which there is a chapel named Mar Elias.

   Elijah. Speculation concerning the name, which means "YHWH is my God," revolves around its echo of the prophet's mission: perhaps it is a "religious alias" (Montgomery and Gehman; cf. Thenius, Gray, Jones), a signal of the supremacy of YHWH over all other gods; however, there is no reason to deny the possibility that he was so named at birth by a family loyal to Israel's God (Šanda).

   "By the life of YHWH. . . ." The invocation of the deity sanctions the oath, asserting the truth of the words spoken, lest there would be punishment for a falsehood (cf. Pope 1962). For the rendition of *ḥay* as "by the life of" (the noun in the construct and not "as YHWH lives"), see Greenberg 1957.

   whom I serve. An affirmation that appears again in 18:15. For the idiom, see 10:8.

   there will be no dew or rain these years, except by my word. Elijah's standing with YHWH is depicted as being of sufficient merit and maturity that by his word alone the drought will be terminated. Drought is not infrequent in Israel and, in modern terms, it means a below-average annual rainfall or an uneven spread of rain during the winter months (November–February), when 70% of the precipitation falls; both circumstances can lead to crop failure (Orni and Efrat 1980, 148–49). Dewfall is known year-round; it is particularly abundant on the coastal plain and helps sustain summer planting (1980, 149). In the present instance, the total cessation of dew and rainfall was interpreted as a divine visitation. Josephus (*Ant.* 8.324) claims that this was the year-long drought during the reign of Ithobaal, reported by Menander.

these years. According to 18:1, the drought extended into a third year. Later tradition speaks of its duration as having been "three-and-a-half years" (Luke 4:25). But in both instances, typological numbers are being used: in Kings, three years signifies a complete, short period of time (cf. 22:1 and the Note there); in Luke, the number is the "stereotyped length of the period of distress in apocalyptic literature" (see Fitzmyer 1970, 537).

2. *The word of YHWH came to him.* In a number of instances, LXX reads *'lyhw,* "Elijah," for MT *'lyw,* "to him" (vv. 2, 8), and *'lyh,* "to her" (v. 11); all are easy transcriptional interchanges so that favoring one or the other seems arbitrary.

3. *hide in Wadi Cherith.* The need for Elijah to hide away is unexplained. The fact that the order follows directly upon v. 1 suggests that Elijah's life was in danger, confirmed later by Obadiah's statement that Ahab searched high and low for the person he considered to have been the source of Israel's troubles (cf. 18:10, 17). The king may have thought that, by ridding himself of Elijah, he could bring about the end of the prophet-induced drought. Angry outbursts by royal personages, threatening prophetic messengers, are not rare; cf., e.g., 13:4; 22:26–28; 2 Kgs 1:9.

Wadi Cherith, east of the Jordan. An unidentified riverbed. The prepositional phrase *'al pĕnê* can mean "east" (cf., e.g., 11:7; Num 21:11; Deut 32:49), as well as the nonspecific "overlooking, in the vicinity of" (e.g., Gen 18:16; Num 21:20; 23:28; see BDB 818b–819a; Drinkard 1979). This ambiguity leads some to seek Cherith west of the Jordan (e.g., Wiseman); most search in Transjordan but can do no better than repeat the generalized location of the verse itself (as did Eusebius, *Onomasticon* no. 966). In this case, Elijah, a Gileadite, returned to what was for him familiar territory. On the other hand, if Cherith is not a proper noun but is taken as an adjective, the root **krt* suggests a place "cut off" from water (Ehrlich) or that Elijah was to hide in the "crags" of the wadi (Qara).

4. *You will drink from the wadi.* This order contains an element of the miraculous, since desert wadis are normally dry most of the year and in a drought year even the pools would give out (cf. Jer 14:3). For the use of *wĕhāyâ* as an introductory formula, see Exod 4:16; Ezek 47:10, 22 (S. R. Driver 1892, §121, obs. 1).

I have ordered the ravens to feed you there. A number of species of ravens inhabit the Holy Land; the short-tailed black *Corvus rhipidurus* makes its nest in the crannies around the Dead Sea and the Jordan Valley. The habit of ravens to store up food and to feed their young who cry aloud when hungry (cf. Ps 147:9; Job 38:41) is likely to be at the base of the present legend. (The classical view that ravens were careless parents, unattentive to their young, is not supported by observation. For God's care of the raven, see Luke 12:24.) In ancient Mesopotamia, ravens were considered ominous creatures and are depicted among the scavengers in the Assyrian battle scenes. Rationalistic explanations that would read *'ărābîm*, "Arabs" or "merchants" (cf. Ezek 27:27), for MT *'ōrĕbîm*, "ravens" (cf. Qimḥi, Thenius), miss the point of the miraculous nature of YHWH's act (and were branded "absurdity" by Skinner); nevertheless, they continue to find their way into more recent commentaries (e.g., Gray).

5. *So he proceeded to do according to the word of YHWH*. For other examples of **hlk* immediately followed by another finite verb, in the sense "to proceed to do," cf. 16:31; 2 Kgs 3:7; and see the Note on 1 Kgs 18:5.

6. *The ravens would bring him bread and meat in the morning and bread and meat in the evening*. The LXX reading (see above, text note b) is preferred by some commentators because "the main meal of Easterners when meat is expected is at evening" (Šanda); but the manna episode in Exod 16:8 could have influenced the Greek rendering (Skinner). In the present instance, YHWH provides "rich nourishment" for his prophet (so Gunkel 1906, 9).

7. *After some time*. Here, as in v. 15, the word *yāmîm* is indefinite (cf. Gen 4:3), unlike other cases, in which it means "a year" (Num 9:22; Judg 17:10; 1 Sam 27:7; 2 Sam 14:26).

9. *Zarephath of Sidon*. For the particle and preposition indicating "belonging to" or "under the jurisdiction of," see 15:27; 19:3; 2 Kgs 14:11. This verse refers to a town on the Mediterranean coast, 13 km south of Sidon; the ancient name is preserved in the nearby village of Sarafend. Zarephath (Akk transcription: *Ṣariptu*) is mentioned together with Sidon in a thirteenth-century BCE Egyptian literary text (ANET, 477a) and was among the Phoenician cities taken by Sennacherib in 701 (Cogan and Tadmor 1988, appendix 1, no. 8). For the archaeological investigation of the site and its finds, see Pritchard 1978, 71–96.

Now I have ordered a certain widow there to feed you. "Because Elijah saw that the widow didn't have enough to sustain herself, moreover to feed him, he knew that what God had meant by 'I have ordered' was to be a miracle" (Qimḥi).

a certain widow. Widowhood was a mark of dependency, since such women often lacked the means to support themselves, even more so in times of famine.

to feed you. For the verb **klkl*, see 4:7; 5:7.

10. *there was a widow*. Elijah is likely to have recognized her by "her widow's garb" (Gen 38:14), dress typically worn long after the mourning period (cf. Jdt 8:5; 10:3; 16:8).

gathering wood. The verb **qšš* is used for gathering straw (*qāš*) (cf. Exod 5:12), as well as for twigs and branches (cf. Num 15:32–33).

"Please bring me a little water in a vessel so I can drink." Elijah's request for drink has been compared to a similar one by Eliezer, servant of Abraham, at the well of the city of Nahor (Gen 24:17); in both instances, the sought-after woman is discovered by the same tactic (Rashi). However, this superficial similarity hides the distinction between the two women: the first one was immediately tagged as the future wife of Isaac; the second had to be convinced to submit to Elijah and his God (Simon 1997, 199).

11. *"Please bring me. . . ."* The imperative *lqḥy*, for the usual *qḥy*, as in Exod 29:1; Ezek 37:16; Prov 20:16.

a bit of bread. The root **ptt* denotes "crumble, break up," as in Lev 2:6; *pat* is "morsel, bit"; cf. Gen 18:5; 1 Sam 2:36; 28:22; *pātōt* are "crumbs"; cf. Ezek 13:19.

12. *She said: "By the life of YHWH, your God. . . ."* The woman's use of the name YHWH is somewhat surprising. That she apparently recognized Elijah as an Israelite, either by his dress or his speech, seems insufficient cause for such a turn of speech; had his behavior somehow led her to suspect that he was a holy man? (cf. v. 24).

I have nothing baked. Like *'ūgâ* (v. 13), the hapax *mā'ôg* is a cake of sorts (Ps 35:16 is generally taken as corrupt). For the mode of preparation of these "round cakes" (from the verb **'wg*), see Note on 19:6.

for myself and my son. For the LXX, "my sons," see Note to v. 15.

14. *"The jug of flour shall not give out. . . ."* The verb *tklh* is pointed as if it were from **klʾ*; see GKC, 75l and rr.

YHWH gives rain. For the anomalous ketib, *ttn*, cf. *lttn* in 6:19.

15. *She ate, she and he and her household.* Up until now, the woman had only spoken of herself and her son. The LXX in vv. 12, 13, and the present verse reads "sons," prompted perhaps by "her household." Many would, therefore, correct *byth* to *bnh*, without textual warrant.

she and he and her household. Read with qere, which is grammatically correct. The alternative order of the pronouns in ketib, "he and she and her household," follows the request of the prophet in v. 13 to bring a bit of bread first to him and then to take some for herself.

for some time. Or "a long time." NAB: "for a year"; see Note above on v. 7.

16. *the flask of oil did not fail.* There is no difference in meaning in the change of gender in the verb from masc., referring to the oil, and the fem., referring to the flask (v. 14).

17. *that he had no breath left in him.* That is, he expired; literally, "until he had no breath left in him." Hebrew *nĕšāmâ* animates all flesh (cf. Gen 2:7), and its loss marks the end of life; cf. Job 34:14–15. Note, too, the hyperbolic use of a similar expression in Dan 10:17. Here also, as is the case in v. 4, the quest for the "factual basis" of the tale in a "matter of simple hygiene"—the child suffered from breathing problems in the stuffy, dusty house (Gray)—misses the point of this hagiographic tale.

18. *"What have I to do with you, man of God? . . ."* An oft-used phrase expressing wonderment and consternation over a new and/or renewed relationship; cf. 2 Kgs 3:13; Judg 11:12; 2 Sam 16:10; 19:23.

Did you come to me to call attention to my sin and kill my son? The woman charges: Your presence in my house has drawn attention to me, so that my faults are now being called to account by YHWH (Rashi; Ehrlich). The MT implies a question, while a number of manuscripts add *kî* at the beginning, subordinating the sentence to the previous one, "that you come to me . . ." (cf. Judg 11:12).

to call attention to my sin. Hebrew **zkr* in *Hiphil* means "to mention, invoke"; cf. Gen 41:9; 1 Sam 4:18; Ps 77:12; Song 1:4; this sense is well established in its

Akk cognate *zakāru* (CAD Z, 16–22). The idiom used here appears again in Ezek 21:28 and 29:16, where it is predicted that the major powers, Babylon and Egypt, will no longer "bring sin to mind," as they had enticed Israel in the past (cf. Greenberg 1997, ad loc.).

and kill my son. Josephus eases the miraculousness of Elijah's deed in the next scene by interpreting: "he ceased to breathe and seemed to be dead" (*Ant.* 8.325).

19. *brought him up to the roof chamber where he was staying.* That Elijah had taken up residence in the widow's house has been withheld from the reader/listener until now; this type of "partial flashback" is a feature of biblical narrative; cf., e.g., Gen 42:21 (on which, see the remarks of Licht 1978, 109–11); [DNF: "In Gen 34:26 the fact that Dinah has been kept in the home of Shechem is not revealed until later."] In like fashion, the Shunamite showed hospitality to Elisha by setting up a room for him in the "roof chamber" (cf. 2 Kgs 4:10–11); note that the same word (*ʿălîyâ*, "roof chamber") is used in both instances.

20. *"YHWH, my God, will you bring harm even to the widow with whom I lodge by killing her son?"* Elijah importunes: Is this woman, who has shown me kindness and taken me in, deserving of punishment as are all the others who suffer from the drought? The prophet's words hint at the unfairness of taking the life of the widow's son and echo the tone of the woman's words (v. 18), which pointed an accusing finger at the prophet and his God.

with whom I lodge. Hebrew *mitgôrēr*, from **gwr*, with the sense of dwelling for a short while; cf. NJPSV: "whose guest I am." In *Qal*, the meaning is "to dwell" over an extended period; cf. Gen 32:5.

21. *He stretched out on the child three times.* Hebrew **mdd* in *Hithpoel* is lit., "measure oneself." The NEB follows LXX, "he breathed deeply upon the child," but this looks like a contextual guess for the unique Hebrew word. A similar act was performed by Elisha upon the dead son of the Shunamite, except that a different verb (**ghr*) is used; the prophet positioned himself directly upon the child, mouth to mouth, eyes to eyes, palms to palms, symbolically transferring his life force to the deceased.

on the child. Hypercriticism sees in the alternate terms "(woman's) son" (vv. 17, 18, 19, 23) and "child" (vv. 21, 23) a sign that the "original kernel" of the tale was secondarily expanded (Jones, with Hentschel 1977, 193). But this interchange of appellations stems from the sensitivity of a single narrator, who expressed in subtle nuances the particular relationship between the lad and the woman as "mother" and "son"; with reference to Elijah, he is "child." Compare the like interchange in Gen 21:1–21 of "child," "lad," and "son," each indicating the relationship of an actor toward the unnamed Ishmael; other examples of the naming of characters as expressing point of view are discussed by Berlin 1983, 59–61, 87–91.

He called to YHWH: "YHWH my God. Let the child's life return to his body." Unlike the complaint expressed in his first call to YHWH (cf. v. 20), in his second address, Elijah pleaded directly for the child's life.

the child's life. That Heb *nepeš* conveys a range of meanings from "throat" to "breath" to "life" (and not "soul") is accepted by all modern scholars (and was recognized earlier by some medieval grammarians; cf. Qimḥi); see Gruber 1987.

22. *YHWH heard Elijah's call.* Whatever the purpose of stretching out upon the child's body may have been, it is YHWH, in response to the prophet's prayer, who brings life back to the dead body.

24. *"Now indeed I know that you are a man of God. . . ."* The gift of life aroused greater awe than the gift of food (cf. v. 16) and, though Elijah's role had already been manifested in his earlier providing for the widow and her son, there she is depicted as unresponsive to the miracle.

Now indeed. For *ʿattâ zeh,* cf. 2 Kgs 5:22.

COMMENT

Structure and Themes

The present chapter is the first part of a larger canonical unit that extends to 1 Kgs 19; it comprises all that remains of the life work of the prophet Elijah, introducing him without fanfare in 17:1 and concluding with the appointment of Elisha as his successor in 19:19–21. (On the position of 1 Kgs 21, see Comment there.) Elijah's defiant opposition to the worship of Baal is the major unifying theme that ties most of the individual episodes, with their several subthemes (e.g., the drought) and subplots (e.g., the stay in Zarephath), into a single whole. Indeed, the main thrust of his ministry, at least in the traditions that have reached us, concerns his struggle with the royal house and its idolatries. But that this was all of the prophet's life work is hard to say; for a survey of the voluminous later legend concerning Elijah, see Ginzberg 1928, 4:195–235; 6:316–42. Much recent discussion has focused on the artfulness of the editorial unit (e.g., Cohn 1982; Simon 1997), reading it as the early biography of the prophet, a "kind of tale of apprenticeship" that portrays the development of Elijah's prophetic personality. Yet the limited selection of traditional material at hand and its narrow focus leave open the question whether this was the original *Sitz im Leben* of 1 Kgs 17.

The questions concerning the transmission of the Elijah tradition remain vexed: Were the individual tales first brought together in an early oral cycle, or is their integration the result of collection into a literary unit prior to their insertion into the narrative of Kings? What was the role of Dtr in shaping the tradition? The disparate nature of the episodes favors taking their present juxtaposition to be a literary compilation removed somewhat from an oral setting among the followers of the prophet. A sign of this is the artful use of "the word" of YHWH and of the "word" of the prophet in vv. 1, 2, 5, 8, (13), 15, 16, 24, which ties all of the parts together. The "word" with which the unit opens, threads its way through two "word"-commands to Elijah to the "word" to the widow, who finally acknowledged the truth of the "word of YHWH" in the mouth of the prophet. This reverberation carries forward the theme of reward for the obedient during the ongoing punishment of the transgressor. On the other hand, the episode of the revival of the dead child (vv. 17–24) is hardly related to the overarching theme of drought; it is recounted here because of its association with the widow of Zarephath, and associative linking is an oral device joining tales (see Comment to 2 Kgs 6:1–7). See further discussion of these issues in the Introduction. Composition.

In the opening verse, 17:1, the prophet Elijah is thrust upon the reader, just as he seems to have been upon Ahab, without setting and with no introduction. This method of presentation is often taken to be characteristic of the prophet himself, who was wont to appear with "eagle-like suddenness" (Skinner) and to disappear just as swiftly and mysteriously (cf. the words of Obadiah in 18:12). More likely, however, it is the juxtaposition of dissimilar literary materials (for which the reader is unprepared) that has engendered this impression. To judge from the story of Elijah's contest with the prophets of Baal on Mount Carmel (1 Kgs 18), the solemn promise of an extended drought is meant to be understood as YHWH's punishment for Ahab's support of idolatry (cf. Deut 11:16–17), which is now described by Dtr in his summary in 1 Kgs 16:30–33. Originally, however, the single opening verse, 17:1, was probably preceded by a scene of confrontation between the two protagonists, now suppressed. (This conjectured scene may also have included more of an introduction to Elijah than the note that he was a Gileadite. The LXX—or its *Vorlage*—seems to have felt this lack and added the title "prophet" after the name *Elijah*. Note also the fabulous context for the meeting of Ahab and Elijah at the house of mourning of Hiel, reported in *y. Sanh.* 10.28b; *b. Sanh.* 113a.) The themes that unite the ensuing episodes are inherent in v. 1: the drought as YHWH's judgment and Elijah as YHWH's faithful servant.

Three separate episodes concerning Elijah's activities, ostensively during the days of the drought, follow on its announcement in v. 1: (1) Elijah in Wadi Cherith (vv. 2–7);[1] (2) Elijah and the Widow of Zarephath: the miracle of food (vv. 8–16); (3) Elijah revives the widow's son (vv. 17–24).

Episode One. Elijah in Wadi Cherith (vv. 2–7). Nowhere is it explained why Elijah was to go into hiding, but YHWH's order, following v. 1 as it does, leads to the surmise that the prophet's life had been threatened by Ahab for having proclaimed the drought (cf. the later hostile encounter between the two in 1 Kgs 18:17–18). For the king to have thought that the much-sought relief could be induced either by forcing Elijah to recant or by removing him altogether may not have been so ill-advised as it seems. If Elijah had been perceived

---

[1] The end of the unit is marked in MT by a Masoretic break (*sĕtûmâ*) between vv. 7 and 8. This understanding is corroborated by the identical opening verses in v. 2 and v. 8. At the same time, the remark that the severity of the famine increased explains the need for the prophet's move to Zarephath; this consideration has prompted some to attach v. 7 to v. 8; e.g., Benzinger, Kittel, Long, Walsh, NAB, NJPSV, NJB.

to have been a wonder-worker, an act of counter-magic on Elijah's part (even though coerced) or the breaking of the spell by Elijah's death would have been conceivable.

The locations and the means by which YHWH sustained Elijah, in a desert wadi and by ravens, accent the miraculous aspect of his gracious care of his servant. Rationalization of the miraculous (see Note on v. 4) misses this point, because it was the prophet's special relationship with YHWH that explains the popularity of this and other such tales in prophetic circles.

Episode Two.   Elijah and the widow of Zarephath: the miracle of food (vv. 8–16). Though unstated, the first round of the contest between YHWH and Baal, which would reach its climax on Mt. Carmel (1 Kgs 18:19–40), was waged in Zarephath. The town, within the territory of Sidon, the kingdom from which Jezebel hailed and in which the god she introduced into Israel was at home, was the apposite setting; it was situated outside the borders of Israel—to some minds, outside YHWH's territory. There in Zarephath, Elijah proved YHWH's omnipotence; he was not limited to one land, because it was he who had brought the drought upon Israel just as he had upon Tyre; and it was he who provided food to those who believed in him (Fensham 1980). The widow of Zarephath proved worthy of YHWH's care by complying with the prophet's request for drink and food, and she was duly rewarded. That she was the unwitting instrument for fulfilling YHWH's promise to the prophet (v. 9) does not diminish her submission to the prophet's word; the story proceeds, as do many biblical tales, on two levels—with YHWH and the human participant acting in tandem (for a thoughtful discussion of this "double causality," see Seeligmann 1992, 62–81).

Episode Three.   Reviving the widow's son (vv. 17–24). The tale of Elijah's revival of a dead child shares common motifs with one told of Elisha in 2 Kgs 4:8–37. In both, the mothers exhibit hospitality to the holy men who have come to stay with them, specifically by setting aside a room for them (1 Kgs 17:19//2 Kgs 4:9–10). Both have a son who falls ill and dies unexpectedly (1 Kgs 17:17//2 Kgs 4:18–20). In both tales, the man of God is the object of a verbal attack, because he is seen to be personally responsible for the child's death (1 Kgs 17:18//2 Kgs 4:28). Finally, Elijah and Elisha both pray to YHWH (1 Kgs 17:20–21//2 Kgs 4:33), as well as perform a magical act that is somehow involved in reviving the child (1 Kgs 17:21//2 Kgs 4:34–35). These striking similarities, however, do not distract from the didactic lesson taught in 1 Kgs 17, one that is lacking in 2 Kgs 4. Elijah's prayer calls for YHWH to deal ethically with the woman who has taken him in during his distress; her act of faith—having kept him alive—is reason enough to bring her son back to life. From another perspective, development can be seen in the concluding statement of the widow acknowledging YHWH (1 Kgs 17:24), altogether lacking in the Shunamite's tale. The widow's words resemble Naaman's declaration that "there is no God in all the world except in Israel" (2 Kgs 5:15); both non-Israelites had been won over by the healing work of a man of God. Such refinements in the Elijah tale as compared to the one told about Elisha may indeed be understood as resulting from the development of a simple legend into an "ethical legend" (Rofé 1988a, 134). Whether the story was "transferred from Elisha to the more illustrious Elijah" (Rofé 1988a, loc. cit.) is another matter altogether, not necessarily related to the issue of thematic change; see Introduction. Composition.

As noted above, Episode 3 is only loosely associated with the preceding one; both concern the widow who was Elijah's host. Though it may have originally circulated as a separate tale, as most hold, its present position resembles a similar juxtaposition in the Elisha cycle: In 2 Kgs 4, a tale concerning the provision of oil for a woman in distress (vv. 1–7) is followed by one telling of Elisha's reviving the son of the Shunamite (vv. 8–37). Associative editing seems to have brought together stories of women in distress in both the Elijah and Elisha literary complexes.

XXXIV. THE CONTEST ON MOUNT CARMEL

(18:1–46)

18 ¹A long time passed, and in the third year, the word of YHWH came to Elijah: "Go, present yourself to Ahab so that I may give rain on the face of the earth." ²So Elijah went to present himself to Ahab.

Now the famine was severe in Samaria. ³Ahab called Obadiah, "Over the Household."—Obadiah greatly feared YHWH. ⁴When Jezebel slaughtered the prophets of YHWH, Obadiah had taken a hundred prophets and hidden them fifty in a cave and continually provided them with bread and water.—⁵Ahab said to Obadiah: "Come, let us go through the land^a to all of the springs of water and to all the wadis. Perhaps we shall find some grass to keep the horses and mules alive and not have to destroy any of the beasts."^b ⁶They divided the land between them to go through it; Ahab went one way by himself and Obadiah went another way^c by himself.

⁷Now as Obadiah was on the way, he was suddenly met by Elijah. He recognized him and fell on his face and said: "Is it you, my lord, Elijah?" ⁸He said to him: "It is I. Go, say to your lord: 'Elijah is here!'" ⁹He said: "What is my sin that you hand your servant over to Ahab to have me killed? ¹⁰By the life of YHWH your God, there is no nation or kingdom to which my lord has not sent there to search for you. And when they said: 'He is not (here),' he had that kingdom or nation swear that they could not find you. ¹¹And now you say: 'Go, say to your lord: "Elijah is here!"' ¹²And it will happen, I leave you and the spirit of YHWH will carry you to somewhere I do not know; and when I come to tell Ahab and he does not find you, he will kill me, though your servant has feared YHWH from my youth. ¹³Has my lord not been told what I did when Jezebel was killing the prophets of YHWH, how I hid a hundred of the prophets of YHWH by fifties in a cave and provided them with bread and water? ¹⁴And now you say: 'Go, say to your lord: "Elijah is here!"' He will kill me!" ¹⁵Elijah said: "By the life of YHWH of hosts whom I serve, today I will present myself to him."

¹⁶So Obadiah went to meet Ahab and he told him; and Ahab went to meet Elijah. ¹⁷When Ahab saw Elijah, Ahab said to him: "Is that you, troubler of Israel?" ¹⁸He said: "I have not troubled Israel, but you have and your father's house, by your abandoning YHWH's commands; you followed the Baals! ¹⁹Now then, send, gather all Israel to me at Mount Carmel, as well as the four hundred and fifty prophets of Baal and the four hundred prophets of Asherah who eat at Jezebel's table."

---

^a With LXX; MT: "Go into the country"; see Note.

^b MT: *mhbhmh*; Qimḥi reports a ketib: *mn hbhmh*; qere: *mhbhmh*.

^c Lit., "one way."

²⁰Ahab sent to all the Israelites and gathered the prophets at Mount Carmel. ²¹Elijah approached all the people and said: "How long will you keep hopping between the two boughs? If YHWH is God, follow him, and if Baal, follow him." But the people did not answer him a word. ²²Then Elijah said to the people:[d] "I alone have remained as a prophet of YHWH, and the prophets of Baal are four hundred and fifty.[e] ²³Let two bulls be given to us; let them choose one bull for themselves, cut it up, and place it on the wood but not set fire (to it). And *I* will prepare the other bull[f] and place it on the wood but not set fire (to it). ²⁴Then you will call on the name of your god, and *I* will call on the name of YHWH, and the god who answers by fire, he is God." All the people answered: "The matter is good!"

²⁵Elijah said to prophets of Baal: "Choose one bull for yourselves and prepare (it) first, for you are many; call on the name of your god, but do not put fire (to it)." ²⁶So they took the bull that was given to them, and they prepared (it), and they called on the name of Baal from morning until noon: "O Baal. Answer us!" But there was no sound and no one answering. They hopped about the altar they had made.[g] ²⁷At noon, Elijah mocked them; he said: "Call loudly. For he is a god. Maybe he is in conversation, or he is occupied, or may be on the way, or perhaps he is asleep and will wake up." ²⁸So they called loudly and they gashed themselves, as was their custom, with swords and spears until blood spilled over them. ²⁹When the noon passed, they raved until the hour of the meal offering. But there was no sound and no one answering and no response.

³⁰Then Elijah said to all the people: "Come up to me." All the people came up to him. Then he proceeded to repair the destroyed altar of YHWH. ³¹Elijah took twelve stones according to the number of the tribes of the sons of Jacob— to whom the word of YHWH came: "Israel shall be your name"—³²and with the stones, he built an altar in the name of YHWH. He made a trough around the altar with a capacity of about two *seahs* of seed. ³³He arranged the wood, cut up the bull, and placed it on the wood. ³⁴He said: "Fill four jars with water and pour (it) on the offering and on the wood."[h] He said: "Do it a second time," and they did it a second time. He said: "Do it a third time," and they did it a third time. ³⁵The water ran around the altar and he also filled the trough with water. ³⁶At the time of the meal offering, Elijah the prophet came forward and said: "YHWH, God of Abraham, Isaac, and Israel! Let it be known today that you are God in Israel and that I am your servant, and by your command I have done all these things. ³⁷Answer me, YHWH, answer me, so that this people will know that you, YHWH, are God, and it is *you* who have turned their hearts backward."

---

[d] A number of MSS add "all" the people, as in v. 21.

[e] LXX adds: "and four hundred prophets of Asherah."

[f] Lit., "the one bull."

[g] Read *'św* (pl.) for MT: *'śh* (sg.), with Sebirin (< *Minḥat Shai*) and many MSS; also Luc., LXX, Vulg., Syr.

[h] LXX adds: *wy'św kn*, "they did so."

[38]Then YHWH's fire descended and consumed the offering, the wood, the stones and the dust, and licked up the water that was in the trough. [39]When the people saw this, they fell on their faces and said: "YHWH, He is God. YHWH, He is God." [40]Then Elijah said to them: "Seize the prophets of Baal. Let no one of them escape." They seized them, and Elijah took them down to Wadi Kishon and slaughtered them there.

[41]Elijah said to Ahab: "Go up, eat and drink, for there is the sound of roaring rain." [42]So Ahab went up to eat and drink, while Elijah went up to the top of Carmel. He crouched on the ground and put his face between his knees. [43]He said to his attendant: "Go up. Look toward the sea." He went up and looked, and he said: "There is nothing." Seven times[i] he said: "Go back."[j] [44]On the seventh time, he said: "There is a cloud as small as a man's hand rising from the sea." He said: "Go. Say to Ahab: 'Hitch up (your chariot) and go down, so that the rain will not stop you.'" [45]By that time, the skies grew dark with clouds and wind; then there was a heavy rain. Ahab mounted up and went to Jezreel; [46]and, as the hand of YHWH had come upon Elijah, he bound up his loins and ran in front of Ahab all the way to Jezreel.

---

[i] Moved up for translation.

[j] Luc. and LXX additions, partially adopted by some commentators and NEB: "he (or: the attendant) returned seven times."

NOTES

18   1. *A long time passed.* Literally, "There were many days"; on the disagreement between the sg. verb and pl. subject, cf. 11:3.

in the third year. That is, at the completion of a short cycle of years, as in 22:1, and see Note there. As a literary device, this number should not be manipulated to "one full year, plus small portions of the preceding and following years" (Walsh), as if this would give the reckoning "three years" more credence.

present yourself to Ahab. The prophet's hiding out (cf. 17:3) had reached its term and a new pronouncement was to be delivered to the king.

so that I may give rain. For the volitional form, see S. R. Driver 1892, 64–69; Waltke and O'Connor 1990, §34.6.

3. *Obadiah, "Over the Household."* The name *Obadiah,* "worshiper of YHWH," expresses the essence of the man's character, illustrated by his brave act related afterward (vv. 4, 13); for the distinction between *ʿōbēd* and *ʿebed,* see Note on 2 Kgs 10:19. On Obadiah's title, see Note on 1 Kgs 4:6; also 16:9. His responsibility for the royal estate seems to explain his personal participation in the search for fodder.

Obadiah greatly feared YHWH. The parenthetical vv. 3b–4 are considered by many to be secondary, anticipating, in contrast to the biblical narrative style, information that is related in context, in v. 13 (Gunkel 1906, 15).

4. *When Jezebel slaughtered the prophets of YHWH.* The verb *hkryt* appears here in close proximity to the *nkryt* in v. 5; further on, Jezebel's murderous ways are described by the verb **hrg*, "kill" (v. 13), the change attributable to the appearance of **hrg* in vv. 12 and 14.

fifty in a cave. The LXX, Tg., and numerous MSS have *ḥmšym ḥmšym*, as in v. 13; MT lost the reduplication by haplography; for the distributive, see Waltke and O'Connor 1990, 288–89. The non-Hebrew adverbial form "by fives" created by Gray may be dismissed.

in a cave. The translation follows English idiom rather than Hebrew, which has "the cave." See Note at 13:14. Nothing can be said regarding the location of these particular caves; some suggest they were in the Carmel range, but this is an unwarranted inference from the later assembly on Mount Carmel.

continually provided them. The perfect after the imperfect (unlike v. 13) indicates the iterative (Burney; Montgomery and Gehman).

5. *"Come, let us go through the land. . . ."* Read with LXX, *lkh wn'brh*, which on the basis of v. 6 (*l'br bh*) looks genuine; cf. the similar forms in 1 Sam 14:1, 6. The retroverted form requires the cohortative after the emphatic imperative, as pointed out by Orlinsky 1940. The MT: *lk b'rṣ* is anomalous; *hthlk b'rṣ* (cf. Gen 13:17) would be appropriate in BH.

we shall find some grass. Hebrew *ḥāṣîr* is synonymous with *'ēśeb, deše'*, and *yereq* (cf. Prov 27:25; Isa 15:6) and often appears as the food of animals (e.g., Ps 104:14; 147:8; Job 40:15).

not have to destroy any of the beasts. The Hiphil of **krt* for destruction of animals is used in Lev 26:22; Mic 5:9; Zech 9:10. Some follow Luc. and LXX and read the verb as Niphal, perhaps *nikkārēt*; others suggest *tikkārēt mimmennû* (Wellhausen 1875; Burney); but MT is intact and echoes *hakrît* in v. 4. The horses and mules were the mainstay of the royal stables; from extrabiblical sources, Ahab is known to have maintained an extensive mounted force and chariot corps; see Comment to 1 Kgs 20. At the same time, the portrayal of the king is rather pitiful; the king was in such straits that he himself undertook to scour the countryside for leftover stubble.

7. *Now as Obadiah was on the way, he was suddenly met by Elijah.* The demonstrative *hinnēh* makes "the narrative graphic and vivid . . . enabling the reader to enter into the surprise" of Obadiah (BDB 244a, sub c); cf. also Gen 37:29; Exod 2:6; Num 12:10.

He recognized him. Elijah's appearance—"a hairy man, girt with a leather belt around his waist" (2 Kgs 1:8)—identified him as the prophetic master.

"Is it you . . . ?" The question is rhetorical, for Obadiah had recognized Elijah. The demonstrative *zeh* adds emphasis, almost "Is it *really* you?" cf. v. 17; Gen 27:21; 2 Sam 2:20 (see Waltke and O'Connor 1990, §17.4.3c).

9. *He said: "What is my sin that you hand your servant over to Ahab to have me killed? . . ."* Obadiah repeats his fear of the king's reaction to the news of Elijah's imminent appearance three times (vv. 9, 12, 14), explaining that his life would be in jeopardy if he were to tell him. Was Obadiah afraid that the king

would suspect him of having made common cause with Elijah, or would he be taken as ridiculing the king?

10. *there is no nation or kingdom to which my lord has not sent to search for you.* In Ahab's eyes, Elijah was a fugitive from justice, inasmuch as his words and deeds had threatened the regime; thus, Ahab could call upon allied kingdoms to extradite Elijah if he were found in their territory (with Montgomery and Gehman). Ahab's reported action recalls ANE practice: clauses respecting the extradition of fugitives were often included in treaty texts, whether they were persons wanted for incitement against the king (see ANET, 660b) or were runaway slaves (Wiseman 1953, 27–32); cf. Rainey 1962, 62. See too 1 Kgs 2:39–40 and Note there.

And when they said . . . he had that kingdom or nations swear. On the double perfect as protasis and apodosis in this frequentative usage, see S. R. Driver 1892, §148.

that they could not find you. For the potential force of the imperfect, cf. 8:5; and see S. R. Driver 1892, §37(b).

12. *the spirit of YHWH will carry you to somewhere.* Or "YHWH's wind," as in 2 Kgs 2:16. "Elijah had so frequently successfully eluded Ahab's officers that he gained a reputation as the possessor of supernatural powers" (Robinson).

15. *"By the life of YHWH of hosts. . . ."* This title appears again in 19:10, 14; 2 Kgs 3:14; 19:31. More properly, the noun *ṣĕbā'ôt* stands in apposition to the divine name and may allude to the armies of Israel or to the heavenly hosts over whom YHWH presides. YHWH of hosts "was conceived as enthroned in visible majesty on the cherubim throne in the Solomonic temple" (DDD col. 1735), expressed in the familiar formula *yôšēb hakkĕrūbîm* associated with the sanctuary at Shiloh (cf. 1 Sam 4:4; 2 Sam 6:2; see Note on 2 Kgs 19:16).

today I will present myself to him. The conjunction *kî* introduces the matter sworn to, as, e.g., in Gen 42:16; 1 Kgs 2:23; cf. BDB 472a (sub 1c).

17. *troubler of Israel.* The basic meaning of Heb **'kr* is "to stir up, disturb," and in MH describes turgid liquids and muddy waters; in BH, it is used mostly with reference to the actions of persons considered to have brought about trouble; cf. Gen 34:30; Judg 11:35; 1 Sam 14:29; here, as in Josh 7:25, the inimical act by Ahab (not Elijah) led to a divine punishment.

18. *by your abandoning YHWH's commands.* The LXX lacks "commands," perhaps reflecting a text in which the struggle was one of recognition of the true God (cf. vv. 21, 39) and not the particulars of his cult. The same charge appears in 2 Kgs 17:16; see also 1 Kgs 19:10 and the Note there.

you followed the Baals! The plural "Baals" is not otherwise used in Kings; in the early histories, it appears only in Judg 2:11; 3:7; 8:33; 10:6, 10; 1 Sam 7:4; 12:10. If not just a derogatory turn of phrase, it may reflect the perception that the Canaanite god Baal had many manifestations.

19. *gather all Israel to me at Mount Carmel.* A mountain range and promontory, 546 m at its height, that juts into the Mediterranean, at the modern city of Haifa. The *Via Maris* turns inland south of Carmel, and crosses into the Jezreel Valley through the Aruna Pass. The mountain's natural beauty became

symbolic of majesty and fertility (cf., e.g., Isa 35:2; Jer 2:7). Early references to Carmel may include the "Antelope's Nose" mentioned in a third-millennium BCE Egyptian text (ANET, 228b) and the "holy mountain" in the vicinity of Acre recorded in an itinerary of Thutmose III (ANET, 243a; Aḥituv 1984, 162–63; see also Cogan and Tadmor 1988, 121 n. 11). After the transfer of the Cabul territory to Hiram (see 1 Kgs 9:11–13), the Carmel range became the border of Israel with Tyre. Activity at the YHWH cult site on the mountain was suspended during Jezebel's purge (cf. 18:30). In Christian tradition, the site of the encounter described here is el-Muḥraqa, at the southeastern edge of the mountain, facing Jezreel, overlooking Tell el-Qasis.

the four hundred and fifty prophets of Baal and the four hundred prophets of Asherah. This is the only biblical acknowledgment of prophecy through non-Israelite gods; Deut 13:2–6 rules against prophecy in the name of foreign gods but is there explained as a test of Israel under YHWH's control.

the four hundred prophets of Asherah who eat at Jezebel's table. These prophets are referred to only in this verse in MT (LXX does mention them in v. 22) and later "escape" the slaughter in v. 40 (see Qimḥi for the fanciful explanation that the queen did not permit them to participate in the contest; for a modern version of this approach, noting Ahab's impotence vis-à-vis his wife, see Provan). In addition, the particle *wĕ'et* expected at the beginning of the entire clause is missing. Thus, following the suggestion of Wellhausen, the clause has been taken as a late addition to the text meant to increase the extent of the prophet's victory; still, a scribal oversight might explain its absence in the concluding scene (Simon 1997, 220 n. 67).

who eat at Jezebel's table. The same expression as in 1 Kgs 2:7; see note there. The NEB's "who are Jezebel's pensioners" is misleading to American readers because these prophets were not retirees.

20. *Ahab sent to all the Israelites.* For MT *bny yśr'l*, LXX reads simply *yśr'l*; some MSS, *bgbl yśr'l*.

21. *"How long will you keep hopping between the two boughs? . . ."* The noun *sā'îp* (here fem. **sĕ'ippâ*) refers to the boughs of a fruit tree (Isa 17:6; cf. Ezek 31:6, 8 [*sĕ'appâ*] of the cedar) as well as the clefts of rocks (Isa 2:21; 57:5). The image seems to suggest the hopping back and forth (of a bird?) between the branches; cf. Tg., Vulg., Ibn-Janah. Others render *sā'îp* (metaphorically from the preceding?) "divided thoughts" (Job 4:13; 20:2); so Rashi, Qimḥi, and many modern commentators; cf. NJPSV: "between two opinions." The NEB offers "sit on the fence," but this is another image. The verb **psḥ*, "skip, hop, limp," is used again in v. 26 for a dance step; see further there.

if Baal, follow him. As suggested above (see Note to 16:32), the Baal referred to is Baal-Shamem, a storm god who was revered under other names: Baal Hadad and Hadad-Rimmon in various Phoenician and Aramean centers. This god continued to be worshiped on Mount Carmel as late as the third century CE in the form of "Heliopolitan Zeus, god of Carmel" (see Avi-Yonah 1952; note that a god "Baal Carmel" is unattested, though it is freely referred to in many discussions). Elijah's challenge to this particular Baal was most apt, because the underlying issue of the contest soon to be waged was the ability of the true god to bring fire, and ultimately rain.

22. *"I alone have remained as a prophet of YHWH. . . ."* The statement is only partly true and should be understood as prophetic hyperbole (so also 19:14). For a hundred prophets had escaped the persecution by hiding in a cave (v. 13), and other prophets of YHWH appear in the stories concerning Ahab's wars with Aram-Damascus (cf. 20:13 and 22:1–28). Yet Elijah's singular campaign against Baal, despite the monarchic reign of terror, marked him off as the era's unequaled man of God.

24. *Then you will call on the name of your god.* The subject can only be the people whom Elijah was addressing (cf. v. 22); yet this direct address is somewhat strange in the description of the projected contest, during which the Baal prophets were to call upon 'their' god. Has the address to them in v. 25 inelegantly been transferred to the present verse (see Simon 1997, 222 n. 74)? More likely is Elijah's identification of the wayward people with Baal.

he is God. Here and in v. 39, Hebrew has *"the God."*

All the people answered: "The matter is good!" The same phrase, indicating assent, was used by Shimei in 1 Kgs 2:38, 42.

25. *"Choose one bull for yourselves and prepare (it) first, for you are many. . . ."* Or, "for you are the majority" (NJPSV).

26. *So they took the bull that was given to them.* This contradicts vv. 23 and 25 and may be the reason that LXX omits the troublesome clause.

They hopped about the altar they had made. A ritual dance of some sort is implied by the hopping, limping step (< *psḥ*; cf. Exod 12:13, 23) of the Baal prophets. For examples gleaned from later sources of ceremonial encompassing of a sacred stone, especially the perambulation of the Ka'aba in Mecca, see Montgomery and Gehman; also de Vaux 1971b, 240–41. In the present instance, the rite, which might have included music and song, was meant to attract the god's attention to his attendants' request; that this was in fact a rain dance (Patai 1939, 255) is a distortion of the terms of the contest (spelled out in vv. 23–24).

the altar they had made. This verse, taken together with vv. 30–32, implies that the place of the contest was not a functioning cult site, though at one time, there had been a high place to YHWH there (otherwise, Alt 1935).

27. *Elijah mocked them.* Hebrew *wayhattēl* is of disputed etymology. The medieval grammarians derive it from **htl*, here in Piel (so Ibn-Janah, Qimhi), though some of the forms lack the *dagesh* (cf. Gen 31:7; Exod 8:25); modern scholars consider this a secondary form of **tll* in Hiphil, uncharacteristically preserving the *he'* (following Gesenius; BDB 1068). In regard to meaning, **htl* conveys dishonesty; it is both "to cheat" (Gen 31:7) and "to lie" (Jer 9:4), even "to be two-faced" (Isa 30:10); thus, rather than the usual translation "mock," perhaps it means Elijah "deluded" the prophets into thinking he was serious when he said Baal was a god (so Simon 1997, 225–26).

"Call loudly. . . ." In the Hittite realm, a table of food and drink was set to attract the god who, though otherwise engaged, was called upon to return to his

temple; might Elijah's taunt, "Shout louder . . . ," be a parody of similar conception? (so Greenberg 1994, 16).

Maybe he is in conversation. The root **śyḥ* is used for talking (Prov 6:22) and musing (Ps 119:15), as well as complaining (Job 9:27; 10:1). Here, as in 2 Kgs 9:11, it means "he is having a word with one of his advisers" (Rashi; so all ancient translations).

or he is occupied. Many follow Ibn-Janah in taking the word as a euphemism; **śyg*, like the root **swg*, indicates "to turn back" (cf. the interchange of *ś* and *s* in 2 Sam 1:22), with the meaning, he is indisposed.

or may be on the way. Note may be taken of the Ugaritic text that tells of the goddess Anath, who comes to visit Baal, only to learn: "The lads of Baal make answer: 'Baal is not in his house, [The God] Hadd in the midst of his palace. His bow he has taken in his hand, also his darts in his right hand. There he is on his way to Shimak Canebrake, the [buf]falo-filled" (ANET, 142a).

or perhaps he is asleep and will wake up. The humanness of the pagan gods can be read in all mythologies, so these words are no more scornful of Baal's divinity than the other mundane activities mentioned in the previous clauses. Further afield is the suggestion that the sleep referred to is the sleep of death; in Ugaritic mythology, Baal descends to the realm of the god Mot (death), bringing grief and mourning to the people (see Ackerman 1992, 84–88; ANET, 139); note also the proposed tracing of this detail, as well as the entire rite on Mount Carmel, to the celebration of "the awakening of Heracles" (attributed to Hiram of Tyre by Menander, quoted in Josephus, *Ant.* 8.146).

28. *they gashed themselves, as was their custom, with swords and spears until blood spilled over them.* The shedding of blood is associated in biblical sources with rites of mourning, probably an expression of extreme grief, and was outlawed for Israelites (Deut 14:1 uses **gdd* in *Hithpael*; Lev 19:28; 21:5: **ntn/śrṭ śrṭ[ṭ]*; cf. Jer 16:6; 41:5). By analogy, the Baal prophets in a moment of great distress resorted to a bloody rite in the hope that it would move Baal to action, thus extricating them from their predicament. Late Hellenistic examples of ecstatic lacerations (de Vaux 1971b, 242–43) can now be supplemented with a poetic line in an Akkadian wisdom text from Ugarit that refers to "ecstatics drenched in their own blood" (CAD M/1, 90a; see Roberts 1970).

29. *they raved.* Literally, "they prophesied"; they worked themselves into a prophetic frenzy; cf. 1 Sam 10:10; 19:20–24; also Num 11:25–26, of persons enthused by YHWH's spirit. For the parade example of frenzied possession of a Canaanite sacrificer reported in the late-eleventh-century BCE Egyptian text of Wen-Amon, see ANET, 26b.

until the hour of the meal offering. The preposition *'ad,* "until," with *lamed* is LBH usage (cf., e.g., 1 Chr 28:20; 2 Chr 32:24), while the older language uses either one or the other (e.g., Gen 32:25; 2 Kgs 20:1). The meal offering was set twice a day (Exod 29:38–42), in the early morning (cf. 2 Kgs 3:20) and in the evening (cf. 16:15), which is the one referred to here. For further use of the phrase as a time marker, cf. Ezra 9:4, 5. The activity of the Baal prophets continued until midafternoon; all the while (see time indication in v. 36), Elijah busied himself with preparing for his sacrifice.

But there was no sound and no one answering and no response. The same phrase as in v. 26 with the additional "and no response" (cf. 2 Kgs 4:31, where it appears with "there was no sound"); also Isa 21:7.

30. *Then Elijah said to all the people: "Come up to me." All the people came up to him.* Their proximity allowed them "to see all that he would do and not suspect him of deception" (Abarbanel; cf. Josephus, *Ant.* 8.340).

Then he proceeded to repair the destroyed altar of YHWH. The assumption seems to be that the altar had been destroyed as a result of Jezebel's hounding of YHWH's cult and its practitioners (cf. 19:10); all that was needed to make it functional again was to reassemble its scattered parts. This appears to be con-tradicted by the following description (vv. 31–32a), in which a new altar is built from scratch. But rather than detecting an early and late stratum in the text (as most commentators do), we may take v. 30b as a general statement, with its spec-ifications in the following verses (rabbinic *kĕlal ûpĕraṭ*; see Burney, Šanda). The rearrangement in LXX, moving v. 30b to follow v. 32, may be an attempt to ease perceived tensions.

Rabbinic exegetes defended the building of the altar as a "temporary regula-tion," suspending the regulation of Deut 12 because of the emergency situa-tion (see, e.g., *b. Yebam.* 90b; Qimḥi); modern commentators use it as marker of the pre-Deuteronomic era, when multiple altars were the rule (see further in the Introduction. Composition).

to repair. Literally, "to heal"; cf. the similar, figurative use in Jer 19:11 for a smashed clay vessel "that cannot be mended."

31. *Elijah took twelve stones according to the number of the tribes of the sons of Jacob.* Elijah's twelve-stone altar joins other symbolic constructions that mark the participation of "all Israel" in the proceedings being commemorated, e.g., Exod 24:4; Josh 4:1–9.

32. *he built an altar.* For the non-apocopated form of the verb, see Note on 1 Kgs 10:29.

He made a trough around the altar with a capacity of about two seahs of seed. The altar area was marked off by the trough that later contained the fire (cf. v. 38); its size is somewhat of a puzzle. Medieval exegetes understood the measure as referring to the area required to sow two *seahs* of seed (e.g., Rashi, Qimḥi). The *seah* is an inexact measure in the Bible, and Mishnaic calculation leads to an unreasonably large tract (1568 m² [Benzinger]) and certainly to a very sizable trench around such a field. If the capacity of the trough (Heb *tĕʿālâ*; translated "conduit" in 2 Kgs 18:17; 20:20) is what is meant, the amount may be insignif-icant; a *seah*-measure is approximately 7.3 liters (see Note on 2 Kgs 7:1), which would give a shallow 15-liter trench, maybe enough to be filled by 12 jars of water (cf. vv. 34–35). The reading by which Elijah is seen to have filled the trench with seed, later watered to make it sprout (so Gray, favored by Jones), in a "rite of imitative magic," requires importation of Palestinian peasant beliefs and much imagination.

He made a trough. The rather mundane Heb *tĕʿālâ*, "trench, channel, ditch" (cf. 2 Kgs 20:20; Isa 7:3; Ezek 31:4) has been caught up in the polemics concerning the date of the Siloam Tunnel, though it is not possible to translate it as "shaft" (as claimed by Rogerson and Davies 1996, 143; and correctly rejected by Norin 1998, 42–44).

34. *"Fill four jars with water and pour (it) on the offering and on the wood."* Elijah's unexplained order has been taken as "a guarantee against fraud" (Gray), as a charm for rain, after the pattern of the water libation at the altar of the Second Temple during the Sukkoth Festival (*m. Sukka* 4:9; see Patai 1939); more basic is the view that Elijah soaked the altar "so as to increase the miracle" (Qimḥi).

"Do it a third time." The verb **šlš* in *Piel* is also "divide into three parts" (Deut 19:3); the "third" activity in 1 Sam 20:19 is unclear.

35. *he also filled the trough with water.* Apparently as a precautionary barrier against the fire (cf. v. 38). The LXX reading of the verb in plural is not preferable, nor is the favored translation in the passive ("the trough *was filled*"); Elijah, together with the people, carried water to the altar site.

36. *Elijah the prophet came forward.* The title "prophet" is used nowhere else in the Elijah cycle. He stepped up to where he could be seen by the assembled crowd and addressed YHWH; cf. similar positioning in Gen 18:23; 44:18 (Simon 1997, 231).

"YHWH, God of Abraham, Isaac, and Israel! . . ." In this invocation of the fathers, the name *Israel* replaces *Jacob*; the formula used here appears again only in 1 Chr 29:18 and 2 Chr 30:6. Coming after v. 31, in which the name change is recalled, this "new" formula is to be expected.

37. *Answer me, YHWH, answer me.* The words are identical to the plea uttered by the Baal prophets (v. 26) and, in both instances, echo the terms of the test: "the god who answers by fire, he is God," as set out in v. 24.

it is you *who have turned their hearts backward.* The inscrutable idiom *hăsibbōtā ʾet libbām ʾāḥōrannît* has been understood in two contrary ways, both presented in NEB: "you have caused them to be backsliders," with the footnote: "Or 'thou dost bring them back to their allegiance.'" The latter sense, that YHWH, by his granting Elijah's request for fire, will bring about the people's "turning back" to him (Tg., Qimḥi [noted, but rejected], Skinner, Šanda, Simon, NAB, NJB), requires taking the verb as future, rather than as past, its most natural sense. In the past-parsing view, Elijah closes his prayer by acknowledging that it was YHWH, after all, who had brought about the people's apostasy, implying that it was in his power to bring about their return, if he so desired (with Greenberg [1981], in his survey of the varied medieval interpretations of this half-verse). For the ascription of man's sinful ways to YHWH, the master of all, cf. Isa 63:17.

38. *Then YHWH's fire descended and consumed the offering, the wood, the stones, and the dust.* The fiery apparition often symbolizes YHWH's presence (e.g., Exod 3:2; 19:18; 24:17), and, with reference to the altar inaugurations (Lev 9:24; 2 Chr 7:3), the fire attests divine approval and acceptance of the worshiper's act (1 Chr 21:26). On Mount Carmel, the consumption of the altar as well as the

sacrifice, all drenched in water, was an impressive show of YHWH's might. The specific notice that the altar was destroyed need not be an addition to the story by a late reader sensitive to the prophet's seeming sanction of a YHWH altar outside of Jerusalem in contradiction of Deuteronomic law (see further in Comment).

and licked up the water that was in the trough. The fire "dried them up, until there was no moisture in the trough" (Qimḥi); in this sense, *lḥk is used of the ox, said "to lick up/clean" the pasture (cf. Num 22:4).

39. *When the people saw this, they fell on their faces.* The awe-struck assembly looked away from YHWH's act of revelation; cf. the similar response at the altar dedications (cited above in v. 38).

"YHWH, He is God. YHWH, He is God." The submission of the people is phrased as an answer to Elijah's initial challenge in v. 24: "The god who answers by fire, he is God."

40. *They seized them, and Elijah took them down to Wadi Kishon and slaughtered them there.* With the people's help, Elijah personally carried out the purge of the Baal prophets. To judge the prophet's act (e.g., Montgomery and Gehman brand it "ugly") or to excuse it as "necessary retribution ordered by Elijah as the 'new Moses' on behalf of God" (Wiseman) or even to remove it as a late element introduced into the story "under the influence of Jehu's massacre of the devotees of Baal" (2 Kgs 10:18–28; Gray)—would be introducing contemporary moral sensitivity foreign to the text. The slaughter at the Kishon is no different than the one over which Moses presided at Mount Sinai (cf. Exod 32:26–28, cf. Simon 1997, 237–40); in his zealousness for YHWH (cf. 1 Kgs 19:10, 14), Elijah outstrips that of Phineas (cf. Num 25:7–8) and Samuel (1 Sam 15:32–33).

Wadi Kishon. The Kishon is identified with Wadi al-Muqatta, which gathers the run-off of many springs and streams in the Jezreel Valley in its course west, reaching the sea on the north side of Mount Carmel. It is mentioned again with reference to the battle of Deborah and Barak with Sisera in Judg 4:7, 13; 5:21; Ps 83:10. The site was chosen "so that their blood would not pollute the land; and on this account, it was spilled into the wadi that would carry it far off" (Gersonides ad 19:1).

41. *Elijah said to Ahab: "Go up, eat and drink. . . ."* Ahab had been a silent witness to the proceedings, both on the Carmel and down in the wadi. He is now bidden to resume his normal pursuits.

42. *He crouched on the ground and put his face between his knees.* A single action, and not two, is here described: Elijah drew up his feet (for *ghr, used in the description of Elisha's revival of the son of the Shunammite, see Note on 2 Kgs 4:34), and, in deep concentration, he apparently prayed for rain. Resort to this meditative position in mystical circles is known in postbiblical and medieval Judaism and in Islamic Sufism, examples of which are collected in Fenton 1994; earlier, by Mach and Marks 1960.

43. *He said to his attendant: "Go up. Look toward the sea."* The prophet's servant was on the mountaintop with him (cf. v. 41); here he is commanded to ascend even higher, to one of the peaks of the Carmel, for the best view.

44. *He said: "Go. Say to Ahab. . . ."* Literally, "Go up"; the sense is not movement from a lower place to a higher one but "present, position oneself," as in Num 16:12; Josh 10:4.

Hitch up (your chariot) and go down. That is, leave the mountain area and descend into the Jezreel Valley toward the town of Jezreel.

so that the rain will not stop you. The extended form of pronominal suffix *-kh* for the common *-k* , exhibited in *yʿṣrkh* is typical of texts written during the late Second Temple period, represented at Qumran; it is rare in MT; cf. Gen 10:19; 27:7. On the orthographical question, see Cross and Freedmann 1952, 65–67.

45. *By that time.* The reduplication of *ʿad kô* "until now" (cf. Exod 7:16) indicates the passage of time during which the prophet's order in v. 44 was fulfilled.

Ahab mounted up and went to Jezreel. The same sequence of verbs is used of Jehu in 2 Kgs 9:16; see Note there for the nuances of *rkb.

46. *and, as the hand of YHWH had come upon Elijah.* Divine possession invigorated Elijah and gave him the strength to run all the way to Jezreel. In other instances, the expression indicates the coming of the divine word to the prophet (2 Kgs 3:15); it is a favorite of Ezekiel, indicating "extraordinary sensory experiences" (Greenberg 1983b, 41–42, ad Ezek 1:5).

he bound up his loins. That is, he wrapped up the outer garment about his loins to leave his legs free for running. The verb *šns appears only here, and it may be related to MH *šnṣ, "to lace, strap (a sandal)"; cf. like expressions with the verbs *ḥgr (e.g., 2 Kgs 4:29; 9:1); *ʾzr (Jer 1:17), all describing action taken in preparation for a vigorous undertaking.

ran in front of Ahab all the way to Jezreel. Elijah took up the role of one of Ahab's outrunners (see Note to 1:5), showing the respect due him as king after the victory over Baal and his worshipers, and Ahab's return to the national God.

to Jezreel. The royal family had an estate at Jezreel, which was about 27 km from Mount Carmel; see further the Note at 21:1.

COMMENT

Structure and Themes

Five scenes of varying lengths follow YHWH's word to Elijah (v. 1) that he appear before Ahab to announce the end of the drought: (1) vv. 2b–6; (2) 7–16a; (3) 16b–19; (4) 20–40; (5) 41–46. Criticism has argued against the unity of the narrative, pointing to major discontinuities between the scenes. For example, the issue of the drought is addressed only in (1) and (5), while the "battle of the gods" directed by Elijah is the subject of the extensive scene (4). The drought seems far from Mount Carmel; the true god, after all, was to make himself known by producing fire, not rain. Furthermore Ahab, with whom Elijah meets and speaks in (3), goes unmentioned throughout (4), only to reappear in (5). That Elijah has a servant at his call is unstated anywhere, until his abrupt introduction in v. 43. The encounter in (2) between Obadiah and the prophet appears secondary to the matter at hand. The conclusion of many, therefore, has been that two or more strands of tradition have been brought together in 1 Kgs 18 (for a short synopsis of the various dissections, see Long, 190; Long's very detailed structural analysis [188–90] "investigate[s] the sense of unity for the final composite form").[1]

But the division of 1 Kgs 18 into two separate stories, their focus being the drought and the contest on Mount Carmel, respectively, is hypercritical. The two foci are not independent of one another but are intimately entwined. The contest, detached from the preceding scenes, is left without introduction and motivation. The competition between YHWH and Baal regarding which of them is the true (and only!) God becomes significant by recalling the story's subtext: the god Baal was viewed in Canaanite mythology as the bringer of rain (among his epithets was *rkb ʿrpt*, "Rider of clouds"), and the cycle of Baal's death and revival (see Note to v. 27) is pertinent to the drought theme no less than it is to the question of his godhead. Consequently, the long-sought reprieve from the drought promised by YHWH in the opening verse materialized once YHWH's supremacy had been manifested and acknowledged on Mount Carmel, and Israel declared its undivided loyalty to YHWH.

The Obadiah–Elijah conversation in (2), rich in background details, provides insight for the hearer/reader into the state of affairs in Samaria during Elijah's absence abroad; the story of loyal Obadiah's saving one hundred prophets underscores the potential danger to Elijah in meeting Ahab. It also reveals Elijah's forceful presence; as in Zarephath, so in Israel, the supporting actors must be won over in order to fulfill the prophet's command.

From the literary perspective, 1 Kgs 18 shares a number of compositional techniques with other biblical narratives. The storyteller moves the plot forward mostly by means of dialogue rather than description; e.g., between Ahab and Obadiah (v. 5), Obadiah and Elijah (vv. 7–15), Ahab and Elijah (vv. 17–19, 41), Elijah and the people (vv. 21–24, 30, 34, 40), Elijah and the prophets of Baal (vv. 25, 27), Elijah and his attendant (vv. 43–44). The detailed description of Elijah's activity in preparing the altar only retards the action (e.g., vv. 31–33, 35). Key words create verbal echoes, further uniting the scenes within themselves, e.g., *bĕhakrît / nakrît* (vv. 4–5); *pōsĕḥîm / waypassĕḥû* (vv. 21, 26); *ʿanēnû / ʿêyn ʿôneh / ʿanēnî* (vv. 26, 29, 37); *wattippôl / wayyippĕlû* (v. 38).

History

The legendary accounts concerning Elijah's activities are not the most desirable source upon which to base a history of the reign of Ahab. In their narrow focus upon the battle against the cult of Baal in Israel, these stories "vilify the enemy," which one expects of partisan literature. Measured speculation can try

---

[1] There are no signs of the editor's working-up of the material, so the present form of the story was probably achieved in the pre-Dtr stage of the tradition.

to rectify the imbalance, remembering all the while that the case for Ahab and Jezebel in the story has not reached us.

King Ahab as portrayed in 1 Kgs 18 does not wholly match the negative image promulgated by Dtr in his epitome (cf. 16:30–33); he is not unswerving in his animosity to Elijah and his God. Thus, at the meeting between Elijah and Ahab when the two adversaries finally faced each other, they exchanged mutual accusations but continued on together to Mount Carmel! The king had acceded to the prophet's demand to arrange the convocation of prophets; at its conclusion, in the victory of YHWH, he would submit to Elijah who, in turn, would display his support of Ahab's rule as one of the king's outrunners. Ahab "the sinner" was won back to YHWH. Other traditions, as well, suggest that the "historical" Ahab had not abandoned Israel's God. In his personal life, the king acknowledged YHWH by giving his sons YHWHistic names (Ahaziah and Jehoram) and, in the public sphere, he is pictured as consulting with prophets of YHWH (cf. 1 Kgs 22), who for their part, supported their king.

The portrayal of Jezebel as a zealot of Baal who undertook to exterminate the prophets of YHWH is a caricature, with little to recommend it.[2] The intolerance that it implies is inconsistent with pagan thought. The exclusiveness of the worship of YHWH to the exclusion of other gods is a feature of monotheism, and it is misleadingly attributed to the cult of Baal (1 Kgs 18:21). Jezebel's behavior becomes understandable when viewed as a political response to the opposition raised by the loyal servants of YHWH to the foreign cults that had been introduced into Israel's capital upon her arrival (Kaufmann 1960, 140).[3] As suggested (in Comment to 1 Kgs 16), the building of a temple of Baal in Samaria followed naturally the joining of the royal houses of Israel and Tyre; the influence of the cult of Baal on the population at large cannot be measured by the heat generated by prophetic propaganda.

There is also no way in which the root of the tradition concerning the contest on Mount Carmel can be recovered. Beyond the recognition that the numbers "four hundred and fifty" and "four hundred" in 1 Kgs 18:19, like the "four hundred" in 22:6, are typological and can surely be reduced, the circumstances under which the king would have condoned the wholesale slaughter described are an enigma. The hypothesis of a "battle and victory at Mount Carmel (including the massacre of the prophets of Baal)" by the "revolutionary," conservative forces led by Elijah (M. A. Cohen 1975, 93*; see also Noth 1960, 242

---

[2] The prophetic view has made its way into many modern readings of the times; see, e.g., Bright 1981, 245: Jezebel was "a strong-minded woman filled with an almost missionary zeal for her god and no doubt contemptuous of the cultural backwardness and austere religion of her adopted land"; also Gray, 390: the persecutions were the result of the "positive policy of the Phoenician queen"; DeVries, 204: "Jezebel was extremely assertive and intolerant"; et al.

[3] The so-called "persecutions" of Antiochus IV against the Jews is another example of the repression of political opponents through the outlawing of the Law of Moses, a reaction to open rebellion (with Tcherikover 1959, 175–203).

n. 5; Alt 1953, 147) reads well but inevitably cannot be substantiated. Whatever success is claimed by the prophetic tradition for Elijah's efforts, it was limited at best; not until the end of the Omride rule and the rise of a new dynasty was the cult of Baal rooted out from Samaria (cf. 2 Kgs 10:18–28).[4]

---

[4] The reading of the Elijah tales by White (1997), which takes the majority of them to be the product of "highly literate scribes of the Jehu dynasty to legitimate its overthrow of the Omrides and to shore up its power" (p. 43), reduces the prophet to a "legendary rain-inducer" (p. 32), not much to go on when seeking the historical Elijah.

XXXV. ELIJAH'S JOURNEY TO HOREB

(19:1–21)

19 [1]Ahab told Jezebel all that Elijah had done and how he killed all the prophets by the sword. [2]Whereupon, Jezebel sent a messenger to Elijah: "[a]May the gods do thus (to me)[b] and even more if by this time tomorrow I have not made your life like the life of one of them." [3]He was afraid,[c] and so he set out to save his life.

He came to Beer-sheba, which is in Judah, and he left his attendant there, [4]while he himself went a day's journey into the steppe. He came and sat down under a[d] broom tree; he prayed that he might die and said: "Enough! Now, O YHWH, take my life, for I am no better than my ancestors." [5]Then he lay down and fell asleep under a broom tree. Suddenly, an angel was touching him, and said to him: "Get up! Eat!" [6]He looked and there, at his head, was a cake (baked on a hot) stone and a flask of water. [e]He ate and drank and then lay down again. [7]The angel of YHWH came back a second time; he touched him and said: "Get up! Eat, for the road is too much for you." [8]So he got up and ate and drank. Then he walked by the strength of that food forty days and forty nights to the mountain of God, Horeb.

[9]There he went into a cave, and there he spent the night. Suddenly, the word of YHWH came to him. He said to him: "What are you doing here, Elijah?" [10]He said: "I have been most zealous for YHWH, the God of hosts, for the Israelites have abandoned your covenant, your altars they have destroyed, and your prophets they have killed by the sword. And I, I alone am left, and they have sought my life to take it." [11]He said: "Go out and stand on the mountain before YHWH. Lo, YHWH is passing by, and a great and mighty wind, rending mountains and shattering rocks is before YHWH. But YHWH is not in the wind. And after the wind, an earthquake. But YHWH is not in the earthquake. [12]And after the earthquake, fire. But YHWH is not in the fire. And after the fire, the sound of sheer silence." [13]When Elijah heard (this), he covered his face with his cloak; he went out and stood at the entrance of the cave. Then a voice came to him and said: "What are you doing here, Elijah?" [14]He said: "I have been most zealous for YHWH, the God of hosts, for the Israelites have abandoned your covenant, your altars they have destroyed, and your prophets they have killed by the sword. And I, I alone am left, and they sought to take my life."

---

[a] LXX adds: "As you are Elijah and I am Jezebel;" see Note.

[b] Added by many MSS and LXX; see Note.

[c] For MT: *wayyar'*, "he saw" read *wayyirā'* with LXX, Syr., and some MSS (a few with plene *wyyr'*).

[d] Ketib *'ht*; qere *'ḥd*; the opposite alteration is noted by Minḥat Shay in v. 5.

[e] LXX adds: "he got up" (as in v. 8).

[15]Then YHWH said to him: "Go, be on your way, toward the wilderness of Damascus. You are to go and anoint Hazael as king over Aram, [16]and Jehu son of Nimshi you will anoint as king over Israel, and Elisha son of Shaphat of Abel-meholah you will anoint as prophet in your place. [17]Whoever escapes the sword of Hazael, Jehu shall kill, and whoever escapes the sword of Jehu, Elisha shall kill. [18]I will leave seven thousand in Israel, every knee that has not bent to Baal and every mouth that has not kissed him."

[19]So he went from there, and he found Elisha son of Shaphat; he was plowing. There were twelve teams ahead of him, and he was with the twelfth. Elijah went over to him and threw his cloak over him. [20]He left the oxen and ran after Elijah and said: "Let me kiss[f] my father and my mother, and then I will follow you." He said to him: "Go. Go back. For what have I done to you?" [21]He turned from him; and he took a yoke of oxen and slaughtered them,[g] and with the ox-gear he boiled their meat;[h] then he gave to the people and they ate. Then he rose and followed Elijah and became his attendant.

---

[f] MT Leningrad and Aleppo Codex read: *'eššĕqâ*; many MSS: *'eššoqâ* (see GKC, 10h).

[g] Hebrew "it."

[h] Lit., "he boiled them, the meat"; see Note.

NOTES

19   1. *how he killed all the prophets.* The MT reads *'t kl 'šr* twice, the second instance of *kl* is redundant, coming before the "all of the prophets"; it is best to omit the word, as do all versions (except Tg.). For *'t 'šr*, cf. 8:31; 2 Kgs 8:12.

2. *May the gods do thus (to me) and even more.* This familiar oath contains the pronoun in most other instances, e.g., 1 Kgs 2:23; 20:10; 2 Kgs 6:31; in 1 Sam 14:44, it is lacking in MT and added by the versions, as here. The addition in LXX, "As you are Elijah and I am Jezebel," is considered original by Thenius, Burney, Gunkel, and Simon; others are impressed by the "fine and unique psychological note" (Montgomery and Gehman) but are puzzled about how it was lost from MT (Stade and Schwally). The imperious sound of these words— You may be Elijah, but I am Jezebel—is in character for this self-confident queen (cf. 21:7, 15; 2 Kgs 9:31; as discussed by Eissfeldt 1967).

3. *He was afraid.* Read *wayyîrā'*, with most versions and some MSS. MT, *wayyar'*, "he saw," is meaningless and, if taken as "he understood" (cf., e.g., Exod 3:4; 8:11), the object of the verb is lacking (cf. Qimḥi: "He saw that he was in danger"). The mistaken vocalization in MT cannot be explained as avoidance of the discrepancy between the present depiction of Elijah and the bravery he displayed on Mount Carmel (Jones); fear for his own personal safety accompanies the prophet throughout the present episode.

he set out to save his life. A pregnant construction. The two verbs *wayyāqom wayyēlek* "he set right out" (see Note on 17:10) have as their object "for the sake of his life"; cf. **nws 'l npš* (2 Kgs 7:7); more frequently **mlṭ 'l npš* (e.g., Gen 19:17; 1 Sam 19:11). There was enough time for Elijah to make his escape, inasmuch as Jezebel did not move immediately to apprehend her enemy; in sending a messenger, the queen so much as suggested to Elijah that he had better be off. Or was this really a "confession of impotence" on her part, as Skinner suggested? After the setback at Carmel, she may have felt that she no longer had a free hand in pursuing her course, as she did when she cut down prophets with impunity.

He came to Beer-sheba, which is in Judah. The note that the town was in Judah (cf. similarly, Beth-shemesh in Judah [2 Kgs 14:11]; Socoh in Judah [1 Sam 17:1]) was meant to indicate that he had left Ahab's realm; moreover, he had reached the border of the kingdom of Judah (note the expression "from Dan to Beer-sheba"). Only the wilderness lay ahead of him.

he left his attendant there. Elijah was accompanied by a personal servant, as befitted a man of stature. But what was to follow was a private matter, between Elijah and his God; so he went on alone, as did Abraham and Isaac in Gen 22:5.

4. *into the steppe.* The translation "wilderness" (NEB, NJPSV), as well as "desert" (NAB, NJB), for Heb *midbār* does not do justice to a term that refers to the steppe, which can sustain nomads and their flocks (cf. Num 14:33). It is the place to which the herds of sheep and goats are "driven" (from **dbr*, with Ibn-Janaḥ and Qimḥi).

a broom tree. A desert shrub (*Retama roetam*) common to the Negev and Sinai, used by nomads as fuel (cf. Ps 120:4), and even eaten in times of great want (Job 30:4).

that he might die. The same idiom appears in Jonah 4:8. Though the narrator described Elijah's leaving of Samaria as a flight for his life (v. 3), he corrects this impression by an ironic touch: Elijah in fact wanted to die but not by the hand of Jezebel (with Zakovitch 1981–1982, 332).

for I am no better than my ancestors. Elijah no longer saw himself as the bearer of a special relationship with YHWH and, in utter despair, asked that he die, as do all men.

5. *fell asleep under a broom tree.* The repetition of "under a broom tree" (as in v. 4) is unusual. The LXX translates "there under a bush," which suggests that the words may have been a marginal gloss to an original "there." The gloss could have arisen in the course of correcting the gender of the adjective *'eḥāt* (v. 4) to *'eḥād* (v. 5); so Stade and many commentators.

an angel was touching him. The same word, *mal'āk*, is translated "messenger" in v. 2; for a similar use of both senses of the word, see 2 Kgs 1:15 and Note there. Further ahead, in v. 7, the divine source of the messenger is identified, as if only then did it become clear to Elijah just who his interlocutor was. The LXX omits "angel" in the present verse and reads simply: "(some)one" (*zeh*), which increases the mystery of the moment.

6. *at his head.* Hebrew *měra'ăšōt* is "the place at the head" used adverbially; cf. Gen 28:11; 1 Sam 19:13.

a cake (baked on a hot) stone. The word for "cake" (*'ūgâ*) is the same one used in I Kgs 17:13. Hebrew *riṣpâ* is properly a "stone," used for paving (Ezek 40:17; Esth 1:6); cf. *mrṣpt* in 2 Kgs 16:17. In the present verse and Isa 6:6, it is a heated stone. For bread baked directly in ashes, see Ezek 4:12 (and the descriptive note in Greenberg 1983b, 107).

a flask of water. Another echo of the earlier drought tale is the unusual word for "flask" (*ṣappaḥat*); cf. 1 Kgs 17:12, 16.

He ate and drank. Miraculous feeding is not unusual in the Elijah tradition; cf. 17:6, 15–16.

7. *The angel of YHWH came back a second time.* The specification that the messenger was from YHWH, which was not noted in v. 5, is not reason enough to think of two separate beings. Only at its second appearance was the divine presence identified.

"Get up! Eat, for the road is too much for you." "The second meal was concerned with future needs [i.e., the long trek to Horeb], the first one was for past needs [i.e., the self-inflicted fast Elijah had undertaken from Samaria to the wilderness of Beersheba]" (Abarbanel).

8. *Then he walked by the strength of that food forty days and forty nights to the mountain of God, Horeb.* Though no direct command had been given, Elijah knew to continue on to Horeb.

forty days and forty nights. The typological number "forty" adds a legendary aspect to the journey, a long distance into the wilderness; it should not be pressed into locating the mountain (contra Šanda). On the echoes of the Moses traditions in this number and in other story elements, see Comment.

to the mountain of God, Horeb. The mountain of YHWH was known in Pentateuchal traditions both as Horeb (e.g., Exod 3:1; 33:6 [the "E" strand]; Deut 1:6; 4:10; cf. 1 Kgs 8:9) and as Sinai (Exod 19:11, 20 [the "J" strand]; Lev 25:1). It seems that the location of the mountain was lost to tradition, since it was not the site of pilgrimage (as sometimes claimed; e.g., Gray citing Noth); therefore, much controversy surrounds the location of Mount Horeb/Sinai. The commonly-held identification with Jebel Musa in the southern Sinai Peninsula, not known earlier than the Byzantine Age, is challenged by other mountain sites farther north and in the Negev, all dependent on the reconstructed route of the Israelite wanderings; see *EncJud* 14:597–600; and Davies 1979, 63–69.

9. *There he went into a cave.* The MT has "the cave"; on the use of the definite in Hebrew, cf. 18:4. It does not refer to a particular cave at Horeb, which some identify with "the crevice of a rock" where Moses had stood (cf. Exod 33:22), though the echo of that earlier stay on the mountain can be heard. See further in Comment.

He said to him: "What are you doing here, Elijah?" A rhetorical question that serves as an opening to the conversation; cf. Gen 4:9.

10. *"I have been most zealous for YHWH. . . ."* For Heb *qinnē*', "to be zealous," see Note on 14:22.

for the Israelites have abandoned your covenant. This is a surprising accusation, following as it does the contest on Mount Carmel, during which the wayward people acknowledged YHWH (cf. 18:39). It is either part of the prophet's exaggerated rhetoric or else indicates that the Horeb tale was originally independent of the one concerning Carmel. Further evidence for separation of the two tales is that the Israelites, not Jezebel, are taken as the perpetrators of the crimes that follow.

your altars they have destroyed. The altar to YHWH on Mount Carmel was noted as having been destroyed; cf. 18:30.

your prophets they have killed by the sword. Jezebel's persecution is referred to in 18:4.

And I, I alone am left. Elijah made this point at Carmel (cf. 18:22), where he also ignored the one hundred prophets saved by Obadiah.

and they have sought my life to take it. Before his victory over the prophets of Baal, Elijah was a wanted person (cf. 18:10); after the slaughter of these prophets, Jezebel warned him that his life was forfeit (19:2).

11–12. *He said: "Go out and stand on the mountain before YHWH. Lo, YHWH is passing by, and a great and mighty wind, rending mountains and shattering rocks is before YHWH. But YHWH is not in the wind. And after the wind, an earthquake. But YHWH is not in the earthquake. And after the earthquake, fire. But YHWH is not in the fire. And after the fire, the sound of sheer silence."* The divine word to Elijah included a full description of the theophany that the prophet would experience from his place on the mountain. Taken this way, the narrative lacks a recounting that this did in fact occur, but the elliptical style familiar from other narratives does not require such a repetition (cf., e.g., 1 Kgs 21:17–20, where the fulfillment of YHWH's command is skipped over); so, with Simon 1997, 265–66; see also Walsh, 274–75. In the present instance, repetition might have spoiled the impact of the scene just described. [DNF: "The explanation given to defend the omission is in defense of the existing text but is dramatically and literarily unsound."]

a great and mighty wind . . . an earthquake . . . fire. The startled and frightened reaction of nature to the appearance of YHWH is a standard image in early poetry (Judg 5:4–5; Hab 3:3–6; taken up in Ps 18:8–10; 68:9) and prose (Exod 19:16, 18; 20:18). In the theophany that Elijah was to experience, the elements precede YHWH, almost like messengers proclaiming the approach of the divine (cf. Ps 104:4).

the sound of sheer silence. So NRSV, a successful approximation of the assonance of the Hebrew text; yet it is hard to relinquish altogether the classic rendition of KJV: "a still small voice." The seemingly contradictory terms "sound" and "silence" appear together (as a hendiadys?) in the apparition described by Eliphaz in Job 4:16. In the utter stillness that followed the storm, Elijah heard a voice and YHWH's speaking to him; the intimation seems to be that this is the desired mode of discourse between the prophet and the divine presence. Some LXX MSS add pedantically, "YHWH is there" (cf. Ezek 48:35).

13. *When Elijah heard (this), he covered his face with his cloak.* Elijah's instinctive reaction to hide from the divine presence is like that of Gideon (Judg 6:22) and Manoah (13:20–22); comparison may also be made between the prophet and Moses, who was sheltered by YHWH as He passed by him (cf. Exod 33:22–23). But while in the case of Moses the concern was viewing YHWH, here it is hearing him in all his power.

he covered his face. Heb **lwṭ*, "to wrap," a rare verb, here in *Hiphil*; cf. also 1 Sam 21:10; 2 Sam 19:5; Isa 25:7.

15. *toward the wilderness of Damascus.* The same form of construct with the *he' locale* occurs in Josh 18:12. The road Elijah was to take in order to reach Damascus is otherwise unknown; perhaps it is a reference to the King's Highway, the north–south pike that reached this oasis-city on the edge of the desert.

anoint Hazael as king over Aram. Elijah had no contact with Hazael; rather, it was Elisha who foretold Hazael's seizing of the throne of Aram-Damascus. For the name Hazael and his identification, see 2 Kgs 8:8 and Note there.

anoint. Anointing was a sign of investiture and was restricted to kings and priests; prophets were never anointed. The verb **mšh* does not mean "to set apart" (so Gray, apologetically redeeming Elijah for his noncompliance with YHWH's order; Simon, too, ascribes a metaphorical meaning to the verb [1997, 267]). Abarbanel suggested that Elijah transferred the tasks to Elisha; cf. 2 Kgs 9:6.

16. *Jehu son of Nimshi.* In 2 Kgs 9:2, Nimshi is Jehu's grandfather; see Note, ad loc.

you will anoint as king over Israel. One of Elisha's attendants anointed Jehu (2 Kgs 9:6), not Elijah.

Elisha son of Shaphat of Abel-meholah, you will anoint as prophet in your place. Prophets were not, as a rule, anointed, and indeed, in the following scene, Elijah does not anoint Elisha (cf. v. 19).

Elisha son of Shaphat. The name *Elisha* is known from Samaria ostracon no. 1 and several seal impressions (WSS, nos. 916 [Ammonite], 975, 979 [Hebrew]); it seems to mean "God saves, delivers" (parsing **yšᶜ* as a verb in *Qal*).

Abel-meholah. Located in the Jordan Valley, south of Beth-shean; see the Note at 4:12.

17. *Whoever escapes the sword of Hazael, Jehu shall kill, and whoever escapes the sword of Jehu, Elisha shall kill.* The course of history as told in the Elisha cycle is much different from the one foretold here. Jehu undertook to root out Baal worship (cf. 2 Kgs 10:18–28); Hazael was responsible for subduing Israel's armed forces (cf. 8:12; 13:3, 22); and Elisha is not known to have been involved in any act, violent or otherwise, against idolators, though he did support the rise of Jehu. On the implications of these discrepancies, see Comment.

18. *I will leave seven thousand in Israel.* This is a round number, based on the number *seven*, and hardly "an authentic note of some census taken of the Zealots" (Montgomery and Gehman). Besides, a slaughter of civilians of such proportion as to leave only seven thousand survivors is unattested, the decimation of the army notwithstanding (cf. 2 Kgs 13:7).

every knee that has not bent to Baal. Kneeling was a sign of submission that often accompanied prayer (e.g., 1 Kgs 8:54; Ezra 9:5; cf. 2 Kgs 1:13); it is not a reference to a rite peculiar to the worship of Baal (contra de Vaux 1971b, 241).

and every mouth that has not kissed him. A similar act of reverence, the "kissing the (molten) calves" was decried by Hosea (Hos 13:2). Kissing the feet of the (statue of the) god is attested in Mesopotamian ritual; for examples, see CAD N/2, 58–60 (*inter alia*).

19. *He found Elisha son of Shaphat; he was plowing.* This detail conveys more than local color; Elisha's prosaic background points up the divine quality of his selection; cf. 1 Sam 11:5–6; Amos 7:14–15.

There were twelve teams ahead of him. The large number of teams is generally taken as a sign of wealth; it was this that Elisha would have to give up if he were to follow Elijah.

Elijah went over to him and threw his cloak over him. Elijah is the first prophet to be identified with a cloak as a sign of his calling (cf. Zech 13:4 and the Note on 2 Kgs 1:8). Persons in positions of authority generally dressed in garb befitting their office (cf., e.g., 1 Kgs 22:10; Esth 6:8); inauguration of a successor sometimes included the symbolic transfer of the predecessor's robes, cf. Num 20:25–28. In the case of Elisha, only later was his master's cloak to be his; cf. 2 Kgs 2:1–15.

20. *He left the oxen and ran after Elijah and said: "Let me kiss my father and my mother, and then I will follow you."* Though no words have been exchanged between them, Elisha understood the significance of having been wrapped in the prophet's cloak.

Let me kiss my father and my mother. This note on leave-taking from loved ones (cf. Gen 31:28) contributes to the characterization of Elisha; the popular tales portray him as the caring and compassionate father to the Sons of the Prophets (2 Kgs 2–8, *inter alia*).

"Go. Go back. . . ." An attempt is made here to capture the sense of the two imperative verbs in the MT; the single command "Go back!"—the rendition of all translations—is less forceful. The prophet sought "to test him, whether he (Elisha) had spoken wholeheartedly" (Qimḥi).

For what have I done to you? Elijah challenged Elisha by denying that there was any significance to the cloak thrown over him or that he had demanded anything of him.

21. *slaughtered them.* The verb *zbḥ* refers here to slaughter for food and not sacrifice, one of the few instances of this meaning; cf. Deut 12:15; 1 Sam 28:24; 2 Chr 18:2.

with the ox-gear. David too used the wood of the yoke for his sacrifice at Araunah's threshing floor; cf. 2 Sam 24:22.

he boiled their meat. Literally, "he boiled them, the meat." The plural suffix after the singular suffix of "he slaughtered it" (i.e., the yoke of oxen); and though there are examples of the pronominal suffix anticipating the object (e.g., 21:13; 2 Kgs 16:15), *habbāśār*, "the meat," is strange. It is lacking in Luc. and LXX and may be a gloss; see also GKC, 131m.

then he gave to the people and they ate. The feast was more than a parting meal with friends; the entire scene is emblematic of Elisha's break with his past, which he gave up to become the prophet's personal servant.

became his attendant. Like Joshua, who served Moses for years prior to being appointed his successor (cf. Exod 33:11; Num 11:28; Josh 1:1), Elisha attended Elijah. The NEB's "disciple" has overtones foreign to Heb *mšrt*, a term for ministering by priests (1 Kgs 8:11), royal servants (10:5; cf. 1:4), and angels (Ps 103:21).

COMMENT

Structure and Themes

This chapter rounds off the cycle of tales concerning Elijah's struggle with Ahab and Jezebel over the worship of Baal in Israel; a new climax, after the victory on Mount Carmel, is reached with the theophany at Horeb and the appointment of a successor to the prophet. At the same time, there is a sense of discontinuity between the business on Mount Carmel and that on Horeb. Elijah ostensively took flight because of the personal threat to his life for having "killed all of the prophets by the sword" (19:1), yet he does not raise this subject with YHWH. Deep despair, expressive of failure, and the rejection of the prophetic office are the paramount themes. The reader is not prepared for the charge brought by the prophet against the Israelites that they, not Ahab (cf. 18:18), had abandoned the covenant, especially after their reported acknowledgment of YHWH as the one and only God on Mount Carmel (18:39). Based on this accusation alone, the punishment of Israel, of whom only seven thousand faithful would be saved (19:18), seems overly severe. Thus, as seen by most critiques, 1 Kgs 19 was originally an independent narrative, now editorially joined to 1 Kgs 17–18 (specifically by 19:1–3aα; note also the linguistic and thematic echoes of 18:4, 10, 22, and 30 in 19:10). The joining of the two units could have been accomplished in the pre-Dtr stage of transmission, when Elijah's trip to Horeb was interpreted as a moment of truth and closure for the prophet.

Among the prominent themes of 1 Kgs 19 is the return of Elijah "on Israel's tracks to the mountain of revelation, and there he receives the revelation" (Buber 1960, 77). Throughout, the narrator has creatively used motifs associated with Moses, enriching his tale with literary allusions that, at times, attain verbal resemblance to the earlier tradition.[1] Elijah journeyed forty days into the desert in order to reach the mountain of God (v. 8), where Moses had spent "forty days and forty nights" receiving the Law (Exod 24:18); during his second stay on the mountain, Moses did not take bread or water (cf. 34:28), while Elijah made his long trek to Horeb sustained only by the food he had consumed in the wilderness near Beer-sheba (1 Kgs 19:8). Elijah cáme to a cave on Horeb (v. 8) and was bidden to take his place on the mountain as YHWH passed by, just as Moses had stood in "the crevice of a rock" for a similar theophany (Exod 33:22). When YHWH "was passing by" (1 Kgs 19:11), Elijah "covered his face with his cloak" (v. 13); Moses was privileged with having YHWH "cover" him with his hand (Exod 33:23; at the burning bush, Moses himself hid his face [3:6]). YHWH's appearance to Israel at Sinai in fire and thunder (Exod 19:18; cf. 3:2) is reenacted

---

[1] The suggestion to take the repetition in vv. 9b–10 and 13b–14 as a *Wiederaufnahme* that marks off the theophany in vv. 11–13a as "a subsequent interpolation" (Würthwein 1983, 160–61) deprives the narrative of many of its ties with the stories of Moses and impoverishes the basic story greatly.

for Elijah (1 Kgs 19:11–12).[2] One may even find an echo of Elijah's zeal for YHWH (vv. 10, 14), if not in Moses himself, then in the act of zeal performed by Phineas when he killed two persons worshiping Baal Peor, an act commended by Moses (Num 25:6–15). And like Moses, who was not permitted to enter the Promised Land but only to see it from afar, Elijah was not to attain the final triumph over Baal but only to know that it would be accomplished by his successors. In sum, Elijah is depicted as having reached the pinnacle of his career, privileged with a personal revelation of Moses-like dimensions.

Yet "Elijah is no new Moses!" (Childs 1980). His confidence in his role as prophet to a wayward people was not restored by his exposure to the power of YHWH or by the divine word. He remained unmoved and repeated his complaints, word for word (vv. 10 and 14); nothing had changed. So, in answer to this continued stubbornness, YHWH ordered him to anoint three aggressive actors, Hazael, Jehu, and Elisha, who would carry out the punishment of the apostate Israelites; the last appointee was to be the prophet's designated successor. Elijah had, in effect, been relieved of his mission, if not altogether dismissed as the prophet of YHWH.[3]

The word of YHWH in vv. 15–18 and Elijah's incomplete execution of His commands in vv. 19–21 suggest that two separate fragments of tradition are juxtaposed in the present text. YHWH bid Elijah to anoint three persons to carry forward his life's work. But Elijah did not anoint any of them; he made no contact with either Hazael or Jehu and, concerning Elisha, he merely threw his wrap upon him (v. 19). Furthermore, these two traditions stand in opposition to others that are preserved in the Elisha cycle. In that cycle, Elisha succeeded to the prophetic office after the assumption of Elijah in a fiery chariot (2 Kgs 2:1–18), and it was Elisha who saw to the anointment of Jehu (cf. 2 Kgs 9:1–13) and met with Hazael in Damascus and forecast the Aramean's rise to the throne (8:8–15). These discrepancies speak to the independence of the Elijah traditions, originating at a time before the Elisha cycle was set; a late tradent would hardly have developed and passed on to posterity prophecies that were contrary to acknowledged "facts." The word of YHWH to Elijah (1 Kgs 19:15–18) provided answers to several issues that must have concerned Elijah's followers.

---

[2] The rejection of storm and fire as indicators of YHWH's presence, in favor of the audible silence, suggests to some that the passage meant to correct, as it were, the revelation at Mount Sinai in Exod 19–20 in its emphasis on the overwhelming power of the deity. Yet if this were the meaning here, it would contradict the following commission of Elijah, which promised vengeful action against all who abandoned YHWH (1 Kgs 19:17–18). Besides, fire from heaven was the confirming sign of YHWH's godhood in 1 Kgs 18. "With an Old Testament theophany everything depends upon the pronouncement: the phenomena which accompany it are always merely accessories" (von Rad 1965, 19). Nor is the preference for silence a polemic against the thunderous voice of Baal, the storm-god (so Cross 1973, 194). The nondivinity of Baal had been proved ultimately on Mount Carmel, and that issue seems extraneous to the present context.

[3] That 1 Kgs 19 describes the effective end of Elijah's career was considered by some medieval commentators (Rashi, Qimḥi, Gersonides); this reading of the story has been adopted in many recent studies (e.g., Childs 1980; Cohn 1982).

The prophet had been only partially successful in his efforts against the spread of the cult of Baal in Israel. But this delay was part of YHWH's plan because He was the master of history. The preservation of both traditions likely goes beyond the desire to affirm YHWH's role in history; rather the commission of Elijah to the two kings and one prophet was seen as associating the master with later chapters in Israel's history: the final battles against Baal worship were set into motion by Elijah.

XXXVI. AHAB AND BEN-HADAD: THE EARLY WARS

(20:1–43)

20 ¹Now Ben-hadad king of Aram gathered all his forces, with him thirty-two kings and horses and chariots. He advanced and laid siege to Samaria and attacked it. ²He sent messengers to Ahab king of Israel within the city. ³He said to him: "Thus says Ben-hadad: 'Your silver and your gold are mine. And your wives and your finest children are mine.'" ⁴The king of Israel replied and said: "As your word, my lord, the king. I and all I have are yours." ⁵The messengers returned and said: "Thus says Ben-hadad: 'I sent to you saying: "Your silver and your gold, your wives and your sons you will give me." ⁶Indeed, this time tomorrow I will send my servants to you, and they will search through your house and the houses of your servants, and all your[a] eyes' delight that they put their hands on they will take away.'" ⁷Then the king of Israel summoned all of the elders of the land and said: "Know now and take note that this fellow is looking for trouble. When he sent to me for my wives and for my sons, for my silver and for my gold, I did not hold back (anything) from him." ⁸All the elders and all the people said to him: "Do not obey and do not consent!" ⁹So he said to Ben-hadad's messengers: "Say: 'To my lord, the king: (According to) all that you sent to your servant the first time I shall do; but this thing I cannot do.'" The messengers went and brought him back this word. ¹⁰Then Ben-hadad sent to him and said: "May the gods do thus to me and even more if the dust of Samaria will be sufficient for handfuls for all the army that is in my train." ¹¹The king of Israel replied and said: "Speak: 'The one who girds up should not boast as the one who unbuckles.'" ¹²Now when (Ben-hadad) heard this word— he was drinking, he and the kings at Succoth—he said to his servants: "Set (the attack)!" And they set upon the city.

¹³Now a certain prophet approached Ahab king of Israel and said: "Thus said YHWH: 'Have you seen this great multitude? I am going to give it into your hands today, and you will know that I am YHWH.'" ¹⁴Ahab said: "Through whom?" He said: "Thus says YHWH: 'Through the attendants of the district officers.'" He said: "Who will prepare the battle?" He said: "You." ¹⁵So he mustered the attendants of the district officers, and there were two hundred thirty-two and, after them, he mustered all the army, all the Israelites, seven thousand. ¹⁶They set out at noon, while Ben-hadad was drinking himself drunk at Succoth, he and the kings, the thirty-two kings who were aiding him. ¹⁷The attendants of the district officers went out first. Ben-hadad sent, and they told him: "Some men have come out from Samaria." ¹⁸He said: "If they have come out for peace, take them alive; if they have come out for war, take them alive."

---

[a] Luc., LXX, Vulg., Syr. read: "their eyes."

SITES OF BATTLES BETWEEN AHAB AND BEN-HADAD I
(1 Kings 20, 1 Kings 22)

[19]When these went out from the city—the attendants of the district officers and the troops that were behind them—[20]each struck down his man. So Aram fled, and Israel pursued them. Ben-hadad king of Aram fled on horse with (some of) the horsemen. [21]The king of Israel set out and attacked[b] the horses and chariots and inflicted a great blow upon Aram.

[22]Then the prophet approached the king of Israel and said to him: "Go, be resolute, and take careful note of what you should do; for at the turn of the year, the king of Aram will march against you." [23]Now the servants of the king of Aram said to him: "Their gods are mountain gods; therefore, they have over-powered us. But if we fight them in the plain, we will surely overpower them. [24]This is the thing you should do: remove the kings, each from his position, and appoint governors in their place. [25]Then you should tally for yourself a force like the force that deserted you, horse for horse, chariot for chariot; and let us fight them in the plain. We will surely overpower them." He listened to them, and he did so.

[26]At the turn of the year, Ben-hadad mustered the Arameans, and he advanced to Aphek to do battle with Israel. [27]Meanwhile the Israelites were mustered and provisioned, and set out to meet them. The Israelites encamped opposite them like two exposed (flocks of) goats, while the Arameans filled the land. [28]Then the man of God approached and said to the king of Israel:[c] "Thus said YHWH: 'Because the Arameans have said: "YHWH is God of the mountains and not God of the valleys," I am going to give all of this great multitude over to you, and you shall know that I am YHWH.'"

[29]They encamped opposite each other for seven days. On the seventh day, the battle was joined and the Israelites struck down one hundred thousand Ara-mean foot soldiers in one day. [30]The remaining ones fled to Aphek into the city; and the wall fell upon the twenty-seven thousand men remaining. Ben-hadad (also) fled and came into the city, into an inner room. [31]His servants said to him: "Now we have heard that the kings of the House of Israel are kings of loyalty. Let us put sackcloth on our loins and ropes on our heads[d] and go out to the king of Israel. Perhaps he will spare your life." [32]So they girded sackcloth on their loins and ropes on their heads and came to the king of Israel. They said: "Your servant Ben-hadad says: 'Please let me live!'" He said: "Is he still alive? He is my brother." [33]The men were looking for an omen and they quickly seized upon it, and they said: "Ben-hadad is indeed your brother." He said: "Go, bring him." Ben-hadad came out to him, and he took him up into his chariot. [34](Ben-hadad) said to him: "I shall return the cities that my father took from your father, and you may set up bazaars in Damascus as my father set up in Samaria." (Ahab said:) "And I, for my part, shall free you under this treaty." He made a treaty with him and freed him.

---

[b] LXX reads "captured" (*wyqḥ*) for MT *wyk*; see Note.

[c] Luc., LXX, Vulg. omit the anomalous *wyʾmr* in MT; see Note.

[d] For MT *brʾšnw* (sg.), read with versions and many MSS (noted by Qimḥi and Minḥat Shay): *brʾšynw* (pl., as in v. 32).

[35]Now one of the Sons of the Prophets said to his fellow, by the word of YHWH: "Do strike me!" But the man refused to strike him. [36]He said to him: "Because you did not obey YHWH, as soon as you leave me, a lion will attack you." He left him, and a lion came upon him and attacked him. [37]Then he met another man and he said: "Do strike me!" The man struck hard and wounded him. [38]The prophet went and waited for the king on[e] the road, and he disguised himself with a wrapping over his eyes. [39]Now, as the king was passing by, he appealed to the king and said: "Your servant went out into the thick of battle. Suddenly a man came over and brought a man to me and said: 'Guard this man. If he is missing, it will be your life for his life, or you will weigh out a talent of silver.' [40]Your servant was busy here and there, and he got away." The king of Israel said: "That is your sentence. You yourself have determined (it)." [41]He quickly removed the wrapping from[f] his eyes, and then the king of Israel recognized him as one of the prophets. [42]He said to him: "Thus said YHWH: 'Because you have freed the man I have doomed, your life shall be for his life and your people for his people.'" [43]So the king of Israel went home, irritated and angry; and he came to Samaria.

---

[e] Some mss read ʿal for MT ʾel.

[f] Ketib: mʿl; qere: mʿly.

NOTES

20 1. *Ben-hadad king of Aram.* An Aramean king of this name is mentioned in 15:18 (see Note there), during the reigns of Asa of Judah and Baasha of Israel. If the battles in 1 Kgs 20 took place early in the days of Ahab, he may be the same king referred to here; if they occurred toward the end of Ahab's reign, perhaps he is another Ben-hadad (II), who bore the same dynastic name; see Comment below.

with him thirty-two kings and horses and chariots. This large number of allied kings cannot be confirmed by extrabiblical sources. Other coalitions were of smaller proportion; e.g., at Qarqar, Adad-idri of Damascus was supported by 11 kings; according to the Zakir stela, Ben-hadad III led a force of 7 kings (ANET, 501). A fragment of a stela from Zinjirli contains a reference to "thirty kings," but the context is not recoverable (KAI 219, line 3). Moreover, the authority that Ben-hadad exercised over these kings (cf. v. 24) indicates that the 32 were most likely tribal chieftains, perhaps in the vicinity of Damascus, rather than heads of large kingdoms. Compare the use of "kings" for sheikhs in Num 31:8; Judg 8:5; Jer 25:24.

He advanced and laid siege to Samaria and attacked it. From the action as it develops, the city does not seem to have come under siege or attack, as this clause seems to imply; rather, this is a general statement of intent, the particulars yet to be played out. That Samaria was open may be deduced from the meeting of the elders with Ahab (v. 7), the unhampered exit of Israel's forces (vv. 17,

19), and the location of the Aramean headquarters camp at Succoth (v. 16), to which the king's messengers travel back and forth.

2. *He sent messengers to Ahab king of Israel.* Hebrew *mal'āk* and its counterpart in Akk *mār šipri*, together with the numerous other terms for persons who served as royal emissaries are studied by Elgavish 1998.

3. *And your wives and your finest children are mine.* In an attempt to sharpen the contrast between the first (v. 3) and second (vv. 5–6) demands of Ben-hadad, emendation of the final clause has been resorted to (Stade and Schwally; earlier Wellhausen); though it has no textual basis and is rejected by most critics, it has reappeared in NJB: "Your wives and children remain yours" (noted as a "conjecture").

4. *The king of Israel replied and said: "As your word, my lord, the king. I and all I have are yours."* Ahab's reply, especially the address "my lord, the king" indicates his readiness to recognize Ben-hadad as his overlord. The threat of military engagement was sufficient for Ahab to compromise his wealth and family, as vassal to Aram.

5. *I sent to you.* The Heb particle *kî* is variously interpreted; it seems preferable to take it here as a sign of direct quotation (cf. Note to 1 Kgs 1:13); otherwise, it may be understood as a strong affirmative (see Waltke and O'Connor 1990, §39.3.4e).

Your silver and your gold, your wives and your sons you will give me. The words "you will give me" were not part of the first demand and reveal Ben-hadad's true intentions. Mere recognition of Aramean hegemony over Israel was not enough; Ben-hadad demanded Israel's wealth.

6. *Indeed.* The particle *'im* appears to strengthen the preceding *kî*; cf. 1 Sam 21:6; Ruth 3:12 (with BDB 475b).

all your eyes' delight. With MT; the reading "their eyes" of some versions softens "the malice" in Ben-hadad's second demand (Montgomery and Gehman). Ahab was unable to comply because it implied the virtual surrender of the city.

7. *Then the king of Israel summoned all of the elders of the land.* The elders, the heads of prominent families in the towns and villages throughout Israel, were recognized by the royal administration of the kingdom as responsible for the daily operation and maintenance of law and order (cf. 1 Kgs 21:8, 11; 2 Kgs 10:1). The present conclave does not imply that they constituted a formal assembly that met regularly to advise the king. The Aramean crisis was the excuse for Ahab to consult with the elders, since the consequences of total submission to Ben-hadad would have to be borne by the populace at large (see Reviv 1989b, 123–24 for another view of this gathering).

this fellow. Literally, "this one"; cf., e.g., 1 Sam 10:27; 21:16; 25:21; 1 Kgs 22:27; 2 Kgs 5:7.

8. *All the elders and all the people said to him.* The people were not previously mentioned (cf. v. 7); the word may be taken together with "the elders," characterizing their advice as expressive of the popular will. Or is "the people" the specific term for the military (cf. Note on 16:15), here their officers?

"Do not obey and do not consent." The interchange of jussive and imperative forms is not usual; cf., e. g., Exod 23:1; Judg 13:4; Amos 5:5; Ezra 9:12.

9. *Say: 'To my lord, the king . . .'* These words were the opening of Ahab's reply to Ben-hadad and not part of his instructions to the messengers ("Say to my lord, the king," as in all translations). For this common ancient Near Eastern epistolary convention, see Speiser 1964, 254, note on Gen 32:5.

10. *Then Ben-hadad sent to him and said: "May the gods do thus to me and even more. . . ."* The oath formula is standard, with the gods (plural, as befits an utterance by a non-Israelite) called upon to enforce sanctions upon the violator; cf. 1 Kgs 19:2.

if the dust of Samaria will be sufficient for handfuls. Audacious hyperbole characterizes Ben-hadad's boast, as did the advice of Ahithophel to Absalom (cf. 2 Sam 17:13, with Montgomery and Gehman). The destroyed city of Samaria, turned to dust, would be carried off by the vast Aramean army and then some. The verb *špq* is taken in the sense it displays in MH, "to provide, be sufficient, enough," evidenced here and perhaps Isa 2:6; cf. Job 20:22. For Heb *šōʿal/šāʿal*, cf. Isa 40:12; Ezek 13:19.

for all the army that is in my train. Literally, "in/at my feet," those that follow me; cf. 2 Kgs 3:9.

11. *Speak.* The imperative *dabbĕru* was likely read by LXX as *rab*, "enough"; but MT is sound, with the verb *dbr* alternating here for the more frequent *ʾmr*.

The one who girds up should not boast as the one who unbuckles. Ahab employs a proverbial saying to remind Ben-hadad that the battle is not won until it is over. The actions depicted are those of a soldier buckling up his sword as he goes to the field (cf., e.g.,1 Sam 17:39; 25:13) and taking it off when he returns (cf. Isa 45:1). For the use of proverbs and parables in diplomatic negotiations, see Note on 2 Kgs 14:9.

12. *he was drinking, he and the kings at Succoth.* Hebrew *bassukkôt* is taken as referring to the town Succoth in the central Jordan Valley (see 1 Kgs 7:46) and not to "booths" (NAB: "in the pavilions"; NEB: "in their quarters"; NJB: "under the awnings"). The description here and in v. 16, in particular, has its parallel in 1 Kgs 16:9; the location of both drinking bouts is specified: Tirzah and Succoth (so Yadin 1955). Succoth also served as the staging area for David's wars in Transjordan (see McCarter 1984, 287).

"Set (the attack)!" In battle contexts, the verb *śym* does not require a specific object to be understood as an order to apply any and all of the devices needed to bring the enemy to its knees; cf. Ezek 23:24. Josephus amplifies: "He at once gave orders to build a stockade around the city and throw up earthworks and not leave any way of besieging untried" (*Ant.* 8.372).

14. *the attendants of the district officers.* Supporting the rendition of Heb *nĕʿārîm* as "retainers" (NAB), "guards" (NJB), "squires" (Gray), "soldiers" (Würthwein), "cadets" (de Vaux 1961, 220) is the assumption that these "young men" were "professional soldiers"; evidence for this meaning goes beyond contextual arguments (cf., e.g., 2 Sam 2:14) and includes the use of the cognate *nʿr* in Ugaritic (Rainey 1975b, 99) and the borrowing of the term into Egyptian (ANET,

256, n. 12; 476, n. 21); see de Vaux 1961, 220–21. Nevertheless, the tenor of the present story calls for a more literal understanding of the word, because only a victory led by a small band of untrained fighters over mighty Aram could prove that it was YHWH who led Israel and caused them to "know that I am YHWH" (v. 13).

district officers. This is the only hint in Kings concerning the organization of the kingdom of Israel; but just what administrative duties — fiscal or military or both — were within the purview of these officers remains conjectural. The term *mĕdînâ* is commonly considered a loanword from Aramaic and appears in LBH; e.g., Esth 1:1; Dan 8:2; Ezra 2:1.

"Who will prepare the battle?" Hebrew *'sr, "to tie, bind," is used for harnessing horses and chariots (cf. Gen 46:29; Exod 14:6), but only in the present verse is the object "war, battle." The meaning of this idiom can be learned from a similar one in Akkadian, *tāḫaza kaṣāru*, "to set up [lit., tie, bind up] a battle (array), to prepare for battle" (CAD K, 260). The rendition "to wrap up the battle" (Provan, Walsh, earlier Gray), as if the final stage was being spoken of, relies on English and not Hebrew idiom; nor is "to attack" (NAB) satisfactory.

15. *So he mustered the attendants.* In military contexts, Heb *pqd, basically "to take note, number," refers to the review and organization of the troops prior to the campaign; cf. e.g., 1 Sam 11:8; 13:15; 2 Sam 18:1.

he mustered all the army. For "the army," see above on v. 8.

seven thousand. This typological number, used in 19:18 with reference to the Israelites who had remained loyal to YHWH, represents a small but complete force as compared to the powerful force that Aram had mustered (cf. v. 1). For a figurative expression of this "few versus many" motif, see v. 27. But in real terms, a force of seven thousand was considerable in ancient times, especially for a small nation; see the figures of the allied kingdoms given in the monolith inscription of Shalmaneser III, Appendix I, no. 2.

17. *Ben-hadad sent, and they told him: "Some men have come out from Samaria."* The LXX smooths to read: "They sent and reported." But the elliptical MT can be construed as: "Ben-hadad sent (a patrol) that reported back to him" (with Montgomery and Gehman).

21. *attacked the horses and chariots.* The LXX reading "captured" (*wyqḥ*) for MT "attacked" (*wyk*), adopted by all translations and commentators, is not preferable; Montgomery and Gehman pointed out the inner-Greek corruption that was the cause of the alteration (also in Josh 15:16). Since "captured" is not preferable, all remarks concerning Ahab's war tactics based on that understanding can be disregarded.

22. *Then the prophet approached the king of Israel and said to him.* Apparently he was the prophet who had earlier given Ahab the encouraging oracle (cf. v. 13). The prophet warns Ahab not to fall prey to overconfidence because of the easily won victory: another encounter with his Aramean enemy awaits him.

Go, be resolute. Hebrew *ḥzq in *Hithpael*, literally "strengthen oneself," conveys the sense of "make an effort" (Num 13:20); "gain power" (2 Sam 3:6); "have courage" (1 Sam 4:9; 2 Sam 10:12), all expressive of the tenor and disposition of the actors. The NAB's "regroup your forces" is too material.

take careful note of what you should do. The verbs **yd‛* and **r'h* are often joined as a hendiadys; cf., e.g., 1 Sam 12:17; 14:38; 23:22–23; 24:11.

at the turn of the year. Literally, "at the return of the year," i.e., the end of one year and the beginning of another. This was the season, "the time when kings go out to battle" (2 Sam 11:1), when it is commonly held that military campaigns were undertaken in the late spring and summer, when weather conditions were favorable for the movement of troops and food stocks were available for their provisioning. Yet winter attacks are not a rare occurrence (cf. e.g., 2 Kgs 25:1; ANET, 564a [Years 4, 6, and 8 of Nebuchadnezzar]).

23. *Their gods are mountain gods; therefore, they have overpowered us. But if we fight them in the plain, we will surely overpower them.* On the level plains, the Israelites would be no match for the Aramean chariot corps.

But if we fight them in the plain. The topographical designation *mîšôr* is sometimes used with specific reference to the high plateau in Transjordan north of Wadi Arnon; cf. Deut 3:10; Josh 13:16; the Golan is never so named (contra Würthwein).

24. *remove the kings, each from his position, and appoint governors in their place.* Ben-hadad was advised to get a firmer grip on his forces by bringing them directly under his authority; rather than being subject to local chieftains (see Note on v. 1), they would be administered by royal appointees.

governors. The Aramaic loanword *peḥâ* (pl. *paḥôt*) appears in 1 Kgs 10:15 with reference to foreign monarchs (cf. also Note on 2 Kgs 18:24). Here it seems to mean "administrator" (the rank is unspecified), as it does in LBH, e.g., Ezra 5:3; 6:7; Dan 3:2.

25. *Then you should tally for yourself a force.* Hebrew **mnh,* "tally," is also used with reference to David's census (2 Sam 24:1), ostensively a count of Israel's fighting strength (cf. v. 9).

like the force that deserted you. For this meaning of **npl* ("desert") and its cognate in Akk *maqātu,* see Note on 2 Kgs 7:4, to which add Eph‛al 1994. Most translations (except NJB) prefer: "that you have lost."

26. *he advanced to Aphek to do battle with Israel.* Of the five or so locations in Israel named Aphek, the one referred to here is probably Aphek in Transjordan, toward the Golan Heights. Tel Soreg, a very short distance from modern Fiq (ABD 1:276), is too insubstantial a site for it to have been a major Aramean stronghold. 'En-Gev, just a short distance from Fiq on the eastern shore of Lake Kinneret, remains a candidate (Aharoni 1979, 335; Kochavi 1996, 197–98; 1998, 31), though the heights overlooking this site on the narrow strand would have been a better location for the use of battle chariots. For a later engagement at Aphek, see 2 Kgs 13:17.

27. *Meanwhile the Israelites were mustered and provisioned.* The perfect with simple *waw* expresses simultaneity (S. R. Driver 1892, §131–32). This sense of concurrence is further achieved by the use of the rare passive forms *kolkĕlû* (GKC, 55f) and *hotpāqdû* (GKC, 54 l).

like two exposed (flocks of) goats. The MT *ḥăśipê ʿizzîm* remains a crux; the ancient versions offer something like "small flocks of goats," adopted by NAB and NJPSV. The adjective *ḥăśîp* from *ḥśp, "to strip, lay bare," may be parsed as a construct governing the substantive with adjectival meaning, like *ḥallūqê ʾăbānîm*, "smooth stones" (1 Sam 17:40); cf. also Isa 29:19; Ezek 7:24.

28. *Then the man of God approached.* He was the same person called a "prophet" in vv. 13 and 22; for a similar interchange of these designations for divine messengers, see Note to 13:18.

and said to the king of Israel. The second occurrence of *wyʾmr* is hard to sustain and may be the reason for its omission in some versions; perhaps it is misread for *lʾmr* (Montgomery and Gehman). Otherwise, it is the first *wyʾmr* that is superfluous (missing from LXX^A, Syr., and one MS); cf. vv. 13, 22.

"YHWH is God of the mountains and not God of the valleys." This repetition of the Aramean rationalization of their loss to Israel (cf. v. 23) changes a single word: "valleys" replaces "plain." The topographical concept referred to is one: level, wide-open spaces that characterize valleys such as the Jezreel Valley.

I am going to give all of this great multitude over to you, and you shall know that I am YHWH. The prophet delivers the identical promise of victory that he had before the first battle with Ben-hadad; cf. v. 13.

29. *They encamped opposite each other for seven days.* Literally, "These encamped opposite those." Unlike the seven days that preceded the fall of Jericho, during which the city was ceremoniously encircled each day (Josh 6), no activity is reported here. The typological number "seven" suggests that a literary device is being used "to delay the progress of the narrative in order to increase its suspense" (Revell 1993, 107).

the Israelites struck down one hundred thousand Aramean foot soldiers in one day. This great number is neither an estimate nor an exaggeration of a real count of the casualties; it is a round number, a mark of the story-like character of the narrative. Reference to the twenty thousand soldiers of Aram-Damascus who, according to the Assyrian approximation, fought at Qarqar (Gray) is of little help in retrieving a realistic number.

30. *the wall fell upon the twenty-seven thousand men remaining.* The oft-made comparison to the collapse of the walls of Jericho (Josh 6:20) is less than apt. No cultic ceremony preceded the taking of Aphek, nor does the storyteller attribute the victory to YHWH's fighting for Israel. At Jericho, the fall of the walls allowed the Israelites to enter the city and slaughter its inhabitants; at Aphek, on the other hand, the Aramean soldiers found their death under the rubble of the town's defenses.

into an inner room. The same idiom appears in 22:25 and 2 Kgs 9:2, where the meaning "the innermost room" is transparent; the drama of Ben-hadad's running "from room to room" (so Šanda, followed by Gray; cf. Josephus, *Ant.* 8.410 [concerning 1 Kgs 22:25]) is unidiomatic.

31. *the kings of the House of Israel are kings of loyalty.* Or "honorable kings." The meaning of the phrase *malkê ḥesed* is enigmatic. If Heb *ḥesed* connotes "loyalty" to assumed obligations and rights between two covenanted parties

(see Note on 1 Kgs 3:6), how could Ben-hadad's servants expect any consideration based on the former vassal relationship between Ahab and their lord, now defunct? Were they counting on the terms of the new relationship that might be established if Ahab accepted their surrender and the submission that would be displayed so prominently by their garb? The NEB's "men to be trusted" tries to capture this sense of *ḥesed*; see also DeVries 1979, 361, "kings who will recognize and respect agreements." The NJB's "faithful and kind kings" and the translation "merciful kings" ascribe to *ḥesed* the late sense of "favor" bestowed by a king, not stemming from mutuality; cf. Esth 2:9, 17.

Let us put sackcloth on our loins and ropes on our heads. As if they were mourners (cf. 21:27) and slaves, they would appear before Ahab, putting themselves at his mercy. Compare the description of the king of Shupria, who beseached clemency from Esarhaddon: he appeared on the walls of his besieged city after "he took off his royal garment and wrapped his body in sackcloth befitting a (penitent) sinner" (CAD A/2, 299b).

ropes on our heads. The symbolism may suggest "that they were ready to be led off as prisoners" (Wiseman).

Perhaps he will spare your life. Literally, "He will keep your person alive."

33. *The men were looking for an omen.* Hebrew *nḥš, only in *Piel*, is "to practice or learn by divination"; cf. Gen 30:27; 44:5, 15; the imperfect used here adds vividness to the scene. The messengers of Ben-hadad took Ahab's words "Is he still alive? He is my brother" as a sign that their mission would succeed. The method by which they divined is an example of cledonomancy, the use of "chance utterances overheard and considered endowed with ominous meanings" (Oppenheim 1954–1956, 55). This procedure was known in both Egypt and Mesopotamia (Oppenheim) and was practiced in the classical world (Greek *kledon*) and in Rabbinic Jewish society (Heb *bat qôl*; see Lieberman 1950, 194–99). Somewhat different is the word sign preselected by Jonathan and his arms-bearer (1 Sam 14:8–10).

He is my brother. As in 1 Kgs 9:13, "brother" is a diplomatic locution used between persons of equal status. The present encounters with Aram began with Ahab as vassal of Ben-hadad; having twice bested his overlord, Ahab could speak of himself as having achieved parity.

they quickly seized upon it. A crux, whose meaning can only be approximated from the context. The MT *wyḥlṭw hmmnw* should be redivided, with all versions and qere (in western Masoretic lists): *wyḥlṭwh mmnw*. The verb *ḥlṭ is otherwise unattested in BH; *ḥlṭ in *Hiphil* means "to pass judgment, validate," in MH, inappropriate in the present instance. Most suggest a meaning "catch, snatch" (as if the verb were related to *ḥlṣ; see Šanda). A Yemenite MS preserves the reading *wymlṭwh*, from which the sense "to catch" might be derived (see Morag 1983).

he took him up into his chariot. This gesture was a public display of recognition of Ben-hadad's continuing royal status. Friendship of this sort was shown by Jehu with respect to Jehonadab son of Rechab (cf. 2 Kgs 10:15).

34. *(Ben-hadad) said to him: "I shall return the cities that my father took from your father, and you may set up bazaars in Damascus as my father set up in*

Samaria." Neither one of these items is referred to earlier in the short report of the reign of Omri (1 Kgs 16:23–27). Many think that the cities were taken during the invasion of the Galilee by Ben-hadad I (15:20), yet Baasha, king of Israel, who reigned at that time was not Ahab's father. See at length in Comment.

you may set up bazaars in Damascus as my father set up in Samaria. These markets are sometimes compared to the *kāru*, the Akkadian term for "harbor, trading station" (CAD K, 231–37), used with reference to the Assyrian colony at Kanish in Cappadocia at the turn of the second millennium BCE, and the Neo-Assyrian commercial settlements founded in conquered territories (see, e.g., Elat 1977, 207–8). But considering that Damascus was not reduced to vassal-age, a minimalist explication seems advisable in the present context: Ben-hadad expressed his readiness to lift the restraints on foreign trade in Damascus in order to allow Israelite merchants free access to the city's markets, which served as a major hub on the Transjordan road to the far north.

bazaars. Hebrew *ḥûṣôt* is the equivalent in BH of later *šûqîn*, "streets, markets" (so Tg.); *šûq* is used only in Qoh 12:4,5; Song 3:2 (// *rĕḥôb*). In reality, these were not market areas in the modern sense but streets along which groups of artisans and tradesmen hawked similar wares, side by side; cf. "the Street of the Bakers" (Jer 37:21). Similar concentration of merchandise and sales can be noted from the names of city gates, e.g., "Fish Gate" (Zeph 1:10); "Sheep Gate" (Neh 12:39).

(Ahab said:) "And I, for my part, shall free you under this treaty." A number of clues indicate that Ahab is the speaker, though the unintroduced shift in subjects is a bit harsh. Only Ahab was in the position to determine the terms of the treaty and conclude it (note the use of the preposition *lamed* in v. 34b); the emphatic use of the pronoun "I" contrasts with the opening of the verse and points to this clause's being a reply to Ben-hadad's offer (G. R. Driver 1966, 1–4; Revell 1993, 112 n. 22).

this treaty. Literally, "the treaty," i.e., the treaty just renegotiated, not the old one.

35. *one of the Sons of the Prophets.* Mentioned here for the first time in Kings, these prophetic brotherhoods figure largely in the Elisha cycle; see Note to 2 Kgs 2:3, to which add Porter 1981.

"Do strike me!" The particle *nā'* may convey emphasis or entreaty. From the result—the wounding of the man (cf. v. 37)—the former seems to have been intended.

36. *"Because you did not obey YHWH, as soon as you leave me, a lion will attack you."* The man of God from Judah was similarly punished for disobeying YHWH's word; cf. 1 Kgs 13:24 and Note there. In these stories, lions are the preferred vehicle for divine judgment; cf. also 2 Kgs 17:25 and, metaphorically, Hos 5:14.

37. *The man struck hard and wounded him.* Literally, "struck him, striking and wounding," with the double infinitive absolute used in combination: the first intensifying, the second indicating the goal or result of the principle verb; cf., e.g., Jer 12:17; see Waltke and O'Connnor 1990, §35.3.2d.

38. *he disguised himself with a wrapping over his eyes.* The disguise served a twofold purpose: it gave the prophet's story a dimension of reality, as if he had indeed just returned from "the thick of battle"; and it hid the speaker's true identity.

a wrapping. Or "bandage." Hebrew *ʾăpēr* is a hapax in BH. In Akk *apāru* is "to provide with a headdress, to put a covering on" (CAD A/2,166–68); for its other Semitic cognates (e.g., Ug, Aram) in which the *ʿayin* is preserved, see Greenfield 1967, 90–91; Ibn-Janah had already pointed to Ar *mġpr*.

waited for the king on the road. The idiom *ʿmd l-* ("wait for") appears again in 2 Kgs 5:9; it means "remain, stay with" in Qoh 2:9.

39. *he appealed to the king.* Literally, "he shouted, called out"; for the technical sense of *ṣʿq ʾl* as appealing for a royal decision, see Note on 2 Kgs 8:3.

you will weigh out a talent of silver. An exorbitant ransom indeed, one hundred times the cost of a slave that went for thirty shekels (cf. Exod 21:32).

40. *You yourself have determined (it).* Hebrew *ḥrṣ* is properly "to cut, sharpen"; cf. Lev 22:22. Like its semantic equivalent in Akk *parāsu* (AHw 830–32), the Hebrew verb developed the meaning "to decide" a case; cf. Isa 10:23; 28:22; Dan 9:26 ("decreed"). In Akkadian glyptic tradition, the sun god Shamash, god of justice, is often depicted holding a saw, with which he "cuts a decision" (e.g., ANEP 683).

41. *He quickly removed the wrapping from his eyes, and then the king of Israel recognized him as one of the prophets.* Prophets seem to have called on Ahab regularly, so it is possible that once the disguise was removed, this fellow's true identity was revealed. There is no evidence for the commonly held view that the prophets "had a distinguishing tattoo or incision on their foreheads, or shaved their heads" (NJB, ad loc., note q). (The oft-cited "mark on the forehead" [Ezek 9:4] is irrelevant to the present circumstances.) Josephus identified him as Micaiah (son of Imlah), apparently on the basis of Ahab's statement that Micaiah never had a good word to say about him (cf. 1 Kgs 22:8); see also Josephus, *Ant.* 8.389; also S. *ʿOlam Rab.* 20.

42. *Because you have freed the man I have doomed.* Literally, "the man of my ban, devoted to destruction." Unlike the account of Saul's war with Amalek, upon whom Samuel announced *ḥerem* before the battle (1 Sam 15:3), Ahab received no such instruction from the prophet in v. 13. The *ḥerem*-ban was a central aspect of Israel's wars with the inhabitants of Canaan (cf., e.g., Num 21:1–3; 1 Sam 15), which later came to be legislated in the laws of war incorporated into the Deuteronomic code (Deut 20:10–18; cf. 7:1–5, 25–26). The present reference to *ḥerem* is the latest one in the narratives concerning the monarchic period; whether this signals the end of its application in Israel's wars is a moot question. Mesha of Moab, Ahab's contemporary, when he fought the Israelites boasts of having doomed them to Ashtar-Chemosh (Moabite stela, line 17; see Cogan and Tadmor 1988, appendix 1, no. 1).

you have freed. The verb *šlḥ* in *Piel* appears only here with the complement *miyyad*, "from (your) hand" (LXX: "from my hand").

43. *irritated and angry.* The expression *sar wĕzāʿēp* appears again in 1 Kgs 21:4 and in the fem. form *sārâ (rûḥăkâ)* in 21:5. The two verbs *srr*, "to be stubborn, rebellious," and *zʿp*, "to rage, be enraged" (cf. Gen 40:6; Dan 1:10), describe sullenness and irritability.

COMMENT

Structure and Themes

The relations between Israel and Aram-Damascus, previously dealt with briefly in 1 Kgs 15:18–20, are the subject of the present chapter and are narrated through the perspective of prophetic narration. The prophet Elijah, Ahab's fierce critic and opponent, is nowhere to be found; other prophets take stage center, one of them supporting the king's actions, another censuring his ways.[1] The major account, vv. 1–34, tells of the failed attempt of Ben-hadad to coerce Ahab into accepting his terms of vassalage (vv. 1–12). In two military engagements that follow Ahab's refusal to submit (vv. 13–21; 26–34), Aram's superior forces are shown to be no match for Israel's small army backed by YHWH. Ben-hadad goes from demanding the surrender of Ahab to imposing upon himself humiliating concessions in order to earn his own release. The descriptions of the two battles are built up of similar elements: a description of the Aramean advance against Israel (vv. 12, 26); a prophetic promise of victory to the king (vv. 13–14, 28); the battle and its outcome in Israel's favor (vv. 20–21, 29–30). The triumph of "the few over the many" manifests, as it does in the other contexts in which this motif is employed (e.g., Judg 7:1–8), that it is YHWH who grants victory to Israel (cf. 1 Kgs 20:13, 28).[2]

A small matter of style has played a significant role in the historical criticism of this chapter. As in many of the prophetic tales of this period, the storyteller does not refer to the king by name but simply as "the king of Israel" (cf., e.g., 2 Kgs 6:24–7:20; 8:4–6). Therefore, the mention of Ahab in vv. 2, 13, 14 is held by some to be a gloss by the late editor who assigned 1 Kgs 20 to Ahab, when it fact, the king of Israel was one of the Jehu dynasty. The same holds true for the identification of Ahab in 1 Kgs 22. However, it is the appearance of the king of Judah alongside the king of Israel in 1 Kgs 22 that confutes the argument of the critics. If Joash son of Jehoahaz is the king of Israel, as proposed (e.g., Miller

---

[1] The LXX presents another order for the last three chapters of Kings; the story of Naboth's vineyard in 1 Kgs 21 is moved up to follow 1 Kgs 19, thus joining it to the other stories concerning Elijah; 1 Kgs 20 and 22 are then read as a continuous narrative on the Aramean wars. There is no consensus among the commentators regarding to the "original" order of these chapters. Montgomery and Gehman's statement still rings true: "But all presumption is against Greek rearrangements in general" (p. 319).

[2] Würthwein's division into profane and prophetic elements, the latter being "interpolations" based upon holy war ideology, is hardly compelling.

1966), then the identity of the God-fearing king of Judah, his loyal ally, would have to be Amaziah rather than Jehoshaphat (cf. 22:4, 7, 8, 10, 18, 29–30, 32). But given the inimical relations between Joash and Amaziah (cf. in particular 2 Kgs 14:8–14), it is hard to believe that the compliant king of Judah was other than Jehoshaphat. Thus, if Jehoshaphat is original to the story line in 1 Kgs 22, the appearance of Ahab in both 1 Kgs 20 and 22 is primary.[3]

A second, shorter tale, vv. 35–43, follows this rather detailed narrative. It recounts the prophetic condemnation of Ahab for his having released Ben-hadad, a man marked for doom by YHWH. Several features suggest affinities with other prophetic tales. For example, the use of a parable, here acted out, is a rhetorical device well known from Nathan's critique of David in the Bath-sheba affair (2 Sam 12:1–6); the punishment of a nonobedient prophet by an attacking lion was also the fate of the man of God from Judah (1 Kgs 13). At the same time, the tale stands at odds with the preceding account of the two Aramean wars; a number of features points to its original independence. The description of Ahab in the war account is sympathetic to the king. Throughout, Ahab has the support of the storyteller, from his brave rejection of the abusive terms of vassalage (vv. 9, 11) through the twice-promised victories over Aram proclaimed by a prophet of YHWH (vv. 13–14; 28). Nowhere is he warned that the battles with Ben-hadad fall under the rubric of *ḥērem*, on the analogy of Samuel's specific instructions to Saul prior to his war against Amalek (1 Sam 15:2–3). But these signs do not necessarily mean that vv. 35–43 must be taken as an editorial creation (so, e.g., Würthwein). They could well represent the displeasure of some prophets with Ahab's politics, the new treaty with Aram, and the release of Ben-hadad. By including this critique of Ahab, Dtr added further lines to the overall negative impression of Ahab and his reign that Dtr wished to convey.

History

The literary character of the present prophetic narratives has not dampened the historical debate, and there is considerable disagreement over the soundness of assigning 1 Kgs 20 (and 22) to the reign of Ahab, in accord with their present placement in Kings; many find that the events depicted cannot be accommodated to the period of the Omrides, "energetic rulers who exerted a great deal of influence in international affairs" (Miller 1966, 443; see earlier, Jepsen 1942; and Noth 1960, 243–44 [with reference to 1 Kgs 22]; also Lipiński 1969; Ahlström 1993a, 575). In particular, the abject king of Israel in 1 Kgs 20 is hardly brave Ahab, who just a year or so later deployed his troops at Qarqar.[4]

---

[3] Another difficulty in taking Joash as the king of Israel in 1 Kgs 20 is the promised punishment of king and people in 1 Kgs 20:35–43; this is inappropriate for someone who was remembered for his successes against Aram (cf. 2 Kgs 13:25).

[4] Miller (1966) suggests that the king of Israel who defeated Ben-hadad three times was Joash son of Jehoahaz, to whom Elisha prophesied three victories (cf. 2 Kgs 13:14–19). Ben-hadad would

Thus, these chapters are read as part of the history of Jehoahaz and Joash, of the dynasty of Jehu. The information garnered from extrabiblical documentation weighs heavily in this debate, since, for the first time, two kings of Israel, Omri and Ahab, are named in foreign monuments. But this testimony, critically evaluated, taken together with the results of the literary analysis of the prophetic narratives, which can be seen to have adjusted factual items to didactic goals, does not require the radical modification of the received history that is sometimes put forward.

Despite the four-year civil war that racked the first third of his reign, Omri was able to achieve stability for Israel on two important fronts: alliance with Tyre added to its economic strength and its international position (see Comment on 1 Kgs 16), while accord with Judah put an end to the decades-long state of conflict between the two sister kingdoms. In both instances, marriage between the royal houses secured the political arrangements (cf. 1 Kgs 16:31; 2 Kgs 8:18). In Transjordan, Omri seems to have ruled Moab with a heavy hand (Moabite Stone, lines 4–5), a state of affairs that lasted at least midway through the reign of Ahab (lines 7–8). Concerning relations with Aram-Damascus, there is no evidence that the rupture between the two kingdoms, which occurred during the reign of Baasha with the Aramean attack on the Galilee (1 Kgs 15:20), was healed; and if the statement concerning Israelite cities captured by Aram refers to deeds during the reign of Omri (cf. 20:34), then Damascus continued to maintain the upper hand on Israel's northeastern border and was even able to establish its commercial presence within Samaria.

The foreign affairs of Ahab's reign are no better documented than those of his father. Mesha of Moab claims to have attained a number of victories over Israelite settlements north of Wadi Arnon, beginning in the days of Ahab down through the end of the Omride dynasty, eventually freeing himself from Israelite vassalage, though the notation at 2 Kgs 3:4–5 assigns the breakaway of Moab to the period following Ahab's death. On the Aramean front, "Ahab the Israelite" joined a broad-based coalition of western monarchs (including token support from Egyptian and Arab interests) led by Adad-idri (Hadad-ezer) of Damascus and Irhuleni of Hamath, which engaged Shalmaneser III at Qarqar in 853 BCE. The Kurkh Monolith Inscription tells of Ahab having sent a considerable contingent: 200 chariots and 10,000 foot soldiers (for this corrected reading, see note to translation in appendix I, no. 2).

Despite the disconnected nature of this picture, the two battles between Israel and Aram-Damascus in 1 Kgs 20, and the associated one in 1 Kgs 22 can be accommodated within the reign of Ahab. Key to the discussion is the matter of chronology. There are no dates in 1 Kgs 20, and though it appears to be chronologically joined to 1 Kgs 22 (cf. v. 1), this joining is not crucial. The joining

---

then be Ben-hadad son of Hazael; this identification eliminates the necessity of identifying him with Adad-idri of Shalmaneser's Monolith Inscription. This also requires the correction (or elimination altogether) of the name of the king murdered by Hazael (Ben-hadad, according to 2 Kgs 8:7, 9), unless a Ben-hadad reigned between Adad-idri and Hazael (see Pitard 1987, 132–38).

is done by use of a literary convention (see, in detail, note to 22:1), which is not a historically viable datum. Once freed from the battle of Ramoth Gilead that took place in 852 BCE, the year of Ahab's death, the events described in 1 Kgs 20 could easily be from an earlier stage in the reign of Ahab (so Bright 1981, 243), prior to his developing a significant military force. Moreover, the didactic quality of the narrative (see above) precludes taking the description of Ahab and his ready capitulation as an objective report that must be brought into line with his appearance in the Monolith Inscription (itself suspect of error and exaggeration).[5] Thus, the reign of Ahab may be seen as one during which Israel emerged from its position as underdog vis-à-vis Damascus, defending its interests on both sides of the Jordan River. This called for constant vigilance, and, despite Israel's participation at the side of Damascus in the anti-Assyrian coalition, local clashes (such as the ones in 1 Kgs 22) continued to haunt the relations between the two whenever the distant threat dissipated.

In regard to the history of Aram-Damascus, the king of Aram in 1 Kgs 20 is Ben-hadad II, referred to as Adad-idri by Shalmaneser's scribes. The reported replacement of the 32 kings by governors (cf. 20:24) may be a recollection of a reorganization by Ben-hadad of his kingdom, in which various Aramean tribal units were brought under a central administration.[6]

---

[5] The emendation of the erroneous number "two thousand" as the size of Ahab's chariot corps at Qarqar (see above) obviates the necessity to assume that other Syro-Palestinian states (e.g., Judah) had sent contingents that were under Israel's command (so, e.g., Malamat 1973, 144).

[6] The reliability of this item should not be doubted on the basis of the use of the number "32" (admittedly high); even prophetic stories incorporate historically sound data, such as the regicide of Ben-hadad II by Hazael (2 Kgs 8:15). Yet v. 24 is too scant a datum to support Mazar's construct of a "great united and sovereign Aramean empire" under Ben-hadad's leadership (B. Mazar 1986, 160).

XXXVII. NABOTH'S VINEYARD

(21:1–29)

21 ¹Sometime afterward. Naboth the Jezreelite had a vineyard in Jezreel next to the palace of Ahab, king of Samaria. ²Ahab spoke to Naboth: "Sell me your vineyard that I may have it as a vegetable garden, for it is next to my house, and I will give you in its place a vineyard better than it. (Or)ᵃ if you like, I will pay you its price in silver." ³Naboth said to Ahab: "Far be it from me by YHWH that I should sell my ancestral inheritance to you."

⁴Ahab came home irritated and angry because of the matter that Naboth the Jezreelite had told him: "I will not sell you my ancestral inheritance." He lay down on his bed, turned his face away, and would not eat. ⁵His wife Jezebel came to him, and she spoke to him: "Why is your spirit irritated and you do not eat?" ⁶He told her: "I spoke to Naboth the Jezreelite, and I said to him: 'Sell me your vineyard, or if you wish, I will give you a vineyard in its place.' But he said: 'I will not sell you my vineyard.'" ⁷Then Jezebel his wife said to him: "Now *you* will exercise kingship over Israel! Get up, eat, and cheer up! *I* will give you the vineyard of Naboth the Jezreelite!"

⁸So she wrote letters in Ahab's name and sealed (them) with his seal; she sent the lettersᵇ to the elders and the nobles of his town, who lived with Naboth. ⁹(Thus) she wrote in the letters: "Proclaim a fast and seat Naboth at the head of the people, ¹⁰and seat two worthless men opposite him. Have them testify against him: 'You have cursedᶜ God and king.' Then take him out and stone him to death."

¹¹The men of his town, the elders and the nobles who lived in his town, did as Jezebel had sent them, just as she had written in the letters she sent them. ¹²They proclaimed a fast and seated Naboth at the head of the people. ¹³Two worthless men came and sat opposite him and testified against him, the worthless men against Naboth in front of the people: "Naboth has cursedᶜ God and king." They took him outside the town and stoned him to death. ¹⁴Then they sent to Jezebel: "Naboth has been stoned to death."

¹⁵When Jezebel heard that Naboth had been stoned to death, Jezebel said to Ahab: "Up, take possession of the vineyard of Naboth the Jezreelite that he refused to sell to you for silver, for Naboth is not alive; he is dead." ¹⁶When Ahab heard that Naboth was dead, Ahab set out to go down to the vineyard of Naboth the Jezreelite to take possession of it.

¹⁷Then the word of YHWH came to Elijah the Tishbite: ¹⁸"Up, go down to meet Ahab, king of Israel, who (resides) in Samaria. He is now in Naboth's

---

ᵃ Perhaps read *w'm* for MT *'m* with three MSS and LXX; *waw* lost through haplography.

ᵇ Read with ketib: *hsprym*; qere: *sprym*.

ᶜ Lit., "blessed"; see Note.

vineyard; he went down there to take possession of it. [19]Tell him: 'Thus said YHWH: "Have you murdered and also taken possession?" Thus said YHWH: "In the place where the dogs licked the blood of Naboth, the dogs shall lick your blood, even yours!"'"

[20]Ahab said to Elijah: "Have you found me, my enemy?" He said: "I have found (you). Because you have given yourself over to doing what displeases YHWH, [21]I will bring[d] disaster upon you, and I will stamp you out. I will cut off (every) male belonging to Ahab, even the restricted and the abandoned in Israel. [22]I will make your house like the House of Jeroboam son of Nebat and the House of Baasha son of Ahijah, because of the provocation with which you provoked (me, i.e., YHWH), causing Israel to sin. —[23]Even against Jezebel YHWH spoke: 'The dogs shall devour Jezebel in the plot[e] of Jezreel.' —[24]Those of Ahab('s kin) who die in the city, the dogs will eat; those who die in the field, the birds of heaven will eat." —[25]Indeed, there was no one like Ahab who had given himself over to doing what displeased YHWH, whom Jezebel his wife instigated. [26]He acted abominably by following the idols, just as the Amorites had done, whom YHWH had dispossessed before the Israelites. —

[27]When Ahab heard these words, he rent his garments and put sackcloth on his body. He fasted and lay in sackcloth and went about subdued. [28]Then the word of YHWH came to Elijah the Tishbite: [29]"Have you seen how Ahab has humbled himself before me? Because he humbled himself before me, I shall not bring the disaster in his days; in the days of his son, I shall bring[f] the disaster upon his house."

---

[d] Read with qere: *mby'* for ketib: *mby*; *'alep* lost through haplography; see Note.

[e] Read with Tg., Vulg., Syr., nine MSS: *ḥlq* for MT: *ḥl* ("rampart"); see Note.

[f] Ketib: *'by*; qere: *'by'*.

NOTES

21 1. *Sometime afterward.* An editorial link (cf. 1 Kgs 17:17), lacking in LXX, in which 1 Kgs 22 follows 20, and ch. 21 is joined to the previous material concerning Elijah, in 1 Kgs 17–19.

Naboth the Jezreelite had a vineyard in Jezreel. The second mention of Jezreel is not superfluous, since the location of the vineyard would not necessarily have been known from Naboth's title "the Jezreelite" (Montgomery and Gehman); it also underlines the fact that the field was in Naboth's hometown, a matter central to the story. That the words *'šr byzr'l* are lacking in LXX is taken by many, along with other "rewritten" verses (e.g., v. 8), as evidence that in the original tale the vineyard was in Samaria (argued anew by Timm 1982, 118–21). This position requires discounting the near-contemporary Jehu tradition in 2 Kgs 9:25–26, which locates the property in contention in Jezreel (cf. also Hos 1:4) in favor of the stereotypical description of Ahab's death in Samaria in 1 Kgs 22:38.

Naboth the Jezreelite had a vineyard. The LXX reads: *wkrm ʾḥd hyh lnbwt,* "Now Naboth had a certain vineyard"; this narrative style resembles other Northern narratives more so than MT; for the introductory *waw,* cf., e.g., 1 Kgs 20:1; 2 Kgs 3:4; 4:1, 38, 42; 5:1, et al.; for the indefinite *ʾḥd,* cf., e.g., 1 Kgs 19:4; 20:13, 35; 22:9; 2 Kgs 4:1; 7:8; et al.

in Jezreel. This town in the tribal holdings of Issachar (cf. Josh 19:18) lies about 15 km due east of Megiddo, at the village of Zerin, overlooking the Valley of Jezreel (from which the town took its name). The early references to Jezreel in 2 Sam 2:9; 4:4 are complemented by the cluster in 1 Kgs 18:45; 21:1; 2 Kgs 8:29, indicative of Omride holdings there—whether of familial or royal origin cannot be said. Excavations at the site have uncovered Early Bronze, Late Bronze, and Iron I settlement levels; significant building took place in the ninth century BCE, especially a large rectangular fortified enclosure, with towers and a gatehouse (Ussishkin 1997, 352–56). But when compared with the size and extent of the construction at Samaria, Jezreel does not compete with the capital, whatever its orientation (contra Alt 1954; Napier 1959). Rather, the city's location—a forward post facing east and Aram (cf. 2 Kgs 9:16–17)— suggests that commercial and military exigencies, which dissipated with the end of the dynasty of Omri, gave it its importance; at the same time, it may have served as the seasonal residence of the royal family (see Timm 1982, 142– 48; and Williamson's [1991, 88–89] cautious conclusions prior to the current excavations).

the palace of Ahab. In 1 Sam 3:3 and 1 Kgs 6:3, Heb *hêkal,* a loanword from Sumerian (é.gal)–Akkadian (*ekallu*), refers to a temple; in the present verse, it has a secular referent, as in 2 Kgs 20:18; Dan 1:4, 2 Chr 36:7.

king of Samaria. To some, the specification of the capital city seems superfluous; yet, as in v. 18, the mention of Samaria stands in sharp contrast to the oft-repeated indication that the vineyard was in Jezreel, at some distance from the king's proper residence. This exceptional title also appears in 2 Kgs 1:3. In neither case can it be used to date the Elijah traditions to the late eighth–seventh centuries, as if "king of Samaria" was coined after the founding of the Assyrian province *Samerina* (contra Rofé 1988a, 36). King Joash is referred to as "the Samarian" in an inscription of Adad-nerari III from the early eighth century (see Cogan and Tadmor 1988: appendix I, no. 3).

2. *Sell me your vineyard.* One of the meanings of **ntn,* "to give," is "to pay (a price, wages)"; cf. Gen 23:13; Num 20:19; Jonah 1:3; "to sell"; cf. Gen 23:9. Its cognate in Akk *nadānu* is similarly used; cf. CAD N/1, 49–50.

its price in silver. Literally, "the silver of the price of this." On *mĕḥîr,* see the Note on 10:28.

3. *Naboth said to Ahab: "Far be it from me by YHWH that I should sell my ancestral inheritance to you."* Priestly legislation viewed the land of Israel as YHWH's possession, and the Israelites as temporary dwellers on it; therefore, it was not theirs to sell in perpetuity or alienate from the family, and the property would revert to its owner in the jubilee year (cf. Lev 25:23–28; Num 36:7). The

only exception were houses in walled cities, which were not redeemable after the first year (Lev 25:29–31).

Far be it from me by YHWH. Others: "The Lord forbid." Hebrew *ḥālîlâ*, "profanation," suggests that the proposed act of sale would be a desecration and so was to be avoided at all costs; cf. Josh 22:29; 1 Sam 12:23; 26:11; 2 Sam 23:17; and without *yhwh*, e.g., Gen 44:7, 17. It sometimes precedes an oath, to strengthen it, as in 1 Sam 24:6–7.

4. *Ahab came home irritated and angry.* Cf. 1 Kgs 20:43. Ahab took Naboth's refusal "as a personal rebuff," for indeed his desire for a vegetable garden seems a "rather trivial" matter (Walsh). "Home" was most likely Samaria, not Jezreel (cf. v. 8).

turned his face away. He sought to brood alone; see 2 Kgs 20:2 for a like turning to the wall, but there for private prayer. The LXX translated "he covered" (*wyks*) his face, a metathesized and misread *k* for *b* in MT *wysb*.

6. *I spoke to Naboth the Jezreelite, and I said to him. . . . But he said. . . .* The unusual syntax of two imperfects followed by an imperfect with *waw*-consecutive adds liveliness to Ahab's description of his negotiations with Naboth, perhaps better translated as : "I am speaking . . . and I say . . . But he said." Cf. S. R. Driver 1892, §27; Ehrlich, ad loc.

But he said: 'I will not sell you my vineyard.' The LXX assimilates MT to the version of Naboth's reply in v. 3 by substituting "my ancestral inheritance" for "my vineyard." Yet the characterizations of the main actors that emerge from these different readings are significant: MT depicts Ahab as seeing no significance to the legal status of the family plot that was the basis for Naboth's rejection of the king's otherwise generous offer (see Würthwein; Zakovitch 1984, 385–88).

7. *Then Jezebel his wife said to him: "Now you will exercise kingship over Israel!* One cannot be sure of the tone of Jezebel's remark. Depicting her as domineering, NJB renders sarcastically: "Some king of Israel you make!" (cf. Šanda). Others take it as exhortative (Stade and Schwally) or even interrogative (Burney, comparing 1 Kgs 1:24; thus, many medieval commentators; NEB: "Are you or are you not king in Israel?"; earlier Moffatt).

exercise kingship. For Heb *ʿāśô mĕlûkâ*, cf. Akk *šarrūtam epēšu*, "to rule, be king" (CAD E, 219–20).

cheer up! For Heb *ṭôb lēb*, lit., "be of good heart," see 1 Kgs 8:66.

I will give you the vineyard of Naboth the Jezreelite! The added pronoun is emphatic and balances the emphatic "you" at the beginning of the verse. The verb **ntn*, translated in vv. 2, 3, 4 as "sell," here carries its basic meaning "give," since Jezebel had no intention of purchasing the vineyard; she would get it by subterfuge.

8. *So she wrote letters in Ahab's name and sealed (them) with his seal.* Though he is depicted as a passive bystander to the plot against Naboth, Ahab was implicated by Jezebel's use of his name and his authority in carrying out her design.

the elders. The elders of Jezreel are mentioned again in 2 Kgs 10:1; cf. also too, 1 Kgs 20:7.

the nobles. It is hard to account for Heb *ḥōrîm,* "nobles" (from **ḥrr*), in the present context, since the word is otherwise attested only in late passages associated with Judah (e.g., Jer 27:20; 39:6; Neh 2:16; 4:13; 13:17), from which the high rank and influence of these persons may be deduced. If the term is not a peculiar "northernism" (Burney), then perhaps it is a gloss on "elders" (see de Vaux 1961, 69–70). Less likely is that "they were state officials who were entitled to preside in court as appointed judges of municipal rank" (Reviv 1989b, 125).

sealed (them) with his seal. Seals of royal personages are a rarity among the over one thousand that have been recovered; only the seals of Kings Ahaz (Deutsch 1997) and Hezekiah (Cross 1999) have survived. The seal bearing the name *Jezebel* (see Note on 1 Kgs 16:31) is not necessarily that of Ahab's wife (as claimed by Wiseman).

9. *Proclaim a fast.* Fasts expressed grief and sorrow and were sometimes accompanied by rites of mourning (e.g., Joel 2:12; Jonah 3:7–8; Neh 9:1); it was believed that, through these acts, YHWH's mercy might be aroused and the transgression forgiven (cf. 1 Sam 7:5–6; 2 Sam 12:22; Isa 58:3). The elders of Jezreel were to announce a public fast, a sign that the town had fallen out of grace. Jezebel seems to have thought that, in this manner, the aroused community would be inclined to believe the lies that would be told concerning Naboth.

seat Naboth at the head of the people. Or "at the front" of the assembly (cf. 1 Sam 9:22). Naboth, as a landowner in Jezreel, likely enjoyed the respect of his townspeople, and so this honor would not have seemed out of line; cf. Job's reminiscence about his former status as landowner and householder (Job 29, especially vv. 7, 25). Josephus amplified: "Hold an assembly over which Naboth, since he came of an illustrious family, was to preside" (*Ant.* 8.358).

10. *and seat two worthless men opposite him.* Two witnesses were required to convict in the courts of ancient Israel; cf. Deut 17:6; 19:15; also Num 35:30.

worthless men. This censorious epithet could not have been in the original letters written by Jezebel; it is likely from the pen of the storyteller, an expression of his evaluation of the action of two false witnesses; cf. v. 13. For another example of such verbal intrusion by the narrator (Dtr?), cf. 2 Kgs 16:8.

Hebrew *bĕlîyaʿal* (Belial) is easier to define than to parse: it refers to an act that is sinful (Deut 15:9) and evil (1 Sam 30:22; cf. Nah 1:11), that upsets "a basic behavioral norm . . . the violation of the covenantal relationship between the individual, community and God" (Rosenberg 1982, 38); cf., e.g., Judg 19:22; 1 Sam 25:17; its performer "mocks justice" (Prov 19:28). Etymologically, the privative *bĕlî,* "without," is joined to either (1) **yʿl* (attested only in *Hiphil* "to be of profit, benefit"), or (2) *ʿlh,* "to arise, go up." A variation of this last proposal takes the non-rising as descriptive of evil persons, whose fate it was to be confined to the underworld, Sheol (cf. Job 7:9); see the survey in T. J. Lewis 1992a, 654–55.

'You have cursed God and king.' The injunction against reviling God and king appears in Exod 22:27, which the present verse seems to echo. In Lev 24:15–16, "expressly uttering" (**nqb*) the divine name in a curse draws the death penalty (see Brichto 1963, 143–47). Thus, the double crime of Naboth would guarantee his execution: he would be accused of an abusive remark against the king reinforced by the name YHWH. Comparison of Naboth's curse to political treason against the king, which was punishable by death in Babylonia (see Ben-Barak 1985), requires secularizing the sacred nature of the biblical violations.

You have cursed. This euphemism, substituting **brk* ("bless") for **qll* ("curse"), is attested again in Job 1:11; 2:5, 9; Ps 10:3. Hebrew **qll* can refer to both verbal abuse (e.g., Judg 9:27; 2 Sam 16:5) and an improper act (cf. 1 Sam 3:13).

Then take him out and stone him to death. Literally, "stone him so that he dies." This punishment was specified for the blasphemer in Lev 24:10–16 (where the verb **rgm*, "stone," is used rather than **sql*, "stone"). Stoning was the method of execution used in a large number of cases, e.g., Lev 20:2 (worshiper of Molech); Num 15:35–36 (Sabbath violator); Deut 21:21 (insubordinate son); Deut 22:21, 24 (sexual offenders). Inasmuch as these crimes "constitute offences against the divinely ordained order, amount to 'high treason' against God" (J. J. Finkelstein 1973, 180), the participation of the public in the stoning gave expression to their disassociation with the crime, thus "purging evil from their midst." In postbiblical Jewish law, an alternate procedure was permissible: the convicted person was pushed off a six cubits' height (*m. Sanh.* 6:4; Würthwein incorrectly attributes this method to biblical practice).

11. *who lived in his town.* See 1 Kgs 12:8 for another example of the definite article after the relative *'ăšer.* The phrase "who lived in his town" (v. 11) is sometimes rendered "who sat in council" with him (NEB), thus magnifying the treachery of the elders who conspired against one of their own. For the sense "to sit (in judgment)," cf., e.g., Ruth 4:1–2.

just as she had written in the letters she sent them. The seeming repetition of v. 13a here is an attempt to make very specific the responsibility of Jezebel and the two scoundrels in the crime. The LXX abbreviates in both cases, but the extra detail in MT recalls the overloaded description of the legal transaction between Abraham and Ephron in Gen 23 (Montgomery and Gehman; see also Würthwein).

12. *They proclaimed a fast and seated Naboth.* The MT *whšybw* is often considered an "ungrammatical blunder" (Stade and Schwally; Burney corrects to *wywšybw*); it may have been caused by the mistaken repetition of v. 9b; see also the Note on v. 6 above.

13. *testified against him . . . against Naboth.* Their claim of blasphemy would have been believable had the disagreement between Naboth and the king over the vineyard been talked about around town (Würthwein).

They took him outside the town and stoned him to death. The execution took place outside the town, perhaps to avoid contamination by contact with the corpse; cf. Lev 24:13, 23; Num 15:35–36. The case described in Deut 17:2–7 suggests that Naboth's accusers were required to take the initiatory role in carrying out the sentence. An alternate tradition held that Naboth's sons were killed along with him (cf. 2 Kgs 9:26; wrongly compared by Gray with the execution of Achan's family in Josh 7:24–25).

stoned him to death. Literally, "stoned him with stones"; cf. v. 10, where "with stones" is omitted but without any change in meaning. Note a similar specification in Lev 24:23, compared with 24:14.

14. *Then they sent to Jezebel: "Naboth has been stoned to death."* Though the letter of instructions had borne the seal of the king, the elders reported back to the queen; obviously, they knew who had penned the letters.

Naboth has been stoned. The verbal form *sūqqal* is Qal passive; cf. Joüon 1923, §58.

15. *"Up, take possession of the vineyard of Naboth the Jezreelite that he refused to sell to you. . . ."* Naboth's vineyard that at one time was not for sale (cf. v. 6) was now his for the taking (see on v. 16).

16. *Ahab set out to go down to the vineyard of Naboth the Jezreelite to take possession of it.* Ahab's "going down" to Naboth's vineyard may be compared to Abraham's "walking through the land" (Gen 13:17; cf. Josh 24:3), both symbolic acts of acquisition through actual traversal of the property newly acquired (so Ehrlich; cf. *b. B. Bat.* 100a).

Ahab's right to the vineyard has been much debated; the only known biblical case of property transferred to the king concerns a person who has left the country; cf. 2 Kgs 8:4–6. Many consider the confiscation to have been within royal prerogative, since Naboth was a convicted criminal. The example of such a procedure recorded on Alalakh tablet no. 17 (ANET, 546b) cited by Wiseman (earlier Loewenstamm 1956, 223–25), however, is too many miles and centuries distant from Samaria to be of relevance. Talmudic discussants note that the "property of those executed by the king is the king's; property of one executed by the court is his [i.e., the criminal's] heir's" citing our passage; they also strained to explain Ahab's "inheriting" by claiming that the king was, in fact, a distant relative of Naboth who merely exercised his legal right (*b. Sanh.* 48b; *t. Sanh.* 4.6).

Ahab set out to go down. The choice of the verb "go down" is governed by strict topographical considerations: Samaria's being located in the hill country of Manasseh; Jezreel, lower down in the Jezreel Valley; cf. Gen 12:10 ("Abram went down to Egypt") and 13:1 ("Abram went up from Egypt").

18. *Ahab, king of Israel, who (resides) in Samaria.* So NJPSV; NRSV: "who rules in Samaria." The specification of Ahab's capital (cf. v. 1) serves as a contrast to his presence in Jezreel; his lawful place is Samaria.

He is now in Naboth's vineyard. For additional examples of *hinneh* without the subject, see 2 Kgs 1:9; 6:13.

19. *"In the place where the dogs licked the blood of Naboth, the dogs shall lick your blood, even yours!"* A "measure for measure" (*talio*) punishment; cf. Nathan's indictment of David in 2 Sam 12:9–11; also 1 Sam 15:33; see Loewenstamm 1962. Behind the prophetic hyperbole may stand the custom of not bringing an executed criminal to burial, his body left unattended and exposed

to the scavenging animals; cf. v. 24. The Luc. and LXX have the additional "and the whores will wash in your blood," based on 1 Kgs 22:38, which describes the scene at the pool of Samaria, not at Naboth's plot (see further there).

In the place where. The noun *māqôm* ("place") always appears in construct form before *'ăšer* (cf., e.g., Gen 40:3; Lev 6:18; Ezek 21:35; Qoh 11:3). On Ahab's death and the nonfulfillment of the prophecy, cf. 1 Kgs 22:37–38 and the Note there.

even yours. Following the particle *gam*, the pronoun picks up the preceding suffix of the noun; cf. 2 Sam 17:5; see GKC, 135f.; for this "slightly emphatic" use, see also Muraoka 1985, 63–65.

20. *Ahab said to Elijah: "Have you found me, my enemy?" He said: "I have found (you). . . ."* The elliptic style of biblical narratives is most blatant at this point: the reader is thrown immediately into the confrontation between Elijah and Ahab, the details of when and how the two met being skipped over as unessential. Nor is there an indication that Elijah related YHWH's message as he was instructed in v. 19. The action continues after its understood delivery. Ahab's response recalls his angry greeting of the prophet in an earlier meeting; cf. 18:17.

Have you found me. Perhaps: "Have you found me out?" See "But he finds reasons to oppose me, considers me his enemy" (Job 33:10; cf. Qoh 7:26).

Because you have given yourself over to doing what displeases YHWH. A Dtr phrase, cf. 2 Kgs 17:17.

21. *I will bring disaster upon you, and I will stamp you out. I will cut off (every) male belonging to Ahab, even the restricted and the abandoned in Israel.* The personal punishment of Ahab (v. 19) is here extended to his entire line, using the stereotypical terms applied to the other Northern dynasties—to Jeroboam in 1 Kgs 14:10–11 and to Baasha in 16:3–4.

I will bring. The qere *mby'* is the preferred reading; though the loss of the *'alep* is explicable by haplography, the following *'lyk* would be better read as *'lyk.* But this is one of any number of cases in Kings where *'l* interchanges with *'l.*

23. *—Even against Jezebel YHWH spoke: 'The dogs shall devour Jezebel in the plot of Jezreel'—.* The verse looks like a late addition based on the Jehu tradition in 2 Kgs 9. Besides the external marker *wĕgam*, which often signals insertions (cf., e.g., 1 Kgs 10:11), the verse breaks up the prophetic denunciation in vv. 21–22, 24.

in the plot of Jezreel. The MT *ḥl*, "rampart," while *lectio difficilior*, is likely to be a correction of the original *ḥlq*, "plot" (so 2 Kgs 9:36; see further in Note there), bringing the prophecy into line with the reported place of Jezebel's death in 9:33, nearby the wall of Jezreel.

24. *Those of Ahab('s kin) who die in the city, the dogs will eat; those who die in the field, the birds of heaven will eat.* The stereotypical curse, as in 1 Kgs 14:11; 16:4.

25–26. *Indeed, there was no one like Ahab who had given himself over to doing what displeased YHWH, whom Jezebel his wife instigated. He acted abominably by following the idols, just like the Amorites had done, whom YHWH had dispossessed before the Israelites.* After having just said that the House of Ahab would meet the same fate as the houses of his predecessors Jeroboam and Baasha, an additional editorial remark sets Ahab apart as the worst of Israel's kings (cf. 16:33); and it is this evaluation that is used by Dtr in describing Manasseh, the worst of Judah's king: he behaved like Ahab (cf. 2 Kgs 21:3).

instigated. The anomalous *hēsattâ* for the expected *hî/êsîtâ*, Hiphil of **sy/wt*, may be due to its assimilation to double-*ʿayin* verbs (cf. Joüon 1923, §80p). The Deuteronomic law against idolatry included a warning of instigation by one's wife; cf. Deut 13:7 (Burney).

26. *He acted abominably by following the idols.* The Hiphil of **tʿb* ("act abominably") is attested again only in Ezek 16:52 and Ps 14:1 (= Ps 53:2) and is here appropriately associated with idolatry; cf. Deut 27:15; Ezek 16:36.

27. *When Ahab heard these words, he rent his garments and put sackcloth on his body. He fasted and lay in sackcloth and went about subdued.* Ahab was overcome with grief and exhibited repentance through these outward signs typical of the mourning period; they are taken by YHWH as a true change of heart (cf. vv. 28–29).

lay in sackcloth. Cf. Joel 1:13.

went about subdued. In the present context, the noun *'aṭ*, "ease, gentleness," may express withdrawal from daily affairs, as is common with mourners; otherwise, cf. Gen 33:14; 2 Sam 18:5. Targum "barefooted" (*yāḥêp*); also Syr.; cf. Josephus, *Ant.* 8.362. The NEB "muttering to himself" associates with the noun *'iṭṭîm* in Isa 19:3 (cf. 8:19), formerly taken as "mutterer" (BDB 31b) but now known to be a loanword from Akk *eṭemmu*, "spirit, ghost" (CAD E, 397–401).

28. *Then the word of YHWH came to Elijah the Tishbite.* As above, in the instruction given to Elijah in v. 19, the present word of YHWH is not followed by a formal address by the prophet to Ahab.

29. *Have you seen how Ahab has humbled himself before me?. . ."* The overt display of grief (cf. v. 27) is interpreted as indicative of submission to YHWH's judgment; see also 2 Kgs 22:19.

has humbled himself. For Heb **knʿ*, Niphal ("humble oneself"), cf. Lev 26:41; 2 Kgs 22:19; 2 Chr 7:14; 12:6; 13:18; 32:26; 34:27.

Because he humbled himself before me, I shall not bring the disaster in his days; in the days of his son, I shall bring the disaster upon his house. The delay in punishment, an expression of YHWH's acceptance of the return of the penitent king, adjusts the prophecy delivered to be against Ahab's offspring in vv. 21–22, 24, bringing it into line with the reported end of the dynasty, the assassination of Ahab's son Joram (cf. 2 Kgs 9).

COMMENT

Structure and Themes

The MT and LXX differ in regard to the placement of 1 Kgs 21 within the history of Ahab's reign. In MT, the three-year respite from hostilities between Aram and Israel (1 Kgs 22:1) serves as the interval during which the Naboth episode takes place; the characterization of Ahab at the conclusion of 1 Kgs 20, moody and disgruntled over the prophetic evaluation of his policies (v. 43), carries over into 1 Kgs 21 (v. 4). On the other hand, LXX joins 1 Kgs 17–19 and 21, creating a single block of stories in which the prophet Elijah is the main actor; 1 Kgs 20 and 22 present the three Aramean wars in sequence, with Ahab's promised death in 20:42 neatly complemented by its fulfillment in 22:37. Yet originality is hard to fix; each arrangement has its own logic (see Gooding 1968). Furthermore, note should be taken of the retroverted LXX text of 1 Kgs 21, which is more concise than MT; older critics have preferred many of these shorter Greek readings to the seemingly pleonastic MT. But recent literary analysis, attending closely to the subtleties of the narrative, has restored confidence in the integrity of MT (see, e.g., Walsh; Zakovitch 1984).

The narrative of the judicial murder of Naboth of Jezreel can be classed with the other Elijah traditions, though the prophet makes his appearance only at the end, in vv. 17–20 (and secondarily in vv. 28–29). Elijah's absence is not sufficient reason to posit the independent existence of an "old, north Israelite, self-contained novella" in vv. 1–16 that was only later associated with the Elijah traditions (Würthwein); the postulated story lacks a denouement (as Würthwein himself admits). A similar narrative construction is observable in the Bathsheba tale, in which the prophet Nathan, who is so vital to the story line, makes his first appearance in 2 Sam 12:1, after the lengthy recital in 2 Sam 11:1–27. The narrative line in 1 Kgs 21 flows smoothly through v. 20bα, at which point it seems to have been curtailed by the introduction of several editorial remarks. The first, vv. 20bß–24, 25–26, condemns Ahab for his practice of idolatry (specifically in v. 26, also metaphorically in vv. 21–22 [in his displeasing and angering of YHWH]) and is not associated with the foregoing Naboth incident. The description of the extirpation of his house from Israel is typical of the prophetic condemnations of the kings of Northern Israel (cf. 1 Kgs 14:9–11; 16:3–5). The parenthetical remark in v. 23 breaks the sequence and extends the punishment to Jezebel and brings the prophecy in line with the fate she met at the hands of Jehu (2 Kgs 9:30–37). The second editorial remark, vv. 27–29, adjusts the immediately preceding prophecy against the House of Ahab by postponing its effective date, a look forward to the events of Jehu's revolt against Joram son of Ahab.

Unlike the other Elijah tales, in which the subject of idolatry is central to the unfolding of the drama, in 1 Kgs 21, it is absent from the main body of the story, appearing only in the editorial additions in vv. 25–26 (and likely vv. 20b–22). Jezebel too is someone else; in the other tales, she is portrayed as the patron of idolatry; in 1 Kgs 21, she is the corrupter of Israel's law and morals through her domination of Ahab and the elders of Jezreel.[1] Of particular note is the

---

[1] Given her central role in the drama, it is indeed surprising that Jezebel does not come in for more criticism than the criticism leveled in the secondary v. 23, to say nothing of the fact that the elders of Jezreel and the false witnesses are completely passed over (it hard to believe that the narrator viewed them as unwilling pawns in the hands of Jezebel).

portrayal of her high-handedness; her fabrication of a crime punishable by the death penalty bears the stamp of monarchic authority.[2] The purpose of this ruse is obscure. At first glance, it might appear that the Israelite king did not have the power to arbitrarily confiscate the desired plot; note Ahab's response to Naboth's refusal to part with his inheritance. Yet it may be that Ahab hesitated to invoke royal prerogative out of respect for the Israelite norm of nonalienation of patrimonies, of which Naboth spoke (v. 3). Jezebel, in turn, may have been fearful that direct action might stir up popular disapproval. At all events, in the present rendition of the tale, Jezebel is absent from the closing sections of 1 Kgs 21 (added only as a footnote in v. 23; see Note); she escapes her fair share of guilt in the crime. The main indictment is delivered against Ahab in the pithy and assonant *hārāṣaḥtā wĕgam yārāštā* ("Have you murdered and also taken possession?" v. 19), an echo of YHWH's commandments at Sinai that enjoined against murder, coveting a neighbor's property, and bearing false witness. He is guilty of complicity in Naboth's murder, whether a willing accomplice or not.[3]

History

The novelistic style of the main body of 1 Kgs 21, especially the tenor of the narrative in its description of the crime perpetrated by Jezebel and her fellow conspirators, has made the Naboth story suspect of being "historical fiction," bearing "little resemblance to the actual historical circumstances" (J. M. Miller and Hayes 1986, 254). These circumstances are then recovered from the version of the events told in the Jehu account: Naboth and his sons were murdered at night, without trial or jury, in order to acquire a plot of ground that was located at some distance from the king's residence (it was not an adjacent vineyard; 2 Kgs 9:25–26).[4] Yet, even if 1 Kgs 21 is taken as prejudicial, "a distorted

---

[2] Jezebel's actions are sometimes interpreted as reflective of foreign conceptions of kingship and royal prerogatives (e.g., Walsh describes Jezebel as "the daughter of the royal house of Sidon [16:31], a society with alien religious and political understandings of the relationship of king and people"), despite the fact that little, if anything, is known about the operation of the monarchy in Phoenicia. More to the point, however, is Jezebel's proceeding in accord with Israelite legal tradition and not by outright seizure. That she was able to find accomplices among the aristocracy of Jezreel speaks as much of the corrupt Israelite society as it does of the supposed corrupt ways of Jezebel's homeland. In both cases, it would be difficult to describe the trial as proceeding from "a kind of lynch law of ancient times" (Rofé 1988b, 92).

[3] At what moment Ahab became aware of his queen's plot and his role in its execution has engaged commentators; see, e.g., Abarbanel on v. 20: "'Because you have given yourself over,' its meaning is that you pretended not to recognize and not to know a thing" about Jezebel's murderous dealings; Wiseman on v. 8: "The use of the king's royal dynastic, administrative or even personal seal to gain his authority would require Ahab's collusion." [DNF: "Ahab manipulated the manipulative Jezebel. He knew exactly what he was doing and what the outcome would be. Elijah's condemnation is corrrectly aimed at the king; the use of his name signet cannot be without his permission and knowledge."]

[4] Seeligmann (1978, 261 n. 16; followed by Rofé 1988b) argues for the priority of the tradition in 2 Kgs 9, mostly on the basis of stylistics and a number of suspected late phrases in 1 Kgs 21 (see above, Notes on vv. 1, 11).

picture" painted to condemn the queen mother during the reign of her son Joram (Ahlström 1993a, 587), it is presumptuous to reconstitute "actual historical circumstances" from the propagandistic version of events in 2 Kgs 9, written to serve Jehu's ends. Both traditions are far from being evidence of a monarchic program of land expropriation or of widespread corrupt dealings between the king and local authorities (as Ahlström correctly warns). Nevertheless, Jehu's use of Naboth's death in his campaign against the Omrides suggests that it had become a national cause célèbre; the denunciation of Ahab's behavior in the sharpest terms by Elijah and the prophetic circles associated with him kept the matter alive until the word of YHWH was accomplished.

The case of Naboth illuminates the operation of the judicial system in ancient Israel, which is touched upon in theoretical legislative fashion in the legal codes of the Pentateuch. Trials of criminals were held in towns and cities under the supervision of the local elders (cf. Deut 16:18), who served as judge and jury, even in matters concerning suspected treason against the monarchy. There is no indication that these respected citizens were state officials; rather, it would seem that the state had recognized a traditional institution of administering justice, a holdover from Israel's premonarchic and preurban past. Court was held in open session "before the people" (1 Kgs 21:13), and procedure required that at least two witnesses appear in order to convict (cf. Deut 17:6). Execution was swift, and appeal in this case does not seem to have been an option.

Concerning land ownership, traditional law protected the rights of the individual against the alienation of family property in perpetuity through the law of Jubilee (Lev 25); in the absence of a male heir, provision was made for female inheritance of ancestral land in order to guard against its transfer outside the tribe (Num 36). In all of these matters, the king had no right of confiscation or preemption. From the Naboth case, however, it does seem that the property of convicted criminals (or perhaps only the property of criminals guilty of lèse-majesté) was transferable to the crown.

XXXVIII. AHAB AT RAMOTH-GILEAD

(22:1–40)

22 ¹They stayed at home for three years, (as) there was no war between Aram and Israel. ²But in the third year, Jehoshaphat king of Judah went down to the king of Israel. ³The king of Israel said to his servants: "Do you know that Ramoth-gilead belongs to us? But we keep silent about taking it from the king of Aram." ⁴He said to Jehoshaphat: "Will you go with me to battle at Ramoth-gilead?" Jehoshaphat said to the king of Israel: "I am (ready) as you are; my forces are as your forces; my horses are as your horses." ⁵Then Jehoshaphat said to the king of Israel: "Inquire of YHWH today." ⁶So the king of Israel assembled the prophets, about four hundred persons, and he said to them: "Shall I go to battle against Ramoth-gilead or shall I refrain?" They said: "Advance! The Lord[a] will give (it) into the hand of the king." ⁷But Jehoshaphat said: "Is there not another prophet of YHWH here that we may inquire through him?" ⁸The king of Israel said to Jehoshaphat: "There is another person to inquire of YHWH through him, but *I* hate him, for he does not prophesy good about me but only evil—(this) Micaiah son of Imlah!" Jehoshaphat said: "The king should not say such a thing!" ⁹So the king of Israel called one of his eunuchs and said: "Quickly bring Micaiah son of Imlah."

¹⁰Now the king of Israel and Jehoshaphat king of Judah were sitting on their thrones, dressed in robes at the threshing floor at the entrance of the gate of Samaria, and all the prophets were prophesying before them. ¹¹Zedekiah son of Chenaanah made himself horns of iron, and he said: "Thus says YHWH: With these you shall gore Aram until their end." ¹²And all the prophets prophesied the same: "Advance to Ramoth-gilead and be successful, for YHWH will give (it) into the hand of the king." ¹³The messenger who had gone to call Micaiah told him: "Look here! The words of the prophets are unanimous in being good for the king. Let your word[b] be like the word of one of them, and speak good." ¹⁴Micaiah said: "By the life of YHWH, only what YHWH says to me will I speak."

¹⁵When he came to the king, the king said to him: "Micaiah, shall we go to battle against Ramoth-gilead, or shall we refrain?" He said to him: "Advance and be successful, for YHWH will give (it) into the hand of the king." ¹⁶The king said to him: "How many times have I put you under oath that you should speak to me only the truth in the name of YHWH." ¹⁷He said: "I saw all Israel scattered on the mountains, like sheep without a shepherd. YHWH said: 'These have no masters. Let each one return to his home in peace.'" ¹⁸The king of Israel said to Jehoshaphat: "Did I not tell you (that) he would not prophesy good about me, but only evil?" ¹⁹He said: "Therefore, hear the word of YHWH. I saw YHWH

---

[a] Tg. and many MSS read: *yhwh*.

[b] Read with qere *dbrk* for ketib *dbryk*.

sitting on his throne and all the host of heaven in attendance to his right and to his left. [20]YHWH said: 'Who will entice Ahab so that he will advance and fall at Ramoth-gilead?' One said thus and one said thus. [21]Then a spirit came forward and stood before YHWH and said: '*I* will entice him.' YHWH said to him: 'How?' [22]He said: 'I will go out and be a lying spirit in the mouth of all his prophets.' He said; 'You will entice, and indeed you will succeed. Go out and do so!' [23]Here, then, YHWH has put a lying spirit in the mouth of these prophets of yours, for YHWH has spoken evil against you." [24]Then Zedekiah son of Chenaanah stepped up and struck Micaiah on the cheek and said: "Which (way) did the spirit of YHWH pass from me to speak to you?" [25]Micaiah said: "You will see on that day when you go into the innermost room to hide." [26]Then the king of Israel said: "Take Micaiah and turn him over to Amon, governor of the city, and Joash, the king's son, [27]and say: 'Thus says the king: "Put this fellow in prison, and feed him scant bread and scant water until I return safely."'" [28]Micaiah said: "If you do return safely, YHWH has not spoken through me." ≪   ≫[c]

[29]So the king of Israel and Jehoshaphat king of Judah advanced to Ramoth-gilead. [30]The king of Israel said to Jehoshaphat: "I will disguise myself and go into battle, but you, wear your robes." Then the king of Israel disguised himself and went into battle. [31]Now the king of Aram had ordered his chariot officers— (there were) thirty-two: "Do not battle with the small or the great but only with the king of Israel." [32]When the chariot officers saw Jehoshaphat, they said: "He is surely the king of Israel." They turned toward him for battle; then Jehoshaphat cried out. [33]When the chariot officers saw that he was not the king of Israel, they turned back from him. [34]But one man drew his bow innocently, and he hit the king of Israel between the joints of the armor. He said to his driver: "Turn your hand[d] and get me out of the camp, for I am wounded." [35]The battle raged that day, and the king was propped up in the chariot facing Aram. He died that evening, and the blood from his wound spilled out into the hollow of the chariot. [36]A cry went through the camp at sundown: "Every man to his city! Every man to his land!" [37]So the king died and was brought[e] to Samaria. They buried the king in Samaria. [38]They washed off the chariot at the pool of Samaria, and the dogs licked his blood, and the whores bathed, in accordance with YHWH's word that he had spoken.

[39]The rest of the history of Ahab and all that he did and the house of ivory that he built and all the cities that he built are indeed recorded in the History of the Kings of Israel. [40]So Ahab slept with his ancestors. Ahaziah his son succeeded him.

---

[c] MT adds: "He said: Hear, all you peoples"; lacking in Luc. and LXX; see Note.

[d] Aleppo and Leningrad codices read *ydk* ("your hand"), as do many MSS; others: *ydyk* ("your hands") (as in 2 Kgs 9:23).

[e] Lit., "he came"; LXX: "they came."

NOTES

22 1. *They stayed at home for three years, (as) there was no war between Aram and Israel.* The verse refers back to 1 Kgs 20:34, which reported the end of the last war between Aram and Israel and the renewal of a treaty between Damascus and Samaria.

They stayed at home. This nuance of Heb *yšb is suggested by the Akk cognate *wašābu*, in such usages as: *ašbāti u qalāti,* "I am sitting doing nothing and saying nothing"; *lā ašbāta ana māt nakri alikma nakra dūk,* "Do not stay at home, go against the enemy country and defeat the enemy" (CAD A/2, 389b).

for three years. A typological number, like "the third day" (e.g., Gen 22:4) and "the third month" (e.g., Exod 19:1), indicating a short period of time; it does not express exact chronological reckoning. For the absolute date, see further in Comment.

2. *Jehoshaphat king of Judah.* The regal formula introducing Jehoshaphat appears in vv. 41–42; it is put off until the death of Ahab.

went down to the king of Israel. A state visit is to be imagined, during which the plans for war against Aram-Damascus were discussed.

3. *Do you know that Ramoth-gilead belongs to us?* For the identification of the site, see Note on 4:13. It is not clear how and when Ramoth-gilead came under Aramean control. According to the terms of the treaty between Ahab and Ben-hadad (cf. 20:34), cities formerly under Israelite jurisdiction should have been returned. Does the status of Ramoth-gilead indicate a breach of the agreement or a new violation on the part of Damascus? See further in Comment.

But we keep silent. Hebrew *ḥšh in *Qal* is "to be silent," e.g., Ps 28:1; 107:29; in *Hiphil*, it can be causative (Neh 8:11), but mostly it is intransitive (e.g., Isa 42:14; Ps 39:3). In this sense, it is an example of an internal *Hiphil* expressing an elative, i.e., "be very silent, motionless"; see Speiser 1967, 482. The preferred modern translation is "we do nothing" (NAB, NEB, NJPSV, NRSV).

4. *"I am (ready) as you are; my forces are as your forces; my horses are as your horses."* The same formulation appears again in 2 Kgs 3:7; see Note there. The deferential tone of Jehoshaphat's response has been the basis for taking him to have been a vassal of Israel, yet the stylized reply could just as well be the court politesse of an independent monarch, allied through marriage with Ahab. See further in Comment.

5. *"Inquire of YHWH today."* Hebrew *kayyôm,* "now, at once, first of all"; cf. Gen 25:31; 1 Sam 9:27; 1 Kgs 1:51. There is no need to eliminate *dĕbar* (with LXX); cf. 1 Kgs 14:5; yet the more common idiom is simply *drš ʾt yhwh as in v. 8; cf. 2 Kgs 8:8; 22:13. The LXX "let us inquire" (followed by NEB) seems to be an assimilation to v. 7.

Inquire of YHWH. The technical term for inquiry of the divine will before battle is most often **šʾl byhwh,* e.g., Num 27:21; Judg 1:1; 1 Sam 23:2; 30:8; in the present case, the term is **drš ʾt (dbr) yhwh,* employed for a prosaic, mundane inquiry in 1 Kgs 14:5. The altered terminology may be associated with the change in the divinatory procedure employed: prophets replace priests as the consultants, and the divine word replaces the mantic oracle. See further in the Comment.

6. *So the king of Israel assembled the prophets, about four hundred persons.* This is the earliest reference to the consultation of prophets prior to battle, a function that had previously been in the purview of priests; cf., e.g., Num 27:21; 1 Sam 30:7–8.

about four hundred persons. The same typological number is used of the prophets of Baal in 1 Kgs 18:19.

The Lord will give (it) into the hand of the king. The prophets' positive response was no doubt given in the name of YHWH, but this has been replaced by the pious surrogate "the Lord" ("to avoid classification of true prophets with false" [Montgomery and Gehman]); many MSS and the Tg. read the tetragrammaton.

7. *"Is there not another prophet of YHWH here? . . ."* The LXX and Vulg. omit the word "another" here and in v. 8, apparently intentionally, so as to divest the 400 of being prophets of YHWH (Stade and Schwally; Burney; Montgomery and Gehman); according to other early readers, they were suspected of being "false prophets" (Josephus, *Ant.* 8.402; see Tg. to v. 10). But there is no indication that they were other than prophets of YHWH.

8. *for he does not prophesy good about me but only evil.* Ahab did not distinguish the prophecies of Micaiah from those of the other prophets; all were ecstatic in their derivation; see below, Note to v. 10.

9. *one of his eunuchs.* On this courtier, see the Note on 2 Kgs 9:32.

10. *dressed in robes.* Literally, "clad in clothes (appropriate to their rank and to the occasion" (see Ehrlich). The LXX rendition "armed," omitting "at the threshing floor," has led to many unnecessary emendations (cf. NEB "in shining armour"); see the next Note.

at the threshing floor at the entrance of the gate of Samaria. The setting of the dramatic scene at the threshing floor has puzzled almost all commentators, who either correct or eliminate the word (see, e.g., Burney). But the specification preserves a small item from the realia of ancient life. The cramped city streets and quarters could not accommodate large gatherings, and the only open space was to be found just inside the city gate or, better yet, outside it; such tracts served as the market and the place of assembly; cf., e.g., the convocation held in front of the Water Gate in Jerusalem (Neh 8:1). At Samaria, the *gōren*, "threshing floor," fulfilled this function; winnowing, after all, was a seasonal activity, which would have made the threshing floor available for the public at other times. A similar scene is depicted in the Ugaritic epic of Aqhat; see ANET, 151, v 7–8; also S. Smith 1953. On this basis, the translation of *gōren* as "open space" (NJB; cf. Gray, "public place;" Jones; Walsh) is expendable; so is taking *bgrn* as an erroneous dittography of the preceding *bgdym*, "robes" (Burney; cf. NEB).

all the prophets were prophesying before them. On the ecstatic behavior of the prophets inherent in the *Hithpael*, see the Note on 1 Kgs 18:29.

11. *Zedekiah son of Chenaanah had made himself horns of iron, and he said: "Thus says YHWH: With these you shall gore Aram until their end."* The

symbolic act of Zedekiah (cf. Jer 27:2) draws its inspiration from the widely known ancient Near Eastern image of animal horns representing might and power. In literature and art, the gods (e.g., Ninlil "gores my enemies with her strong horns" [CAD Q, 136a]), and their royal protégés (e.g., Thutmose, "the young bull, firm of heart, sharp of horns, who cannot be felled" [ANET, 374b]) are regularly endowed with horns. See also the iconographic representations of horned crowns in ANEP 475, 486, 498. In biblical verse, horns are the proud symbols of strength; cf. Deut 33:17; also Jer 48:25; Zech 2:1–2; Dan 8:3–7.

had made himself horns of iron. Verse 11 is bracketed by vv. 10 and 12, both of which use participles to describe the ongoing action; the spotlight in v. 11 focuses upon Zedekiah, one of the 400, whose distinctive conduct caught the narrator's attention. The horns he was wearing had been prepared in advance of the gathering.

12. *And all the prophets prophesied the same: "Advance to Ramoth-gilead and be successful, for YHWH will give (it) into the hand of the king."* If there were any lingering doubts that Ahab would triumph at Ramoth-gilead (the word "success" is not expressed in v. 6), after Zedekiah's display, all were convinced of the king's victory. Note that, unlike v. 6, this verse retains the tetragrammaton.

13. *The messenger who had gone to call Micaiah.* This scene, at Micaiah's dwelling, did not follow the one at the threshing floor (vv. 10–12) but took place simultaneously, as the syntax indicates. Walsh aptly suggests adding "Meanwhile." On the syntax of simultaneity, see Talmon 1978; Berlin 1983, 126–28.

The words of the prophets. Other versions support MT *dbry* against LXX *dbrw* ("they spoke"), adopted by NAB, NEB, and many older commentators.

unanimous. Literally, "one mouth" (*peh 'eḥad*) has its cognate in Akk *pû ištēn*, which connotes action in unison and common cause; see AHw 872b–73a; CAD Š/1, 140b–41a. Rabbinic exegesis (in the name of R. Isaac) took this unanimity as a sure sign of false prophecy, since "no two prophets prophesy in the same style" (*b. Sanh.* 89a).

14. *Micaiah said: "By the life of YHWH, only what YHWH says to me will I speak."* An echo of Micaiah's reply to the king's messenger can be heard in the Balaam narrative; cf. Num 22:38; 23:12, 26; 24:13.

15. *"Micaiah, shall we go to battle against Ramoth-gilead, or shall we refrain?"* The LXX reads the plural verbs in MT in the singular, as in v. 6, explained as the plural of majesty (Montgomery and Gehman). Note that, if Ahab meant to include Jehoshaphat in his question, Micaiah directed his answer to Ahab only.

16. *The king said to him: "How many times have I put you under oath that you should speak to me only the truth in the name of YHWH."* Micaiah's reputation for presenting contrary prophecies seems to have raised the suspicion that this time he was lying.

17. *like sheep without a shepherd.* Implied in Micaiah's words is Ahab's neglect of his people, since "shepherding" was the task of the righteous king (cf. 2 Sam 5:2; 7:7). Here it was Israel's army that was destined to become the proverbial leaderless flock; cf., e.g., Num 27:17; Jer 23:1–2; Ezek 34:1–6; Zech 13:7;

and the same image in a bilingual Sumerian-Akkadian proverb collection: "A people without a king (is like) sheep without a shepherd" (Lambert 1960, 232, iv 14–15).

19. *Therefore, hear the word of YHWH.* The MT is preferable to the double reading in LXX: for MT *lkn*, first *l' kn*, "Not so!" (adopted by Skinner, Gray), and second *l' 'nky*, "Not I" (i.e., this word is not mine but YHWH's).

all the host of heaven in attendance to his right and to his left. In Deuteronomistic writings, the heavenly host is the term for the celestial bodies worshiped by the foreign nations (cf., e.g., Deut 4:19; 17:3; 2 Kgs 17:16; 21:3; Jer 8:2; 19:13; 33:22), forbidden to Israel. In Micaiah's vision, the host takes on the quality of attendants in the heavenly court, where the outcome of the battle is to be decided on; cf. the divine beings in Job 1:6 and the seraphs in Isa 6:2; cf. also Ps 103:21; 148:2. YHWH's council as the counterpart of the earlier council of the Canaanite god 'El is discussed by Cross 1973, 186–90; Mullen 1992.

20. *'Who will entice Ahab so that he will advance and fall at Ramoth-gilead?'* The enticement was to guarantee that Ahab would fall in battle. In many biblical circles, it was held that YHWH led evildoers to their own downfall by turning them stubborn (as in the case of Pharaoh; cf. Exod 14:1–4) or by sending "an evil spirit" to incite persons one against another (such as the citizens of Shechem against Abimelech, Judg 9:23). Ezekiel spoke of another kind of baiting of prophets; he understood YHWH as adding to the punishment of the false prophets by misguiding them to evil acts (cf. Ezek 14:9–10); see Greenberg 1983b, 253–54.

One said thus and one said thus. The unique adverb in MT, *bkh . . . bkh*, is read in 2 Chr 18:19 *kkh . . . kkh*, an example of *beth* and *kap* interchange, due to their similarity in late Hebrew script.

21. *Then a spirit came forward.* Literally, "the spirit (the one who volunteered) went out" from among the crowd of divine beings.

24. *Then Zedekiah son of Chenaanah stepped up and struck Micaiah on the cheek.* The idiom **hkh 'l lhy* is a gesture of humiliation (cf. Lam 3:30; also Mic 4:14; Ps 3:8; Job 16:10); in Babylonia, the act was punishable by the payment of a fine or even stripes (see Code of Hammurabi 202–5 [ANET, 175]); cf. also at the interrogation of Jesus in John 18:22.

"*Which (way) did the spirit of YHWH pass from me to speak to you?*" The word "way" is added in 2 Chr 18:23, just as it appears in the same expression in 1 Kgs 13:12. The LXX interpreted *'y zh* as "Where?" (cf.1 Sam 9:18). In either case, Zedekiah called Micaiah's very words into question, implying that he spoke lies in YHWH's name.

25. *into the innermost room.* Compare with 1 Kgs 20:30; 2 Kgs 9:2.

26. *Amon, governor of the city.* Amon is not known from any other source. For his title, see the Note on 2 Kgs 23:8.

Joash, the king's son. The literal translation of the title *bn hmlk* masks a scholarly debate: Were the bearers of this title of royal stock, or were they ordinary court officials? Since most of the "sons of the king" known from textual references (cf., e.g., Jer 36:26; 38:6) and stamp seals (WSS, nos. 412–16) are not attested in the genealogical lists in the Bible, some consider these "sons" to be low-ranking officers, perhaps with police duties (de Vaux 1961, 119–20). Because Joash appears only in the present verse, he is considered by some to be a "deputy" (see NEB, note, ad loc.) But the biblical registers are far from complete and the royal harems large, so the "king's sons" could actually have been part of the extended royal family. For the use of the equivalent term *mār šarri* in Mesopotamia, most often "prince," see CAD Š/2, 105–12.

27. *Put this fellow in prison.* Persons could be confined until their case was decided; e.g., the Sabbath violator (Num 15:32–36) and the blasphemer (Lev 24:10–12). In the present instance, Micaiah was detained until his prophecy could be verified, unlike Jeremiah, who was adjudged harmful to society and so constrained (Jer 37:15; 38:6). The ancient Near Eastern practice of imprisonment is surveyed in van der Toorn 1992a.

this fellow. See the Note on 1 Kgs 20:7.

scant bread and scant water. Micaiah's meager prison fare was to be no better than that available during a drought or siege; cf. Isa 30:20. On this appositional construction, see Waltke and O'Connor 1990, §12.3c.

safely. Or "unscathed" [DNF]; for *šālôm* in the sense of "health, welfare," see Gen 43:27; Exod 18:7; 2 Kgs 10:13.

28. *Micaiah said: "If you do return safely, YHWH has not spoken through me."* Micaiah's final words reflect the Deuteronomic criterion by which a true prophecy may be recognized; cf. Deut 18:21–22. The MT has the additional clause, omitted by Luc., LXX: "He said: Hear, all you peoples." This annotation, of uncertain date (see Ball 1977 for the unlikely suggestion that it stems from Dtr), sought to identify Micaiah with the late-eighth-century prophet, Micah the Morashtite, by quoting the opening phrase in Mic 1:2.

30. *"I will disguise myself and go into battle, but you, wear your robes."* Did Ahab really "think that he could escape God's decree by his changing clothes" (Qara)? Just as other royal personages who sought to hide behind disguises (e.g., Saul in 1 Sam 28:8 and Jeroboam's wife in 1 Kgs 14:2), Ahab also was found out. The Neo-Assyrian ritual practice whereby a substitute king (*šar pūḫi*) was appointed to protect the real king from harm on inauspicious days and was put to death when the dangerous term passed (see Parpola 1983, xxii–xxxii) has been compared to Ahab's disguise (so Naʾaman 1997a, 166–68); but the ruse on the battlefield at Ramoth-gilead through which Ahab sought to escape his fate was unlike the foreign practice, which was of a different nature.

I will disguise myself and go into battle. The infinitive absolute verbal forms (cf. other examples in 2 Kgs 3:16; 4:43) are translated by first-person sg. in the LXX and Tg.

but you, wear your robes. Jehoshaphat is portrayed as not being very keen, since his compliance with Ahab's suggestion put his life in jeopardy (as later seen in vv. 32–33). Josephus pictures Jehoshaphat as donning Ahab's royal garments in an attempt to trick fate (*Ant.* 8.412; apparently following Luc. and LXX). But would Jehoshaphat have agreed with such a scheme?

31. *(there were) thirty-two.* The irregular syntactical position of the number, lacking in 2 Chr 18:30, suggests that it may have been derived secondarily from 1 Kgs 20:1.

"Do not battle with the small or the great but only with the king of Israel." An illogical order for a military operation, except that, within the context of the story, it directs the reader's attention to YHWH's determination to bring about his word concerning Ahab's death.

32. *then Jehoshaphat cried out.* The Chronicler took this to mean that Jehoshaphat called upon YHWH, "and YHWH helped him" (2 Chr 18:31; added by the LXX in Kings). The more earthly view sees Jehoshaphat as shouting the "Judaic war-cry" (Stade; Montgomery and Gehman) in order to make his identity known.

34. *But one man drew his bow innocently.* The archer took aim, but he did not know that he had targeted the king of Israel; cf. the 200 Jerusalemites who accompanied Absalom "in all innocence, not knowing anything of the matter" (2 Sam 15:11).

between the joints of the armor. Hebrew *širyôn* (also 1 Sam 17:5; Neh 4:10; 2 Chr 26:14), a coat of mail, used for protection of both humans and animals, is a loanword (from Hurrian?), as is Akk *siriam* (CAD S, 313–15; see Speiser 1950). Examples of scale-armor have been recovered in excavations (see, e.g., ANEP 161; Yadin 1963, 1:196–97). On an exterior panel of the chariot of Thutmose IV, an enemy chariot driver is depicted shot through by an arrow that has pierced his armor at a weak point, the joints that allowed for flexibility of movement by the wearer (ANEP 314, at no. 11).

"Turn your hand. . . ." By pulling up on the reins, the driver signaled a change of direction to the team; cf. 2 Kgs 9:23 for a similar movement of the hand.

get me out of the camp. For MT *hmḥnh*, LXX reads: *hmlḥmh*, "the battle, war" (so NRSV); but the following *hmlḥmh* in v. 35 may have interfered. The NJPSV has "'behind the lines' (note f: Lit. 'outside the camp')."

35. *The battle raged that day.* This sense of Heb **ʿlh*, "raged, rose," may be compared to the "rising waters" that flood the land (Jer 47:2; with Qimḥi, Burney). The MT *wtʿlh*, for the expected apocopated form *wtʿl* (as in 2 Chr 18:34), is due to dittography.

36. *A cry went through the camp at sundown: "Every man to his city! Every man to his land!"* Micaiah's prediction comes to pass; the army of Israel returns home like a leaderless flock (v. 17).

A cry went through the camp. The disagreement of gender between *wayyaʿăbōr*, "went through" (masc.), and *hārinnâ*, "the cry," (fem.), is overcome in all versions by translating "the herald went through the camp" (so NEB), though *rinnâ* never has this meaning; on the lapse of agreement when the verb precedes the subject, see GKC, 145o; Waltke-O'Connor 1990, §6.6.

37. *So the king died.* For MT *wymt hmlk*, Luc. and LXX read *ky mt hmlk*, "for the king is dead," the words being part of the cry that ran through the camp.

38. *They washed off the chariot at the pool of Samaria.* This spot has provisionally been identified with the small pool (5 × 10 m) excavated in the northwest corner of the royal quarters at Samaria (NEAEHL 1303).

They washed off. Hebrew **šṭp,* "flow, wash," is used of rivers in flood (e.g., Isa 8:8; Jer 47:2) and a driving rain (Ezek 13:11, 15); NJPSV: "flushed out."

the dogs licked his blood, and the whores bathed, in accordance with YHWH's word that he had spoken. Because of the contradiction between the present verse and Elijah's promised punishment of Ahab, which was to take place in Jezreel (21:19), as well as the novel bathing by the whores, the verse has been suspect of being the "clumsy attempt of a pious editor" at writing about the fulfillment of prophecy (Robinson; earlier Skinner marked it as "so strained and so disparaging"). Yet this alternate tradition on the demise of Ahab remains just that: a description of the king's disgraceful end that was not harmonized with the Elijah tales.

the whores bathed. A crux variously solved. The Tg. and Syr. interpreted it as "washed his armor" (*mānê zēnā²* [for Heb *zōnôt,* "whores"]); the entire phrase is taken as an intrusion from the preceding "dogs," understood in the derogatory sense as male prostitutes (cf. Deut 23:19; so Montgomery and Gehman; Provan). Perhaps the LXX addition (here and in 1 Kgs 21:19) of "pigs" to the dogs who licked the blood points up a possible solution. Dogs and swine were the scavengers of ancient cities, and they appear together in formulaic curses from the ancient Near East, as in the Esarhaddon oaths: "Let dogs and pigs eat your flesh" (ANET, 538b). Might the scene at the pool of Samaria originally have been a scene of dogs licking and pigs wallowing/bathing in Ahab's blood ("whores" [*hazzōnôt* for *ḥăzîrîm*] somehow being a copyist's error)?

39. *the house of ivory that he built.* A luxury item, ivory carvings were used to decorate furniture (cf. Amos 6:4); the reference here may be to a building that was particularly ostentatious, with wall panels as well as appointments in ivory (cf. 3:15). At Samaria, a large group of ivories (over 500 fragments), many carved in Phoenician style, was discovered in a burnt building on the acropolis, the dating of which is disputed (see Kenyon 1971, 83–89; Barnett 1982, 49).

all the cities that he built. Archaeologists have redated the architectural remains at many Northern sites, formerly held to be tenth-century Solomonic constructions, to the ninth century and the Omride kings, especially Ahab; see A. Mazar 1990, 406–16. Compare the notice in 1 Kgs 16:34.

40. *So Ahab slept with his ancestors.* This phrase, indicating the peaceful death of a monarch, is first used concerning David (see Note on 1 Kgs 2:10) and thereafter in the closing formula of all of the kings of Judah and Israel in a consistent manner; it is lacking with respect to kings who lost their lives in coups or on the battlefield. The present notice concerning Ahab is the one exception, since the king's violent death (v. 37) should have ruled out the use of the phrase. That Dtr made an exception for Ahab (so Na'aman 1997a, 167) does not seem likely, considering his view of this arch-sinner. It may be that the editorial framework for Ahab's reign was composed prior to insertion of the

prophetic story in 1 Kgs 22:1–38 (see Halpern and Vanderhooft 1991, 230–35); see further in Comment.

COMMENT

Structure and Themes

The reign of Ahab that had been introduced in 16:29–33 is brought to its conclusion in 1 Kgs 22 with a tale that leads to the king's death and burial (vv. 1–38), rounded off by the Dtr closing formula of his reign (vv. 39–40). The tale itself picks up the narrative of the Aramean wars that was interrupted at the end of 1 Kgs 20 and tells of a third military encounter between Ahab and Ben-hadad.[1] The same literary issues raised in those earlier episodes, especially the anonymity of the Israelite king and the reconstructed history of the relations between Samaria and Aram-Damascus, have led many to transfer 1 Kgs 22 (together with 1 Kgs 20) to a later Omride king or to one of the Jehu dynasty. However, in this case, the site of Ramoth-gilead (cf. 22:3, 6, 29), part of the original kernel by most estimates, makes transfer to a king other than Ahab unsuitable; Joram son of Ahab held Ramoth-gilead, from which he fought Aram (cf. 2 Kgs 8:28; 9:1); and Joash son of Jehoahaz fought Aram at Apheq, not Ramoth-gilead (2 Kgs 13:17). Besides, neither of these later kings died in the manner described in 1 Kgs 22. The irreverent events at the pool of Samaria (22:38) realize the promised punishment of Ahab (20:42) and, even without his name expressly mentioned throughout most of 1 Kgs 22 (except for v. 20), tradition seems to have justly assigned the tale to this son of Omri, after which it was an easy step to identify the king of Judah with Jehoshaphat.[2]

Regarding the hostilities: in the present developed literary form of 1 Kgs 22, details concerning the battle at Ramoth-gilead—the enlistment of the troops, the engagement, the outcome—are curbed; the issues of conflicting prophetic viewpoints and the royal response to the word of YHWH dominate (vv. 5–28). Thus, for example, Jehoshaphat of Judah, who willingly agreed to join forces with Ahab (v. 4) to the point of endangering his own life (vv. 30–33), disappears in the midst of the battle report; similarly, the reader is left to infer from the scattering of the Israelite army (v. 36) in realization of the prophecy (v. 17) that the goal of recovering Ramoth-gilead (v. 3) was not achieved. But these and

---

[1] At the beginning and the end of 1 Kgs 22:1–38, there are editorial markers linking the tale to the Ahab cycle: 22:1–2a point back to 1 Kgs 20:34 and the treaty imposed by Ahab on Ben-hadad; 22:38 echoes (somewhat imperfectly) 1 Kgs 21:19.

[2] The inappropriateness of the notice of Ahab's peaceful demise in v. 40 (see Note on v. 40 above) is taken by many as proof positive of the incorrect identification of the anonymous "king of Israel" as Ahab. But the prophetic story may have entered the Ahab cycle after the composition of the regnal framework. This discord is no greater than the inconsistency between the description of the king's disgrace in 1 Kgs 22:38 and the prophecy in 21:19. Ancient editors (as well as late annotators) do not seem to have found it necessary to iron out all creases.

other loose ends (e.g., the assumed vindication and release of Micaiah) are not sufficient cause to parcel out 1 Kgs 22:1–38 between two, three, or more separate narrative levels, each one being a successive addition or commentary to the earlier tradition (see, e.g., Würthwein; DeVries 1978; H. Weippert 1988; see Roth 1982 for an instructive methodological review of seven historical-critical exegeses of 1 Kgs 22); readings of this sort deprive the tale of its essential unity (so Long 1983). Prophets and prophecy provide this unity.

Divination prior to battle was an established procedure in Israel, and recourse to its priestly practitioners is often noted (cf., e.g., Judg 20:27–28; 1 Sam 23:9; 30:7; and the instances in which only the query is recorded, e.g., Judg 1:1; 20:18, 23; 1 Sam 23:2, 4). Consequently, the consultation with prophets rather than priests in preparation for the attack on Ramoth-gilead comes as a surprise. Ahab's inquiry may be formulated in the traditional fashion (e.g., "Shall I . . . or shall I not?"; "Will so and so do . . . or will he not?"), but ecstatics who brandish symbolic tools (1 Kgs 22:11–12) have replaced the venerable mantics of the Urim and Thummim. The 400 prophets are spoken of as "his (i.e., Ahab's) prophets" (cf. 22:22), indicating that they can be counted on to support the king, and from the advice of the king's messenger to Micaiah, these men of God were viewed as pliable (v. 13). Jehoshaphat's suspicion concerning their unanimous prediction of victory, which ultimately led to the altercation between Zedekiah son of Chenaanah and Micaiah son of Imlah, draws the reader to the heart of the matter: two views of prophecy, divination by "YHWH's spirit" and divination by "YHWH's word," contend for authority. The narrator comes down on the side of "the word" that issues from YHWH in his divine council; true prophecy is rational and unaffected by the deceptive spell of the "spirit." And in conformity with Deuteronomic doctrine, the word that YHWH has truly spoken will be known when it comes to pass (cf. 1 Kgs 22:28 and Deut 18:21–22).

The issue of true and false prophecy is a major point of contention at the end of the Judean monarchy, and the fortunes of Micaiah and the later Jeremiah seem remarkably similar. Like Micaiah, Jeremiah was challenged by a prophet who proclaimed a contradictory message in the name of YHWH (cf. Jer 28); in reply, Jeremiah suggested that true prophecy was identifiable by its substance: the warning call for repentance was YHWH's true word, while the promise of well-being had to pass the "wait and see" test (28:8–9). On another occasion, Jeremiah's life was threatened because of his critical words, and he was thrown into prison to keep him from spreading his defeatism (cf. Jer 37:12–21). For some, these similarities suggest that 1 Kgs 22 was written toward the end of the period of classical prophecy, its author having "employed historical sources" to create an *exemplum* in which Micaiah is "a true prophet on all counts" (Rofé 1988a, 149–52; Na'aman 1997a, 166–68 takes vv. 19–28 as a Dtr interpolation). Still, the distinctiveness of 1 Kgs 22 remains; among its unique features is its negative stand on the ecstatic experience. While the spirit of YHWH is attested as the animating force of early prophets, it plays no role in the lives of their successors, the literary prophets (see Mowinckel 1934). In their view, the spirit is mere wind (cf. Mic 2:11; Jer 5:13), the mark of a madman (cf. Hos 9:7). The issue confronting Jeremiah is that both he and the false prophets claim to have received the word of YHWH. Thus, the vision of Micaiah in 1 Kgs 22:19–23 remains singular in its discredit of the spirit as a source of divine knowledge and is, perhaps, the expression of an earlier transitional stage in the development of Israelite prophecy.[3]

History

If we accept the identification of the king of Israel in 1 Kgs 22 as Ahab, the battle of Ramoth-gilead took place in 852 BCE, in the year following the allied expedition against Shalmaneser III at Qarqar.[4] The participation of Israel with Aram-Damascus in that battle did not affect the long-term relations between the two states; with the passing of the crisis and, energized by his success in halting Assyria's advance, Ben-hadad reasserted his presence in Transjordan to Israel's discomfiture. A seesaw state of affairs characterized most of the next decade, its ups and downs determined mostly by the recurrent efforts of Shalmaneser to reach Damascus. In 849, four years after the indecisive outcome at Qarqar, the Assyrian king engaged the western league once more; he did so again in 848 and 845, and only in 841 did he reach the environs of Damascus. Whether Israel renewed its alliance with Ben-hadad after the death of Ahab is unclear (see Comment to 2 Kgs 7, 9–10 in Cogan and Tadmor 1988, 84, 120–21) but, as 1 Kgs 22 shows, it was ever ready to turn the preoccupation of its powerful northern neighbor to advantage.

However his spotted military record is to be evaluated, Ahab left his mark in stone and mortar. Excavations at Samaria, Megiddo, Hazor, and Dan have uncovered evidence of significant construction and fortification in the mid–ninth century, illuminating the half-verse that credits Ahab with building "the house of ivory . . . and all the cities" (see the Note on v. 39a).

---

[3] Micaiah does not claim that the 400 prophets are self-deluded or that they are motivated by personal gain; they appear as pawns, serving YHWH's ends. In this respect, as well, they are unlike the false prophets denounced by the literary prophets.

[4] The sole consideration in fixing this date is the death of Ahab, determined on the basis of the overall chronological scheme of the Israelite monarchy. The "three years" of peace in v. 1 is of no significance, being a typological number (see the Note on v. 1).

XXXIX. THE REIGN OF JEHOSHAPHAT (JUDAH)

(22:41–51)

22 ⁴¹Jehoshaphat son of Asa became king over Judah in the fourth year of Ahab king of Israel. ⁴²Jehoshaphat was thirty-five years old when he became king, and he reigned twenty-five years in Jerusalem. His mother's name was Azubah daughter of Shilhi. ⁴³He followed all the way of his father Asa; he did not stray from it, doing what was pleasing to YHWH. ⁴⁴ᵃBut the high places were not removed; the people continued to sacrifice and make offerings at the high places. ⁴⁵Jehoshaphat made peace with the king of Israel. ⁴⁶The rest of the history of Jehoshaphat and the exploits he undertook and how he fought are indeed recorded in the History of the Kings of Judah.

⁴⁷He stamped out from the land the rest of the male prostitutes who remained from the days of his father Asa. ⁴⁸There was no king in Edom; a prefect was king. ⁴⁹Jehoshaphat builtᵇ Tarshish ships to go to Ophir for gold; but he did not go, for the ships were wreckedᶜ at Ezion-geber. ⁵⁰Then Ahaziah son of Ahab said to Jehoshaphat: "Let my servants go with your servants in the ships." But Jehoshaphat did not consent.

⁵¹So Jehoshaphat slept with his ancestors, and he was buried with his ancestors in the City of David his ancestor. Jehoram, his son, succeeded him.

[1 Kgs 22:52–54 is treated in *II KINGS*, Anchor Bible volume 11.]

ᵃ Some translations (e.g., RSV) combine vv. 43 and 44, renumbering the remainder of the chapter accordingly.

ᵇ Read with qere *ʿśh* for ketib *ʿśr*; also many MSS and versions.

ᶜ Qere *nšbrw* for ketib *nšbrh*; see Note.

NOTES

22 42. *Jehoshaphat was thirty-five years old when he became king, and he reigned twenty-five years in Jerusalem.* Jehoshaphat reigned from 870 to 846 BCE.

45. *Jehoshaphat made peace with the king of Israel.* Hebrew **šlm* in *Hiphil* conveys the sense of surrender; cf., e.g., Deut 20:12; Josh 10:1; 11:19; if so, was this note intended as criticism of Jehoshaphat? Some translations seem to have understood the verb as reflecting 1 Kgs 22:1 and thus render "remained at peace" (NEB); "was at peace" (NJB); but cf. "submitted" (NJPSV). The formal end to the state of war that prevailed between Judah and Israel from the early days of the secession of the Northern tribes (cf. 1 Kgs 14:30; 15:16, 32) was marked by the marriage of Athaliah to Jehoram (2 Kgs 8:18). See further in the Comment.

47. *He stamped out from the land the rest of the male prostitutes who remained from the days of his father Asa.* See the Note on 1 Kgs 15:12.

male prostitutes. For these hierodules, see the Note on 1 Kgs 14:24.

48. *There was no king in Edom; a prefect was king.* The kingdom of Edom was last referred to in 1 Kgs 11:14–22, where the rebellious activity of Hadad the Edomite against Solomon was reported. The present note on Judah's (continued? or renewed?) rule over Edom introduces the following note concerning Jehoshaphat's maritime activities at Ezion-geber, an Edomite port.

a prefect was king. The term *niṣṣāb* (LXX transcriptions vocalized it *nesîb*; see the Note on 1 Kgs 4:19) is the same one used for Solomon's district governors (cf. 1 Kgs 4:5, 7; 5:7). Many object to this two-word clause on syntactical as well as substantive grounds and follow Stade's emendation joining it to v. 49, thus obtaining: "The deputy of king Jehoshaphat built Tarshish ships . . ."; the deputy becomes, then, the subject of the next clause (cf. Burney; Skinner; NEB, NJPSV [note]). That an appointee could be considered both prefect and king at the same time is strictly a question of the perspective of the reporter (Šanda); this is borne out by the two titles of Hadad-yisʾi of Gozan, who in the bilingual inscription on a statue from Tell Fekheriyeh is both *šākin māti* (Akk "governor") and *mlk* (Aram "king, ruler"); see Millard and Bordreuil 1982, 139.

49. *Jehoshaphat built Tarshish ships to go to Ophir for gold.* The terms echo the earlier description of Solomon's sea trade; see the Notes on 1 Kgs 9:26–28; 10:11, 22. The text tradition is divided over a number of readings, as seen by the qere notations. The LXX insertion of 22:41–51 at 16:28 reads "ship" (cf. Tg.), suggesting that the pl. "ships" may have arisen from the miscopied "ten" (MT ketib).

but he did not go, for the ships were wrecked at Ezion-geber. The subject seems to be Jehoshaphat, unless the reference is to the "ship(s)" that "did not go" (revocalized as *halĕkâ/û*), so Stade, Burney, NAB, NEB. The MT has *nšbrh ʾnywt*; qere *nšbrw* corrects to late vocalization. However, the ketib preserves the archaic form of 3d fem. pl. with a final *heʾ*; cf., e.g., Gen 49:22; Deut 21:7; 1 Sam 4:15; the article *heʾ* before *ʾnywt* has dropped out by haplography. The cause of the shipwreck goes unnoted; "inexperienced sailors" (J. Robinson) and a sudden violent storm (Šanda) are frequent guesses. A novel suggestion limits Jehoshaphat's shipbuilding "to a makeshift renovation of Solomon's old and now rotted merchant ships" (Donner 1977, 392).

50. *Then Ahaziah son of Ahab said to Jehoshaphat: "Let my servants go with your servants in the ships." But Jehoshaphat did not consent.* The short, two-year reign of Ahaziah (cf. 1 Kgs 22:52) permits dating the affair between the 17th and 19th year of Jehoshaphat (ca. 852–851 BCE). Though the present sequence might lead one to think that Ahaziah offered assistance after the wreck, the editorial link *ʾāz*, "then," does not require such a conclusion; see the Note on 1 Kgs 3:16. Accordingly, the Chronicler was able to reorder and reinterpret the entire episode: the initiative for the joint venture issued from Jehoshaphat, who was condemned by the prophet Eliezer son of Dodavahu for joining up with Ahaziah, a condemnation that was followed by YHWH's wrathful destruction of the ships (2 Chr 20:35–37); for this original use of the story elements of Kings to create the theological pattern sin-prophecy-punishment, see Japhet 1993, 801–2.

COMMENT

Structure and Themes

The 25-year reign of Jehoshaphat is treated in just 11 verses, mostly brief head-lines; perhaps it was felt that the king's appearance in the two prophetic stories (1 Kgs 22:2–38; 2 Kgs 3:4–27) gave sufficient indication of his righteous char-acter (cf. 1 Kgs 22:7; 2 Kgs 3:11–14). The LXX[B] places 1 Kgs 22:41–51 after 1 Kgs 16:28 and repeats 1 Kgs 22:41–46 again following 1 Kgs 22:40; the alternate chronology followed by Luc. is behind this alternate location of the summary of the reign of Jehoshaphat. The LXX tradition is discussed in the Introduction. Chronology.

It is somewhat unusual to find a lengthy string of notices, as in vv. 47–50, placed after the closing formula "The rest of the history of Jehoshaphat . . . are indeed recorded . . . ," though a single verse (cf. 1 Kgs 14:30; 15:23, 32; 2 Kgs 15:16, 37) or even more (cf. 2 Kgs 12:21–22; 14:19–22) in such positions is attested.

History

The major achievement of Jehoshaphat's reign was peace with Israel, the impli-cation of which is disputed. All options have been posited, from informal union between the two kingdoms (Miller and Hayes 1986, 275) expressive of Judah's submission to Israel, to its equal and independent status as "full ally" of the Omrides (Bright 1981, 251). The end of hostilities between the kingdoms of Judah and Israel was formally expressed in the marriage of the two royal houses (cf. 2 Kgs 8:18; 2 Chr 18:1). Jehoshaphat chose to take part in two military cam-paigns initiated by Israel, one against Aram-Damascus (1 Kgs 22), the other against Moab (2 Kgs 3). Judah may have chosen to cooperate in wars that touched upon Israel's position in Transjordan because of the potential benefit to its own extraterritorial interests. The southern kingdom of Edom was under the thumb of Judah (1 Kgs 22:48), which probably meant that the Red Sea trade moving north through the Negev was also under Judean supervision. But it is hard to understand how Judah thought that it could renew maritime activ-ity through the port of Ezion-geber without the help of more experienced sea-men. Does Jehoshaphat's turning down the offer of help from Israel's King Ahaziah (1 Kgs 22:50) mean that he thought to take advantage of his own con-tacts with Tyre rather than use the connections that ran through Samaria? Whatever the case, he fell upon some bad times that ended the matter (1 Kgs 22:49).

APPENDIXES

◆

APPENDIX I: A SELECTION OF EXTRABIBLICAL TEXTS RELATING TO 1 KINGS

1. SHOSHENQ I (Shishak), King of Egypt (945–924 BCE)

Selection from the list of cities in Philistia, Judah, and Israel incised on the southern wall of the Temple of Amun at Karnak; arranged in rows (of which ten are extant). The numbering of the city names follows the placement of the hieroglyphs on the relief and is read from right to left.

Text: G. R. Hughes, ed. 1954; *Treatments*: B. Mazar 1957; Kitchen 1973, 432–47; Aharoni 1979, 323–30; Aḥituv 1984; Naʾaman 1998. *Photograph*: ANEP 349.

Row I	Row III (cont.)	Row IV
1–9 "Nine Bows" (traditional enemies of Egypt)	17 Rehob	40 Abel
	16 Beth-shean	41–52 little legible
	15 Shunem	
	14 Taanach	Row V
10 Copy of Asiatics		53 [Pe]nuel
11 Ga[za]/Ge[zer] (?)	Row III	54 [ḥ] d š t
12 m [ ]	27 Megiddo	55 p-n Succoth
13 Rubuti	28 Adar	56 Adam
	29 Yad-hammelek	57 Zemaraim
Row II	30 [ḥ b] r t	58 [Mi]gdol
26 Aijalon	31 ḥ n m	59 [ ] r d
25 Qiryathaim	32 ʿAruna	60 [ ] n r
24 Beth-horon	33 Borim	61–63 [lost]
23 Gibeon	34 Gath-padalla	64 ḥ [ ] p n
22 Mahanaim	35 Yaḥam	65 The Valley
21 š w d	36 Beth-ʿr/l n	
20 [lost]	37 k q r y	
19 Adoraim	38 Socoh	
18 Hapharaim	39 Beth-tappu[ah?]	

2. SHALMANESER III, King of Assyria (859–824 BCE)

The Kurkh Monolith (lines 78–102)
Latest edition: Grayson 1996, 11–24;
Translations: ARAB 1. 610–11; ANET, 278–79; DOTT, 47
Photograph: ANEP 443
[Note: Errors in the poorly inscribed cuneiform text on this provincial stela are indicated in parentheses, alongside the suggested corrections.]

In the eponymy of Dayan-Ashur, on the fourteenth of Adar, I set out from Nineveh and I crossed the Tigris River. I approached the cities of Giammu that were on the Balih River. They (his subjects) were afraid of my awe-inspiring lordship and the splendor of my fierce weapons, and with their own weapons, they killed Giammu, their lord. I entered the cities Sahlala and Til-sha-Tirahi and brought (the images of) my gods into his palaces; I celebrated the *tašiltu*-festival in his palaces. I opened his storehouses and beheld his treasures. I plundered his possessions and carried them off to Ashur, my city.

I set out from Sahlala and approached Kar-Shalmaneser. I crossed the Euphrates River at its flood for the second time on rafts of goatskins. In the city Ana-Ashur-utir-asbat that is on the other side of the Euphrates on the Sagur River—that the Hittites (i.e., north Syrians) call Pitru—(there) I received the tribute of the kings of the other side of the Euphrates: Sangar of Carchemish, Kundashpi of Kummuh, Arame son of Gusi, Lalli of Melid, Haiani son of Gabari, Kalparuda of Pattin, Kalparuda of Gurgum, silver, gold, tin, copper, copper bowls. I set out from the Euphrates and approached Aleppo. They (the people of Aleppo) were afraid to do battle and so grasped my feet. I received silver and gold as their tribute and offered sacrifices to the god Adad of Aleppo.

I set out from Aleppo and approached the cities of Irhuleni of Hamath. I captured Adenni, Barga (and) Argana, his royal city and carried off his spoil, his possessions, and the contents of his palaces. I set fire to his palaces. I set out from Argana and approached Qarqar. Qarqar, his (text: my) royal city, I destroyed and wasted and set afire.

1,200 chariots, 1,200 horsemen, 20,000 foot soldiers of Adad-idri of Damascus

700 chariots, 700 horsemen, 10,000 foot soldiers of Irhuleni of Hamath

200 (?) (text: 2,000) chariots, 10,000 foot soldiers of Ahab the Israelite

500 foot soldiers of Byblus (text: Gua)

1,000 foot soldiers of Egypt

10 chariots, 1,000 (?) (text: 10,000) foot soldiers of Irqata (text: Irqanata)

200 foot soldiers of Matinu-baal of Arvad

200 foot soldiers of Usanata

30 chariots, [ ]000 foot soldiers of Adunu-baal of Siana (text: Sizana)

1,000 camels of Gindibu of the Arabs

[ ]000 foot soldiers of Baasha son of Rehob from Mount Amana

—these twelve kings came to his aid. They set out against me to do battle. I fought with them with the exalted strength that the god Ashur my lord gave me, and the mighty weapons that the god Nergal, who goes ahead of me, granted me. I defeated them from Qarqar to Gilzau (or: Dilziau). I struck down 14,000 of their warriors with the sword. Like the god Adad, I rained down upon them a flood. I scattered their corpses and filled the steppe with his vast army. With my weapon, I let their blood flow into [ ]. The plain was too small to hold (all) the bodies, and the broad field was insufficient for their burial. On the corpses, like a bridge, I reached the Orontes River. In that battle, I took from them their chariots, their stallions, and their horses broken to the yoke.

3. HAZAEL, King of Aram-Damascus (ca. 845–810 BCE)
Tel Dan Aramaic Inscription
Text edition: Biran and Naveh 1995

1. [   ] and cut [   ]
2. [   ] my father went up [against him when] he fought at [   ]
3. My father lay down; he went to [his ancestors?]. Then the king of Is-
4. rael entered Qedem in my father's land. Hadad made me king.
5. Hadad went in front of me and I departed from [the] seven [   ]
6. . . . of my kingdom, and I killed [seve]nty kin[gs], who harnessed thou [sands of cha]
7. riots and thousands of horses. [I killed Jeho]ram son of [Ahab]
8. king of Israel, and [I] killed [Ahaz]iahu son of [Jehoram, kin]
9. g of the House of David. I set [their towns into ruins and turned
10. their land into [desolation . . .   ]
11. other [. . .   and Jehu ru]
12. led over Is[rael . . .   and I laid   ]
13. siege to [. . .   ]

APPENDIX II: THE CHRONOLOGY OF ISRAEL AND JUDAH

David ca. 1005–965
Solomon ca. 968–928

JUDAH		ISRAEL	
Rehoboam	928–911	Jeroboam I	928–907
Abijah	911–908	Nadab	907–906
Asa	908–867	Baasha	906–883
		Elah	883–882
		Zimri	882
		Tibni	882–878**
		Omri	882–871
Jehoshaphat	870–846*	Ahab	873–852
Jehoram	851–843*	Ahaziah	852–851
		Jehoram	851–842
Ahaziah	843–842		
Athaliah	842–836	Jehu	842–814
Joash	836–798		
		Jehoahaz	817–800*
		Jehoash	800–784
Amaziah	798–769		
Azariah	785–733*	Jeroboam II	788–747*
Jotham	759–743*	Zechariah	747
		Shallum	747
Ahaz	743–727*	Menahem	747–737
		Pekahiah	737–735
		Pekah	735–732
Hezekiah	727–698	Hoshea	732–724
Manasseh	698–642		
Amon	641–640		
Josiah	639–609		
Jehoahaz	609		
Jehoiakim	608–598		
Jehoiachin	597		
Zedekiah	596–586		

* Includes years as co-regent
** Rival rule

The dates follow the reconstruction in M. Cogan, "Chronology," *ABD* 1:1002–10. In a few instances, these dates differ from those that appear in Cogan and Tadmor 1988, 350.

APPENDIX III:
CHRONOLOGIES OF THE ANCIENT NEAR EAST

1. *Kings of Assyria*

Ashur-rabi II	1012–972
Ashur-resh-ishi	971–967
Tiglath-pileser II	966–935
Ashur-dan II	934–912
Adad-nirari II	911–891
Tukulti-Ninurta II	890–884
Ashurnasirpal II	883–859
Shalmaneser III	858–824
Shamshi-Adad V	824–811
Adad-nirari III	811–783
Shalmaneser IV	783–773
Ashur-dan III	773–755
Ashur-nirari V	755–745
Tiglath-pileser III	745–727
Shalmaneser V	727–722
Sargon II	722–705
Sennacherib	705–681
Esarhaddon	681–669
Ashurbanipal	669–627
Ashur-etil-ilani	
Sin-shum-lishir	627–612
Sin-shar-ishkun	
Ashur-uballit II	612–609

2. *Kings of Babylonia:*
The Chaldean Dynasty

Nabopolassar	625–605
Nebuchadnezzar II	605–562
Amel-Marduk	652–560
Neriglissar	560–556
Labashi-Marduk	556
Nabonidus	556–539

3. *Kings of Egypt*

21st Dynasty

Amenemope	1033–981
Osochor	984–978
Siamun	978–959
Psesennes II	959–945

22d Dynasty

Shoshenq I	945–924
Osorkon I	924–889
Shoshenq II	c. 890
Takeloth I	889–874
Osorkon II	874–850

25th (Nubian) Dynasty

Pi(ankhy)	747–716
Shabako	716–702
Shebitku	702–690
Tarhaqa	690–664
Tantamani	664–656

26th Dynasty

Psammetichus I	664–610
Necho II	610–595
Psammetichus II	595–589
Apries	589–570
Amasis II	570–526
Psammetichus III	526–525

---

* The dates of the kings of Assyria and Babylonia given here are reckoned from their accession year; the native Mesopotamian practice was to count from the first full year following the accession, which begins in Nisan (= March/April). J. A. Brinkman (in A. L. Oppenheim, *Ancient Mesopotamia* [rev. ed.; Chicago: University of Chicago Press, 1977] Appendix: Mesopotamian Chronology of the Historical Period, pp. 335–48) follows the Mesopotamian practice.

INDEX OF SUBJECTS

♦

INDEX OF SCRIPTURAL AND OTHER ANCIENT REFERENCES

◆

INDEX OF HEBREW AND OTHER ANCIENT LANGUAGES

◆

I. AKKADIAN

aḫāzu, 241
aḫḫūtu, 299
ammatu, 237
apāru, 470
apsû, 271
arrat la napšuru maruštim, 174
ašbāti u qalāti, 489
askuppu/askuppatu, 238
bamâtu/bamtu, 184
beḫēru, 354
burāšu, 88, 228
dikut māti, 401
eber nāri, 213
ekallu, 237, 477
elammakku, 313
ellamu, 237
emēdu, 314
eṭemmu, 483
Garasu, 337
gidlu, 262
gillatu, 397
gullatu, 268
gullulu, 397
gušūrē erēni ṣirūti, 241
ḫazan(n)u, 400
ḫiādu, 311
ḫilāni / bīt ḫilāni, 238, 256–8, 268
Ḫumri / bīt Ḫumri, 416
ḫupšu, 401
idī petû, 283
[ina muḫḫi bī]ti isappid u'i iqabbīma, 372
ina pān uzzuzzu, 156
ina uzni rapaštim ḫasisi palkê ša išruka apkal ilāni, 187
karābu, 244
kāru, 469
kiddinūtu, 348
kimta rapaštum, 343
kiūru, 267

kuribu, 244
kurru, 212
lā ašbāta ana māt nakri alikma nakra dūk, 489
lam/wû, 265
leqû, 261
libbu rapšu la kāṣir ikki, 221
līmu, 101, 201
maḫīru, 321
maqātu, 466
marāṣu, 174
mār šarri, 493
mār šipri, 463
marû, 158
maškanu, 303
massu, 204
māti, 211
minamma qātka ana muḫḫija tadka, 338
mišarum, 348
muškēnu, 303
nadānu, 194, 477
nāgiru, 202
nakāru, 379
našû-nadānu, 341
nēmedu, 314
nīru, 347
nišek šēni, 402
pagû, 320
pānam šakānu, 176
parakku, 281
parāsu, 470
patāḫu, 245
pû ištēn, 491
pūtu, 270
qanê, 381
qaran ṣubāti, 339
qāta našû, 283
qātam dekû, 338
qātam mullû, 373
qinnaz zaqtum, 349
rakāsu, 215
râmu, 226

VI. HEBREW

א

ʾāb, 261
ʾābâ, 349
ʾabî-haʿêzrî, 421
ʾăbŏy, 372
ʾădonî, 194
ʾahāh, 372
ʾaḥî, 421
ʾak, 304
ʾākēn, 326
ʾālâ, 284
ʾalgûmmîm, 313
ʾalmūggîm, 88, 313
ʾālôn, 370
ʾāmar lĕ, 281
ʾammâ, 237, 239
ʾanšê hattārîm, 317
ʾăparsĕmôn, 311
ʾăpēr, 470
ʾarbeh, 285
ʾarmôn, 413
ʾăšer / ʿal ʾăšer, 194, 348, 480, 482
ʾăšērâ, 398
ʾăšer bilĕbab, 282
ʾašrê, 312
ʾaštart, 327
ʾaṭ, 483
ʾatta, 186
ʾattâ, 380
ʾay, 372
ʾayîl, 246
ʾāz, 193, 277, 304, 307, 500
ʾbl, 163
*ʾby, 194
ʾeben massāʿ, 231
ʾēbûs, 213–4
ʾel, 284, 409
ʾĕlōhîm, 196
ʾên, 319, 349
ʾerez, 228
ʾet, 246, 306, 331, 416
ʾēt ʾăšer, 284
ʾēzôb, 223
ʾezraḥ, 222
ʾḥd, 477
*ʾḥz, 241
ʾim, 160, 284, 463
ʾimrê ʾemet, 332
ʾîš ḥayil, 163
ʾiṭṭim, 483
ʾiwwâ, 341
ʾIyyar, 237

ʾkl (ʿl) šlḥn / ʾōkĕlê šulḥan, 214, 370
ʾlhym, 163
*ʾmn, 162
*ʾmr, 162
*ʾnp, 287, 328
ʾomēr, 227
ʾŏnî, 305
ʾôt, 368
ʾôy, 372
ʾoyâ, 372
ʾrwn hbryt / bryt yhwh, 279
ʾrwn hʿdwt, 279
ʾrwt, 214
*ʾsr, 465
ʾth, 174
*ʾṭm, 238
ʾûpāz, 318
ʾūrwâ, 214
ʾwlm/ʾlm/ʾûlām, 237, 248
ʾylm, 237
ʾy zh, 492
*ʾzr, 445

ב

bāʾammâ, 239
baddîm, 280
*bāʿēr, 379
bāʿēt hatî, 304
bāmâ/bāmôt/bāttê habbāmôt, 184–5, 359–60
bāqār, 213
barbūr, 213
barûk, 282
bassukkôt, 464
bat qôl, 468
bayit, 203
bᵊʾ bymym, 155
bᵊʿby, 268
*bdʾ, 367
*bdd, 280
bĕʿîr, 380
bĕlî, 479
bĕlîyaʿal, 479
ben, 205
ben-haymînî, 421
ben ʾiššâ ṣĕrûʿâ, 337
ben ʾišša zônâ, 337
bĕrît, 284, 328
bĕrôš, 88, 228
bêt-hallaḥmî, 421
bêt-haššimšî, 421
bĕyad, 409
*bḥr, 354
bî, 194
bišnayîm, 195

THE ANCHOR BIBLE
Commentaries (C) and Reference Library (RL) volumes on the Old and New
Testaments and Apocrypha

THE CONTRIBUTORS

Susan Ackerman, Dartmouth College. RL17

William F. Albright, Johns Hopkins University. C26

Francis I. Andersen, Professorial Fellow, Classics and Archaeology, University of Melbourne. C24, C24A, C24E

Markus Barth, University of Basel. C34, C34A, C34B

Adele Berlin, University of Maryland. C25A

Helmut Blanke, Doctor of Theology from the University of Basel. C34B

Joseph Blenkinsopp, University of Notre Dame. C19, RL5

Robert G. Boling, McCormick Theological Seminary. C6, C6A

Raymond E. Brown, S.S., Union Theological Seminary, New York (Emeritus). C29, C29A, C30, RL1, RL7, RL15

George W. Buchanan, Wesley Theological Seminary. C36

Edward F. Campbell, Jr., McCormick Theological Seminary. C7

James H. Charlesworth, Princeton Theological Seminary. RL4, RL13, RL14

Mordechai Cogan, Hebrew University, Jerusalem. C10, C11

John J. Collins, University of Chicago. RL10

James L. Crenshaw, Duke Divinity School. C24C, RL16

Mitchell Dahood, S.J., The Pontifical Biblical Institute. C16, C17, C17A

Alexander A. Di Lella, O.F.M., Catholic University of America. C23, C39

David L. Dungan, University of Tennessee, Knoxville. RL18

Joseph A. Fitzmyer, S.J., Catholic University of America. C28, C28A, C31, C33, C34C

J. Massyngberde Ford, University of Notre Dame. C38

Michael V. Fox, University of Wisconsin, Madison. C18A

David Noel Freedman, University of Michigan (Emeritus) and University of California, San Diego. General Editor. C24, C24A, C24E

Victor P. Furnish, Perkins School of Theology, Southern Methodist University. C32A

Jonathan A. Goldstein, University of Iowa. C41, C41A

Moshe Greenberg, Hebrew University, Jerusalem. C22, C22A

Louis F. Hartman, C.SS.R., Catholic University of America. C23

Andrew E. Hill, Wheaton College. C25D

Delbert R. Hillers, Johns Hopkins University. C7A

Luke Timothy Johnson, Candler School of Theology, Emory University. C35A, C37A

Craig R. Koester, Luther Seminary. C36

Bentley Layton, Yale University. RL11

Baruch A. Levine, New York University. C4, C4A

Jack R. Lundbom, Clare Hall, Cambridge University. C21A

P. Kyle McCarter, Jr., Johns Hopkins University. C8, C9

John L. McKenzie, De Paul University. C20

Abraham J. Malherbe, Yale University (Emeritus). C32B

C. S. Mann, formerly Coppin State College. C26

Joel Marcus, Boston University. C27

J.Louis Martyn, Union Theological Seminary, New York. C33A

Amihai Mazar, Institute of Archaeology of Hebrew University, Jerusalem. RL2

John P. Meier, Catholic University of America. RL3, RL9

Carol L. Meyers, Duke University. C25B, C25C

Eric M. Meyers, Duke University. C25B, C25C

Jacob Milgrom, University of California, Berkeley (Emeritus). C3, C3A, C3B

Carey A. Moore, Gettysburg College. C7B, C40, C40A, C44

Jacob M. Myers, Lutheran Theological Seminary, Gettysburg. C12, C13, C14, C42